CW01191777

Nachtjagd, Defenders of the Reich 1940-1943

Martin W. Bowman

Pen & Sword
AVIATION

First Published in Great Britain in 2016 by
Pen & Sword Aviation
an imprint of
Pen & Sword Books Ltd
47 Church Street, Barnsley, South Yorkshire S70 2AS

Copyright © Martin W Bowman, 2015
ISBN 9781473849839

The right of Martin W Bowman to be identified as author of this work has been asserted by him in accordance with the Copyright, Designs and Patents Act 1988.

A CIP catalogue record for this book is available from the British Library.

All rights reserved. No part of this book may be reproduced or transmitted in any form or by any means, electronic or mechanical including photocopying, recording or by any information storage and retrieval system, without permission from the Publisher in writing.

Typeset in 10/12pt Palatino
by GMS Enterprises PE3 8QQ

Printed and bound in England by
CPI Group (UK) Ltd, Croydon, CR0 4YY

Pen & Sword Books Ltd incorporates the Imprints of Pen & Sword Aviation, Pen & Sword Family History, Pen & Sword Maritime, Pen & Sword Military, Pen & Sword Discovery, Wharncliffe Local History, Wharncliffe True Crime, Wharncliffe Transport, Pen & Sword Select, Pen & Sword Military Classics, Leo Cooper, The Praetorian Press, Remember When, Seaforth Publishing and Frontline Publishing.

For a complete list of Pen & Sword titles please contact
PEN & SWORD BOOKS LIMITED

47 Church Street, Barnsley, South Yorkshire, S70 2AS, England
E-mail: enquiries@pen-and-sword.co.uk
Website: www.pen-and-sword.co.uk

Contents

Acknowledgements		4
Chapter 1.	'Night Fighting! It Will Never Come To That!'	7
Chapter 2.	The Early Experten	35
Chapter 3.	'The Other Prinz'	43
Chapter 4	Defence Of The Reich 1942	61
Chapter 5.	Under Cover of Darkness	77
Chapter 6.	The Common Danger	99
Chapter 7.	'Das Nachtgespenst'	107
Chapter 8.	The 'Wilde Sau'	121
Chapter 9.	'Emil-Emil'	149
Chapter 10.	Gomorrah	165
Chapter 11.	Deadly Nacht Musik	183
Chapter 12.	Hydra	191
Chapter 13.	'Zahme Sau'	201
Chapter 14.	Once The Most Beautiful City In The World	221
Appendix I	German ranks and their Equivalents	241
Appendix II	The 100 Highest Scoring Nachtjagd Pilots	242
Glossary		248
Bibliography		251

Acknowledgements

I am indebted to all the contributors for their words and photographs, in particular Nora Norgate; Jim Moore DFC and The 49 Squadron Association. I am equally grateful to Theo Boiten for information, images and invaluable reference work. And to everyone connected with the Kracker Archive, Simon Parry and John Foreman.

Thanks also go to my fellow author, friend and colleague, Graham Simons, for getting the book to press ready standard and for his detailed work on the photographs; to Pen & Sword and in particular, Laura Hirst; and Jon Wilkinson, for his unique jacket design once again.

'Pauke! Pauke!' ('Kettledrums! Kettledrums!'): the Leutnant had obtained visual contact of his target. It was a 'Lanki', crossing gently from port to starboard. His bordfunker immediately transmitted 'Ich beruhe'. Then they closed in rapidly for the kill - 300, 200, 150 metres, finally opening fire from 100 metres.

Strikes peppered the fuselage and danced along the wing root. Another two-second burst and the four-engined bomber burst into flames. Doomed, it fell away to port in a flaming death dive, impacting in a German forest. Gouts of fuel from ruptured tanks ignited and lit up the night sky with a reddish hue. The engines buried themselves deep into the earth. 'Sieg Heil!' said the pilot over R/T to ground control. The British bomber crew had unwitting been 'homed in' on: its H_2S set had been picked up by the night-fighter's 'Naxos Z' FuG 250, while Flensburg FuG 227/1 homed in on the bomber's 'Monica' tail-warning device.

On another night it would be the turn of the Leutnant and his Unteroffizier to be the preyed-upon. It was all part of a deadly and sophisticated electronic game in which the RAF, the Luftwaffe, aided by the scientists, pitted their wits in an ethereal, nocturnal battleground. One side gained the ascendancy until the inevitable counter-measure was found.

Confounding the Reich: The Operational History of 100 Group (Bomber Support) RAF.

Chapter One

'Night Fighting! It Will Never Come To That!'

Josef Kammhuber was born in Tüssling, Bavaria on 19 August 1896, the son of a farmer. At the beginning of World War I he was 18 and joined a Bavarian engineer battalion. He experienced the Battle of Verdun in 1916 and was promoted to Leutnant in 1917. He was allowed to remain in German's tiny post-war army and in 1925 was promoted to Oberleutnant. Between October 1926 and September 1928, he received division-level leadership training. From 1 May to 30 September 1930 he was sent to the USSR for secret pilot training. On his return he joined the staff of General Walter Wever, chief of staff of the Luftwaffe. He was promoted to Hauptmann on 1 February 1931. Wever was in the process of attempting to set up a strategic bomber command but in June 1936 Wever was killed in an air crash. Kammhuber had continued to rise in the ranks, promoted to Major on 1 October 1934, Oberstleutnant on 1 October 1936 and then Oberst on 1 January 1939. Kammhuber had put in a request in February 1939 for active duty. Promoted to Generalmajor, he was assigned as chief-of-staff of Luftflotte 2 and was in this position at the start of the war in September. In January 1940 he was transferred to the Western Front where he became Geschwader-Kommodore of KG51, a tactical bomber unit. During the French campaign he was shot down and captured and interned in a French PoW camp at the age of 44. He was released at the end of the Battle of France in July 1940 and returned to Germany where he was placed in command of coordinating flak, searchlight and radar units. At the time these were all under separate command and had no single reporting chain; so much of the experience of the different units was not being shared. The result was XII Fliegerkorps, a new dedicated night-fighting command.

Patrick Foss was born in Ketton, Rutland on 8 November 1913. When he was about nine years old he decided he wanted to go to sea in the Merchant Navy. He searched a reference book of schools and found the Nautical College, Pangebourne. His mother, who ran the Linden Hall Hotel in Bournemouth, agreed that she would send him there when he was thirteen. At the end of his first year, aged fourteen, he spent his summer vacation signing on a tramp steamer on the run from Cardiff to Oporto in Portugal as a shilling a month steward. He slept late and ate in the officers' quarters, but did any work that needed doing, from scraping paint to taking a turn at the steering wheel. When he was seasick the Captain sent him down to the engine room where he was put to work greasing the steel piston rods as they reciprocated out of the cylinders. It was at that point in the ship where the movements were minimal. A year later Foss signed on for another trip with his brother Denis, this time from Barry Docks in South Wales to Nantes on the River Loire in France, conveying coal dust to a power station.

Returning to Barry Docks he glimpsed dimly the dimension of the vast unemployment gripping Britain. These were the early days of the Great Depression and something like two million were registered unemployed. Then and there he decided that for an ambitious lad like him the sea was not his profession. His thoughts turned to the sky.

While he waited for work at Saunders Roe, which had no work, Foss worked at a garage near the Linden Hall Hotel, pumping petrol into the customers' cars. He ground in valves and helped skilled men work on jobs and learned a great deal. He felt sure that he was headed on his chosen road of aviation. Then came the next step along the aviation path. A young aviation engineer visited the hotel. He told Foss that if he wanted to learn to fly, the most inexpensive way was to go to Germany where he could get cheap flying instruction, especially on gliders, because of the high rate of exchange of the Travellers Mark. Foss at once booked the first course in the spring of 1931 on the Wasserkuppe in Bavaria. Germany led the world in the art of gliding. This was no accident. Under the Versailles Treaty, following World War One, Germany was forbidden to train military pilots and so men who looked ahead to the building an air force used gliding to create a reservoir of men skilled in the basics of flying.

After a long rail journey down the Rhine and into the hinterland Foss reached the mountain, Wasserkuppe, upon which the gliding school stood. He found a number of German youth milling around the station and they clubbed together to hire a taxi. The school consisted of long, low army huts, divided into small rooms sleeping two each. Other huts were a dining room, cook house and workshops, with hangars alongside. The whole place was under several feet of snow and a blanket of fog. There was no possibility of gliding. They were given some ground instruction and sat around and filled the day as best they could. Foss found two Britishers on the course, one a dance band drummer in his mid-thirties and the other a student aged twenty-one.

Foss flew gliders during the day and found someone to give him lessons in German in the evenings. He became very good friends with Günther Groenhoff, who was a test pilot for the remarkable designer, Dr. Alexander Lippisch who had an experimental glider workshop nearby.[1] Groenhoff was the national sail-planing champion who held several long-distance and height records. Foss graduated to the small Klemm low-wing monoplane with a 60 hp engine.

That summer of 1931 in Marburg many of the students were being enrolled in the Sturm Abteilung Hitler legions. His friend Hans Stech was among them and he took Foss along to the parades - 'hundreds of marching youth in their brown shirts and swastika armbands, singing through the streets'. The young Englishman could see that the Nazis (National Socialists) were 'going places and capturing the youth with big aims and demanding discipline and sacrifices'. He was impressed, as most youngsters of seventeen would be. Foss wrote: 'At that time in England there was little get up and go spirit and young people yearned for it. In both Germany and Britain at that time there were growing unemployment and hopelessness, while politicians manoeuvred and denounced and looked out for their own interests.

'There were at least thirty political parties in Germany that year and I went to some of their parades. The most impressive and frequent were the Nazi parades, with hundreds of students in their brown shirts and breeches moving with discipline. The Nazi challenge was along the lines of an appeal to sacrifice and patriotism. Nazi posters proclaimed: 'The German youth does not smoke' and 'The German girl does not make up her face'. I saw little evidence of the evil thing Nazism was to become. One incident which I put down at the time to student high spirits happened at a lecture I attended at which a Jewish professor was shouted down and driven out of the hall with blows.'

In 1932 Foss returned to Germany to take an advanced gliding course near Kassel and he returned to Germany twice more before war closed the frontiers. He found a number of German soldiers enrolled on the course. He got on well with them and they with him and was invited into their barracks and saw the 'not permitted' tanks and other military equipment that they manned. 'I still did not realise the significance of their involvement in the gliding as a means of bypassing the ban on military flight training, as Germany began its building of an air force' he wrote. 'Nine years later, as I flew over Germany at night on bombing raids, I wondered if the German fighter pilots hunting me might be the same men with whom I learned to fly in Kassel. I comforted myself with the thought that those men had probably by now been promoted to Generals.'

He returned to Germany twice more before war closed the frontiers. As he travelled, his German had improved sufficiently for him to be taken as a German, though they detected something different from his accent. Germans from the south would ask, 'Aren't you from Hamburg?' or, in northern tones, 'Aren't you from the Black Forest?' Yet he could barely write a word and I had no grammar. In 1935 Foss had an added incentive to visit Germany. While ice skating at an ice rink, he met a delightful girl from the Harz Mountains in middle Germany named Renate. She was a blonde beauty and he became very fond of her and she of him. He went to her home and met her family. Nearby an air force flying school had been opened and he heard that they had lost eighteen pupils in flying accidents in the previous weeks. He thought that they must have been working under a great deal of pressure. One day Renate took Foss for a walk in the woods. She suddenly stopped, told him to stand still and went and looked around behind all the trees. Then she sat down and to his surprise, for he was expecting something different, began to whisper about a terrible place near there which she called a 'concentration camp'. 'Clearly it distressed and frightened her, but its horror did not impinge on my mind' wrote Foss. 'I was equally obtuse when I was travelling through the country and stayed the night in Bremen in the home of a young woman I had met. The family was Jewish and well-to-do. In the late evening we heard marching feet in the street below the flat, stamping, singing and shouting. The family were clearly mortally afraid and told me it was the SS (Hitler Bodyguard men). Then came terrifying sounds; glass smashing, the crash of doors being broken down, cries, shrieks and drunken oaths. I wanted to look out of the window, but the family begged me not to or make any sign that the flat was occupied. I had never seen people in such terror, but I didn't draw any conclusions from the incident, certainly not that such scenes would be allowed to grow in Germany and other countries until war became inevitable.'

Back in Britain Foss applied for a short service commission of six years as a pilot in the RAF and from a crowd of applicants he was one of just two who were selected. The selection board was no doubt impressed that both applicants stood out as a result that they had done something unusual. In the 1930s Foss had become a recruit to the Oxford Group (later Moral Re-Armament) which had challenged him to make a daily practice of 'trust and teamwork, coupled with asking God to show what is right,' as he put it. From this, he claimed, sprang much of his initiative and willingness to carry responsibility. Foss had trained as a sailor and had completed glider training in Germany and the other applicant had flown light aircraft in northern Canada; summer and winter. The RAF would teach them to fly all over again but first they had to wait nine months before the Service took them for training.

Foss went on to fly elderly biplanes like the Armstrong Whitworth Atlas and Siskin, of metal and fabric before progressing to the Handley Page Hinaidi biplane developed from the WWI Handley Page HP 500, at Upper Heyford. Early in 1934 he was posted to 7 Squadron at Worthy Down near Winchester in Hampshire to fly the Vickers Virginia biplane bomber. In 1935, when the squadron was first beginning to equip with Heyfords, it was thought for a time that they might have to fly them into combat after

Benito Mussolini, the Italian dictator invaded Ethiopia. Although Mussolini's invasion of Ethiopia did not involve Britain, in 1936 7 Squadron moved to one of the airfields under construction at Finningley near Doncaster in South Yorkshire with the promise of re-equipment with Wellesley bombers. In 1937, with about eighteen months of his short service to go before transfer to the Reserve, Foss - now a flight lieutenant - was posted to Andover, Hampshire, to 142 Squadron, equipped with Hawker Hinds and commanded by Squadron Leader Edward Collis de Virac Lart.[2]

Early in 1938 Foss flew to Manchester to collect the squadron's first Fairey Battle bomber and his next task was to convert all the pilots on to the low winged monoplane which had a crew of three. In May that same year they were ordered hurriedly to disperse their Battles into the fields around the airfield at Andover. Eighteen months later the Battle squadrons were sent to stop German tanks invading Belgium and Holland with disastrous results. The Battle squadrons were decimated and the aircraft was never heard of again as a fighting plane. On 3 September 1939 war with Germany was declared and Foss became a flying instructor.

In the late 1930s the RAF considered that bombers like the twin-engined Hampden, Wellington, Whitley and Blenheim with machine-gun turrets and flying in close formation to maximize defensive fire power against attacking fighter aircraft were unbeatable: It was even assumed that these aircraft did not need any form of fighter escort to reach and destroy their assigned targets. Events would soon shatter this illusion but in the 1930s for anyone who wanted to fly, the RAF was considered to be the best 'Flying Club' in which to do just that. In Germany however, the mood was quite different. During the Spanish Civil War of July 1936 to March 1939 volunteers from the Luftwaffe and the Wehrmacht Heer served with General Franco's Nationalists. Hugo Sperrle commanded the unit's aircraft formations. The 'Legion Kondor', upon establishment, consisted of the Kampfgruppe 88, with Ju 52 bombers and the Jagdgruppe 88 with Heinkel He 51 fighters, the reconnaissance Aufklärungsgruppe 88 (supplemented by the Aufklärungsgruppe See 88), an anti-aircraft group, the Flakbteilung 88 and a signals group, the Nachrichtenabteilung 88. Overall command was given to Hugo Sperrle, with Alexander Holle as chief of staff.[3] The Legion Kondor developed methods of terror bombing which were used widely in the Blitzkrieg tactic in World War II. The destruction of Guernica a town in northern Spain in Operation 'Rügen' at about 1630 on Monday, 26 April 1937 by waves of Ju 52 and He 51s commanded by Wolfram Freiherr von Richthofen resulted in perhaps 200-300 people killed but the number reported dead by the Basques was 1,654 dead and 889 wounded. In his journal for 30 April, von Richthofen wrote: 'When the first Junkers squadron arrived, there was smoke already everywhere (from the VB [VB/88] which had attacked with three aircraft); nobody would identify the targets of roads, bridge and suburb and so they just dropped everything right into the center. The 250s toppled a number of houses and destroyed the water mains. The incendiaries now could spread and become effective. The materials of the houses: tile roofs, wooden porches and half-timbering resulted in complete annihilation. Most inhabitants were away because of a holiday; a majority of the rest left town immediately at the beginning [of the bombardment]. A small number perished in shelters that were hit.'

When Britain declared war on Germany in September 1939 young RAF bomber pilots were enthusiastic and confident in their aircraft and equipment. The RAF believed that modern aircraft like the twin-engined Hampden, Wellington, Whitley and Blenheims with machine-gun turrets and flying in close formation to maximise defensive firepower against attacking fighter aircraft were unbeatable. The strategy was that these aircraft did not need fighter escort to reach and destroy targets but as the Luftwaffe would discover in the Battle of Britain (and much later the Americans from 1942 onward), this was all wishful thinking. The Handley Page Hampden and the Vickers Armstrong Wellington, Armstrong Whitworth Whitley and Bristol Blenheim, all twin engined bombers, were the mainstay of Bomber Command early in the war.

Like many of its genre, the Wellington was weakly armed but quite often it was this bomber's exploits, which featured in the headlines in the British press and sometimes in German papers as well. During the first month of the war the RAF mostly focused its bomber attacks against anti-shipping operations on the German Bight. Operations by 24 Wellingtons against elements of the German fleet at Heligoland on 3 September 1939 met with stiff opposition from fighters and flak. Although 'Freya' radar had warned the German gunners of the impending raid the thick cloud at their bombing altitude fortunately had hidden the Wellingtons from view. Four Messerschmitt Bf 109Ds of 1 Gruppe Zerstörergeschwader 26 at Jever led by Hauptmann Friedrich-Karl Dickore climbed and intercepted the bombers after they had bombed but their aim was spoiled by cloudy conditions. Even so, the two pairs of Bf 109Ds damaged two of the Wellingtons in the attack. One pair attacked from above and the other pair from below. Leutnant Günther Specht, who damaged one of the Wellingtons, was shot down by return fire. Specht ditched in the sea and he was later rescued. The German had been wounded in the face and later had to have his left eye removed.[4] Luckily for the Wellington crews, the three remaining Bf 109Ds were low on fuel and they broke off the engagement, while sixteen Bf 109D/Es and eight of I./ZG26's new Bf 110Cs arrived too late to intercept the bombers.

Continued bombing operations by the inexperienced Wellington crews were brave but foolhardy; especially when one considers that many of their battle-hardened opponents had honed their fighting skills in the Legion Kondor in Spain. On 14 December twelve Wellingtons on shipping searches were attacked Bf 109Es of II./JG77 that had taken off from Wangerooge together with four Bf 110s of 2/ZG26 at Jever and five Wellingtons were shot down. Air Vice-Marshal John Eustace Arthur 'Jackie' Baldwin, AOC 3 Group was compelled to compare it to the Charge of the Light Brigade. Worse was to follow. RAF bombers mounted a heavy attack against shipping off Wilhelmshaven on 18 December in what came to be known as the 'Battle of the Heligoland Bight'. Twenty-four Wellingtons on 9 Squadron, 37 Squadron and 149 Squadron formed up over Norfolk heading for the island of Heligoland. Two aircraft aborted the operation due to mechanical defects, but the remaining 22 pursued the attack and as the Wellingtons approached the German coast near Cuxhaven, Bf 109 and Bf 110 fighters of Jagdgeschwader 1, guided by radar plots of the incoming formation made by the experimental 'Freya' early warning radar installation at Wangerooge and directed by ground control, were waiting. The Wellingtons were easy pickings and the RAF crews were caught cold as the cunning German fighter pilots made beam attacks from above. Previously, attacks had been made from the rear but now the German pilots tore into the bombers safe in the knowledge that the ventral gun was powerless at this angle of attack. They knew too that the front and rear turrets could not traverse sufficiently to draw a bead on them. For almost half an hour 44 Luftwaffe fighters tore into the Wellingtons. In addition to the twelve Wellingtons lost and the two written off in crashes, three others were damaged in crash landings in England. Luftwaffe fighter claims for aircraft destroyed on the raid totalled 38, which later, were pared down to 26 or 27. Among these, Oberleutnant Johannes Steinhoff's claim for two destroyed was reduced to one.[5] Hauptmann Wolfgang Falck of 2./ZG76 who claimed two Wellingtons, force-landed his aircraft on Wangerooge after return fire from the bombers damaged his engines. Only two of I/ZG76's sixteen claims were disallowed, one of which was Falck's second. Falck's wingman, Unteroffizier Fresia, was credited with two confirmed destroyed. Leutnant Uellenbeck limped back to Jever with no fewer than 33 bullet holes in his 110.

'I was with the second formation on a course of 120 degrees, about fifty kilometres to the north of Ameland. Suddenly we came upon two Wellingtons flying 300 metres beneath us, on the opposite heading. I attacked the leader from the side and it caught fire. Then I opened fire on the second one, from the left and above. When he didn't budge I moved into position 300 metres behind him and opened up with everything. The nose of the bomber fell and it dived towards the sea. It was at this time that I was hit by a bullet, between my neck and left shoulder; the round went clean through me and hit Unteroffizier Dombrowski the radio operator on his left wrist.'

Uellenbeck's claims for two destroyed was upheld. Though RAF crews claimed twelve German single and twin-engined fighters, just three Bf 109 fighters were lost and a handful damaged or hit.

Wolfgang Falck, born on 19 August 1910 in Berlin, had begun his pilot training at the Deutsche Verkehrsfliegerschule (German Air Transport School) at Schleissheim on 7 April 1931. The course he and 29 other trainees attended was called Kameradschaft 31 among whom were men like Hannes Trautloft and Günther Lützow. Falck graduated from the Deutsche Verkehrfliegerschule 19 February 1932. In February 1933 he attended the Infantry School at Dresden for officer training and made Leutnant in October 1934. In March 1935 Falck became an instructor at the Deutsche Verkehrsfliegerschule at Schleissheim and in April 1936 he was promoted to Oberleutnant and transferred to JG132 'Richthofen' at Jüterbog-Damm as Staffelkapitän of 5 Staffel. In July 1938 Falck was appointed Staffelkapitän of 8 Staffel of the new JG132 at Fürstenwalde. The new unit was later redesignated I./ZG76 and equipped with the Bf 110 Zerstörer fighter. Falck led 2./ZG76 during the Polish campaign from Ohlau in Silesia, gaining three victories over Polish Air Force aircraft. The unit was then relocated to Jever to protect the northern seaboard and the Kriegsmarine naval bases.

As well as Falck the 'Battle of the Heligoland Bight' also produced another pilot destined to find fame with the Nachtjagd, although success at night at first seemed to elude him. Leutnant Helmut 'Bubi' ('Nipper') Lent of 1./ZG76 in a lone Bf 110 Zerstörer was one of the pilots ordered to intercept and engage the attacking bomber force and he put in claims for three of the Wellingtons when he landed at Jever. Two of these, which were shot down at 1430 and 1445, were later confirmed. Both aircraft were on 37 Squadron and were captained by Flying Officer P. A. Wimberley and Australian Flying Officer Oliver John Trevor Lewis respectively and they crashed in the shallow sea off Borkum. Wimberley survived but his crew died. Lewis and his crew were killed also. It is likely that his third claim may have been Wellington IA N2396 LF-J on 37 Squadron, piloted by Sergeant H. Ruse, which he crash-landed on the sand dunes of Borkum with two men dead. Lent was refused the victory over Wimberley, as the Wellington was attacked by Lent after it had already been badly damaged and was about to crash. The Wellington was credited to Carl-August Schumacher. Lent later flew combat operations in Norway with 1./ZG76, where he scored seven victories and was awarded the Iron Cross 1st Class.

Blenheim light bombers fared no better than the Wellingtons on daylight shipping searches in the North Sea. In the first and only encounter between Blenheims and Bf 110s, on 10 January 1940 in mid-morning, nine Blenheims on 110 Squadron led by Squadron Leader Ken Doran DFC took off from Wattisham in Suffolk in three 'vics' for a North Sea shipping reconnaissance. At roughly the same time, Hauptmann Wolfgang Falck led four Bf 110s of 2./ZG76 from Jever airfield near Wilhelmshaven on a westerly course over the North Sea for a routine patrol. When flying 200 kilometres north of Terschelling Island, one of the German pilots spotted a handful of specks on the horizon and warned his leader on R/T. Swiftly, the sleek Zerstörers curved onto the course of the British intruders. Within seconds, Falck identified the dots as Bristol Blenheims and ordered his Flight to attack. At 1152 the fighters dropped onto the tails of the Blenheims, which at that time, having no under armament, were very vulnerable to attack from below so Doran led the formation of three vics of three aircraft down to sea level in plus 9 boost. It was to no avail - Schwarmführer Falck's cannon shells struck home and Blenheim P4859 of 110 Squadron exploded on the surface of the sea. Twenty-six year old Sergeant John Henry Hanne, married, of Maida Vale, London, his 23-year old observer, Sergeant George Llewelyn Williams, of Ynsddu, Monmouthshire and nineteen-year old AC1 Edwin Vick, WOp/AG of Morecombe, Lancashire, were killed. Two other Blenheims on 110 Squadron were badly shot up during the 25 minute engagement. N6203 crashed on return at Manby in Lincolnshire and N6213 was written off at Wattisham. These were claimed destroyed by Leutnants Helmut Fahlbusch and Maximilian Graeff. After expending all their ammunition, the four German fighter pilots broke off the fight and jubilantly flew back to Jever, all with slight damage. Following this encounter Doran continued with the reconnaissance, which earned him a bar to his DFC. [6]

During the period from 14 February to the end of March 1940 Blenheims of 2 Group completed another 250 North Sea shipping sweeps, which resulted in the loss of only four aircraft and their crews. They all fell victim to German fighters. One of these was N6211 on 110 Squadron, shot down by Hauptmann Falck of 2./ZG76 on 17 February north of the Dutch Frisian Islands. Sergeant Frederick John Raymond Bigg, the 27-year old pilot, Sergeant William Barnard Woods, the 21-year old observer and AC1 Jack Orchard the 20-year old WOp/AG were reported missing and are commemorated on the Memorial at Runnymede for those members of the RAF and Commonwealth Air Forces who have no known grave.[7] That same month Hauptmann Falck was appointed Gruppenkommandeur ZG1 at Düsseldorf. The Gruppe was relocated to the Baltic coast in April and on 9 April Falck led the unit during the invasion of Denmark. He recorded his seventh (and final) victory, shooting down a Danish Fokker C.V taking off from Værløse.

Serious losses finally convinced the Air Staff that a profound change of its daylight policy was necessary. Following heavy Wellington and Blenheim losses in daylight the elderly Whitley squadrons were immediately employed in night leaflet dropping operations and made no appearance in daylight at all. When RAF Bomber Command took the decision in May 1940 to start strategic bombing of Germany by night, there was little the Luftwaffe could do to counter these early raids. The subject of night fighting was raised at a conference of German service chiefs just before the war and according to Kommodore Josef Kammhuber who was present at the conference it was dismissed out of hand by Hermann Göring with the words, 'Night fighting! It will never come to that!'

Up until May 1940 the night air defence of the Reich was almost entirely the province of the flak arm of the Luftwaffe. No specialised night fighting arm existed though one fighter Gruppe (IV./(N)JG2) was undertaking experimental 'Helle Nachtjagd' (illuminated night fighting) sorties with the aid of searchlights in northern Germany and in the Rhineland. IV./(N)JG2 flew the Bf 109D with the cockpit hood removed as a precaution against the pilots being blinded by the glare of the searchlights.

On the night of 25/26 April Oberfeldwebel Hermann Förster of the 11th Staffel NJG2 shot down a Hampden on a mine-laying operation near Sylt, the first Bomber Command aircraft to be shot down by a fighter at night. The aircraft was L1319 on 49 Squadron. Pilot Officer Arthur Herbert Benson and crew were killed. Forster went on to claim two Fokker G.Is in Raum ('Box') 'Rotterdam' on 10 May and Hampden P4286 on 44 Squadron at Oosterhout on 14/15 May. Pilot Officer Leslie James Ashfield and his crew were killed. On 24 May Förster destroyed a Blenheim at Borkum. Förster also claimed Hampden I P1178 on 83 Squadron at Often near Aachen on 3/4 June. Flying Officer Francis John Haydon and crew were killed. On 9 July he destroyed a Whitley twenty kilometres north of Heligoland. Forster joined 2./JG27, scoring another six daylight victories. Hermann Förster was killed in action on 14 December 1941 flying with JG27 Afrika in North Africa. His last victory was on 10 December when he shot down a Boston III fifteen kilometres east of Bir Hacheim to take his final total to twelve Abschüsse.

On 22 June 1940 Hauptmann Wolfgang Falck, Kommandeur, I./ZG1 who had some experience with radar-directed night-fighting sorties in the Bf 110 flying from Aalborg in northern Denmark that April, was ordered to form the basis of a Nachtjagd, or night fighting arm, by establishing the first night fighter Gruppe, I./NJG1. While at Aalborg Falck had prepared a comprehensive tactical appraisal report on night interception. Thus after I./ZG1's participation in the Battle of France General Albert Kesselring ordered Falck to take his unit to Düsseldorf and reform for the night fighter role. On 26 June Falck was appointed Kommodore of NJG1 and IV./(N)JG2 was incorporated into the first Nachtjagd Geschwader as III./NJG1. From Düsseldorf airfield Bf 110s and Do 17Zs of NJG1 undertook experimental night-fighting sorties in defence of the Ruhr with the aid of one flak searchlight regiment. In July the creation of a true night air defence for the Third Reich was dramatically accelerated when Göring ordered Josef Kammhuber to set up of a full-scale night fighting arm. Within three months, Kammhuber's organisation was remodelled into Fliegerkorps XII and by the end of 1940 the infant Nachtjagd had matured into three searchlight battalions and five night fighter Gruppen.[8] Major Falck received the Ritterkreuz in October 1940. He was to command NJG1 for three years and in partnership with General Josef Kammhuber develop a highly effective night fighter force.

Kammhuber organized the night fighting units into a chain known to the British as the 'Kammhuber Line', in which a series of radar stations with overlapping coverage were layered three deep from Denmark to the middle of France, each covering a zone about 32 kilometres long (north-south) and twenty kilometres wide (east-west). Each control centre or zone was known as a 'Himmelbett' (literally translated, 'bed of heavenly bliss' or 'four-poster bed' because of the four night-fighter control zones), consisting of a 'Freya' radar with a range of about 100 kilometres, a number of searchlights spread through the cell and one primary and one backup night fighter assigned to the cell. RAF bombers flying into Germany or France would have to cross the line at some point and the radar would direct a searchlight to illuminate the aircraft. Once this had happened other manually controlled searchlights would also pick up the aircraft and the night fighter would be directed to intercept the now-illuminated bomber. However, demands by Bürgermeisters in Germany led to the recall of the searchlights to the major cities. Later versions of the 'Himmelbett' added two Würzburg radars, with a range of about thirty kilometres. Unlike the early-warning 'Freya' radar, Würzburgs were accurate (and complex) tracking radars. One would be locked onto the night fighter as soon as it entered the cell. After the Freya picked up a target the second Würzburg would lock onto it, thereby allowing controllers in the 'Himmelbett' centre to obtain continual readings on the positions of both aircraft, controlling them to a visual interception. To aid in this, a number of the night fighters were fitted with a short-range infrared searchlight mounted in the nose of the aircraft to illuminate the target and a receiver to pick up the reflected energy known as 'Spanner' or 'Spanneranlage' ('Spanner' installation) literally translated, a 'peeping Tom'. 'Spanner I' and 'Spanner II', a passive device that in theory used the heat from engine exhausts to detect its target, were not very successful.

Nachtjagd's first official victory over the Reich was credited to Oberfeldwebel Paul Förster of 8./NJG1 when off Heligoland at 0250 hours on 9 July he destroyed Whitley V N1496 on 10 Squadron at Dishforth. Flight Lieutenant D. A. Ffrench-Mullen and his four crew who were on a bombing operation to Kiel, survived and were taken prisoner. Förster was a former soldier who trained as a pilot in 1936 and as a Zerstörer pilot he scored three day victories in 1940. After he was shot down and wounded he was assigned to the role of flying instructor and later served as a staff officer. In 1943 he retrained as a night fighter pilot and on 1 June 1943 he joined 1./NJG1 where Förster achieved four more night victories.

Often called 'Father of the Nachtjagd' Werner Streib, born on 13 June 1911 in Pforzheim, helped develop the operational tactics used by the Nachtjagd during the early and with the likes of Wolfgang Falck made the Luftwaffe's night-fighter arm an effective fighting force against the RAF bombing offensive. After a spell in banking and finance, Streib had joined the Wehrmacht as an infantryman. A transfer to the Luftwaffe, as an observer in a reconnaissance unit followed and later he trained as a fighter pilot. In 1937 he was assigned to Jagdgeschwader 2 'Richthofen' at Jüterbog-Damm. He then became a Bf 110 Zerstörer pilot in Wolfgang Falck's ZG1 as the war began. The first of Streib's 66 Abschüsse and the only one in daylight was a Bristol Blenheim on 10 May 1940. By the end of July I./NJG1 operating from Gütersloh airfield near Münster had a fortunate spell of operations, destroying six bombers in the 'Helle Nachtjagd' system. Streib, now Staffelkapitän, 2./NJG1, shot down Whitley V P5007 on 51 Squadron in the early hours on 20 July 25 kilometres northwest of Kiel. Flight Lieutenant Stephen Edward Frederick Curry and three others on his crew were killed and one was taken prisoner. This was followed on 21/22 July by Whitley V N1487 on 78 Squadron flown by Sergeant Victor Clarence Monkhouse ten kilometres north of Münster. All the crew were killed. Streib soon added to his score, claiming two Wellingtons on 30/31 August and three bombers on 30 September/1 October. Kammhuber realised that 'Helle Nachtjagd', entirely dependent as it was on weather conditions and radar-guided searchlights was only a short-term solution; it simply could not penetrate thick layers of cloud or industrial haze over the Ruhr and other industrial centres in the Reich. He soon concentrated all his energies in developing an efficient radar-controlled air defence system.

In July 1940 Patrick Foss was promoted Squadron Leader and he joined 115 Squadron at Marham in Norfolk which was equipped with Wellingtons. 'At the time' wrote Foss[9] 'there were three RAF Groups operating night bombers, mainly against Germany. The Wellingtons were in 3 Group, Whitleys in 4 Group and Hampdens in 5 Group. Other Groups controlled the light bombers, fighters, coastal reconnaissance and so on. All three Groups of night bombers had twin-engined aircraft with crews of between four and six. Bomber Command's attack plan called for raids each night, if weather allowed, on such 'military' targets as oil plants, factories, harbours and railway marshalling yards. When the moon was minimal one Group would fly each night. When there was a moon the three Groups doubled up, which meant we did a raid every other night. A raid was a major operation; a station complement of two thousand or more was needed to launch up to twenty Wellingtons on one night.

'Aircrews lived a strange life. On our off days, on these comfortable, long-established stations, we lived like country gentlemen in a fair degree of luxury and almost as if the war did not exist. On flying nights, we stole out like cat burglars to venture out, each aircraft singly, over the seas and into enemy territory, where we felt hunted and watched every minute. We flew in a high degree of tension. The sight of shells bursting in the sky ahead, often seen for an hour or more before we reached a target, had a mesmeric effect on me as my imagination leaped around. Highly subjective feelings kept me thinking more about my skin than about the people in the dark far below me. I did not want to die, nor have my courage tested by a shell burst or a fighter's attack.

'I realised somehow I had to conquer this deep desire for self-preservation and treat the whole business as a surgeon would an operation. As each trip brought more near-misses by shells or close encounters with fighters, I became more and more conscious of the dangers and I also began to question whether what we were doing was of any real use in the war. This helped me to understand why some men, their fear building up raid after raid, failed to press home attacks on their targets and instead dumped their bombs in the area before turning for home. It meant, of course, that they told lies to the debriefing officers and their aircrew went along with them because they, too, were afraid.

'It was the responsibility of a flight and squadron commander to know his men and understand the build-up of pressures, raid after raid. Each captain was different and the commander had to judge when each crew should come off operations to allow them to rest and re-think, as well as to train new crews in all that they had experienced. At this time Command had set a tour of 31 trips. The average loss rate was around 25 trips, so every raid over 25 gave a crew the sense they were lucky to be still alive.

'During World War I men were treated as cowards when they lost their nerve; and some authorities took the same line early in World War II. It proved to be a useless course; it encouraged no one to do better. The desirable way was to get a man to be honest and admit his fears and seek the support of his brother officers. When I did this with men, particularly when I became squadron commander in Malta, it seemed to have a profound effect on them and on me too. I learned that the more afraid the average man is, the more likely he is to push home attacks and take risks, if only to prove he is not afraid. The bravest men, I found, were those who conquered their fear by facing it, not those who had no idea of the danger of what they did.

'I could see that we lived double lives - our 'gentlemen's lives' and our almost secret nefarious outings to Germany. It was a very personal war. If we did not fight it, no one else would. Almost all of us experienced 'twitch' and other symptoms of stress in the eyes, the lips or the bowels. But the stress did not lead us to dump bombs or pull away from attack. It boosted morale in a remarkable way, so long as it was contained by a relationship with each other which was honest and caring. Looking back at the raids we flew in the early days to attack 'military' targets, the marshalling yards and factories, I shudder at how amateur we were. The targets for new crews were the big railway yards at Hamm and Soest, on the edge of the Ruhr industrial area - Ham and Eggs was the obvious crew slang for them.[10] They were large area targets and not so heavily defended as was the Ruhr area itself. There were planners who believed that bombing a railway yard would cause delays and disruption of communications. My own experience in 1938, before the war, of trial bombings of railway lines at the Army Corps of Transport railway experimental centre had convinced me - and the Army - that damage could be repaired in a few hours and did not cause much delay in a marshalling yard. These attacks were rather artificial, by low-flying Battles, but war experience confirmed that without continuous bombardment the yards were an unproductive target. However, our new crews did gain the experience of flying over Germany, of being shelled and hunted by fighters and of just how difficult it was to identify a military target from a great height in European weather.

'My first bombing raid was on Gelsenkirchen in the Ruhr - the target was a factory. When we arrived in the target area thick smoke and layers of cloud made it impossible to identify anything as small as a factory. I was very suspicious of our visual navigation, although I had an excellent navigator and had myself been an experienced navigator in peacetime. Since we left England we had seen nothing to pinpoint our position. We could only release our bombs in the general area and turn for home. The German reaction with anti-aircraft flak and searchlights was strong and accurate. As we flew towards Marham, 300 miles distant, our crew talked about the experience. Our conclusion was that if that was the worst we would meet, we had some chance of surviving our tour of operations. But in my mind was the question whether we had bombed the right town, let alone the specific factory. On this and other raids our great problem was finding and identifying a military target by our available means of navigation - map-reading, calculation and hoping to find some identification near our target. Our weather forecasters had only a general and limited idea of the local conditions 300 miles from the UK. They seemed unable to forecast smog or the height of cloud layers.

'On this first raid my navigator and I had hoped that we might see the river Rhine and get a fix from that, but we never saw the river. There was one aid on which we came to rely heavily, the German range-type wireless stations, which they switched on to aid their own aircraft. We took bearings with our loop aerial. But these only helped us to get into a four or five mile area around the target. There came a night when we filed into the briefing room before a raid and were horrified to be told that no German radio station was on the air. It would not have surprised me to learn that each of our aircraft hit a different target that night.

'On my next raid, to an oil processing plant at Wesseling, near Cologne we carried a photo flash bomb with our other bombs so that we could photograph our target. My navigator and I worked out a track to strike the Rhine at its junction with the Moselle. From there we would count the loops in the Rhine until we reached the one on which Wesseling lay. As we approached the Wesseling curve, my bomb aimer lay below me, looking down through the aiming window, directing me by intercom, while the other four crew manned the fore and rear gun turrets and the look-out in the upper astrodome. The second pilot sat beside me, acting as counsellor, lookout and ready to take over the controls, should I be wounded. In order to get a good photograph, the flash bomb had to be dropped at a precise height and the camera, fixed in the aircraft, had to be aimed so that the lens did not pick up the direct light of the flash, when the bomb burst after falling to about one thousand feet above the ground. The flash activated a photo cell which closed the camera shutter. This photography required that the Wellington be flown straight and level on a long run in. Straight and level at a precise height was a delight for German flak gunners!

'This was another murky night, with a layer of cloud at the height we had planned to drop the flash bomb. We could see a Whitley bomber caught in the beams of searchlights, directly above our target, lit up by the reflection from the clouds as though in bright moonlight. Shells were bursting all round him. We decided to glide in below him, hoping the defences would not pick us up while they concentrated on the Whitley. We arrived over the target without being picked up and let go our bombs and the flash bomb. When the flash went off it seemed as though the defences were blinded for a few seconds. Then all hell was let loose at us. Shells began to burst around us; we could hear the explosions and see the black puffs of smoke. Our rear-gunner called that he thought he saw the lights of a fighter nearby. The searchlights bracketed us and I threw the Wellington into twists and turns to try to throw them off. They did not let go. Any moment could be our last. I sweated with fear as I pulled and twisted the controls. Then I offered up a prayer to be shown what to do.

'At that moment an extraordinary impression came over me. I seemed to be outside the Wellington, away in the sky. I could see the aircraft in the lights and shell bursts, as though I were a spectator. Then I saw how I might break out of the defences if I made a highly dangerous manoeuvre. As I saw this, I had a feeling of confidence that what I should do was right. Then I was back in the Wellington, frightened and heaving at the controls. I pulled the aircraft up into a big stall turn, fell over and spiralled down towards the earth. Almost at once the lights shut off and we were falling in utter darkness. I eased the aircraft out of the dive to be parallel with the unseen ground. At that moment a single searchlight came on and lay along our track, showing us that we were a few hundred feet above the countryside and lighting up hills ahead of us. The light went out and we climbed to avoid the hills and return to operating height for the flight home.

'Back in the interrogation room at Marham we commented, rather smugly, the Commander-in-Chief calls our bombing 'gardening' [not to be confused with minelaying operations which were called 'Gardening']. Air Marshal Sir Charles Portal, Chief of Bomber Command, had been invited by our Station Commander to witness a demonstration of dive bombing by a Wellington. Afterwards the C-in-C talked to us about the pin-pointing of targets by night. He said we were digging up the German countryside with our bombs. It was not until 1942 with the introduction of the pathfinder force, which used radar to fix their positions and marked them with fires that the main force bombers could be sure where the area of the target of the night lay. A few minutes after our 'gardening' the print of our flash photo revealed a factory in a curve of the Rhine with four bombs bursting on the roof! Unfortunately, when we compared the photo with our detailed map of the target, it in no way fitted. Someone suggested that perhaps the map was wrong. Wearily, we trailed off to bed. Three weeks later a report arrived from the Photo Interpretation Unit. They had identified the place where our bombs had fallen - a tank factory in Cologne, ten miles from our intended target!

'When the Luftwaffe made their bombing attacks on London in July 1940, the Prime Minister ordered us to attack Berlin. This was the longest trip we had ever attempted in the Wellington, close to our maximum range with full tanks and minimum bomb load. We set off for Berlin with half a gale blowing from the west, low and middle cloud and murk on the ground. We were given strict instructions to turn back after three and three-quarter hours flying, wherever we were, to be sure of returning to Britain against the gale. As I reached three and three-quarter hours we thought we might be in the Berlin area. We had failed to get any fixes on the route and the weather was heavy cloud and total blackness. We glimpsed below us lakes and forests, but never a light or other indication of a city. There was nothing worth bombing and no time for a search. We turned for home and began to plug back against the gale. After an hour or so we saw lights on the ground, which we identified as an airfield working night fighters. We made to bomb them but our bomb releases failed to work. We plugged on and finally, over the North Sea, succeeded in losing our bomb load, saving us some petrol. We landed at Marham with less than thirty minutes of fuel remaining after eight and a half hours in the air. Our other crews returned with similar stories. No one was sure he had hit Berlin. We hoped other stations had had more luck.

'A few days later, we were ordered to bomb the Channel ports, Calais and Le Havre, our shortest trips ever. They were on brilliant moonlit nights and we could clearly see the lines of barges waiting to carry the German army to invade Britain. From 6,000 feet they looked like match sticks. We had filled every hook with high explosives and fire bombs. The Germans had only deployed light flak guns and these were less accurate at our height. I saw fires break out along the docksides and in the barges, followed by many explosions. On one raid I saw quite clearly water jets being played by fire-fighters - the first time we had seen a result of our attacks. Thanks to the efforts of our fighters, the Germans never achieved the air supremacy over southern England which they needed for a successful invasion. However, the destruction wrought by our bombers on the ports and barges must also have played a part in their decision to call off the invasion. That decision ultimately meant losing the war.

'In August 1940 we made a long trip towards Magdeburg to attack an aircraft factory at Bernberg. The night was clear and moonlit and I could see the Hartz Mountains where I had visited friends in 1932. We passed near Goslar, the home of Renate, my pre-war girl friend. When we reached our estimated time of arrival we were delighted to see below us a cross of big runways and sheds, but I was not sure that this was our target so put the second pilot in my seat and went down to lie beside the bomb aimer to have a better look. I had been troubled by seeing, five miles to the south, bombs bursting and flak coming up and wondered if that was the right target. As we lay there, trying to decide, suddenly our Wellington went into a steep dive and then we saw our bombs leave and crash through the roofs of the sheds. As we pulled out of the dive, chunks of the roofs flew past us, very close. At once guns opened fire and I could feel strikes on our aircraft. At the same time a force, like a giant hand, seized our Wellington and threw it upwards. Once we were away from the target area the second pilot started making excuses for the attack, saying we were running out of time and he was sure that we had found the right target.

'I went all around the aircraft to see what damage we had sustained and found nothing that was serious. However, I was very troubled that each of our three compasses seemed to be giving a different reading. We attempted to verify them by the moon, but without moon tables or a sextant we failed. So we averaged the three readings and steered a general westerly direction. Clouds now prevented us from fixing a position. When we expected to reach the coast we saw a coastline and a flashing beacon. In a discussion with the crew, one of them thought the beacon might be on the English coast, so we flew close and fired our recognition signal, a very light giving the colours of the day. It was answered by light flak and we dashed out to sea. In a couple of minutes we passed over a bund and then wave crests. This convinced me we must have crossed a part of the Dutch Zuider Zee and if so we were embarking on a flight of about 150 miles across the North Sea.

'I checked our fuel gauges and found several were showing nil and others only small amounts of fuel, maybe half an hour's running, certainly not enough to get us beyond the middle of the North Sea. We seemed bound for an emergency landing at sea, something none of us had rehearsed; indeed, I had no idea even how to activate the dinghies. I doubted whether air/sea rescue boats operated so far out. I asked the crew for their suggestions. One option was to turn back and land on the beach and surrender ourselves. No one would hear of that. So we continued westwards. As we strained our eyes looking for land, we kept seeing it, only to find it was cloud on the water.

'When I asked the wireless operator to try and get a bearing from the Direction Finding service in England, he told me his wireless was playing up, but he would try. Then he told me he could hear several SOS calls and that meant that the D/F stations would concentrate on them. I insisted he keep trying and he finally received a bearing. I plotted it on the chart; it was almost due north and put us out in the English Channel.

'I couldn't believe it. I asked our operator if the bearing could be a false one put out by a German station. They were known to give false bearings to our aircraft in distress. If we were half way across the North Sea and turned north we would go down in the cold sea en route to Iceland. The operator assured me it was a good bearing from an English station. I swallowed my doubts and turned north. The sun was up, but cloud was solid below us. Suddenly there was a gap and I saw a green field. I pulled back the engines and dived for this break. I saw fields dotted with high posts and other anti-invasion obstructions; it must be the south of England. I gingerly opened up our engines again, noting that every fuel gauge registered empty.

'Suddenly, right ahead, appeared a grass airfield, apparently empty. I dared not circle to look more closely because if we banked our wings the petrol might run away from the outlets and stop the engines. I shut down and went straight in. As we ran across the field I noted large piles of earth dotted about. We came to a halt beside a flying control building with no sign of life. We got out and began to look for someone. We came upon a sandbagged shelter and out of it peered a steel-helmeted RAF figure, a Pilot Officer.

'What's this place?' we asked. 'This is West Malling' (in mid-Kent).

'Funny sort of airfield,' I commented, 'full of molehills.'

'Not moles' he replied, 'unexploded bombs; they've been going off all through the night.'

'We jumped down into his hole, telephoned Marham and requested to be re-fuelled.

'I went and looked over the Wellington and decided it was safe to fly on. A refueller arrived, manned by some very nervous airmen. We had never been refuelled so fast; then they were gone. We learned that on the previous day a big raid by German bombers flying towards London had been met by RAF fighters over West Malling and had dumped their bombs before turning back to France. The airfield had been evacuated, its fighters sent elsewhere. Only this one flying control officer had been left. We rumbled across the airfield to take off, my heart in my mouth, fearing our vibration might set off an explosion.

'Back in the interrogation room at Marham our plots and timings were carefully analysed. Another crew had claimed to have hit the target factory and set it on fire. It was probably the fire we had seen to the south of us. The other Captain was a very experienced pilot from civil aviation and he was convinced he had hit the right place. We put a bold face on our story, although I had doubts. To complicate matters, the Group Air Vice-Marshal had telephoned to congratulate the station and added, 'There is an immediate award of a Distinguished Flying Cross in this, please give me the name.' Both crews were bone weary and it seemed impossible to decide who had hit the right target. The Station Commander invited us to toss a coin and the other Captain won. I was glad of it, especially when, a few days later, he was shot down. His wife had something to show off his gallantry.[11]

'Operations over Europe became steadily more hazardous week by week as the Germans developed their air defence from the coast to Germany, with permanent sites for radar, searchlights, flak and night fighters with their elaborate control. One night, as we returned from a raid on the Ruhr, our rear-gunner reported that he could see a fighter following us. He had first reported its white downward recognition light (which helped his gunners on the ground.) Then he reported blue and gold lights in the cockpit and he could count two heads. I asked him to keep giving me their distance behind us, estimated with his gunsight, but on no account to fire. I reckoned our firing would give our enemy a pinpoint to aim at and his cannons were much more deadly than our two Vickers guns firing at a head-on fighter. He crept up on us slowly. I turned left, he followed us. I turned right and dived and again he followed us. It was clear he could not see us, but had some device by which he could follow us. Before the war I had exercised with ground operators who listened to aircraft approaching England for air defence purposes and I had helped them to calibrate. In the course of doing this I heard a hint that there were other ways of picking up and fixing aircraft flying in. So I had a suspicion that this German fighter might be carrying similar equipment.

'As we made our way to the Belgian coast we played a cat and mouse game. I could not throw him off and he did not have enough confidence to open fire. Finally I instructed the rear-gunner to aim and, when the fighter came within 150 yards, to shout. At once I pulled the Wellington up into a high stall. We hung there on the engines and then fell out of the stall, to find that the fighter was about one hundred yards ahead of us. He immediately began hunting around to find us on his screen, but he couldn't see backwards. At the coast he dived away and we continued on our way to Marham.

'Our Intelligence people appeared to be very interested in our report of this encounter. One hinted that this was a very early report of German airborne radar in use. The RAF had its own disinformation campaign about radar. Before each sortie bomber aircrews were handed red lozenges - we called them cat's eyes - and were informed that they were carrots, to help us see better in the dark. After the war, I heard that the Germans, after many interrogations of shot-down crews, had put scientists to work to investigate the powers of the carrot, perhaps to explain their own bomber losses by night over Britain.'

On the other side of the North Sea Nachtjagd pilots began to rack up high scores. Oberfeldwebel Paul Gildner of 3./NJG1 claimed three aircraft over the Netherlands during September 1940. Gildner, born on 1 February 1914 in Nimptsch (Silesia), had volunteered for the Wehrmacht in 1934 as an infantry officer but had transferred to the Luftwaffe. Gildner was already serving as a Oberfeldwebel Zerstörer pilot when war began in September 1939, flying the Messerschmitt Bf 110 with 1/ZG1. Gildner flew intensively during the European campaign in May-June 1940 and also flew sorties during early stages of the Battle of Britain. In August 1940 after training in night flying he was transferred to 4./NJG1). He scored his first Abschuss on 3 September 1940 when he shot down Hampden I P4370 on 144 Squadron (which he identified as a Whitley) and which was detailed to bomb Ludwigshafen. The bomber crashed near Sittard just on the German side of the border with Holland at 0045 hours on the night of the 2nd/3rd when 84 aircraft of RAF Bomber Command attacked a wide variety of targets in Germany, France, Holland and Italy. Pilot Officer R. S. A. Churchill and one crewmember were taken prisoner; the two others were killed. On the night of 18/19th at 2230 hours near Groenlo, Gildner shot down Whitley V P5008 on 58 Squadron, which had been detailed to bomb Hamm. Sergeant Albert Alfred Ellis Crossland and crew were killed. Two hours later, at Zieuwent, Gildner shot down another Whitley, N1425 on 77 Squadron, which was detailed to bomb Soest. Pilot Officer Peter Ernest Eldridge and his crew were killed. After Falck and Streib, Gildner was the third Nachtjagd pilot to be awarded the Ritterkreuz, on 9 July 1941 after his 14th Abschuss.

On the evening of 16 October 1940 Leutnant Ludwig Becker of 4./NJG1 and his bordfunker Unteroffizier Josef Staub claimed Nachtjagd's first ground radar-directed kill at Oosterwolde. Ludwig Becker was born on 22 August 1911 in Dortmund-Aplerbeck in the Province of Westphalia, a province of the Kingdom of Prussia. Joining the Luftwaffe volunteers in 1934, by 1939 he was a test pilot and a Leutnant in the Luftwaffe reserve. Serving with NJG1, he crashed a Messerschmitt Bf 110 near Winterswijk on 30 August 1940. On what was a perfect moonlight night on the 16th of October flying a Dornier Do 17Z-10 equipped with the experimental 'Spanner' night-vision device they were guided onto the tail of a Wellington by Jägerleitoffizier (JLO or fighter-control officer) Leutnant Hermann Diehl of the experimental 'Freya' station at Nunspeet in Holland. The Wellington, L7844 KX-I on 311 Czechoslovak Squadron at East Wretham, was being flown by Pilot Officer Bohumil Landa. Becker reported:

'At about 21.20 I was controlled by Leutnant Diehl at Nunspeet using Freya mit Zusatz and Würzburg, using Morse on the tactical frequency. I was guided very well at the correct height of 3300 metres with constant corrections towards the enemy at his starboard rear and suddenly saw, about 100 metres to my left and above, an aircraft in the moonlight, which on approaching closer I recognized as a Vickers Wellington. I closed in slowly behind him and gave a burst of about five of six seconds, aiming at the fuselage and wing roots. The starboard engine caught fire at once and I drew my machine up above him. For a while the Englishman [sic] continued, rapidly losing height; then the fire went out and I watched him spinning downward and finally crash. I observed no one bailing out. I returned to my standby area.'

The Wellington crashed at 2145 hours near Oosterwolde/Doornspijk. Landa and three crew were killed. Sergeants Emanuel Novotny and Augustin Sestak bailed out safely before their aircraft was completely destroyed in the crash near Oosterwolde at 2145. Landa and three of his crew were found dead in the wreckage the next day. It was Becker's first Abschuss. Becker, born on 22 August 1911 in Dortmund-Aplerbeck in the Province of Westphalia, a province of the Kingdom of Prussia, had volunteered for the Luftwaffe in 1934 and became a Stuka pilot before joining the Bf 110 Zerstörer and becoming a night fighter pilot in July 1940. Serving with NJG1, he crashed a Messerschmitt Bf 110 near Winterswijk on 30 August 1940. In 1941-42 Becker became one of the leading 'Experten' in the Luftwaffe night fighter arm. He shot down forty bombers in 1942 and taught the new and young crews from his experiences. To them Becker 'The Night Fighting Professor' was an inspiring fatherly figure. Instrumental in introducing the Lichtenstein AI radar into the night fighter arm in 1941 though most night fighter aircrew were sceptical about it (they liked to rely on the 'Mk I Eyeball'). Becker had one of the still experimental sets installed in his Do 217Z night fighter at Leeuwarden, 161 kilometres (100 miles) north of Arnheim on the Friesland coast. Guided by the revolutionary radar, his and Nachtjagd's first AI victory was in the early hours on 9 August 1941 in a Do 215B-5 night fighter version of the Do 215 reconnaissance-bomber when 44 Wellingtons of Bomber Command attacked Hamburg. Becker shot down six RAF night bombers 8/9 August-29/30 September 1941. He was awarded the Knight's Cross in July 1942 and he then served as a Staffelkapitän in 12./NJG1. By the end of the year, Becker had forty victories to his credit. Becker and his bordfunker Oberfeldwebel Josef Straub (who had taken part in forty victories) were posted missing in action on 26 February 1943 in a Bf 110G-4 while on a daylight sortie intercepting a Boeing B-17 formation over the North Sea and crashing north of Schiermonnikoog in the Netherlands. All his 46 victories were at night.

At midnight on 1/2 October 1940 Leutnant Hans-Georg Mangelsdorf of the 2nd Staffel NJG1 shot down a Whitley V near Hummelo, 21 kilometres east of Arnhem. His victim was P4964 on 78 Squadron at Dishforth which crashed at Sterkrade with the loss of New Zealand Pilot Officer Neville Halsey Andrew and crew. Two weeks later, on the 14/15th, Mangelsdorf was killed during aerial combat with a Hampden on 44 Squadron, crashing eight kilometres west of Gardelegen airfield. I./NJG1 at Venlo, Netherlands in order to more easily intercept the known RAF bomber routes into targets in the Ruhr, claimed five 'Helle Nachtjagd' kills. These included Hampden Is X2910 on 44 Squadron piloted by Sergeant Leonard John Burt and X2993 on 50 Squadron flown by South African Pilot Officer Arthur Howell Davies on a bombing operation on Berlin. Burt and two of his crew were killed, one being taken into captivity. Davies and one of his crew were killed, two others being taken prisoner. Three of I./NJG1 's victories were credited to Oberleutnant Streib, a feat which earned him the award of the Ritterkreuz on 6 October with eight victories claimed. He was the first night fighter pilot to be honoured with the Knight's Cross.

Nachtjagd's final kills over the Continent during 1940 went to 4./NJG1. Oberleutnant Egmont Prinz zur Lippe Weissenfeld destroyed Wellington IC P9286 on 115 Squadron ten kilometres west of Medemblik on 16/17 November, the aircraft going down in flames at 0205 hours to crash near Winkel, Holland and with the loss of

Sergeant Donald Ewart Larkman and crew. Twenty-nine year old Feldwebel Hans Rasper of the same Staffel destroyed Whitley V P5012 on 102 Squadron on 15/16 December ten kilometres northwest of Petten off the Dutch coast at Egmond. Flight Lieutenant Kenneth Thomas Hannah and his crew were killed. Rasper's bordfunker, Erich Schreiber was killed in 1942. Rasper was taken prisoner on 26/27 April 1945 after he was shot down in Mittelfels, near Cham, by American ack-ack during a strafing run. He had seven Abschüsse.[12] At least nineteen Bomber Command aircraft were destroyed July-December 1940 in the 'Kammhuber Line', as the continuous belt of searchlights and radar positions between Schleswig-Holstein and northern France was christened by the British bomber crews. About thirty bombers were brought down by flak during the same period. Apart from organising an effective short-range defensive Nachtjagd, Kammhuber also appreciated the value and effectiveness of 'Fernnachtjagd' (long-range night intruding) over Britain but the 'Intruder' force was never raised beyond one single Gruppe (I./NJG2) which operated the Ju 88C-6 and Do 17 from Gilze-Rijen in the Netherlands. It never exceeded 21 aircraft but despite this and severe operational losses (21 aircraft alone during 1940) 'Fernnachtjagd' made a promising start. The Gruppe's first intruder victories were two Wellingtons destroyed by Feldwebel Otto Wiese 100 kilometres west of Texel and Georg 'Gustav' Schramm over the North Sea on the night of 22/23 July 1940. Weise was killed on 21/22 June 1941, shot down over Peterborough by Beaufighter R2277 on 25 Squadron piloted by Flying Officer J. M. Herrick and he crashed at Deeping St James.[13] By December 1940 claims for another sixteen bombers followed. (By October 1941 the handful of crews in I./NJG2 had claimed more aircraft destroyed than all other Nachtjagd units combined). On 20/21 October 1940 when 139 bombers went to many targets in the occupied countries, Italy and Germany, a Whitley, 'O-Orange' on 58 Squadron at Linton-on-Ouse, which crashed on fire, on the slopes of the Cleveland Hills near Ingleby Greenow in Yorkshire, was claimed shot down by Hauptmann Karl Hülshoff commanding I./NJG2, the specialist German intruder unit. Pilot Officer Ernest Henry Brown and two of his crew were killed. Two were injured, one of whom died two days later. Hülshoff claimed the Whitley as a 'Hereford'. He destroyed four more aircraft over England during 1940-41, adding another seven victories before the end of the war. Hülshoff was awarded the Deutscheskreuz in Gold. He was taken prisoner on 10 March 1941.

Hamburg, the second largest city of the Reich, with a population of just over a million and a half, was one of many targets bombed on 24/25 October when 113 aircraft tried to reach many targets in the Reich. One Wellington was lost on the raid on Hamburg. At Linton-on-Ouse nine Whitley Vs on 102 Squadron were detailed to bomb the Air Ministry Building in the Leipzigstrasse in Berlin. Pilot Officer A. G. Davies took off at 2202 hours and just six minutes later he was shot down in flames near Tholthorpe by 21-year old Feldwebel Hans Hahn of III./NJG2 who claimed it as a 'Wellington' for his first victory. Davies was injured and the second pilot and the observer died in the aircraft. Sergeant Angus Stewart Wilson and Pilot Officer Terence Edward Lee died of their injuries on 2 November.

On 28 October Leutnant Heinz Völker flying a Ju 88C-4 attacked two Hampdens on 49 Squadron as they were returning from Hamburg to Lindholme. The first Hampden was damaged but was able to land safely. Völker then attacked a second, which went down in the North Sea half a mile off Skegness with the loss of all Pilot Officer John Raymond Bufton's crew.[14] Völker scored a total of twelve victories and was awarded the Ritterkreuz. He and his two crew were killed on 22 July 1941 when over Ashwell, Hertfordshire, their Ju 88C-4 collided with a Wellington of 11 OTU. All eight men on the Wimpy were killed.

Victory claims submitted by night-fighter crews in the Reichsverteidigung (Air

Defence of Germany) coupled by the long-range intruder operations over the UK and the North Sea grew steadily. During January 1941 eight bombers were destroyed by Nachtjagd. Six were by the intruders of I./NJG2. The two others - Whitley V T4203 on 78 Squadron by 23-year old Oberleutnant Reinhold Eckardt of II./NJG1 on the night of 9/10th, which went down between Millingen and Kekerdom, Holland with the loss of Sergeant Charles Arthur Smith and crew - and Whitley V N1521 on 58 Squadron by Oberleutnant Egmont Prinz zur Lippe-Weissenfeld of 4./NJG1, which crashed near Callantsoog, Holland on the 15/16th. Pilot Officer William Edgar Peers and his crew also died.[15]

Sir Richard Peirse committed a total of 222 aircraft to oil targets in Hannover on 10/11 February, which fell during the February new moon. The previous highest Bomber Command sortie rate was 135, to Gelsenkirchen in the January 1941 moon period. The bulk of the Hannover force was made up once again of Wellingtons, of which 112 took part.[16] Sergeant pilot Bill Garrioch and his crew on 15 Squadron took off from RAF Wyton near Huntingdon in Wellington IC T2702 'H-Harry' for their 16th operation of the war as he recalls:

'The briefing officer announced the target, the route in and out and the bomb load - 4,000lb made up of seven 500lb bombs and the balance in incendiaries. The Met Office forecast clear skies, strong westerly winds, a full moon and very cold. The CO, Group Captain Forster said that this was to be the biggest show of the war to date, wished us all the usual good luck and told us to beware of moving stars (night fighters)! This great man, a First World War pilot, still wore a steel brace on his back caused by spinal injuries received in a crash. Even so, he flew with us occasionally. Take-off was timed for 1730 hours and the flight duration expected to be about seven hours. Then followed the usual pre-flight planning between pilot, navigator and crews. We then went to the mess for our tea of bacon and eggs, back to our quarters to change into warmer clothing and of course to empty our pockets. The ritual of this act always gave me a momentary feeling of apprehension until I put some small change back into my pocket in case we had to land away from base on return. The funny thing is I had only half a crown in small change, which I put into my pocket; that being the only article carried on my person.

'We boarded the Bedford crew bus for the six-mile journey to Alconbury our satellite airfield. Generally during these bus journeys there was the usual chatter, pocket chess or cards but on this occasion everyone seemed quiet and preoccupied with their thoughts, so much so that our navigator Sergeant Bob Beioley remarked on it. Bob and Sergeant Glyndwr 'Taffy' Rearden, WOp/AG had completed twelve operations with me on Blenheims prior to converting to the 'Wimpy'). Prior to air test in the morning Taffy expressed the wish to be front gunner that night as a change from being cooped up inside the cabin. I agreed, as WOp/AG Sergeant George Hedge RNZAF was also a fully qualified WOp/AG. Soon we arrived at our dispersal. I signed the Form 700 and as I climbed the ladder into the aircraft Chiefy Wright said to me, 'If you break this one; don't bring it back!' ('H-Harry' was Flight Lieutenant Morris's aircraft but my 'D-Dog' was being repaired after I had accidentally hit my wingtip on the control caravan during a previous take-off). I laughed and said that I would be a good boy and nurse his precious 'Wimpy'. I glanced at my watch and at the other aircraft around the dispersal area.

'Time to start up. Fuel on, first port and the starboard engines coughed, burst into life and warmed up at 1,000 rpm. Soon we ran each engine up to take-off rpm (2,650), tested the magnetos, oil pressure and temperature and cylinder head temperature and checked and set the gyro, cooling gills, flaps, etc. All the crew reported ready. The time was now 1725 hours. I gave the signal and with a final wave to our much-appreciated ground crew, we moved out towards our take-off position near the end of the runway. We were No.2 to go. At precisely 1730 hours No.1 started his take-off run and as he reached the end of the runway I lined up and got my green light from the caravan. Brakes off, I opened the throttle slowly to maximum power as we started rolling. As we gathered speed the noise was deafening and seemed to reach a crescendo that vibrated throughout the loaded aircraft. I kept the nose down until the last bit of the all-too-short runway loomed up, then, pulling up; she lifted clear, a light kiss on the concrete and off. Wheels up and nose kept down to increase flying speed. I throttled back to climbing rpm to reach operating height and the engine noise now changed to a welcome hum. All was well.

'Bob gave me the course, which I confirmed from my kneepad. As the snow-covered countryside receded far below in the darkness, Sergeant Bill Jordan, the 2nd pilot who was on his second trip with me for familiarization, flew the aircraft and the gunners entered their turrets while I visited each member of the crew to ensure that all was in order. Soon we reached the coast at Orfordness and levelled off at 11,000 feet. The navigator and the wireless operator were at their stations and the lighting was very subdued, creating an eerie yet efficient atmosphere tinged with the smell of dope and fuel, amid the roar of the smooth-sounding Pegasus engines. When we were over the sea Taffy and Sergeant Jock Hall, rear gunner, a Scotsman with many trips in Coastal Command, test-fired their guns. From now on we were on the alert for night fighters. It was cold and clear. The patches of white cumulus would make us an easily identified target seen from above. I took over before we reached the Dutch coast, which we crossed at 1850 hours - another 213 miles and 65 minutes to the target. We had a very strong tail wind and ground speed was nearly 200 mph. Bob got a pinpoint. We were almost dead on track - a slight course alteration and all was well. We were lucky so far.

'It was unbelievably quiet. We flew towards the target and still there was no flak. We were very much alert but it was the easiest run-in so far and the ground was easily identifiable. Only five minutes to the target. Then we saw it. Bob was a good navigator - we were almost spot on. On the eastern horizon the rising moon assisted target identification. With bomb doors opened and bombs fused Bob went down to the bombsights. He saw the target nestled in the crook of the 'Y'-section of a big road junction. We had a following wind so I throttled back a little and kept the aircraft steady. Right a little ... I did not see any activity at all, not even a little flak. The first Wimpy's bombs burst. Then suddenly there was a series of flashes close to Gilmore's aircraft. Bob called, 'Left... left ... left ... a bit more ... steady now ... steady.' Flak now curled lazily up towards us and then there was heavy ack-ack to our left. It was accurate for height but was not near us. Must be the other aircraft in trouble. Bob called 'Bombs gone!' and I immediately turned steeply to port. Jock in the rear turret watched our bombs burst. There were only six flashes. Where was the seventh? Gilmore's aircraft started a fire and our incendiaries were well alight. Ack-Ack was almost non-existent with us but as we flew away we saw other aircraft getting a hot reception and the sky was full of flak. All this time the fires seemed to grow in intensity - Hannover was visible forty miles away. The moon was up and it was like daylight. We watched for enemy fighters but all was quiet and we could not even see other aircraft.

'Against a strong head wind our ground speed was now only 85 knots; it was going to be a long haul home. Large white cumulus clouds were building up below. As we crossed the eastern coast of the Zuider Zee at Kempen, Jock suddenly called out, 'Fighter below and behind!' I put the engines to cruising revs and steep turned to starboard to face him. As I turned I saw a Me 110, which was turning to meet me. I turned violently to port to avoid him. Jock gave him a long burst but he still attacked, hitting the aircraft in the fuselage and port engine. I put the flaps down and soon the shooting stopped. He had overshot. I heard the cannon fire hit the aircraft somewhere behind me. Jock said that he had been hit. Could we get him out of the turret? The port engine was on fire. I turned off the fuel and full throttle. Bob called, 'Are we on fire?' Bob's sudden announcement on the intercom must have paralyzed my senses if only for a fleeting instant because as I was looking through the cockpit window, superimposed in space, just outside the windscreen was a very clear picture of my grandfather and a great uncle looking directly at me. It was so clear that I even recognized my uncle's old tweed jacket! Then it was gone and I was back to reality. It frightened me because these two much-loved relatives had been dead for about seven years. Much later George told me that cannon shells came through the fuselage and exploded in his radio equipment. How he and Bob were not hit I'll never know. I was saved by the armour plate behind my head. At that moment I knew we had to survive and I seemed to find added strength and courage to risk anything that would bring us out of this alive. I looked back and the fuselage was full of smoke. I could not see anyone. Perhaps a flare was burning. Taffy moaned faintly saying, 'Get me out' and I saw the fighter turn to port over our port wingtip. Bill Jordan went forward to open the escape hatch and to get Taffy out of the turret. I told the crew to prepare to bail out and raised the flaps.

'We were diving now. The fighter came in again and once more I put the flaps down and the aircraft yawed violently to port while I throttled back and side slipped to almost stalling speed. Cannon and machine-gun tracer went just over the top of us but miraculously we were not hit. This time, as the fighter went over the top of us I raised the flaps and control was easier. I think only the starboard flap worked. I told Taffy to shoot the fighter down, position 10 o'clock. He did not answer. Bill Jordan tried desperately to operate the turret door release and get him out. George Hedge was standing beside me ready to help when Bill opened the floor escape hatch. Bob and Jock were still back in the smoke-filled fuselage. Were they alive? I did not know. I decided that unless we bailed out or landed quickly we would all die. We were blazing very badly now. I signalled to George not to jump as I had not given the order and I dived for the ground in the hope that a crash landing might save some of us. The aircraft persisted in turning to port. We were diving very steeply and fast, over 300 knots. Through the cockpit window I saw the port engine and that the inner wing was now on fire. Off all fuel and full throttle starboard engine. The frozen expanse of the Zuider Zee was hurtling towards us. I tried to level off but the elevators were sluggish and we hit the ice slightly nose down and skidded for what seemed to be miles. Then, suddenly, she broke through the ice and the nose filled up with water and ice through the open escape hatch. Then the aircraft stopped. We must have crashed at about 2230.'

'Taffy' Rearden died trapped in his front turret, which sank beneath the ice. Jock Hall was badly injured with his foot almost severed and he had bullet holes in his burned clothing but surgery at the Queen Wilhelmina hospital in Amsterdam was successful and he survived. 'H-Harry' was one of four losses on the Hannover raid and was credited to Hauptmann Walter Ehle of Stab (staff flight) II/NJG1 from Middenmeer north of Schiphol for his fifth victory. Ehle poured 560 rounds of 7mm machine gun and 100 rounds of 20mm cannon into Wellington T2702, which crashed on the frozen Ijsselmeer about seventeen kilometres west of Kempen. Walter Ehle was born on 28 April 1913 at Windhoek in German West Africa (now Namibia). At the start of World War Two Ehle flew with 3./ZG1 and was credited with three daylight victories before the unit was re-designated 3./NJG1 and he became a night fighter. Ehle would become one of the longest serving Gruppenkommandeur in the Luftwaffe, leading II./NJG1 from October 1940 until his death in November 1943. His sixth night victory was a Bristol Blenheim shot down on 2 June 1942 and he had sixteen victories in total by the end of 1942.

Three other bombers were lost on 10/11 February and included Hampden X3001 on 49 Squadron at Scampton, which was shot down by Austrian-born Leutnant Leopold 'Poldi' Fellerer of 5./NJG1 north of Bergen-Alkmaar for his victory.[17] Pilot Officer J. H. Green and two of his crew were taken prisoner; one crewmember being killed. Dornier Do 17Z and Ju 88C-2 Intruders of NJG2 claimed six aircraft over England: Oberleutnant Albert Schulz and Hauptmann Rudolf 'Rolf' Jung of 2./NJG2 claimed a 21 Squadron Blenheim and a Wellington near West Raynham in Norfolk respectively. The Blenheim, which Schulz shot down on its return to Watton, was the Oberleutnant's third victory having shot down two Blenheims at Church Fenton airfield on 16 January. Pilot Officer Albert Chatteway and Pilot Officer George Eltham Sharvell were killed. Schulz was shot down and killed by B-17 return fire on 30 January 1944. (Feldwebel Heinz Krüger his bordfunker was killed and Unteroffizier Georg Frieben, bordshütze, bailed out safely). Wellington IC R1084 piloted by Sergeant Harold Humphrey Rogers, crash landed at Narborough without injury to the crew.[18] Twenty-five year old Oberleutnant Paul Semrau of 3./NJG2 claimed two Blenheims near Feltwell for his first and second Night-Abschüsse. As a destroyer pilot, he had destroyed six aircraft on the ground). Oberleutnant Kurt Hermann and his bordfunker Unteroffizier Englebert Böttner of I./NJG2 claimed two Hampdens near Waddington for their 5th and 6th victories. Their first victim was AD719 on 49 Squadron piloted by Sergeant G. M. Bates who was returning to Scampton. A burst of fire set the aircraft on fire. Bates and one of his crew bailed out safely but the other two perished in the aircraft which crashed at Langworth, Lincolnshire. A few minutes later Herrmann attacked a 144 Squadron Hampden piloted by Sergeant William Alexander McVie who was flying with his navigation lights on. Herrmann's fire hit the aircraft's hydraulics, undercarriage and flaps. The lights went out and the Hampden dived away to land safely at Hemswell.[19]

Another 144 Squadron Hampden flown by Sergeant E. Dainty orbited Hemswell but was refused permission to land because of the intruder activity and eventually, low on fuel, the crew abandoned the aircraft, which crashed at Snettisham, Norfolk. After attacking three airfields with incendiary bombs and chasing an unidentified aircraft without result, Hauptmann Rolf Jung, Staffelkapitän 2/NJG2 saw a Wellington with its navigation lights on. It was a 115 Squadron Wellington returning to Marham and flown by Sergeant Harold Humphrey Rogers. He had narrowly missed colliding with two other aircraft and was intent on avoiding a similar situation. Rogers had attacked Rotterdam as strong winds had prevented him reaching his target at Hannover. He had also machine-gunned two airfields in Holland on the return. Near a flashing landmark beacon at Swaffham, Rogers switched on the Wellington's navigation lights. Almost immediately the port engine was hit and Sergeant Hill the rear gunner was wounded in his left arm. The aircraft began to lose height rapidly but Rogers was able to make a successful forced landing on a railway cutting at Narborough.[20] The intruders of I./NJG2 claimed twelve bombers destroyed on intruding operations over England during February.

Despite these highly efficient intruder operations Hitler soon put a stop to 'Fernnachtjagd'. He told Kammhuber: 'If the long-range night-fighting really had results, the British would have copied it a long time ago, as they imitate anything good that I do.' 'And' he added, 'The German citizen, whose house has been destroyed by a British bomber, would prefer it if the British aircraft were shot down by a German night-fighter to crash next to his burning house.' This decision allowed Bomber Command (and later the 8th Air Force) to build up and launch a crushing strategic bombing offensive against Germany virtually undisturbed over the British Isles and it undoubtedly was a decisive factor in the outcome of the war.

On the night of the 14/15 February Whitley V T4164 on 77 Squadron at Topcliffe was shot down by Major Hans Jüsgen of Stab I./NJG3 eight kilometres south of Nijmegen. Pilot Officer C. R. Hubbard and his crew were taken into captivity. On the night of the 15/16 February Wellington IC T2847 on 15 Squadron went down near Barchem in Holland to Feldwebel Ernst Kalinowski of 6./NJG1 for his second victory. (His first had been a Wellington on 18 December 1939, during the Battle of the Heligoland Bight). Pilot Officer Cyril Bertie Dove and three members of his crew were killed; two others were taken prisoner. On the night of 28 February/1 March Oberfeldwebel Paul Gildner of 4./NJG1 destroyed Blenheim IV T1895 on 105 Squadron at Swanton Morley at Oosterhoogebrug. The Blenheim exploded in mid air and crashed at Oosterhogebrug. Twenty-seven-year old Sergeant John S. H. Heape was taken prisoner; Sergeant Sylvester Jones of Manchester the 26 year old observer and 32-year old Sergeant John Bimson the WOp/AG were killed. It was Gildner's sixth confirmed Abschuss. On 2/3 March Gildner claimed another Blenheim IV when he shot down Z5901 on 21 Squadron at Watton at 2248 hours. The aircraft crashed at Tolbert killing the pilot, Flight Lieutenant John Dickinson DFC and his two crew, the 29-year old observer, Sergeant Charles W. Fry of Whipton, Exeter and Sergeant Robert Mower the WOp/AG. All three airmen were buried at Groningen.[21]

In March Nachtjagd claimed twenty victories, including fourteen over the continent. On 27/28 March 38 Wellingtons and a Short Stirling I set out to attack Cologne and 39 aircraft - 22 Hampdens, thirteen Whitleys and four Manchesters - set out for Düsseldorf. One of the Manchesters, L7307 EM-P on 207 Squadron at Waddington was piloted by Australian Flight Lieutenant Johnnie Aloysius Siebert. On his crew were Sergeants P. C. Robson, second pilot, George Fominson, navigator/bomb aimer/front gunner, Warrant Officer1 J. A. 'Jim' Taylor, Sergeant W. J. J. McDougal, 2nd WOp/AG in the mid-upper-turret and Sergeant Peter Gurnell, rear gunner. The crew had recently recommenced operations following a tour on 44 Squadron on Hampdens and had already visited Cologne, Brest, Lorient and La Rochelle. Group Captain John Nelson Boothman the station CO saw the crews off at around 1930 hours.[22] His parting words, as the crews climbed into the lorry, which took them to their dispersed aircraft, were to the navigator, who was wryly advised to be sure to 'pick out a nice, fat maternity hospital' in Düsseldorf as his aiming-point. This was a sarcastic jibe at 'Lord Haw Haw' who was claiming in propaganda broadcasts at that time that the RAF only bombed hospitals and non-military targets. Their route took them over Holland again. In Eindhoven, on the bombers' route to and from the Ruhr, Kees Rijken, who was twelve when the Germans attacked his country and thus about 14 when the air war really started, was an avid watcher:

'Almost every day and night the allied bombers came over Eindhoven. Most nights my father and I stood in the garden, watching, listening and sometimes sheltering from the shell splinters of the German ack-ack with a pan on our heads. When the ack-ack stopped we knew that the German fighters were airborne. From our house we could see the sky in the direction of Germany start to light up and eventually turn red. When we were standing in the garden my father had the habit of signalling the 'V for Victory' sign to the overflying aircraft with his pocket lantern. The impact of the great numbers of bombs that were dropped upon targets in the Ruhr was so great that sometimes the doors in our house started clattering.'

Düsseldorf was bombed at around 2230 hours in two approaches, dropping eight bombs of 500lbs on each run over the target area. Very intense flak was encountered and one shell burst beneath L7307 and buffeted the starboard wing up in the air. Level flight was resumed and as they set course for England the crew speculated as to whether they had experienced a near miss or whether any damage had occurred on the starboard side. Approaching the searchlight belt on the Dutch border the flak died down and fighter attacks were expected. At this moment the starboard engine began to smoke, lost power and had to be stopped. Immediately the Manchester began to lose height and the port engine started to lose power too. The notorious Vulture engines were proving inadequate to the task. Johnnie Siebert called that he couldn't hold them up any longer and the aircraft fell into a sideslip to port, nose down but still under some semblance of control. Taylor in the wireless operator's position slammed the switch of his W/T set over to transmit and without waiting for the fifteen seconds necessary for the set to warm up began transmitting their position to base. As he did this he suddenly noticed tracer passing on their port side. The Manchester had been intercepted by a Bf 110 night fighter piloted by Oberfeldwebel Gerhard Herzog of 2/NJG1. The time was 2330 hours. L7307, which was shot down at 2350 hours one kilometre west of Hertogenbosch, was credited to 29-year old Oberleutnant Walter Fenske of I/NJG1. Herzog had shot down a Whitley on 78 Squadron at 2305 hours at Helenaveen and at 2330 hours he claimed a Wellington at Bakel, ten kilometres southeast of Helmond.

    Taylor was temporarily cut off from the intercom as he transmitted and missed the captain's first order to abandon the aircraft. The starboard engine had by now caught fire and a hydraulic failure was experienced in the aircraft. Neither of these were unusual experiences in Manchesters at this time and it is not absolutely certain that Fenske's fire actually hit the crippled Manchester. Taylor was then slapped firmly on the shoulder as the second WOp/AG, Sergeant McDougal, hastened forward to the escape hatch beneath the nose, struggling into his parachute as he went. Taylor slipped the clip over his Morse key to clamp it on 'transmit', ripped out his intercom lead and oxygen tube and followed McDougal. By this time the aircraft was side-slipping viciously, diving steeply and one engine was racing. The hydraulic failure had severed power to the rear turret and the main undercarriage had flopped down. As Taylor dived through the hatch Pete Curnell, the rear gunner, who had been unable to rotate his turret by hand, closely followed him. The starboard main wheel narrowly missed Taylor and Curnell as the aircraft side-slipped over them. They were the last crewmembers out alive. It is likely that Siebert escaped the same way but was hit by the main wheel. The Australian's body was located next day some distance from the wreckage of his aircraft in a depression, which testified to the force of the impact. His parachute had not fully opened and it was surmised that he might have been stunned as he left the aircraft or did not get out soon enough.

    Herzog had attacked the Manchester from below and as he broke away he observed the parachutes of the five remaining aircrew in the glow of the searchlights. The aircraft dived away beneath them, an engine still racing and crashed on a farmhouse at Bakel, northeast of Helmond, near Eindhoven, killing some cows. None of the family of nine was killed or injured. Herzog then dropped a flare, which burst beneath the descending airmen. In its glow they could see that they were falling into an area of open water. Taylor and Curnell were feverishly blowing up their Mae Wests when they splashed down into four inches of water overlying a further two feet of mud. Taylor sprained an ankle in the landing and after disposing of his 'chute waded for about an hour before reaching firm ground and discovering a pub in the village. He was given first aid and fed, before being sent on his way with the 'name' of a contact in the underground movement in Eindhoven. Early next morning he was spotted and arrested by a German patrol who took him to the airfield of Eindhoven nearby, where he was reunited with the survivors of his own crew and that of one of the Wellingtons shot down. By a strange coincidence one of the two pigeons carried in L7303 arrived back in its loft in the early hours of 28 March in the very street in Lincoln, where Taylor's' girlfriend of the time, later his wife, then lived. How the pigeon managed to escape may never be known.

At the airfield the surviving RAF crewmembers met Oberfeldwebel Gerhard Herzog, who described to them his combat with their 'Wellington'. Many glances were exchanged among the crew, as they knew that no Manchester had previously fallen in occupied territory. Following this meeting Taylor and Curnell had the tragic task of identifying the body of their pilot, brought in by the Germans and were later kept in solitary confinement, deprived of cigarettes and interrogated for almost three days. The Germans must by then have inspected the wreckage of the aircraft and in the absence of any of the distinctive geodetic structure must have suspected that they had not shot down another Wellington.

Kees Rijken concludes: On 29 March 1941 a staff member of the Ortskommandantur asked my father to see that a grave be dug in the 'Ehrenfriedhof (military part) of the municipal cemetery. An RAF flight lieutenant would be buried at 1500 hours. The German official showed my father the identity disc of the fallen airman, who appeared to be John Siebert RAAF and RC, No.36155. At the town hall the officials did not know what the second 'A' in RAAF meant but the letters 'RC' were understood. Though the Germans had forbidden any public gathering the rumour that an 'English' airman would be buried that afternoon had spread quickly and thousands of inhabitants assembled around the cemetery. A German chaplain, a military band, a firing squad and a Roman Catholic Dutch priest were present. Luftwaffe personnel carried the coffin, covered with the British flag, to the grave. The German military band played 'Ich hatte einen Kameradan' (I had a comrade') and a salute of honour was fired. After the funeral the Dutch people crowded round the grave and clearly showed their sympathy with the fallen airman and their antipathy to the Germans by wearing red, white and blue or orange knots. Many flowers were laid on John Siebert's grave.'

On 30/31 March 109 aircraft including fifty Wellingtons were ordered to attack the two German battle cruisers, *Scharnhorst* and *Gneisenau* - nicknamed 'Salmon & Glukstein' (a famous London department store) lying in dock at Brest on the French coast.

Meanwhile, some Wellington crews on 99 Squadron were having mixed emotions.

Sergeant Alf Jenner, a WOp/AG had flown nine operations and was crewed up with Squadron Leader David Torrens, a new flight commander. 'As he was new to Bomber Command it was decided to give him the most experienced crew. I was by now something of a veteran with twelve ops and I became Torrens' front gunner. First WOp was Arthur Smith, a splendid wireless operator who had served in the pre-war RAF in Iraq. The second pilot was Eric Berry, who came from a well-off Yorkshire family and who had flown private aircraft before the war. His wartime training had been short, converting straight from a Tiger Moth to a Wellington. Although he had only flown two or three ops he was well thought of and was about to skipper his own crew. Our rear gunner was Pilot Officer Palmer and our observer, Flying Officer Goodwyn, was from Ipswich:

'At Waterbeach we played a guessing game. If there was a 'breeze' that an op was on that night we would watch the petrol bowsers refuelling the Wimpys and note the number of gallons. If it was about 400 gallons that meant a trip to the Ruhr; if it was over 650, it must mean Berlin! Everyone was worried but did not show it. We had things to do to pass the rest of the afternoon. The wireless had to be checked and guns cleaned. At five o'clock on the afternoon of 9 April we entered the briefing room and sat down.[23] At the end of the room was a large map, covered with a curtain. The Briefing Officer dramatically pulled the curtain aside and we were startled to see a red ribbon that seemed to go on forever! It was Berlin, then the longest trip in the RAF repertoire. The RAF hadn't been to the Big City since the previous September. We all thought, 'Jesus Christ! Why me?' The trip would take the clumsy, over-laden Wellington nearly five hours just to get there and each machine followed the other at intervals of about five minutes. The theory presumably was that the German civilians would be scared out of their wits by the thought that the RAF had unlimited supplies of heavy bombers. In fact there were ninety aircraft from several stations that night.

'After briefing finished we ate our flying supper in the mess. It was rather poor fare, usually corned beef and chips, bread pudding and tea. Everyone was in a high state of nervousness and excited hysteria, although no one showed any sign of despondency. We were quite well trained and highly motivated. It was really dark, cold and clear. A bomber's-moon shone overhead. I climbed into the astrodome area of 'M for Mother' and stowed my parachute. Our pilots wore theirs in flight. As we taxied out and lined up on the new tarmac runway I gripped the astrodome hatch clips, in case I needed to get out quickly, as I always did. We were away first. Torrens thundered down the runway (our bomb load was small because of the need for extra fuel). With flaps full on we climbed slowly into the sky above Waterbeach. I climbed into the front turret immediately (enemy fighters might already be about). Grinding away slowly we headed for Southwold, our point of departure.

'Nearing the coast of Holland I exclaimed, 'Enemy coast ahead!' As usual on any night raid, the first sign of enemy activity as our Wellington crossed the Dutch coast was a burst of flak from the ground, fired it seemed with the intention of letting the RAF know that the defenders were alert. There were a few shots and all was quiet again. The captain talked quietly to us, telling us to keep our eyes peeled. There followed a nerve-wracking three hours during which very little anti-aircraft fire was encountered.

Instead, as the lone bomber edged its way towards Berlin at about 120 mph, it was passed in silence from one searchlight to the next until we could see the multitude of coloured flak bursts over Berlin. We had been told that there were 1,000 guns at Berlin. Field Marshal Göring had only recently announced that the RAF would never get through to Berlin. Because a few had, he was determined to claw down every one in future. No land warfare was going on at that time. (The French had been defeated and the Russians were still nominally their allies). So Göring was able to concentrate as much heavy flak as he wished and from less than 15,000 feet, which was as high as most laden Wellingtons could fly, that looked plenty. And to make his task easier, we were going over one at a time. They couldn't all fire at us but it felt like it. We could actually smell flak. The Germans were very good gunners. Down below Lake Wannsee shone in the moonlight. Buildings or imagined buildings appeared in the Berlin suburbs below and at any moment an attack by night fighters was expected. One of my tasks when over the target was to report heavy flak bursts on the ground to enable the pilot to take evasive action in the time it took the shells to lift themselves up to our level. For a while this ploy worked and our bombs went down, hitting the opera house we were later told. Then it happened.

'There was a loud explosion in one of the engines. Fortunately, it did not catch fire. Torrens feathered the prop but 'M for Mother' could not maintain height and, though it succeeded in flying out of the heavy barrage, was down to 1,000 feet within half an hour. Nearing Brunswick Torrens came on the intercom.

'Sorry to tell you chaps but we will not make it back. You will each have to decide if you want to bail out or stay in the aircraft for a crash-landing.'

'I had previously decided that should such an occasion occur, then I would jump. I looked at the altimeter. It read 1,100 feet (300 feet less than recommended). The ruddy bulkhead at the front prevented me from turning the turret door handle. (To bail straight out of the turret would have taken me into the turning props.) To my relief, Eric Berry opened it from the other side. Flying Officer Goodwyn and I bailed out. The remaining four crew, including Pilot Officer Palmer, rear gunner and Sergeant Albert Smith, WOp/AG stayed with the aircraft and crash-landed at Wolfenbüttel near Hannover. They set fire to the aircraft before being captured and taken prisoner. Goodwyn and I joined them.'

On 9/10 April also, two other Wellingtons on 99 Squadron failed to return from a raid on Vegasack by nine aircraft. Wellington II W5375 on 12 Squadron, which was being flown by Wing Commander Vivian Q. Blackden the CO, which crashed in the Ijsselmeer north of Harderwijk on a raid of Emden by seven aircraft was claimed shot down by Oberleutnant Egmont Prinz zur Lippe Weissenfeld of 4./NJG1 for NJG1's 100th victory at 0059 hours. Wing Commander Blackden and his crew were killed. Blackden, who had flown Fairey Battles in 1940, was buried at Lemsterland in Holland. Nachtjagd crews actually claimed seven Wellingtons, three of them over England. Stirling I N6011 on 7 Squadron at Newmarket was claimed by Feldwebel Karl-Heinz Scherfling south-west of Lingen at 2335 hours. Flight Lieutenant Victor Fernley Baker Pike DFC and all except one of his crew were killed. A Whitley was claimed by Oberfeldwebel Wilhelm Beier near Chelmsford at 0235 hours. Beier was born on 11 November 1913 at Homberg in Niederrhein. At the age of twenty-seven he made his first claim for an aircraft destroyed when, on 18 December 1940 he reported the destruction of a Hurricane near Lowestoft at 0636 hours. In the following six months he made five more claims and on 6 July 1941 he claimed four bombers destroyed. These were a Wellington, a Blenheim and two Whitleys, all of which were said to have fallen into the North Sea. On 8 August he claimed to have destroyed three more bombers: a Blenheim, a Halifax and a Wellington. Unlike his fellow pilots, Beier seemed not to venture over the British coast, preferring to stay over the North Sea. Nevertheless, he had some close calls. On one occasion, the right main-wheel tyre of his Ju 88 burst when he was taking off and caused the undercarriage to collapse. The aircraft slid to a halt in front of the control tower at Gilze-Rijen and all three crew were able to escape unhurt. Beier's reputation as a night fighter pilot was rapidly established and with a total of fourteen claims, he was awarded the Ritterkreuz on 11 October but his former bordfunker Kurt Bundrock, who had flown with Beier after Reinhold Knacke's death in February 1943 said Beier missed several good opportunities to shoot down a bomber to such an extent that it became clear, both to Bundrock and ground control officers, that Beier did not want to engage English bombers anymore. Soon after Beier was transferred to Jagdgruppe Ost and became a flight instructor. [24]

On 10/11 April 53 bombers comprising 36 Wellingtons, twelve Blenheims and five Manchesters headed for Brest to try and finish off the Gneisenau which had been recently damaged by a Coastal Command torpedo bomber. Meanwhile 29 Hampdens and 24 Whitleys went to bomb Düsseldorf and minor operations were flown to Bordeaux/Merignac airfield and to Rotterdam. Four hits were claimed on the Gneisenau. One Wellington failed to return while five Hampdens were lost on the raid on Düsseldorf. Two were shot down by Hauptmann Werner Streib of Stab I/NJG1 who by May would have 26 confirmed victories and one by Oberfeldwebel Gerhard Herzog of 2./NJG1. Leutnant Hermann Reese of 2./NJG1 and Leutnant Hans-Dieter Frank of Stab I./NJG1 claimed the other two. Frank had joined the Luftwaffe in 1937 and was introduced to night-fighting in the spring of 1941. The Bf 110C-4 (3300) flown by Reese collided with his victim southwest of Beesell/Limburg and he bailed out. His bordfunker, Unteroffizier Wilhelm Roitczak was killed. On 7 August 1942 Reese was forced to bail out a second time, with injuries, after being shot down by fighters.

Forty night bombers were claimed destroyed during April 1941 (including 25 by

I./NJG2, 6 by I./NJG1 and two by III./NJG1. But Nachtjagd would not always be able to rely on the 'Himmelbett'. Soon would come a time when the 'Bed of Heavenly Bliss' would turn into a bed of nails.

Endnotes Chapter 1

1   Alexander Martin Lippisch (2 November 1894-11 February 1976) was a German pioneer of aerodynamics. He made important contributions to the understanding of flying wings, delta wings and the ground effect. His most famous design is the Messerschmitt Me 163 rocket-powered interceptor. His interest in aviation stemmed from a demonstration conducted by Orville Wright over Tempelhof Field in Berlin, in September 1909. During his service with the German Army from 1915-1918, Lippisch had the chance to fly as an aerial photographer and mapper. Following the war, Lippisch worked with the Zeppelin Company and it was at this time that he first became interested in tail-less aircraft. In 1921 his first such design would reach production in as the Lippisch-Espenlaub E-2 glider, built by Gottlob Espenlaub. This was the beginning of a research programme that would result in fifty designs throughout the 1920s and 1930s. Lippisch's growing reputation saw him appointed the director of the Rhön-Rossitten Gesellschaft (RRG), a glider research group. Lippisch's work led to a series of tail-less designs. In early 1939, the Reichsluftfahrtsministerium (RLM, Reich Aviation Ministry) transferred Lippisch and his team to work at the Messerschmitt factory, in order to design a high-speed fighter aircraft around the rocket engines then under development by Hellmuth Walter. In 1943, Lippisch transferred to Vienna's Aeronautical Research Institute (Luftfahrtforschungsanstalt Wien, LFW), to concentrate on the problems of high-speed flight. Like many German scientists, Lippisch was taken to the United States after the war under Operation Paperclip. Lippisch died in Cedar Rapids on 11 February 1976.
2   KIA 13 August 1940 while leading a formation of Blenheims on 82 Squadron in an attack on Aalbirg airfield in Denmark..
3   General Hugo Sperrle had at his disposal 48 Heinkel HE 51s and 48 Junkers Ju 58 bombers. The force also had some Me 109s. Those who flew in combat were required to send written data to Sperrle about what went well and what did not. By doing this, Sperrle hoped to end up with almost perfect tactics for any aerial assault used by the Luftwaffe in what might prove to be future conflicts. The leadership of the 'Condor Legion' was rotated so that more than just one senior Luftwaffe officer all gained experience of modern aerial warfare. After Sperrle, the 'Condor Legion' was commanded by Helmuth Volkmann who in turn was succeeded by Wolfram Freiherr von Richthofen. Other notable participants included Hermann Aldinger, Oskar Dirlewanger, Rudolf Demme, Adolf Galland, 'Hajo' Herrmann, Werner Mölders, Hannes Trautloft, Heinrich Trettner, Wilhelm Ritter von Thoma and Hellmuth Volkmann.
4   Later, in May 1943, after a long convalescence and post in fighter training schools, Specht became Gruppenkommandeur, II./JGII. He scored 32 confirmed victories, including 15 Viermots and was awarded the Ritterkreuz (Knight's Cross) before being reported MIA on 1 January 1945 during the disastrous Bodenplatte operation.
5   Johannes 'Macky' Steinhoff (15 September 1913-21 February 1994) was one of very few Luftwaffe pilots who survived to fly operationally through the whole of the war period 1939-45. He was also one of the highest-scoring pilots with 176 victories and one of the first to fly the Messerschmitt Me 262 jet fighter in combat as a member of the famous aces squadron Jagdverband 44 led by Adolf Galland. Post war Steinhoff became a senior West German Air Force officer and military commander of NATO. He played a significant role in rebuilding the post war Luftwaffe, eventually serving as chief of staff from 1966-1970 and then as chairman of NATO's Military Committee 1971-1974. In retirement, Steinhoff became a widely read author of books on German military aviation during the war and the experiences of the German people at that time. Steinhoff was decorated with both the Oak Leaves and Swords to the Knight's Cross of the Iron Cross. He played a role in the so-called Fighter Pilots Conspiracy when several senior air force officers confronted Hermann Göring late in the war.

6   *Blenheim Strike* by Theo Boiten (ARP 1995).
7   *Blenheim Strike* by Theo Boiten (ARP 1995).
8   II., III./NJG1,1./NJG2 and I./NJG3.
9   *Climbing Turns: A Pilot's story in war and peace* (Linden Hall 1990).
10   Marham's Wellington Squadrons were operational on eleven nights in July 1940, with a raid by 24 Wellingtons on the night of the 27/28th being the biggest so far in the war when Cologne, Hamm, Soest and Hamburg were attacked, with nineteen Hampdens assisting. *RAF Marham: Bomber Station* by Martin W. Bowman (The History Press, 2008).
11   Possibly this was Pilot Officer Alexander John Roberts Pate who was killed when he crashed near Iver, Buckinghamshire on 30 October 1940 during the ferry flight to Malta.
12   He died on 16 June 1999. (Boiten).
13   One other unnamed crew KIA and one PoW. From research by Theo Boiten.
14   *Intruders over Britain: The Luftwaffe Night Fighter Offensive 1940 to 1945* by Simon W Parry (ARP 2003).
15   Reinhold Eckardt (born Bamberg 26 March 1918) was KIA on 30 July 1942 after combat with a 102 Squadron Halifax at Kampenhout, 9 km N of Melsbroek, near Brussels after his third Viermot victory of the night. He had to bail out and became entangled in the tailplane. His bordfunker, Feldwebel Frank, bailed out safely.
16   Four-engined bombers went into action for the first time when 43 aircraft, including 3 Stirling Is on 7 Squadron, led by Acting Squadron Leader J. M. Griffith-Jones DFC bombed oil storage tanks beside the Waal at Rotterdam in a separate operation. Each Stirling carried 16 500lb bombs and they dropped a total of 46 500lb bombs (2 hung up). 7 Squadron had been the first squadron in the RAF to receive the four-engined bomber, in August 1940.
17   Fellerer was born in Vienna, Austria on 7 June 1919. In November 1940 he was posted as a bomber pilot, before being assigned as Technical Officer to II./NJG1. He claimed his first victory on 11 February 1941, a Hampden on 49 Squadron north of Bergen-Alkmaar. He was transferred to 4./NJG1 in June. In October 1942 Fellerer was made Staffelkapitän of 3./NJG1 before being posted to NJG5 in December that year. Promoted to Hauptmann, he became Gruppenkommandeur of II./NJG5 in December 1943. During this period, Fellerer raised his score to 18 victories. In January 1944 he claimed a B-24 Liberator on 4 January and a B-17 Flying Fortress on 11 January. On the night of 20/21 January he claimed five RAF Viermots. He was then awarded the German Cross in Gold in February and after 34 victories was awarded the Knight's Cross on 8 April. Fellerer then moved to command III./NJG6 in May. During August-October 1944 Fellerer and III./NJG6 also flew operations to counter supply operations from Italy to the Polish Home Army uprising in Warsaw. He claimed two Douglas DC-3s and two Liberators during this time, his final kill coming in October. In 450 sorties Leopold Fellerer claimed 41 aerial victories, 39 of them at night.
18   *Intruders over Britain: The Luftwaffe Night Fighter Offensive 1940 to 1945* by Simon W Parry (ARP 2003). Flying Officer Harold Rogers DFM was KIA on 8/9 April 1943 on 76 Squadron on the operation on Duisburg when he was flying as 2nd dickey to Flying Officer Maurice Alec Stanley Elliott. All 8 crew died.
19   McVie was KIA on the night of 15/16 May 1941 on the operation on Hannover. One other crew member was killed and two were taken prisoner.
20   Intruders over Britain: The Luftwaffe Night Fighter Offensive 1940 to 1945 by Simon W Parry (ARP 2003). F/O Harold Rogers DFM was KIA on 8/9 April 1943 on 76 Squadron on the operation on Duisburg when he was flying as 2nd dickey to F/O Maurice Alec Stanley Elliott. All 8 crew died.
21   *Blenheim Strike* by Theo Boiten (ARP 1995).
22   In 1931 Flight Lieutenant J. N. Boothman, flying Supermarine S.6B S1595 won the Schneider Trophy outright for Britain setting an average speed of 340.08 mph (547 km/h). Air Chief Marshal Sir John Nelson Boothman, KCB KBE DFC AFC died in 29 December 1957.
23   On 9/10 April 80 a/c - 36 Wellingtons, 24 Hampdens, 17 Whitleys and 3 Stirlings - went to Berlin. 6 FTR.
24   Quoted in *Intruders Over Britain* by Simon Parry (ARP 1987, 2003). Beier died on 12 July 1977.

Chapter Two

'The Early Experten'

War is a horror, but if it has to be, then it should be fought in fairness, with honour and chivalry to preserve something human among the horror. Attacks on women and children, air mines and phosphor dropping on our peaceful population in cities and small towns - all that is unbelievably foul.

Leutnant Helmut 'Bubi' ('Nipper') Lent.

When World War II had begun at 0445 on Friday 1 September 1939 with German forces crossing the Polish border, Leutnant Lent, flying a Bf 110 marked M8-DH with Walter Kubisch as his wireless operator and rear gunner took off from Ohlau at 0444 to escort Heinkel He 111 bombers of I. and III./Kampfgeschwader 4 (KG4) attacking the airfields at Krakow. The German plans for the invasion of Poland were conceived under the codename 'Fall Weiss' ('Case White'). This operation called for simultaneous attacks on Poland from three directions, the north, the west and the south, beginning at 0445 on the early morning of 1 September. At 1630 on 2 September, the second day of the German attack, Lent took off in the direction of Lódz and claimed his first aerial-victory of the war, shooting down a PZL P.11. At this point of the campaign the Bf 110s switched from bomber escort to ground-attack since the Polish Air Force was all but defeated. In this capacity Lent and Kubisch destroyed a twin-engined monoplane on the ground on 5 September and another aircraft, a PZL P.24, on 9 September. On 12 September 1939 he was attacked by a Polish aircraft which shot out his starboard engine. Lent made a forced landing behind German lines. He flew five more sorties during the Polish campaign, destroying one anti-aircraft battery. For his actions in the Polish campaign Lent was awarded one of the first Iron Cross 2nd Class of the war on 21 September. I./ZG76 relocated to the Stuttgart area on 29 September to defend the western border against the French and British, who had been at war with Germany since 3 September 1939. From early October to mid December I./ZG76 operated from a number of airfields in the Stuttgart and Ruhr areas before relocating north to Jever on 16 December.

Oberst Helmut Lent was born on 13 June 1918 at Pyrehne, district of Landsberg an der Warthe, Province of Brandenburg (now Pyrzany, Lubusz Province, western Poland) and christened Helmut Johannes Siegfried Lent. He was the fifth child of Johannes Lent, a Lutheran minister and Marie Elisabeth, née Braune. Helmut Lent had two older brothers, Werner and Joachim and two older sisters, Käthe and Ursula. His family was deeply religious; in addition to his father, both of his brothers and both grandfathers were also Lutheran ministers. From Easter 1924 until Easter 1928, Lent attended the local public primary school at Pyrehne. His father and oldest brother Werner then tutored him at home in preparation for the entrance examination at the public secondary school at Landsberg. In February 1933 Helmut joined the Jungvolk, the junior branch of the Hitler Youth. From March 1933, he acted as a youth platoon leader, or Jungzugführer (1 March 1933-1 April 1935) and flag-bearer, or Fähnleinführer (1 April 1935-9 November 1935) until he left the Jungvolk to prepare for his diploma examination. Helmut passed his graduation examinations at the age of seventeen on 12 December 1935. On 2 February 1936 he began the eight-week compulsory National Labour Service (Reichsarbeitsdienst) at Mohrin. He showed an early passion for glider flying; against his father's wishes, he joined the Luftwaffe as a Fahnenjunker on 1 April 1936. Lent's military training commenced on 6 April at the 2nd Air Warfare School (Luftkriegsschule 2) at Gatow on the south-western outskirts of Berlin at Berlin-Gatow. He swore the National Socialist oath of allegiance on 21 April. Flight training began on Monday, 7 August at Gatow. His first flight was in a Heinkel He 72 Kadet D-EYZA single engine biplane. Lent logged his first solo flight on 15 September in a Focke-Wulf Fw 44 Stieglitz. By this time, Lent had accumulated 63 flights in his logbook. In conjunction with flight training, the students also learned to drive motorcycles and cars and during one of these training exercises, Lent was involved in a road accident, breaking his upper leg badly enough to prevent him from flying for five months. This did not adversely affect his classroom training and on 1 April 1937, after taking his commission examination, he was promoted to Fähnrich. On 19 October Lent completed his flight training and was awarded the A/B Licence. He earned his wings on 15 November. On 1 February 1938 he was promoted to Oberfähnrich and on 1 March to Leutnant. By this time, he had made 434 flights in eight different types of aircraft and had accumulated 112 hours and 48 minutes flying time, mostly in daylight flights, in single engine training aircraft.

After leaving Gatow, Helmut Lent was posted to the Heavy Bomber Crew School, or Grosse Kampffliegerschule at Tutow in northeast Germany. He spent three months training as an observer (1 March-30 May 1938). Prior to completing this course Lent was again involved in a motor vehicle accident and this resulted in a broken lower jaw, concussion and internal bleeding. He was hospitalised for three weeks. On 1 July Lent was posted to III./JG132 'Richthofen' at Jüterbog-Damm flying on 19 July for the first time after his injuries. In early September 1938 Lent participated in armed patrols, flying Arado Ar 68 fighters in support of Germany's occupation of the Sudetenland. Then Lent's staffel, 7./JG132, relocated to Grossenhain near Dresden in preparation and support of the annexation of Czechoslovakia. Lent flew a number of operational patrols in this conflict until his Staffel relocated again to Rangsdorf on 29 September. After the tension over the occupation of the Sudeten territories eased, Lent's unit began a conversion to the Messerschmitt Bf 108 Taifun. On 1 November 1938 III./JG132 moved to Fürstenwalde, between Berlin and Frankfurt an der Oder and was renamed II./JG141, which changed its designation to I./Zerstörergeschwader 76 (I./ZG76) on 1 May 1939 at the same time relocating to an airfield at Olmütz, Czechoslovakia. The gruppe was being re-equipped with the Messerschmitt Bf 110 Zerstörer and Lent made his first flight in the Bf 110 on 7 June. Lent was granted his Luftwaffe Advanced Pilot's Certificate (Erweiterter Luftwaffen-Flugzeugführerschein), also known as 'C'-Certificate, confirming proficiency on multi-engine aircraft, on 12 May. While converting to the Bf 110, Lent did not have a regular Funker in the rear gunner's seat, but on 14 August he was accompanied in M8+AH for the first time by Gefreiter Walter Kubisch. On 25 August I./ZG76 deployed to an airfield at Ohlau to the southeast of Breslau. Lent participated in the attack on Poland. He destroyed several aircraft on the ground and a PZL P.24 fighter in the air on 3 September 1939 for his and I./ZG76's initial victory. However, on 12 September, following the destruction of an aircraft on the ground he was attacked by another fighter and his starboard engine was hit and put out of action. This necessitated a forced-landing, fortunately behind his own lines, in which he received minor injuries. On 29 September I./ZG76 was withdrawn to the Stuttgart area of Germany to provide Reichsverteidigung(Air Defence of Germany), against France and Britain.

Dashing night fighter pilots and national heroes like Helmut Lent attracted large amounts of fan mail, mainly from young girls and women. In Lent's case one of them was Elisabeth Petersen. Lent replied to her letter and he and Elisabeth met on a blind date at the Reichshof hotel in Hamburg, after which they enjoyed a skiing holiday in Hirschegg in February 1940. All German officers were required to obtain official permission to marry; however, this was usually a bureaucratic formality. When Lent decided to marry Elizabeth Petersen his case was more complicated. 'Elisabeth Petersen' was in fact Helene (Lena) Senokosnikova, born in Moscow in April 1914. She had been afraid to reveal her true identity, since Russians were not popular in the Third Reich, but after a thorough investigation into her background and racial ancestry, she received her German citizenship on 15 March 1941. They were married on 10 September 1941 in Wellingsbüttel, Hamburg. The marriage produced two daughters. Christina was born on 6 June 1942; the second, Helma, was born on 6 October 1944, shortly after her father's fatal crash. Both of Helmut's older brothers, Joachim and Werner, as members of the Bekennende Kirche (Confessing Church), encountered trouble with the Nazi party. The Confessing Church, led by Pastor Martin Niemöller, was a schismatic Protestant church which opposed the Reich's efforts to 'Nazify' Germany's Protestant churches. It stood in outspoken opposition to National Socialist principles, particularly those embodied in the Aryan Paragraph. Through the Barmen Declaration, the church condemned the national German Evangelical Church as heretical. Werner Lent, an adherent to the Confessing church, was arrested for the first time in 1937 after preaching an anti-Nazi sermon. In June 1942, his brother Joachim was arrested by the Gestapo after reading the so-called Mölders letter from the pulpit. The Mölders letter was a propaganda piece conceived by Sefton Delmer, the chief of the British black propaganda in the Political Warfare Executive (PWE) to capitalize on the death of Germany's fighter ace Werner Mölders; this letter, ostensibly written by Mölders, attested to the supreme importance of his Catholic faith in his life - by implication, placing faith above his allegiance to the National Socialist Party.

By June 1940 RAF Bomber Command penetrations of German airspace had increased to the level that Hermann Göring decreed that a night-fighter force should be formed. The officer tasked with its creation was Wolfgang Falck, Gruppenkommandeur of the I./ZG1 who had eight victories and received the Ritterkreuz. The night-fighter force began to expand rapidly, with existing units being divided to form the nucleus of new units. Helmut Lent briefly participated in the Battle of Britain when on 15 August twenty-one Bf 110s from I./ZG76 escorted He 111 bombers of KG26 on their attack on Yorkshire and the Newcastle/Sunderland area. I./ZG76 lost seven aircraft on this raid, which was Helmut Lent's 98th and final sortie as a Zerstörer pilot. In August Lent and his faithful Kubisch were transferred to the Nachtjagd. Born on 7 September 1918 in Helbigsdorf in Saxony, the son of a machine fitter, Kubisch had served his apprenticeship as a blacksmith before volunteering to join the Luftwaffe. Lent completed night fighter training at Ingolstadt in south-western Germany and was appointed Staffelkapitän of the newly formed 6./NJG1 on 1 October at Fliegerhorst Deelen, 12.5 kilometres (8 miles) north of Arnhem. By October 1940 NJG1 comprised three Gruppen, while NJG2 and NJG3 were still forming. It was during this period that Helmut Lent reluctantly became a member of the night-fighter force. At the end of August Lent wrote home, 'We are currently converting to night fighting. We are not very enthusiastic. We would sooner head directly for England.' Eventually, after 24 sorties without success, he sought an interview with Major Wolfgang Falck and requested a transfer to day fighters. Falck rejected the request as he was to recall:

'After we converted to night fighting, Lent's pilots were getting kills but he as the staffel leader was not scoring. He became so angry that he actually lost his nerve. In spite of the difference in ages [Falck was eight years older than Lent] and positions, we had a very fine personal relationship because he came from the same part of Germany where my family lived. In addition, we were both sons of Protestant ministers. I liked him, understood him and liked to fly with him. Because of this relationship, he came to me when his pilots were scoring at night and he was not.

'I cannot carry on in this position under these circumstances,' he said. 'I want to be transferred to the day fighters again.'

'His case was not unlike that of Steinhoff, who also did not want to be a night fighter.

'Stay here another month' I said. 'If you are not successful I will see what I can do about having you transferred. But if you are successful, as I know you will be, you will stay here with NJG1. In those four weeks he was indeed successful and rose later to Kommandeur and Geschwader Kommander. He had the education, background and bearing of a man who can carry responsibility. And more importantly, he realized the responsibility of leadership. He was a great young man and was one of our greatest 'Experten'.[25]

On the night 11/12 May 1941 Lent claimed his first night victories when he shot down two Wellington ICs on 40 Squadron on the raid on Hamburg. BL-H R1330 piloted by Sergeant Roderick William Finlayson, a New Zealander, was shot down at 0140 near Süderstapel and BL-Z R1461 which was being flown by Sergeant Frederick Tom Luscombe at 0249 near Nordstrand. Only one crewmember survived from both the Wimpys. In May 1941 Nachtjagd claimed 41 bombers destroyed. Fourteen victories were credited to I./NJG2 and six to 4./NJG1 including Stirling I N3654 on 15 Squadron flown by Wing Commander Herbert Reginald Dale (all KIA) by Oberleutnant Egmont Prinz zur Lippe Weissenfeld on the 10/11th near Spanbroek and four to I./NJG1. Operating from Schleswig airfield in northern Germany, 5. and 6./NJG1 destroyed twelve bombers in the 'Helle Nachtjagd' over the Grossraum Hamburg on the nights of 9, 11 and 12 May.

In June Nachtjagd destroyed 66 aircraft, 22 of them by I./NJG2. This included the intruder Gruppe's 100th victory, an unidentified Wellington seventy kilometres east of Great Yarmouth by Oberfeldwebel Hermann Sommer of 2./NJG2 at 2355 hours on 27 June. During 1940-41, Sommer claimed eight aircraft over England including, on 29/30 April 1941 four Blenheims, as he recalled: 'I saw an English aircraft fire recognition signals and flew toward it where I found an airfield, illuminated and very active. I joined the airfield's circuit at between 200 and 300 metres [altitude] at 0015 hours and after several circuits a aircraft came within range. I closed to between 100 and 150 metres and fired. After a short burst the aircraft exploded in the air and fell to the ground. At 0020 hours I saw another aircraft landing with its lights on which I attacked from behind and above at roughly 80 metres. The aircraft crashed after my burst of fire and caught fire on hitting the ground. In the light of the flames from the two wrecks, I could see fifteen to twenty aircraft parked on the airfield. I dropped my bombs on these.'

Sommer claimed nineteen Abschüsse in NJG2, NJG1 and NJG102 1940-early 1944. He was killed during a daylight sortie on 11 February 1944.

II./NJGI claimed 13 and I./NJG1 8. I./NJG3 at Werneuchen near Berlin for protection of the Reich capital, scored five kills during June. One of these victories was achieved by Feldwebel Ernst Kalinowski and his bordfunker Unteroffizier Zwickl of

2nd Staffel who destroyed Stirling W7430 on 7 Squadron over the 'Big City' in a 'Helle Nachtjagd' sortie on 2/3 June. The Stirling crashed northwest of Luckenwalde. The pilot, Flying Officer John Mitchell and five of his crew were killed. Only Sergeant W. S. Bellow the rear gunner survived.

On 26/27 June when Bomber Command raided Cologne, Kiel and Düsseldorf weather conditions were appalling and prevented good bombing. Two Wellingtons and two Manchesters were lost. One of the Manchesters, L7304 on 61 Squadron flown by Flying Officer Kenneth Gordon Webb, was shot down at Adolf Hitler Koog by Hauptmann Walter Fenske of I/NJG1. The Manchester crashed near Brunsbuttel with the loss of all the crew. Fenske was shot down and crashed at Kröppingen on 26 March 1944 during aerial combat. He died of his wounds on 28 March at Brodenbach. He had twelve Abschüsse. The other Manchester, L7374 on 97 Squadron which crashed off Westerhever, was lost with New Zealand Flying Officer Francis Edwin Eustace DFC and crew.

On 27/28 June Oberleutnant Reinhold Eckardt of 6./NJG1 destroyed four bombers in 46 minutes, including Whitley V Z6647 on 77 Squadron, during a 'Helle Nachtjagd' sortie in the Hamburg area. Southwest of Bremervörde at 0158 Oberleutnant Helmut Lent, Staffelkapitän 6./NJG1 claimed Whitley V T4297 on 102 Squadron - one of eleven Whitleys that failed to return - for his third night - Abschuss. Sergeant J. M. Culley's crew were all marched off into captivity. In the same area the following night, Lent destroyed Stirling I N3664 on 7 Squadron with the loss of everyone on the crew of Flying Officer Valentine Ronald Hartwright DFM. South of Wesermünde he claimed another 7 Squadron Stirling - N6001 flown by Squadron Leader William Terrance Chambers Seale, which was also lost with no survivors. Altogether, Nachtjäger destroyed ten bombers on the continent on the night of 28/29 June.

Britain's highest award, the Victoria Cross, was awarded to a Wellington crewmember after his actions on 8 July on a raid on Münster. Squadron Leader R. P. Widdowson captained one of the 75 Squadron RNZAF crews that attacked the city and was fortunate to return. Their Wellington was badly damaged by a Bf 110 night-fighter, which hit the starboard engine and put the hydraulic system out of action, with the result that the undercarriage fell half down. The bomb doors fell open too, the wireless sets were put out of action and the front gunner was wounded in the foot. Worst of all a fire was burning up through the upper surface of the starboard wing where a petrol-feed pipe had been split open. The crew thought that they would have to bail out so they put on their parachutes. Some got going with the fire extinguisher, bursting a hole in the side of the fuselage so that they could get at the wing but the fire was too far out along the wing for them to do any good. They tried throwing coffee from their flasks at it but that did not work either. By this time the Wellington had reached the Dutch coast and was flying along parallel with it, the crew waiting to see how the fire was going to develop. Finally Sergeant James A. Ward, the second pilot thought there was a sporting chance of reaching the fire by getting out through the astrodome, then down the side of the fuselage and out on to the wing. His courage was to earn the VC. Ward recalls: 'Joe, the navigator, said he thought it was crazy. There was a rope there; just the normal length of rope attached to the rubber dinghy to stop it drifting away from the aircraft when it's released on the water. We tied that round my chest and I climbed up through the astrodome. I still had my parachute on. I wanted to take it off because I thought it would get in the way but they wouldn't let me. I sat on the edge of the astrodome for a bit with my legs still inside, working out how I was going to do it. Then I reached out with one foot and kicked a hole in the fabric so that I could get my foot into the framework of the plane. I punched another hole through the fabric in front of me to get a handhold, after which I made further holes and went down the side of the fuselage on to the wing. Joe was holding on to the rope so that I wouldn't sort of drop straight off.

'I went out three or four feet along the wing. The fire was burning up through the wing rather like a big gas jet and it was blowing back just past my shoulder. I had only one hand to work with getting out, because I was holding on with the other to the cockpit cover. I never realized before how bulky a cockpit cover was. The wind kept catching it and several times nearly blew it away and me with it. I kept bunching it under my arm - then out it would blow again. All the time, of course, I was lying as flat as I could on the wing but I couldn't get right down close because of the parachute in front of me on my chest. The wind kept lifting me off the wing. Once it slapped me back on to the fuselage again but I managed to hang on. The slipstream from the engine made things worse. It was like being in a terrific gale, only much worse than any gale I've ever known in my life. I can't explain it but there was no sort of real sensation of danger out there at all. It was just a matter of doing one thing after another and that's about all there was to it. I tried stuffing the cockpit cover down through the hole in the wing on to the pipe where the fire was starting from but as soon as I took my hand away, the terrific draught blew it out again and finally it blew away altogether. The rear gunner told me afterwards that he saw it go sailing past his turret. I just couldn't hold on to it any longer.

'After that there was nothing to do but to get back again. I worked my way back along the wing and managed to haul myself up on to the top of the fuselage and got to sitting on the edge of the astrodome again. Joe kept the dinghy rope taut all the time and that helped. By the time I got back I was absolutely done in. I got partly back into the astro hatch but I just couldn't get my right foot inside. I just sort of sat there looking at it until Joe reached out and pulled it in for me. After that, when I got inside, I just fell straight on to the bunk and stayed there for a time.

'Just when they were within reach of the English coast the fire on the wing suddenly blazed up again. Some petrol, which had formed a pool inside the lower surface of the wing, had caught fire. However, after this final flare-up the fire died right out much to the relief of all the crew. The crew pumped the wheels down with the emergency gear and Widdowson decided that instead of going to Feltwell, he'd try to land at another aerodrome nearby which had a far greater landing space. As he circled before landing he called up the control and said, 'We've been badly shot up. I hope we shan't mess up your flare-path too badly when we land.' He put the aircraft down beautifully but the Wellington ended up by running into a barbed-wire entanglement. Fortunately nobody was hurt.'[26]

Squadron Leader Ray Glass DFC a pilot in 214 Squadron was one of 57 Wellington crews despatched to Osnabrück two nights later, on 9/10 July, in a Merlin engined Wellington II:

'We carried a 4,000lb 'Dustbin' bomb. In a Wimpy the bomb doors and floor were removed and the bomb attached by a one-inch wire hawser and toggle to a metal beam introduced under the main spar. An axe was supplied to cut the hawser in case it hung up. So much for technology! We reached the Zuider Zee but with a full moon silhouetting us from above and below, we were a sitting target. We were attacked by a Me 109 and 110, which were beaten off by the rear gunner who claimed the 110 as a 'probable'. Our port engine was hit so we bombed Bergen airfield and observed a huge smoke ring of debris and the runway lights went out.'[27]

On 11 July Leutnant Wilhelm Johnen and his 'sparker' bordfunker Gefreiter Risop, a Berliner, took off on their first operational sortie in 3./NJG1 at Schleswig. Johnen, born on 9 October 1921 in Homberg at the Niederrhein (Lower Rhine region), had, in June 1941 been posted to 3./NJG1 at Schleswig commanded by Hauptmann Werner

Streib.[28] Mild, briny, sea-air greeted him as he landed in the black out and opened the cockpit roof of his Bf 110. Now, on his first sortie, bombers were reported flying singly over the North Sea. The target for three dozen Hampdens were the shipyards at Wilhelmshaven. Without radar Johnen and his 'sparker' relied on instructions from 'Meteor' the Westerland ground station giving the course and altitude of the bombers and their own night vision. Although they saw two bombers they dived in to the cover of cloud each time Johnen cocked his cannon and the night-fighter crew returned to Schleswig without firing their guns in anger. But they had been blooded. 'Good bombing' was claimed by the attackers with no aircraft lost.

In the summer of 1941 ground trials of the new radar navigational aid 'Gee'[29] were in progress at Marham, Norfolk. Twelve pilots and twelve observers on 115 and 218 Squadrons were involved in the trials and had been informed they would not be undertaking operational flying until these were completed. Understandably they were surprised to be notified of briefing for an attack on Sunday 13 July 1941. It was to be a 'maximum' effort consisting of 69 Wellingtons, 47 of which were targeted on Bremen, twenty on Vegasack and two on Emden. All crews would encounter heavy cloud and icing. Sixteen aircraft would claim to have bombed Bremen. Two Wellingtons would fail to return from the Bremen attack.[30] On 115 Squadron the all-sergeant crew of Wellington IC R1502, W. J. Reid, pilot and captain, Geoff T. Buckingham, observer, M. B. Wallis wireless operator, M. G. Dunne, front gunner and T. W. Oliver, rear gunner were short of their regular second pilot. He had been sent to London to attend a Commission Board. 27-year-old Sergeant-pilot Frederick Birkett Tipper, who was regarded as a jinx on the Squadron, took his place. The crew that he had flown with on his first sortie had suffered a very shaky 'do'. On his second operation the aircraft had crashed on take-off, fortunately with no fatal result. Bremen would be his third operational flight.

The observer's chair in a Wellington moved backwards and forwards in tracks firmly fastened to the floor of the aircraft. When he boarded the aircraft Buckingham found to his intense annoyance that the tracks to his chair were broken leaving it free to slide all over the place in the event of violent evasive action. Furthermore, the chair cushion was missing. Instead of throwing his parachute pack on the bed as he usually did - he would have to sit on it in lieu of the cushion. Little did he realize that before the night was out the object of his annoyance would save his life.

The sky was clear in England but over the North Sea thick cloud was encountered. As they approached the enemy coastline there was a partial thinning of the cloud and Sergeant Tipper was able to pass a pinpoint on the Dutch Coast to his observer. Tipper then left the cockpit and made his way aft to the astrodome where he would keep a constant vigil for night fighters. The Wellington was now at 9,000 feet. Buckingham had just spotted Texel Beacon and was returning to this station from the cockpit when Sergeant Oliver in the rear turret yelled over the intercom, 'Fighter'. Simultaneously he opened up with his guns raking the fuselage with vibration and filling it with the fumes of cordite. Oberleutnant Egmont Prinz zur Lippe-Weissenfeld, the Austrian Prinz and Staffelkapitän, IV./NJG1 had just made his initial strike, setting the starboard engine of the bomber on fire. He was now somewhere out in the darkness manoeuvring for a second attack. Buckingham rushed forward to the cockpit and pressed the starboard engine fire extinguisher button. This put out the fire. Next he jettisoned the bombs and gave the pilot a reciprocal course to fly. He then returned to the cabin to check his log. At this moment the second attack occurred and it was far more devastating than the first. Cannon fire from beneath the bomber raked the whole length of the fuselage wounding all members of the crew, some more seriously than the others. Buckingham blacked out. When he came round he was lying across the step, adjacent to the forward escape hatch. As the aircraft had gone into a dive the loose seat, which he had cursed so roundly at the beginning of the flight, had slid to the nose and deposited him on the floor by the escape hatch. His parachute pack, which he had used as a cushion, was lying on top of him. He took stock of the situation. The bomber was on fire and he was wounded in the face and arm with cannon shrapnel. There was a hole in the back of his leg, which was bleeding profusely. The door to the front turret was wide open. There was no sign of the pilot. Fastening his parachute pack to the harness he found that one J-clip had been- smashed by the cannon fire. He used the remaining clip then heaved on the edge of the escape hatch. In an instant he was out and away into the night. Hanging awkwardly beneath his parachute, suspended at an angle by one clip only, he made a bad landing injuring his anklebone. Tipper's body was recovered from the wreckage.[31] It was assumed that Tipper had been killed by the second burst of fire from the night fighter. Later Prinz zur Lippe-Weissenfeld visited the crew in hospital and expressed his regret that a member of the crew had died. He said he was after the bomber not the crew.

Endnotes Chapter 2

25   Quoted in *Horrido!* by Colonel Raymond F. Toliver and Trevor J. Constable (Bantam 1968).
26   Ward was KIA on 15/16 September 1941, shot down in a 75 Squadron Wellington over Hamburg.
27   2 FTR. 82 a/c bombed Aachen 1 Hampden and 1 Whitley FTR. Three crews of NJG1 claimed 3 of these losses.
28   By October 3./NJG1 was re-designated 1./NJG5 and then in December again re-designated, this time to 5./NJG5.
29   A navigational and blind-bombing device, which was introduced into RAF service during August 1941. It consisted of the reception by equipment in the aircraft of transmission from a 'master' ('A') and 2 'slave' stations ('B' and C) situated on a base line about 200 miles long. The difference in the time taken by the 'A' and 'B' and 'A' and 'C' signals to reach the aircraft were measured and displayed on a CRT of the navigator's table in the aircraft. From then on the aircraft could be located on 2 position lines known as 'Gee' coordinates. Accuracy of a 'Gee' fix varied from less than ½ a mile to about 5 miles, depending on the skill of the navigator and the strength of the signal. 'Gee' range varied with the conditions from 300-400 miles.
30   The starboard engine on a Wellington IC on 75 Squadron flown by Sergeant F. I. Minikin cut as the bomber crossed the coast at 6,000 feet and crashed in the sea near Corton, 2 miles N of Lowestoft. Both pilots, who were injured, were picked up. Rest KIA.
31   R1502 had crashed at 0028 on 14 July at Onderdijk, 5 km S of Medemblik.

Chapter Three

'The Other Prinz'

Prinz zur Lippe-Weissenfeld was born on 14 July 1918 in Salzburg, Austria and as a member of a cadet line of the aristocratic House of Lippe. His father was Prinz Alfred zur Lippe-Weissenfeld and his mother Anna Weissenfeld, née Countess Goëss. Egmont was the only son of four children. His sisters Carola, Sophie and Dora were all younger than Egmont. The family lived in an old castle in Upper Austria called Alt Wartenburg. At birth he had a remote chance of succeeding to the throne of the Principality of Lippe, a very small state within the German Empire. However, only months after his birth, Germany became a Republic and all the German royal houses were forced to abdicate. Prinz zur Lippe-Weissenfeld in his younger years was very enthusiastic about the mountains and wildlife. From his fourteenth year he participated in hunting. At the same time he was also very much interested in music and sports and discovered his love for flying at the Gaisberg near Salzburg. Here he attended the glider flying school of the Austrian Aëro Club. He attended a basic flying course with the second air regiment in Graz and Wiener Neustadt even before he joined the military service. Prinz zur Lippe-Weissenfeld never married or had children. In January 1941 he became acquainted with Hannelore Ide, nicknamed Idelein. She was a secretary for a Luftgau. The two shared a close relationship and spent as much time together as the war permitted, listening to music and sailing on the Ijsselmeer.

At the age of 18 Prinz zur Lippe-Weissenfeld joined the infantry of the Austrian Bundesheer in 1936. In the aftermath of the 1938 Anschluss, the incorporation of Austria into Greater Germany by Nazi Germany, he transferred to the German Luftwaffe and was promoted to Leutnant in 1939. He had earned his Luftwaffe Pilots Badge on 5 October 1938 and underwent further training at Fürstenfeldbruck, Schleissheim and Vienna-Aspern. His Luftwaffe career started with II./ZG76 before he was transferred to NJG1 on 4 August 1940. The unit was based at Gütersloh where he familiarised himself with the methods of the night fighters. He claimed his first aerial victory, a Vickers Wellington on 115 Squadron at 0205 hours, on the night of 16/17 November 1940. His second victory was claimed on the night of 15 January 1941 when he shot down an Armstrong Whitworth Whitley N1521 on 58 Squadron at Linton-on-Ouse over the northern Netherlands, near the Dutch coast in the Zwanenwater at a nature reserve at Callantsoog. He was wounded in action on 13 March, while flying a Bf 110 D-2 of 4./NJG1 with his bordfunker Josef Renette when he made an emergency landing at Bergen after their aircraft was hit by the defence fire, wounding them both. By the end of March 1941 he had accumulated 21 aerial victories for which he was awarded the Knight's Cross (Ritterkreuz des Eisernen Kreuzes) on 16 April 1942. Shortly after midnight on 10 April 1941, Prinz zur Lippe-Weissenfeld claimed a 12 Squadron Wellington over the Ijsselmeer, raising NJG1's victory score to 100. This achievement was celebrated at the Amstel Hotel in

Amsterdam with General Josef Kammhuber, Wolfgang Falck, Werner Streib, Helmut Lent and others attending.

On 30 June 1941 while flying a Bf 110C-4 on a practice intercept mission over Noord Holland, he collided with a Bf 110C-7 piloted by Leutnant Rudolf 'Rudi' Schoenert of 4./NJG1 and crashed near Bergen aan Zee. On 19 June 1941 he earned his first of four references in the daily Wehrmachtbericht, a daily radio report made by the Oberkommando der Wehrmacht (High Command of the Armed Forces) regarding the military situation on all fronts. By July 1941 his number of aerial victory claims stood at ten. Promoted to Oberleutnant he became Staffelkapitän of 5./NJG2 on 15 November 1941. By the end of 1941 he had claimed a total of fifteen aerial victories. He was awarded the German Cross in Gold (Deutsches Kreuz in Gold) on 25 January 1942 and the Knight's Cross (Ritterkreuz des Eisernen Kreuzes) on 16 April 1942 after he had shot down four RAF bombers on the night of 26/27 March, his score standing at 21 aerial victories. This feat earned him his third reference in the Wehrmachtbericht on 27 March 1942. In July he was one of the leading German night fighter aces with 37 aerial victories.

Promoted to Hauptmann, Prinz zur Lippe-Weissenfeld was made Gruppenkommandeur of the I./NJG3 on 1 October where he claimed three further aerial victories. He was transferred again, taking command of III./NJG1 on 31 May 1943. One month later he claimed his 45th aerial victory for which he was awarded the Knight's Cross with Oak Leaves (Ritterkreuz des Eisernen Kreuzes mit Eichenlaub) which he received on 2 August. After a one month hospital stay, Prinz zur Lippe-Weissenfeld was promoted to Major and made Geschwaderkommodore of NJG5 on 20 February 1944. He and his crew, Oberfeldwebel Josef Renette and Unteroffizier Kurt Röber, were killed in a flying accident on 12 March on a routine flight from Parchim to Athies-sous-Laon. Over Belgium they appear to have encountered low cloud and a dense snowstorm and it was assumed that the aircraft hit the high Ardennes ground after being forced to fly lower because of ice forming on the wings. Bf 110G-4 C9+CD crashed in the Ardennes Mountains near St. Hubert where the completely burned-out wreck was found the following day. The funeral service was held in the city church of Linz on 15 March. Prinz Egmont zur Lippe-Weissenfeld and Prinz Heinrich zu Sayn-Wittgenstein are buried side by side at Ysselsteyn in the Netherlands. Lippe-Weissenfeld, who in life was often referred to as 'the other Prinz', is credited with 51 aerial victories, all of them claimed at night.

By the end of the war, the 4./NJG1 was one of the most successful Nachtjagdstaffel of the Luftwaffe. Other members included such night fighter pilots as Oberleutnant Helmut Woltersdorf, Leutnant Ludwig Becker (44 victories, killed February 1943); Leutnant Leopold 'Poldi' Fellerer (41 victories); Oberfeldwebel Paul Gildner (46 victories, killed in a flying accident at Fliegerhorst Gilze-Rijen in the Netherlands in February 1943) and Unteroffizier Siegfried Ney (twelve victories, KIA February 1943).

On 30 August 1941 Helmut Lent received the Knight's Cross (Ritterkreuz des Eisernen Kreuzes) for seven day and fourteen night victories. On 1 July he had taken command of 4./1 NJG1 at Fliegerhorst (airfield) Leeuwarden. During the month he claimed seven kills to take his score to twenty victories. He claimed his tenth Night-Abschuss on 12/13 July when 33 Hampdens and 28 Wellingtons raided Bremen. He destroyed Hampden AE226 on 50 Squadron at 0055 on the morning of the 13th. The bomber crashed at Veendam in Holland; there were no survivors on South African Pilot Officer Edward Douglas Vivian's crew.

On 14/15 July 78 Wellingtons and nineteen Whitleys were dispatched to Bremen where they were given three aiming points; the shipyards, the goods station and the Altstadt. One of the Wellington ICs that took part was 'T-Tommy' on 9 Squadron at

Honington with an all-sergeant crew captained by 20-year old Sergeant Jack Cyril Saich, who came from Dunmow, Essex. Robert Douglas Telling, who was from Epsom, Surrey was the second pilot. Navigator was Smitten, a Canadian from Edmonton, Alberta, while the three remaining members were an Englishman, Sergeant Eric Trott, from Sheffield and two more Canadians - Hooper from Vancouver, the front gunner and Sergeant English the rear gunner was from Picton, Nova Scotia. 'T-Tommy' (T2619) took off at 2330 on 14 July with seven 500lb bombs on board. It seemed at first that Bremen would prove hard to find for the weather was very thick. Just before 'T-Tommy' reached the city, however, it came out of the clouds into a clear sky carved by the sharp blades of searchlights. There was a slight haze over the rooftops 11,000 feet below but Smitten found the target and Saich began his bombing run. It was just twenty minutes to two in the morning. One bomb was released, when the wheeling searchlights caught and held 'T-Tommy' in a cone of light which grew in size and intensity as more and more beams concentrated upon the aircraft. Two heavy anti-aircraft shells burst just behind and below the rear turret and inside the fuselage itself level with the leading edge of the tail plane. The first shell wounded English in the shoulder and the hand and cut the hydraulic controls to the turret so that it could no longer be turned except by the slow process of cranking it. Fragments of the other shell riddled the rear part of the fuselage and set on fire the fabric covering it and the tail fin. Saitch said, 'The flames seemed to be the signal for every anti-aircraft gun in the target area to give full and uninterrupted attention to us.'

And all this time, be it remembered, the rear gunner was in the blazing end of the torch. Saich took violent evasive action and succeeded in throwing the German gunners momentarily off their aim. While he was doing so Smitten went to the help of English in the rear turret. He made his way down the rocking, shell-torn fuselage till he was brought up short by the fierce fire separating him from the turret. Here for the moment he could go no further. He crawled back a little way, snatched a fire extinguisher and returned to the fire in the fuselage, which he presently subdued. Above him the fin still flamed. He sprayed it with all that remained of the methyl bromide in the extinguisher, thrusting it through the hot framework of the fuselage from which the fabric had burnt away. He was able at last to reach the turret.

English was still there but he had made preparations to abandon the aircraft by swinging the turret round into the beam position and opened the doors to throw himself out backwards. The doors now refused to close. Back went Smitten and returned with a light axe. He leant out through a hole beneath the fin, which he had just saved from burning, the wind of the slipstream tearing at him and hacked away at the doors till they fell off. English was then able to rotate his turret by means of the hand gear and as soon as the gaping hole, where once the doors had been, coincided with the end of the fuselage, he extricated himself and entered the aircraft.

While this was going on astern more trouble broke out forward. The Wellington was hit again and a shell splinter set light to the flares carried in the port wing. These are for use in an emergency, when a forced landing has to be made in darkness. They burned brightly - so brightly that Saich thought the port engine was on fire. He promptly turned off its petrol, opened the throttle fully and switched off. Soon, however, the flames died down, for the flares had burnt their way through the fabric of the mainplane and fallen from the aircraft. Realising what had happened Sergeant Saich turned on the petrol again and restarted the engine. At his orders Telling was crouched beside the main spar behind the wireless cabin pumping all the oil which could be extracted from a riddled auxiliary tank. 'T-Tommy' was still under intense anti-aircraft fire and the shell splinters, one of which wounded him, were described by Telling as 'angry hail tearing through the aircraft.'

One further misfortune had befallen the Wellington. At the moment when the Germans scored their first hit, the bomb doors were open, for the aircraft was completing its first bombing run-up and one of the bombs had just been released. The damage caused by the anti-aircraft shell was such as to make it impossible either to close the bomb doors or to release the remaining six bombs, since the hydraulic pipes had been punctured and the electrical wiring to the slips had been severed. As well as this and the damage to the fuselage, the rear turret, the rudder and the fin, there was a large hole knocked by a shell in the starboard wing. It had just missed the petrol tanks.

In this condition 'T-Tommy' was headed for base. The chances of making it did not appear bright. The aircraft with bomb doors open and a heavy load still on board was very hard to control and Saich's task was not made easier by the hole in the wing through which the draught rushed, blanketing the starboard aileron which was for all intents and purposes useless. Nevertheless be held sternly to the homeward course given him by Smitten and at 0535 hours on 15 July 'T-Tommy' crossed the English coast dead on track. Its speed had been much reduced and the petrol gauges had been registering zero gallons for two hours out of the four on the return journey from Bremen, over nearly 300 miles of sea. With dry land beneath him once more Saich determined to make a forced landing, for he thought that at any moment the engines would stop for lack of fuel.

The sky was now 'pale as water before dawn' and he picked out a barley field where it seemed to him that a successful landing might be made. In the half-light he did not see the obstruction poles set up in the field to hinder an airborne invasion. He set about making his perilous descent. The flaps would not work and when he came to pump the undercarriage down with the emergency hydraulic band pump he found that, owing to loss of oil, it would only push the tail wheel and one of the main wheels into their positions. 'T-Tommy' came in to land, lop-sided a little to take full advantage of the one sound wheel. On touching down, the aircraft swung round but its motion was violently arrested by an obstruction pole. It shuddered and then came abruptly to rest on its belly with its back broken. Save for many bruises none of the crew sustained further hurt. 'T-Tommy' was little more than a wreck. It had flown to that East Anglian barley field with a huge hole in its starboard wing, with uncounted smaller holes in its fuselage, with nine feet of fabric burnt entirely away forward from the rear turret, with half the fin and half the rudder in the same condition. Yet it flew home. The operative word is 'flew.' Saich and Smitten were awarded the DFM.[32]

Crews reported the 'whole of Bremen was ablaze'. Four Wellingtons were lost on the Bremen raid and one crashed at Stiffkey in Norfolk. Unteroffizier Benning of l./NJG3 destroyed either T2737 on 149 Squadron which was ditched in the North Sea (all of Pilot Officer O. L. Dixon's crew were rescued) or W5726 on 305 Squadron flown by Flying Officer Jerzy Janota-Bzowski. He and five crew were killed. Leutnant Eckart-Wilhelm 'Hugo' von Bonin of 6./NJG1 destroyed R1613 on 214 Squadron flown by Pilot Officer J. G. Crampton (PoW). Born in Potsdam on 14 November 1919, von Bonin joined the Luftwaffe in November 1937. His first victory had come on the night of 10/11May 1941 when he destroyed a Wellington. Two Stirlings returning from Hannover crashed in England and a Wellington crashed near Veendam. Two Wellingtons were shot down. Oberleutnant Helmut Lent's victim has been identified as Wellington II W5513 on 104 Squadron flown by Pilot Officer William George Rowse which was lost with all six crew.

On the night of 24/25 July 1941 34 Wellingtons and thirty Hampdens were detailed to raid Kiel and 31 Whitleys and sixteen Wellingtons were dispatched to bomb the docks at Emden. A Hampden and a Wellington were lost on Kiel. Two Wellingtons that failed to return from the attack on Emden were shot down by night fighters of 4./NJG1. At Boazum Helmut Lent, who was flying alone that night, shot down Wellington IC R1369 on 57 Squadron piloted by Sergeant F. L. Green which crashed off the Frisian Islands. Green and three of his crew were killed, two crew were taken prisoner. The other Wellington was R1397 on 103 Squadron which had taken off from Elsham Wolds with five other Wimpys at about 2330 hours. R1397 was captained by Mervyn Lund, the 23-year-old pilot from New Zealand. His four other crewmen were also in their twenties. Rear gunner Frank Walker from Yorkshire was the oldest member of the crew at 30. There was some light fog over the North Sea but visibility was good and their flight went well; the crew had flown on six previous sorties together and when they turned for home the dockyards were ablaze. Then, at about 0400, high over the fields of Holland, they were spotted by a night-fighter pilot who made an attack. The Wellington fought him off and took evasive action but the German pilot dived and attacked again from below. This time he crippled the Wellington, which crashed in flames in a pasture close to a farm near the village of Kleiterp. Bas van Gelder, a vicar, recalled: 'Suddenly there was a tremendous roar and a black shadow passed before a fierce jet of fire sprayed the air. Out of the sky a flaming, smoking wreck appeared. There was a tremendous bang and then the darkness returned.' The impact blew a thirty feet crater into the ground and people from the village quickly gathered, before a squad of German soldiers appeared, clapping and cheering when they saw the devastation. Soon though, they were dodging and ducking the shrapnel from the wrecked plane. 'They looked like rabbits fleeing from fireworks,' joked the Dutch villagers. The dead RAF men were not identified and their remains were buried in a single, anonymous grave in the nearby town of Leeuwarden, although none of this was known back in Britain. Seventy years after the event, the RAF still acknowledged only that the men were 'missing presumed killed in action'.[33]

The following night, 25/26 July, thirty Hampdens and 25 Whitleys were despatched to Hannover and 43 Wellingtons visited Hamburg. Two Whitleys on 10 Squadron were lost to crews of 1./NJG1 and 4./NJG1. One of the Whitleys went down in the North Sea; the other crashed at Koresel in Belgium. There were no survivors on either aircraft. Leutnant Lothar Linke of 4./NJG1 destroyed Hampden AD835 on 83 Squadron at Scampton over Schiermonnikoog at 0357 hours for his third Abschuss. The skipper, Sergeant P. H. Draper was injured but his three crew, including 27-year old air-gunner, Sergeant Edwin Marsden were killed. In 1948 his grieving parents Mr. and Mrs. Marsden of Blackburn visited their only son's grave at Vredenhof cemetery on Schiermonnikoog. Altogether during July, 63 Bomber Command aircraft were claimed shot down.

Lothar Linke was born on 23 October 1909 at Liegnitz in Schlesien. Pre-war he was a flying instructor. At the outbreak of World War II, Oberfeldwebel Linke was serving with 3./ZG76. He participated in the invasions of Poland and Norway. He recorded his first victory on 19 April 1940 when he shot down Blenheim IV P4906 on 107 Squadron at Lossiemouth, flown by Sergeant Peter Chivers near Stavanger in Norway. The aircraft was lost without trace and all three crew are listed on the Runnymede Memorial. Linke transferred to the Nachtjagd in August. Following conversion training, he was posted to II./NJG1 and was assigned to 4./NJG1. Linke gained his first night victory on the night of 11/12 May 1941 when he shot down a Wellington near Osterfelde. On 1 November 4./NJG1 was re-designated 5./NJG2. On 26 June 1942 he destroyed a Wellington and on 27 July he scored his seventh Abschuss when he shot down Lancaster R5748 on 106 Squadron Rottevalle. On the 13/14

September raid on Bremen when training aircraft from the OTUs were included in the 446 aircraft dispatched, he shot down Wellington IC HD991 flown by Sergeant George Stanley Bickerton RCAF on 22 OTU which had taken off from Stratford. Bickerton and two of his crew were killed. Two others were taken into captivity. It was a bad night for 22 OTU which lost three Wimpys in total. Twenty-one year old Pilot Officer Frank H. de Nevers RCAF from Vandura, Saskatchewan and his crew were killed. So too were 22-year old Sergeant John Hywell Davies and crew on R1658. (Altogether, thirteen bombers were lost from various OTUs and two from conversion units).

By the end of the year Linke had increased his victory total to eleven. Also, 5./NJG2 had been re-designated 11./NJG2 on 1 October. On 27 February 1943 Linke was appointed Staffelkapitän of 12./NJG1. On the night of 4/5 May he claimed five RAF bombers destroyed to record his 20th to 24th Abschüsse. His first was a Wellington, followed by a Halifax, Lancaster and two more Halifaxes. Linke was credited with 27 victories in over 100 sorties. He recorded 24 victories at night, including twelve Viermots and a Mosquito IV (DZ386 XD-H) on 139 Squadron flown by Wing Commander Peter Shand on 21 April 1943 at North Ijsselmeer. Linke was shot down on the night of 13/14 May 1943 after downing two Lancasters when his Bf 110G-4 was hit by return fire from Halifax II BB252 on 10 Squadron at Melbourne flown by 32-year old Sergeant Eddie Fish, from Blackpool who left a widow, Clara Jane, northwest of Lemmerwegen. Six of Fish's crew were killed. Sergeant Michael John Boyle, air gunner of New Malden, Surrey was critically injured in the crash and died on 15 January in Leeuwarden Hospital. Linke and his crewman bailed out but Linke struck the tail unit of the aircraft and fell to his death. Walter Czybulka landed safely by parachute. He was wounded and taken to a hospital in Leeuwarden. Oberleutnant Linke was posthumously awarded the Ritterkreuz on 19 September 1943. Of his three victories recorded by day, two were recorded flying as a Zerstörer pilot.

On 6/7 August 1941 two Wellingtons and two Whitleys failed to return. Hauptmann Werner Streib, Kommandeur of 1./NJG1 shot down Whitley V Z6488 on 51 Squadron south-east of Eindhoven and Feldwebel Reinhard Kollak, Wellington IC X9633 on 149 Squadron at Thorembais East of Wavree. Kollak was born at Frogenau in East Prussia on 28 March 1915 and began his military career by joining the Reichswehr. In 1935 he was transferred to the Luftwaffe where he trained as a fighter pilot. Upon completion of his training in the spring of 1940 Kollak was posted to I./ZG1 and participated in the campaigns in France and the Battle of Britain. In October 1940 he joined the newly formed 1./NJG1 and claimed his first night victory while flying as a Feldwebel when he destroyed a Whitley in the early hours of 17 June 1941. Destined to become the highest scoring non commissioned Nachtjagd pilot, by all accounts Reinhard Kollak was a modest man who shared the credit for his successes with his bordfunker Hans Herman and was credited with 49 victories in over 250 sorties, all at night. Herman had joined the Luftwaffe in 1938 at the age of nineteen and served as Kollak's bordfunker until the war's end.

In August a record 67 RAF bombers were shot down by flak and fighters. They included fifteen by I./NJG2, twelve by 4./NJG1, another twelve by I./NJG1 and one by III./NJG1. On the night of 12/13 August when seventy RAF bombers were detailed to attack Berlin only 32 of the aircraft reached the capital and got their bombs away on the aiming point at the Reichsluftfahrtministerium (RLM or Reich Air Ministry) building in the Alexander Platz and nine aircraft were lost. Manchester L7381 on 207 Squadron was brought down with the loss of Flying Officer William Michael Ronald Smith DFC and all his crew. Leutnant Hans Autenrieth and his bordfunker, Gefreiter Rudolf 'Rudi' Adam and gunner Unteroffizier Georg 'Schorsch' Helbig flying a Bf 110D-3 of 6./NJG1 took off from Stade on a 'Helle Nachtjagd' interception sortie in search of their first night-Abschuss. Autenrieth was born on 15 March 1921 in Weiler. From 1939 to June 1941 he completed training at Erganzungstaffel./NJG1. Adam, who was born on 21 July 1919, had been a trumpeter in a dance-band before the war. Georg 'Schorsch' Helbig was born on 29 June 1920. Autenrieth recalled his experiences that night:

'I had taken off with the first wave to area 2A on my third operational flight but, having had to abandon this sortie due to malfunction of the oxygen system, I thought myself to be dogged by bad luck. Fortunately, however, this proved not to be the case, for it gave me the opportunity to take the place of another crew of the second wave and, using their machine, to operate in area 2C which had the reputation of being the most successful one. Having orbited the radio beacon for about half an hour, I received the report 'Otto, Otto' from ground control. I flew towards the searchlight cone but was unable to recognize the target within it. As I was only a little above the target; it took a long time before I was close enough to make out the coned aircraft in the haze. I watched the enemy machine trying to escape the searchlights by diving and twisting. When at last I had approached to within about 500 metres, I was able to make out that it was a four-engined machine. As the searchlights were already at a very low angle and I was worried that the Tommy would soon have escaped from them and also from me, I opened fire. I fired short bursts at the wildly twisting Tommy who then succeeded to get out of the searchlight's cone.

'I was of course very disappointed at this failure. But this disappointment was not to be the only one this night. Whilst still blaming myself for this missed opportunity, I received the report of a second sighting which I was able to spot at once. I was about 2000 metres above him and tried to reach him as quickly as I was able. Only after having dived down some 1000 metres and having to steepen my dive even more in order to keep him in my sights, did I realize that the Tommy was on an opposite course and that I had been in an ever steepening dive. My engines screamed, I never got a chance to fire and I levelled gently out. The air-speed indicator showed almost 700km/h and I thought the aircraft would break up. I forgot all about the Tommy. Whilst I dived past him through the searchlights, I was blinded by one of them which shone directly in my face. When I again looked out I saw the beams hanging above me and to my left. Only then did I realize where was up and where was down. When I was at last back to level flight I found myself 1000 metres below the still coned enemy machine. I climbed back after him with full power. I closed steadily in, it was a Vickers Wellington. When I was about 150 metres behind him, the rear gunner of the Wellington suddenly opened fire at me. But the bullets passed to port of my cockpit. I pressed all the buttons at once and aimed the first burst at the rear turret. When this had been silenced, I went for the starboard engine and wing. The hits could be made out clearly and a long trail of smoke appeared. As my Me 110 was considerably faster than the Wellington, I was soon so close that I had to pull up above it.

'Then I heard ground control shout 'Sieg Heil' and immediately after my radio operator as well. I went into a turn to port to take a look at the burning Tommy, but to my disappointment could see nothing at all. Shortly afterwards ground control reported: 'Machine descended burning with smoke trail in direction 3.' My disappointment at this misfortune was great, in which my radio operator joined me. When I was directed at a new sighting at only 1000 metres' height I was certain that it would be the Wellington I had just fired at. I went for him angry as hell. But when I was still at 2000 metres the Tommy had escaped the searchlights and I climbed back to 6000 metres and called it a day.

'Towards 3 o'clock I was directed to another Tommy who was flying 10-12 kilometres away and 1000 metres below me. With my advantage of height I soon closed on the four-engined enemy aircraft from his rear and above. At about 100 metres I opened fire on his starboard engines and wing with machine guns and cannon and turned away to port and above for a second attack. When I had done my 180-degree turn the Tommy was no longer being held by the searchlights. But I saw a long trail of smoke which I now followed. The controller asked me whether I was still able to see the enemy aircraft. Unfortunately I had to say no. But at almost the same moment I spotted the British bomber on my starboard bow, huge and only some 100 metres below. I reduced power to adjust to the Tommy's speed and make my second attack from his port quartet and above. Unfortunately, one cannon had failed during my first attack and I no longer had full firepower. I was unable to observe the effect on the Tommy as I had to break off in order not to ram him. After this second attack I was unable to see either the Tommy or a smoke trail. Some ten minutes later my radio operator and I observed the fire of a crash. We had both guessed correctly: it was our first Abschuss. This was confirmed at once by the controller who reported over the radio that the Tommy had been held by the Würzburg radar right up to his crash. We were very pleased by this first success and returned home with two enemy contacts and one kill. It transpired that the Halifax had continued to fly for another twelve minutes after my two attacks, until it finally went down from 1000 metres height [500 metres north-east of Wittstedt and fifteen kilometres SSE of Bremerhaven] at 0316.'[34]

The crew on Halifax L9531 MP-R on 76 Squadron at Middleton St. George piloted by Sergeant Clarence Emerson Whitfield bailed out safely but Whitfield and four others fell into a swamp and were drowned. Flight Sergeant William Andrew Irving Bone the rear gunner was one of two who were taken into captivity but he was shot and killed on 19 April 1945.

In England on the night of 12/13 August German Intruders attacked targets in Cambridgeshire. One of them, a Ju 88G flown by Oberfeldwebel Rolf Bussmann of 3/NJG2 headed towards Weston-on-the-Green where he shot down two Avro Ansons assigned to 15 Service Flying Training School. Flight Sergeant E. Julin-Olsen from Norway was killed just after midnight. His Airspeed Oxford 2 aircraft was shot down at 4,000 feet. A few moments later Bussmann shot down another Oxford 2, which crashed a mile north of Tackley killing LAC C. P. Blair, from Portugal. Bussmann also dropped six 50 kilogram bombs and machine gunning Weston-on-the-Green aerodrome, damaging seven parked Oxford aircraft. His aircraft might also have been responsible for dropping eight bombs on Kidlington aerodrome and nine on Chipping Norton aerodrome the same night. Heading back east near Ely another target was spotted, this time a Blenheim on 17 OTU, which had just taken off from Upwood for night flying practice. Bussmann fired a single burst and the Blenheim fell in flames to crash near the village of Wilburton. There were no survivors. Bussmann and his crew returned to Gilze-Rijen where they landed very heavily, which caused the undercarriage to collapse and their aircraft to slew off the runway. The crew only just managed to vacate the night fighter before it burst into flames.

On 14/15 August Oberfeldwebel Robert Lüddecke of 3/NJG2 flying a Bf 110 claimed two Wellingtons twenty kilometres east of the Humber Estuary for his second and third Abschüsse. He had previously destroyed a Wellington forty kilometres southeast of Eastbourne on 27 June. North east of Barrington on the night of 19/20 August 21-year old Feldwebel Alfons Köster of NJG2 shot down Wellington IA N3005 on 11 OTU as 26-year old Flight Sergeant Cyril George Andrews began his approach at Bassingbourn. Nineteen year old Sergeant Richard Henry Hazell was killed. Eighteen year old Sergeant Ronald George Peter Capham suffered minor cuts and bruises and the after-effect of shock. Andrews and Sergeant Frederick Guttridge later died of their injuries in Addenbrookes Hospital. Before NJG2 departed into the dark skies above they circled around again coming in at low level to strafe a stationary Wellington at the base.[35] The Wellington was the seventh aircraft on 11 OTU to be destroyed by NJG2.

Oberleutnant Ludwig Becker and his Bordfunker Unteroffizier Josef Staub of 4./NJG1 flew Do 215 G9+OM, the first Fu 202 Lichtenstein AI-equipped night-fighter on operations from Leeuwarden during late summer 1941. With the use of this revolutionary radar set and skilfully guided by the fighter controller of 'Himmelbett' box 'Lowe' ('Lion') they claimed six bombers west of Groningen. At this time the Nachtjagd had devised the simple but effective system of dividing their airspace into boxes, each of which was patrolled by night fighters that were warned of the approach of enemy bombers by ground radar interpreted by a ground controller. Once the aircraft had entered the 'box', the night fighter used its on-board radar to track it and hopefully shoot it down. Throughout the war, this system was improved and revised as both sides found counters for the other's new equipment, but generally it always ended with the fighter crew being the last link between the bomber and its fate. The long loiter time of aircraft like the Bf 110, Ju 88 (and later the He 219), enabled the crews to intercept the RAF night bomber streams over very long distances and there were many occasions when bomber crews relaxed their vigils just that little bit too soon and paid the ultimate price. It required a considerable amount of fortitude and self-discipline to stay alert at the controls of a heavy fighter for several hours, listening to the ground controller, the aircraft's radar operator and peering into the darkness to spot tell-tale flames from exhausts or the sudden burst of fire as another night fighter made an interception. Some crews flew several months without victories and some were content with downing one bomber then relaxing their own vigil.

On 8/9 August Oberleutnant Ludwig Becker and his bordfunker Unteroffizier Josef Staub shot down Wellington IC T2625 on 301 'Pomeranian' Squadron piloted by Flying Officer M. Liniewski who was killed, as were three of his crew. Only two crew survived to be taken into captivity. On 14/15 August when Hannover was the target for 152 RAF bombers, Oberleutnant Ludwig Becker and his Bordfunker Unteroffizier Josef Staub of 4./NJG1 shot down Whitley V Z6842 on 102 Squadron which crashed at Terwispel in Holland. Flight Lieutenant D. N. Sampson and crew were taken into captivity. Helmut Lent claimed his thirteenth Night-Abschuss when Whitley V Z6819 on 51 Squadron crashed off Schiermonnikoog with the loss of Sergeant Peter Ryland Griffin and crew. On 17/18 August when Bremen was the target for 39 Hampdens and twenty Whitleys, Hampden I AE185 on 50 Squadron at Swinderby was Ludwig Becker's next victim. Pilot Officer E. C. Maskell and his three crew were rescued. The aircraft crashed at Paterswolde in Holland. On 6/7 September on a raid on Hüls by 86 aircraft, Whitley V Z6478 on 10 Squadron at Leeming was brought down by Becker and crashed at Oldebroek in Holland. There were no survivors on Sergeant Aubrey Poupard's crew. Becker's sixth victim, on 29/30 September, when the target for 93 aircraft was Hamburg, was Wellington IC X9910 on 115 Squadron at Marham. Sergeant Arthur Robert Hulls and all his crew were killed.

The chance of a RAF bomber crew finishing a tour of thirty operations was remote but by mid-August 20-year old Sergeant Basil Sidney Craske, a Whitley pilot on 10 Squadron at Leeming Bar in North Yorkshire had completed 26 and the 27th, to Cologne on the night of 16/17 August was viewed as 'relatively easy'. Craske's crew on Whitley V Z6805 'G-George' consisted of 34-year old Sergeant Harold P. Calvert, navigator, Sergeant King, WOp/AG and Sergeant Bruce Robertson, rear gunner. In view of promised cloud cover from the Dutch coast to the target Craske and Calvert agreed upon a track to the target as opposed to 'going in by the back door'. Craske was to recall:

'It was a relatively calm night and after a bit of a stooge across the North Sea we obtained a good fix and some flak around the Hook of Holland. It was fairly obvious by this time that the promised cloud cover was a figment of the Met man's imagination, as it was as clear as a bell. But our die was cast, our course plotted, so we continued as planned. The searchlights were obviously working overtime and it was not going to be easy to sneak through by playing the waiting game. However, this was our best bet and sure enough the dancing beams of light merged into strong cones both to port and starboard, balancing an aircraft in full glare on the tip of the cone like a jet of water holding a Ping-Pong ball on a fairground rifle range. Our chance had arrived and with all the power that 'G-George' could muster I went for the gap. Alas, not much progress had been made through the searchlight belt when the cockpit was filled with dazzling light. Normally, with a few hectic manoeuvres there was a fair chance of losing the lights but on this occasion the centre' light had a bluish colour and had fastened on to 'G-George' and no amount of twisting and turning could shift it and its accompanying beams. I was so occupied with trying to get out of the illumination that it was something of a surprise to hear and to see cannon tracer shells flying around the aircraft and in particular flashing up through the unoccupied front gun turret. The attack was from below and mercifully the rear turret was missed but gaping holes were blasted in the underside of the fuselage even to the extent of losing the Elsan (I wonder who the lucky recipient was beneath). I concluded that the bombs, positioned beneath the cockpit, acted as armour plating and had saved the three of us in the cabin - a sobering thought. I had no doubt in my mind what to do next. I put the nose straight down and kept it that way. The ASI registered 320 mph. In the meantime Robbie in the rear turret was more than a little disturbed and was yelling all sorts of things into the intercom. He thought we had all 'had it' and certainly I was not able at that time to put his mind at rest. We had been at our usual 12,000 feet and at about 7,000 feet I tried to get back on an even keel, which was easier said than done. The port wing had dropped and the only way I could get sufficient purchase on the 'stick' (a large wheel) was to put my feet against the dashboard and heave like blazes with the wheel turned as far to the right as I could get it. With some relief I got 'George' out of the dive and regained straight and level flight once again.

'I calmed Robbie with the news that I was still alive and flying and took stock of our situation. The engines were sounding good and while we were somewhat battered, there seemed no reason not to go to the target. However, a further attack from the starboard saw cannon shells whistling through the starboard engine, through the cockpit and within inches of my feet and out the other side. The starboard engine caught fire. I managed to extinguish it but the port engine sounded a bit sick to say the least. It was amazing to me that the pilot of the night fighter did not finish us off but presumably he lost us in the darkness.'

Oberleutnant Wolfgang 'Ameise' ('Ant') Thimmig of 2./NJG1, who was born on 4 October 1912 at Dresden/Saxonia is credited with shooting Craske's Whitley down at 0230 hours near Winterswijk twenty kilometres northeast of Bocholt. Thimmig's kill was one of the earliest 'Dunkel Nachtjagd' ('dark night fighting') victories, being achieved in complete darkness and under the guidance of ground radar. The crew jettisoned the bombs and everything removable but Craske was unable to maintain height and he ordered his crew to bail out. Everyone survived and they were made PoW. (Harold P. Calvert was later shot in cold blood by a member of the Polizei after escaping from Stalag IIIE). In all seven Whitleys and a Wellington failed to return from the raid on Cologne, the majority of these losses being due to night fighters of I./NJG1. Three Hampdens and two Manchesters meanwhile failed to return from a raid on Düsseldorf by 52 Hampdens and six Manchesters and one Wellington was lost on the raid against rail targets at Duisburg by 54 Wellingtons.

Rail targets at Duisburg were attacked again on 17/18 August when the weather was bad and bombing was poor and again on 18/19 August when the weather was clear and the bombing results were good. Raids were mounted against Kiel, Mannheim, Düsseldorf, Karlsruhe and Cologne until on 28/29 August rail targets at Duisburg were once again the objective of Bomber Command. The force this time was made up of sixty Wellingtons, thirty Hampdens, thirteen Stirlings, nine Halifaxes and six Manchesters. Furthermore, six Hampdens on 49 and 106 Squadrons made searchlight suppression sorties near the target, as Sergeant George Luke, WOp/AG on Sergeant Eric Robert Holmes Lyon's crew on AE193 ZN-A, one of the three Hampdens of 106 Squadron used in the operation, explains:

'The apprehension felt at the possible danger involved was counteracted to a degree by the feeling of pride, rather like being chosen for the first eleven at school. We 'intruders' were to take off early and reach the target fifteen minutes ahead of the main force. We carried a small load of incendiary bombs to release at 14,000 feet and additional ammunition for the machine guns, which, after diving to low level, we would use against the searchlights on the target route. We were to continue to harass the searchlights, hopefully keeping them out of action for one hour allowing the main force to bomb, leave the target area and be well on route for home and then they would regain height and return to their bases. This would enable the main bomber force to avoid the searchlight cones and the resulting attention of the German fighter and flak concentrations.

'We released the incendiary bombs, surprisingly meeting little opposition en route, then dived to low altitude and commenced our attack on the searchlights. I felt great exhilaration during the low level attacks, the sense of speed being much greater and in my position as under gunner in the Hampden I was kept extremely busy firing away left and right at searchlights as they were switched on. They were extinguished immediately, whether by our marksmanship or intentionally by the Germans, we were not sure. We continued our attack with the wireless operator firing from the upper gun position. I felt that we were successfully achieving our purpose, although in the hectic activity taking place I caught sight of one of the main force bombers, which was caught in a cone of searchlights, receiving a pasting from the flak batteries. We were meeting only light flak and machine gun fire from the searchlight defences.

At low level and in the dark you are upon your target and gone almost before they can react. The pace of events was so fast that the hour-long attack seemed to last but a few minutes. Then we regained height and set course for base. We had crossed the Dutch coast at about 10,000 feet and were approximately forty miles northwest of Texel, when because of a technical inability to switch fuel tanks, we lost both engines and we were forced to ditch. We all survived but after drifting in a dinghy for three days we were in such poor physical condition that when we were found by a Dutch fishing boat they had no choice but to hand us over to the German Naval authorities in the small harbour of Zoutkamp.'[36]

On the night of 28/29 August Helmut Lent claimed his 14th Night-Abschuss when he destroyed Hampden I AE126 on 49 Squadron which crashed off Ameland with the loss of Pilot Officer Bernard Maurice Fournier and crew. In September Lent claimed three bombers destroyed. His fifteenth Night-Abschuss came on the night of 6/7 September when he shot down Whitley V Z6881 on 78 Squadron which crashed at Bergum, Holland with the loss of Pilot Officer Francis Bernard Thorpe's crew. The night following, 7/8 September, he destroyed Wellington IC Z8845 on 9 Squadron which was being piloted by Sergeant Jack Cyril Saich who had been awarded the DFM for bringing 'T-Tommy' back against all odds from Bremen on 15 July. Saich and all his crew including Sergeant Eric Trott were killed. Lent claimed Wellington IC R1798 on 115 Squadron also. The Wimpy crashed near Drachtstercompaignie with the loss of Flight Sergeant John Gerald O'Hara Keating RCAF and crew. That night they were among 197 bombers that went to three aiming points in Berlin while another 51 bombers headed for Kiel. The Berlin force comprised 103 Wellingtons, 43 Hampdens, 31 Whitleys, six Halifaxes and four Manchesters. One of the Manchesters was EM-W L7380 on 207 Squadron which was flown by Flight Lieutenant Wilfred John 'Mike' Lewis DFC. Born in Durham Country, Ontario on 24 March 1918, 'Mike' served in the Durham Militia from 1936 to 1938 as a machine gunner. He first applied to join the RAF on 1 May 1937, was eventually selected and on 15 July 1938 he took the SS *Alaunia* to England. He completed his pilot training and was commissioned on 17 September. He joined 44 Squadron, flying his first op on 4 December 1939. By August 1940 Pilot Officer Lewis had carried out 35 operational flights over enemy territory with conspicuous success and gallantry, totalling over 200 hours operational flying. On the night 17/18 September he successfully pressed home a dive bombing attack on a concentration of barges in Antwerp docks. During the preliminary reconnaissance over the target area, the aircraft was subject to intense and accurate enemy anti-aircraft fire and searchlights. During the dive bombing attack, intense anti-aircraft fire and tracer severely damaged the tailplane in seven places, the starboard engine and the fuselage, causing the aircraft to be temporarily out of control. This action earned 'Mike' the award the DFC on 8 October 1940. He then went on to serve on 97 and 207 Squadrons. Now, a year later, on 7 September, a day or two after the completion of his second tour, the 207 Squadron CO saw Mike packing to go on leave and said, 'We're short one pilot for tonight. Would you mind doing one extra trip?' Mike agreed. This one extra op would cost him his freedom for three years and eight months, as Sergeant Charles Hall, his WOp/AG recalls:

'The outward flight was uneventful until about midnight when at about 13,000 feet over the sea near Tonning in Schleswig-Holstein, Sergeant 'Dusty' Miller the rear gunner shouted, 'Night fighter astern!' This was accompanied by a stutter of machine gun fire, which hit our aircraft in the area of the port engine. As Miller opened fire the night fighter continued over the top of the Manchester enabling me, from my mid upper gunner's position, to fire into the belly of the enemy aircraft at very short range. Flight Lieutenant Lewis had immediately dived our aircraft and sought cover of thick cloud and contact was lost with the enemy fighter. There were no casualties but we had a serious fuel leak so after dropping our 4,000lb bomb and incendiaries on a searchlight concentration at Wilhelmshaven (which had given us much trouble in previous operations) we set course for Waddington. The port engine cowling began to glow red-hot, then white hot in turn. Lewis shut down the engine, feathered the airscrew and activated the fire extinguisher within the engine cowling. This seemed to extinguish the fire but thereafter twelve very anxious eyes were focused on the port engine for signs of further trouble! It soon became apparent that we were not capable of maintaining height on the one remaining Vulture engine so we gradually lost height. With the gunners keeping a sharp lookout we descended through cloud emerging at 1,500 feet over Holland with the inhospitable grey-black waters of the North Sea clearly visible. At this point Lewis decided that we were not going to make the English coast and turned south aiming to reach the Friesian Islands. The Friesians eventually came into view and turning westward again Lewis kept the aircraft parallel to the shore. We took up our crash positions. Amidst noise, water and mayhem we hit, bouncing several times before settling in what turned out to be the surf of the North coast of Ameland.'

Lewis put the Manchester down safely on the beach in about five feet of water at 0010 hours. The crew took to their dinghy and got ashore. As they had previously agreed not to compromise any Dutch civilians, they were taken prisoner. Their attacker was Feldwebel Siegfried Ney of 4./NJG1 who successfully claimed this as his fifth Abschuss.[37] In all, 137 crews claimed to have bombed their allotted targets in Berlin. Fifteen bombers were missing and at least ten, including two Wellingtons on 115 Squadron at Marham, are thought to have been shot down by night fighters. R1772 piloted by Sergeant Rowland Bertram Dunston Hill was shot down over Kiel Bay by a Bf 110. All five of Hill's crew bailed out safely and were taken prisoner. R1798 flown by Sergeant Ian Patrick McHaffie Gordon was shot down on its return from Berlin by Oberleutnant Helmut Lent of 4./NJG1 as his 23rd Abschuss at 0458 hours near Drachtstercompagnie in Friesland province with the loss of all the crew.

In September Nachtjagd shot down 34 aircraft, including four by the intruders of I./NJG2 and nine by III./NJG1. II./NJGl's tally rose to over 100 kills on 15/16 September when Unteroffizier Walter Geislinger of the 6th Staffel destroyed Stirling I N6021 LS-O on 15 Squadron at Hemslingen, Germany with the loss of Pilot Officer Edward John Douglas Guild and his crew. In October Nachtjagd shot down twenty more Viermots, including two by I./NJG2, ten by 4./NJG1 and four by I./NJG1 including Manchester L7373 on 207 Squadron at 0530 on 14 October by Gefreiter Erhard Brühnke, which crashed two kilometres south of Gorssel near Beverlo, Belgium. The skipper, Pilot Officer Lionel Arthur Paskell DFM and four of his crew were killed. One man evaded and one was taken into captivity.

Over East Anglia on the night of 3/4 October Feldwebel Alfons Köster of 3./NJG2 flew low over Oakington, opening fire on a Wellington on 101 Squadron that had just landed. Three crew members were injured. Köster, was born on 6 February 1919 in the city of Hüingsen (Sauerland) and joined the Luftwaffe as Unteroffizier in 1938. After completing his training in the late 1940s, Köster was appointed to serve on the 3./NJG2. His first night victory, a Defiant, came on the night of 9/10 April 1941 in the skies over England. In July of the same year, he was promoted to Feldwebel. On 15 July Köster shot down two Blenheims for his fifth and sixth victories. On 20 August he was awarded the Trophy of Honour after eight confirmed kills. In late 1941 he was transferred along with his Gruppe to the Mediterranean where he shot down another four aircraft at night, plus a fifth victory during the day.

A short while after attacking the Wellington on 101 Squadron at Oakington Köster and his crew intercepted Short Stirling I N6085 MG-H on 7 Squadron, which had taken off from Oakington and was heading home after failing to find Brest in occupied France. At 2230 hours, just as they were approaching the area of Bourn airfield from the south, the sound of cannon fire could be heard above the roar of their engines. Köster had spotted the huge bomber and brought his night-fighter to bear on the target. The giant four engined bomber was covered in white flashes from cannon shells exploding as they slammed into one of the Stirling's wings. Immediately one engine caught fire and the conflagration quickly spread to the entire wing. Fortunately the night fighter broke off the engagement. Squadron Leader Donald Ian McLeod the Stirling pilot gave the order to bail out, one crew member shouting for the pilot, who was still at the controls, to get out too. However McLeod remained at his controls to give his six crew time to get out. Only Sergeant I. Hunter

RNZAF and Pilot Officer J. R. Alverston got out safely. The burning aircraft was seen flying over Papworth. It passed west over the church and carried on, approaching Kisby's Hut area near Bourn. It gradually lost height, crashed through a line of trees and smashed into a field where it broke apart. At first locals thought it was German aircraft down, but as they neared the scene from amidst huge sheets of flame the unmistakeable tail fin of a Short Stirling was evident. It was possible to see the dead pilot still in his seat. Tom Ford, a local ARP warden, managed to retrieve his body from the flames using a long stick. A policeman arrived with one of the crew who had bailed minutes before; this man told them that there were still several bombs on board. In the crash the bombs had been torn out of the bomb bay and had been thrown a considerable distance forwards. The bombs were discovered a short while later, lying on the surface of the field.[38]

On the night of 12/13 October Helmut Lent claimed his 18th and 19th Night-Abschüsse when he destroyed two Wellington ICs over Holland. His first victim was X9822 BL-J on 40 Squadron flown by Sergeant George Frederick Bateman, which crashed at Westergeest at 0006 with the loss of all the crew. Hampden I AD965 on 144 Squadron followed at 0033 and crashed in the Ijsselmeer with the loss of Rhodesian Sergeant Herbert Edward Chamberlain and crew. On 15/16 October when 27 Wellingtons and seven Stirlings were dispatched to bomb Cologne three Wimpys were shot down. Feldwebel Heinz Meier of 2/NJG1 in a Bf 110 claimed one of the Wellingtons for his first victory when he shot X9916 on 75 Squadron RNZAF down at Gravenbicht/Limburg at 2117 hours. Sergeant John Anthony Matetich, a Rhodesian and crew were killed. Oberleutnant Reinhold Knacke also claimed a Wellington for his thirteenth Abschuss. On 26/27 October when 115 aircraft attacked the shipyards and two city aiming points in Hamburg Unteroffizier Alfred Brackmann of I./NJG3 claimed a 'Manchester' (possibly a Hampden, which limped home and crashed near Whitby) for his second victory SSE of Bremervoorde. Two Wellingtons were shot down; one ditched in the North Sea, 120 miles off Cromer and another crash-landed in Suffolk.

Warrant Officer J. W. B. Snowden and the crew of Wellington X9873 on 115 Squadron joined the grim reaper's toll on 31 October/1 November 1941 when they failed to return from a raid on Bremen. X9873 was the only aircraft lost. Four Whitleys were lost on Hamburg, one being claimed by Oberleutnant Paul Gildner of 4./NJG1 operating from Leeuwarden in a Bf 110. X9873's observer, Albert E. Robinson, recalled: 'The Bf 110 made a copybook attack from astern and below on our Wellington at 1930 hours. We never saw him until it was too late. We were never in with the chance of a shot. He just loomed up out of the murk with a startling suddenness and opened up with a prolonged and devastating burst of cannon fire. It was all over in a matter of seconds. No time to consider. One minute we were happily of course and the next we were plunging down and about to crash, ironically, on Schiermonnikoog itself.' Fate decreed that he should survive the shoot down by Gildner, all five crew being taken prisoner plus some 'enlightening even if somewhat dreary years' in German prison camps before liberation by Russian troops in May 1945' It was Gildner's 20th victory and the Whitley later that same night - probably Z9141 MH-J on 51 Squadron piloted by Flight Lieutenant Eric Arthur Barsby - was his 21st. Barsby and his crew were killed. Unteroffizier Heinz Grimm of 5./NJG2 destroyed one of the other Whitleys north of Nordeney for his second Abschuss. Oberleutnant 'Rudi' Schoenert of 4./NJG1 claimed two Halifaxes and Oberfeldwebel Siegfried Ney of the same unit claimed a Wellington west of Callanstoog.

On 1 November 1941 Lent became acting Gruppenkommandeur of the newly formed II./NJG2. His twentieth night Abschuss and his last that year came during the night of Friday 7 November/Saturday 8 November. He shot down a Wellington IC heading for Berlin, which came down near Akkrum. The six-man all-New Zealander crew of X9976 on 75 Squadron RNZAF which was being flown by Sergeant John William Black were killed in the action. This achievement earned Lent a reference in the Wehrmachtbericht (his first of six in total), an information bulletin issued by the headquarters of the Wehrmacht. To be singled out individually in the Wehrmachtbericht was an honour and was entered in the Orders and Decorations' section of one's Service Record Book.

In December 1941 Nachtjagd claimed thirteen Viermots including three by 4./NJG1 and another three by I./NJG1 on the 27/28th. On 28/29 December 61 Hampdens of the 81 detailed reached their target, the Chemische Werke, a synthetic rubber plant at Hüls west of Duisburg. The target was clearly identified in the moonlight and the factory was thoroughly bombed, fired and photographed. Four Hampdens were lost. P1165 on 408 'Goose' Squadron RCAF at Balderton, flown by Pilot Officer Stuart Bruce Keigh Brackenbury RCAF, who was on his eighth trip, fell to the guns of Oberleutnant Helmut Woltersdorf of 7./NJG1 and the Hampden crashed two kilometres west of Winterswijk (Gelderland). Woltersdorf was born on 15 November 1915 in Friedberg. Brackenbury had reached the target and bombed it. The flare they could have used to illuminate the target had not been needed so they were still carrying it when a Bf 110 night fighter attacked them while at 15,000 feet. The flare was hit and ignited. Brackenbury bailed out. He was free for four hours before being found by some Dutchmen who led him down back streets to the police station, which was manned by Germans. He was taken to meet Major Wolfgang Falck, Kommandeur NJG1 at Twente. Falck apologized and treated him well before he was taken to a prisoner of war camp.[39] Helmut Woltersdorf was killed at Twente on 2 June 1942 when he crashed into parked aircraft after being attacked by an enemy aircraft while landing with his bordfunker Heino Pape, who was wounded in the crash.

On the night of 30 November/1 December when 181 bombers attacked Hamburg, losing thirteen aircraft, Leutnant Ludwig 'Luk' Meister of 5./NJG1 claimed his first victories; a Halifax, five kilometres south of Bramstedt at 2221 hours, a Whitley thirty kilometres northwest of Stade four minutes later and a Wellington at Hamburg at 2325. However, only two victories are confirmed. Ludwig 'Luk' Meister was born on 14 December 1919 at Rohrmühle near Erbendorf in Bavaria. He joined the Luftwaffe in October 1939 and learnt to fly at 4./Flieger-Ausbildungs-Regiment 51 at Weimar/Nowra before transferring to the A/B Schule at Dresden/Klotzsche in November. Further training at Flugzeugführerschule C9 at Altenburg followed from 30 June 1940. On 21 February1941 he arrived at Blindflugschule 1 at Brandis and, finally, Zerstörerschule at Neubiberg where he received his operational training on the Bf 110. In mid-June he was posted to NJG1 and was assigned to the Ergänzungsgruppe to gain an appreciation of Nachtjagd tactics. In September he was transferred to II./NJG1 operating from Stade near Hamburg. In February 1942 II./NJG1 relocated to St. Trond in Belgium. Here, between 11 and 13 February, Meister participated in Operation 'Donnerkeil': the aerial protection of the battleships *Scharnhorst* and *Gneisenau* and the battle cruiser *Prinz Eugen* on their dash through the English Channel to Norway. His bordfunker was Feldwebel Hannes Forke.

On 20 January during a 'Himmelbett' sortie over the North Sea to the north of Terschelling, Oberleutnant Ludwig Becker of the 6th Staffel NJG2 destroyed three Wellingtons in 37 minutes: Z8370 on 12 Squadron flown by Flight Lieutenant W. H. Thallon, who was taken prisoner; Z1110 on 101 Squadron flown by Sergeant Peter Lewis Chapman and Z1207 on 142 Squadron flown by Pilot Officer John Grant Scott

RCAF with the loss of both crews. Paul Gildner claimed Hampden I AT148 on 49 Squadron flown by Flying Officer Alexander Muir Harvey. There were no survivors. Mainly because of a lull in Bomber Command operations just sixteen bombers were claimed destroyed by Nachtjagd in January 1942. Twelve of these went to II./NJG2 at Leeuwarden, which 23-year old Hauptmann Helmut 'Bubi' ('Boy') Lent, innovator of the night fighter arm had established on 1 November 1941. On the night of 17 January he claimed his 21st Night-Abschüsse when he shot down Whitley V Z9301 on 51 Squadron at Terschelling at 2145 hours. Sergeant James Thomas Thom and crew were killed. A few nights later, on 21/22 January at 2228 Lent claimed another Whitley, Z9311 MH-J on 51 Squadron at Dishforth. There were no survivors on Pilot Officer Bernard Sides crew. A mere seven victories were claimed by Nachtjagd in February, all by II./NJG2. Hauptmann Helmut Lent destroyed Hampden AE308 on 455 Australian Squadron at Swinderby in daylight west of Terschelling on the 6th for his 30th day-Abschüsse. Sergeant Bernard Edward Brown's crew, who were one of 33 Hampdens on 'Gardening' operations off the Frisians were lost without trace. Small numbers of aircraft often made themselves useful sowing their 'vegetables' on 'Gardening' sorties to 'regions' that stretched from the French Atlantic coast to as far as the Kattegat. Each 'region' had codenames like 'Spinach' (the area off Gdynia in the Baltic); 'Geraniums', 'Tangerines', 'Sweet Pea' and 'Silverthorne'.

On 24/25 February Oberleutnant Egmont Prinz zur Lippe Weissenfeld, Staffelkapitän, 5th Staffel II./NJG2 claimed two Hampden Is on 144 Squadron which were one of 44 Hampdens on 'Gardening' operations in the Frisians. The first was an uneven duel with X2969 flown by 21-year old Flight Sergeant Bruce Thomas Dundas, son of the second Marquess of Zetland. In the battle between the two aristos, there was only one outcome. Hardly a noble death, all four crew were lost without trace. AT194 flown by Sergeant Karl Hugo Eklund RAAF also vanished into the North Sea with the loss of the entire crew. On the 27th Whitley Z9280 on 77 Squadron went down to Unteroffizier Heinz Vinke at Driesum at 2258 hours (the first of his 54 night victories). Squadron Leader Leslie Hugh William Parkin DFC and three of his crew died, one man surviving to be taken into captivity. Destruction of two other 77 Squadron Whitleys, Z6943 piloted by Flight Lieutenant Donald Atherton Irving RAAF and Z9148 flown by Pilot Officer Morris Donald Darwin McCarthy RNZAF, were credited to Leutnant Leopold 'Poldi' Fellerer and Oberfeldwebel Berthold 'Petz' ['Sneak'] Ney respectively. There were no survivors on either aircraft.

21-year-old Leutnant Dietrich 'Dieter' Schmidt, who was born on 17 June 1919 at Karlsruhe, had initially been posted from the Zerstörerschule at Neubiberg to 8./NJG1 at Twente in the Netherlands in September 1941 before joining III./NJG1. He comments on the early wartime Nachtjagd procedures:

'The Third Gruppe of NJG1 was at Twente, an airfield to the north of Enschede in Holland. The Gruppe was carrying out Helle Nachtjagd in a sector of the night-fighting defences reaching from the Heligoland Bight to Belgium, together with the searchlight and fighter control units stationed there: when approaches by enemy aircraft were reported, a number of night fighters were sent up to readiness positions, then shoot down any enemy aircraft caught in the searchlights. At the time, the British used almost exclusively twin-engined aircraft, Wellingtons, Whitleys or Hampdens, flying loosely on a broad front, i.e. practically singly. In our opinion, we young crews had been over-trained for our task as night fighters: to begin with, we were only permitted to take off for practice flights, especially for searchlight target indications and sometimes we were ordered to cockpit readiness for the more senior crews. So two months passed before I had my first operational flight and another two-and-a half months passed before I had my second one. But at that time the night air war was a slow business. Crews were trained for the 'Himmelbett' method of the 'Dunkle' ['Dark'] Nachtjagd'. In that, the abilities of the Jägerleitoffizier [JLO, or GCI-controller] were critical, as he directed the fighter to a position behind and a little below the enemy aircraft with a succession of courses, heights and speeds to fly, until he was able to make him out as a dark shadow against the lighter night sky. During the first half of 1942 we received the first Bf 110s specially built for night-fighting, recognisable by the large propeller spinners. Each DB601F motor delivered 1300 hp but suffered frequent engine trouble and caused some losses. New British aircraft such as the twin-engined Avro Manchester and the Short Stirling began to appear. One Manchester its engines damaged by flak, had force-landed in Holland on its return and we had taken a good look at it.'

It had soon become obvious that the 'Helle Nachtjagd' with searchlights could only function in more or less clear weather. At the beginning of 1942 therefore, fighter controllers were equipped with radar sets, one 'Freya' early warning one and two Würzburg 'Riese' ('Giant Würzburg') for individual guidance and the crews trained for the 'Himmelbett' method of the 'Dunkle' Nachtjagd. In that, the abilities of the controller were critical, as he directed the fighter to a position behind and a little below the enemy aircraft with a succession of courses, heights and speeds to fly, until he was able to make him out as a dark shadow against the lighter night sky. Kammhuber's system resembled the British GCI-system and it took full advantage of Bomber Command's tactic in sending bombers singly and on a broad front and not in concentrated streams. All approaches to Germany and its main industrial centres were divided into 'Himmelbett Räume' ('four poster bed boxes'), circular and partly overlapping areas in which one to three fighters orbited a radio beacon. Individual 'Himmelbett' positions were equipped with a long-range 'Freya' AN early warning radar, two Würzburg Riese radar with a range in the direction-finding mode of 31½-37½ miles (50-60 kilometres), a ground to air transmitter, one-two radio beacons and a visual beacon. Positions near the coast were additionally equipped with a Wassermann or 'Mammuth' long-range search installation. When approaching bombers were located by 'Freya' radar its Jägerleitoffizier would vector an individual Nachtjagd crew towards a single bomber with one of the Würzburg radars at his disposal. The bomber was simultaneously plotted on a Seeburg Tisch (an accurate plotting table with a radius of 36 kilometres) by the second Würzburg. Night fighters were at first restricted to activity within the area of their boxes. Procedure was for one night fighter to be taken under GCI control in each 'Himmelbett' Box affected by the raid, while any other night fighters available orbited the radio beacon at different heights in the waiting area. The first night fighter was vectored towards the bomber formation until such time as it picked up the enemy in its Lichtenstein B/C, whereupon it was released from control and the remaining aircraft were called up and sent into action one by one. Lichtenstein B/C airborne interception radar had been given industrial priority No.1 in July 1941 and the first four Lichtenstein B/C sets were installed in aircraft of NJG1 at Leeuwarden in February 1942. Such was their effectiveness that by the spring successes obtained through the searchlight and GCI techniques were about equal.

These therefore, were the defences which confronted crews in Bomber Command at the beginning of 1942 but a new and dynamic leader and the arrival of a new aircraft which was to prove the most successful bomber of the war, were about to usher in a new era in RAF Bomber Command.

Endnotes Chapter 3

32   Telling was killed 6 months later on 19 January 1942 when his Wellington broke up during a training flight near Thetford, Norfolk. Saich and 5 others on 'T-Tommy's crew, including Sergeant Eric Trott, KIA on the Berlin raid on 7/8 September 1941 when their Wellington was shot down in flames by a German night fighter, believed to be flown by Oberleutnant Helmut Lent of 4./NJG1 near Terwispel in Holland. Fifteen bombers FTR.

33   Including 21 by I./NJG2, 16 by 4./NJG1,14 by I./NJG1 and 5 by III./NJG1.

34   Quoted in *Night Airwar* by Theo Boiten (The Crowood Press 1999).

35   See *War-Torn Skies of Great Britain: Cambridgeshire* by Julian Evan-Hart (Red Kite 2008).

36   3 Wellingtons, 1 Halifax, a Hampden and 1 Stirling, were lost. The 2nd and 3rd searchlight suppression Hampdens (AD971 EA-O and AE126 on 49 Squadron), which FTR on 28/29 August were shot down and crashed into the Waddenzee, south of Ameland. Oberleutnant Helmut Lent, 4./NJG1, shot down AD971 at 0340 hours for his 21st victory. Pilot Officer Bernard Fournier and his 3 crew KIA. They were buried in Nes General Cemetery. Ten minutes earlier AE126 piloted by Pilot Officer Thomas Pratt had gone down in the same area, probably shot down by flak at 0043 hours in the Waddenzee. 3 of the crew were buried on Vlieland and Texel Islands and Sergeant A. Willis, under gunner, at Harlingen. In addition to the searchlight suppression losses, 3 Wellingtons, 1 Halifax, a Hampden and a Stirling on the Main Force on Duisburg were lost probably all to flak.

37   Siegfried Ney's eleventh and final Abscuss seems to be a Hampden I on 408 Squadron north of Petten on the night of 27/28 March 1942 when he was killed after being struck by debris from a Whitley on 138 Squadron. Returning to Canada in 1945, 'Mike' Lewis continued to serve in the RCAF until his retirement in 1965. He died on 17 July 2009 at Dorothy Ley Hospice (Toronto) in his 92nd year.

38   See *War-Torn Skies of Great Britain: Cambridgeshire* by Julian Evan-Hart (Red Kite 2008). Oberfeldwebel Alfons Köster was finally awarded the Knight's Cross on 29 October 1942 after 16 confirmed victories. In the spring of 1943 he was transferred to the Stab I/NJG1 and in September of that year, promoted to Leutnant. Köster would claim 26 aerial victories, 25 of them at night, before he and his crew, Leutnant Bodusch and Unteroffizier Lingen, were killed on the night of 6/7 January 1945 when their Ju 88C-6 (wrk nummer 621499 D5+PX) was shot down and over Varel. Köster was posthumously promoted to Hauptmann.

39   Hampden IAD804 on 144 Squadron crash-landed only 30 kilometres from the site of the crash of P1165, at Gaanderen, 6 kilometres east of Doetincham (Gelderland). Emergency landing was made to save the life of Sergeant Cheesman, seriously WIA over Germany and who died in hospital shortly after his arrival.

Chapter Four

The Defence of the Reich 1942

Düsseldorf was not made up of little houses - it was high flats. One cellar was made into an airraid shelter and fortified - they made a soft wall in them so that if something happened, you could knock through to next door or the other way around. It wasn't so bad until 1942 and then it really started. Don't forget, we had three enemies, the Americans in the daytime, the British at night and the Gestapo every day. If you saw a stranger, you treated him with mistrust - say even someone who came from a different part of Düsseldorf. You never knew, if you said, 'This damn war,' if they would report you. People had been arrested for showing a bit of light in the blackout. They were accused of guiding the RAF in - but we didn't need to tell them - they knew where we were. All they had to do was find the cathedral of Cologne, go up the Rhine and there they were. Everything you said was picked up - even if you grumbled about the food. You had to be careful - you were really afraid. In the factories they put Gestapo in among the workers in boiler suits. If there was a meeting, if someone voiced a wrong opinion, they were arrested. Within yourself you felt resentful about having to suffer the war, but you could only talk to the family - but sometimes you couldn't even trust them. There were no squeakers in my family, but there were occasions when children had reported their parents.

The drive to recruit young people was towards the end of the war. I was involved in that. I learned to shoot after the war I could go to the fairground and win prizes and I taught my children to shoot with air rifles. But I never fired a shot in anger.

The difference between our two countries was not hate. The British always classed the army as the Nazi Army but we looked on the Nazi Army as the SS. Even the Germans were afraid of them. The Wehrmacht was just the same as your army - conscripted people. You would hear old soldiers after the war saying that the SS stood behind them and pushed them into the front line. Officers had been shot for disobeying orders from the SS. You nursed the myth that all Germans were bad but we didn't want the war. I didn't want to lose my friends. When the bombings started I went down to the Rhine where I felt safe. I didn't want to be buried alive. I was in a flat with an air-raid shelter underneath, but it was claustrophobic, which was why I wouldn't go down there. As soon as the siren went, it was only five minutes to the Rhine and there was a big green there where we felt safe. If a bomb dropped it was a million to one chance it would drop on you but for a big house to drop on top of you, that's a bit different. I had no hate, even in those days and I have none now. We knew that someone had been given a job to do and they were doing it. The Americans came over during the day at the sort of height that you see aeroplanes flying over now. They always did carpet bombing - never target bombing. In the winter you would see a great vapour trail and then you knew there was a load coming towards you. If you heard something whistling while they were coming towards you, you ducked. If they were passing you, you knew you were safe. The RAF tried to hit the target, but my school was bombed - in my street there were 144 houses and after the war there were just three shells left. Two streets further down were the barracks, but it was our street which was obliterated. We all said we thought it was the bomb aimer's fault. It's an easy mistake, at night in a wind. We put it down as a mistake.

When you came out after a raid, the first thing you did was make sure who was underneath, who you could help to get out and you counted your friends - so and so had not come out - they must be under the rubble. The soldiers in the barracks came and helped - an elephant from the zoo came and helped - and the zoo was bombed too. Police, air-raid wardens, army, civilians, anybody who could possibly help, helped. If a dog heard a knocking, you'd dig until you found where that knocking was coming from. Quite a few got killed, but you tried to get out as many as you possibly could. The only places where the cellars were actually damaged were where the landmines went. We lost our water supply and had to go down to the Rhine to get a bucket of water to wash. The Rhine was beautiful in those days - but I wouldn't put my toe in it now. We call it a cesspit now, but in my days it was really lovely.'

Eleven-year old Angelica Sohn. The bombing of her home town was so traumatic that she could not hear a thunderstorm without the old fear returning, just as it did in the war.

On 22 February 1942, having been recalled from the USA where he was head of the RAF Delegation, Air Marshal Sir Arthur T. Harris arrived at High Wycombe, Buckinghamshire, to take over as Commander-in-Chief of RAF Bomber Command from AVM J. E. A. 'Jackie' Baldwin, who had, since 8 January been standing in for Sir Richard Peirse, who had been posted to India. Harris was directed by Marshal of the RAF, Sir Charles Portal, Chief of the Air Staff, to break the German spirit by the use of night area rather than precision bombing and the targets would be civilian, not just military. The famous 'area bombing' directive, which had gained support from the Air Ministry and Prime Minister Winston Churchill, had been sent to Bomber Command on 14 February, eight days before Harris assumed command. Harris warmed to his task and announced:

'The Germans entered this war under the rather childish delusion that they were going to bomb everybody else and nobody was going to bomb them. At Rotterdam, London, Warsaw and half a hundred other places, they put that rather naive theory into operation. They sowed the wind and now they are going to reap the whirlwind.'

As one Halifax bomber pilot recalled: 'Butch' Harris, as his crews were to call him, was a rough, tough, vulgar egomaniac. He was just what Bomber Command needed. He feared no foe, senior officers or politicians. He brooked no arguments from juniors and pooh-poohed any from those of equal or senior status who held a contra opinion. Harris knew what he was going to do and proceeded to move Heaven and earth to do it. Woe-betide anyone who stood in his way. He was a firm believer in the Trenchard doctrine and with it he was going to win the war.'

Bombing German cities to destruction was not an entirely new concept. Ever since October 1940 crews were instructed to drop their bombs on German cities, though only if their primary targets were ruled out because of bad weather. During 1941 more and more bombs began falling on built-up areas, mainly because pinpoint bombing of industrial targets was rendered impractical by the lack of navigational and bombing aids. Following the analysis of the Butt Report, the British High Command made a number of decisions in February 1942 that changed the nature of the bomber war against Germany. On 14 February Air Chief Marshal Norman Bottomley issued the 'Area Bombing Directive', which lifted the restrictions placed on the bombers in 1941. Harris saw the need to deprive the German factories of its workers and therefore its ability to manufacture weapons for war. From 1942 onward mass raids would be the order of the day, or rather the night, with little attention paid to precision raids on military targets.

One of the men in Great Britain responsible for recommending the bombing raids on German cities was Professor Frederick A. Lindemann. Born in Baden-Baden in 1886, he was the son of building contractor Samuel Lindemann. His scientific work in Berlin brought him a chair in physics at Oxford in 1919. In 1921 he met Winston Churchill and became his intimate friend. Churchill made Lindemann his special scientific adviser and later, head of the statistical department with cabinet rank. In 1942 King George VI elevated him to the peerage and he became Lord Cherwell. Hardly a secret committee or advisory staff existed of which Lord Cherwell was not a member, working behind the scenes of politics and science. He was very likely the most successful court politician of our times and had more direct access to power than any other scientist in history. Mostly on Lord Cherwell's advice and guided by his questionable calculations, Churchill initiated an all-out bombing war on German cities. In a note sent to Churchill on 30 March 1942 Lord Cherwell wrote to the Prime Minister on 30 March 1942.

'The following seems a simple method of estimating what we could do by bombing Germany. Careful analysis of the effects of raids on Birmingham, Hull and elsewhere have shown that, on the average, one ton of bombs dropped on a built-up area demolishes 20-40 dwellings and turns 100-200 people out of house and home.

'We know from our experience that we can count on nearly 14 operational sorties per bomber produced. The average lift of the bombers we are going to produce over the next fifteen months will be about three tons. It follows that each of these bombers will in its lifetime drop about forty tons of bombs. If these are dropped on built-up areas they will make 4,000-8,000 people homeless.

'In 1938 over 22 million Germans lived in fifty-eight towns of over 100,000 inhabitants, which, with modern equipment, should be easy to find and hit. Our forecast output of heavy bombers (including Wellingtons) between now and the middle of 1943 is about 10,000. If even half the total load of 10,000 bombers were dropped on the built-up areas of these fifty-eight German towns the great majority of their inhabitants (about one-third of the German population) would be turned out of house and home.

'Investigation seems to show that having one's house demolished is most damaging to morale. People seem to mind it more than having their friends or even relatives killed. At Hull signs of strain were evident, though only one-tenth of the houses were demolished. On the above figures we should be able to do ten times as much harm to each of the fifty-eight principal German towns. There seems little doubt that this would break the spirit of the people.

'Our calculation assumes, of course, that we really get one-half of our bombs into built-up areas. On the other hand, no account is taken of the large promised American production (6,000 heavy bombers in the period in question). Nor has regard been paid to the inevitable damage to factories, communications, etc, in these towns and the damage by fire, probably accentuated by breakdown of public services.'

At the end of March 1942 the new head of Bomber Command, Air Marshal Harris, changed his offensive tactics. Instead of deploying several waves of aircraft on each raid, as he had been doing, he despatched strong single formations to carry out area bombing raids. In these raids, large numbers of bombers made concentrated attacks on an area target within the shortest possible time span. However, 'Bomber' Harris did not possess the numbers of aircraft necessary for immediate mass raids. On taking up his position he found that only 380 aircraft were serviceable and only 68 of these were heavy bombers while 257 were medium bombers. Salvation though was at hand. In September 1941 the first of the new four-engined Avro Lancasters, a heavy bomber in every sense of the word, had been supplied to 44 (Rhodesia) Squadron at Waddington for Service trials. In early 1942 deliveries began to trickle through to 44 Squadron and on the night of 3/4 March four aircraft flew the first Lancaster operation when they dropped mines in the Heligoland Bight. That same night Harris selected the Renault factory at Billancourt near Paris, which had been earmarked for attack for some time, as his first target. A full moon was predicted so Harris decided to send a mixed force of 235 aircraft, led by the most experienced crews in Bomber Command, to bomb the French factory in three waves. It was calculated that approximately 121 aircraft an hour had been concentrated over the factory, which was devastated and all except twelve aircraft claimed to have bombed.[40]

During March also the first 'Gee' navigational and target identification sets were installed in operational bombers and these greatly assisted bombers in finding their targets on the nights of 8/9 and 9/10 March in attacks on Essen. On the latter, 187 bombers including 136 Wellingtons bombed the city, which without 'Gee' had been a difficult target to hit accurately. 44 Squadron flew the first Lancaster night-bombing operation of the war when two of the Squadron's aircraft took part in the raid by 126 aircraft on Essen on 10/11 March. Despite the new technological wonder the bombing was scattered on all three raids on the city which was covered alternately by industrial haze and unexpected cloud. The same month 97 Squadron moved from Coningsby to Woodhall Spa nearby and became the second squadron to convert from the Manchester to the Lancaster but the early Lancasters gave some trouble, as David Penman[41] recalls:

'Flight Lieutenant Reginald R. 'Nicky' Sandford DFC of 44 Squadron flew a Lancaster in to convert a few pilots. Conversion consisted of one circuit by Nicky followed by one circuit each for the pilot to be converted. We then climbed into a Manchester and went to Woodford where we collected six Lancasters. I still remember with pleasure the surge of the four Merlins and the tremendous acceleration of the lightly loaded Lancaster after the painfully underpowered Manchester. Unfortunately, the Lancaster had teething problems and the first was a main wheel falling off Flying Officer Deverill's machine when he took off from Boscombe Down. Then an outboard engine fell off after a night landing on the grass at Coningsby. More serious trouble came when six aircraft took off on the first operational sortie loaded with six 1,500lb mines. Over Boston Flying Officer Rodley looked out to see first one and then the other wing tip fold upwards. Even at full power he was descending but luck was on his side, as he dropped the aircraft in the Wash without injuring the crew. A second aircraft diverted to a strange airfield and overshooting the runway ended in a quarry. Engine trouble, maladjusted petrol cocks and upper wing skin buckling restricted flying but all were overcome in the end. The Lancaster was easy to fly and after the Hampden and Manchester it was like stepping from an ancient banger into a Rolls Royce. After the wing tip failures, bomb load with full fuel was reduced from 9,000lbs to 6,000lbs and we stopped doing circuits and bumps with a full bomb load! It had always been customary to do night flying tests before operations with bombs on, though it was stopped on the Hampdens at Waddington when one enthusiastic low flyer skidded to a halt in a field with 4 x 500lb bombs on board.'

Leutnant Wilhelm Johnen finally gained his first victory on 26/27 March 1942 when 104 Wellingtons and eleven Stirlings attacked Essen. Ten Wellingtons and a Stirling were lost. Johnen and Gefreiter Risop's victim was Wellington III X3589 KO-F on 115 Squadron which Sergeant Harry Taylor had taken off from Marham in Norfolk at 1953 hours. The Wellington was flying at about 14,500 feet and Taylor took no avoiding action. His gunners made Johnen's Messerschmitt 110D-3 their target but they were shooting too far ahead. Johnen decided to attack. Risop quickly transmitted the code word: 'Pauke, Pauke' to 'Wolfsburg' their ground station. Johnen dived from his superior altitude and got the Wellington in my sights. The air speed indicator needle rose to 330 mph and the bomber grew ever larger in his sights. Now he could clearly see the tall tail unit and the rear gunner's Perspex turret which was occupied by Sergeant James Herbert Watkinson. The Bf 110 came into the searchlight area and a few well-aimed bursts lashed the Wimpy's fuselage, tearing off huge pieces of the fabric. The Wellington was on fire and turned over on its back. Everything happened in a flash. At incredible speed Johnen streaked past the burning bomber and zoomed high into the sky to escape the threatening flak bursts.

'Good stuff, Herr Leutnant. Good stuff,' shouted Risop and reported their first victory to the ground station:

'Wolfsburg from Buzzard 10. A Vickers Wellington shot down.'

'Congratulations, Herr Leutnant, carry on the good work and perhaps we'll get another.'

Risop suddenly called out: 'There's one above us.'

Johnen could only vaguely recognise the outlines of an enemy aircraft. 'What a miracle! We had spotted him without a searchlight, without radar and without direction. The bomber was flying at a fairly high speed on a northerly course. My nerves were on edge.'

It was a Short Stirling. Johnen aimed vertically at his fuselage in order to put the tail gunner out of action.

'It's time to fire' said Risop. 'Otherwise he'll spot us. Put your trust in God and wade in Herr Leutnant.'

They were the last words the Viennese bordfunker spoke. The Bf 110D-3 was hit by return fire and scores of litres of petrol were alight. In a fraction of a second Johnen's aircraft was transformed into a flaming torch. The flames were already licking the cockpit and a machine gun salvo grazed Johnen's leg and tore away a bundle of recognition flares attached to his left leg. The cockpit roof was torn away by the weight of the explosion and flew away. At this moment of almost instant death, Johnen cast a glance at Risop. He had slumped forward, lifeless, over his radio. The machine gun bursts had killed him. Johnen's hope of getting out of the burning aircraft as it fell vertically into the yawning depths was very slight but he made it. He crashed heavily into the water of a flooded meadow and sank up to his neck in the mud. The cold water completely revived him. Johnen spent some time in hospital for second degree burns to his face and his wounded leg. Risop had gone down with the 110 and deep into a marsh 'like a torpedo' and there was great difficulty in recovering the bordfunker's body. Sergeant Harry Taylor and his crew lay dead in a field east-south-east of Goch Germant. Risop's replacement was Facius, a Viennese. In June Johnen and Facius claimed four Abschüsse over the Netherlands.

On 26/27 March also, at 2357 hours, Oberleutnant Paul Gildner of II./NJG2 claimed one of two Blenheims on 114 Squadron that failed to return from raids by eleven Blenheims from West Raynham in Norfolk on airfields at Schiphol, Soesterberg and Leeuwarden in Holland. Z7700/Q of Flight Lieutenant Martin Bury and crew disappeared without a trace in the North Sea off the Dutch coast. Martin and his crew are commemorated on the Runnymede Memorial. Gildner's victim was Z7307/L of Canadian Flight Sergeant Bill Popplestone and crew which crashed into the Waddenzee

North of Wieringen with no survivors. William Maurice Popplestone, 'a good-natured chap, pleasant features and a moustache of sorts, in order to make himself look older than his 22 years' was from Pilot Mound, Manitoba. He and Cyril White his WOp/AG were both washed ashore and were laid to rest in the Harlingen war cemetery. Pilot Officer William George Francis Hawkins, the 34 year old observer, married of Bromley, Kent was the third member of the crew.[42]

On 28/29 March 234 bombers, mostly carrying incendiaries, went to Lübeck, an historic German town on the Baltic, with thousands of half timbered houses and an ideal target for a mass raid by RAF bombers carrying incendiary bombs. Eight bombers were lost but 191 aircraft claimed to have hit the target. A photo-reconnaissance a few days later revealed that about half the city, 200 acres had been obliterated. The increase in RAF night bombing raids in the more favourable spring weather met with a rapid rise in Nachtjagd victories. In March 1942 41 bombers, including 27 by II./NJG2 with 6 of these being credited to Oberleutnant Ludwig Becker and four each by I. and III./NJG1 were brought down by German night fighters. And in April 46 bombers, including twelve by II./NJG2, nine by I./NJG1 and four by III./NJG1, were destroyed. II./NJG1, which had recently moved to Sint-Truiden/Sint-Trond, scored its first six victories from this Belgian base during the month. On the night of 6/7 April 157 bombers went to Essen but the crews encountered severe storms and icing and there was complete cloud cover at the target. Only 49 aircraft claimed to have reached the target area and there was virtually no damage to Essen. Five aircraft were lost[43] and Pilot Officer Mike Evans' Wellington crew on 149 Squadron[44] had a narrow escape as Sergeant Jim Coman, the WOp/AG, recalls:

'We were returning from Essen when we were attacked by a Messerschmitt 110 over the Dutch coast just south of the Friesian Islands at about 18,000 feet. The 110 hit us in our port wing, holing one petrol tank and causing us to lose about 400 gallons of fuel. The gunners returned fire and it broke off the attack and dived back through the clouds trailing smoke. Before landing at base we lowered the undercarriage to examine the port wheel for damage but nothing appeared amiss. However, the pilot decided to keep the weight off the wheel for as long as possible and landed port wing up but on reaching stalling speed and the wheel touching the ground, it collapsed. The wing hit the ground and swung us round 180 degrees and the wing broke across one of the fuel tanks. We all evacuated the aircraft quickly, as we could hear the engine sizzling in the petrol spillage. Fortunately, it did not catch fire.'

97 Squadron operations finally recommenced in earnest on the night of 8/9 April when 24 Lancasters carried out a minelaying operation in the Heligoland Bight. The main Bomber Command thrust by 272 aircraft was aimed at Hamburg. On 11 April 44 Squadron was ordered to fly long distance flights in formation to obtain endurance data on the Lancaster. At the same time 97 Squadron began flying low in groups of three in 'vee' formation to Selsey Bill, then up to Lanark, across to Falkirk and up to Inverness to a point just outside the town, where they feigned an attack and then back to Woodhall Spa. Crews in both the squadrons knew that the real reason was that they were training for a special operation and speculation as to the target was rife. Training continued and early in April rumours of some special task for the Lancasters were confirmed when eight crews were selected to practice low level formation flying and bombing. On the 17th at briefing at Woodhall Spa when the curtain was drawn back at the briefing there was a roar of laughter instead of the gasp of horror. The target was the diesel engine manufacturing workshop at the MAN (Maschinenfabrik Augsburg-Nurnberg Aktiengesellschaft) factory at Augsburg. No one believed that the RAF would be so stupid as to send twelve of its newest four-engined bombers all that distance inside Germany in daylight. Crews sat back and waited calmly for someone to say,

'Now the real target is this' but Augsburg was the real target. Air Marshal Harris wanted the plant raided by a small force of Lancasters flying at low level (500 feet) and in daylight despite some opposition from the Ministry of Economic Warfare, who wanted the ball-bearing plant at Schweinfurt attacked instead. Sixteen Lancaster crews, eight each on 44 and 97 Squadrons were specially selected and South African Squadron Leader John Dering Nettleton, who had already completed two tours, was chosen to lead the operation. Squadron Leader J. S. Sherwood DFC* would lead 97 Squadron. Crews were ordered to take their steel helmets on this raid.

Just before the Lancasters took off, thirty Bostons bombed targets in France in a planned attempt to force hundreds of German fighters up over the Pas de Calais, Cherbourg and Rouen areas. This was designed to draw the enemy fighters into combat so that the passage of the Lancasters would coincide with their refuelling and rearming. Unfortunately it had the opposite effect and the incursion put the Luftwaffe on the alert.

Nettleton flying R5508 took his formation flying in vics of three down to just fifty feet over the waves of the Channel as the French coast came into view. Five minutes later, Nettleton's first two sections were intercepted by fighters in a running fight that lasted an hour. The Lancasters tightened formation, flying wingtip to wingtip, to give mutual protection with their guns as they skimmed low over villages and rising and falling countryside. The Bf 109s of II./JG2 were forced to attack from above. L7536/H, flown by Sergeant George Thomas Rhodes was first to go down, a victim of Spanish Civil War veteran Major Walter 'Gulle' Oesau, Kommodore, JG2.[45] None of the crew stood a chance at such a low altitude in an aircraft travelling at 200 mph. The whole of 44 Squadron's second 'Vee' were shot out of the sky. R5506 flown by Flight Lieutenant Nicky Sandford DFC fell victim to the guns of Feldwebel Bosseckert. L7548 piloted by Warrant Officer H. V. Crum DFM was shot down by Unteroffizier Pohl of II./JG2 and L7565 flown by Warrant Officer John Frank Beckett DFM was destroyed by Hauptmann Heine Greisert of II./JG2. All the crew were killed. Crum's crew survived and they were taken prisoner. Nettleton and Flying Officer A. J. Garwell DFM piloting R5510 continued to the target alone, flying low in the afternoon sun across southern Germany until the South African sighted the River Lech, which he followed to the target. Coming over the brow of a hill on to the target the two Lancasters were met with heavy fire from quick-firing guns. The bomb aimers could not miss at chimney-top height on a factory covering an area of 626 x 293 feet. Nettleton and Garwell went in and dropped their bomb loads but Garwell's Lancaster was hit and set on fire. He landed in a field two miles west of the town and the fuselage broke at the mid-turret. Garwell and three of his crew survived and were taken prisoner.

The six Lancasters on 97 Squadron had flown a slightly different route and had avoided the fighters in France. The target was easily picked out but the flak gunners were ready for them and it was as 'hot as hell for a few minutes.' L7573 flown by Squadron Leader Sherwood was hit and went down, the port wing striking the ground and the aircraft exploding in a ball of flame. Miraculously, Sherwood was thrown out of the aircraft, still strapped in his seat and was the sole survivor. R5513 flown by Warrant Officer Thomas James Mycock DFC received a shell in the front turret, which set fire to the hydraulic oil and in seconds the aircraft was a sheet of flame. It was on fire over a mile from the target but Warrant Officer Mycock continued on to drop his bombs on the factory before the Lancaster went into a climb with bomb doors open, finally burning from end to end to plunge into the ground. There were no survivors. It was close fighting; one rear-gunner spotted a German behind a machine gun on the roof and saw him collapse under his return fire. 'We must plainly regard the attack of the Lancasters on the U-boat engine factory at Augsburg as an outstanding achievement of the Royal Air Force' wrote Winston Churchill in a message to Arthur T. Harris. 'Undeterred by heavy losses at the outset, the bombers pierced in broad daylight into the heart of Germany and struck a vital point with deadly precision. Pray convey my thanks of His Majesty's Government to the officers and men who accomplished this memorable feat of arms in which no life was lost in vain.'[46] Five of the 17 bombs dropped did not explode and although the others devastated four machine shops, only 3 per cent of the machine tools in the entire plant were wrecked. Squadron Leader Nettleton, who landed his badly damaged Lancaster at Squires Gate, Blackpool ten hours after leaving Waddington, was awarded the VC for his efforts.[47]

Bomber Command continued its usual routines and for four consecutive nights, beginning on the night of 23/24 April, it was the turn of Rostock, a port on the Baltic coast, to feel the weight of incendiary bombs. By the end only 40 percent of the city was left standing.[48] Australian Sergeant Cal Younger, navigator/bomb aimer on Australian Flying Officer Russell A. R. Jones's crew on 460 Squadron RAAF[49] flying Wellington IVs from RAF Breighton recalls:

'Rostock on 26/27 April was one occasion in my fairly brief aircrew career when pity almost overwhelmed me. Because so many of its buildings were old and built of timber, we carried incendiary bombs. We could see the blazing city from 140 miles away as we flew home in relative safety. True, night fighters claimed some victims but we did not see one and the flak over the target had worried us little. There had been no challenge, no battle to carry out on our mission and so there was awe and pity and guilt. In the years since the war many aircrew who survived must have looked at their consciences many times and looked away again. Certainly, I wondered how much blood I had on my hands, or whether I had any at all. After all, in early 1942 RAF chiefs were worried about the lack of accuracy of the bomb aimers of whom I was one. The bomb aimer was also the navigator at that time. Later the two tasks were separated. On several occasions I brought back photographs which proved that we had been on the target, so it is likely that I caused some deaths at least. Mostly one felt dispassionate about bombing. Our job was to bomb a target and to do so we had to contend with fighters and flak and searchlights (which could be very unnerving). One did not really give much thought to people below. I suppose their chances of survival were better than ours.

'In the air, on operations, we were in danger from the moment we took off until the moment we landed. Statistically we had small hope of surviving even one tour of operations. We became impersonal. We had been given a target and we faced, in most instances, an awesome challenge from night fighters and from flak. Frequently we were pinned in the sky by a cone of searchlights, often consisting of one hundred or more beams. We felt naked and as vulnerable as a butterfly. The target, even if it was a city like Essen, became for us almost an abstract, engendering no more emotion than a clay pigeon. That ordinary people were below us seeking what shelter they could from our dreadful cargoes did not impinge on our minds. Over the target the battle was usually intense. We saw our friends shot down in flames and our relief when finally we left the target was immense. There was no room for regret. There was little if any discussion of feelings on the squadron at the time; just an occasional, 'I felt sorry for the sods' or some such remark. There were some sensitive types who must have suffered conscience but they kept their feelings to themselves. It is difficult to convey the atmosphere in the Mess. We all knew we were very likely to die. We had only to watch our friends disappearing. We lived on a permanent 'high' and did not talk about death except in joke. When we were not on ' ops' we headed for York. Most went to pubs and bars. I always went to the cinema, more often than not by myself. Some became regulars at the local village pub.'

Halifax W7653 DY-A was taking off from Dalton airfield in Yorkshire on 27 April with a heavy bomb-load scheduled for Cologne. It was the second operation since the squadron had converted from the Whitley bomber to the Halifax. Twenty-two-year-old Flight Sergeant Lawrence 'Larry' William Carr, who was from Green Walk in Crayford, Essex and his crew - all sergeants - were one of 97 aircraft - 76 Wellingtons, 19 Stirlings and two Halifaxes detailed for the raid.[50] The night of 27/28 April was the Squadron's second night of operations on the Halifax. It was the very first night Carr's crew had set off on a major operational trip in a Halifax and it was his 14th operation since joining 102 Squadron. With his engines wide open at full boost, Larry Carr tried to make 'A-Apple' take off and saw that he was running out of runway fast. It was not until disaster seemed absolutely certain that he felt the wheels sluggishly leave the surface. Even so he had an uncomfortable feeling that they were going to hit the boundary hedge which was racing towards them. He was right. They did. With a shudder the big aircraft bashed its undercarriage wheels through the aerodrome hedge, sending up a spectacular shower of broken bushes and twigs in the slipstream. This interesting display was observed at close quarters by Sergeant G. H. 'Dixie' Lee on 102 Squadron in his rear gun-turret. He was the first man on the tense crew to break silence since the aircraft had started rolling. Over the North Sea they were dead on course for the target. 'Dixie' Lee began crooning a blues. In the navigator's position, Sergeant Ronald B. 'Ronnie' Shoebridge indicated the general relief with a cheerful remark. 'Well' he said, 'Cologne may be a stinking target but the stink will smell nice to me when we've pranged it up and turned for home again.'

'Odour Cologne,' said someone else. 'Listen to the sound of broken glass when we shake up the scent-bottles.'

By that time the Halifax was crossing the French coast at about 12,000 feet and the moon above was shining, silvery and serene. 'Dixie' noticed that there was hardly anything coming up in the way of flak and that there were only a few searchlight beams. He didn't care for it and stopped singing to speak to the 21-year old mid-upper gunner, 'Jimmy' Garroway. 'Jimmy', I don't like this much' he said. 'They're too quiet down below and that bloody moon's too damned bright. Better keep your eyes skinned for fighters.'

He had hardly finished speaking when a black shape flicked across the moon and he saw the unmistakable silhouette of a fighter about 600 yards away. 'Jimmy' also spotted it. Both yelled 'Fighter to starboard, Skipper' at the same time and swung their guns. But Larry Carr at the controls tossed the big Halifax into weaving evasive action at their warning and in a minute or so it seemed that he had shaken the enemy off. Even so, 'Dixie' felt that it was only a foretaste of plenty of bother to come. The brilliant moonlight conditions were all in favour of any attacker since the slower moving bomber was illuminated almost as clearly as by day and the vast dim cavern of the sky would give an attacker every chance of making an unexpected pounce; which was exactly what happened a few minutes later.

Tense, keyed up and straining his eyes 'Dixie' Lee suddenly saw a Bf 110 whipping out of the void and diving straight upon them. Their attacker was Oberleutnant Reinhold Eckardt of 7./NJG3. On the night of 27/28 June 1941 he had destroyed four bombers in 46 minutes during a 'Helle Nachtjagd' sortie in the Hamburg area where five bombers fell to night-fighters. 'Dixie' Lee yelled a warning to Carr, who again threw the Halifax into a violent weave, but the approaching Eckardt knew his business. He kept dead on his target and when he was about 350 yards both he and 'Dixie' Lee opened fire at each other almost at the same instant. Amidst the terrific din that filled 'Dixie' Lee's gun turret he was suddenly half-blinded by a brilliant flash. At the same time he felt a sharp, stabbing pain in one foot. One of the 110's cannon shells had scored a square hit on the turret, striking his ammunition feed. But the rest of the burst had also scored. A matter of seconds later the whole port-side of the Halifax was a roaring mass of flames which swept back in the slipstream. The shaken and wounded 'Dixie' heard Carr shout the order over the intercom for the whole crew to bail out. At the same time he realized that the aircraft had gone into a headlong dive. Dazedly he groped for his parachute pack, but as he did so he suddenly saw that the 110 was coming in for the kill. As was so often the case in actions of this kind, Eckardt was over-confident. He flew in dead close, thinking that he could be in no possible danger from his falling and blazing victim. But 'Dixie' Lee was ready for him. As Eckardt closed in Lee had his gun-sights dead on and let fly with a burst that poured squarely into the approaching German. The fighter immediately burst into a blaze and spun over, to dive earthwards. 'Dixie' Lee, Ronnie Shoebridge, Larry Carr and the second pilot, Flight Sergeant J. William Ralston RCAF bailed out safely.[51] 'Jimmy' Garroway, Thomas Kenneth Robinson the flight engineer and Sergeant Iorweth Edwards the tail gunner had died in those few minutes of action.

Between 11 May 1940 and 31 May 1942, of the principal targets in the Ruhr, Essen had been attacked 89 times, Duisburg 93 and Dortmund 33. Of the main German cities outside that great industrial area, Bomber Command had been to Cologne 144 times, to Mannheim 68, to Hannover 64 and to Magdeburg 26. The four German ports most directly concerned with the Battle of the Atlantic were heavily attacked. Targets in Bremen were bombed 110 times, Wilhelmshaven 88 and Kiel and Emden 82 each. Hamburg was attacked 115 times. And yet, in August 1939 Hermann Göring, as Reichs Minister for air, he had convinced himself 'personally of the measures taken to protect the Ruhr against air attack. In future I will look after every battery, for we will not expose the Ruhr to a single bomb dropped by enemy aircraft.'

On 19/20 May 197 aircraft raided Mannheim and eleven bombers failed to return. Seven of these were claimed by Nachtjagd. In 9./NJG4 Oberleutnant Hubert Rauth claimed a Wellington and Hauptmann Wilhelm Herget, a Halifax northwest of St. Hubert for their third victories. 'The Little Kadi' as he was known, was born on 30 June 1910 in Stuttgart. He trained as a pilot prior to the outbreak of war and was serving with II./ZG76 flying the Bf 110 with 6 Staffel. Though only 5 feet four inches tall - the minimum height for a pilot was 5 feet 6 inches - Herget received special permission to become a pilot though he was unable to reach the rudder pedals and an engineer had to fit wooden blocks, much like you would on a child's bicycle. In intensive operations during the 1940 campaign in Western Europe he scored his first air victories, with three Spitfires downed during May and a Curtiss Hawk in June; he was also awarded the Iron Cross 2nd Class. During the Battle of Britain he claimed two Hurricanes on 30 August and a Spitfire the following day. Three more Spitfires were claimed on 1 September and another on 2 September. By the end of 1940 he had amassed fourteen air victories before converting to the night fighter role with NJG1.

Four Stirlings were claimed by Oberfeldwebel Heinz Strüning, Oberfeldwebel Wilhelm Engel, Hauptmann Erich Simon and 26-year old Oberleutnant Friedrich 'Fritz' Gützeit of 6./NJG1. Early in the morning of 1 September 1939 Gützeit was the first to score a victory during the Polish campaign when he shot down a P-24 fighter of the Polish Pursuit Brigade before he was shot down in the Warsaw area and held prisoner for a time. Stirling W7520 MG-S on 7 Squadron which Gützeit claimed on 20 May 1942 was his second and last Abschüsse. He collided with the aircraft and was killed. The Stirling crashed at Brustem, one kilometre east of St.Trond with the loss of the New Zealand skipper, Flight Lieutenant Hector Garrick Pilling DFC and crew.

On 29 May Sergeant Calton 'Cal' Younger, navigator/bomb aimer on Flying Officer Russell A. P. Jones RAAF's crew on 460 Squadron RAAF, prepared for his 13th operation.

1n 1939 Calton had heard Prime Minister Menzies on the radio tell Australians that Britain had declared war on Germany and therefore Australia was at war with Germany. 'I was in bed with measles, but I got out of bed and drafted a letter to the Navy. I was that keen. Eventually I got an answer saying that I would be called up in due course but they started up the Empire Air Training Scheme and my father had a friend in the air force who suggested I might like that. So Cal, who had yet to receive his call-up from the Navy, volunteered to train for aircrew. 'The Empire was much more important to the dominions than to English people. It was the Empire that I came over to fight for.'

At the end of August 1941 he arrived in Bournemouth with nine fellow navigators after a ninety-three-day voyage. 'There were ten of us who had stuck together from training. We became a unit. We were on the same ship. Eight were killed and two became prisoners.'

Shortly after his arrival at Bournemouth and having volunteered for Bomber Command, Cal was sent to Lichfield and 27 OTU to become part of a crew and gain experience on Wellingtons. It was at Lichfield that the first of Cal's navigator friends became a casualty - his roommate Hal Rogerson. 'I was walking the three miles back to the airfield. I had three-penn'orth worth of chips which I was eating. It was thick fog. I could hear a plane circling. I got home and was lying on my bed reading when a couple of my friends came in and told me that Hal had been killed. They had crashed into a hill in the fog.'[52]

In February 1942 Cal joined 460 Squadron RAAF and his first raid on Germany came at the end of March - to Essen. 'I've never seen such a sight in my life. We were caught in a cone of searchlights. We saw an aircraft on each side of us go down. They were chucking all sorts of stuff up at us. The second pilot was in the astrodome and he saw a chance to get out. He told the skipper and we did get out of it. They had to put a new wing on the plane.

'Ironically, the target which caused me to jump for my life was believed to be more or less undefended. Nor, it was hoped, were French civilians in danger. It was the Gnome-Rhône factory at Gennevilliers, near Paris. At briefing on 29 May we were told that our squadron was to provide four of twelve Wellingtons, which were to attack from 2,000 feet and illuminate the target for the heavies who would bomb from 8,000-10,000 feet.[53] The four navigators worked out their flight plans together. Some time before midnight the four Wellingtons followed each other into a moonlit sky. I had a strange feeling, a presentiment of disaster. As we flew over Northampton, its roofs shining in the moonlight, I suggested to my wireless operator (Sergeant Kenneth Reginald Mellowes) that he should go to the astrodome to look at his home city. We flew over Reading, crossed the coast at Beachy Head then set course for Paris.

'As we neared our target we were stunned to see this extraordinary pyramid of searchlights and light flak; a network of tracer, a fireworks display on a scale I had never imagined. It was pretty obvious we were in for a hiding. Perhaps we were unwise to stick to the height we had been given. It looked suicidal in the scintillating moonlight. We did not hesitate. As I prepared to go to the bombsight I heard a crunching sound behind me. We had been hit and the intercom had failed. I told the skipper we would bomb on the red and green. A blue, master beam of a searchlight had fastened on us and our rear gunner (Sergeant G. H. Loder RAAF) fired down the beam. Eventually he put it out but not before a red line of tracer traversed the length of our starboard wing, almost as if the gunners were operating a garden hose. This stream of light flak appeared to go through the nose - but it must have been in front. It went right along the starboard wing and set it on fire. We were only at 2,000 feet.

'Standing beside the pilot I could see that we were doomed. I took his parachute from its container and put it on his knee and then released the front gunner (Sergeant George Houghton) from his turret, gave him his parachute, opened the hatch and told him to jump. I clipped on my own parachute as I returned to the skipper. He had managed to clip on one side of his parachute. I did the other for him. He asked, 'Was there any chance? I told him 'No'. He smiled a gentle, almost serene smile and told me to jump. At that moment the aircraft went into a steep dive, screaming as if in agony or from some terrible frustration. I could see that the skipper did not intend to bail out. He really had no time but also he did not know what had happened to the wireless operator and the rear gunner and would never have abandoned them. The latter had bailed out when he saw flames streaming past his turret. To this day I do not know what happened to the wireless operator. He had been standing, watching from the astrodome and I think the burst of fire amidships had killed or badly wounded him.

'I felt a strange calm and I am sure I would have gone down with the skipper had I not seen the front gunner standing by the open hatch. As he stepped down I yelled to him to jump. He didn't. I wasn't going to either because I didn't think there was a chance. I, too, felt an amazing serenity, but I had nothing to lose so I obeyed orders. Another second would have been too late. I jumped. I felt the heat of the fire above me and then the jerk as my parachute opened, just missing a tree. I heard the Wellington crash at the same moment. I went straight into the ground on my chin and knocked myself out for about half an hour - silly as a two-bob watch being dragged by my parachute. When I was coming to I thought, 'Where are all the others. This is a funny sort of heaven.' Then gradually things cleared. The parachute just broke my fall. I had landed in a commercial vegetable garden. I was unconscious for a time but suffered no injury. Eventually I got up and walked away. Eight days later, after many hard hours of walking at night, I was arrested by French police and handed over to the Germans. Several years later I repeated my trek and discovered from a hotelier who had been chief of resistance in the area that the police should have handed me over to him, I should have been hidden until flown to England in a surreptitious Lysander, perhaps to join in the battle once more and to add to my guilt'.[54]

Top-level consultations between Harris and his subordinate commanders had revealed that the raids on Rostock had achieved total disruption. Whole areas of the city had been wiped out and 100,000 people had been forced to evacuate the city. The capacity of its workers to produce war materials had therefore been severely diminished. Harris had for some time nurtured the desire to send 1,000 bombers to a German city and reproduce the same results with incendiaries. Although RAF losses would be on a large scale Churchill approved the plan. Harris, (now Sir Arthur), gave the order 'Operation Plan Cologne' to his Group Commanders just after mid-day on 30 May so that 1,000 bombers would be unleashed on the 770,000 inhabitants. Some 599 Wellingtons, including four of Flying Training Command, made up the bulk of the attacking force, which also included 88 Stirlings, 131 Halifaxes and 73 Lancasters. The rest of the force was made up of Whitleys, Hampdens and Manchesters. All bomber bases throughout England were at a high state of readiness to get all available aircraft airborne for the raid. 12 Squadron at Binbrook, for instance, put a record 28 Wellington IIs into the air. To accomplish this task, however, all aircraft had to fly without second pilots and this placed added strain on the crews.

Only ninety minutes would be allowed for 1,000 plus aircraft to pass through the target area. The main danger was the prospect of collision but this was an acceptable risk to get the bomber stream through the night-fighter boxes as quickly as possible. The bombers had to swamp the anti-aircraft defences and put down such a concentration of HE (High Explosive) and incendiaries in a short period that the fire services would be overwhelmed and large areas would be consumed by the fires. The

OTU Groups were providing 365 aircraft, including Wellingtons, Hampdens and Whitleys. It was suggested that the loss factor of 10% or about one hundred aircraft would be acceptable for this size of operation. With the late withdrawal of the Coastal Command contribution it was necessary to make up numbers with totally trainee crews. The total dispatched was 1047 aircraft. For 98 minutes a procession of bombers passed over Cologne. Stick after stick of incendiaries rained down from the bomb bays of the Wellingtons, adding to the conflagration. Almost all aircraft bombed their aiming point as briefed. The defences, because of the attacking forces size, were relatively ineffective and flak was described variously as 'sporadic' and spasmodic'.

It was announced that the raid had been a success. Amazingly, Cologne Cathedral had survived and losses totalled 41 aircraft - 3.9% of the total force operating. A cryptic announcement in the *Daily Telegraph* the following day said: 'At a Bomber Command Station. Sunday. On the 1,001st day of the war more than 1,000 RAF bombers flew over Cologne and in 95 minutes delivered the heaviest attack ever launched in the history of aerial warfare.'[55]

The majority of the Luftwaffe night-fighter effort on 30/31 May was concentrated in the 'Himmelbett' boxes on the coast and in the target area. The German defences were locally swamped by the mass of bombers and Nachtjagd crews destroyed relatively few. Of the 43 RAF losses it is estimated that thirty were shot down by 'Himmelbett' operating night-fighters, these were mainly achieved on the return journey when the bomber stream had been more dispersed than on the way in and was easier for the Jägerleitoffizier (JLO, or GCI-controller) to pinpoint individual target aircraft. Eight claims were submitted by four crews of II./NJG1 at Sint-Truiden/Sint-Trond, including three by Oberleutnant Walter Barte and his Funker Unteroffizier Pieper of the 4th Staffel, seven of which were later confirmed by the Reichsluftfahrtministerium (RLM or Reich Air Ministry). Barte's first claim on the night for a Wellington shot down north of Maastricht was later officially turned down. Of the remaining RAF losses, sixteen or seventeen were downed by flak over Cologne and twelve were shot down by anti aircraft fire on the legs to and from the target. At Venlo three victories (two Wellingtons and Halifax L9605 on 1652 Conversion Unit crashed near Weert) were awarded to Oberleutnant Reinhold Knacke, Staffelkapitän, 1/NJG1 for his 18th-20th victories. Two III./NJG1 Experten operating from Twente were successful on 30/31 May. Oberleutnant Manfred Meurer destroyed Hampden P2116 on 14 OTU near Diepenveen. The pilot, Pilot Officer T. E. P. Ramsey, was taken prisoner; his three crew were killed. In all, four Hampdens on 14 OTU failed to return to Cottesmore. Oberleutnant Helmut Woltersdorf claimed Wellington IA N2894 of the Central Gunnery School (a veteran on 403 flying hours) near Apeldoorn with the loss of Pilot Officer D. M. Johnson and crew and Wellington IC DV715 on 156 Squadron at Vorden. Sergeant P. G. A. Main and crew were killed.

Four Wellington Ic's on 22 OTU at Elsham Wolds were lost. One of these, DV843, was shot down at about 2340 hours by Oberleutnant Wilhelm Beier of I./NJG1 at Dinteloord in Holland. Pilot Officer William Arthur Fullerton DFM and his crew were all killed. Four Wellingtons on 26 OTU at Graveley were lost. One of these, W5704, was shot down at about 0130 hours by Hauptmann Werner Streib and crashed at Middelberg with the loss of all five men on Flying Officer William Robert Humphrey Whiting's crew. DV740 'O-Orange' flown by Warrant Officer Freddie Hillyer was possibly destroyed by thirty-year old Oberleutnant Horst Patuschka of 4./NJG2 in a Bf 110, crashing at Alem in Gelderland. 'O-Orange' was hit in the port engine over Cologne and was flying at barely 90 mph when Patuschka delivered the coup de grace. He set the Wimpy's rear fuselage on fire and Hillyard gave the order to bail out. Just before he left the cockpit he glanced down and saw that the front turret guns were pointing sideways. The power for the hydraulics came from the dead port engine. This meant that 22-year old Pilot Officer Cyril White, the son of a parson and the youngest man on the crew was trapped in the turret. The diminutive pilot from Alresford in Hampshire, who had joined the RAF as a trainee flight mechanic before becoming a fitter and when war came and who had re-mustered as a pilot, fought his way through to the turret and banged on the door as he grabbed the dead man's handle and tried to wrench the doors open. But it was jammed. There was no answer from the turret. White must be dead. Hillyer got out before the Wellington crashed. Next day he was taken prisoner and driven to nearby Utrecht. Before being taken into captivity his captors drove him to the scene of the crash. He could see that all his crew had been killed in the fighter attack. They included Sergeant Dave Vincent the navigator, bomb aimer and Sergeant Hector Smith the rear gunner, the only married man on the crew and the oldest. Short and tubby he would sit in his turret smoking his pipe in spite of repeated warnings from Hillyer.

DV707, flown by 31-year old Flight Sergeant Edwin John Ford DFM, a former motor salesman, was shot down by Leutnant Helmut Niklas and his bordfunker, Unteroffizier Wenning of 6./NJG1, crashing at Leeveroi near Venlo where Ford and three of his crew were first laid to rest. Warrant Officer Denis W. Caswell was taken into captivity with quite severe burns and wounds caused by cannon shell splinters. Niklas also claimed Wellington IC R1791 on 15 OTU at Harwell which was being flown by Warrant Officer Jack Paul DFM, a tall solid Midlander from Coventry; a veteran of over thirty operations, who had returned from one week's leave and his honeymoon with his wife Joyce just the day before. He had completed a bombing tour on Wellingtons in the Middle East before becoming an instructor. Niklas and Wenning intercepted the Wimpy on the bomber's way home near Charleroi in Belgium. On the approach of the bombers Niklas had taken off from St-Trond and flew to the radio beacon just to the north-west of their allocated fighter control station. Wenning later recalled:

'In our area we did not have long to wait. At 3000 metres we encountered the first, which we recognised as a Wellington, 500 metres away. At almost exactly the same time the Tommy spotted us. He made a sudden turn to the right and then turned away from us. We went after him, but his fire was so strong that we could not get into a firing position and we overshot the Wellington. Again we moved into a position behind the target and, from short range, we pumped shells into the bomber's left wing. It caught fire and we could see the flames. By this time our victim was down to 2000 metres. Again we closed in. We fired another burst into the fuselage and wings and the flames burnt brighter. Then we moved out for a while, waiting to see whether it would be necessary to go in again.'

The Wimpy's intercom was rendered useless and 'Bunny' Evans' rear turret was badly damaged. The turret could not be turned fully and one of the guns was useless. Paul pulled the bomber into a hard turn and the fighter overshot allowing the student front-gunner, a pupil named Sergeant James McCormack, to open fire. When the Bf 110 returned for a second attack Evans opened fire with his one serviceable gun, but he was wounded in the hand. The Wellington suffered further damage, with fire breaking out near the port engine and this quickly spread. Without the intercom, further instructions could not be passed so Paul shouted to Flight Sergeant Tommy Lyons the wireless operator to tell the crew to bail out. After the second attack 'Bunny' Evans realised that the aircraft was severely damaged. He opened his turret door and crawled into the fuselage. He could see flames but no sign of life up front. Without communication he assumed that they had bailed out. (His pilot was slumped over the control column, unconscious). Evans grabbed his parachute, clipped it on and as the Wimpy passed through 2,000 feet he dropped through the diamond-shaped escape hatch in the rear of the aircraft, kicking it out as he went.

Niklas and Wenning watched for a short time as the Wellington flew on, the blaze growing the whole time. Then it flipped over and went down, trailing sparks like a comet. Close to the ground it exploded, lighting up the surrounding countryside. Niklas climbed back up to his operational altitude and reported to their ground station that they were ready for the next target. Almost immediately they were guided into position behind a second Wellington and sighted it 700 yards in front. 'He was weaving but he did not open fire. Had they seen us? We went straight into the attack. The target grew larger until, suddenly, it seemed enormous. My breath almost stopped: we were going to ram him. From short range we opened fire, hitting him on the wings and on the fuselage. We could see the glow of the flashes on the rear fuselage. I was about to call out 'He's on fire!', when suddenly Leutnant Niklas shouted 'I've been hit, breaking off immediately!' I had mistaken the muzzle flash from the rear turret for the glow of hits. We could not bother with the Tommy any more - we had our own problems.'

Niklas's left arm had been smashed and was unusable and also it was bleeding profusely. Unable to reach the controls from his position in the rear of the 110, Wenning improvised a tourniquet and tied it round Niklas's arm; then he set about the difficult task of directing his pilot back to Sint-Trond while the latter drifted in and out of consciousness. Wenning continues: 'That was how we flew back to our airfield. Leutnant Niklas was almost over the lights before he caught sight of them. It was too late to land on the runway. So, with a sideslip, he tried to get down on the emergency strip. Trees passed just below us. 'We're too low!' Niklas murmured, 'I can't go on any longer' and slumped forward. There was a scraping sound and soil was flung against the cabin. We skidded over the ground for what seemed an eternity. I sat there tensely. So this was what a crash landing was like; I had always imagined that it would be different. The crashing and splintering grew louder; there was a jerk and everything was still. Then Niklas shouted: 'Let's get out of here!' He had hit his head but had regained consciousness. He leapt from his seat, trying to run and at the same time to release his parachute harness. But it was no good and he fainted. I laid him out gently on the grass and opened his blood-soaked flying suit. Soon a doctor and others appeared and they carried him away. I was surrounded by a lot of people, who began to ask questions; I realised just how lucky I had been.'[56]

Niklas had shot the aircraft down at 0246 and it crashed in the southwest outskirts of Charleroi. Paul was taken prisoner and one of his crew evaded. The other three were killed. A second Wellington on 15 OTU, W5586, piloted by 26-year old Warrant Officer Jack Hatton, an ex-Cranwell apprentice is believed to have been shot down by Oberleutnant Reinhold Knacke of 3./NJG1 at Waasmont Brabant in Belgium at 0215 hours. Hatton and three crew were taken prisoner. Hatton's wireless operator, Sergeant Bob Collins, an Australian from Brisbane, reached Gibraltar and he was flown home on 21 July.[57]

In all, 898 crews claimed to have hit their targets. Post-bombing reconnaissance certainly showed that more than 600 acres of Cologne had been razed to the ground. The fires burned for days and almost 60,000 people - the Ausgebombten - had been made homeless. Thirty-one bombers were lost. The day after the raid on Cologne, at Hitler's 'Situation Conference', 43-year old General Hans Jeschonnek, Chief of the General Staff of the Luftwaffe, stood up to read out the official report given to him by Reichsmarschall Göring. His hands were shaking. 'According to preliminary reports we estimate that 200 enemy aircraft have penetrated our defences. The damage is heavy... we are still waiting for final estimates.' Hitler exploded. He ranted and he raved. He pounded the table with his fist and poured scorn on the evasive report. 'You are still waiting for final estimates?' he cried. 'And the Luftwaffe thinks there were only

200 aircraft? The Luftwaffe has probably been asleep last night ... but I have not been asleep. I stay awake when one of my cities is under fire. And I thank the Almighty that I can rely on my Gauleiter, even if the Luftwaffe deceives me. There were a thousand or more English aircraft... do you hear? A thousand, twelve hundred... maybe more!'[58]

Hitler was not interested in defence. He wanted revenge.

Endnotes Chapter 4

40   It was reported that 300 bombs fell on the factory destroying 40% of the buildings. Production was halted for 4 weeks and final repairs were not completed for several months. A post-war American estimate said that the production loss was almost 2,300 vehicles. Just 1 aircraft (a Wellington) was lost but 367 French people were killed, 341 were badly injured and 9,250 people lost their homes.
41   Later Wing Commander Penman DSO OBE DFC.
42   *Blenheim Strike* by Theo Boiten (ARP 1995).
43   2 of them Hampdens, a Manchester on 61 Squadron, 1 Stirling and a Wellington.
44   N3726 OJ-G.
45   Oesau had shot down 10 a/c in Spain and was the 3rd German pilot to reach 100 victories, on 26 October 1941. He was shot down and killed in air combat with P-38 Lightnings SW of St. Vith, Belgium on 11 May 1944 in his Bf 109G-6. At the time of his death, his score stood at 127 aerial victories, including 14 four engined bombers.
46   37 aircrew were lost, of which 12 were made PoW and 36 returned.
47   Although also recommended for a VC by Air Marshal Harris, Sherwood was awarded the DSO. After a brief spell instructing with 1661 HCU and being promoted to Wing Commander, Nettleton returned to 44 Squadron as OC in January 1943. He FTR from a raid on Turin on 12/13 July 1943.
48   The raids on Lübeck and Rostock prompted the Luftwaffe into reprisal, or Baedeker raids, after the German guide book to English cities, on Canterbury, Exeter, Norwich and York.
49   First RAAF Squadron in Bomber Command and which carried out its first operation on 12/13 March.
50   *The Bomber Command War Diaries; An Operational reference book 1939-1945* by Martin Middlebrook and Chris Everitt (Midland Publishing Ltd 1985, 1990, 1995).
51   Six Wellingtons and the Halifax W7653 on 102 Squadron FTR. *The Bomber Command War Diaries; An Operational reference book 1939-1945* by Martin Middlebrook and Chris Everitt (Midland Publishing Ltd 1985, 1990, 1995).
52   Quoted in *The Bomber Command Memorial* (Fighting High Ltd 2012).
53   65 Wellingtons, Lancasters, Halifaxes, Hampdens and Stirlings.
54   Cal and his rear gunner were the only survivors on Wellington Z1391 UV-R that night.
55   Stiles' navigator, Squadron Leader T. Hillier-Rose recalled that Stiles was 'ticked off for having flown on the raid. At the time he was recovering from a severe wound to an arm, sustained in a crash whilst flying a Mosquito.
56   Niklas recovered from his wounds, but he was killed in January 1944 after an engagement with USAAF bombers on a daylight raid.
57   *RAF Bomber Command Losses; Operational Training Units 1940-1947* by W. R. Chorley Midland Publishing 2002).
58   Quoted in *Operation Millennium* by Eric Taylor (Robert Hale Ltd 1987).

Chapter Five

Under Cover of Darkness

Major Heinrich Prinz zu Sayn-Wittgenstein was one of the most successful night-fighter pilots and his name was bracketed with those of Major Streib and Lent. But the ambition of this eager and outstanding airman was to be head of the night-fighter elite. Spurred on by his need for action, the young Gruppe Kommandeur shot down 83 enemy bombers in tough air battles. But his 83rd Abschuss, actually his fifth kill on the night of the 21st January 1944, led him not to his coveted position but to his death. Directly after his fifth victory that night he was attacked and shot down by a British night-fighter. The Prinz gave orders to his crew to bail out and tried to save his aircraft. He failed. Recognising the danger too late, he bailed out just before the burning machine crashed. On the following day his body was found near the wreckage. Major Heinrich Prinz zu Sayn-Wittgenstein, born on the 14th August 1916 in Copenhagen, decorated with the Ritterkreuz des Eisernen Kreuzes mit Eichenlaub und Schwertern will be remembered by all night-fighter pilots as a courageous and exemplary airman.

Duel Under The Stars **by Wilhelm Johnen**

In 10 Downing Street in London on Sunday morning 31 May, Winston Churchill was triumphant on receiving the details of the raid on Cologne. He had been prepared for losses of up to one hundred aircraft on Cologne but to lose only forty was providential. Immediately he sent a signal to 'Bomber' Harris: 'I congratulate the whole of Bomber Command upon the remarkable feat of organization which enabled you to despatch over a thousand bombers to the Cologne area on one night without confusion to concentrate their action over the target in so short a time as one hour and a half. This proof of the growing power of the British bomber force is also the herald of what Germany will receive city by city from now on.'

These were fighting words but as Squadrons repaired and patched their damaged bombers for the second 'Thousand Bomber Raid' within 48 hours, this time against Essen on the night of 1/2 June, a force of 956 bombers was only achieved by using OTU crews and aircraft once more, as Flight Lieutenant John Price at 10 OTU confirms:

'We had only 700 first line bombers. To make up the difference the other 300 were drawn from the OTUs. I was doing my usual so called 'rest' period of six months between ops. The idea being to give seasoned aircrew a brief respite from real operations and also to teach others. I found it ironic that so many of us got killed on these OTUs. Pilot error (the pupil was flying), navigational errors, bad weather over England in wintertime - the losses were horrendous. To return to the thousand-bomber raid on Essen, at briefing we were told our part in the operation was to kill as many of the workers as possible. Other bombers would go for the Krupps factory itself. Real bombs were not used on an OTU station so I was a bit shaken to see them rolling onto our airfield at Harwell. We had Whitley aircraft, which were unbelievably slow and climbed at about 125 mph with a full bomb load. They had the same turrets as the Wellington. There was no protection for the poor old air-gunners front and rear, just perspex. I felt very sad. As an instructor I had been ordered to go but as there were not enough instructors to fill the aircraft pupil pilots were called upon - ditto navigators and air gunners. My pupils - 18-year old boys - pleading with me to let them go besieged me. I knew that half of them would not come back but I chose my dozen or so then prayed for their safety. None came back.'

'We got a course to steer from ground control. Clouds were beneath us. Moon very big, very clear sky.'

'Kurier[59] still far away to the west. We approached him on incoming heading. Picked it up in Li-set at a distance of 4.5 kilometres [2.8 miles]. We turned round and chased him.

'Marie 2,[60] slow down, slow down, can't see anything.'

'We've overtaken the Kurier. Start the whole procedure again.'

'Marie 4, Marie 3. Pick him up in Li-set at 2.6 kilometres [1.6 miles]. Height 3000 metres [9,700 feet].

I lead my pilot towards him. Marie 300 metres [970 feet].'

'Karl-Heinz: 'I have him!'

'We lose height. Underneath Kurier. It's a Hampden. Dangerous. Can see and fire downwards. We climb ever more. Distance 100 to 150 metres [110 to 160 yards].

'Attack.

'Keep firing. Burst of fire aimed very well. Kurier is burning.

'Sieg Heil! [Bomber destroyed!]'

'Karl-Heinz congratulates me: a Lichtenstein victory! I am feeling very pleased.'

Vollkopf and Huhn's victim was Hampden AT191/A on 408 Squadron, which they hit at 0006 hours north of Harderwijk. Pilot Officer William Frederick Dixon Charlton had taken off from Balderton at 2258 hours. After the night-fighter attack the Hampden crashed in flames into the Ijsselmeer with the loss of the crew. Flight Sergeant F. J. E. Womar DFM, one of the gunners, was flying his 56th operation. On 2 June Hauptmann Lent presented Huhn with the EK1 (Eisernes Kreuz I or Iron Cross, First Class). Other victories were credited to Hauptmann Walter Ehle of II./NJG1, who destroyed a Wellington on 16 OTU piloted by Flying Officer Ronald James Robinson DFC and Hauptmann Alfred Haesler of III./NJG1 who claimed a Whitley on 10 OTU flown by 26-year old Squadron Leader Dennis Brendan Geoffrey Tomlinson DFC. Tomlinson and his crew were killed, as were Robinson and one of his crew.[61]

Although seemingly lacking the concentration of the earlier raid on Cologne the bombing nevertheless was effective enough to saturate the defences. One skipper went as far as to say that the fires were more impressive than those on Cologne were. A belt of fires extended across the city's entire length from the western edge to the eastern suburbs. Many fires were also spread over other parts of the Ruhr.

After Cologne and Essen, Harris could not immediately mount another 1,000-bomber raid and he had to be content with smaller formations. On the night of 3/4 June 70 bombers were despatched on the first large raid to Bremen since October 1941. Eleven aircraft failed to return - eight of them shot down by Nachtjäger. They included Stirling I W7474 HA-K on 218 Squadron flown by 29-year old Pilot Officer James Garscadden and 19-year old Pilot Officer John Richard Webber, which was shot down by Unteroffizier Heinz Vinke of II./NJG1 south of Den Helder at 0032 hours. All seven crew were killed. Another was Manchester I L7432 on 50 Squadron at Skellingthorpe flown by Flying Officer John Frankland Heaton, which took off at 2110 hours on 3 June. The Manchester lost power crossing the Dutch coast and refused to climb higher than

9,000 feet but Heaton still managed to bomb the target and even completed two circuits to obtain the mandatory photographs. On the way home over the Veluwe in central Holland the Manchester was attacked and set on fire by a Bf 110 night fighter and crashed near Apeldoorn. Sergeant Ken J. F. Gaulton RAAF, wireless operator, recalls:

'I switched to the aircraft inter communication system to advise the pilot that we were cleared to return to our base, this information having been received on the 0230 broadcast from Group HQ. A Messerschmitt 110 attacked us. The starboard wing of our aircraft was burning and the pilot advised that he was going to dive in an attempt to 'blow out' the fire. This did not succeed. The German aircraft did a victory roll near the tail of our aircraft and Sergeant Peter Buttigieg our tail gunner shot him down. I was amazed to hear the yelling from the tail gunner who was engaging the Me 110 with his guns. After diving for thousands of feet I requested the pilot's permission to have the tail gunner and mid-upper gunner join me to prepare the rear escape hatch for evacuation. This was done and we jumped in turn; firstly the tail gunner (the only married man in the crew) then the mid-upper gunner and then came my turn. The aircraft kept on diving and crashed, killing Heaton, Pilot Officer John Ross Steen, 2nd pilot, Pilot Officer Harold William Sheen, navigator and Sergeant Stan Thomas, front gunner, all of whom were in the front of the aircraft. I left the aircraft when it was slightly under 1,000 feet, quickly pulled the ripcord and was promptly knocked out by the chest parachute striking me under the jaw. I landed in the Zuider Zee on an ebbing tide and speared up to my chest in mud. An Alsatian dog woke me by licking my face and its owner took me to a medical doctor at about 0530 am. I was unable to walk. The doctor quickly established that the man was a collaborator and was therefore unable to hide me. I was transported by car to Arnhem where I was interrogated by the Gestapo and then by train to Amsterdam, where I was gaoled in the Amsterdam watchtower for four days. While I was there a German captain from the fighter squadron visited me about 6 June and advised me that our aircraft had crashed on a hunting lodge owned by the Dutch Royal family near Apeldoorn. He told me that we had shot down one of his aircraft, killing two airmen. He claimed the Germans were two up as four of our crew had been killed.'[62]

On the night of 6/7 June three more Manchesters, three Wellingtons, two Stirlings and one Halifax were lost from the 233 aircraft despatched to Emden. A 9 Squadron Wellington crashed and caught fire shortly after taking off from Honington and burnt out but the crew were safe.[63] One of the three Wellingtons that were shot down on the operation was a 150 Squadron Wimpy flown by Flying Officer Malcolm James Larke Blunt RAAF, which was downed by Oberleutnant Ludwig Becker of 6./NJG2 and crashed into the North Sea off Ameland. All the crew perished. Becker was also credited with shooting down a 7 Squadron Stirling, one of two that failed to return. All of Flying Officer N. L. Taylor's crew survived and were taken prisoner. The other Stirling, a 214 Squadron aircraft flown by 26-year old Flight Lieutenant Reginald Turtle DFC who was a veteran of 46 ops, was shot down by Oberleutnant Prinz Egmont zur Lippe-Weissenfeld of II./NJG2 and crashed off Terschelling with no survivors. Turtle was posthumously awarded the DFC.

Two of the missing Manchester Is were on 50 Squadron. Sergeant Leonard Thomas Baker's aircraft was shot down by Oberleutnant Ludwig Becker at 0044 hours and crashed into the North Sea off Ameland. Pilot Officer A. D. 'Don' Beatty and his all RAAF crew ditched their Manchester I off the coast of the Dutch Friesians after their Manchester developed engine problems. Beatty recalls:

'We could only climb to 9,000 feet with a bomb load, when bombs dropped on target we always put the nose down and headed for the deck to avoid night fighters and flak and to also fire at searchlights when necessary. We flew north of the Friesian Islands at low altitude when one engine packed up. The propeller would not feather, causing excessive drag and as I was in the front turret and the ocean getting too close I climbed back up behind the pilot while the two pilots struggled to control the aircraft. We were perhaps only 200 feet above the water and could not gain height, when the port engine stopped and the aircraft crashed nose first into the drink.

'I saw the second pilot [Sergeant Ronald Burton] hit the dashboard and then we were under water. Both he and I were not strapped in. I picked myself up off the floor and got kicked in the face by the navigator [Pilot Officer Fred W. R. Allen] as he pushed open the escape hatch. I followed him and was about to jump into the water when I saw the navigator's curtain bobbing up and down in the escape hatch. I tore it off and helped the pilot who was badly injured out and helped him swim around to the dinghy on the starboard side of the aircraft, which was half submerged. The tail section had broken behind the mid-upper gunner's turret. The dinghy had inflated upside down and the mid-upper gunner cut it free, which was probably just as well as the aircraft sank in a couple of minutes. I heard the wireless operator [Sergeant Arthur G. Tebbutt] calling in the dark that he could not see so I swam to where he was calling from and brought him back to the dinghy. We all got in the dinghy, which was upside down, as we did not want to lose anybody in the dark. We spent a wet and most uncomfortable night, as there were six of us who had survived. The 2nd pilot had a horrific head wound [Burton died from his injuries on 10 September]. The navigator, we found later, had a broken thigh. The wireless operator had a split lip and eyebrow and I had a head wound and badly bruised left side, arm and leg.

'When daylight finally arrived we had to all get back into the water and the two uninjured gunners turned the dinghy over and helped us all back in stiff and sore. About an hour after daylight two Me 109s on patrol spotted our florescent trail in the water, flew low over us, waggled their wings and disappeared. A very old biplane seaplane arrived, landed and picked us up. The injured were put on stretchers. The dinghy was slashed to sink it and we were flown to Nordeney where we were put into the Luftwaffe hospital for a week and were very well treated. We were covered in oil and florescence. The two uninjured were put in the cooler until we were fit to travel. One of the blond 109 pilots came to see me, gave me cigarettes and shook hands. As neither of us understood each other, I tried to thank him for his courtesy and in saving us. We joined the two gunners and were then taken under escort by train to Frankfurt to Dulag Luft for interrogation. There we joined up with a number of Commonwealth and RAF aircrews and placed on a guarded train to Stalag Luft III at Sagan in Silesia, where we arrived 16 June 1942.'

On the night of 17/18 June 24-year old Oberleutnant (later Hauptmann) Walter Knickmeier at the 'Berta' ground station expertly directed Wilhelm Johnen and Facius his Viennese bordfunker to their prey. Facius had replaced Risop, Johnen's original bordfunker who had been killed on 26/27 March when Johnen bailed out and was hospitalised with second degree burns and injuries to his left leg. Although he suffered a great deal of pain his health had improved day by day and the new skin gradually replaced the old. During his convalescenece at Bad Schachen his thoughts had turned to his staffel at Venlo and to his comrades. He had wondered if he would ever fly again.

'Buzzard 10 from 'Berta' radioed Oberleutnant Knickemeier. The JLO was a trained pilot and former Armament Officer as well as a reknowned Fighter Controller, guiding night fighters to the Viermots throughout the war. He participated in 24 Abschüsse with Werner Streib, Wolfgang Thimmig and Reinhold Knacke.

'Bank to port on course 280. Kurier at your altitude one mile to stern. Give it full throttle and keep your eyes open.'

Almost at stalling speed Johnen let his adversary approach, keeping his eyes on the bright horizon to the north. At last he saw a small shadow ahead. He dived immediately and got below him. Once he had sighted his quarry he felt quite calm. He was in no hurry and he crept in closer and closer. The enemy bomber was a Wellington. It was trundling wearily homewards after bombing Cologne. Oberleutnant Knickemeier reported that a second bomber was flying further to the north out of Johnen's sector. At this moment Facius said on intercom: 'Herr Leutnant, fire into his wings. I'm sorry for those poor fellows.' Johnen had little sympathy with them and aimed the cross of his sights on the enemy's port engine. The distance decreased rapidly and the rear gunner had already fired a few bursts, but he could not aim properly because his pilot was taking avoiding action. 'The tracers flew across the sky like a necklace of broken beads; wrote Johnen later. 'I stuck close on his tail and waited for a favourable moment'. Now the Wellington's wings were spread out against the northern sky as the pilot went into a left-hand turn. As this moment Johnen levelled his Bf 110 and let the bomber pilot fly into the cross wires of his sights. The left aileron appeared and Johnen gave the Wimpy a burst and set his port engine on fire. Johnen waited for the crew to bail out but nothing happened. Then the fire appeared to have gone out. The pilot had probably cut his port engine and was trying to get away on one. Johnen made a second attack and had to lower his wing flaps to keep at the bomber's speed. Johnen thought that the bomber pilot must be a wily old fox and tried to shake him off by stalling. Now, Johnen was hanging like 'a limp feather' in the sky. Each of them was trying to fly even slower. Johnen grew impatient and rashly attacked from the rear. The rear gunner was waiting for him to approach and as he drew closer Johnen's two cannon and four machine guns were pointed at the enemy bomber's turret. The rear gunner and Johnen opened fire at the same moment before the burning Wellington turned onto its back and dived earthwards to its doom. Johnen could smell burning in his cockpit but he could not see any flames. Suddenly, his elevator jammed and he dived steeply. Johnen let fly a 'juicy oath' and his bordfunker must have taken this as an alarm signal because Facius bailed out. Johnen finally landed the Bf 110, happy but sweating profusely in the early morning hours at Venlo.[64] That same month Johnen and Facius destroyed a Halifax and a Wellington on the night of 21/22 June when 44 bombers were shot down on the raid on Krefeld and they shot down another Halifax on the 24th of the month when 34 bombers were lost on Wuppertal.

On 22/23 June 227 aircraft attacked Emden again for the third night in a row. Good bombing results were claimed by 196 crews but decoy fires are believed to have diverted many bombs from the intended target. Six aircraft - four Wellingtons, one Lancaster and a Stirling - were lost while Emden reported that fifty houses were destroyed, 100 damaged and some damage caused to the harbour. Six civilians were killed and forty were injured. Then, on the night of 25/26 June the third and final 'Thousand Bomber Raid' in the series of five major saturation attacks on German cities took place when 1,006 aircraft, including 102 Wellingtons of Coastal Command, attacked Bremen. One of the many instructors involved in the 1,000 Plan was Flying Officer Harry Andrews. After completing an anti-shipping tour of ops flying Hudsons of 224 Squadron, Coastal Command he was posted to 1 (C) OTU at Silloth as an instructor on Hudson's in early 1942:

'The monotony of training was temporarily broken for us when thirty or so Hudsons took part in the 1,000 bomber raid on Bremen. The instructors flew the aircraft but most of the crews were trainees, many of them from establishments in Canada. The Bremen raid was their first taste of operations. I think that many of us welcomed the news of the operation as a break from months of instructing. The ceaseless 'circuits and bumps', the constant reminders to student pilots to lead with the port throttle to prevent swing (and, to the over-confident type, a graphic description of the burn-up that often followed an uncontrolled swing). The warnings to 'watch your airspeed' on the approach, the fighting down of one's reaction to take over the controls when the student was holding off too high at nearly stalling speed and, not least, an encouraging word to the student whose white knuckles gripping the controls too tightly and whose knee tremours indicated both stress and determination. And later on when the student pilots had soloed on Hudsons teaching them low flying over the sea and holding one's breath at their first attempt to fly at fifty feet or so. Certainly we had no conception of the seriousness and moment of the 1,000-bomber raids operation.

Looking back I find it almost unbelievable how ignorant we all were on what was happening: in short, what it was all about and what part we were playing in the overall plan.

'After the abortive stand-by for the Cologne raid in May no one really took the orders for special operations on 23 June seriously until we flew to Squires Gate late on that day for bombing-up: ten 100lb GP bombs - the maximum load a Hudson could take with the fuel required. We then flew on to Thornaby arriving late at night. The next day (24 June) was spent in the seemingly inevitable hanging about and it was not until the late afternoon that we were released from standby: another anti-climax. On the morning of 25 June we were briefed that Bremen was the target: 1,000 aircraft would be taking part, the risk of collisions over the target was virtually nil if everyone kept to their timings and flight paths. Briefing included weather, night fighter tactics, anti-aircraft flak concentrations and other standard Bomber Command data. All of us had a Coastal Command background involving anti-U-boat, reconnaissance and anti-shipping operations. The Bomber Command type of briefing was entirely new to us. Many of the student navigators had been trained overseas and had little or no experience of night flying or European weather. The specific briefing for the Hudson crews was to climb to 10,000 feet after take-off, cruise at 140 knots to the target, bomb and then immediately descend to 1,500 feet and return to base at that level, if I remember correctly, the designated targets were the Focke-Wulf aircraft works and the U-boat construction yards at Deschimag in the waterfront area of Bremen.'

Flight Lieutenant The Honourable Terence Mansfield, 419 Squadron RCAF Bombing Leader; 'Moose' Fulton the CO's navigator/bomb aimer, who was on the 30th and final operation of his tour, recalls:

'We took off at 2325 hours. Although briefed for a greater height, we found the target area completely covered by cloud and came down to 12,000 feet in the hope of getting some visual identification from which we could start a timed run. We ended up doing what others did, namely bombing what we thought was the most likely place. Not very satisfactory and nor were the results.'

The heavy bomber crews were given the opportunity of bombing the red glow of the fires, using 'Gee' as a check, or proceeding to a secondary target in the vicinity of Bremen. The cloud conditions prevailed at many of the targets of opportunity and many crews, unable to bomb, brought their lethal cargoes home. Flying Officer Harry Andrews continues:

'The old Hudson I had, like many others, suffered from the faults brought by the hard usage from OTU training. Rate of climb at full throttle was something less than 1,000 feet a minute and 3 or 4 degrees of lateral trim was required to fly level. Weather was good for the first 200 miles or so. The sky was clear and the surface of the North Sea was dark against the lightness of the sky. With some envy I could see the silhouettes of Halifaxes and the odd Stirling flying high above us and overtaking on a roughly parallel course. The weather then turned treacherous (as was not uncommon over the North Sea). Low stratus covered the entire sea long before we reached the enemy coast and medium and heavy cloud developed in layers. We were navigating solely on dead reckoning and had only a general idea of our position, flying in and out of cloud (no radar, 'Gee', Loran or H$_2$S^{65} in those days at least for our Hudsons). We saw groups of light and medium flak to port and starboard with a heavier concentration ahead, which we assumed to be Bremen (a pious but hopeful assumption since we had not been able to fix our position on crossing the coast). In a somewhat detached frame of mind I noticed the coloured AA tracer start slowly then corkscrew past one's line of sight almost unbelievably quickly. Cloud cover was such that no positive identification of the target could be made.

'A few minutes after our dead reckoning time over target the turret gunner shouted that a night fighter with an orange light was astern of us (we had been warned at briefing that some German night fighters carried a red/orange light - purpose unknown). It disappeared as quickly as it came and it may well have been the exhaust flame of one of our own aircraft. However, at that time violent evasive action seemed to be the prudent order of the day. Some minutes later we saw through a gap in the clouds a port complex which, from its geographical features, we took to be Wilhelmshaven. Since we were now well behind our scheduled time over target and Wilhelmshaven was a designated alternative target and, not least, mindful of the other 999 (theoretical) aircraft milling around in the general area we released the bombs. With some relief we dived to just above the lowest layer of stratus and set course for home. Fifteen or so minutes later a gap in the cloud layer showed us for a fleeting moment to be over a coastal airfield with one runway lit by flares. A few minutes on we had a glancing sight of one of the islands off the coast but we were too low to identify it and an uneventful flight home was made at low level. Not a heroic flight or one that made even a minuscule contribution to the defeat of Germany. The contribution made by Coastal Command OTU Hudsons in the main must have been to public morale - the 'magic' figure of 1,000 bombers had simultaneously attacked a German city.'

The risk of collision and enemy fighter activity proved a constant threat and crews had to be ever watchful. Squadron Leader Wolfe's Wellington of 419 'Moose' Squadron RCAF was involved in an engagement with a Bf 110 night fighter north of Borkum at 4,200 feet over the North Sea. Sergeant D. R. Morrison opened fire and the enemy fighter's port engine was seen to burst into flames, which almost at once engulfed the entire wing. It dived into the sea, leaving a large circle of fire around the point of impact.

Although the raid on Bremen was not as successful as the first 1,000-bomber raid on Cologne, large parts of the city, especially in the south and east districts were destroyed. The German high command was shaken but 52 bombers were claimed destroyed by the flak and night fighter defences for the loss of just two Bf 110s and four NCO crewmembers killed or missing. The actual total of 48 aircraft lost (including five Coastal Command aircraft) was the highest casualty rate (five per cent) so far. Of the 31 No.1 (C) OTU Hudsons on the Bremen raid, two returned early owing to cowling and engine trouble and three were lost. Twenty-nine crews reached the target area. All except three, one of which, AM794, was shot down by Oberleutnant Egmont Prinz zur Lippe-Weissenfeld, Staffelkapitän 5./NJG2 east of De Kooy airfield, returned safely, two with minor shrapnel damage.

A total of 1,123 sorties (including 102 Hudsons and Wellingtons from Coastal Command) had been despatched and fifty Bomber Command aircraft and four from Coastal Command were lost. A Hudson flown by Flight Lieutenant Derek Hodgkinson (later Air Chief Marshal Sir Derek Hodgkinson, KCB CBE DFC AFC) on 220 Squadron, CO of the temporary Operational Hudson Squadron, was shot down by two unidentified Bf 110s attacking simultaneously on the return leg over the Dutch coast. Hodgkinson skilfully ditched his burning aircraft off Ameland, where he and his badly wounded navigator were taken prisoner next day. Hudson V AM762 VX-M on 206 Squadron crashed at Frel near Heide; it was shot down by Oberleutnant Werner 'Red' Hoffmann, Staffelkapitän 5./NJG3 for his first night victory of the war. The pilot, 22-year old Flight Sergeant Kenneth Douglas Wright, the WOp/AG and an air gunner were killed. Two other crew were taken prisoner. Hudson V AM606 VX-S flown by 29-year old Squadron Leader Cyril Norman Crook DFC which crashed into the sea south of Fehmarn Island fell victim to 20-year-old Leutnant Hans-Heinrich 'Kegel' [Skittle'] König who had two Blenheim day Abschüsse in 1941 with 5./ZG76 before his unit was incorporated into Nachtjagd in November as 8./NJG3. An unidentified war reporter flew with König on 25/26 June:

'Far, far away the thin white fingers of the searchlights rise up. The first flashes of exploding shells flicker in the sky. Now the multi-coloured streams from the light flak join in. 'Take off!' The cabin windows slam closed. With one leap the mechanic jumps off the wing. The fuselage shudders in the slipstream of the propeller. The chocks are snatched away. We sweep over the concrete runway into the thick wall of cloud and climb and climb...We have reached our ordered altitude. Far below us the milky-grey mass of cloud shimmers, in many places already clearly marked by the muzzle flashes of the flak guns, the bomb explosions, the searchlights and the core of raging red fires over my home town. And now, suddenly, we receive the call from afar! We commence our hunt. The moon is our guiding light.

'King' [König] is sitting forward at the controls. The left hand on the throttle, the right on the button for machine guns and cannon. The head flashes to the left, to the right, the eyes bore into the night. 'There he is, ahead! Can you see him?' Throttle closed. It is a Lockheed Hudson; it is much slower than we and has not spotted us. The black camouflage shimmers in the silvery light of the moon. This is the attack: the fighter is snatched upward and fires from all barrels. The dull sound of the engines is overlaid by the clear crackling of the guns. For a moment we gaze into a fountain of deadly fireworks, we're then pressed unremittingly backwards. The Lockheed had swung desperately away, we dive down after it. The Tommy must still have his machine under control. He twists cleverly and then we have him and are set for another merciless attack. Bright yellow, bright red, thin tracer at eye level, directed at the belly of the British bomber. He doesn't defend himself. Has the gunner been eliminated already? Now small flames appear on the port wing! 'He's burning, King, he's burning!' He is still diving down towards the layer of cloud which could be his salvation if he reaches it unscathed. We make another attack; a burst goes into his starboard wing. As the machine disappears reeling into the white veil there is a flash. We have to abandon our opponent to his inevitable fate. A fresh call has reached us. We turn in.

'How ghost-like is the confrontation with the enemy in the sky at night! Like a black shadow which discloses its bodily shape only in the aftermath, the duck-like profile of a Vickers Wellington suddenly appears before us. 'I am attacking!' says King and snatches the machine steeply upwards. But before the deadly fire leaves the fighter's barrels, a pulse beat ahead; there are flashes above us from the rear guns of the British bomber. Just tiny sparks, like someone striking matches far away. At the same time our guns sound with ear-splitting crashing; it must be boring like red hot steel into the enemy's belly, who spreads his wings seemingly within one's reach. Missed.

'Like a plaintive call from far away I hear the words on the intercom: 'I am wounded! I'm finished! Get ready to jump!' My hand goes at once to the emergency lever. I take one last querying look at the radio operator. King also turns his head. Both have blood running over their faces. King must have a severe injury. To his right there is a gaping hole in the glass cockpit roof. Leaden silence. The hands are on the parachute straps. The body is tense. Then the releasing words. 'My right eye is gone,' says King, 'but I can still hold the machine. I will try to get you home.' The radio operator appears to have been only slightly wounded. Now that the immediate threat has been removed, the steady sound of the engines sounds like soothing music. What is the Wellington doing? Is this attack to have been in vain? It has been heavily hit. Then I see it tottering not far away to aft. 'King, it's burning! It's going down over the port wing! It's exploding!' I must have shouted this into the throat mike. I have to repeat it before they understand it up front. When King replies - in monosyllables, without pleasure at his success, I realize for the first time and with stifling certainty that the fight is not over yet. Now our lives are at stake and they are in his hands. If the left half of the face has also been hit, if the blood runs into the other eye, then we are lost.

'All around the lone aircraft, which had already sent out its emergency call, the battle continued with undiminished intensity. We are in deep shadows beneath the clouds; the muzzle flashes of the flak only intermittently interrupting the darkness. Somewhere a blazing fire. Our comrades at the base would certainly be following our progress with all their good wishes. Only now, as the airfield appears before us with all its lights, we feel a certainty that we would master our fate. King approaches for landing. The pneumatics lower the undercarriage. A small bounce on the grass, then the machine completes its run and stops. We only heard later on that, after landing, the last drops of coolant were dripping out of the damaged tank. Twice, three times King nearly collapsed on the way to operations. Time and again he rallies under our helping hands. Warm light receives us as we enter the hut. There is absolute quiet in the bright room; twenty-thirty pairs of eyes gaze at the young pilot. Upright, with tousled fair hair and face covered in blood he stands before his commander: 'Obediently report: Leutnant König returned from enemy encounter. One certain Abschuss in area Anton Two!'

König lost sight in his right eye, which made him unfit for further night-fighting duties but he persuaded his superiors to allow him to join a day-fighting unit (Jagdstaffel Heligoland) in March 1943 and he soon made a name for himself in the air battles against the American combat boxes. He destroyed eight Viermots during the ensuing summer months and rose to command 3./NJG11 in October. In April 1944 he was appointed Kommandeur I./JG11, claiming four American bombers shot down on 29 April. After shooting down his 28th Viermot - a B-17 - over Kaltenkirchen on 24 May the ensuing explosion ripped off the left wing of his FW 190A-7 and König crashed to his death. He was posthumously promoted to Hauptmann and decorated with the Ritterkreuz 19 August 1944.

The bomber OTUs of 91 Group suffered particularly heavily, losing 23 of its 198 Whitleys and Wellingtons. Altogether, 29 Wellingtons, four Manchester Is, three Halifaxes, two Stirlings, one Hampden and one Whitley were lost. Flying Officer Leslie Thomas Manser on 50 Squadron at Skellingthorpe piloted L7301, one of the Manchesters lost. Manser's Manchester was caught in a searchlight cone and seriously damaged by flak on the approaches to Cologne. Manser held the bomber steady until his bomb load was released and despite further damage, set course for England although he and his crew could have safely bailed out after leaving the target area. The Manchester steadily lost height and when it became clear that there was no hope of reaching England, Manser ordered the crew to bail out. Oberleutnant Walter Barte of 4./NJG1 intercepted the Manchester at low level in Nachtjagd Box 6A and delivered the coup-de-grace with a burst in the right Vulture engine for his fifth victory. Manser, who went down with the aircraft and was killed, was awarded a posthumous Victoria Cross on 20 October after testimonies from five of his crew who evaded. Barte also claimed a Wellington thirty kilometres north of Hasselt and a Wellington NNE of Maastricht. Oberleutnant Heinrich Prinz zu Sayn-Wittgenstein claimed a Manchester and a Wellington. Stabsfeldwebel Gerhard Herzog of I./NJG1 claimed two Wellingtons as did Oberleutnant Helmut Woltersdorf of 7./NJG1. Nachtjagd claimed thirty Abschüsse in total.⁶⁶

Wellington IC T2723 on 20 OTU at Lossiemouth flown by Sergeant N. W. Levasseur was shot down into the sea off Terschelling in an encounter with Oberleutnant Egmont Prinz zur Lippe Weissenfeld of 5./NJG2. All six crew were killed. 24 OTU sent sixteen aircraft this night and three failed to return. Whitley V BD266 on 'B' Flight flown by Pilot Officer J. A. Preston was shot down in the North Sea North of Vlieland at 0254 hours by Major Kurt Holler of II./NJG2 for his second victory. All five crew died. Leutnants' Lothar Linke, Robert Denzel and Hans-Georg Bötel of II./NJG2 claimed four Wellingtons; Bötel's claim were for his first two combat victories. Denzel was killed on 25/26 June 1943. He had ten Abschüsse. Whitley V BD379 piloted by 21-year old Flying Officer James Brian Monro RNZAF was hit by flak from 5./Marine Flak Battery 246 and was finished off by Leutnant Günther Löwa of 5./NJG2. The Whitley crashed into the sea off Terschelling at 0418 hours with the loss of all six crew, all of whom were OTU instructors. Three members of the crew were removed from the wrecked aircraft on 26 June and buried next day. Pilot Officer Ian Patterson Clark, WOp/AG was washed ashore on 27 June and buried on 29 June. Löwa was killed on 29/30 June when he is believed to have collided with Stirling I N3076 on 7 Squadron flown by Flight Sergeant M. G. Bailey RCAF which crashed off Borkum. Bailey and two others were taken prisoner. Five of his crew were killed. Löwa's Bf 110F-4 crashed into the North Sea.

Although the raid was not as successful as the first 1,000-bomber raid on Cologne, large parts of Bremen, especially in the south and east districts were destroyed.⁶⁷ The German high command was shaken but at Leeuwarden airfield in northern Holland at least, morale soared. II./NJG2 claimed seventeen of the 48 bombers shot down. Hauptmann Helmut 'Bubi' ('Boy') Lent, who claimed nine aircraft during June to take his score to 48 Abschüsse, destroyed a Wellington and an OTU Whitley. Wellington IC T2612 on 18 OTU was shot down at 0237 hours on 26 June and crashed near Andijk with the loss of Pilot Officer Maksymilian Niemczyk and his all-Polish crew. Whitley V BD2612 on 24 OTU flown by Sergeant Frederick Marsden Cole RCAF was shot down into the sea at 0256 hours. All the crew were killed. III./NJG1, operating from Twente aerodrome, claimed seven RAF aircraft. Twenty-two year old Leutnant August 'Gustel' Geiger of the 9th Staffel shot down three of these bombers: Wellington IC R1078 on 11 OTU piloted by Pilot Officer S. G. King RCAF crashed near Rheine with the loss of three of his crew; Whitley V AD689 on 10 OTU flown by Sergeant Norman Maxwell Oulster RCAF crashed in the vicinity of Lingen-Ems with no survivors and Stirling I N3754 on 7 Squadron, which came down at Bimolton between 0120 and 0158 hours. Geiger was born on 6 May 1920 in Überlingen, near Lake Constance. He joined the Luftwaffe in late 1939 and was posted in mid-1941 as Leutnant to 8./NJG1.

Oberleutnant Werner 'Red' Hoffmann, Staffelkapitän, 5./NJG3, operating from Schleswig, scored his first two night kills by shooting down a Coastal Command Lockheed Hudson and a Whitley. The Hudson was shot down six kilometres southeast of Heide and the Whitley in 'Himmelbett' box Heide ['Heather'] six kilometres east of Büsum. Born on 13 January 1918 at Stettin, Hoffmann began flying gliders in 1932 and he joined the Luftwaffe in December 1936, learning to fly with the Luftkriegschule near Potsdam. He was awarded his pilot's badge in June 1938 and was then sent to 7./JG234. III./JG234 was eventually re-designated I./ZG52 in May 1939 and was equipped with the new Bf 110 Zerstörer fighter. Leutnant Hoffmann was assigned to 4./ZG2 in early 1940 and he participated in the Battle of France. He claimed his first victory, an RAF fighter over Calais, on 24 May. He was slightly wounded in June and spent some time in hospital. In July Hoffmann was transferred to Ergänzungs-Zerstörergruppe Værløse (top left) Squadron Leader Patrick Foss.

(top right) Hauptmann Wolfgang Falck Kommandeur of NJG1.

(left) Hauptmann Ludwig Becker. 44 night victories in NJG1 and NJG2.

(right) Major Werner Streib of 1./NJG1. 67 Nachtjagd victories (including 30 Viermots).

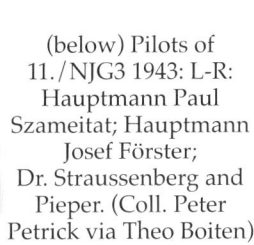

(below) Pilots of 11./NJG3 1943: L-R: Hauptmann Paul Szameitat; Hauptmann Josef Förster; Dr. Straussenberg and Pieper. (Coll. Peter Petrick via Theo Boiten)

(Above left) General Joseph Kammhuber.

(Above right) Oberleutnant Paul Gildner of 3./NJG1.

(Bottom) Bf 110 night fighter. The twin Mk.108 cannon tray beneath the forward fuselage was omitted when FuG 202 Lichtenstein BC radar was carried.

(Left) Oberleutnant Egmont Prinz zur Lippe-Weissenfeld, 51 victories in NJG1 and 5.

(Right) Oberleutnant Reinhold Eckardt, 22 night and 3 day victories in ZG76, NJG1 and NJG3.

(Above) Feldwebel Hermann Wischenski of 3./JG300.

(Left) Oberfeldwebel Heinz Gossow of 1./JG302.

(Right) Feldwebel Anton Benning of 2./JG300.

Hauptmann Leopold 'Poldi' Fellerer, Kommandeur, NJG5.

L-R: Oberleutnant Reinhard Kollak, 8./NJG4; General Kammhuber and Major Walter Ehle, Gruppe Kommandant II./NJG1 at St. Trond on 29 August 1943 on the occasion of the award of the Ritterkreuz to Kollak and Ehle.

(Above) Major Walter Ehle.

(Left) Wolfgang Schnaufer lays a wreath at Walter Ehle's funeral on 19 November 1943. He was killed on the night of 17/18 November.

(Below) Leutnant Klaus Bretschneider and Lofgen of 5./JG300.

Nachtjagd night fighter pilots' briefing, 1942.

Propaganda leaflet dropped over France referring to the bombing of Düsseldorf.

150 Bombes de deux tonnes s'abattent sur la cité allemande de DUSSELDORF en 50 minutes

A gauche est une photographie montrant la taille gigantesque des bombes britanniques. L'explosion de l'une de ces bombes sème la dévastation dans tout un quartier.

Major Helmut Lent with Hauptmann Heinrich Ruppel, Area Controller at Leeuwarden in 1943. Raumführer Ruppel had been a pilot on the Western Front in WW1.

Nachtjagd Experten at St. Trond, early spring 1944: L-R: Major Helmut Lent (Kommodore NJG3); bandmaster; Oberleutnant Heinz-Wolfgang Schnaufer (Kommandeur IV./NJG1) and Hauptmann Hans-Joachim Jabs (Kommodore NJG1). (Coll. Martin Drewes via Rob de Visser/Theo Boiten)

(Right) Feldwebel Erich Handke, Heinz-Wolfgang Schnaufer's bordfunker.

(Below) Avro Manchester L7465 of 207 Squadron being shot down near Bocholt by Oberleutnant Helmut Woltersdorf of 7./NJG1 on 26 March 1942.

(Left) Hauptmann Paul Semrau, 46 night victories in NJG2 and NJG6.

(Right) Oberleutnant Wilhelm Telge of Stab II./NJG1.

(Left) Hauptmann Reinhold Knacke, 44 night victories in NJG1.

(Below) Hauptmann Hans-Joachim Jabs. 28 night and 22 day victories in ZG76, NJG3 and NJG1.

Lübeck in flames.

(Above) Hauptmann Ludwig 'Luk' Meister, 38 night and 1 day victories in NJG1 and NJG4.

(Below) Flight Lieutenant John Siebert RAAF.

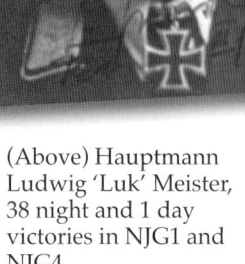

(Above) Oberleutnant Lothar Linke. 24 night and 3 day victories in ZG76, NJG1 and NJG2.

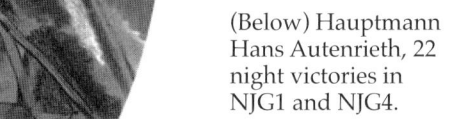

(Below) Oberleutnant Wilhelm 'Wim' Johnen. 34 night victories in NJG1, 5 and 6.

(Below) Hauptmann Hans Autenrieth, 22 night victories in NJG1 and NJG4.

(ABove left) Oberfeldwebel Gerhard Herzog of 2./NJG1 on his wedding day. (via Kees Rijken)

(Above right) Feldwebel Heinz Vinke, 54 victories in NJG1.

(Below) Leutnant 'Rudi' Röhr and his Funker, Unteroffizier Erwin Cobi.

(Above left) Major Heinrich Prinz Zu Sayn-Wittgenstein, 83 Nachtjagd victories (including 23 on the Eastern Front) in 170 sorties with NJG2, 3 and 5.

(Above right) Leutnant Hans-Heinrich 'Kegel' [Skittle'] or 'King' König.

(Below) Oberleutnant Eckart-Wilhelm 'Hugo' von Bonin of 6./NJG1 (32 night victories) inspecting his first victim, Wellington Ic R1379 on 115 Squadron on 11 May 1941.

Messerschmitt Bf 110G-4 of II./NJG6 with FuG 220 dipoles associated with Lichtenstein SN-2 AI radar and Schräge Musik installation behind cockpit at Grossachsenheim airfield on an airfield at dusk.

L-R: Hauptmann Paul Semrau; Leutnant Heinz Strüning; Oberfeldwebel Alfons Köster; Leutnant Wilhelm Beier on 9 November 1942 on the occasion of the award of the Ritterkreuz to Struning and Köster. (Coll Hans-Jakob Schmitz via Theo Boiten)

(Above) Leutnant Heinz Strüning, 56 Nachtjagd victories in NJG1 and 2 in 250 sorties.

(Left) Doktor Goebbels the German Propaganda Minister in the ruins of Cologne Cathedral.

(Below) Oberfeldwebel 'Rudi' Köhler, Oberleutnant Werner 'Red' Hoffmann's funker.

(Above) From left: Oberleutnant Walter Barte, Staffelkapitän 4./NJG1; Unteroffizier Pieper, his Bordfunker and Oberwerkmeister Adam (ground crew).

(Above) Oberleutnant Werner 'Red' Hoffmann, Staffelkapitän 5./NJG3.51 victories in NJG3 and 5, plus 1 Zerstörer victory in ZG2.

(Right) Oberleutnant Hans Krause, 25 night victories in NJG3 and NJG2.

(Above left) Hauptmann Werner Baake, 41 night victories from 195 sorties in NJG1.

(Above right) Leutnant August 'Gustel' Geiger of 8./NJG1, 53 victories in NJG1.

(Left) II./1NJG5 Experten at Parchim, spring 1944: R-L: Oberleutnant Josef Kraft; Oberleutnant Helmuth Schulte; Hauptmann Leopold 'Poldi' Fellerer; Leutnant Peter Spoden; u/k.

as an instructor with the rank of Oberleutnant and appointed Staffelkapitän. He remained with the unit until 3 August 1941 when the unit was disbanded and became Staffelkapitän of 5./NJG3 at Schleswig. On the night of 25/26 June 1942 Hoffmann and his bordfunker, Oberfeldwebel 'Rudi' Kohler shot down two Zweimots during the 1,000-bomber raid on Bremen. By the eve of the Battle of Hamburg they had scored eight night-Abschüsse in the illuminated and 'Himmelbett' night fighting. Hauptmann Hoffmann served with I./NJG1 at Sint-Truiden/Sint-Trond in May 1943 and was appointed Gruppenkommandeur of I./NJG5 on 5 July, one of the Gruppen of NJG5 stationed in the vicinity of Berlin. He and Kohler claimed a Lancaster North of Berlin as their ninth Abschuss at 0032 hours on 4 September (Lancasters on eight different Squadrons crashed in this area during the raid). Their first 'Tame Boar' kill was followed by nineteen more Lancasters and Halifaxes, half of them in the Berlin area, in six months September 1943-February 1944.

Fifty-two bombers were claimed destroyed by the flak and night fighter defences on the Bremen raid for the loss of just two Bf 110s of 4./NJG2 and 4./NJG3 and four NCO crewmembers killed or missing. Oberleutnant Reinhold Knacke and his funker, Unteroffizier Günther Heu of 1./NJG1 at Venlo shot down three Viermots; a Halifax three kilometres ESE of Weert, a Wellington ten kilometres east of Weert and a Wellington three kilometres southwest of Middelbeerer.

In June 1942 no less than 62 RAF bombers (including twelve Halifaxes) were claimed shot down by II./NJG2, the top-scoring night fighters based at Leeuwarden. On 31 June Hitler decreed that all searchlight regiments except one (which was kept in action in the Venlo area for experimental purposes against the possible resumption of the searchlight techniques at some later date) should be given up to the flak for the protection of special industrial and urban targets, which eliminated any further use of the 'Helle Nachtjagd' technique. Kammhuber, who strongly contested the decision (though he later decided that the step proved beneficial to the development of the 'Himmelbett' system) compensated by further extending the existing radar positions. This had the double aim of leaving no gap through which attacking aircraft might penetrate and to put fighters into a position to attack bombers continuously along the penetration and return flights. By early 1942 'Himmelbett' was so advanced that all that was necessary to make good the loss of searchlights was the further extension of the existing radar positions. To achieve greatest density of interception, Kammhuber retained these positions intact, though for more coverage he might have spread them more widely apart. Further positions were equipped, first covering the entire foresector up to the coast and then gradually taking in the main target areas in the rear. The old Grossraum was combined with new positions to form the new Nachtjagdgrossraum under the command of a Nachtjagdführer. Night fighter divisions eventually consisted of four to six of these night fighting areas. The Bomber Command tactics of staggered approach, involving a period of long duration (between one and one and a half hours) over a target were ideal for the successful operation of the 'Himmelbett' system. From June 1942 until the British introduction of 'Window' in July 1943 German night fighters inflicted heavy losses on the bomber forces. Leutnant 'Dieter' Schmidt of III./NJG1 comments:

'The British began now not only using heavier machines, they also changed their tactics by no longer approaching loosely on a broad front but, in order to overwhelm the defences, coming tightly packed in what became known as a 'bomber stream'. The first of these attacks was the famous 1,000 bomber raid on Cologne in the night of 30/31 May 1942. We responded with a defence network of night-fighting areas, the 'Dunkle Nachtjagd', which was independent of searchlights, reaching from the coast far back into the hinterland. The growing intensity of the air war but especially the difficulty of air operations at night resulted in the first and for us young ones hard to bear losses of experienced crews: after 23 victories Oberleutnant Woltersdorf, Kommandeur of the 7th Staffel was killed in a belly landing on 2 June. On 30 June Oberleutnant Werner Rowlin lost his life while bailing out[68] and Feldwebel Richard Philipp of the 9th Staffel, who landed his aircraft on 9 June in spite of being shot through the lung, was out of action for a long time.

'In mid-1942 our Gruppe not only got a new commander in Hauptmann Thimmig, our equipment was also significantly improved by aircraft fitted with radar, the Lichtenstein BC, which had been developed since August 1941 by IV./NJG1. Until now, the success of the 'Dunkle Nachtjagd' had been entirely dependent on the skill of the ground controller to direct the fighter accurately, especially during the final phase of the approach to the enemy aircraft. Now it would suffice to guide the crew close enough to be able to pick up the target with their on-board radar. Also, the aircraft were no longer painted black but in a light colour and by the end of the year our Bf 110Fs with their unreliable engines were replaced by the G4 night fighter version, which was to serve us well until the end of the war.'

On the night of 29/30 June Bomber Command dispatched 253 aircraft to Bremen. Eleven aircraft failed to return. Nine were shot down by night-fighters including six by II./NJG2. Three of these were Halifax IIs on 405 'Vancouver' Squadron RCAF. W1113 LQ-G piloted by Pilot Officer Henry Adolphus Echin RAAF (who served as Chinn) was shot down at 0148 hours by Oberleutnant Rudolf Sigmund of II./NJG2 and crashed between Wolvega and Noordwolde. There were no survivors. W7714 flown by Warrant Officer Lawrence Sidney RCAF was shot down at 0214 hours by Oberstleutnant Alfred Helm of Stab IV/NJG1 and crashed at Sybrandaburen with the loss of all the crew. W7715 LQ-H flown by Flight Lieutenant Harold Liversidge was claimed by two pilots within one minute of each other: Leutnant Rolf Rüssmann of III./NJG3 into the Borger swamps south of Papenburg at 0145 hours and Unteroffizier Alfred Brackmann of 2./NJG3 at Bimolton, seven kilometres NNW of Nordhorn at 0146 hours. Only the rear gunner survived. Wellington III X3539 on 75 Squadron RNZAF was shot down at 0308 hours by Oberleutnant Egmont Prinz zur Lippe Weissenfeld of II./NJG2 and crashed in Waddenzee south of Ameland. Pilot Officer Walter Jack Monk RNZAF and crew were killed. A Wellington III on 57 Squadron, which returned to Methwold, carried the dead body of Pilot Officer Buston the rear gunner who was killed in a night fighter attack. Stirling I N3076 MG-S on 7 Squadron was probably shot down at 0233 hours by Leutnant Günther Löwa and Feldwebel Möller of 5./NJG2 in Bf 110F-4 R4+JN. The bomber crashed in the North Sea 35 kilometres northwest of Vlieland. Flight Sergeant M. G. Bailey RCAF and his two gunners were taken prisoner. The five others were killed. Löwa probably collided with the bomber and crashed in the sea near his final victim and he and Möller were killed. Stirling I BF310 OJ-H on 149 Squadron was shot down at 0302 hours by Oberleutnant Leopold 'Poldi' Fellerer of 5./NJG2. It also crashed in the Ijsselmeer off Schellingwoude. Pilot Officer Cecil William Simmons RCAF, an American from Winston-Salem, North Carolina and his crew were killed and are buried at Amsterdam.

Warrant Officer Len Collins RAAF a Stirling gunner on 149 Squadron at Lakenheath who had completed his tour and was awaiting a posting to an EFTS to train as a pilot volunteered for an extra op. He stood in for the mid-upper-gunner, who was ill, on the crew of Squadron Leader George William Alexander, who would be flying N6082. It would be Collins' 33rd trip. He recalls:

'Other than the second pilot, Flying Officer William George Barnes, on his first trip to gain experience, the remainder of the crew were on their thirtieth. All were RAF. I was the only Aussie. The trip to Bremen was uneventful. Conversing with the squadron leader I found that he was most interested with the pyrotechnic display from the flak and the colours of the searchlights as we crossed the enemy coast. I predicted we were in for trouble when a blue one slid off our wing tip. However, either our doctored IFF did not work or the Germans were given a tip-off. Over Bremen we received a direct hit from flak on our inner starboard engine, killing Alexander and Pilot Officer Cyril William Dellow, observer and injuring the wireless operator, Philip Frank Hickley. The bombs were dropped live, a photo taken and we headed for home on three engines. Over the Zuider Zee a night fighter [a Bf 110 of 6./NJG2 flown by Leutnant Hans-Georg Bötel] appeared. I can still recall the flash of his windscreen in the darkness as he opened fire. As I was speaking to the rear gunner, Sergeant [Richard Thomas Patrick] Gallagher he was blown out of his turret. I was ringed with cannon shells and injured in the leg by shrapnel. Owing to the electrical cut out which protected the tail of the aircraft from the mid-upper guns, I was unable to fire on the fighter attacking us. Fortunately, the turret became jammed in the rear position, allowing me to vacate it. Forward, the aircraft was burning like a torch. I could not contact any crewmember. The position was hopeless. I felt I had no option but to leave the aircraft. My parachute was not in its storage holder. I found it under the legs of the mid-upper turret with a cannon shell burn in it. I removed the rear escape hatch, clipped on the parachute and sat on the edge of the hatch. I pulled the ripcord and tumbled out. The parachute, having several holes from the shell burn, 'candlesticked' (twirled) as I descended and I landed in a canal. I was apprehended the following day and was taken to Leeuwarden airfield for interrogation. Here I met the pilot of the Messerschmitt 110 who claimed to have shot us down. I abused him in good Australian. He understood, having spent three years at Oxford University.'

N6082 was shot down at 0204 hours and crashed in the Ijsselmeer near Wons south of Harlingen. Collins was the only survivor. The others who were killed were Flight Sergeant Leslie Wiltshire and Sergeant Leslie Shearer. Bötel was killed on 3 July 1942 when his 110 crashed at Britswerd Holland, north of Sneek on his final approach to Leeuwarden airfield. He had three victories.

A record 147 Bomber Command aircraft were destroyed by Nachtjagd in June 1942 and in July 102 heavies were shot down. On the night of 19/20 July nineteen Wellingtons laid mines off Lorient, St. Nazaire and La Pallice. One Wellington on 12 Squadron failed to return. A few aircraft short of a hundred RAF heavies were to attempt to bomb the Vulkan U-boat yard at Vegesack if clear, or the town if there was cloud-cover at the shipyards. The target area was found to be cloud-covered and all aircraft bombed Vegesack by Gee but no bombs fell on the target. Three Halifaxes were lost. Oberleutnant 'Rudi' Schönert of 5./NJG2 claimed one of them near Borkum and Oberleutnant Lippe-Weissenfeld claimed another north of Terschelling. Pilot Officer Horace James Skelly and his crew on W1179 NP-S on 158 Squadron were killed. Oberstleutnant Alfred Helm of Stab IV/NJG1 claimed the other 158 Squadron Halifax when he shot down W1162 NP-D which crashed into the Waddenzee with the loss of Sergeant Patrick Joseph Dillon and crew. Helm was the oldest night fighter pilot in World War Two being born on 16 January 1894. The 48 year old had fought in WWI and scored at least three air to air victories while serving with Kampfstaffel 30 of KG5. He was a holder of the Military St. Heinrich Order and was awarded the EK1 and 2 and EP. He began WW2 in 1939 by flying the Ju 52 before progressing onto Bf 110 night fighters. He ended the war with three victories.

On the night of 21/22 July 1942 of 291 bombers despatched to bomb Duisburg again ten Wellingtons, one Halifax and a Hampden failed to return. Two of the missing Wellingtons - both on 115 Squadron - were claimed by Oberleutnant Reinhold Knacke, Staffelkapitän, Stab I/NJG1: X3561 five kilometres southeast of Roermond and X3750 eight kilometres east of Eindhoven for his 22nd and 23rd victories. Two nights later when 215 aircraft bombed Duisburg again, seven aircraft failed to return. Oberleutnant Prinz Sayn-Wittgenstein claimed a Lancaster for his thirteenth victory. Leutnant Hans Joachim Witzleb of I./NJG3 claimed a Blenheim 'Intruder' on 18 Squadron northeast of Vechta for the first of his six Abschüsse. Flight Lieutenant Fred Martyn Thorne and his two crew were killed. Two Stirlings that were lost over Holland this night were claimed by Hauptmann Herbert Bönsch, five kilometres southwest of Oss and Unteroffizier Heinz Oloff of 3./NJG1, at s'Hertogenbosch.

When RAF heavies attacked Duisburg for the third time that month, on the night of 25/26 July, twelve aircraft failed to return. Oberleutnant Reinhold Knacke claimed three Abschüsse. At Schandeloo he shot down Blenheim IV R3837, one of three 114 Squadron Intruder's that were lost, killing Sergeant Leonard Causley and crew. Twelve minutes later Knacke shot down Stirling I W7576 on 15 Squadron piloted by Pilot Officer Wilbert Andrew Shoemaker DFC RCAF three kilometres north of Horst. The skipper and two of his crew were killed; four men were taken into captivity. Knacke's third victory was a Wellington at Repelen. Among the other claimants were 22-year old Oberleutnant Kurt Loos of 1./NJG1 who claimed a Halifax and Oberfeldwebel Heinz Strüning of 8./NJG2 who claimed a Wimpy northeast of Amersfoort. Feldwebel Heinz Pahler of 2./NJG1 claimed a Wellington also and Oberleutnant Rolf Bussmann of 9./NJG2 claimed a Wellington west of Bergen am Zee and a 'Stirling' north of Goeree.

On the night of 26/27 July, again in full moonlight, the target was Hamburg and 115 Squadron suffered worse losses. At Marham Wing Commander Frank W. Dixon-Wright DFC the 31-year-old CO led the briefing. Popular with his crews, he had already completed a tour of operations. Some members of his crew on Wellington BJ615 were second tour men. They too were well respected. At around 2200 hours 115 Squadron BJ615 and thirteen other Wellington crews began taking off. In all, 403 Wellingtons, Hampdens, Lancasters, Halifaxes and Stirlings were despatched. Hamburg suffered its most severe air raid to date and widespread damage was caused, mostly in the housing and semi-commercial districts. The Fire Department was overwhelmed and forced to seek outside assistance for the first time. 337 people lost their lives, 1027 were injured and 14,000 people were made homeless. Damage amounted to the equivalent of £25,000,000. Night fighters were active because of the clear moonlight conditions along most of the route and over the target flak was accurate. Eight of the 29 bombers shot down were by night fighters of II./NJG1 at Leeuwarden. Many of the missing aircraft came down off the northwest German coast, in the northern part of The Netherlands and in the Friesian Islands area. Oberleutnant Lothar Linke of 5./NJG1 shot down Lancaster R5748 on 106 Squadron at 0205 hours and it crashed at Rottevalle in Friesland. Rhodesian Squadron Leader Francis Harold Robertson DFC and three of his crew were killed. Three crew were taken into captivity. Four of the fifteen missing Wellingtons were on 115 Squadron. Hauptmann Helmut Lent of II./NJG1 was patrolling over the North Sea north west of Vlieland in a Bf 110 night fighter looking for Viermots to further his score. At the end of June his tally stood at 39 night and eight day victories when he had been presented with the Ritterkreuz des Eisernen Kreuzes mit Eichenlaub at the Führerhauptquartier at Rastenburg. Two Wellington victories followed on the 3rd and 9th of July an now, on the night of 26/27 July, at 0235 hours he claimed a Halifax northwest of Vlieland. Four minutes later a dark shape loomed into his line of sight. Quickly closing the gap between himself and the other aircraft he perceived the unmistakable bulky outline to be a Wellington bomber. Not wishing to overshoot and lose the enemy aircraft in the darkness Lent eased back on his throttles. Wing Commander Dixon-Wright and his crew were doomed. Their aircraft went into the sea near the crash position of Lent's Halifax victim at 0239. The only body recovered from the water was that of 25-year old Pilot Officer George Whittaker DFM the WOp/AG.

Bomber Command was stood down on 27/28 July but this was the full moon period and on 28/29 July a return to Hamburg was announced at briefings. Crews were told that the raid would be on a far bigger scale than two nights before. At Oakington, Pilot Officer Leslie R. Sidwell, rear-turret gunner in 23-year-old Flight Lieutenant Douglas W. Whiteman's crew of Stirling IW7565, 'B-Beer' on 7 Squadron made a note that said it was another 'Thousand Raid'. He surmised, correctly, that the number was again being made up with OTU crews.

'Out at dispersal we got everything finally checked and ready in the sweltering heat inside the aircraft before climbing out into the oh-so-welcome cool night air. It was lovely to relax outside on the grass and smoke casually before reluctantly putting on the flying kit which I knew would be badly needed for the cold later on, after the muck-sweat had gone. I donned flying kit, regretfully and knowing full well it would be freezing at height was soon in another sweat in the aircraft. We took off at 2229 hours. The weather was good. We passed over Cromer and out over the North Sea. I spent the time taking the usual sightings from my rear turret on flame-floats we'd dropped to check drift for the navigator. We'd been briefed to cross the German coast north of the Elbe estuary and then to turn south twenty miles north of Hamburg to run up to the target.

'There was heavy flak and we were hit just before the run up. Just after we'd bombed, someone on the intercom reported tracer coming up from below and we were hit by night-fighter attack from underneath. I reported a decoy headlight out on the starboard quarter and searched around for other fighters. I reported one coming in from above on the port side and told the skipper to turn to port. I think I hit him with a burst before my power went off. A fighter came in again from the rear and continued firing. My turret was shattered and we seemed to be in a steady dive. The skipper gave the emergency bail-out order, quickly followed by what sounded like his cries of pain. Then the intercom abruptly cut off and we were on fire.

'When my turret power had failed I'd been left partly on the beam. I started to operate the dead man's handle (emergency winding gear) to centralize my turret so that I could get back into the fuselage to grab my parachute and bail out. (Chutes could not be stored in the rear turret as one did in earlier two-engined jobs, which were dead easy for rear gunners to quit in a hurry). I wound away like mad at the hand-winding gear behind me, very conscious that we were losing precious height. As if in a dream, I saw a Me 110 closing in from astern with his guns blazing away. I wound away as I watched him through the shattered perspex. My painfully slow progress was like a nightmare. I was conscious of the EBO order given in what seemed some time ago ... Would I be in time? He was extremely close to me when he eventually broke away and I finally managed to move the turret sufficiently to fall back hurriedly into the fuselage. I grabbed my 'chute from the stowage outside the turret doors, forced open the nearby emergency exit door and as quickly as I could, jumped out into space. In those seconds I was conscious of flame and smoke up front in the fuselage. I gave no thought at all to any dangers of bailing out, or that I'd had no practice in jumping. I just concentrated in getting out of a doomed aircraft. In my haste to get out I banged my head on something as I quit poor old 'B-Beer', partly knocking myself out. I pulled the ripcord without counting as you were normally told to do. I must have done the right thing because I came to swinging in the air. I could see the waters of the Elbe shining below, with the full moon bright towards the south.

'After all the turmoil I was now swinging gently in a strangely contrasting silence, floating down and rather higher than I'd expected. This peace was suddenly interrupted by a dazzling searchlight, which probed around as if looking for me. It held me in its blinding beam. I felt naked, vulnerable and powerless hanging there, not knowing what to expect. I raised my arms and wondered, 'Is this It?' But it soon switched off, as if satisfied that I'd been located and I was left to watch the Elbe more clearly as I lost height and to worry about landing in the wide waters. I'd never fancied coming down in the water and I pulled the rigging lines as instructed, hoping to spill air from the 'chute to alter my course. Probably more by luck than anything else, the Elbe disappeared and I braced myself for a landing, south of the river. The ground seemed to loom up very quickly in the moonlight and it wasn't possible to judge my first parachute landing expertly. I landed rather clumsily and hurt my right ankle on the hard ground but tall growing crops helped to cushion me. I remembered that my first duty was to hide my chute. As I struggled to gather it all up I thought I'd have a good view of a big 'Thousand Raid' but I was surprised. Little was seen or heard and I wondered, 'Where are they?' My watch showed 0110 hours just after landing.'[69]

Bomber Command casualties were heavy, Twenty Wellingtons and nine Stirlings were lost and a Whitley had ditched in the North Sea crashed in the sea. During the course on the night Nachtjagd claimed an estimated 24 aircraft destroyed, mainly in 'Himmelbett' fashion. Of the fourteen aircraft of 75 Squadron RNZAF, only eight returned to Feltwell. Five went down in northwest Germany: X3452 in the mouth of the Eider River to an unidentified night-fighter with Sergeant C. Croall RNZAF and crew being taken into captivity; Z1570 was shot down by Leutnant August 'Gustel' Geiger of 8./NJG1 at Hastenkamp near Neuenhaus with the loss of Flight Sergeant Arthur Grahame Johns RNZAF and crew; BJ661 was destroyed at 0305 hours on its way back over the Ijsselmeer in a surprise attack from below and behind by Leutnant Wolfgang Küthe of 5./NJG2 with the loss of Flight Sergeant John Edward Gilbertson RNZAF and two of his crew.

On 29/30 July, 291 RAF bombers were despatched to Saarbrücken, which suffered severe damage and casualties in the centre and northwest districts. Nine aircraft failed to return. Hauptmann August 'Gustel' Geiger of 9/NJG1 in a Bf 110G-4 claimed Whitley V Z9230 NF-N on 138 Squadron flown by Squadron leader William Twiston Davies DFC which crashed WNW of Rijssen on SOE operation 'Lettuce 5'. All seven men on the aircraft were killed. On the night of 5/6 August when RAF Bomber Command dispatched small numbers of aircraft to attack Essen and Bochum, Gieger destroyed Halifax II W1180 on 158 Squadron at Oldebroeke, twelve kilometres NNW of Erpe in Holland. Sergeant J. C. Stevens and three of his crew were taken prisoner; the three others were killed. Only three aircraft bombed at Bochum and only one at Essen. Three Halifaxes and a Lancaster and one Wellington failed to return and a further aircraft crashed in England. Wellington IV Z1216 on 142 Squadron flown by Sergeant George Camps Hooper RCAF was shot down by Leutnant Eckart-Wilhelm 'Hugo' von Bonin of 6./NJG1. (By the end of 1942 he would have a total of nine Night-Abschüsse). Stirling R9161 on 149 Squadron flown by Flight Lieutenant Frederick George Neate and Lancaster I R5728 were claimed destroyed by Oberleutnant Reinhold Eckardt. Twenty-eight year old Hauptmann Ludwig Bietmann of 5/NJG1 claimed Wellington III X3712 on 419 Squadron flown by American Warrant Officer1 Noel McHenry Moore RCAF. Bietmann shot down three Wellingtons on the night of 28/29 August and his seventh and final victory, a Halifax, followed on 8 September. He was killed on the night of 10/11 September.

For the next Main Force raid, on Düsseldorf on 31 July/1 August, 630 aircraft were despatched. Again Bomber Command's operational training units made up the numbers, which were deprived of 29 aircraft - eighteen of which were shot down by 'Himmelbett' night-fighters - but some extensive damage was inflicted. Two aircraft, a Blenheim 'Intruder' on 18 Squadron and a Wellington on 21 OTU at Edgehill, were shot down by Hauptmann Werner Streib Kommandeur I./NJG1. The crew on Blenheim IV V6432 skippered by Wing Commander Christopher Hastie Jones DFC the 18 Squadron CO, had taken off from Wattisham in Suffolk and was shot down at 0015 hours. It crashed at Kevelaer killing Jones, 22-year old Sergeant Kenneth M. Waylett, observer of Sholing, Southampton and 30-year old Sergeant Austen D. Evans the married WOp/AG of Amblecote, Stourbridge in Worcestershire. All three men were laid to rest in Reichswald cemetery.[70] Wellington Ic X9983 skippered by Sergeant Brian Robert Anstee crashed near Helden in Holland with loss of all except two of the crew. Seven aircraft were destroyed by II./NJG1. Leutnant Heinz-Wolfgang Schnaufer of Stab II./NJG1 claimed three aircraft to add to his first kill on 1/2 June when he destroyed a Halifax south of Louvain. In Düsseldorf and Neuss 453 buildings were destroyed and more than 15,000 damaged with 279 people killed and over 12,000 Ausgebombten - 'bombed out'.

And so ended the month of July and the 'moon' period. Twenty-nine of the 102 bombers shot down during the month were credited to Hauptmann Helmut Lent's crack II./NJG2 at Leeuwarden, ten to I./NJG1 and seven to III./NJG1. On 5/6 August 22-year old Oberleutnant Kurt Loos of 1./NJG1 claimed his ninth Abschüsse when he shot down Halifax R5761 EM-T on 207 Squadron at Altforst twenty kilometres west of Nijmegen. Flight Lieutenant Gerald Antony Ings and crew were killed. On the night of the Frankfurt raid on 24/25 August Loos claimed his tenth and final victory, shooting down Lancaster I R5537 OF-B on 97 Squadron at Westmalle (Antwerpen), 17 kilometres northwest of Herentals in Belgium. Canadian Flying Officer Gilbert Campbell Hooey DFC and crew were killed. (Kurt Loos was killed on 24 March 1945 in aerial combat with American fighters over Göttingen). Major Kurt Holler of Stab NJG4 claimed two Stirlings near Thynes SSE of Namur and by Givet-Pondrome and a Wellington four kilometres southeast of Rheine for his 3rd-5th victories. The first of his two Stirling victories was W7562 on 218 Squadron piloted by Flight Sergeant Robert Yates which was lost with all eight crew. Among the other claimants were Unteroffizier Eduard Kleinert of 5./NJG1 who claimed a Lancaster (W4105 KM-X on 44 Squadron) northeast of Felmy in Belgium for his first Abschuss. South African Pilot Officer Denis Franklin Nicholson and his crew were killed. Kleinert scored his second and final Abschuss on 8/9 September when he shot down Wellington III X3745 on 150 Squadron at Sart-St-Laurent southwest of Namur. Sergeant John Glaves and his crew were killed. (Kleinert was killed in a crash at Wimmertingen on 25 January 1943 after his Bf 110F-4 (4708) suffered an engine failure). Twenty-eight year old Feldwebel Heinrich 'Heinz' Macke of 7./NJG4 claimed a Stirling at Hélenne-en-Temps for his first and only victory. (Macke was killed on 24/25 February 1944 when his Bf 110 crashed at Juvincourt on return from a night sortie). Oberleutnant Kurt Martinek of 9./NJG4 claimed a Stirling (W7616 MG-G on 7 Squadron) near Thy-le-Château for his first Abschuss. The skipper, Flight Sergeant William Nelson Shumsky RCAF and four of his crew were killed; two were taken prisoner. Feldwebel Fritz Schellwat of 5./NJG1 claimed a Wellington twenty kilometres east of Leuven for his fourth Abschuss.

One hundred 'Himmelbett' kills were claimed by Nachtjagd in August 1942 with II./NJG1 at Sint-Truiden/ Sint-Trond, Belgium, recording the most with 25 confirmed victories. Much of the success in the 'Himmelbett' night-fighting was achieved by excellent ground-to-air and air-to-ground communication using a combination of R/T codes and plain language. On 12 August Leutnant Hans Autenrieth, adjutant of II./NJG1 and his regular bordfunker Unteroffizier Adam worked in concert with the Ground Controller of Raum 6B during a successful interception on Wellington BJ767 on 75 Squadron RNZAF, which crashed in flames 700 metres southwest of Vaals, the Netherlands at 0133; Autenrieth and Adam's fourth confirmed kill. The Skipper, Flight

Lieutenant Laurence St. George Dobbin RNZAF and one of the crew were killed; three others were taken into captivity. Leutnant Autenrieth's first night Abschuss was Halifax I L9531 on 76 Squadron on 12/13 August 1941. By 26 November 1943 he had claimed fourteen 'Himmelbett' Abschüsse.

On the night of 24/25 August 1942 'Douggie' Baker captained Stirling W7572 OJ-R for the raid on Frankfurt when 226 aircraft - 104 Wellingtons, 61 Lancasters, 53 Stirlings and eight Halifaxes were dispatched. The main point of interest about that summer night was its beauty. The sky was absolutely clear as Baker's Stirling, having completed the operation, crossed the border between Germany and Belgium on its course back to Lakenheath. High above, the full moon hung like a great silver ball spreading its soft radiance over the sleeping world and the crew hated every square inch of it. This was because a full moon in a clear sky was just about the most dangerous thing that any bomber crew could encounter. It made their aircraft a silhouetted dead-duck target for any fighters approaching from below. Moreover, it was almost impossible for the bomber's gunners to pick out the small shape of a fighter rising from the green-grey expanse of the ground below until it had got perilously close. Baker therefore was taking his crew home with 'the wicks turned fully up' and with everybody tense and the gunners alert for trouble. When trouble came none of them actually saw Oberfeldwebel Reinhard Kollak's Bf 110C fighter of 7./NJG4 which launched it, aided by the prevailing fine weather with good visibility, an almost full moon and no cloud. With a nice, clear target in his sights Kollak must have enjoyed himself as he came up for his first attack from below and dead behind. Even so, he seems to have been a little over-confident, for his first burst did no more than put Sergeant T. J. Jenkins' rear gun-turret out of action, produce a small fire and an equally warm stream of remarks from the flight engineer, Sergeant F. J. Berthelsen RNZAF, who jumped violently and winced over a wounded arm. Baker, at the controls, immediately flung 'R-Robert' into evasive action, but within his heart of hearts he knew that he hadn't a hope. Once again Kollak came into the attack and once again the Stirling shuddered as a burst of cannon shells smashed into the starboard wing-tanks, setting up a blaze of fuel which whipped back in the slipstream. It was Kollak's tenth victory. Baker now had to make a decision. It was obvious they would have to abandon aircraft, but it would be best for all concerned if they could get as near to home as possible before doing so. Meanwhile, the fire was gaining, so he had to decide how long the wing structure would stand up to the terrific heat before it finally collapsed and put the aircraft into a spin from which it might be impossible for anybody to get clear. However, the only thing to be thankful for was that Kollak had sheered off, obviously satisfied now that his 'kill' was burning. Baker put 'George', his automatic pilot, into action and as his crew came tumbling forward to go out through the escape hatch, he unbuckled his safety harness and heaved himself out of his seat. Then he went aft along the fuselage to make a final check and satisfy himself that all of them had got away.[71]

Sixteen aircraft - six Lancasters, five Wellingtons, four Stirlings and one Halifax were lost on the raid on Frankfurt; all of whom were shot down by night-fighters. Crews of NJG1 and NJG4, patrolling in the 'Himmelbett' boxes in Belgium and Northern France were credited with fourteen victories.

Wellingtons came in for high losses on 27/28 August when a mixed force of 306 aircraft were despatched to bomb the German army headquarters and garrison at Kassel. 142 Squadron lost five of the fifteen Wellingtons despatched from Waltham. At least one of these (Z1396 flown by Flight Sergeant Alan Harker) was shot down by a night-fighter on its way back from Kassel by Oberleutnant Rudolf Altendorf of 2./NJG3 at Erika, northwest of Meppen on the Dutch-German border. There were no survivors.

Thirteen year old Hendrik Kleinsman and his family in the Dutch village of Bentelo in the province of Overijssel regularly watched the nightly procession of RAF Bomber Command aircraft roar overhead towards the German border. Near Bentelo at just after midnight the Kleinsman family watched thunderstruck as they saw a bomber crash in a fireball after it was attacked by a night-fighter. It is believed that the German pilot was Oberleutnant Viktor Bauer of III./NJG1. Hendrik recalls. 'It was a giant ball of fire. The huge bomber hit the ground with such force that its cockpit, engines and four bombs were driven up to fifteen metres into the sodden earth.' One of the crew bailed out before the crash at Delden, five kilometres west of Hengelo. Thirty-one bombers, 21 of them Wellingtons, were lost and a Lancaster crashed at Waddington on return. Nachtjagd was responsible for the majority of these losses, being credited with 23 confirmed kills during the course of the night.

On the night of 28/29 August Leutnant 'Luc' Meister, now of 8./NJG4, claimed another triple Abschüsse to take his score to six. His first kill was a Wellington NNE of Worms at 0012, followed by a second Wimpy at Bad Kreuznach three minutes later and finally, a Stirling at Arlenbach at 0043. Meister transferred to I./NJG4 in October to take up the post of Adjutant to Hauptman Wilhelm Herget, the newly appointed Gruppenkommandeur. By the end of 1942 Meister's score stood at eight. Oberleutnant Kurt Martinek of 9./NJG4 claimed his second Abschuss, shooting down Wellington III DF665 VR-Q on 419 'Moose' Squadron RCAF at Petit-Doische (Namur). Sergeant Peter Karil Zaparynuk RCAF and three crew were killed; a fifth crewmember evaded. Martinek claimed a triple victory on the night of 2/3 September to take his final score to five Abschüsse. He shot down Halifax II DT487 on 405 'Vancouver' Squadron RCAF at Lesve, twelve kilometres southwest of Namur. Flight Lieutenant Lawrence David Hillier RCAF and crew were killed. Next he shot down Wellington III X3711 on 419 'Moose' Squadron RCAF at Warnant near Dinard, killing Canadian Wing Commander Archibald Philip Walsh DFC AFC and crew. Lastly, he destroyed Lancaster I R5763 on 49 Squadron at Abee twelve kilometres southeast of Huy. Flight Sergeant Ronald George Lewis and his two gunners were killed; three were taken prisoner and one evaded. Martinek was killed in a flying accident on 3/4 November at Neudorf near Stendal.

During September 1942 86 heavies were shot down by the Nachtjagd with 22 victories credited to II./NJG2, fourteen to I./NJG1, nine to II./NJG1 and eight to III./NJG1. Twelve bombers failed to return from the 4/5 September raid on Bremen by 251 Wellingtons, Lancasters, Halifaxes and Stirlings. IV./NJG1 claimed three Halifaxes and five Wellingtons. Oberleutnant Ludwig Becker, Hauptmann Helmut Lent, Oberleutnant zur Lippe-Weissenfeld and Unteroffizier Karl Heinz Vinke of II./NJG2 at Leeuwarden claimed seven bombers including four Wellingtons destroyed. Heinz Vinke was born on 22 May 1920 in Barby, in the Province of Saxony, a Free State of Prussia. He joined the Luftwaffe in 1938, where he was trained as a Zerstörer (destroyer) pilot. Serving in NJG2 over Northern Europe, his first air victory was on 27 February 1942; an Armstrong Whitworth Whitley 22 kilometres (14 miles) north-east of Leeuwarden. His next claim was filed on the night of 3/4 June when he shot down a Short Stirling at 0216 over the Zuiderzee. His fourth victory was a Vickers Wellington shot down on 28 June at 0054 east of Enkhuizen. Vinke shot down his fifth victim, a Wellington, on the night of 27/28 August at 0232. He transferred to NJG1 in early 1943.

Night fighter pilots rarely witnessed death at close quarters in the sky over Germany and were only usually made aware of the destruction meted out by RAF bombing raids when they went off on home leave. On 3 September a night fighter pilot in 'Wim' Johnen's Staffel in NJG1 at Venlo returned from Karlsruhe and gave his own account of the raid by 200 bombers which started an estimated 200 fires in the city at the same time and caused much residential and some industrial damage. He was no doubt chagrined by the fact that only eight of the bombers were shot down.

'At 0210 hours the sirens wailed. Very few of the townspeople stumbled out of their warm beds and sought the protection of the air raid shelters. What was the good? In comparison with the big industrial cities Karlsruhe was unimportant and the British would at the most be making a feint or a nuisance attack. But suddenly, even the most cool-headed citizen felt anxious as a deafening roar of engines made the air above this old Residenz town quiver. 'The Tommies are over the city,' ran the alarm cry through the streets and houses. The first bombs exploded in the centre of the city causing a panic among the population. Everyone rushed in despair to the air raid shelters and the wardens had the greatest difficulty in keeping order. Our flak gunners fired like maniacs into the night sky without inflicting any serious damage on the bombers. Street after street went up in flames. Tears stood in the eyes of the citizens on the following morning when they saw the tragic damage. The first doubts as to our war leadership began to rise and many people lost their faith in the Hitler regime. Wild rumours ran round the city. 'I think,' my friend who had returned from leave said at the end of his shattering report, 'that the enemy has achieved his first objective: to destroy the morale of the home front.'[72]

On 6/7 September, when 207 bombers raided Duisburg for the loss of eight aircraft Leutnant Wilhelm Beier of III./NJG2 scored a triple victory over southern Holland. Flight Lieutenant Leonard Charles Pipkin DFM was the navigator and one of eight men on a 103 Squadron Halifax at Elsham Wolds flown by Squadron Leader Clive Saxelby that took part in a raid on Duisburg. The Halifax was shot down over the outskirts of the town while the raid was still in progress, killing Sergeant Charles Edward Benstead, 28, one of the air gunners. 'Bix Sax' and five others survived to be taken into captivity but Pipkin,[73] who bailed out as bombs were bursting around him, had other ideas. With the help of Comète he got across the frontier with Belgium and finally, on 24 October, Pipkin reached Gibraltar. He was the 62nd 'parcel' sent along the escape line to successfully make a home-run'.[74] On the same day that Pipkin reached Gibraltar, another navigator on 103 Squadron at Elsham Wolds, 21-year old Warrant Officer Herbert John 'Dizzy' Spiller DFM and Squadron Leader Sidney Horace Fox DFM's crew on Halifax W1188 'D-Donald' were shot down by Oberleutnant Gerhard 'Gerd' Friedrich of Stab II/NJG4 at 2150 near Bar-le-Duc in the Meuse for his fourth victory. Friedrich, who was born on 16 September 1917 at Berlin-Johannisthal, initially served as a transport pilot and he participated in the invasion of Crete. He underwent conversion training as a night fighter pilot and was posted to III./NJG1 at the beginning of 1942. 'Sid' Fox, Henry Wood, 'Fitz' Fitzsimmons, 'Phil' Heath and 'Jock' Mercer were killed. 'Peewee' Maddocks was captured the day after bailing out and spent the rest of the war in prisoner of war camps. 'Woolly' Woollerton also was captured shortly after bailing out. At Elsham Wolds there had never been any lectures on escape and evasion or how to make contact with the Resistance or how to get out of an area, how to hide, what to avoid but Spiller reached Paris and was fed into the 'Comète' Line. Spiller travelled south with Sergeant R. P. 'Smitty' Smith, a Canadian Wellington pilot on 115 Squadron at East Wretham who had been shot down on the raid on Turin on 9/10 December. They were joined later by Sergeant W. McLean an air gunner and the only survivor on a 7 Squadron Stirling which crashed in Belgium on 6/7 December 1942 on Manheim. All three men were smuggled out of Spain aboard a British orange boat that took them to Gibraltar and they docked at Gourock in Scotland on 26 January 1943.

On 8/9 September 249 aircraft were dispatched to Frankfurt-on-Main. Five Wellingtons and two Halifaxes were lost, four of them to night-fighters. On 10/11 September training aircraft of 91, 92 and 93 Groups swelled the numbers in a 479-bomber raid on Düsseldorf. Thirty-three aircraft failed to return and the OTUs were hard hit. At least sixteen aircraft were shot down by night-fighters of NJG1 and NJG2.

These included eight OTU Wellingtons. 16 OTU at Upper Heyford lost five of thirteen Wellingtons dispatched. I./NJG2, the former intruder Gruppe flying the Ju 88C-6, had returned from North Africa earlier that month to resume 'Himmelbett' night-fighting duties in the west from Gilze-Rijen and Oberleutnant Schultz destroyed Wellington Ic R1616 on 22 OTU at Stratford at 2345 hours near Biervliet. Sergeant John Daniel Williams RCAF and his crew died in the aircraft. Again, many training aircraft from various OTUs and Conversion Units were included in the force of 446 bombers which attacked Bremen on 13/14 September. Twenty-one aircraft - fifteen Wellingtons, two Lancasters, a Halifax, a Whitley and a Stirling - failed to return. Six of the Nachtjagd's thirteen confirmed kills were claimed by six crews of II./NJG2, all but one of these achieved over the Netherlands and the Dutch coast. On the night of 14/15 September 202 aircraft attacked Wilhelmshaven for the loss of two Wellingtons. This was the last raid by Hampdens and all four aircraft of 408 Squadron RCAF returned safely.

On an airfield in Holland on the evening of 6 October General Kammhuber organised a 'kill-feast' to celebrate Nachtjagd's 1,000th Abschuss of the war (on 10 September) and to which every Nachtjagd pilot with one or more victories was invited. As the only pilot in his Staffel without any kills, 21-year old Leutnant Johann 'Hans' Krause of 1./NJG3 had to remain behind at Münster-Rheine. Leutnant Hans Krause had joined I./NJG3 as Technical Officer in November 1941. During the ensuing few months, the twenty-one-year-old pilot flew the Bf 110 on 'Himmelbett' sorties, but in June 1942 he completed a conversion course at Gilze-Rijen on the Dornier Do 217, with which his Staffel at Rheine airfield was subsequently equipped. In his capacity as Technical Officer, he and his Funker Unteroffizier Otto Zinn spent July 1942 at Berlin-Diepensee airfield test-flying and calibrating the 'Lichtenstein'- equipped Do 217 night fighter version.

Now, at dusk on the evening of 6 October Hans Krause and his crew could only sit it out as steady rain pelted the windows of the almost elegantly furnished common room where the Met briefing at 1700 hours confirmed bad weather everywhere and icing at certain levels. The only exception seemed to be between 22.00 and midnight when a break in the clouds between two fronts was forecast. With a sardonic grin the meteorologist bade them a quiet night, which is what Krause and his crew expected. With their chief mechanic as a fourth they settled down to game after game of cards. From time to time they nibbled from the dishes of carrots on the tables. Quite apart from the fact that he liked them, they were supposed to be good for night vision. It began to get boring. Now and again someone looked out at the weather but it was still driving rain and quite cold. Suddenly, towards 1900, the telephone rang.

'Herr Leutnant for you' the operator said. It was their Staffelkapitän, Hauptmann Walter Milius who was calling from the victory celebration in Holland in order to check that all was as it should be.[75]

Endnotes Chapter 5

59 Bomber.
60 Luftwaffe code for distance to target.
61 *RAF Bomber Command Losses; Operational Training Units 1940-1947* by W. R. Chorley Midland Publishing 2002).
62 Peter Buttigieg, a Maltese national, Gaulton and Flight Sergeant John Farquhar, WOp/AG bailed out and Manchester VN-Z L7432 crashed in flames at Beekbergen near Apeldoorn at 0233 hours. German radio traffic on the morning of 4 June referred to a Bf 110 crashing at Deelen. Buttigieg tried to get back to England but was betrayed and fell into the clutches of the Gestapo. He survived the war.
63 A Halifax on 405 Squadron was abandoned on the return to Pocklington due to both outer engines losing power and crashed near Binbrook. All the crew bailed out successfully. *RAF Bomber Command Losses of the Second World War, Vol.3 1942* by W. R. Chorley (Midland 1994)
64 Adapted from *Duel Under the Stars* by Wilhelm Johnen.
65 H_2S was a navigational radar developed by Dr. Lovell at the TRE (Telecommunications Research Establishment) at Malvern, Worcestershire, which produced a 'map' on a CRT display on a 360° arc of the ground below the equipped aircraft. The TRE and its airfield at Defford nearby was the centre of all wartime RAF radar research. In 1941 it had begun work on jammers to counter the 'Freya' early-warning ground radar, which was first discovered at Auderville on Cap de La Hague in February. After the famous raid on Bruneval on 27/28 February 1942 in which British paratroopers and an RAF radar technician dismantled a complete Würzburg radar installation and removed it to England along with one of its operators, TRE developed jammers for the Würzburg also.
66 Gerhard Herzog was KIA on 20 October 1943 at Kettenburg, near Visselhövede in ramming an RAF aircraft. He had nine Abschüsse.
67 5 Group destroyed an assembly shop at the Focke-Wulf factory when a 4,000lb 'Cookie' scored a direct hit. Six other buildings were seriously damaged.
68 Rowlin was killed during an attack on a 78 Squadron Halifax. His bordfunker-gunner, Feldwebel Heinz Werner bailed out safely. Rowlin had four Abschüsse.
69 Sidwell, Sergeant W. F. Carter, flight engineer and Sergeant A. L. Crockford a new pilot on the Squadron who joined the crew late on to fly as 'second dickey' for experience, survived and were soon captured. Flight Lieutenant Whiteman, Sergeant Albert Bates, a replacement for Sergeant Paddy Leathern, the mid-upper gunner who had reported sick late on, Sergeant Frank McIntyre, WOp/AG and Sergeant John Boyle, navigator were KIA.
70 *Blenheim Strike* by Theo Boiten (ARP 1995).
71 Sergeants J. B. Downing, 2nd pilot and G. Robinson and Flight Sergeant V. S. Wood the MUG, who broke his ankle on landing, were taken prisoner. Berthelsen, Williams and Jenkins evaded capture. Baker, Berthelsen, Jenkins and Williams eventually reached Gibraltar where they were put aboard the submarine, HMS *Seawolf* on 12 October for the sea-crossing to England. The submarine docked at Poole on the 19th. Adapted from *Chute Open - Inside the Aircraft, Jump for it!* by Gerald Bowman. Reinhard Kollak was awarded the German Cross in Gold on 12 April 1943 and the Knight's Cross he received on 29 August 1943 when his tally had increased to 29 victories. Kollak was the most successful pilot of III./NJG4.
72 *Duel Under The Stars* by Wilhelm Johnen.
73 Saxelby was sent to Stalag Luft III and was one of the officers who took part in *'The Great Escape'*. Whilst waiting in the tunnel close to the foot of the final ladder, shots were heard, upon hearing them the waiting party turned and went back along the tunnel expecting to be shot at any moment. He was not one of the fifty who were murdered by the German's following the escape, Clive Saxelby died on 22 March 1999.
74 Pipkin was flown to Mount Batten the following day. He was awarded the DFC on 10 November. Squadron Leader Pipkin died in a shooting accident on 30 August 1944. See *RAF Evaders: The Comprehensive Story of Thousands of Escapers and their Escape Lines, Western Europe, 1940-1945* by Oliver Clutton-Brock (Grub Street 2009).
75 See *Night Airwar* by Theo Boiten (The Crowood Press 1999)

Chapter Six

The Common Danger

By the light of their torches they could still see traces of blood and hair on the propeller. Strips of uniform were hanging on the antennae of the Li.

In the early morning at Venlo on 16 September 1942 Oberleutnant Reinhold Knacke, Staffelkapitän and his funker, Unteroffizier Günther Heu and crews of 1./NJG1 at readiness waited for the order to take off. Twenty-two years old, Knacke had been born in Strelitz, Mecklenberg on New Year's Day 1919. On 28/29 June he had been the first Nachtjagd pilot to claim a Mosquito kill, when he shot down DD677 on 23 Squadron at Haps, South Holland. Continual combat eventually had begun to fray the night-fighter pilot's nerves. Knacke led an incredibly ascetic life. He neither drank nor smoked and in the rest periods kept fit by playing games with his fellow pilots. Operations lasted from four to six hours. The exhausted crews fell into their bunks and slept, until the Americans arrived in their B-17s and B-24s. Alert - the night fighters also had to take part in the daylight defence. Until dusk they had a few hours rest and relaxation and then the performance began again. Hardly had they slept a few hours to rest their nerves after the excitement of the night than the air raid sirens roused them. Tired and sleepy, the crews slumped in their armchairs. Chess boards lay abandoned and only soft music could be heard on the wireless during the night hours. The hands of the clock wandered towards 2300 hours. A few of the crews had returned to their bunks in full flying kit, ready at any moment to run to take off. A dim red light gave a cosy tone to the room and accustomed the night-fighter pilots' eyes to the darkness. In this way the human eye needed but five minutes to adapt itself to complete darkness whereas normally the eye needs twenty minutes. Some of the men had fallen asleep with their heads on the table and one pilot was still holding the book he had been reading when he dozed off. All tension had disappeared from their features. At 2345 hours the telephone rang. A messenger picked up the receiver.

'Bomber formations are reported assembling in Map Square 23. Strength, 400 aircraft. Altitude 4600 metres. All aircraft proceed to Beacon 'Li' at Scheveningen on the Channel coast.'

In a flash the messenger's words had been grasped by the crews.[76] A 369 aircraft strong Bomber Command force was en route to bomb the Krupp works in Essen but many of the Wellington and Whitley aircraft and crews were from the training groups.

Reinhold Knacke and Günther Heu were the first crew in 1./NJG1 to take off, at 2346 hours. The engines roared and a dense rain of sparks swirled in the slipstream behind them, making the Schwarzemänner (ground crews) or 'black men', so-called because of the colour of their tunics, shield their eyes.

Knacke turned on to course 200 without making a circuit round the airfield. He switched off his navigating lights and his Bf 110 was swallowed up in the darkness. A clear starry sky lay over Holland. Ideal weather for night fighters. Knacke climbed rapidly and Heu called his Staffel on the intercom. 'Buzzard 5' from 'Buzzard 1'. Come in.'

'Buzzard 1' from 'Buzzard 5'. Victor, message received. Am on course 200.'

One after the other the fighters reported. Knacke called up Hauptmann Streib who ordered complete radio silence to prevent the RAF bombers having any suspicions of their presence. The ground station reported three other night-fighter gruppen in the air. At 2410 hours Knacke received orders to attack. 'All aircraft fly on course 180. The leading Viermots are flying over the coast west of Rotterdam on course 90. Probable objective the Ruhr. Enemy altitude 16,500 feet.'

Knacke turned on his radar, set his course at 180 and came down to 16,500 feet. Within five minutes he would meet the leading bombers. Heu picked up blips on the cathode ray tubes and wild with excitement immediately gave his pilot a change of course to 900. As he turned the 110 from the altitude and distance tubes he knew that a bomber was directly ahead. His nerves were at breaking point. The enemy pilot took no avoiding action and Knacke gave full throttle. Suddenly Heu reported a new contact crossing slowly, from north to south. For a moment Knacke was uncertain which opponent to pursue; then he decided upon the nearest Viermot. Cautiously he throttled back and Heu gave him the final Li readings. Then they saw their quarry; it was a Short Stirling. Knacke opened fire and hit the engines and petrol tanks. A second burst tore open the fuselage and probably killed the crew. The Stirling exploded with a bright scarlet flash in the harbour of Rotterdam.

Within half an hour Knacke had shot down four bombers. Then Unteroffizier Heu reported another contact. Knacke attacked at full speed, caught up his opponent and fired immediately into the full petrol tanks. Knacke's five victories took his score to 38. Eighteen of the 21 Wellingtons that were missing were on the OTUs. Whitley V P4931 on 10 OTU at Abingdon flown by Warrant Officer L. A. D'eath RNZAF were last heard on w/t transmitting 'SOS' before they bailed out and were taken prisoner. The kill was claimed by Oberleutnant Gerhard Stammler of 8./NJG2 at 0212 for his first victory. Stammler was killed in action flying a Ju 88C-6 on 5 December. The rest that were missing were nine Lancasters, five Stirlings and three Halifaxes. Nineteen Abschüsse were claimed by the Nachtjäger. Oberleutnant Albert Schultz of II./NJG2 probably shot down Wellington IC DV941 on 26 OTU at 0010 hours two kilometres west of Egmont. Sergeant Lawrence William Streeter RNZAF and his crew were killed. Hauptmann Horst Patuschka of 8./NJG2 claimed a Wellington and a Stirling for his 15-16 Abschüsse. Patuschka and his crew were killed in combat in Tunisia on 7 March 1943 when his Ju 88C-6 crashed following engine failure. Hauptmann Werner Streib claimed a Wellington for his 38th Abschuss. About fifteen minutes before reaching Essen a flame damper on the port inner engine of Halifax II W7770 on 405 Squadron RCAF burned through and later, on the bombing run, the oxygen supply failed. Despite these problems Flight Sergeant William Frederick Murray RCAF the 20-year old skipper carried on and bombed the target and course for Topcliffe was made at 16,000 feet. Then Oberleutnant Paul-Hubert Rauth of 5/NJG4 attacked at 0037 hours and set the bomber's port wing on fire. Murray gave the order for the crew to abandon but the escape hatch was jammed.

Pilot Officer Lorne Edward Kropf, the 27-year old wireless operator recalled: 'I heard bullets thump into the aircraft but I had no idea how badly we were hit until I heard [22-year old Sergeant Ron Barnicoat] the flight engineer ask 'Do we really have to jump?' And the skipper said, 'Yes, the whole port wing's on fire. But the escape hatch was jammed. We couldn't get out. We had gone into a spin and I guessed the force of our falling wouldn't let it open. We had fallen about 10,000 feet when the gas tanks exploded. I could hear air whistling past and with all my might I pushed with my hands and feet and got loose. Maybe I escaped through a hole in the fuselage; I don't know. Below me I saw another parachute open and I learned afterward that it was the flight engineer. And not far away I saw our aircraft, a mass of flames, falling, falling. The next thing I knew I had landed. I had only a scratch on my forehead. I could see the flames from the plane lighting up the sky and I knew it was too late to help anyone. The flight engineer was between me and the plane. I didn't want to try to join him for fear that I'd be seen. Perhaps it's just as well I didn't try because he was taken prisoner. The rest of the crew were dead.'[77]

W7770 went down in flames east of the airfield at Maubeuge (Nord) in France. It was Rauth's fifth Abschuss. Kropf was reported missing for six weeks but he evaded capture and was taken across the Spanish border on 19 October. He left Gibraltar for England on the 31st was awarded the DFC and he later completed a tour on 432 Squadron.

On the night of 19/20th September 118 aircraft were dispatched to Saarbrücken and 68 Lancasters and 21 Stirlings went to Munich. At Saarbrücken the Path Finders had to mark two targets but ground haze caused difficulties and the bombing was scattered to the west of the target. Five aircraft failed to return. At Munich about 40 per cent of crews dropped bombs within three miles of the city centre and the remainder dropped them in the western, Eastern and southern suburbs. Four bombers went missing in action.

On 23/24 September 83 Lancasters bombed Wismar for the loss of four aircraft and 28 Halifaxes attacked Flensburg, losing five aircraft. Meanwhile, 24 Stirlings went to Vegasack and another eight Stirlings and 25 Wellingtons laid mines between Biscay and Denmark. Two Wellingtons failed to return from the 'Gardening' sorties. Stirling I R9187 on 218 Squadron flown by Squadron Leader Cuthbert Raymond DFC, a New Zealander serving in the RAF, which crashed forty kilometres north of Nordeney on the Vegasack raid was shot down by a Bf 110 flown by Unteroffizier Karl-Georg Pfeiffer of 6./NJG2. It was his first victory since joining the Gruppe at Leeuwarden in late April. Pfeiffer had been banished to Wittmundhafen as a punishment for failing to lower the undercarriage of a new FW 190 when landing on his first or second training flight. Four FW 190s had been allocated to NJG2 for day operations against Coastal Command aircraft that were becoming a nuisance to shipping and coastal targets in the Dutch coast area. Major Helmut Lent, the Gruppenkommandeur was so angry that he told Pfeiffer he did not want to see him again. Pfeiffer recalls:

'The Leeuwarden Gruppe was commanded by Major Lent and was considered to be the best night fighter unit, especially as their aircraft, mostly Me 110, were already equipped with Lichtenstein radar. Staffelkapitän Oberleutnant Ludwig Becker's bordfunker, Feldwebel Josef Staub, was a master in the operation of this highly sensitive device and unceasingly instructed the other radio operators in the finer points of its use. My bordfunker was Gefreiter Willi Knappe from Berlin. After I shot down the Stirling I was recalled to Leeuwarden and a great victory party of the Abschuss tyro with my comrades! It had been a textbook Abschuss, ideal for a beginner: bright moonlight, white cumulus clouds and the island of Heligoland clearly visible below. The crew must have been asleep not to have seen me, especially as my guns had been badly sighted and my first burst missed. But then the Short Stirling burst into flames and several white parachutes emerged. The first Abschuss was always a psychological hurdle for a crew. Now we had taken it.'

A Bomber Command directive was now issued whereby crews stood down from night flying would be employed on daylight intruder sorties to keep the German sirens wailing and disrupt industry by driving the workers into air raid shelters. The RAF crews' only protection was cloud cover and it was essential that there was sufficient cloud to hide in. A Wellington was no match for a German fighter and all aircraft captains had strict orders to return to base if the cloud cover broke up. On Monday 28 September three Wellingtons on 115 Squadron were detailed for a 'cloud cover' daylight bombing attack on Lingen on the Dortmund-Ems Canal. As the aircraft made their way east the cover thinned out rapidly to a scattering of isolated clouds. Sergeant Crimmin in BJ695 decided to turn back. Squadron Leader Sandes in BK272 made a similar decision. Squadron Leader Robert James Sealer Parsons in Z1663 decided to press home the attack but eight kilometres south west of Urk over the Zuider Zee, he was attacked by Unteroffizier Kurt Knespel of 10./NJG1 in a FW 190. As his cannon shells tore through the fuselage Flight Sergeant John Austin Parker, the Canadian WOp/AG was hit and died instantly. Flames from the ruptured wing gasoline tanks, fanned by the slipstream, spread rapidly. Parsons shouted over the intercom that he would try to ditch the bomber. The front-gunner, Sergeant Gilmour, entered the cockpit from his turret and saw Flight Sergeant William Leonard Clough, the 31-year-old observer with the cabin fire extinguisher in his hand vainly trying to subdue the raging furnace. The aircraft hit the sea and only the Canadian gunners, Sergeants Gilmour and Stansell emerged.

With the coming of autumn weather and a decrease in Bomber Command activity during October 1942 38 bombers were destroyed by Nachtjagd. Twenty of these victories were credited to I./NJG1 at Venlo and nine to II./NJG2. Four aircraft were claimed by II./NJG1 including two by Leutnant Hans Autenrieth. The first of these was on 5/6 October when 257 Main Force bombers were detailed to attack Aachen. That morning crews awoke to the sound of distant thunder. At RAF Elsham Wolds, Flight Sergeant Gordon Mellor, navigator on Warrant Officer Kenneth Fraser Edwards' Halifax crew on 103 Squadron 'rather thought ops were going to be scrubbed'.

'The Met Officer said we would get a few bumps and the air was quite unstable - rather rough weather for quite a way, though we would possibly have it clear over the target. Everyone gave him a rousing cheer. It was part of the build-up. We had the final meal, got kitted out and waited to be taken to the aircraft. In the Halifax normal checks were carried out and off we went. We were routed southerly to go across the English Channel just east of London, then a turning point in France and a straight run to Aachen. Suddenly, over Belgium, the weather cleared. It was a brilliant night and we saw a magical display of the Northern Lights. We saw activity either side of us - one or two planes went down. There were fighters about.'

One of them was a Bf 110F-4 flown by Leutnant Hans Autenrieth and his bordfunker Unteroffizier Rudolf 'Rudi' Adam who had five Abschüsse to their name. Autenrieth's and Adam's first victory was on 12/13 August 1941 but further kills were hard to obtain. In 1942 Autenrieth had an indecisive exchange of fire with a Wellington over Maastricht on 1 June and five other Feindberührungen, or 'contacts with the enemy' during the next eleven months but none resulted in confirmed victories. Only on the night of 31 July/1 August 1942 did he finally add to his score when he shot down two Wellingtons, which crashed near Titz and Berg, Germany. Two more Wellingtons fell to his guns on the nights of 11/12 and 12/13 August before he and Adam were shot down by return fire from Wellington III Z1594 on 101 Squadron on 24/25 August. The Wellington crashed at Ougrée, a southern suburb of Liège, 30 kilometres south of where Autenrieth and Adam came down after they had bailed out of their brand new Bf 110G-4 safely.[78] Their unit lost the crew of Leutnant 'Rudi' Röhr and his Funker, Unteroffizier Erwin Cobi who were killed when their Bf 110F-4 crashed 800 metres north-east of the railway station at Kottenfirst.[79]

Warrant Officer Kenneth Edwards' Halifax crew on 103 Squadron headed to the target at Aachen and got their bombs away. 'We had gone in at about 12,000 feet' continues Gordon Mellor 'and by the time we came out we were down to 10,000 feet. We were trying to avoid the light flak beneath us and the heavier flak that went up to about 15,000 feet - flying between the two. Four or five minutes out of the target area the rear gunner called out: 'There is a fighter behind us. It's a Me 110. He's sitting there shadowing us.' We had a conference over the intercom. A general discussion followed and it was the pilot's decision finally, we would try and scare him off. The rear gunner and mid-upper gunner let fly. The night fighter was 500 yards or so back, rather a long way for a .303 machine gun. The night fighter pulled in a bit closer and started pumping cannon shell at us, causing damage and hitting the rear gunner. There were two further attacks. He was no beginner, he knew what he was doing and the inboard engines on both sides were set on fire. You could see the tracer whizzing past. None of us in the front of the aircraft was hit. Neither was the mid-upper gunner, so it was the poor rear gunner who took the packet.

'We were beginning to lose power, the wings and the inboard engines were in flames and we were going down at quite a rate. We were twisting and turning - whatever the pilot could do to try and avoid the attacks. The Me 110 disappeared from our view. We were getting quite low. Our speed had been terrific on the down gradient. The pilot said everybody out - abandon aircraft. The escape hatch was right underneath my seat, which I whisked away. We passed the main pilot's parachute up and then it was time to be out - he said 'Come on, hurry up.' I got my parachute on, swung my legs out over the opening and was dropping my bottom on to the edge when I felt a shove on my shoulders. I was gone. The slipstream caught me. I slid underneath, more or less horizontal and the tail of the plane passed over. That was the last I saw of it. I was supposed to count to ten but having seen the tail plane go I thought the parachute was not going to foul, so I pulled the ripcord.

'I came to a sudden sort of rest. The parachute was tight - quite a jolt in the nether regions. I didn't see what happened to the aircraft. I tried to swing round but by that time I was in the tops of trees. I was very lucky. I stayed there swinging in the trees for a couple of minutes, to gather my senses. I thought, 'Right I've got to get down. I've got to hide the parachute.' I pressed the knob on the box where the parachute harnesses joined. They fell apart, the harness virtually fell off and I fell. It was all of twelve inches at the most. I was fine. The only problem was the parachute in the tree.'[80]

Oberleutnant Eckart-Wilhelm 'Hugo' von Bonin of 6./NJG1 claimed a Wellington northeast of Maastricht for his ninth Abschüsse. Twenty-nine year old Oberfeldwebel Gerhard Jecke of 2./NJG4 flying a Bf 110D (3193) claimed a Halifax at Marquillies for his first and only victory. He was killed by return fire from the Halifax (W1047 on 35 Squadron) before the bomber crashed killing Squadron Leader Jack Gordon Kerry DFC and the rest of the crew.

At Münster-Rheine on the evening of 6 October Leutnant Johann 'Hans' Krause of 1./NJG3, Oberfeldwebel Otto Zinn his bordfunker and Obergefreiter Friedrich Specht his bordshütze were not expecting to take off on their twenty-fifth sortie in search of their first victory because of the bad weather but the steady rain had ceased and now there were only intermittent showers. At 2000 a telephone call reported that strong enemy radio tuning was taking place in England. It could only be that RAF Viermots (237 aircraft including 101 Wellingtons were taking off for a raid on Osnabrück) were on their way. Krause and his crew went to thirty minute readiness and then full of anticipation if not a little trepidation, they were ordered to their aircraft. At first a red flare seemed to indicate that it was all in vain but then a green flare signalled them to take off and their disappointment was forgotten. 'First night nerves' turned to determination as the adrenaline rush began. Krause and his crew were soon scanning the sky for their first contact. The sky now was mainly cloudless and spangled with stars. It boded well. Even when contact was lost with their JLO and the radio beacon too had gone off the air Krause and his crew were successful. They returned at 2355 with claims for two Wellingtons destroyed; one at Ülzen and the other six kilometres north of Hagenau. Their first victory was Wellington III BK313 on 115 Squadron that was on its way home to Mildenhall with 22-year-old Flying Officer Leonard Ian Smith RCAF and crew, all of whom were killed. Krause's second victory was Wellington III DF639 on 75 Squadron RNZAF which crashed at Hardenberg killing Sergeant George William Rhodes and his crew.[81] As well as the two Wimpys, Nachtjäger destroyed two Halifaxes and two Lancasters. Oberleutnant Herman Greiner of 11./NJG1 claimed a Halifax 25 kilometres west of Harlingen for his second Abschüsse. Oberfeldwebel Karl Wieland of 1./NJG1 flying a Bf 110F-4 claimed a Halifax for his third victory. (Wieland and his funker Unteroffizier Günther Heu, were killed on 13 January 1943 when their 110 suffered engine damage during aerial combat and crashed and exploded at the Rielse dijk near Gilze-Rijen airfield). One of the Halifaxes was W1189 on 103 Squadron which crashed off Ameland with Sergeant James Porter and his crew, five of whom were lost without trace. The second Halifax that was lost was W7763 on 405 'Vancouver' Squadron RCAF which crashed at Prattenburg, Holland. Pilot Officer T. W. Stewart RCAF and crew were taken into captivity.

A few nights later, on 15/16 October Leutnant Hans Autenrieth, his gunner Unteroffizier Georg 'Schorsch' Helbig and his bordfunker Unteroffizier Rudolf 'Rudi' Adam claimed their eighth Abschuss when east of Roerdorf they shot down another Halifax, which failed to return from a raid on Cologne. Victories that month by IV./NJG1, Hauptmann Helmut Lent's Gruppe at Leeuwarden (previously II./NJG2, which had been renumbered on 1 October) included four victories by Leutnant Wilhelm Beier of Stab IV./NJG1 on 15/16 October, which took his total to 36 kills. Whilst flying from Melsbroek near Brussels and patrolling in 'Himmelbett' box 'Hamster' on 23/24 October, Oberfeldwebel Robert Lüddecke of 3./NJG2 claimed a Stirling destroyed. A few days later I./NJG2 moved further south and in February 1943 began flying 'Himmelbett' sorties in Italy.

In November 1942 just ten victories (three by IV./NJG1 at Leeuwarden) were claimed by Nachtjagd. On the night of 16/17 November Oberleutnant Reinhold Knacke and his bordfunker, Unteroffizier Heu of 1./NJG1 destroyed a Short Stirling when 65 aircraft were engaged in 'Gardening' operations from Lorient to the Friesian Islands. Short Stirling I W7566 OJ-C on 149 Squadron flown by Sergeant Thomas Anderson West and two Wellingtons failed to return from the night's operations. The Stirling had taken off from Lakenheath at 1721 hours. Leu picked it up on his Li set at 16,350 feet at 4,000 yards distant. Knacke peered out in the direction of the plot but could not see him for the vision of the human eye in the dark is not more than 100 to 200 yards. His nerves were at breaking point but West was still flying calmly towards the defence zone and would only be at action stations once the first searchlight was turned on. West was taking no avoiding action. Knacke gave full throttle and rapidly closed the distance. Suddenly Heu reported a new contact at 2,000 yards distance as another Viermot crossed their field slowly, from north to south. For a moment Knacke was undecided which opponent to pursue and then he decided on the nearest Viermot. The enemy machine had begun to weave and was now travelling on the Li set alternately from port to starboard and back. Heu gave Knacke the final Li readings but three pairs of eyes scanned the sky in vain for his shadow. Knacke finally shot the Stirling down into the sea off Vielle-Ste-Gironde. In his excitement Knacke fired immediately into the full petrol tanks. Flight Sergeant Cecil Robert McMullin RCAF the rear gunner lost his head, abandoned his machine guns and bailed out, landing right in the propeller of Knacke's

110. There was a dull thud, which made the Messerschmitt shudder. The engine began to vibrate so badly that Knacke had to shut it down. He landed his clumsy 110 at Venlo on one engine. Mechanics rushed over and lit up the machine. By the light of their torches they could still see traces of blood and hair on the propeller. Strips of uniform were hanging on the antennae of the Li. The fate of the Canadian gunner upset everyone. McMullin was buried at Hourtin Communal Cemetery while the body of Sergeant Herbert Carter, the only other body that was recovered from the sea was laid to rest at Vielle-Ste-Gironde Communal Cemetery. All the other members of the crew have no known grave and are commemorated on the Runnymede Memorial.

During December 37 Viermots were claimed by Nachtjagd. On the night of the 17/18th Hauptmann Helmut Lent of Stab IV./NJG1 shot down two Lancasters for his 55th and 56th kills. Lancaster I ED355 KM-D on 44 (Rhodesian) Squadron at Waddington piloted by Flight Sergeant John Glen Dening RAAF was claimed at 2022 hours at Woudsend. Then he shot down Lancaster I ED333 OF-B on 97 Squadron flown by Flying Officer Samuel Lorne McBurney RCAF into the Ijsselmeer off Urk sixteen minutes later. All the men on both aircraft were killed. In all, IV/NJG1 claimed five of the thirteen bombers destroyed by the Nachtjagd from the 104 heavies that were dispatched. Eighteen aircraft in fact failed to return. All Major Helmut Lent's first 65 night victories (May 1941-July 1943) were claimed whilst flying from Leeuwarden. By the end of 1942 Lent had 48 Night-Abschüsse and was the top German night-fighter 'Experten'.

Oberleutnant Hans-Joachim Jabs downed an unidentified Stirling and a Lancaster; probably W4382 on 50 Squadron, off the Dutch coast. Born in Lübeck on 14 November 1917, Jabs had joined the Luftwaffe in 1937. Originally trained as a Bf 109 pilot, he was posted to Zerstörergeschwader 76 (ZG76), flying the Bf 110, in March 1940. A member of II./ZG76, Jabs operated over France in mid 1940, claiming four French aircraft and RAF fighters. He then flew in the Battle of Britain. Despite the vulnerability of the Bf 110 against the more nimble RAF aircraft and the heavy losses incurred, Jabs claimed eight Spitfires and four Hurricanes destroyed. By the end of the year Jabs was one of the top scoring Zerstörer (destroyer) pilots, with sixteen victories. Decorated with the Ritterkreuz in October 1940 he thereupon successfully led his 6./ZG76 during the campaign in Crete. In 1941 most of the Bf 110 units were withdrawn from daylight fighting and Jabs was transferred to night fighting. His Staffel became 9./NJG3 near Hamburg in November and on completion of night fighter training Jabs became an operational night fighter pilot helping to protect the port and Kriegsmarine installations. He went on to claim his first night-Abschuss (an unidentified Stirling) on 25/26 June 1942 and was appointed Staffelkapitän of the elite 11./NJG1 at Leeuwarden that November. By the end of 1942 he had shot down four RAF Viermots. Most of his victories during the war would be shared with his bordfunker, Erich Weissflog.

II./NJG1 claimed three bombers during December 1942. Hauptmann Werner Streib destroyed Wellington III BJ589 on 156 Squadron near Heijen on 20/21 December. Flight Sergeant G. A. Proudfoot and one of his crew were taken prisoner. The three others were killed. On the 21st III./NJG1 at Twente claimed three victories and I./NJG1 one. At 2353 hours that same night a Lancaster on 106 Squadron was claimed shot down at Poelkappelle, Belgium by a night fighter pilot who would become Germany's greatest 'Experte' of the night air war.

Endnotes Chapter 6

76 Adapted from *Duel Under the Stars* by Wilhelm Johnen.
77 Murray's 20 year old brother Flight Lieutenant John Richard Murray RCAF, navigator on 524 Squadron, Coastal Command was killed flying a Wellington on 4 October 1944.
78 The pilot, Flight Sergeant Clarence Scott Elkington RCAF and his rear gunner, Sergeant John Henry Garland were killed and were buried in Heverlee. The three other crew members survived and were taken into captivity. *Night Airwar: Personal recollections of the conflict over Europe, 1939-45* by Theo Boiten (The Crowood Press, 1999).
79 *Night Airwar: Personal recollections of the conflict over Europe, 1939-45* by Theo Boiten (The Crowood Press, 1999).
80 Quoted in *The Bomber Command Memorial* (Fighting High Ltd 2012). Ten bombers were lost on the raid on Aachen. A further six crashed in England. Unable to retrieve his parachute and with dogs barking, Gordon Mellor moved off. Three of the eight-man crew including Warrant Officer Kenneth Edwards, were killed aboard the Halifax, which crashed at Rosmeer in Belgium. Four men were taken prisoner. Gordon Mellor evaded capture. In Paris he was met by Dédée de Jong who ran the Comète Escape Line and was taken to Bayonne and Ste-Jean-de-Luz where he and three other evaders, led by 'Florentino' Goïcoechea and Albert Johnson, made it across the Pyrénées on 19 October. The airmen were taken into San Sebastián and transported to the British Embassy in Madrid before being put on an aircraft at Gibraltar and flown home on 31 October. Gordon Mellor arrived at his home in Wembley on 1 November; his birthday! *RAF Evaders* by Oliver Clutton-Brock (Grub Street 2009).
81 By the beginning of April 1944 Hans Krause had doubled his score to four, all except one of his victories achieved while flying the Do 217-N2, a SN-2 radar-equipped night-fighter variant of the Dornier bomber armed with four cannon and four machine guns in the nose. Krause became Staffelkapitän of 6./NJG101 at Parnsdorf in Austria in the summer of 1943. He would finish the war with 23 RAF Viermots of Bomber Command and 205 Group in Italy and five Soviet Abschüsse. Otto Zinn survived 150 night fighter sorties with Krause.

Chapter Seven

'Das Nachtgespenst'

The British propaganda radio station Soldatensender Calais (Soldiers' Radio Calais) congratulated Schnaufer on account of his 23rd birthday on 16 February 1945. The radio station explicitly addressed the soldiers of NJG4 stationed in Gütersloh followed by the song 'Das Nachtgespenst' [The Bogeyman] praising him for the honorary title given to him by the British bomber crews 'The spook of St. Trond'.

On the afternoon of 13 July 1950 a distinguished German businessman on a wine buying visit to France headed south on the Route Nationale 10 Biarritz to Bordeaux in his Mercedes-Benz 170V cabriolet. Strikingly handsome, dark-haired and olive-complexioned his arresting appearance was the outer manifestation of a strong personality and powerful will. He was endowed with the qualities of intelligence and character that produce successful men in all walks of life. Just south of Bordeaux,[82] at about 18:30, he was involved in a collision with a Renault 22 truck driven by Jean Antoine Gasc, who was carrying a six metric tons load of empty gas cylinders. The Mercedes overturned, hurtling the driver into a ditch. The collision ruptured the fuel tank of the Mercedes and ignited the petrol. Witnesses to the accident quickly put out the flames. Alice Ducourneau gave first aid to the German, who was bleeding from a wound from the back of his head. The police appeared at the scene of the accident at about 1930 followed by an ambulance shortly after. Suffering a fractured skull, the wine producer was then immediately taken to the Saint-André Hôpital in Bordeaux. He never regained consciousness and succumbed to his injuries at the hospital two days later on 15 July. The investigation into the accident concluded that though the impact of the two vehicles was severe, it seemed unlikely that the collision itself was the cause of his injuries. It was speculated that at least one of the truck's cargo of thirty empty gas cylinders, which were thrown off by the collision, had struck the Mercedes driver on the head. Subsequently the truck driver was charged with manslaughter and breach of traffic regulations before a court at Jauge, Cestas. The hearing began on 29 July and concluded with his conviction on 16 November. It was ruled that as a consequence of not observing the law, he involuntarily caused the death of the Mercedes driver. Jean Antoine Gasc was probably unaware that Heinz-Wolfgang Schnaufer was the top-scoring night fighter pilot of World War II, credited with 121 aerial victories claimed in just 164 combat sorties. Schnaufer claimed 32 of his all-time record total whilst serving with the Leeuwarden Gruppe.

Following his release from the hospital and as a prisoner of war in 1945 Schnaufer had reluctantly taken over the Schnaufer-Schlossbergkellerei ('Schnaufer's Castle Mountain Winery') in the Lederstrasse, Calw, which his father Alfred, a mechanical engineer (Diplom-Ingenieur) and merchant and his grandfather, Hermann Schnaufer had founded in 1919, shortly after World War I. Heinz-Wolfgang Schnaufer was born on 16 February 1922 in Calw in the Free People's State of Württemberg of the German Reich during the Weimar Republic era; the first of four children. At the age of six, Heinz-Wolfgang went to the local Volksschule (primary school) at Calw. After completing his fourth grade, he received two years of schooling at the Oberschule, also in Calw. Following the death of his grandfather in 1928 the winery was run by his father alone. When he unexpectedly died in 1940 Heinz-Wolfgang's mother Martha, née Frey ran the business until Heinz-Wolfgang, his brother Manfred, his sister Waltraut and his brother Eckart took over the winery after World War II. The company then expanded the business and in addition to the winery offered wine imports, sparkling wines and a distillery for wine and liqueur. The distribution channel worked with agents and sales offices throughout Germany. He had never planned to run the family winery as his ambition had always been to pursue an officer's career in the Luftwaffe. However, in the immediate aftermath of World War II the business had virtually ceased to exist and Schnaufer was tasked with rebuilding it from scratch. He had to re-establish business links to suppliers and customers and to consolidate them. Then he had to expand and grow the business by making new contacts. Lastly, he had to create an infrastructure which supported the growth of the business.

As the wine business began to prosper, Schnaufer also gave thought to alternative employment possibilities in peacetime aviation. On 23 September 1946 with his wartime friend Hermann Greiner, he travelled from Weil am Rhein to Berne in Switzerland to meet South American diplomats; the two hoped to find employment as pilots in South America. In World War Two Georg-Hermann Greiner flew a total of 204 sorties and shot down 51 enemy aircraft, of which 47 were at night and four were during the day. On 1 November 1944 Hauptmann Greiner was appointed Gruppenkommandeur of IV./NJG1, replacing Hauptmann Heinz-Wolfgang Schnaufer who had been promoted to Kommodore of NJG4. Greiner's flying career had ended in March 1945 when injuries he sustained in a crash were sufficient for him to see out the remainder of the war in hospital. Following a period of imprisonment by the Allies at a camp in Schleswig-Holstein, Greiner was discharged and returned to his mother's home near Stuttgart. Greiner wished to continue in a career involving flying and agreed to join Heinz-Wolfgang Schnaufer on the expedition to try and earn a living flying in South America.

To get to Berne they crossed the Swiss-German border illegally. The meeting was a failure. As they returned to Germany, they were caught by Swiss border guards attempting to make a second illegal border crossing. The Swiss handed them over to the French occupation authorities and they were imprisoned in Lörrach, where they remained until Schnaufer managed to make contact with a French general, who was a customer of the Schnaufer winery and had them released. This misadventure kept him away from his business for about six months. Greiner then moved to Bonn where he studied law. He married in 1949 and became a sales representative for a textile factory. In August 1957 he joined the Bundesluftwaffe with the rank of Hauptmann. He served seventeen years rising to the rank of Oberstleutnant. He retired in 1972 and in 1980 moved to Wangen.

At an early age Heinz-Wolfgang had expressed his wish to join an organisation of military character and joined the Deutsches Jungvolk (German Youth) in 1933. After completing his sixth grade at school he took and passed the entry examination at the Backnang National Political Institutes of Education (Nationalpolitische Erziehungsanstalt - Napola), a secondary boarding school founded under the recently established Nazi state. The goal of the Napola schools was to raise a new generation for the political, military and administrative leadership of the Third Reich. Schnaufer learned to fly gliders and he was considered a very good student, finishing top of his class every year. Aged seventeen he graduated with his Abitur (diploma) in November 1939 with distinction. At the Napola school he also received the Reich Youth Sports Badge (Reichsjugendsportabzeichen), the base-certificate of the German Life Saving Association (Deutsche Lebens-Rettungs-Gesellschaft), the bronze Hitler Youth-Performance Badge (HJ- Leistungsabzeichen) and completed his B-licence to fly glider aircraft. In 1939 Schnaufer was one of two students posted to the Napola in Potsdam. The Flying Platoon (Fliegerzug) stationed in Potsdam centralised all the destined flyers from all the Napolas. Here he learned to fly glider aircraft, at first short hops on the DFS SG 38 Schulgleiter and later on the two-seater Göppingen Gö 4 which was towed by a Klemm Kl 25. During his stay at Potsdam, the film producer Karl Ritter was making the Ufa film Cadets in Potsdam. The Napola had detached two companies to work on the film, among them Schnaufer. It remains unclear exactly what role he played in this film. Following his graduation from school, Schnaufer passed his entry exams for officer cadets of the Luftwaffe. He joined the Luftwaffe on 15 November 1939 and underwent his basic military training at the Fliegerausbildungsregiment 42 (42nd Flight Training Regiment) at Salzwedel.

Schnaufer was appointed as Fahnenjunker (cadet) on 1 April 1940. He then received his flight training at the Flugzeugführerschule A/B 3 (FFS A/B 3 - flight school for the pilot licence) at Guben, now the Cottbus-Drewitz Airport. He completed his A/B flight training on 20 August 1940. He was trained to fly the Focke-Wulf Fw 44, FW 56 and FW 58 and the Heinkel He 72, HD 41 and He 51, the Bücker Bü 131, the Klemm Kl 35, the Arado Ar 66 and Ar 96, the Gotha Go 145 and the Junkers W 34 and A 35.He was then posted for ten weeks to the Zerstörerschule (destroyer school) at Wunstorf near Hannover. At Wunstorf, Schnaufer and the bordfunker, Friedrich Rumpelhardt were assigned as an aircrew team on 3 July. Schnaufer's previous radio operator had proved unable to cope with aerobatics and Schnaufer thoroughly tested Rumpelhardt's ability to cope with aerobatics before they teamed up. Here the two decided to volunteer to fly night fighters. Following their training at Wunstorf, they were sent to Nachtjagdschule 1 at Schleissheim near Munich to learn the rudiments of night-fighting on the Arado 96 and the FW 58. Training at night focused on night takeoffs and landings, cooperation with searchlights, radio-beacon direction finding and cross country flights. In April 1941 Leutnant Schnaufer was posted to Schnaufer then attended the advanced Flugzeugführerschule C 3 (advanced flight school) at Alt Lönnewitz near Torgau and the Blindflugschule 2 (BFS 2) at Neuburg an der Donau from August 1940 to May 1941. This qualified him to fly multi-engine aircraft.

Unlike many of the 'Experten', Schnaufer joined the Nachtjagdflieger straight from training in November 1941 to fly 'Himmelbett' sorties with II/NJG1 at Stade near Hamburg. Schnaufer was assigned to 5./NJG1. The Bf 110s of II./NJG1 at the time were not equipped with airborne radar such as the Lichtenstein radar. Night fighter intercept tactics had matured since their early beginnings in July 1940 and II. Gruppe had already been credited with 397 victories. Sorties against enemy bombers at the time were usually flown by means of ground-controlled interception, although the Luftwaffe was already experimenting with airborne radar. This air defence system, consisting of a series of radar stations with overlapping coverage, layered three deep, was conceived by Generalleutnant Josef Kammhuber and was organised in the so-called Kammhuber Line. Conceptually, the system was based on a combination of ground-based radar stations, search lights and a Jägerleitoffizier (fighter pilot control officer). The Jägerleitoffizier had to vector the airborne night fighter by means of radio communication to a point of visual interception of the illuminated bomber. These interception tactics were referred to as the 'Himmelbett' procedure.

On 15 January 1942 II./NJG1 moved to Sint-Truiden/Sint-Trond in Belgium. Schnaufer entered front-line service at a time when the RAF was reassessing the air offensive against Germany. The effectiveness of Bomber Command to accurately hit German targets had been questioned by the War Cabinet Secretary David Bensusan-Butt who published the Butt Report in August 1941. The report in parts concluded that the RAF crews failed to navigate to, identify and bomb their targets. Although the report was not widely accepted by senior RAF commanders, Prime Minister Winston Churchill instructed Commander-in-Chief Richard Peirse that during the winter months only limited operations were to be conducted. Flight operations were also hindered by bad weather in the first months of 1942, so II./NJG1 saw only very limited action during that period.

On 8 February 1942 II./NJG1 was transferred to Koksijde without having scored any victories while at Sint-Truiden. The objective of this assignment was to give the German battleships *Scharnhorst* and *Gneisenau* and the heavy cruiser *Prinz Eugen* fighter protection in the breakout from Brest to Germany. The Channel Dash operation (11-13 February) by the Kriegsmarine was codenamed Operation 'Cerberus' by the Germans. In support of this, the Luftwaffe under the leadership of General der Jagdflieger (General of the Fighter Force) Adolf Galland, formulated an air superiority plan called Operation 'Donnerkeil' for the protection of the three German capital ships. II./NJG1 was briefed of these plans on the early morning on 12 February. The plan called for protection of the German ships at all costs. The crews were told that if they ran out of ammunition they must ram the enemy aircraft. To the relief of the night fighters they were assigned to the first-line reserves. The operation was successful and the night fighters were kept in their reserve role. On the evening of 12 February II./NJG1 was relocated to Schiphol. On the afternoon of 13 February Schnaufer flew a reconnaissance mission over the Zuiderzee and the North Sea and then relocated to Westerland on the island of Sylt. They then relocated again to Aalborg-West in Denmark from where they made a low-level flight in close formation over the Skaggerak, landing at Stavanger-Sola. Over the following days they operated from the airfield at Forus, making a short term landing at Bergen-Herdla. In total, Schnaufer made two operational flights without contact with the enemy. Following this assignment they relocated to 5 Staffel's new base in Germany at Bonn-Hangelar via Oslo-Gardermoen, Aalborg and Lüneburg.

Prior to Operation 'Millennium' on the night of 30/31 May when the RAF targeted and bombed Cologne, Schnaufer had been appointed Technischer Offizier (TO - Technical Officer) on 10 April and was located at Sint-Truiden again. As a Technical Officer, Schnaufer was responsible for the supervision of all technical aspects such as routine maintenance, servicing and modifications of the Gruppe. In this role he was no longer a member of 5 Staffel but was then a member of Stab II./NJG1. Schnaufer did not participate in the defence of Cologne. The 'Himmelbett' procedure had limitations in the number of aircraft which could be controlled. Therefore only the most experienced crews were deployed and Rumpelhardt and Schnaufer had yet to achieve their first aerial victory. However, the 20-year-old Leutnant had all the attributes of a top-class night fighter pilot and these soon became evident on the night of 1/2 June one day after the 1,000 bomber raid on Cologne when he recorded his first kill on his and Rumpelhardt's thirteenth combat sortie.

In the early hours on 2 June at a height of 3500 metres they fired a burst of cannon fire into Halifax II W1064 on 76 Squadron, which was flying home on three engines. At 0155 the aircraft crashed near Grez-Doiceau, fifteen kilometres (9.3 miles) south of Louvain, Belgium, with the loss of Sergeant Thomas Ronald Augustus West and Sergeant John Robert Thompson his air gunner. Four crew bailed out safely, two of which evaded. This victory was achieved by ground-controlled interception through the Kammhuber Line. Once near to the target, Rumpelhardt had visually found the bomber and directed Schnaufer into attack position from below and astern. The Halifax caught on fire after two firing passes. During this mission the 'Himmelbett' flight officer vectored them to a second bomber, a Bristol Blenheim. The attack had to be aborted after Hauptmann Walter Ehle shot down the bomber from a more favourable attack position. Shortly before 0300, they were then flying in the vicinity of Ghent, they spotted another target. Schnaufer made two unsuccessful attacks. During their third attack, which closed the distance to twenty metres (66 feet), they were hit by the defensive gunfire. Schnaufer was hit in his left calf, the port engine was burning, the rudder control cables were severed and an electrical short circuit caused the landing lights to be permanently on. Rumpelhardt and Schnaufer considered bailing out but decided to make an attempt for their home airfield after they managed to put out the flames and restart the engine. While Rumpelhardt made radio contact with Sint-Truiden, Schnaufer landed the aircraft without rudder control and on ailerons and engine-power alone. This was the only time that their aircraft sustained damage in combat or any member of the crew was wounded. Both Rumpelhardt and Schnaufer were awarded the Eisernes Kreuz 2. Klasse (Iron Cross 2nd Class) for their first aerial victory. Schnaufer had hoped that he could remain on active duty and that the bullet lodged in his calf would isolate itself but he had to be admitted to a hospital in Brussels from 8-25 June for surgery. Rumpelhardt was given home leave until 26 June while Schnaufer was in the hospital.

Schnaufer had to wait two months to achieve another victory, claiming the destruction of two Wellingtons and a Whitley within the space of 62 minutes in the early hours of 1 August. At 0247 he destroyed Wellington Ic DV439/H on 25 OTU at Finningley one kilometre (0.62 miles) southwest of Loon op Zand, Netherlands. Pilot Officer P. P. L. Welch and his crew were taken into captivity. At 0317 he shot down Wellington Ic DV552/N on 27 OTU at Lichfield, the bomber crashing at Huldenberg. Flying Officer Mervyn George McNeil RNZAF and his crew were killed. And at 0345 he destroyed Whitley V BD347 on 24 OTU at Honeybourne at Gilly, Charleroi, Belgium. The aircraft crashed at Fleurus. The skipper, Pilot Officer G. Silva RAAF and two of his crew evaded capture. Sergeant William Thomas Whiting, the rear gunner, was killed.

Rumpelhardt and Schnaufer flew their first combat sortie with the Lichtenstein radar on the night 5/6 August. Though they managed to make contact with an enemy aircraft they failed to shoot it down. On the night of the 24/25 August, Schnaufer scored his fifth aerial victory, when he claimed Wellington III BJ651 JN-M on 159 Squadron near Loonbeek, Belgium. This was the first time Rumpelhardt had guided him into contact using the Lichtenstein airborne radar. His next claim was made on the night of 28/29 August. This was probably Halifax II W7089 on 78 Squadron piloted by Sergeant John Alexander Brock Marshall RAAF on a secondary attack against Saarbrücken. The primary attack force was targeting Nuremberg that night. On the night of the 21/22 December 1942 Leutnant Schnaufer claimed a Lancaster and the bomber crashed at Poelkapelle. It was Schnaufer's first victory against this type and his seventh overall. Schnaufer may also have been responsible for the destruction of another Lancaster that night. Rumpelhardt and Schnaufer had attacked a Lancaster and observed it catching fire followed by the aircraft plunging earthwards. Hauptmann Wilhelm Herget of I./NJG4 who had also attacked a Viermot in the same vicinity was given credit for the destruction of the Lancaster.

By the end of 1942 Schnaufer's total stood at seven, with three victories recorded on one night, 1 August, which earned him the Iron Cross 1st Class (Eisernes Kreuz 1.

Klasse). From 29 November to 16 December Rumpelhardt was confined to the hospital bed with high fever. Rumpelhardt then attended various officer training courses from February to October 1943. Schnaufer was promoted to Oberleutnant in July 1943, when his total was seventeen. Total Nachtjagd claims for 1942 were 687 aircraft destroyed. Between 14 May to 3 October 1943, Schnaufer claimed 21 further aerial victories in Rumpelhardt's absence; twelve with Leutnant Dr. Leo Baro, five with Oberfeldwebel Erich Handke, two with Oberleutnant Freymann and two with Unteroffizier Heinz Bärwolf as his radio operators. Unteroffizier Heinz Wenning had also flown with Schnaufer on three flights while Rumpelhardt was ill.

II./NJG1 saw little action in the first few months of 1943 and Schnaufer did not claim his next aerial victory until 14 May 1943. II./NJG1 'Himmelbett' control areas were located to catch the bombers heading for the Ruhr Area. Bomber Command had only had ten major attacks in that region from January to April 1943. Consequently, II./NJG1 claimed no victories in January, two in February, one in March and three in April. Schnaufer's number of aerial victories increased again during the Battle of the Ruhr. Schnaufer, with Baro as his radio operator, shot down a 214 Squadron Short Stirling (R9242) at 0214 on 14 May on the raid on Bochum. Four members of the crew, including the Sergeant pilot Raymond Mordue Gibney, lost their lives. His next victory was at 0307, his 9th overall; a 98 Squadron Halifax JB873 returning from Bochum. The captain, Pilot Officer Gerald Herbert Dane MiD and 2nd pilot Sergeant James Howard Body were killed in the crash.

On the moonless night of 29/30 May Bomber Command flew one of the most significant raids of the Battle of the Ruhr. The area bombing of the Barmen northeastern end of the long and narrow town of Wuppertal involved 719 aircraft in five successive waves. The town, which had been formed in 1929 by the union of the adjacent towns of Elberfeld and Barmen in the Upper Wupper Valley, was within easy 'Oboe' range and eleven of the Mosquito markers were dispatched. Sixty-two of the aircraft turned back early with technical problems. In all 150 individual aircraft were plotted on the Würzburg radars flying through the 'Himmelbett' boxes in eastern Belgium. Altogether, II/NJG1 put up a total of thirteen Bf 110s and three Dornier 217s. Leutnant Heinz-Wolfgang Schnaufer and his bordfunker Leutnant Baro took off from St. Trond at 2351 on 29 May for a night operation in the area of 'Lurch' ('Amphibian') just to the north of Liège. At 0222 Schnaufer shot down Stirling III BK688 HA-A on 218 Squadron piloted by Flight Sergeant William Arthur Mathias Davis RAAF flying at 14,800 feet above the small village of Schaffen-Diest in Belgium. Able crashed and exploded adjacent to the Luftwaffe airfield at Schauffen. The crew of seven was blown to pieces. The remains of the crew were placed in three coffins. At the time the Germans thought there was a crew of five on Able and not the seven who crewed the aircraft.[83]

'At about 0035 hours' recalled Schnaufer 'I was directed on to an in-flying enemy aircraft at an altitude of 3500 metres. It was located on the Fu SG 202 [Lichtenstein airborne radar] and after further instructions [from Dr. Baro] I made out a four-engined bomber [Stirling III HA-H BF565 flown by Pilot Officer Sidney Gordon Allan RAAF] at 0045 hours, about 200 metres away above and to the right. I attacked the violently evading bomber from behind and below at a range of 80 metres and my rounds started a bright fire in the left wing. The blazing enemy aircraft turned and dived away steeply, hitting the ground and exploding violently at 0048 hours; the position of the crash was 1.5 kilometres to the south of Belven, five kilometres north-west of Eupen.' The Australian pilot and his crew were all killed. At 0143 hours Schnaufer then shot down Halifax II DT804 on 35 Squadron flown by Flying Officer Ronald Hoos, who was killed along with five of his crew; one man being taken prisoner. Schnaufer and Baro returned at 0231 hours on the 30 May with claims for three Viermots. For the loss of thee aircraft and two aircrew killed six II./NJG1 crews scored eleven victories. Thirty-three bombers failed to return, 22 of these shot down by night-fighters.

In June 1943 Schnaufer claimed a further five aerial victories. Schnaufer and Baro were scrambled on 11/12 June in Bomber Command's attack on Düsseldorf and on 16/17 June in defence of Cologne. However, on both occasions they failed to make contact with the enemy. Their next success came on 21/22 June. Schnaufer described his encounter at 0133 with Stirling III BK712 on 218 Squadron flown by Pilot Officer William Golder Shillinglaw RAAF (all KIA), which resulted in his 13th victory:

'I recognized 500 metres above and to the right, a Short Stirling, and succeeded in getting in an attack on the violently evading enemy aircraft. It caught fire in the fuselage and the wings and continued on, burning. Then it went into a vertical dive and crashed three kilometres to the northeast of Aerschot.' All seven crew were found dead in the wreckage.

With Baro on the radio and radar, they managed another victory over a Wellington on 25 June at 0258. On 29 June they shot down three bombers in another attack on Cologne, a Lancaster and two Halifax bombers at 0125, 0145 and 0155 respectively. This brought the number of aerial victories Schnaufer was credited with to seventeen. On 28/29 June Schnaufer and his funker, Leutnant Dr. Baroof destroyed Lancaster III LM323 OF-U on 97 Squadron at 0125. Flight Lieutenant Frederick Phillip Seward and his crew were all killed. Twenty minutes later, Schnaufer destroyed the first of two Halifaxes. At 0145 he shot down HR812 on 35 Squadron flown by Pilot Officer Graham Thomas Beveridge, who was killed. North of Liège at 0218 he shot down DK137 on 76 Squadron. Twenty-two year old Sergeant Geoffrey Charles Parritt and crew were killed.

Schnaufer was promoted to Oberleutnant on 1 July 1943. He had been eligible for this promotion since April, why he was overlooked at the time remains unknown. Schnaufer claimed his last two aerial victories with Baro operating the radio on the night of 3/4 July, Bomber Command had again targeted Cologne. Their victims were a 196 Squadron Wellington shot down at 0048 and a 149 Squadron Stirling at 0233, taking his total to nineteen victories. His next bordfunker was Oberleutnant Freymann, the signals operator of II Gruppe. Under 'Himmelbett' control they shot down a 49 Squadron Lancaster on another raid on Cologne on 9 July at 0233. Schnaufer was awarded the Ehrenpokal der Luftwaffe (Honour Goblet of the Luftwaffe) on 26 July. His next success came when he and Freymann shot down a Lancaster on 10/11 August 1943 at 0032. The target that night was Nuremberg and it was the first aerial victory of the entire German night fighter force achieved by Y-Control. This was also the last victory with Freymann and Schnaufer's last as a member of II.Gruppe.

On 13 August Schnaufer was transferred to IV./NJG1 at Leeuwarden, where he was appointed Staffelkapitän of 12./NJG1. He took over command from Oberleutnant Eberhard Gardiewski, who had been taken prisoner of war. At the time IV./NJG1 was under the leadership of Gruppenkommandeur Hauptmann Hans-Joachim Jabs, whose first impression of Schnaufer was not entirely favourable. Shortly after Schnaufer's arrival, on one of his first sorties from Leeuwarden, Schnaufer had taken right of way during taxiing. This forced Jabs into second place in order of take-off, an act of insubordination and perceived as arrogant by Jabs. Whilst Hans-Joachim Jabs, who was both a day and night fighter ace and Helmut Lent, were somewhat reluctant convertees from day to night fighting, the same cannot be said of Heinz-Wolfgang Schnaufer who took to night fighting like the proverbial duck to water.

Schnaufer, who had received the Deutsches Kreuz in Gold on 16 August, flew his first operational sortie with 12./NJG1 on the night of 17/18 August. Although uncertain, it is assumed that Handke was Schnaufer's radio and radar operator on this sortie. Bomber Command had targeted Peenemünde and the V-weapons test centre that night. Schnaufer, who had been tasked with leading one of the first 'Zahme Sau' sorties under Y-Control, had to abort the mission early due to engine trouble. By now his score had reached 23. At about this time he teamed up with bordfunker Leutnant Friedrich 'Fritz' Rumpelhardt with whom he developed an almost telepathic understanding and shared 100 victories. Prior to this Schnaufer had had two regular operators, Dr. Baro, with whom he shared twelve victories and Erich Handke, eight. Schnaufer's secret was superb aircraft handling combined with marksmanship and Rumpelhardt on the radar.

Schnaufer flew only the Bf 110. Around mid-September 1943 the two-man Bf 110 crew was increased by a third member, sometimes referred to as bordmechaniker or bordschütze. The reason for this was that the decline of the 'Himmelbett' procedure, the introduction of the broadcast procedure 'Zahme Sau' and the growing threat of RAF intruder night fighter operations, had necessitated the need for another pair of watchful eyes to the rear. Unteroffizier (later Oberfeldwebel) Wilhelm Gänsler, who had formidable night vision, had previously flown with Ludwig Becker and had shared in seventeen Abschüsse with him and had been awarded the Ritterkreuz. After joining Schnaufer's crew Gänsler shared in 98 victories. With Handtke and Gänsler as his crew, Schnaufer claimed his 26th aerial victory on 23 September, a 218 Squadron Stirling III (EJ104 HA-G on 218 Squadron) five kilometres (3.1 miles) south of Kirchheimbolanden during a 'Wilde Sau' ('Wild Boar') intercept sortie. The Stirling exploded and crashed in the Bauwaldthal with no survivors on the crew skippered by Flying Office Adrian Colebrook Brace.

In the second half of 1943 Schnaufer and his crew began experimenting with upward-firing cannon, otherwise known as 'Schräge Musik' ('Oblique or 'slanting' Music'). This device was in fact a modernized version of a combat technique used in 1916 by Gerhard Fieseler, then a front-line pilot in Macedonia. His friends used to call it 'fieseling.' With this tactic Fieseler was able to stand up to overwhelming odds and scored 21 Night-Abschüsse without receiving a single machine-gun hit. In spring 1918 when Fieseler was a pilot on the Balkans Front, he took a round-turreted Lewis machine-gun from a Breguet he had shot down and mounted it in the upper wing indentation of his Fokker D VII, in front of the pilot's seat, so that he could fire it upward at an angle. Each time he attacked he would fly underneath the enemy aircraft and his slanted MG rarely missed its target.

Oberfeldwebel Paul Mahle, an armourer attached to II./NJG5 at Parchim, worked closely with Rudolf Schönert and built his own working prototype of 'Schräge Musik', which was soon fitted to all of the Gruppe's aircraft. 'Schräge Musik' comprised two Oerlikon MG/FF 20mm cannon installation mounted behind the rear cockpit bulkhead of the Bf 110 and Ju 88 night fighters and was arranged to fire forwards and upwards at an angle of between 70° and 80°. Fighter pilots whose aircraft were fitted with 'Schräge Musik' did not need to attack 'von unten hinten' ('underneath, behind'). They could attack from the blind spot underneath the bomber with cannon raked at 15°, fired by the pilot using a Revi C/12D reflector sight. On a light night the German pilot would open fire at about 200 yards, but if it was dark engagements closing to thirty yards were not uncommon. An attack by a 'Schräge Musik'-equipped night fighter typically came as a complete surprise to the bomber crew, who only realised a night-fighter was close by when they came under fire. Also known as 'Jazz Musik' the name was ironic because Doktor Goebbels' Propaganda Ministry would not permit this American deep-south styled music to be broadcast in Germany. 'Rudi' Schönert was the driving force behind the introduction of 'Schräge Musik' in night fighter aircraft, the first prototype of which he introduced into his own Dornier Do 17 in 1942. Initially, 'Schräge Musik' was rejected by Helmut Lent and Werner Streib but Schönert claimed the first aerial victory with upward-firing guns in May 1943. It is not exactly known when Schnaufer's Bf 110 was equipped with 'Schräge Musik'. Rumpelhardt stated that the weapons system was installed prior to his return from officer training. It is also not exactly known how many of his victories had been claimed using the upwards firing canons. According to Fritz Engau, who had known Schnaufer since Flugzeugführerschule C 3, twenty to thirty of Schnaufer's aerial victories had been claimed using upwards firing guns.

Rumpelhardt had returned from his officer training courses in early October 1943 and rejoined Schnaufer's crew. Gänsler, Rumpelhardt and Schnaufer claimed aerial victories 29 and 30 on 9 October when there was a heavy raid on Hannover. Near Schwaförden, nine kilometres (5.6 miles) north of Sulingen at 0113 Schnaufer shot down Halifax II HR945 NP-Y on 158 Squadron. All of Sergeant D. C. E. Cater's crew bailed out and were taken into captivity. Schnaufer's second Viermot went down at 0142 near Holtensen, southwest of Hannover.

If the bomber went into a corkscrew after being attacked from below it was possible for a good night-fighter pilot - if the manoeuvre was not too violent - to formate underneath the bomber and continue the attack with 'Schräge Musik'; Schnaufer destroyed three bombers in this way. German pilots agreed that a violent corkscrew, begun early, was the most effective evasive manoeuvre for a bomber. If the bomber was hit at all, it was usually when it was changing direction at the top. The general view was that an evading Halifax was an easier target than an evading Lancaster, though the latter usually caught fire more easily when it was hit. Schnaufer was most impressed by the general manoeuvrability of the Lancaster and the violence of the manoeuvres flown by these aircraft never ceased to amaze him. If a bomber crew opened fire or initiated a corkscrew before they were in position to open fire themselves, the 'Experten' would often break away rather than enter a long and usually fruitless chase; once in the bomber stream, there was every chance of finding another bomber whose crew would prove less vigilant. The less experienced German pilots, however, keen to get a 'kill' and lacking the confidence to break away and seek other targets, would often press on with their attack regardless - and achieve nothing.

On the night of Thursday 16th/ Friday 17th 12./NJG1 at Leeuwarden were grounded because of dense fog. At first no enemy bombers had been reported but suddenly Viermots were reported crossing the North Sea. The route taken by 482 Lancasters and ten Mosquitoes again led directly to the Reich capital across Holland and Northern Germany and there were no major diversions. Oberleutnant Schnaufer jumped into action. He and his crew took off in their 'Schräge Musik'-equipped Bf 110 and climbed through the low cloud and icing which persisted up to 15,000 feet. Widespread mist and fog at 150-300 feet in the North German plains reduced the overall effectiveness of the fighter defence and 23 aircraft, mostly Bf 110s had to abandon their sorties prematurely but Schnaufer continued until he burst through the murk to find that it was 'crystal clear' at altitude. The German controllers planned the course of the bombers with great accuracy. Aided by Leutnant Lübke, Jägerleitoffizier of 'Himmelbett' box 'Eisbär' ('Polar Bear') at Sondel, Northern Holland, at 1801 hours near Follega, Schnaufer closed on a lone Lancaster far ahead of the bomber stream which had been reported crossing the North Sea when he took off. German radar had begun picking up J beams at 1800 hours and the assembly of the RAF formations, their leaving England and approach, were all plotted correctly by H$_2$S bearings. It could only be a Path Finder. It was. Lancaster III JA853 MG-L on 7 Squadron flown by Warrant Officer Wallace Arthur Watson RAAF who had taken off from Oakington at 1624. Schnaufer closed to 4000 metres, fired and the 'Lanki' exploded into a thousand pieces sending debris and burning pieces of pyrotechnic flares in all directions. JA853 was one of four Lancasters lost on 7 Squadron.

Next, at 1812 hours Schnaufer picked out another Viermot. It was Lancaster I DV300 SR-W on 101 Squadron flown by Flight Lieutenant Ronald Ernest MacFarlane DFM RCAF. Schnaufer positioned the 110 under the bomber and fired his 'Schräge Musik' cannon. Sergeant Eric Ronald Edward Jordan the rear gunner had spotted the 110 and he was still hosing tracer at his attacker when the bomber was finally engulfed in flames. The stubborn gunner and the rest of the crew were killed when the Lancaster exploded over Banco polder near Lemmer. Next, at 1823 Schnaufer singled out Lancaster III JB545 EA-O on 49 Squadron, fired his 'Jazz Musik' guns again and 'O-Orange' disintegrated in a fireball before crashing at Sonnega southwest of Wolvega with the loss of all of Flying Officer Gordon Lennox Ratcliffe's crew. The heat engulfed Schnaufer's 110, his wings seemed to catch fire momentarily and then the fighter lost 1,500 feet of altitude before he could finally recover. It was a near thing. Then Gänsler reported on intercom: 'Lancaster at 6800 metres (19,700 feet south of Leeuwarden)'. It was now 1841 hours. Lancaster II DS831 QO-'N-Nuts' on 432 'Leaside' Squadron RCAF was being flown by 23-year old Flying Officer William Charles Fisher the American skipper from Missouri. He had wanted to become an engineer but due to the war enlisted in the RCAF because many of his family were living there. His wife was eight months pregnant at the time. Schnaufer made a firing pass at the 'Lanki' but his tracer went wide. Flight Sergeant Herbert Albert Turner the Canadian rear gunner fired a hail of bullets at the 110 and Fisher put 'N-Nuts' into a corkscrew manoeuvre. Schnaufer could only admire the guts of the enemy pilot. After waiting patiently for the diving and climbing to ease off the bomber reached the top of one of its corkscrews and he closed to thirty metres behind and slightly below and fired into the 'Lanki's fuel tanks. DS831 careered over Leeuwarden trailing a sheet of flames and completely disintegrated on impact at Wytgaard south of Leeuwarden at 1841 hours followed by the explosion of the bomb load.

Fisher, Sergeant Raymond Hughes RAFVR the 18-year old flight engineer from Bangor, Caernarvonshire; Flight Sergeant James Stuart Briegel RCAF the navigator; Warrant Officer Raymond Kenneth Saunders RAAF the 23-year old air gunner of East Guildford, Western Australia; and Flight Sergeant Herbert Albert Turner the 24-year old air gunner of London, Ontario and 22-year old Flight Sergeant Thomas Walter Pragnell RAFVR were killed. Tom's twin brother Jack was also a member of a Bomber Command crew. Before enlisting, Tom had been working at Mansfield's shoe factory in Northampton. They came from a large family; George and Sarah Ann Pragnell had borne Elsie, Noreen, Stan and Doris. Only Flight Sergeant Montagu Brudell RAAF the 21-year old wireless operator and Sergeant Owen D. Lewis RCAF the 'second dickie' survived and they were taken prisoner. Schnaufer had to make five attempts to land back at Leeuwarden and then only by a fortuitous hole in the cloud. The four victories took Schnaufer's total to forty victories.[84]

Twelve nights later on 29 December Schnaufer claimed two more Viermots. At 1850 five kilometres (3.1 miles) northeast of Meppel in the Netherlands he shot down Halifax II JD314 ZA-X on 10 Squadron at Melbourne which was being flown by Sergeant Walter Douglas Hall. The skipper and all his crew on 'X-X ray' were killed. At 1945 hours near Wietmarschen, west of Lingen, Germany he destroyed Lancaster II DS718 EQ-R on 408 'Goose' Squadron RCAF at Linton-on-Ouse. Sergeant Bert Henry Fearn and his crew on 'R-Robert' died also. Oberleutnant Schnaufer was awarded the

Ritterkreuz des Eisernen Kreuzes for 42 victories on 31 December. On 3 January 1944 the presentation was made by Generalmajor Josef 'Beppo' Schmid, commanding I Jagdkorps.

On the night before his 22nd birthday, on 15 February, Schnaufer and his crew claimed aerial victories 45 to 47. Bomber Command had sent 561 Lancasters and 314 Halifaxes, supported by Mosquito night-fighters and bombers, destined for Berlin. Schnaufer, who had been suffering from stomach pains all day, and his crew returned to Leeuwarden at 0014. Rumpelhardt had been the first to congratulate him on his birthday over the intercom. Their fellow airmen had prepared a birthday celebration. The stomach pains had become unbearable and Schnaufer was taken to a hospital with appendicitis. He stayed in the hospital for about two weeks before, together with Rumpelhardt, he went on leave at home. Carelessly lifting his suitcase the stitches burst and he required further hospitalisation and he did not fly again until 19 March. Schnaufer had been appointed Gruppenkommandeur IV./NJG1 on 1 March, taking over command of the Gruppe from Jabs who was given command of NJG1. On 25 March at 0012 Schnaufer claimed a Viermot east of Dortmund. Nine minutes later at Neuwarendorf east of Münster he shot down Lancaster HK539 on 626 Squadron at Wickenby to take his score to fifty. Wing Commander Quentin Weston Aldridge Ross and his crew were killed.

Schnaufer was promoted to Hauptmann on 1 May. On 25 May when enemy bombers targeted the railway marshalling yard at Aachen, he claimed five Abschüsse over the Netherlands in quick succession between 0115 and 0129 for victories 70 to 74. The first four of these were Halifaxes. He shot down LK885 on 51 Squadron three kilometres (1.9 miles) northwest of Eindhoven and it crashed at Acht with the loss of Pilot Officer Wilfred Carroll Lawson RCAF and two of his crew. LW653 on 158 Squadron piloted by Flight Sergeant John Seymour Macleod Clarke followed three minutes later two kilometres (1.2 miles) NNW of Tilburg. There were no survivors. The third Halifax, MZ622 on 76 Squadron, went down at 0122 1.5 kilometres (0.93 miles) west of Goirle. There were no survivors on the crew of Flight Sergeant Peter Stuart Wade RAAF. Three minutes later LW124 on 429 'Bison' Squadron was destroyed between Dongen and Tilburg. Warrant Officer2 Mario Alfred Fernandez de Leon RCAF, who was from Guatemala and three of his crew were killed. Finally, at 01.29 Schnaufer shot down a Lancaster seven kilometres (4.3 miles) southwest of Tilburg.

On the night of 12/13 June Schnaufer claimed three bombers shot down, the first as a Lancaster and the second and third as a Lancaster or Halifax, between 0027 and 0034. Another victory followed on 17 June and on the 21st/22nd when the bombers were detailed to bomb Wesseling he claimed four Lancasters over Holland and Belgium to take his total to 84 victories. At 0125 he destroyed Lancaster III LM592 'Q-Queenie' on 44 Squadron which exploded over Riethoven with the loss of Pilot Officer Edwin Albert Canty RAAF and his crew. Over Belgium five minutes later he shot down Lancaster I ME683 EM-W on 207 Squadron two kilometres (1.2 miles) south of Meeuwen, Pilot Officer Alvin Van Dyke Corless RCAF and crew were killed. Six minutes later he destroyed Lancaster LM434 on 44 Squadron five kilometres (3.1 miles) south of Opoeteren. Pilot Officer Neville John Wingrove Scholtz, a Rhodesian and one crewmember were killed; four were taken prisoner and one evaded. Finally, at 02.05, six kilometres (3.7 miles) south of Hamont, Schnaufer shot down Lancaster I ME843 on 630 Squadron. There were no survivors on the crew of Pilot Officer Robert Cecil Hooper DFC.

Hauptmann Schnaufer was awarded the Knight's Cross with Oak Leaves (Ritterkreuz des Eisernen Kreuzes mit Eichenlaub) on 24 June. For Schnaufer July 1944 was less successful than the previous three months. He claimed two bombers on the night of 20/21 July and three on 28/29 July, taking his total to 89 aerial victories. On 30 July he received a letter from Göring telling him that he had been awarded the Knight's Cross with Oak Leaves and Swords (Ritterkreuz des Eisernen Kreuzes mit Eichenlaub und Schwertern). Hitler himself made the presentation. It is said that when he came to the presentation his first words were, 'Where is the night fighter?' Shortly following the presentation of the Schwerter both Rumpelhardt and Gänsler received the Knight's Cross on 8 August. His crew was the only night fighter crew in the entire Luftwaffe of which all crew members wore this decoration.

In early September NJG1 was forced to abandon its airfields in the Netherlands and Belgium. Continuous heavy attacks by RAF and USAAF bombers and strafing by Allied fighter-bombers rendered the airfields unsuitable for operations. On 2 September VI./NJG1 relocated from Sint-Truiden to Dortmund-Brackel. Schnaufer achieved his 100th victory on 9 October when he claimed two Viermots during a raid by 415 bombers on Bochum. In recognition of this achievement, he was honorably mentioned in the Wehrmachtbericht, an information bulletin issued by the headquarters of the Wehrmacht on 10 October, and awarded the Knight's Cross with Oak Leaves, Swords and Diamonds (Ritterkreuz des Eisernen Kreuzes mit Eichenlaub, Schwertern und Brillanten) on 16 October.

Schnaufer was appointed Geschwaderkommodore of NJG4 at Gütersloh on 20 November; the youngest Geschwaderkommodore in the Luftwaffe at the age of 22. He flew his first combat sortie as Geschwaderkommodore on 22 November and claimed two victories in the area of Dortmund. Of the bombers shot down by the crews of NJG4, four-fifths did not open fire or manoeuvre before being attacked; this would seem to indicate that their crews had no inkling of the approach of the night-fighter. Two-fifths of the bombers shot down did not even fire or manoeuvre after the night-fighter had opened fire. Almost all of the bombers shot down by night-fighters fell in flames. Schnaufer recalled two occasions when a bomber's fire had surprised him; on both occasions the fire had been accurate and he did not attempt to press an attack. On two other occasions his fighter suffered serious damage from return fire and on many others he landed to find that his aircraft had been holed.

Schnaufer and his crew flew from Gütersloh to Berlin-Staaken on 27 November for the official presentation of the Diamonds to the Knight's Cross with Oak Leaves and Swords by Hitler. Following the official photo session by Hitler's photographer Heinrich Hoffmann, Schnaufer met with Oberst Nicolaus von Below, Hitler's Luftwaffe adjutant, at the Reichsluftfahrtministerium (Ministry of Aviation). Here Schnaufer and his crew were filmed for the German newsreels Die Deutsche Wochenschau. Three days later they returned to Gütersloh.

Schnaufer became the leading night fighter pilot on 6 November when he surpassed Oberst Helmut Lent's record of 102 night-Abschüsse after he claimed three Viermots shot down from a force of 235 Lancasters which attacked the Dortmund-Ems Canal. Schnaufer, whose victory total stood at 106 at the end of 1944, failed to shoot down a single bomber in January 1945. It was his first month without filing a claim since April 1943. He was ordered to Carinhall, the residence of the Reichsmarschall Hermann Göring, on 8 February 1945. Göring informed him about the intent to appoint him as Inspekteur der Nachtjäger (Inspector of the night fighter force), a role held by Oberst Werner Streib at the time. Schnaufer, not wanting to oust his friend and mentor from this position, argued that he would better serve the German cause fighting the enemy. Göring was convinced and Schnaufer remained in his position as Geschwaderkommodore.

The British propaganda radio station 'Soldatensender Calais' (Soldiers' Radio Calais) congratulated Schnaufer on account of his 23rd birthday on 16 February 1945.

The radio station explicitly addressed NJG4 at Gütersloh followed by the song 'Das Nachtgespenst' [The Bogeyman] praising him for the honorary title given to him by the British bomber crews 'The spook of St. Trond'.[85] During the last seven months of the war NJG4 had lost about fifty fighters in action. Of these five had fallen to return fire from the bombers, thirty to Mosquito attack and fifteen had fallen to unknown causes. When jamming rendered Schnaufer's radar equipment useless he would fly towards the strongest jamming and there search visually. Once in the bomber stream, on a moonlight night, there were occasions when the streams were short and very concentrated when he had as many as twenty-five bombers simultaneously in view; on a dark night it was rare for more than three bombers to be in sight at the same time. Schnaufer's greatest one-night success was on 21 February when he claimed nine Lancaster heavy bombers in the course of one day. Two were claimed in the early hours of the morning and a further seven, in just nineteen minutes, in the evening between 2044 and 2103. On 7/8 March he claimed three RAF four-engine bombers for victories 119 to 121. These were his last victories of the war. He was then banned from further combat flying and was tasked with evaluating the then new Dornier Do 335, a twin-engine heavy fighter with a unique 'push-pull' layout, for its suitability as night fighter. Disobeying his ban from combat flying, he flew his last sortie of the war on 9 April 1945. Attempting to chase a Lancaster, he took off from Fassberg at 2200 and landed after 79 minutes at 2319 without success.

Schnaufer was taken prisoner of war by the British Army in Schleswig-Holstein in May 1945. Interrogation had begun in late May 1945 by a team of twelve officers from the Department of Air Technical Intelligence (DAT), led by Air Commodore Roderick Aeneas Chisholm. The German prisoners were brought to Eggebek. Here they conducted a number of interviews with various members of the night fighter force. Friedrich Rumpelhardt was released on 4 August 1945 and soon after Schnaufer was admitted to a hospital in Flensburg, ill with a combination of diphtheria and scarlet fever. Rumpelhardt, who was the most successful bordfunker in Nachtjagd being credited with 100 abschussbeteiligungen, or 'contributions to claims and who had taken part in 100 successful attacks with Schnaufer (and 98 with Oberfeldwebel Gänsler) became an administrative officer at an agricultural college in West Germany. After his recovery Schnaufer arranged for Wilhelm Gänsler to move from East Germany and found employment for him in the family's business. Meanwhile, their Bf 110 had been evaluated by the RAF and was later included in a display of captured German aircraft in Hyde Park in London. It was eventually broken up, but one of its fins, showing Schnaufer's tally of 121 victories, was put on display at the Imperial War Museum in Lambeth, while the other was displayed in the Australian War Memorial Museum in Canberra.

Endnotes Chapter 7

82 *Horrido!* by Colonel Raymond F. Toliver and Trevor J. Constable (Bantam 1968).
83 The remains of the crew were buried at the village cemetery at Schaffen. The committal service was taken by the Luftwaffe padre of the neighbouring airfield and a photograph of the service was taken at the request of the Padre and a copy given to the grave digger. There was a story circulating at the time of the crash that two crew members had bailed out, it was not until the Casualty Inquiry Report was published on 9 July 1945 that the story was finally laid to rest. Until then the crew's families had remained in hope that two of the crew might be alive.
84 After the war at a ceremony to mark the 50th anniversary of the crash seven kilometres south of Leeuwarden Jack Pragnell met one of the survivors of the crew who told him that a decision was made to guide the plane to an area away from the town as they had a full bomb load to cause the least damage to the town; a decision that would cause six of the crew to lose their lives. Fisher rests in the US Military cemetery at Neuville-en-Condroz Cemetery in Belgium while his five crew rest in the Leeuwarden Protestant Churchyard. See *The Loss of Lancaster DS831 16/17 December 1943* by Dutch student Mr Marvel M. Huizenga.
85 Broadcasts from the secret British 600-kilowatt radio transmitter, the most powerful in Europe, code-named 'Soldiers' Transmitter Calais' had begun on Sunday 24 October 1943 with German-language propaganda broadcasts to the continent to supplement the operations of the earlier-established German Short-Wave Transmitter Atlantic. The operations were supervised by Sefton Delmer. The transmitter studio in Milton Bryan in Bedfordshire broadcast a regular programme aimed at members of the Luftwaffe and was intended to weaken German morale. The broadcasts were supported by the German air crew who had landed their Ju 88 in Britain in May 1943 and who regularly closed the programme by inveighing against the British for imposing such impossible conditions on German fighters in their struggle against an overwhelming enemy. The broadcast team had their own wing commander, N. Roffy of Air Intelligence 3, who kept them informed about the most up-to-date technical innovations being used by the Luftwaffe. Part of the programme was a running commentary on the most recent Allied air raids and included extremely precise details - lists of specific German streets destroyed; the names of individual targets, even the house-numbers of buildings. Germans were strictly forbidden to listen to these broadcasts, but there were many unlicensed listeners who concluded that they were surrounded by on-the-spot British agents who immediately reported the results of British raids back to their headquarters.

Chapter Eight

The 'Wilde Sau'

Mitten in dem starksten Feuer
Swischen Fliegern, Flak und Mordsradau,
Ja, das wird dem Tommy teuer:
Die Horridos der 'Wilden Sau'

Das Lied von der Wilden Sau **by Peter Holm.**

By early 1943 Kammhuber's 'Himmelbett' defences had been completed and the Lichtenstein AI (Airborne Interception)-equipped Nachtjagd aircraft were now capable of exacting a toll of up to six per cent bomber casualties on any deep penetration raid into the Reich. Thus, Bomber Command losses rose rapidly during the first few months of 1943 although in early January operations were, of necessity, on a limited scale, normally to the U-boat bases on the Atlantic coast. On 16/17 January Berlin was bombed for the first time in fourteen months by 190 Lancasters and eleven Halifaxes.[86] Air Marshal Sir Arthur Harris, C-in-C Bomber Command sent them on their way with the words, 'Tonight you are going to the big City. You will have the opportunity to light a fire in the belly of the enemy that will burn his black heart out.' Only one Lancaster was lost but the raid was a disappointment. Thick cloud en route and haze over the target caused problems and the bombing was scattered. The Berlin flak had proved light and ineffective and it was assumed that the greater altitude of the attacking force had surprised the German gunners.

Harris repeated the raid on Berlin, sending 170 Lancasters and seventeen Halifaxes back to the 'Big City' the following night, 17/18 January, when the weather was better. The routes taken by the bombers to and from Berlin were the same as those followed on the previous night and German night-fighters were able to find the bomber stream. Nineteen Lancasters and three Halifaxes that were lost were claimed by 'Himmelbett'-operating Nachtjäger. Unteroffizier Karl-Georg Pfeiffer of 10./NJG1 claimed one of the Lancasters (probably W4772 on 1654 HCU at Swinderby, which was being flown by Pilot Officer Frederick Arthur Read DFC) over the North Sea ten kilometres west of Vlieland at 2329 hours in bitterly cold weather as his second Abschuss:

'The 10th Staffel (Oberleutnant Sigmund) to which I had been assigned had recently returned to Leeuwarden from Gilze-Rijen. (The Staffel had been sent to Gilze-Rijen for a few weeks because attacks had been expected on the towns of Tilburg, Breda and Eindhoven. The attack on the Philips works at Eindhoven had actually taken place on a bright Sunday [6 December 1942]. By the time we night fighters had arrived it was all over.) We took off at 2201 hours and flew to the operational area 'Tiger' (around the Dutch Frisian island of Terschelling) and orbited for hours over the radio beacon. The Jägerleitoffizier announced monotonously at regular intervals:

'No Kuriere in sight' and we had to continue orbiting. We were at about 6000 metres.

'Suddenly the Jagerleitoffizier shouted, 'Have Kurier for you, Kirchturm [Church Tower'] 10 (1000 metres), course 300°, Kurier flying from two to eleven.[87]

'So power off quickly and I dived from 6000 to 1000 metres. Meanwhile ground control reported 'Kirchturm 5' so the Britisher was down to 500 metres over the water on course for home. Unfortunately the visibility at this height was extremely hazy; no more than 500 metres in good but diffuse moonlight. Then it was 'Kirchturm 2', so I went down even lower. Attack was impossible at this height and also, the Lichtenstein radar gave no indications close to the ground.

'We were now flying at no more than one hundred metres over the North Sea and strained our eyes. According to the information from the Jägerleitoffizier we were a little offset behind him: '1000 metres, 800 metres, 500, 400, 300 metres!' Power off and minimum speed in order not to overtake him. We had to attack from behind and wase dangerous because of the rear turret of the 4-mots. Suddenly I saw about 200 metres on my starboard bow something grey in the thick soup. So he had not spotted us yet. Calm now! Guns armed? Night sight switched on? Everything OK! Now I could see that it was an Avro Lancaster. I applied a little more power and approached him cautiously. No sudden movement that attracted their attention!

'Now I was exactly behind him at about 100 metres range. The rear turret was clearly recognisable. My radio operator kept silent. Suddenly the rear turret was lit up in a flickering light. The head of the gunner with his helmet appeared and I realized that the poor fellow was lighting a cigarette. He felt he was already safely home. Any further delay would be crazy. I pressed the gun button on the stick and was startled at the rattle of the cannon. I stayed behind him firing and observed the projectiles striking the rear turret and the fuselage. Suddenly both inner engines caught fire. The great night bird dipped down and crashed into the sea. The escaping petrol spread fire over the water and was still alight as we reported our success and set course for Leeuwarden, where I landed at 2346 hours. For a beginner with only one Abschuss this was a precarious situation but at the time we were still optimistic and trusted that only the other one would suffer.'[88]

The next Main Force raids were on Lorient and Düsseldorf on 23/24 January when just over 200 bomber sorties were flown. A Stirling was lost on the raid on Lorient where successful bombing was claimed and two Lancasters failed to return from the operation on Düsseldorf where some bombs fell in the south of the city. One of the Lancasters was 'C for Charlie' on 460 Squadron RAAF at Breighton flown by Squadron Leader Richard Osborn DFC the 'A' Flight commander. The route to the target began with a climb to 20,000 feet from Breighton and course set for Mablethorpe and across the North Sea to Holland. At ETA the target was cloud covered and no 'Oboe' placed markers were seen. The bombs, therefore, were dropped blind on ETA and heading set for home. Estimating a coast-out at Noordwijk, a diversion signal was received to proceed to Bradwell Bay but instead of coasting out over Noordwijk 'C-Charlie' was attacked over the Ijsselmeer about fifty miles to the North East by Oberleutnant Wolfgang Kuthe and Unteroffizier Helmut Bonk of IV./NJG1 in a Bf 110F-4 night-fighter. Kuthe approached 'von hinten unten' (from behind and below) and raked the Lancaster with cannon fire. Osborn was hit in his left upper arm by a shell and a deafening roar filled the cockpit. The intercom was put out of action and the T1154/R1155 transmitter/receiver, which was the standard radio set in use by Bomber Command, was knocked out while the fuel tank between the two starboard engines was soon ablaze and a sheet of flame stretched back towards the tail-plane. Badly wounded and with the aircraft on fire, the decision was made to turn back, lose height rapidly and force-land in Holland.

Kuthe closed in and delivered a second attack, which ruptured the hydraulic system and killed the rear gunner, Pilot Officer Stuartson Charles Methven RAAF. Executing a 270° turn to port, Osborn put the Lancaster into a rapid descent. By now he had no reference to his flight instruments but, by the light of the flames, sensed the ground coming up rapidly, and levelled off. Unable to lower the undercarriage or lower the flaps he cut the throttles. The Lancaster ploughed through a dyke and moments later slithered to a halt near Stavoren and the de Boer farm just west of the village of Warns. Rapidly evacuating the aircraft through the various upper surface hatches, five of the crew gathered on the soft turf, the wounded mid-upper gunner helped by the wireless operator. 'C-Charlie' was now burning fiercely from the cockpit area to the tail. Of the bomb aimer Sergeant John Vincent Conlon RAAF there was no sign. Presently Harmen de Boer, his son Meindert and his daughter Maria appeared and ushered the five into their farmhouse bearing the mortally injured rear gunner on a tarpaulin sheet and began to tend the crew. Any hopes of escape for the others were dashed by the swift arrival of a party of German soldiers from the 'Eisbär' ('Polar Bear') sector control station at Sondel. Dr. Tromp Visser was summoned to tend to the wounded and then an ambulance arrived and the two were driven off with the doctor to St. Bonifacius hospital in Leeuwarden. Conlon's body was found with unopened parachute the next day 500 metres east of what remained of the Lancaster. A fire extinguisher bottle, which Martje de Vries-Jagersma, pregnant with her first child, 'liberated' from the wreckage was adapted with a screw-top to use as a hot water bottle for her new baby's cot and later for her nine siblings! Following spells in hospital (osteomeyelities having set in) and in PoW camps, Richard Osborn was repatriated in a prisoner exchange in September 1944.[89]

On 30 January Mosquito B.IV crews of 2 Group Bomber Command raided Berlin to disrupt speeches in the main broadcasting station by Hermann Göring and Dr. Joseph Goebbels for this was the 10th anniversary of Hitler's seizure of power. Three Mosquitoes on 105 Squadron arrived over Berlin at exactly 1100 hours and the explosion of their bombs severely disrupted the Reichsmarschall's speech. In the afternoon, three Mosquitoes on 139 Squadron arrived over Berlin at the time Göbbels was due to speak. However, the earlier raid alerted the defences and flak brought down a Mosquito. Other RAF bomber crews were dispatched to various targets in Germany in daylight 'to cause despondency and despair among the refugees from Cologne'. Of the nineteen Wellingtons and seventeen Bostons which went to many places in Germany and Holland, only two Wellingtons and one Boston found targets to bomb. Four Wellingtons failed to return. In a raid on Emden by eight Wellingtons on 466 Squadron RAAF, Pilot Officer Mackeldon aborted the operation and five crews returned. Flight Lieutenant Cyril John Simmons and the crew on HE397 and Sergeant Leslie Frederick Axby and crew on HE471 did not return. Leutnant Wolfgang Kuthe of 11./NJG1 shot HE397 down over the North Sea off Terschelling at 1314 hours. He crashed his Bf 110F-4 after this victory at Ameland Island, most likely as a result of return fire.

In January 'Himmelbett' Nachtjagd destroyed 44 bombers (including nine by I./NJG1, two by III./NJG1 and 16 by IV./NJG1) and in February 61 aircraft were shot down. On 2/3 February when 161 aircraft went to Cologne, the night was cloudy and a further experiment was made using a four-engined bombing force with various forms of Path Finder techniques. Markers were dropped by two 'Oboe' Mosquitoes and H_2S heavy marker aircraft. Damage was caused right across the city. Five aircraft failed to return. Stirling I R9264 MG-L, a Path Finder aircraft on 7 Squadron flown by Squadron Leader W. A. Smith DFC MiD,[90] which was shot down by Oberleutnant Reinhold Knacke Staffelkapitän 1./NJG1 and a 44 victory 'Experte' crashed near Rotterdam was examined by the Germans who retrieved the H_2S set from the bomber. This was only the second night that this new device was used. The set was damaged but Telefunken in Berlin were able to reassemble it. This gave them an early indication of the operational use of H_2S and eventually it led to the development of a radar device known as 'Naxos', which would enable night fighters to home on to a bomber emitting H_2S signals. On the night of 3/4 February meanwhile, Hauptmann Reinhold Knacke was killed in his Bf 110F-4 by return fire from his second victim that night, an unidentified Halifax, near Achterveld, Holland. The rear gunner opened fire at exactly the same moment as Knacke and the bursts on both sides were fatal. In the early morning German troops found the crews and debris of both aircraft lying next to each other in a field. A posthumous award of the Oak Leaves was announced three days after his death. On the 1/2 March 1943 raid on Berlin, some bombs hit the Telefunken works and the H_2S set was completely destroyed but Halifax II W7877 TL-O on 35 Squadron with an almost intact H_2S set, which was shot down by Leutnant August 'Gustel' Geiger of III./NJG1 crashed in Holland on this night with the loss of all but one of Squadron Leader Peter Campbell Elliott DFC and crew and the Germans were able to resume their research into H_2S immediately.[91]

On the 14th the RAF returned to Cologne again. Over the target sky markers were used once again and this time crews had more time to line up before they dropped below cloud. The results however, were 'unsatisfactory', as there were no photographs because of the cloud cover. Nine aircraft were lost to night-fighters, three of which were Wellingtons and two were claimed by Ritterkreuzträger Paul Gildner, who after the death in combat of Reinhold Knacke had been given command of 1./NJG1 at Gilze-Rijen airfield. Gildner's score stood at 38 Abschüsse, two in the Battle of France and 36 at night. Unteroffizier Heinz Huhn, his experienced radar operator recorded:

'On 14 February we destroyed a Wellington and a Boeing [sic] in sector 'Hamster' [Domburg/Holland]. There was no radio beacon in operation and we flew without being able to orientate ourselves. Our bearing set was unserviceable. Thank God we could still communicate over R/T with the ground station. Finally, a thought crossed my mind: could it be the Lichtenstein that was jamming our bearing set? I switched off the Li-set. Sure enough, I could then obtain a bearing. We proceeded towards the box flying at a height of 3000 metres [9,700 feet]. We received a course to steer straight away but the Lichtenstein was not in operation. We flew between two layers of cloud; above us the clouds were very thin. We therefore climbed above these clouds and got a visual on a Wellington.

'I am engaging', Gildner announced and he attacked directly from behind. Its left engine and wing on fire, the enemy pulled up steeply and plunged down. We observed it crashing into the water: 'Sieg Heil!' [Bomber destroyed!]

'Immediately, we received a new course to steer from the ground station. The moon brightly illuminated the sky as if it were daylight. I experienced interference in the R/T communications with ground control. At last we obtained visual contact.

I am engaging' Gildner said, as he got into an attacking position and opened fire. The Kurier was identified as a Boeing [sic]. It was burning in the left engines and dived down out of control. It crashed into the sea. 'Sieg Heil!

'We were vectored onto another aircraft. We got a visual but we were too fast. We turned around to get into a good attacking position but contact was lost with the Kurier in the process. We were low on fuel so we set course for home right away. It was a smooth landing. Oberleutnant Gildner's 39th and 40th night victories.'

His 39th victim was Wellington HE169 on 196 Squadron, which crashed into the North Sea at 2148 hours twelve miles (twenty kilometres) west of Schouwen. Flight Lieutenant Roderick Fairweather Milne, a New Zealander in the RAF and crew were killed. The 'Boeing' was Stirling I BF438 WP-D on 90 Squadron flown by Sergeant Lionel William Tabor RNZAF, which crashed thirty miles (45 kilometres) west of Flushing

(Vlissingen) at 2207 hours with the loss of the whole crew. All nine aircraft lost were claimed by night-fighters. Leutnant Johannes Hager of 6./NJG1 flying a Do 217 claimed Halifax II DT694 on 158 Squadron flown by Squadron Leader William Fletcher DFC DFM near Mechelen. Fletcher and four crew were killed: one PoW; one evaded. Oberfeldwebel Fritz Schellwat of II./NJG1 claimed Stirling I BF449 on 15 Squadron three kilometres NNW of Hechteren. He would finish the war with 17 Abschüsse. Flight Lieutenant Owen Cecil Chave and crew were killed. Oberleutnant Manfred Meurer, Staffelkapitän 3./NJG1 destroyed three bombers on their homeward flight, including Wellington III X3420 on 426 'Thunderbird' Squadron RCAF between Beegden and Heel to take his score to fourteen. Wing Commander Sedley Stewart Blanchard RCAF and crew were killed. I./NJG1 claimed another Stirling and a Wellington destroyed.

Despite the dreadful weather conditions on 19/20 February, three experienced crews were given permission to take off from Leeuwarden to try and intercept the returning Wilhelmshaven force. Twelve bombers failed to return. In adverse weather conditions Oberleutnant Hans-Joachim Jabs, Staffelkapitän, II./NJG1 destroyed three Stirlings on 15 Squadron in 44 minutes over the North Sea operating in 'Himmelbett' box 'Schlei' at Schiermonnikoog Island to take his score to 29 victories. Stirling III BF457 on 15 Squadron (at 2100 hours) flown by Flying Officer David Joseph Hopson, Stirling I BF378 on 15 Squadron (at 2114 hours) flown by Flying Officer Bernard Verdun Crawford RNZAF and Stirling I BF411 on 15 Squadron (destroyed at 2145 hours) flown by Pilot Officer John Charles Monteith RCAF. There were no survivors on any of these aircraft, Oberleutnant Paul Gildner, Staffelkapitän, 1./NJG1 was also victorious, as Unteroffizier Heinz Huhn recalled in his diary:

'We're in the Operations Room that night. A thick layer of mist and bad ground visibility prevail. Enemy bombers are reported approaching Wilhelmshaven. We can't take off. Still, Gildner wants to get after the bombers, if necessary he will fly the Dornier. The bombers fly back through the boxes in our area. We decide to take off all the same. There's a full moon. The Dornier is not fitted with flame dampers, so from the engine exhausts long flames trail back. The radio and radar equipment of the aircraft is completely worn out. I switch off the Lichtenstein and we have to search without it. We immediately get a course to steer for a mission in box 'Tiger'. The first Kurier is a Halifax. Suspecting no attack, its crew must feel quite safe. Gildner attacks, the 'Kurier' starts to burn and at 2105 hours it crashes into the North Sea. Sieg Heil.

'The reflector sight has broken down and only one cannon still fires. We are guided onto another aircraft. At 2110 hours we obtain visual contact. A Halifax. A giant pillar of smoke from our first kill rises from the water. An attack, the Kurier trails a long banner of smoke; it explodes and crashes into the sea. Time is 2116 hours.

'We are vectored onto another aircraft, this time we engage a Boeing [sic]. R/T connection is very bad, as a transmitter on the ground has broken down. I am dripping with sweat, have to switch all the time and tune the radio set. And my helmet fits miserably. Nevertheless, were still in business and remain in visual contact with the enemy bomber. We get into attacking position. Gildner opens fire; only three machine guns are still working. The aircraft is not burning yet. We charge in again and fire another burst, then have to turn away as a second Kurier is flying only 200 metres away from us. So, this one is getting away. We can only claim a damaged. Our own aircraft has been hit by return fire in the propellers.

'We immediately turn back for home and safely touch-down. In the Operations Room we have a big party that same night with champagne and red wine. Jabs has shot down three bombers, all Short Stirlings. Our third probably didn't make it back home either as it sent off an SOS. In the afternoon of the 20th our lightning visit to Leeuwarden comes to an end and we fly back to Gilze.'

Both 'Halifaxes' which Gildner claimed were Lancasters, on 156 Squadron and 467 Squadron RAAF, both crashing into the North Sea, twenty and fifteen kilometres north of Vlieland respectively. The 'Boeing' was a Stirling, probably BK627 on 90 Squadron.

On the evening of 24 February Oberleutnant Paul Gildner, Staffelkapitän, l./NJG1, whose score stood at 44 victories, was killed when his Bf 110G-4 crashed on final approach to Gilze-Rijen following an engine fire. He had been in charge of the Staffel for just three short weeks since the death of his friend Reinhold Knacke. A force of RAF Viermots set out to attack Wilhelmshaven and Gildner and his Funker, Unteroffizier Heinz Huhn, were ordered off to the close-control area 'Hamster' above the Scheldt Estuary. They obtained a Lichtenstein contact on a bomber but they suffered an electrical fault and a loss of power on the port engine and failed to complete the interception. Gildner decided to return to Gilze but the airfield was shrouded in mist, so the Staffelkapitän ordered Huhn to take to his parachute. After some difficulty, Huhn managed to bail out at low level and landed safely but Gildner was unable to get out of his stricken Messerschmitt and died in the crash.

At Leeuwarden on 26 February, thirty-year-old Hauptmann Ludwig Becker, Staffelkapitän 12./NJG1 a great night fighting tactician with 44 night victories, waited to fly his very first daylight sortie. Shortly before taking off from Leeuwarden 1135 hours in a formation of twelve Bf 110s of IV./NJGI led by Hauptmann Hans-Joachim Jabs, in pursuit of American daylight raiders Becker was informed of the award of the Eichenlaub (Oak Leaves) to his Ritterkreuz (Knight's Cross), which had been bestowed on him on 1 July 1942 after his 25th night victory for his leading role in the development of the night fighter arm. They intercepted the B-17s and B-24s, returning with claims for two shot down but Becker's Bf 110 was lost without a trace. Completely at ease and master in the night battle against the British bombing offensive, the 'Night Fighting Professor' and his Funker Feldwebel Josef Staub fell victim to the gunners of B-17s or B-24s of the 1st and 2nd Bomb Wings. Losses to 'Experten' like this were not good for German morale, which was under pressure due to the intensifying air war over Europe, as Oberleutnant 'Dieter' Schmidt of NJG1 recalls:

'The fall of Stalingrad [in February 1943] resulted in a change of fortunes in the east. For us operations became more difficult and stressful too. Not only did the night attacks of the British become increasingly heavy during 1943. On 27 January the Americans, who so far had only appeared over occupied territory, attacked a German town without fighter escort. They maintained these attacks and, as there were only very few day fighter units stationed in the west, our past as Zerstörer units was remembered and we were called upon to confront these attacks. The 3rd Gruppe took part in a number of these operations but had only had one major engagement with the enemy on 4 March near Texel. The successive re-equipment of the aircraft and the operational readiness by day and night proved a considerable strain. Also, the night fighter version of the Bf 110 had become cumbersome through additional equipment for day-fighting and the crews no longer had the necessary experience of formation flying and attacking tactics. So, losses of highly specialised and experienced night fighters could not be avoided. In the hitherto quiet Holland, where a large part of NJG1 was stationed, the efforts of the resistance increased in 1943. It was necessary to guard the widely dispersed aircraft and hangars against possible sabotage. Shooting down single four-engined British aircraft dropping sabotage material from low level was also part of our task.

'The British intensified their bomber stream tactics and used four-engined aircraft - the Short Stirling, Halifax and the Lancaster - almost exclusively: the different performance of these three types and the different height of the individual waves were well known to us. On operations over the north German plain especially, one could choose the type to confront; but there was no difference in the defensive power of the three types. The tight British bomber stream and the radar equipment of our own machines resulted in a change in our tactics. We became more independent of our controllers and we succeeded in shooting down several enemy aircraft in succession more frequently. The bomber stream required a concentration of the night-fighters on the supposed approach route, which could frequently be determined by our early warning radar on the coast and the monitoring of radio traffic. Now began the time of operational deployments at short notice, most frequently to Sint-Truiden/Sint-Trond in Belgium. Also, during the short summer nights we would be reinforced by crews from Geschwader stationed in the hinterland.'

March 1943 came in with a roar, when on the 1st RAF Bomber Command was briefed for Berlin - 'The Big City' as they knew it. Counting the cost next day, it was found that of the force of 302 aircraft setting out, seventeen were lost: a nasty 5½%. IV./NJG1 destroyed five of the nineteen aircraft that failed to return. These included Halifax II DT641 on 419 'Moose' Squadron RCAF flown by Pilot Officer Arthur James Herriott DFM over the North Sea eight kilometres north of Ameland by Major Lent and Stirling I EF347 on 15 Squadron flown by Flight Sergeant Harold Stanley Howland by Leutnant Wolfgang Kuthe of 11./NJG1 at Schillaard. There were no survivors on either of these aircraft. Kuthe was killed on 14 April 1944 after gaining his eighth victory when his Bf 110G-4 crashed at Leeuwarden airfield. Most likely he had been hit by return fire. Three Halifaxes were credited to III./NJG1, 2 of which - Halifax II BB223 on 51 Squadron flown by Flight Sergeant John David William Stenhouse at Voorst and Halifax II W7877 on 35 Squadron flown by Squadron Leader Peter Campbell Elliott DFC at Oost-Stokkum - went to Leutnant August 'Gustel' Geiger. Again, there were no survivors on either aircraft. By the start of 1943 Geiger had ten victories and had been awarded the Iron Cross First Class. In early 1943 Geiger was promoted to Oberleutnant and transferred to 7./NJG1, becoming Staffelkapitän in May 1943 with forty confirmed victories. Oberleutnant Herbert Heinrich Otto Lütje claimed Halifax II DT797 on 408 Squadron flown by Sergeant Arnold Wallace Cochrane RCAF (six killed; one PoW) at Zuidloo.

The night of 5/6 March has gone into history as the starting point of the Battle of the Ruhr. Essen, the city of Krupp steelworks, was on the receiving end of a heavy raid when fourteen out of 442 aircraft failed to return, six of which were shot down by five IV/NJG1 crews. Major Helmut Lent shot down Halifax BB282 on 76 Squadron (Flight Sergeant Clifford Arthur Milan RCAF and crew KIA) and Lancaster I W4847 on 83 Squadron (Flight Sergeant Henry Albert Partridge RCAF and crew KIA) into the Waddenzee and the Ijsselmeer respectively. Hauptmann Herbert Lütje of 8./NJG1 destroyed Halifax II HR687 on 78 Squadron near Staphorst, the aircraft crashing on Leidijk Dekkerweg. Flight Sergeant John Rawson Thompson and two of his crew were killed.

On 8/9 March 335 bombers went to Nuremberg and eight aircraft failed to return. On 9/10 March 264 aircraft of Bomber Command attacked Munich and eight aircraft were lost. On 11/12 March 314 Lancasters, Halifaxes and Stirlings were despatched to Stuttgart. Eleven aircraft failed to return. On this night, 21-year old bordfunker Unteroffizier Karl-Ludwig Johanssen of 11./NJG4, flying with the experienced Leutnant Johannes Engels because his pilot, Leutnant Martin 'Tino' Becker (who he had teamed up with in January 1943) had gone sick, scored his first victory but at a cost as Johanssen recalls:

'At Gilze Rijen we collected a new machine, a Bf 110F with the markings 2Z+IU and equipped with Lichtenstein, a radar set I had never seen before. A local flight of forty minutes and then on 11 March cockpit readiness and take-off at 2143 hours for the box 'Bergziege' (near Bergzabern). We had good radio contact with the Jägerleitoffizier (JLO, or GCI-controller) while climbing at maximum rate to our operational height of 5300 metres. The equipment was checked and the four machine guns and two MG-FF 2cm cannon, loaded and cocked. At my feet were the ammunition drums of the two 2cm cannon with 75 rounds each. The screen of the Lichtenstein was aglow with the green time base and the ground blips, which also showed our altitude. Our aircraft was over the radio beacon 'Bergziege'. We were directed to the north-west corner of the box and waited there flying in large circles. At last we got directions from the controller. Course and height were changed as in the exercises, using brief coded expressions.

'2 times Lisa - Marie 7 - Hanni 5, 2 - 1 times Rolf -Marie 6 - Rolf - Lisa - Marie 5'.

No indication yet on the Lichtenstein. We hoped to reach the 'Fat Car' before it left the range of the Würzburg ground radar.

'Rolf - Marie 4'. A slipstream shook our machine. There, a new blip on the screen. That must be the enemy aircraft. The controller continued with his orders but now the pilot only responded to my instructions:

'Rolf - more Rolf - Stop - Marie 2 - a little Lisa - same height - Lisa - Marie 1, 5 - Rolf - Marie 1 a little Siegfried (climb) - Rolf - Marie 1 - Lisa - Lisa - Stop -Marie 0, 8 - a little Rolf'. With a jerk of the controls the pilot called, 'There he is!' To ground control: 'Making 'Pauke-Pauke' [Kettledrums-Kettledrums' - going into attack].

'Our eyes looked out and clung to the black shape. Small, bluish exhaust flames made it easier to keep the target in sight. Four engines, twin tail, were recorded almost subconsciously. From about 200 metres aft and to starboard we fired our first burst but apparently without effect. But we had been spotted and the Viermot fired and took evasive action. Second attack: the tracer disappeared into its wing and fuselage. He must have been hit!

'Continued twisting and turning; another burst but on breaking off the rear gunner had us in his sights. There was a crackling in our aircraft. The starboard engine trailed white smoke. Coolant! But it was still running. I tried to change the ammunition drums. Impossible! Our twisting made them either a ton weight or they flew up around my head. Another attack from the port rear. The shots from the four machine guns were on target. Breaking off to starboard below the Viermot we got so close to that, as he went down, at the same time our port wing tip touched his starboard wing. A brief strike but we were still flying. The starboard engine now packed up and stopped.

'The Viermot had turned off to port and while I tried to contact control and give the pilot a course for the radio beacon Bergziege, the cockpit was suddenly lit up by flames. The enemy aircraft had crashed and its fire lit up the wooded and hilly countryside. Our altitude was still 800 metres. Rounded peaks were below us and above a star-lit sky with a half moon. These impressions were interrupted by the order over the intercom.

'Jump Johanssen! I cannot hold the machine.'[92]

'Released by the emergency lever, the cabin roof disappeared to the rear. Now out! My brain worked precisely. Best chance to starboard where the engine has stopped! Careful, you must get past below the tailfin! I climbed, no, rolled out of the cabin, still holding on as the pilot called over the intercom: 'Are you out?'

'Then I noticed that the cable from the helmet and the oxygen mask with its tube were still connected to the aircraft. I let myself fall back and disconnected the joints, although these should have released on their own. But one had heard of exceptions. Back on the wing alongside the fuselage. The front cabin cover opened, was flung backwards by the slipstream, the aerial mast disintegrated and at the same moment I let go. Slip along the wing, under the tailplane and count 21-22-23, before I pulled the ripcord of the parachute. Once clear of the machine it was suddenly quiet while doing a couple of somersaults in free fall. Tense expectation happened next. It was the first time, for bailing out is not done as an exercise. First there was a rustling on my back (the parachute was worn like a rucksack), then a zishing noise and a heavy jerk. It had opened! Whatever now followed would not matter. Hanging on the 'chute I observed the crash of our aircraft and at almost the same moment, a parachute glided past. The thought came as a relief: Engels, the pilot, had got out.

'But something else occupied my mind during these seconds. Down below, a river silvery in the moonlight, but directly beneath me, two similarly bright rectangles. Carp ponds? The thought had barely occurred to me when there was a swishing and the surroundings grew huge. A heavy impact. I was sitting on the ground, on garden soil, the rear parts somewhat bruised and I was amazed and almost frightened. Two metres away, silvery in the moonlight, there was the wall of a glasshouse and thirty metres further another such 'carp pond'. Swimming would have been no problem, but this?!

'It was deathly quiet now, around midnight, with no one in sight. I sent up a green signal light as a sign for my pilot that I was safely down. I left my parachute where it was and, following the next wider path, reached a busy street. The air raid warning was still on. A soldier showed me the way to a telephone in a market garden. Picking up the receiver I heard two men talking. The conversation was about the events of the last minutes and about the parachutists, who they did not know whether they were friend or foe. As I made myself known as a friend there was silence on the line.

'Finally: 'Who's there?' After a brief reply and the request to look for my pilot, it was confirmed that Engels got out all right and was now in Weiblingen at the Gasthof zum Ochsen hostelry. The garrison doctor at Heidelberg, one of the speakers, invited me to go to his home close by. The soldier took me there and explained where I was and what he had seen of the fight. At the doctor's home I got a friendly reception from his family and was able to phone our base at Mainz-Finthen. Comrades congratulated me and said that they had already spoken with Engels. We were to be picked up the following day by a Fieseler Storch.

'After a quickly improvised meal a policeman suddenly appeared and asked for my identification. I had to decline, for at the alert I had put on my flying overall only and had left my uniform jacket containing my identity card hanging in the crew room. With his hand on my shoulder he declared that I was under arrest and required me to surrender my arms. The signal pistol was taken from its lanyard and placed, together with the remaining cartridges, upon the table. It must be said that during the preceding nights some British crews had bailed out and had not been found. The tension gradually subsided and I watched further developments almost with amusement. But for the authorities it was bitter earnest. My notebook did not count as evidence, neither the mention that I had just telephoned my unit. Finally Doctor 'B' had a word with the policeman in an adjoining room. After several phone calls I was informed that a civil defence duty car would take me to the Großdeutschland barracks. They were already expecting me in the mess. I was offered a glass of wine but the fact that I did not know that Heidelberg had an airfield, was suspicious. I recounted my experiences but these were discounted. In the end I spent a sleepless night in an Unteroffizier's room whose usual occupants happened to be on leave. In the morning, having reported to the clerks' office, I was taken in a motorcycle side car to Wieblingen. We met Leutnant Engels by the wreckage of our aircraft. The remains were hardly recognisable as an erstwhile Bf 110. The Storch, with our Staffelkapitän at the controls, landed close by and took us first to the crash site of the Halifax in the Odenwald. The place was recognisable from afar. A new clearing had been made by the fire and the exploding bombs. Part of the crew had escaped by parachute. Beside the wreckage we found tins containing jam and other victuals. For a long time I kept *The Story of the Naked Man*, a well known English novel I believe, as a souvenir. Our take-off in the Storch from the small meadow and under a telephone line was criminal. The overloaded kite got airborne at the very last moment. Flowers and cigarettes from the enthusiastic spectators of Wieblingen and Odenwald covered the floor of the cabin.'

Engels and Unteroffizier Karl-Ludwig Johanssen's first victory was most probably Halifax II BB212 on 405 'Vancouver' Squadron RCAF, which was shot down by a Bf 110 at 17,000 feet and came down near Schonau in the Odenwald. Flight Sergeant G. T. Chretien DFM and five of his crew had bailed out safely and were taken prisoner. The rear gunner, Sergeant Robert Moore, was killed and later buried in Durnbach War Cemetery. The Stuttgart raid was 405 'Vancouver' Squadron RCAF first in Bomber Command and four of its fifteen aircraft despatched failed to return to Leeming. At least three were shot down by night fighters of NJG4.

At the 6./NJG4 base at St. Dizier on the night of 11/12 March 1943 Feldwebel Gerhard Rase and his radar operator Unteroffizier Rolf Langhoff and the other German crews went out to their Bf 110 night fighters. Rase and Langhoff were still waiting to achieve their first night Abschuss. On the other hand, their Staffelkapitän, Oberleutnant Hans Autenrieth, was almost into double figures. NJG4 Bf 110 crews had been quite successful on the night of 9/10 March when they destroyed six Viermots over France. Three of them were Lancasters and Oberfeldwebel Reinhard Kollak destroyed two of these. Rase was no doubt anxious to emulate Kollak and his Staffelkapitän and the other high-scoring pilots in the Gruppe. There would be plenty of opportunities because just over 300 Lancasters, Halifaxes and Stirlings were given Stuttgart as their target on 11/12 March. The Main Force would be led by a dozen PFF Lancasters equipped with H2S and sixteen 'backers-up' whose task was to maintain landmark illumination in passing, along the route Châlons-sur-Marne-Bischmiller-Stuttgart-Baden-Baden and return.

At Wyton at 14.30 that afternoon Acting Squadron Leader Norman Mackie DFC on 83 Squadron went to the briefing which was conducted by Wing Commander Gillman the CO. Our target was Stuttgart with zero hour 22.45. The raid was to consist of 300+ heavy bombers (Lancasters, Halifaxes and Stirlings) led by twelve 'Y' aircraft and backed up by sixteen other Pathfinders. The 'Y' aircraft, fitted with the blind-bombing aid H_2S, were each to drop one SBC (small bomb container) of 4lb incendiaries over Baden-Baden on the outward journey and this landmark illumination was to be maintained by the 'backers-up' in passing. On reaching the target the 'Y' aircraft were to mark the aiming point blindly with red TIs at zero -1, releasing sticks of illumination flares at four-second intervals after continuing on the same heading. The 'backers-up' were to aim their green TI's at the aiming point if able to identify it visually by the light of the illumination flares, otherwise at the centre of the concentration of red TI, or, if these had ceased to burn, at the green TI already dropped. The 'backers-up' were to attack at intervals of one or two minutes from zero +1 to zero +22. On the homeward route, aircraft of PFF were again each to drop one SBC of 41b incendiaries at Baden-Baden as a navigational aid to aircraft of the Main Force. The route was Châlons-sur-Marne-Bischmiller-Stuttgart- Baden-Baden-return. The route was straightforward and the met forecast very reasonable. And so we were briefed - not being at all unhappy with the target, as generally speaking, anything in southern Germany was preferable to the Ruhr, Hamburg or the 'Big City'.

Mackie had started his first tour on the Squadron at Scampton in May 1941, completing a total of twenty-three ops on Hampdens before converting to the Manchester on the squadron and finally finishing his tour of 200 hours in March 1942. The award of a DFC was gazetted in May 1942, whilst he was 'on rest' instructing at 29 OTU. Norman rejoined 83 Squadron for a second tour in November 1942. In the meantime, his squadron had been incorporated into the new PFF, flying Lancasters at

Wyton. Norman Mackie vividly recalls his twentieth Lancaster sortie, as a 'backer-up' to Stuttgart on 11/12 March:

'After main briefing we had our usual general crew chat before dispersing either to the sections for a further specialist briefing or back to the mess to rest up before our ops meal of egg and bacon. Our take-off was scheduled for about 20.00 and since I always liked to have plenty of time to dress and so on, I wandered down to the flight in good time. The inevitable chat and wisecracks and then we were aboard the garry for dispersal. Our usual pre-flight external check of the aircraft and a few quick words with the ground crew and we were aboard. My aircraft was ED312 OL-'F for 'Freddie', which had been allocated to us when it arrived new on the squadron in November 1942. We had done thirteen out of our nineteen trips on this aircraft and loved it dearly. However, 'F for Freddie' was in for inspection on this day and since John Hurry, another Squadron Leader pilot on 'A' Flight, was on leave I was given his aircraft ED313 OL-B.

'The rear gunner was usually first in because with his unwieldy electrically heated suit it was a fair struggle before he eventually got comfortable with his four .303 Browning guns. Of all aircrew I reckon the rear gunner required most guts. The turrets were the coldest spots, particularly the rear gunner's position, where temperatures of -40°C could be experienced and frostbite was a common occupational hazard. Also, he was isolated from the rest of the crew and if his intercom failed he could do nothing but wait for someone to come to his rescue and see what the matter was! Ken Chipchase, aged twenty-one and the youngest of the crew was our rear gunner. 'Jock' Lynch, our mid-upper gunner, at thirty was the oldest member of the crew. Flight Sergeant Alexander Lynch had a DFM, which I understood he won by downing a couple of night fighters on his first tour with 144 Squadron.

'So, after settling ourselves and checking with the ground crew that the starter battery was plugged in, we carried out the usual intercom check; but all was not well, there was something wrong with Lew Humber's (Flight Sergeant L. E. J. Humber, WOp) headset in the wireless op's position! After a quick check it was found that his helmet was at fault and there was nothing else but for this to be changed. With a mad dash he was out of the aircraft and on his way to the engineer officer's van to see what could be done. As customary, each aircraft had their own start-up time and knowing which aircraft was immediately ahead, watch was kept usually by the mid-upper gunner with his better all round vision to see when this kite started up - and then we knew it was our turn for sure. However, as engines were bursting into life all around and some started to taxi out it was clear we had missed our scheduled place in the queue. Nevertheless, to save time we started up our engines and did the cockpit checks. So when the flight van was seen tearing back and Humber scrambled aboard the aircraft, the ladder was quickly stowed, door closed and we were taxiing out, the very last as the rest of the squadron were now well on their climb away from base. Some people always wore certain items of clothing on ops and I clearly remember that Lew Humber always wore a forbidding pair of black gloves, which he said brought him luck!

'A quick 'green' from the caravan and we were soon airborne. Unfortunately our route, with pretty straight legs, did not give us much opportunity to cut corners and so it was necessary to pile on 'Merlin' power (as the squadron song went - 'I like Merlin music, good old Merlin music, played by the Rolls-Royce Merlin band') and try to make up time as best we could. This was essential because being a 'backer up' we had to keep the TI's going in the target area for the Main Force, as well as the route-marking at Baden-Baden for others on their way in. The weather had been clear on take-off, but further southeast the cloud became 10/10ths with tops about 8,000 feet over France before quickly breaking up to nil shortly before Châlons-sur-Marne. After sporadic bursts of flak on crossing the French coast, we were flying at about 18,000 feet and in the Châlons-sur-Marne-Nancy-Metz area when we saw three aircraft shot down on our port beam. There was no flak, so clearly fighters were around and I started to weave the aircraft around with our gunners on the alert.

'There was a one third moon and visibility was excellent as the aircraft smoothly purred along at about 180 knots. It seemed so peaceful and on seeing each aircraft go down I can well remember the feeling of most aircrew when they saw the same thing: 'Poor buggers - it can't happen to us!' However, there was another feeling I had that night of being isolated - probably because of the late rake-off and knowing my squadron friends were well ahead of us. Of course, we weren't all that alone as witnessed by the aircraft going down and the Main Force of 300 heavies following the same track behind. As we proceeded we could see small bursts of flak in different areas and the occasional searchlight, but nothing was so near as to cause any concern. Flight Sergeant Barrett (Flight Sergeant W. E. Barrett DFM) was our bomb-aimer and the closer we got to the target the more important his job became. Laying in the nose of the aircraft his task at this time was to assist the navigator, Joe Ogilvie (Flight Lieutenant Allan M. Ogilvie DFC), by map-reading and getting an accurate ground fix if possible. Pre-war, Barrett had been to Germany where he had acquired a Nazi dagger with the inscription Blut und Gott, which he always carried in his flying boot when going on ups.

'Our main target of Stuttgart lay only forty miles from Baden-Baden and the usual searchlights and flak peppering our boys ahead could be seen. The met forecast of 2/10ths to 5/10ths medium cloud at about 18,000 feet and ground haze was fairly accurate. The ground haze, however, was sufficient to prevent accurate pinpointing so, as instructed at briefing, we proceeded to add our green TI to others seen in the target area. The heavy flak, which engaged us, was inaccurate and slight to moderate in intensity, with some light flak hosing up periodically a little way below.

'After bombing we set course for Baden-Baden where with other PFF aircraft we were to deposit our incendiaries to provide route-markers as a navigational aid to aircraft of the Main Force and so prevent them from straying over Karlsruhe or Strasbourg. Furthermore, numerous searchlights were exposed at Karlsruhe and adjacent areas with some intermittent flak, which indicated that some aircraft had already wandered off track and were possibly being harried by night fighters. I could not help thinking it was rather cruel to set fire to an ineffectual little spa town like Baden-Baden but, as Jock Lynch remarked: 'They would at least have some bloody water to put the fires out!'

'Leaving Baden-Baden behind, we set course for Châlons-sur-Marne about 180 miles distant. Contrails had been forecast and we had noticed them in evidence above 17,000 feet, so decided to keep below this height. There was patchy cloud and we were well settled with the occasional gentle weave for the gunners to scan around. Little was being said on the intercom and our thoughts as usual after leaving the target safely were that another op was now thankfully under our belts.

'Even under ideal conditions at night the gunners could see no further than 300 yards or so and now, with the thinnish wisps of alto-stratus, from time to time this distance could be somewhat reduced. However, it was equally to our advantage that any fighters would have similar sighting problems. We now had about eight minutes to run before reaching our turning point at Châlons-sur-Marne and Joe Ogilvie decided to ask if he could take some astro-shots. However, it wasn't far from here that we had seen an aircraft shot down when we were on our way to the target. So I told him that as I wanted to keep a bit of a weave going in what could be a fighter belt, it would be better to delay his wish. Also, one of the engines was running a bit rough with the revs tending to fluctuate from time to time. It was about two minutes after I had refused Joe his astro-shot and I was again glancing at the rev counters when suddenly the aircraft gave a violent shudder as cannon shells thudded into the starboard wing from below, bursting the starboard engine into flames and shaving the canopy, as they whipped by in a reddish stream!

'Almost instinctively, before Jock Lynch yelled, 'Fighter-Fighter, Corkscrew Starboard-Corkscrew Starboard' as he opened fire and the tracer ripped into the metal, I was diving to starboard but not quick enough to avoid being hit. Also, on now seeing the starboard inner engine had caught fire I yelled at the flight engineer (Sergeant Ralph Henderson, a new pilot on the squadron who went on the trip instead of the crew's regular flight engineer, Flight Sergeant Geoff Seaton, to get the feel of ops) to take extinguishing action. At the same time I realized that my dive to starboard was far too steep and on trying to lift the wing up and roll into the corkscrew climb, the ailerons didn't appear to be responding. I then noticed that the flight engineer had mistakenly pulled back the starboard outer throttle and not the starboard inner as he should have done and was about to feather the good engine! There was no time for pleasantry. Knocking his hands away I powered the starboard outer engine to full boost and revs and quickly dealt with the starboard inner myself. I then noticed that all the cowlings had disappeared from the starboard inner engine, which was now enveloped in flames and belching smoke back in the slipstream across the wing. Although feathering had stopped the engine, the prop continued to slowly rotate and the controls felt very spongy. However, the wing had now started to come up and I attempted to continue a corkscrew as best I could. We had originally been flying at 16,000 feet, but with the weave and associated variation in altitude, the first attack caught us a little below this height. Having been briefed on numerous occasions that the German night fighters stuck religiously to their assigned height bands, I decided to dive to about 11,000 feet and hope the change of altitude might lose the fighter. Both gunners had started firing after the first attack commenced and Jock Lynch was trying to give me instructions as to which way to turn so that he could find the fighter. Chipchase had just said he reckoned the fighter was a Me 110 when a second attack developed and tracer was again whistling into and around our aircraft from the starboard quarter. Jock Lynch at the same time yelled 'Corkscrew-Corkscrew; I see the bastard' and the whole aircraft vibrated as he let go with his guns! I was now attempting to throw the aircraft around using my throttles and flying controls as best I could, but the aircraft continued to lose height which I was unable to stop in spite of getting as much power as possible out of the good engines. On this second attack the tracer seemed again to hit the burning starboard inner engine and I well recall thinking that the fighter must be aiming at the flames, which must be so obvious and make us a sitting target whichever way we went. Every cowling now seemed to have disappeared from the starboard inner, as had also the leading edge of the inboard wing. Tongues of flame were licking around No.1 tank, which still had a fair quantity of fuel and there was a horrible acrid smell wafting about in the aircraft.

'Thinking there would be a big explosion at any moment and with recollections of the theory that you might put an engine fire out by diving, I stuck the nose down with some vague hope that this could do the trick. But at 6,000 feet this clearly wasn't working and I levelled out. Jock Lynch was trying to give me instructions so that he could find the fighter, but once again we were attacked from directly underneath and to port. I heard the staccato clunks as more shells whipped into the metal and then heard Jock Lynch saying in his Scottish brogue:

'I think I've got the bastard!' But now the port inner engine was obviously hit in the last attack as it starred to splutter and bang with the revs gyrating all over the place. There was therefore no alternative but to quickly press the fire extinguisher and feather.

Fortunately, Henderson reacted quickly to my instructions and this action was accomplished rather better than before! Realizing that we were now a sitting duck and to prevent any further blind attack developing, I dived down to about 4,000 feet. However, the whole aircraft now started to vibrate badly and although there was smoke and a strong smell of fumes in the aircraft, none of the crew reported any internal fire. My main worry, however, was that the aircraft controls didn't seem to be responding properly and made me think they were badly damaged.

'Up to that point I had given no thought to abandoning the aircraft, but with the fire spreading along the starboard wing and licking around the cockpit together with the fact that the aircraft was rapidly becoming uncontrollable, I suddenly decided THIS IS IT! and I shouted: 'BAIL OUT; BAIL OUT!' An immediate 'Oh my God!' came over the intercom from someone whom I thought was Chipchase. I tried desperately to get the aircraft straight and level for the bail-out, but even with the aileron control hard over we continued in a slow spiral descent. The bomb-aimer, Eric Barrett, was responsible for removing the escape hatch in the floor of the nose of the aircraft, so that he could lead the bale-out followed by the other members of the crew. When he tried to eject it through the opening, it jammed and it took him several moments to free. With Henderson breathing down his neck, he lost no further time in bailing out.

'Being rather occupied trying to prevent the aircraft from sliding further out of control, I hadn't given a thought to baling out myself My parachute was stowed behind my seat and the responsibility for recovery and help in hooking it on to my chest harness lay with the flight engineer. However, when I looked for him I found that he had already departed and someone I thought to be Humber was quickly passing by toward the front. There was no sign of the gunners and not unexpectedly when I called them the intercom seemed to be dead. There being no reply, therefore, I assumed they must have gone out of the main door at the back. At the same time I had the impression that Joe Ogilvie then went by and I yelled out to him to get me my parachute which he went back to do. In fact I can clearly recall him messing around behind my seat to get it. Joe certainly risked his chance of escape and, therefore, his life by spending time in both recovering the parachute and then fitting it on the hooks of my harness. The latter action was no mean feat. Not only was the control column well back (trying to hold the nose up), but with my right arm and shoulder half-raised to hold the aileron control hard over to port, there was little space to get the parachute pack near, let alone on to my chest. I don't know how he managed it but remember that it was a great struggle which seemed to take some time before he had it finally clipped on and then he was gone!

'With Joe away, I was now alone and a most eerie sensation came over me as the slipstream whistled through the open hatches like a banshee and the flames enveloping the starboard side splayed back in a great big gush. I wasn't certain what the aircraft would do as soon as I released the control column and took my feet off the rudder pedals. But obviously it would spin starboard and so I extracted my legs and put them together to the right of the control column, slammed the throttles back to even any torque and simultaneously let go of the aileron control which was hard over to port. I then started to slide feet-first down into the well, but having forgotten to take my helmet off I found my head jerked back by the oxygen and intercom connections. However, lightning couldn't have been quicker as I pushed the helmet off and let my feet continue heading toward the void of the open hatch. As I suspected the aircraft had started a violent gyration to starboard and I was propelled through the opening into the night air.

'Before I left I knew my altitude was about 2,500 feet and so I didn't waste time before pulling the rip-cord and then suddenly, a jerk and I was just dangling in space.

It was pitch black but I could see the canopy above and wondered if I could manoeuvre myself. But on pulling the lines all I seemed to do was lift myself up to the side as opposed to the canopy spilling out air and my sliding in the direction I wanted. Suddenly I saw a big fireball explosion, which I assumed was the aircraft exploding some distance away. Other than this I couldn't see anything below, but all of a sudden my feet and body were carving their way through trees before coming to an unexpected halt and I was hanging in mid-air. My immediate thought was to get out of my harness and so I twisted and banged the release knob. Unfortunately, I hadn't thought of judging how far I was off the ground, which I couldn't see, but soon realized it had been higher than I imagined when my legs struck the ground and a stab of pain shot through my thigh.'

Norman Mackie's Lancaster had been shot down by Feldwebel Gerhard Rase and his radar operator Unteroffizier Rolf Langhoff, a Bf 110 crew with 6./NJG4 who claimed ED313 OL-B destroyed as their first combat victory. Langhoff died in air combat over Châlons-sur-Marne on 16/17 April 1943, whereas Feldwebel Rase survived the war with four Abschüsse to his credit. Their unit, operating from St. Dizier, had a field day on 11/12 March 1943, with nine crews claiming nine heavies destroyed, plus two probables. In all, eleven Bomber Command aircraft failed to return from the Stuttgart raid, plus two crashed on return in England. Oberleutnant Hans Autenrieth, Staffelkapitän of 6./NJG4 recalls:

'According to a special report of our Geschwader we achieved our greatest success up till that time on the night of 11/12 March, being credited with nine definitive and two probable kills. I personally flew two sorties, which was something we only did very infrequently and scored my tenth kill, a Short Stirling at 0018, which crashed three kilometres southwest of Châlons-sur-Marne [BF469 BU-M on 214 Squadron, Pilot Officer Alexander Carruthers RCAF who was an American and his crew died]. Other successful NJG4 pilots who were mentioned in the special report were Hauptmann Otto Materne, Oberleutnant Hans-Karl Kamp, Oberleutnant Kornacker, Leutnants Jakob Schaus and Wilhelm Engels, Oberfeldwebel Reinhard Kollak and Feldwebel Rase. The remains of this Lancaster were damaged but recognizable and were sought out and photographed by Feldwebel Rase and myself a few days later. None of the Lancaster crew could be found at the site of the crash, so we assumed that they had bailed out by parachute and subsequently escaped capture. Possibly, however, the dead crew members had been recovered and buried by the Recovery Team from the local Luftwaffe airfield sector. The operational units were never tasked with these duties. It was the policy in those days to keep our flying personnel away from the crash sites until any victims had been recovered and taken away. Understandably, one wanted to spare the crews from the sight of the often gruesome scenes at these crash sites!'

As for Norman Mackie's adventures after being shot down, he went on to extract his parachute from the trees and bury it. Nearby, at Sogny-en-l'Angle (Marne), 37 kilometres southwest of Châlons-sur-Marne, his Lancaster had crashed in flames. Ralph Henderson and Joe Ogilvie managed to escape capture, returning to the UK on 6 June 1943. Barrett and Humber were taken prisoner. Lynch and Chipchase were killed and laid to rest in Sogny-en-l'Angle. Following his evasion and safe return to England, Henderson was awarded the DFM on 23 July 1943. As captain of Lancaster JB424, he and his crew were all killed in action during a Berlin raid exactly four months later, on 22/23 November. Mackie was captured by a Wehrmacht patrol on the second night after baling out and was imprisoned alone in a room adjoining their control post with his flying boots removed. Undaunted, he managed to force a boarded-up window and to escape without raising alarm. With the help of various French Resistance fighters, Norman reached Switzerland in early April. At first, he was imprisoned in the Prison de St. Antoine, Geneva, but was later released and classed as an Internee. During the second half of 1943 he worked for the British Air Attaché, before making a clandestine departure from Switzerland on 6 December 1943. In the company of Captain Jeff Morphew SAAF (a fighter pilot who had flown Tomahawks in the Western Desert before becoming a PoW in Italy and escaping to Switzerland in March), the two men escaped through France to reach Spain on 20 December. A short spell of imprisonment followed in Figueras, but eventually Norman was released, safely reaching England via Gibraltar on 17 January 1944. He briefly served as Lancaster Flying Instructor at PFF NTU before he was appointed as Squadron Leader Flight Commander to form a new LNSF Mosquito Squadron, 571, in 8 Group on 23 April 1944. He went on to complete another forty ops, being awarded a DSO before he was finally rested from operational flying in December 1944.

On 12/13 March 1943 the target for 457 aircraft (158 Wellingtons, 156 Lancasters, 91 Halifaxes and 42 Stirlings and ten Mosquitoes, the latter acting as Path Finder markers) was Essen. The weather was good and the pathfinders were using the new 'Oboe'[93] technique of marking the target with special flares dropped by the Mosquitoes, directly controlled by radio beams from England. Crews learned the next day that 23 aircraft, five per cent of the force, some 140 aircrew, were missing. Oberleutnant Manfred Meurer of 3./NJG1 claimed two Halifaxes, a Lancaster and a Wellington to take his score to 23 Abschüsse. Leutnant Oskar Köstler of 10./NJG1 claimed two Wellingtons and a Lancaster to take his score to five victories. Hauptmann Wilhelm Dormann of 9./NJG1, a pre-war Lufthansa pilot destroyed a Stirling to take his score to four Abschüsse. Oberleutnant Horst Pause of Stab I/NJG1 flying Bf 110G-4 4882 was shot down and killed by return fire from a Stirling on 15 Squadron at Lachären, 21 kilometres northeast of Hertogenbosch. He had four Abschüsse.

The night following there was no Main Force activity and 51 Wellingtons and seventeen Lancasters carried out minelaying in areas between Lorient and the Kattegat. Two Wellingtons claimed by Unteroffizier Robert Karl Franz of 10./NJG5 and 23-year old Oberleutnant Paul Anton Guido Zorner of 2./NJG3 and a Lancaster on 9 Squadron (ED494) piloted by American Warrant Officer Howard Clark Lewis RCAF failed to return. There were no survivors on any of the aircraft. Zorner, born Paul Zloch at Roben bei Leobschütz Schlesien in Upper Silesia (now Poland) on 31 March 1920, had joined the Luftwaffe in October 1938. After flying Ju 52 transports between Sicily and North Africa he had begun night fighter training in October 1941. In July 1942 he joined 2./NJG2 flying Ju 88s, making his first attack on the night of 17 August over Holland. By the end of September he had made six more attacks with the Ju 88 and then changed to the Dornier 217 and went to Grove at Jutland. He made a further six attacks with the Do 217 but it was too 'clumsy' for a night fighter, though it could stay in the air for five hours. On 17 January 1943 he shot down a Halifax over the Friesian Islands. In March he made attacks on American bombers; on one attack he was shot up and had to make an emergency landing. Zorner returned to night fighting and it was after 38 attacks that he shot down his second Halifax (his 11th Abschüsse), on 24/25 July, though he was hit by return fire and he and his bordfunker Oberfeldwebel Heinrich Wilke had to bail out. Wilke received the Knight's Cross of the Iron Cross on 6 December 1944. Paul Zorner would finish the war with the Knight's Cross of the Iron Cross with Oak Leaves.

On 13/14 March also Ju 88C-6 C9+FU in 10/NJG5 piloted by Unteroffizier Karl Robert Franz was shot down by return fire from Wellington III BK516 on 300 Squadron before the Polish Wimpy went down to Franz's guns. Franz was killed and his Ju-88 crashed into the English Channel fifty kilometres north of Morlaix-Bretagne. Sergeant Tadeusz Kuzminski the captain of the Wellington and his crew perished also.

Wellington III BK296 on 420 'Snowy Owl' Squadron RCAF flown by Flight Sergeant Charles Harrison Tidy RCAF was claimed by Oberleutnant Zorner three kilometres north of Nordeney for his sixth Abschüsse. Tidy and his crew were killed. Oberleutnant Martin Drewes of 7./NJG3 claimed a Halifax at Store Heddinge on 14/15 March for his second Abschüsse. Halifax II DT620 on 138 Squadron was one of three that was lost on SOE/SIS operations from Tempsford that night. It crashed southeast of Koge in Denmark with the loss of Flight Sergeant Leslie Rowland Smith's crew. A fourth Halifax crashed at Fawley in Buckinghamshire.

On the night of 24/25 March Oberleutnant Dietrich 'Dieter' Schmidt's name appeared on the 8./NJG1 battle order for a different type of mission:

'During 1942-43 the British often penetrated with single, low flying aircraft over Holland to drop sabotage equipment, weapons and at times secret agents, to aid the Resistance. Dutch liaison people called in the material by radio and three or four simple lamps marked the dropping zones. For some time the Abwehr had succeeded in turning the whole thing around and the radio traffic was now almost completely controlled by German posts. Thus, the material, including the agents, could be collected immediately at the dropping zone. In order to make sure that the whole game looked real we received orders from time to time to shoot down one of the Special Operations machines. The whole exercise was difficult for us insofar as it was hard to track down machines by radar because of their low flying height. These sorties were relatively unattractive for the 'old hands'. For us 'young hands' however, they were a welcome practice. We were briefed on the place and time of the established drop and we take off as soon as the intruder was confirmed.

'Shortly after midnight, as expected, the radio connection with the Jägerleitoffizier (JLO, or GCI controller) faded out relatively soon. The last message we received was that the aircraft was homeward bound at a height of 200 metres. We proceeded at a height of one hundred metres in the direction of the Zuider Zee and beneath us - the night is not too dark - we saw the newly reclaimed land to the east of the Zuider Zee. Then suddenly my bordfunker discovered him above - definitely four-engined. I sneaked up on him from behind. A short burst in the left wing. I could see hits registering but despite the low-level, at which we flew, he immediately peeled off to the right and levelled off just over the water. I could only continue to chase him because of a fire in his left engine, the glow of which reflected on the water. Immediately after everything was dark. Over and out? A red Very light, which a few minutes later was fired into the sky from the spot, confirmed that it had crashed.

'Therefore we were deeply disappointed when on our return at the Operations Room we were greeted with the news that the intruder's outward flight had been reported over Northern Holland. Empty handed again! I gathered that I had, out of inexperience and for fear of detection, opened fire at much too long a range and with far too short a burst! With the obvious mixed feelings we drove to our quarters and tried to sleep. At dawn the phone rudely awakened me:

'My congratulations on your first kill.'

'Are you trying to pull my leg?' On the other end of the line was my friend Werner Rapp, who was duty officer and still in the Operations Room. He informed me that the crew of seven had been picked up in their dinghy between Enkhuizen and Stavoren. So the aircraft did crash! The report on the outward-bound machine was a second enemy aircraft.'

Schmidt's first victory was Halifax HR665 NF-L on 138 Squadron that had taken off from Tempsford for dropping at three different DZs. Flying Officer E. Clow RNZAF was at the controls and on board were two secret agents, Gerbrands (code-name 'St. John') and Bergman ('St. Andrew') and containers with supplies for the Dutch

Resistance ('Leeks 5/Catarrh II'). Two containers were successfully dropped near Limmen 25 kilometres northwest of Amsterdam and then Clow set course for Friesland to drop the two agents. While flying low over the Zuider Zee they were hit in the left wing by Schmidt's gunfire at 0036 hours. Bergman was killed by the burst of fire and the aircraft was so heavily damaged that Clow had to ditch in the sea east of Enkhuizen. The crew managed to escape from the aircraft before it sank and set sail in their dinghy but were soon picked up by the Germans. A second SD Halifax, on 138 Squadron, flown by Flying Officer Rutledge successfully made two drops in Holland, at 'Lettuce 10' and 'Parsnip 5' before returning to Tempsford.

On 26 March RAF Bomber Command went back to the Ruhr, this time to Duisburg and then, they were briefed for Berlin on 27 March. There were 396 aircraft going. Post war analysis showed that the raid on Berlin that night was a failure. The pathfinders marked two areas but they were short of their aiming points by five miles. Consequently, none of the bombs came within five miles of the target area in the centre of the city. Out of 396 aircraft despatched nine were missing.

Nachtjagd scored 96 victories during March 1943. These included eighteen by III./NJG1 and nine by I./NJG1. On the night of 29/30 March, when 329 aircraft of Bomber Command raided Berlin, 21 aircraft - eighteen of which were shot down by 'Himmelbett'- operating night-fighters over the Netherlands and Germany, failed to return. One of the losses was Lancaster I W4327 UV-S on 460 Squadron RAAF flown by Flight Lieutenant K. H. Grenfell RAAF which was shot down by Unteroffizier Christian Koltrinmger of 7/NJG1, an Austrian born in Salzburg, for his third and final Abschüsse. He and his bordfunker Unteroffizier Willi Voght were killed when the Bf 110F-4 was hit by fire from the rear turret gunner, Sergeant Sidney George Webb who at least had the satisfaction of sending the Messerschmitt 110 down to crash at Kloosterhaar before he died.

A total of 149 'Oboe'-guided Wellingtons bombed Bochum; twelve Wellingtons failed to return. Major Lent shot down Wellington BJ762 on 426 'Thunderbird' Squadron flown by American Flight Sergeant Richard Earl Todd RCAF at Nije-Mirdum. Todd and two of this crew were killed. Two others were taken prisoner. Feldwebel Vinke claimed Wellington III X3965 on 166 Squadron flown by Sergeant Owen Eastwood Collins RNZAF. There were no survivors. Major Werner Streib Geschwaderkommodore of NJG1 who on 26 February had been awarded the Oak Leaves to his Knights Cross for 42 confirmed victories, claimed Wellington X HE545 on 166 Squadron piloted by Pilot Officer James Robert Arthur Hodgson, which went down near Deelen airfield with the loss of the crew. Oberleutnant Martin Bauer of I./NJG1 claimed Wellington MS484 on 420 'Snowy Owl' Squadron, which went down near Wanrooy with the loss of all on Flying Officer Bruce Angus Grant RCAF's crew. III./NJG1 claimed nine Wellingtons, five Lancasters and a Halifax destroyed. Leutnant August 'Gustel' Geiger, Staffelkapitän, 7./NJG1 flying Bf 110G-4 G9+ER and guided by 'Himmelbett' box 'Krote' ('Toad') over the Dutch-German border was the night's top-scoring pilot with five victories in two sorties. At 2252 hours he shot down Wellington X HE182 on 431 'Iroquois' Squadron RCAF near Ahaus. The skipper, Sergeant Ernest Joseph Aspden and all except one of his crew were killed. At 2315 hours Wellington HE385 on 196 Squadron went down near Barchem. Flying Officer Edward Richard Culff and his crew were killed. On his second sortie of the night at 0347 hours Geiger destroyed Halifax II BE244 on 51 Squadron, which was returning from Berlin and it spun in at Vorden with the loss of all of Flying Officer Raymond George Harris' crew. At 0427 hours this was followed by Lancaster ED596 on 106 Squadron at Delden. Squadron Leader Eric Lewis Hayward DFC and crew were killed. Seventeen minutes later Geiger shot down Lancaster I W4327 on 460 Squadron RAAF, which crashed at Kloosterharr in Holland with the loss of Flight

Lieutenant Kenneth Hugh Grenfell RAAF and his crew. These victories took Geiger's score to nineteen.

During April 1943 Nachtjagd claimed 161 bombers destroyed in the 'Himmelbett' system. At least eighteen of these were by IV./NJG1 at Leeuwarden, thirteen by I./NJG1 at Venlo, five by III./NJG1 at Twente and three by II./NJG1 at St. Trond. Essen was bombed by 348 aircraft on 3/4 April for the loss of fourteen Halifaxes and nine Lancasters. Four victories were credited to IV./NJG1. Oberleutnant Eckart-Wilhelm 'Hugo' von Bonin, Staffelkapitän 6./NJG1 downed Lancaster ED694 on 9 Squadron at Stevensbeek in Holland. Pilot Officer William Hallewell Swire and his crew were killed. I./NJG1 destroyed a Lancaster and four Halifaxes, three of them by Gruppen Kommandeur Major Werner Streib, including DT808 on 405 'Vancouver' Squadron RCAF, which came down at Vierlingsbeek. The skipper, Warrant Officer William James McAlpine RCAF and his crew were killed. Hauptmann Herbert Lütje, Staffelkapitän 8./NJG1 claimed Lancaster ED334 on 83 Squadron at 2245 hours at Winterswijk and Halifax DT617 on 419 'Moose' Squadron RCAF at 2337 hours, the aircraft coming down at Olst. Squadron Leader Frank Thompson Flower and crew were killed, as were Flying Officer Peter Delamere Boyd's. Leutnant August 'Gustel' Geiger and Unteroffizier Emil Henzelmann both of III./NJG1 destroyed an unidentified Lancaster at Gemen and Halifax II DT795 NP-N on 158 Squadron at 2350 respectively; the aircraft crashing at Wapenveld. Twenty-six year old American Warrant Officer Frederick Henry Blake RCAF and crew were killed. Blake, who was from Oregon, left a widow, Barbara. Henzelmann was killed on 13/14 December 1944 after a failed belly landing during a practice flight after an engine fire.

On the night of 4/5 April, 577 bombers were dispatched to Kiel and twelve aircraft failed to return. NJG3 'manning' the 'Himmelbett' in northwest Germany and Denmark claimed six kills. Nineteen bombers were lost on the Duisburg raid of 8/9 April from a force of 392 aircraft. Only one was shot down by a night-fighter. Another eight Lancasters failed to return from a force of 104 Lancasters and five Mosquitoes that went to Duisburg on 9/10 April. IV./NJG1 destroyed five Lancasters. Three of these were credited to Oberfeldwebel Heinz Vinke of 11./NJG1. ED554 on 207 Squadron at Langar piloted by Sergeant Harold Arthur Healey RCAF went down at Jisp at 2242 with the loss of all the crew. ED566 on 9 Squadron at Waddington piloted by 22-year old Sergeant Arthur Roy Hobbs, husband of Gladys Mary at Boultham went down in the North Sea at 2345 hours fifty kilometres west of Castricum with the loss of all the crew who are commemorated at Runnymede.

ED724 on 103 Squadron, which Oberfeldwebel Vinke claimed destroyed over the North Sea west of Alkmaar at 0014 was flown back to England by Flight Lieutenant E. G. Bickers with the body of the rear gunner, Sergeant Richard Herbert Howell in his turret. Attempting to land near Bodney airfield, the bomber was wrecked but there were no injuries. ED502, another 9 Squadron Lancaster, came down at 2345 hours at Snelrewaard near Utrecht. There were no survivors on the crew skippered by 23-year old Warrant Officer Arthur Mills White RNZAF who was from Waikato, New Zealand. The crew are buried at Oudewater Protestant Cemetery. Major Werner Streib of I./NJG1 claimed Lancaster ED806 on 9 Squadron at Nistelrode. Twenty-four year old Pilot Officer Arthur Frederick Paramore, a married man from Fishponds and his crew were killed. Oberst Werner Streib would score 67 Nachtjagd Abschüsse (including thirty Viermots) in 150 sorties with NJG1.

Leutnant Oskar Köstler and Unteroffizier Heinz Huhn were ordered off from Bergen in a Bf 110G-4 for a patrol in 'Himmelbett' box 'Hering'. Köstler and original bordfunker Unteroffizier Voller were one of the newly-trained Nachtjagd crews posted to 10./NJG1 in the Netherlands in the summer of 1942. They operated from

Leeuwarden and its satellite Bergen/Alkmaar airfields, claiming their first victory on 1/2 March 1943. Within five weeks they were aces with two Wellingtons and two Lancasters destroyed, plus a B-17 in daylight on 4 March. Voller had fallen ill early in April and was replaced by Huhn, whose two previous pilots were killed in action. Huhn recorded his experiences on 9/10 April in his diary:

'Almost cloudless, moon, take-off at 2150. To begin with flying on radio beacon. After an hour, at last, contact with Lichtenstein at 2.2 kilometres. Köstler: I have him at 200 metres distance'. Sitting below him. Halifax or Lancaster at forty metres. I have to call out the speed. At last! Attack! The cannons start firing. Suddenly a blow from ahead, bright as day, boiling hot. What was that? Have we been hit? No, Tommy's exploding. Splinters rain onto our machine. We are burning. In front of me flames, a bright flood. We are going down. Heat is beating into my face. Leutnant Köstler is silent. I reach for the cockpit roof jettison lever. Helmet is singed; have to close eyes. At last the handle! Roof flies away. I rise up and shove myself off. Get away. Machine going down, burning. I somersault, cannot find the rip-cord. At last, a jerk, I float. Around me burning parts. I find that I am over water. Unlock parachute safety catch. I believe to be carried further out to sea, so I pull the parachute lines. Parachute collapses, falls. Icy cold, hands freezing. I notice that I'm drifting towards land. How high might I be? Attack was at 5500 metres, jumped at 5000? I reach for the signal pistol but it is not secured and my hands are almost rigidly stiff.

'Am over land ... pain, hang uncomfortably in the 'chute. Hands are stiff and without feeling. I had lost my boots during the jump. Bright patch below me. A lake? Would I drown in a puddle after all this? But I'm still very high. Swinging violently. At last the earth is coming up towards me. Woods, trees. Splintering, I am hanging between two trees. Helpless. No strength left and my hands frozen stiff. Parachute straps cutting into my flesh. Must wait until my hands have warmed. Pain. At last feeling returns to my fingers. I swing myself towards a tree trunk, am about four-five metres above ground. I grip the trunk. Release straps! Won't work. Lock frozen? With a final effort I clamber a little higher. Fortunately there is a branch which gives support, otherwise no strength left and fall down. Not to break my neck now, after all this! A little higher. Straps loosening at last. Chest straps are free but leg straps still pulling me upwards. A little higher still. At last the leg straps are released too. Climb, slide, fall down the trunk. Moss at the bottom. Dinghy off. I feel faint. Struggle up. Limbs unharmed. Signal pistol and torch still there. Have three red cartridges left. Must not use them senselessly.

'Start walking through the forest. Fall down again, get up, stumble, lose signal pistol, search for it and find it again. Move on. Feet cold, socks wet through the damp ground. Face burning, skin singed. Find a track, then past a meadow, finally a good road. Tread on sharp metal fragments of the Tommy lying around on the road everywhere. March on, pass a lone building. Fire one red. See no telephone wire in the bright light, so carry on. After an hour a railway crossing. Change direction and follow the rails. Painful for the feet due to sharp stones. Half an hour's laborious tramping along the rails. No signal cabin. Suddenly a noise behind me: a train. Load the last red cartridge. A shot in front of the engine. Brakes squeal. Train stops. Flash SOS. Freight train. Have to identify myself, get aboard. Face burning, eyebrows crusted over. Try to phone from next station. No connection. Continue on train to Harderwijk. Get out there. At the unit there I hear: Leutnant Köstler dead. Call Bergen: they think I'm a ghost as I had been reported dead. Karl Vinke had shot down three this night. Then into sick quarters. Eat, ointment on the forehead, sleep. In the morning I was taken to the crash site. Had spoken during the night with Hauptmann Heinrich Ruppel [Raumführer Ruppel had been a pilot on the Western Front in WWI and he was acknowledged to be one of the most skilful fighter controllers in Nachtjagd] and made my report. At crash site. Bits from the Tommy strewn around for miles. Pieces of bodies everywhere. At the crash site of our machine also bits everywhere. Must have exploded in the air. Leutnant Köstler with open parachute dead beside the wreckage. Only the bloody head is put into the coffin. Then a car arrives from Leeuwarden to fetch the coffin. I go with it.'

There were no survivors on Flight Sergeant John David Steele RCAF's 101 Squadron crew when Lancaster III ED618 exploded at 2243 hours. Leutnant Oskar Köstler and Unteroffizier Heinz Huhn's Bf 110 crashed a few kilometres further north at Elburg.

On 10/11 April a force of 502 Lancasters, Halifaxes, Stirlings and Wellingtons were detailed for a raid on Frankfurt. Twenty-two aircraft failed to return, ten of these losses due to crews of NJG4. Hauptmann Wilhelm Herget, Kommandeur, I./NJG4 claimed his sixteenth night kill when he downed Wellington X HE652 on 426 Squadron flown by Pilot Officer John Henry Sammet RCAF at Virelles (Hainaut). There were no survivors. Halifax II DT806 on 35 Squadron flown by Flying Officer G. F. Lambert was shot down by Leutnant Helmut Bergmann of Stab III./NJG4 for his sixth confirmed kill. The aircraft crashed at Fleigneux, Luxembourg. Lambert and all his crew were killed. Halifax II JB871 'V-Victor' on 76 Squadron flown by Flight Lieutenant Arthur Horace Hull was at about 15,000 feet near Hirson (Aisne) in Belgium when glowing balls of tracer streamed out of the darkness behind and the port wing flooded with fire as the tanks went up. They had been attacked by Stabs Feldwebel Walter Piwarz of 3./NJG4 who claimed his first victory. Hull said quite calmly, 'Bail out! Bail out!' He held 'Victor' steady and the crew and Group Captain John Rene Whitley the station commander of RAF Linton on Ouse, who was along for the ride, clipped on their parachutes and crawled to the hatches. Hull was later found dead in the cockpit. But his sacrifice had not been in vain. Whitley and three of the crew evaded and three were injured but alive and were taken into captivity. (Piwarz was killed on 14/15 October 1944; shot down northwest of Gütersloh by a Mosquito on 85 Squadron piloted by Squadron Leader B. A. Burbank).

Stirling III BK760 on 7 Squadron flown by 32-year old Squadron Leader Humphrey William Albert Chesterman AFC had arrived over fifteen minutes early over the target and was immediately hit several times by flak but the crew continued with their attack and bombed the target from 17,000 feet. Returning home they were then hit over the village of Bree by Major Walter Ehle of Stab II./NJG1 who claimed the bomber as his 19th Abschüsse of the war. The Stirling crashed at 0345 hours, one kilometre south west of Tongelo. The skipper and four of his crew were killed and two evaded.

Nachtjagd lost two Bf 110s of NJG1 and two Do 217s of NJG4 and three crews, at least two due to accidents. Halifax II DT775 'F-Freddie' on 78 Squadron at Linton on Ouse was caught by a night fighter from below and it crashed in a field in Eastern France, where it burned out. Warrant Officer Jack Adams and five of his crew bailed out safely and all were taken into captivity. Sergeant Joe Enwright, a married man with a small daughter, was killed by cannon fire and his body was found near the remains of his rear turret the next day. Of the ten crews on 78 Squadron who returned to Linton on Ouse from Frankfurt, six were shot down on ops 16 April-15 July 1943.

On the night of 14/15 April Stuttgart was the destination for 462 Wellingtons, Halifaxes, Lancasters and Stirlings. Twenty-four bombers failed to return. Nachtjäger claimed seventeen Viermots. Among the claimants were Hauptmann Heinrich Wolters of Stab IV.NJG4 with a Stirling and two Halifaxes. Oberleutnant Rudolf Altendorf of 2./NJG4 claimed a Stirling and a Halifax for his 10th and 11th Abschüsse. Hauptmann Hans-Karl Kamp of 7./NJG4 claimed a Wellington and a Halifax. Leutnant Helmut Bergmann of Stab III/NJG4 claimed a Wellington and a Halifax. Stirling III BF462 on 90 Squadron captained by Pilot Officer R. J. Beldin was attacked by a Bf 110 and a Ju 88 and was claimed shot down by Hauptmann Otto Materne of 4./NJG4 for his second

Abschuss. Beldin was the only survivor. Materne went on to claim a further three Abschüsse before he was killed on 6 September 1944. Major Kurt Holler of Stab NJG4 claimed a Stirling and a Wellington for his 10th and 11th victories. Holler destroyed another Stirling south of Sedan two nights later. On 22 June he destroyed a Wellington for his 18th and final Abschuss when his Bf 110E-2 was hit, presumably by return fire and he was killed. His bordfunker, Feldwebel Robert Gotha was wounded but survived after bailing out. Flight Lieutenant 'Ben' Benson DFC and Flight Lieutenant 'Brandy' Brandon DFC on 157 Squadron in Mosquito NF.II DD739 destroyed a Do 217 at Layer Breta Heath for their third victory. On the night of 3/4 July they shot down another Dornier at Sint Trond for their fourth victory. Do 217N-1 G9+HN was flown by 28-year old Oberleutnant Hans Helmut Fuchs of 4/NJG1 who was killed.

On 16/17 April 327 Lancasters and Halifaxes were detailed to bomb the important Skoda armaments factory at Pilzen in Czechoslovakia. Thirty-seven aircraft failed to return. A force of 271 bombers bombed the AG Farben Industrie on the banks of the Rhine at Mannheim-Ludwigshafen. Bombing was reasonably concentrated causing extensive damage but clear conditions made it ideal for the single-engined fighters. Twenty-four aircraft failed to return, one Wimpy was abandoned over Surrey and two other aircraft crashed on return. Nachtjäger claimed 35 Viermots destroyed. Leutnant Norbert Pietrek of 2./NJG4, who had completed his night-fighter pilot training in January, returned to Florennes airfield in southern Belgium in his Bf 110F-4 with claims for two bombers, the first of which, was a Lancaster. Pietrek and Otto Bauchens his bordfunker had been ordered to patrol in 'Himmelbett' box 'Kater' ('Tomcat') near their airfield. Pietrek chased the Lancaster until it crashed into a hill on the banks of the River Meuse. As he headed for a radio beacon Bauchens tried to make radio contact with Oberleutnant Brockmüller their Jägerleitoffizier (JLO, or GCI-controller) but jamming prevented the bordfunker from re-establishing contact. Nonethless Pietrek, open-mouthed, unexpectedly spotted an enormous 'barn door'. It was a Stirling.

'A for Apple' on 214 Squadron. flown by Flying Officer D. E. James RCAF had taken off from Chedburgh at 2150. While flying at 9,000 feet in bright moonlight and good visibility just south of Ste-Quentin a Bf 110 was seen approaching on the starboard beam at the same level as the Stirling at a range of 800 to 1,000 yards. James immediately began corkscrewing, starting with a diving turn to starboard and, shortly afterwards, Sergeant Eric Markham Lee, the rear gunner, reported a 110 coming in to attack from astern. Almost at once the Bf 110 was seen attacking from the port beam and level. The 110 opened fire and hit the wings of the Stirling, apparently with no serious effects but it seems probable that the turret hydraulics may have been damaged as the rear turret became unserviceable after a 2-3 second burst had been fired. Lee was dead. James jettisoned his bombs and continued evasive action, picking up speed by diving and at times the Stirling reached a speed of 300mph. The 110 opened fire at 800 yards and then came in very close, almost colliding with the Stirling. A stream of bullets passed through the window between James and the navigator; the mid-upper turret was damaged and the centre section and rest position riddled. The intercom and all electrical services failed. The mid-upper gunner fired all his ammunition in two or three long bursts. Pietrek pressed home his attacks and fired many bursts of tracer and HE shells at the Stirling. A-Apple's Nos. 5 and 6 starboard wing tanks were holed and petrol was leaking out and there was a fire beyond the starboard outer engine with burning petrol coming from the trailing edge of the wing. Two engines were out of action. Pietrek and Otto Bauchens were completely exhausted and the Stirling was no longer a threat so Pietrek broke off. It was thought by the crew that it was because the night-fighter was out of ammunition but it was quite clear to Pietrek that the 'Tommy' would not make it home. Sure enough, it got as far as Crèvecoeur-le-Grand in the Oise and James gave the order to abandon the aircraft. Two of the crew were taken prisoner but James and four others evaded capture and returned to England. Pietrek's claim was confirmed but he did not receive confirmation for the Lancaster that crashed. It had come down in the area of a neighbouring 'Himmelbett' box and was awarded to another fighter pilot who claimed a Lancaster in the area around that time.

Sergeant S. T. 'Tom' Wingham, bomb-aimer on Sergeant Dave Hewlett's Halifax II crew on 102 Squadron at Pocklington, Yorkshire, flew his 16th op on 20/21 April when the moon was still full so it was with some trepidation that he realized, from the petrol and bomb loads, that he was in for another long trip. All told 339 aircraft were to visit Stettin, an 8½ hour round trip, while 85 Stirlings were despatched to bomb the Heinkel factory near Rostock. Wingham recalled that: 'With briefing came enlightenment. Bomber Command had come up with a new plan to beat the German GCI - a low-level trip.' His Halifax climbed on take-off and crossed the North Sea at 10,000 feet, reaching the Danish coast near Esbjerg where they descended to 700 feet. 'Now began one of the most exhilarating trips I took part in as 350 heavy bombers streamed across Denmark between 400 and 700 feet. Lying in the nose map reading did feel a bit hairy as we were constantly being hit by the slipstream from other unseen aircraft. In the brilliant moonlight all the ground detail was clear and Danes came out of their houses flashing torches and waving. Occasionally, a little light flak came up to port or starboard as aircraft strayed off course or the sky was lit up as an aircraft hit the deck. We continued low level across the Baltic doing a cruise among the islands until, on our last leg with the North German coast on our starboard, we climbed to a bombing height of 14,000 feet. As we approached the target, Stettin was well alight and in the glare from the fires below and the brilliant moonlight. It was like carrying out an aircraft recognition test. It was the first time I had seen FW 190s and Me 109s as well as 110s and Ju 88s, all clearly visible flitting about among the silhouettes of Lancs and Halifaxes. Somehow we were not singled out for attention as we went in and bombed. Immediately after completing the bomb run we dived for the deck and went out the same way we had come.

'For such a long-range target, over 600 miles from England and well outside the range of 'Oboe' it was probably the most successful raid during the Battle of the Ruhr. There were a lot of very tired pilots when we got home. We still lost between 6-7%, which was the going rate for the job, so presumably Harris felt there was nothing to be gained by repeating the exercise. As far as I know this was a one-off and the tactic was never used again on such a large scale.'

Altogether, 21 aircraft - thirteen Lancasters, seven Halifaxes and one Stirling - failed to return from Stettin. NJG3 was credited with twelve and NJG5 with another six confirmed victories. Flight Lieutenant Charles Woodbine Parish was killed when he was shot down over Denmark by Unteroffizier Berg of 7./NJG3 at Kastrup who claimed the 7 Squadron Stirling as a 'Boeing' on the operation to Stettin. It was the RAF pilot's 54th operation of the war. Five Lancasters and three Halifaxes were claimed shot down by Nachtjäger crews who also claimed five of the eight Stirlings lost from the 86 sent to bomb the Heinkel factory at Rostock. Stirling III BF506 AA-P on 75 Squadron RNZAF which crashed at Boegballe in Denmark was shot down by Oberfeldwebel Rudolf Manglesdorf of 12./NJG3. Pilot Officer Alan Gray Tolley RNZAF and crew were killed. Manglesdorf ended the war with ten Abschüsse.

As was usual on nights when the heavies were operating, the German defences could expect 'night nuisance' raids on Berlin and other targets as a diversion for the Main Force operations, but on 20/21 April Mosquito operations were also designed to 'celebrate' Hitler's birthday. Mosquito light bomber and night-fighter versions were a thorn in the side of the German air defence and usually the Bf 110 and Ju 88, the standard night-fighter types then in Nachtjagd service, lacked the speed to successfully intercept the 'Wooden Wonder'. An exception was on 19/20 April, when there were no Main Force operations and Major Helmut Lent, Kommandeur IV./NJG1 claimed to be the second Nachtjagd pilot to destroy a Mosquito (NF.II DZ694 on 410 Squadron) whilst flying a standard Bf 110.[94] Guided by Leutnant Lübke, Jägerleitoffizier of 'Himmelbett' box 'Eisbär' ('Polar Bear') at Sondel, Northern Holland, Lent power-dived onto the Mosquito west of Stavoren from superior altitude and at 500 kph fired a burst of cannon shells at the 'Wooden Wonder'. Flight Sergeant W. J. Reddie and his navigator Sergeant K. Evans who were on a Night Fighting Patrol over Holland were killed. Lent was noted for experimenting with new methods of attack. He would practice and perfect a diving attack, which would give him sufficient speed to overtake a Mosquito and shoot it down. For being one of the first German pilots to overcome this versatile aircraft he received special praise from Göring. Lent eventually rose to the rank of Oberst with a position of high command in the night fighter arm. He would achieve 102 night-victories and eight day-victories before being killed in a flying accident on 5 October 1944. The experiment was repeated the following night, this time with Oberleutnant Lothar Linke, Staffelkapitän 12./NJG1 in the leading role when nine Mosquitoes of 105 Squadron and two of 139 Squadron led by the CO, Wing Commander Peter Shand DSO DFC in DZ386 with Pilot Officer Christopher D. Handley DFM as navigator, carried out a bombing attack on Berlin. Over the target it was cloudless with bright moonlight and bombs were dropped from 15,000-23,000 feet. Flak was moderate and quite accurate but the biggest danger proved to be night-fighters. Linke, again led by 'Eisbär' overtook Shand's Mosquito in his Bf 110G-4 from high altitude and at high speed in a power dive and sent his quarry down over the northern part of the Ijsselmeer at 0210 hours. Shand remained missing while the body of his navigator was washed ashore at Makkum. Linke, with 24 night and three day victories was killed on the night of 13/14 May 1943. After shooting down two Lancasters (W4981 on 83 Squadron flown by Sergeant Anthony Stephen Renshaw and ED589 on 9 Squadron piloted by Sergeant George Henry Saxton) and Halifax DT732 on 10 Squadron flown by Flight Sergeant John Franklin Mills RAAF - all without any survivors - over Friesland, his Bf 110G-4 (G9+CZ) suffered an engine fire and he bailed out near the village of Lemmer in Friesland but he struck the tail unit of his Bf 110 and was killed. Linke's bordfunker Oberfeldwebel Walter Czybulka bailed out safely. In mid-July 1943 three FW 190s for Mosquito hunting were stationed at Bonn-Hangelar, which came under operational control of 'Himmelbett' Box 6 in eastern Belgium. The subsequent Mosquito-hunting sorties by these single-engined fighters were without result.

No more Main Force operations were flown until the night of 26/27 April when the target was Duisburg again. Altogether 561 aircraft were despatched, seventeen of which were lost - ten of them to 'Himmelbett' Nachtjäger of NJG1 operating over the Netherlands.

On 4/5 May 596 aircraft of Bomber Command carried out a heavy raid on Dortmund; of which 31 aircraft or 5.2% of the bombing force failed to return - 22 of them destroyed by 'Himmelbett' Nachtjäger of NJG1. All but three of these were achieved over the Netherlands and the Dutch coastal waters. Ninety Stirlings had been part of the Dortmund force.[95] Six crews in IV./NJG1 destroyed twelve of the bombers. Gruppenkommandeur Major Lent claimed two Stirlings; BK773 on 7 Squadron flown by Pilot Officer William Holden RCAF at 0008 hours over the Ijsselmeer south of Enkhuizen and Stirling I EF343 on 149 Squadron flown by Flying Officer Walter Edwin Davey ten minutes later at Heeg) to take his score to 66 victories. There were no survivors on either crew. III./NJG1 claimed six bombers. One - Stirling III BK658 on 15 Squadron flown by Sergeant W. M. McLeod RNZAF was shot down by Unteroffizier

Karl-Georg Pfeiffer of 10./NJG1 for his third victory:

'The Jagerleitoffizier (JLO, or GCI-controller) called, 'Have Kurier. But your time is up; make quickly Reise-Reise [literally 'journey'. R/T code as in 'Machen Sie Reise-Reise! - Break off engagement]. Your relief is already on his way.'

'My radio operator asked, 'What is Kurier doing? We are not thirsty yet!' We wanted to tell our controller that we still had fuel for a good half-hour. As the relief had not yet arrived, we were directed to the Kurier, flying south-easterly in the direction of Dollart, probably in order to drop bombs on Emden. It was a pitch-black night and we had to do the entire sortie on instruments. At last ground control 'Schlei' placed us behind the Kurier and my radio operator picked him up on his radar. He brought me ever closer to the target until the target and ground blips converged. But I could see nothing. The enemy must have been very close. He must be visible from below against the stars. So I went down 200 metres but still nothing. At long last I saw exactly and about fifty metres above me, with little stars moving along with us. They were the exhaust flames, damped like ours. I carefully placed myself in an attacking position, exactly below him as Oberleutnant Becker had taught us. I pulled slowly up behind him. Now was the moment when, using appropriate deflection, I would be able to fire without getting into the arc of fire of the rear turret (but don't forget to dip down again, otherwise we would get too high and give the rear gunner a perfect target). I pressed the firing button for one or two seconds but nothing happened. At last one cannon began to stutter. I caught my breath. A small fire started in the starboard inner engine but it did not get bigger.

'The Tommy now pushed his machine down onto me. He must have noticed where the enemy must be. I reduced power and remained, as if in formation, below and to the rear of him. The one cannon continued to stutter. Now we both increased speed and then the pilot of the Short Stirling suddenly pulled his machine upward. I followed all his moves. The one cannon (the others continued to remain silent) fired intermittently but struck home now and then. I wondered how much longer he would pull up his heavy machine. By now we were on our backs and had practically done a looping in formation. Now he was in a vertical dive and the speed increased from 450 to 500, 550, 650 and more. At this moment many searchlights lit up (probably from Emden) and had both of us brightly illuminated. I was blinded and did not even notice that we were still in a dive towards the ground behind the bomber. The good people on the searchlights had probably meant to do us a favour, perhaps even to assist us but the opposite was the case. As thanks, I wished they would go to the devil. Then my radio operator shouted, 'Watch the altimeter!'

'He was right: it showed only 2000 metres, 1500, 1200, 1000. I pulled the stick back as hard as I could. At last the good 'Casar X', as my 110 was known, pulled slowly out and we levelled out at about 400 metres at probably 650 km/h. Now there was a heavy explosion beside us. The Short Stirling had struck the ground [at Midwolda, 31 kilometres east of Groningen]. We had probably been chasing a dead crew all this time or they had not been able to recover from the looping. My knees were still trembling as we gave our Abschuss report to 'Schlei'. The JLO congratulated us and gave us the shortest course to Leeuwarden, for now all four red lights of the fuel tanks were lighting up. But we made it and landed at 0120 hours. The Abschuss had been at 0100 hours precisely. Later the flak tried to lay claim to the Abschuss but the required witnesses on the ground were able to confirm our claim, if with only one cannon and a stuttering one at that.'[96]

It was Duisburg again on 12/13 May in bright moon with no cloud and excellent visibility. The target was clearly identified visually which was a rarity. As usual, the flak was intense and accurate. Of 572 aircraft that set out for Duisburg 34 aircraft or

5.9% of the force failed to return. Twenty-four of these losses are attributed to 'Himmelbett'- operating night-fighters of NJG1; all these victories being achieved over the Netherlands. I./NJG1 at Venlo destroyed ten bombers; III./NJG15, including two Halifaxes on 35 and 77 Squadrons and Wellington X HE321 on 428 'Ghost' Squadron RCAF skippered by Flight Sergeant Alan Edgar Hatch RCAF (all of whom were killed) by Oberleutnant August 'Gustel' Geiger. These were Geiger's 24th-27th official victories.

On 13/14 May 442 aircraft were sent to bomb Bochum while 156 Lancasters and twelve Halifaxes set off on a long haul to bomb the Skoda armaments factory at Pilzen in Czechoslovakia. The raids on Pilzen and Bochum cost 33 bombers. Bochum cost 24 aircraft (thirteen Halifaxes, six Wellingtons, four Stirlings and a Lancaster). Pilzen cost nine aircraft. Twenty-seven aircraft were shot down by Nachtjäger patrolling in the 'Himmelbett' over the Netherlands, Belgium and Germany. I./NJG1 claimed nine bombers, including Stirling III BF479 on 149 Squadron at Lakenheath by Leutnant Walter Schön of the third Staffel at Kasterlee (Antwerpen). Flying Officer Leslie Cyril Martin and his crew were killed. Schön and his bordshütze, Unteroffizier Georg Marotzke were killed on 20 October when their He 219A-04 was shot down in air combat at Klein Ballerstedt/Stendal. Schön had seven Abschüsse.

III./NJG1 at Twente destroyed ten Lancasters, Halifaxes and a Stirling over the Dutch-German border. Hauptmann Herbert Lütje, Staffelkapitän 8./NJG1 claimed six victories. His first three claims were against Pilzen-bound bombers, the first at 2332 hours: Lancaster III ED667 W-Willy' on 57 Squadron at Scampton flown by 23-year old Pilot Officer Jan Bernard Marinus Haye, who had completed 22 bombing operations. Born at Pehalongon in Java, of Dutch parents who divorced in 1929, he attended school in Hilversum and The Hague. After his mother remarried in 1938 and went to live in England he visited her on holidays and from 1939 he went to schools there. 'Dutchy' or 'Bob', as he was known, went down at Albergen, followed ten minutes later by Lancaster I R5611 on 106 Squadron at Syerston, which crashed at Rossum/Weerselo. Sergeant Francis James Howell and crew were killed.[97] Six minutes before midnight Lancaster I W4305 on 44 Squadron at Waddington went down between Bevergem and Horstel. Flying Officer J. G. McD Olding RCAF survived and was taken prisoner. His six crew died.

When the Bochum raiders were on their return leg, Lütje destroyed Halifax JB966 on 405 'Vancouver' Squadron RCAF near Oud Avereest at 0225 hours. Flying Officer Hugh Donald Beattie RCAF and one of his crew died; the others were taken prisoner. At 0245 Lütje destroyed Halifax JD113 on 419 'Moose' Squadron RCAF at Dalton. Flying Officer Walter Herbert Secretan Buckwell and three of his crew were killed. The three others were taken prisoner. Seven minutes later Lütje shot down Halifax II JB892 on 77 Squadron, which crashed into woods near Noordsleen. All of Flying Officer Dennis Percival Puddephatt's crew were killed. These took Lütje's tally to 28 victories. He was awarded the Ritterkreuz two weeks later and appointed Kommandeur of IV./NJG6 in Rumania. Lütje ended the war as Kommodore of NJG6 with fifty kills.

Unteroffizier Karl-Georg Pfeiffer of 10./NJG1 was another of the successful fighter pilots on 4/5 May:

'We headed for night-fighting area 'Löwe' ['Lion'] (between Leeuwarden and Groningen). Very soon the Jägerleitoffizier (JLO, or GCI-controller) announced a Kurier flying over the Zuider Zee in a north-easterly direction. At last an incoming aircraft, which had not yet dropped his bombs. Ground control directed us to the target and Unteroffizier Willi Knappe my bordfunker soon had it on his Lichtenstein radar. As we got closer, we noticed that the Britisher [sic] [Lancaster W4110 on 44 Squadron flown by Rhodesian Flying Officer William Douglas Rail] was constantly altering his course. Obviously an old hand who knew that he was passing through the German night fighter belt. I placed myself exactly beneath him and tried to follow his regular weaving movements. That was no simple matter. At long last we were weaving in unison like dancers to music and the time had come when I had to pull up. My neck was almost stiff through constantly staring upward. I pulled up quickly and was no more than 25 metres below and behind his tail. Then I remembered that I had not armed the cannon. Down quickly and away. He had not noticed us and I was able with shaking hands to repair my lapse. Now the manoeuvre had to be done all over again. I followed his movements, climbed a little, pulled up and fired! I intended to make certain by cutting through the fuselage from front to rear, when I realized that he would still have all his bombs on board. On firing I gave a little left rudder and the projectiles did not strike the fuselage but the port wing with the two engines, which caught fire at once. That was enough. Now away to the side and down I went. As I turned I noticed that the bomb doors were open and the whole load went down, narrowly missing my Me 110. We saw the Lancaster burning brightly. One could already see through the skeleton of the fuselage and still it continued to fly. Did the crew manage to bail out? They certainly had sufficient time. [All seven on Flying Officer Rail's crew were killed]. Suddenly the aircraft exploded and the burning parts fell into the North Sea, twenty kilometres west of Den Helder.

'We landed at about 0437 hours after a half-hour flight and were glad that the night with its terrors was over. Once again all had gone well. The cockpit-clock showed 0329 hours. Willi also gave a sigh of relief and remarked dryly, 'Congratulations on your EK I'.[98] It was my fourth Abschuss, for which a pilot received this decoration (the radio operator after the 6th). During May the well-known dance band Barnabas von Gecy was playing in the 'Harmonie' in Leeuwarden. Some of us got tickets and we hoped that we were not on the battle order that night. I was in luck and it turned out to be a wonderful evening. As I lay in bed later, still dreaming of the lovely melodies, the telephone suddenly rang. 'Unteroffizier Pfeiffer report at once to the officers' mess!' I dived into my uniform, thinking that nothing good would come of this. When I arrived I found a party in progress, with ladies and many civilian guests. Major Lent came up to me and said, 'I hereby invest you with the EK I for your victories. Carry on like that!'[99]

'I was amazed and happy and only noticed now that the officers had invited the entire orchestra Barnabas von Gecy to join in the celebrations. I was allowed to remain and enjoy the party for the rest of the night. The next morning each and every hair on my head ached. A terrible hangover. But it had been worth it.'

Endnotes Chapter 8

86 The Stirlings were withdrawn from an original plan so that only the higher-flying heavies would participate and most of the force came from 5 Group.
87 Figures on a clock face, i.e. East to West in the northern part of the night fighting area.
88 All the crew were lost without trace and are commemorated on the Runnymede Memorial. On both raids - 16/17th and 17/18th January the Path Finders were unable to mark the centre of Berlin and bombing was inaccurate. The experiments with the Lancaster-Halifax force using TIs against the 'Big City' now ceased until H2S became available. 35 major attacks were made on Berlin and other German towns during the Battle of Berlin between mid-1943 and March 1944; 20,224 sorties, 9,111 of which were to the big City. From these sorties (14,652 by Lancasters), 1,047 aircraft FTR and 1,682 received varying degrees of damage. AM Sir Arthur Harris said later, 'We can wreck Berlin from end to end if the USAAF will come in of it. It will cost between 400-500 aircraft. It will cost Germany the war.
89 Adapted from the *Bomber Command Assoc Newsletter, No.28* February 1995.

90   All except two of his crew survived.
91   *The Bomber Command War Diaries* by Martin Middlebrook and Chris Everitt (Midland 1985)/*The Lent Papers* by Peter Hinchliffe.. NJG1 were credited with thirteen kills. Three crews of IV./NJG1 destroyed four bombers over the northern province of the Netherlands.
92   The Bf 110F was unable to fly on one engine when carrying night fighting equipment.
93   'Oboe' was the most accurate form of high-level blind bombing used in World War II and it took its name from a radar pulse, which sounded like a musical instrument. The radar pulses operated on the range from 2 ground stations ('Cat' and 'Mouse') in England to the target. The signal was heard by both pilot and navigator and used to track the aircraft over the target. If inside the correct line, dots were heard, if outside the line, dashes, a steady note indicated the target was on track. Only the navigator heard this signal. When the release signal, which consisted of 5 dots and a 2-second dash was heard, the navigator released the markers or bombs. In April 1942 109 Squadron was established at Stradishall, Suffolk to bring 'Oboe' into full operational service as a navigation aid for Bomber Command before moving to Wyton in August, where at the end of the year, it received the first 'Oboe'-equipped Mosquito BIVs. 'Oboe' was first used on 20/21 December 1942 when the CO, Squadron Leader H. E. 'Hal' Bufton and his navigator, Flight Lieutenant E. L. Ifould and 2 other crews, bombed a power station at Lutterade in Holland. On 31 December 1942/1 January 1943, on a raid on Düsseldorf, sky-marking using 'Oboe' was tried for the first time when 2 Mosquitoes on 109 Squadron provided the sky-markers for 8 Lancasters on the Path Finder Force. 'Sky markers' were parachute flares to mark a spot in the sky if it was cloudy. The PFF markers' job was to 'illuminate' and 'mark' targets with coloured TPs (target indicators) for the Main Force and other 8 Group Mosquitoes. Air Commodore (later AVM) Donald C. T Bennett's specialist Path Finder Force formed in August 1942 achieved Group status on 13 January 1943. 109 became the premier marking squadron in the RAF, carrying out the most raids and flying the most sorties in 8 Group, which it joined on 1 June 1943. On 10 December 109 Squadron at Marham received the first BX.VI for the RAF, although 692 Squadron were the first to use it operationally, on 5 March 1944. In addition to its flare marking duties for the heavies, 109 Squadron's Mosquitoes carried bombs. On 23 December 1944 Squadron Leader R. A. M. Palmer DFC lost his life in an 'Oboe'-equipped Lancaster borrowed from 582 Squadron when he led a formation-attack on the Cologne railway marshalling yards. His Lancaster was hit by flak and set on fire but Palmer got his bombs away before his aircraft went down out of control. He was awarded a posthumous Victoria Cross. On 21 April 1945 109 Squadron dropped the last bombs to fall on Berlin in World War II.
94   On 28/29 June 1942 Oberleutnant Reinhold Knacke, Staffelkapitän, l./NJG1 had been the first Nachtjagd pilot to claim a Mosquito kill.
95   Another seven bombers crashed in England in bad weather.
96   McLeod and five others were taken prisoner. Sergeant Peter McNulty was KIA.
97   Two of 'Dutchy' Haye's crew were killed and 4 were taken prisoner. 'Dutchy' successfully evaded capture and reached Amsterdam on foot and by bicycle where he received help from the Dutch Underground and he was hidden in The Hague for the next 8 weeks. During that time he met and fell in love with 22-year old Elly de Jong, one of the Underground workers. On 26 July Haye reluctantly said goodbye to Elly and sailed to England on a barge with other evaders. He eventually returned to operations on 83 (Path Finder) Squadron. After VE Day he returned to Holland to find Elly de Jong. She and other members of the Underground had been betrayed and arrested and sent to Ravensbrück concentration camp under sentence of death. Elly was transferred to Mauthausen from where she was liberated before the sentence could be carried out. On 8 November 1945 she married her RAF pilot and they lived happily for over fifty years.
98   Eisernes Kreuz I or Iron Cross 1st Class.
99   Pfeiffer scored his 5th victory when he shot down Stirling BF405 on 218 Squadron 70 km north of Terschelling on 27/28 May. Flight Sergeant William David Mills and his crew, who were on a Gardening operation, were lost without trace.

Chapter Nine

'Emil-Emil'

'Marie-5,' sounded in the earphones of the bordfunker crouched in the cockpit of the Bf 110G-4a night-fighter. The codeword, sent from the ground controller, indicated that the night predator was only 5 kilometres behind a British bomber. It had been picked up on German ground radar, fixed on the Seeburg plotting table and transmitted to the Leutnant and his Unteroffizier stalking the bomber on their Helle Nachtjagd. As soon as the bordfunker picked up contact on his Lichtenstein C-l weitwinkel (wide-angle) radar, he transmitted 'Emil-Emil' to alert his controller.

Confounding the Reich: The Operational History of 100 Group (Bomber Support) RAF.

At 1640 hours on Saturday 9 May 1943 the radar station at Grove in Denmark intercepted a distress call from the three man crew of a Ju 88C-6/R-1 which had taken off from Aalborg to intercept a BOAC Mosquito en route from Scotland to Stockholm's Bromma Airport in Sweden. D5+EV reported fire in its left engine and a short time later said that it had to make an emergency sea landing. Oberstleutnant von der Pongartz at once ordered a rescue aircraft to Quadrant 88/41; it sighted three empty inflatable rubber dinghies and radioed for a sea rescue speedboat. At 1805 Flight Lieutenant Roscoe piloting a Spitfire on 165 'Ceylon' Squadron and accompanied by another fighter flown by Sergeant Seaman, was making a patrol flight along the coast of northern Scotland between Peterhead and Aberdeen when he sighted a German aircraft. Roscoe gave this account:

'The aircraft reported to me by our radar station was about fifteen miles from Peterhead, heading west. I flew towards it at top speed to intercept it before it reached the coast. About five miles off the coast it changed course and flew south. When I managed at last to cut off its eastward flight path, the plane was already one mile inland. By this time I had identified it as a Ju 88 and was preparing to attack, when suddenly I saw that it had let down its landing gear and was firing a series of red signal flares. Then it began to wave its wings up and down. I came nearer and motioned with my hand for the plane to follow me, at the same time ordering Sergeant Seaman to stay on the other side of it and escort it toward Dyce, a small Scottish airstrip about fifteen miles northwest of Aberdeen. At the airfield the Ju 88 again sent out red signal flares, curved around and landed. I followed it until it switched off its engines and halted just at the edge of the airfield and took the three Germans prisoner.'

While Oberstleutnant von der Pongartz at Grove was reporting the disappearance of the Ju 88 to NJG3, the missing German air crew were scrambling out of the Ju88 at Dyce. The aircraft was at once rolled into a hangar and Group Captain J. W. Colquhoun the airfield commander, sent several top-priority coded telegrams to London. No one at Dyce was aware that this event marked a major coup for the British Secret Intelligence Service, the SIS, in its campaign against the Luftwaffe. The Ju 88 was carrying the top secret FuG 202 Lichtenstein BC AI radar set. The fiancée of the pilot, Flugzeugführer Oberleutnant Herbert Schmidt was Jewish and had been arrested and transported to a concentration camp while his bordfunker, Oberfeldwebel Paul Rosenberger was of Jewish descent. Bordschütze Oberfeldwebel Erich Kantvill, a Nazi, went along with the defection. Herbert Schmidt was in reality an SIS agent who had been recruited by his father, a Social Democrat at that time living underground and the former personal adviser of German Chancellor Stresemann who had died in 1929.

The British had spared no effort in uncovering the secret of Würzburg radar and had devoted equal zeal to investigating the new German target-locator system. They had learned of its existence through their radio monitoring stations, which repeatedly picked up the codename 'Emil-Emil' being passed between the German night fighters and their ground controllers. Special operators aboard aircraft on 1473 Flight subsequently detected transmissions on the 490 megahertz band on 'Ferret' flights over occupied Europe - proof was needed that they came from enemy night-fighters. Dr. R. V. Jones, chief of the scientific branch of the secret service in the Air Ministry obtained Churchill's permission to send a Wellington bomber full of measuring instruments to Frankfurt am Main on 3 December 1942, six months after the investigation began, to be used as a decoy in the hope that the crew could find out at least the megahertz frequency of the menacing German radar. A Wellington IC on 1473 Flight flown by Pilot Officer Edwin Paulton RCAF went with the bomber stream to Frankfurt to pinpoint the source of the transmissions. If they did in fact come from German night-fighters, the crew were to allow the enemy aircraft to close in to attack and to follow his radar transmissions throughout. Pilot Officer Harold Jordan, the special wireless operator, picked up a signal, which came closer until it was so loud that it nearly deafened him. It was a Ju 88. Jordan warned the crew that an attack was imminent and Flight Sergeant Bill Bigoray RCAF, the wireless operator, sent out signals to base. The 'Wimpy' took evasive action as the Ju 88 made ten to twelve attacks. Four of the crew were wounded. Jordan was hit in the arm and jaw in the first two attacks but continued to work his set. In the third attack, he was wounded again, this time in the eye. Almost blind, he explained the operation of the wireless set to the navigator. Bigoray, although badly wounded in both legs, had persisted in passing on the messages from Jordan. Edwin Paulton managed to fly the badly damaged Wellington to England and ditched off Walmer Beach near Deal and the crew were saved at the last minute and reported: 'It was 490 megahertz.' [100]

On 10 May, a German-speaking RAF interrogation officer arrived at Dyce and Herbert Schmidt gave him a detailed report on the organization, structure and tactics of the German night fighter zones in Denmark, as well as suggestions as to how Bomber Command could better protect its bombers from night interceptors and avoid detection by 'Freya' and 'Würzburg' radar. Air Marshal Harris gained other first-hand tips that only a German night-fighter pilot could know. On Monday 11 May Dr. Jones left London and arrived at Dyce to take charge of the Ju 88. Dr. Jones, one of the top British radar specialists, was initiated into the secrets of Lichtenstein BC and ordered a series of test flights. The unit codes of the Ju 88 were painted over and replaced with the RAF badge and the serial number PJ876; then it flew to Farnborough with a Spitfire for escort. Here Squadron Leader Charles Hartley and Wing Commander D. A. Jackson took charge of it. The British wanted to see Lichtenstein radar working under realistic conditions, so they carried out the tests at night and arranged for the German plane to fight a duel with a Halifax bomber. The two planes fought their improvised battle with such zeal that they almost collided. The Halifax could not shake off the German night fighter no matter how it manoeuvred; but the experimental flights revealed that the correct use of continuous vertical flight curves - corkscrew curves - made it hard for the pursuer to come into firing position.[101]

Examination by TRE (Telecommunications Research Establishment) scientists at Malvern in Worcestershire developed a homer using a receiver known as 'Serrate', which actually homed in on the radar impulses emitted by the FuG 202 Lichtenstein BC and Lichtenstein FuG 212 ('Emil-Emil') interception radars. 'Serrate' got its name from the picture on the cathode ray tube (CRT). When within range of a German night-fighter, the CRT displayed a herringbone pattern either side of the time trace, which had a serrated edge. 'Serrate' came to be the code name for the high-level Bomber Support operations. 'Serrate' could only home in on Lichtenstein AI radar and then only if it was turned on. RAF Beaufighters would also be equipped with Mk.IV.AI radar, which would be used in the closing stages of a 'Serrate' interception because 'Serrate' could not positively indicate range. The Mk.IV was also needed to obtain contacts on enemy night-fighters that were not using their radar.[102]

On 12/13 May 1943, 238 Lancasters, 142 Halifaxes, 112 Wellingtons, seventy Stirlings and ten Mosquitoes were detailed for an operation on Duisburg-Ruhrort. Thirty-four aircraft failed to return. One of the nine Halifaxes that were lost was DT801 TL-A on 35 Squadron at Graveley piloted by 29-year old Ontario-born and Toronto-educated Squadron Leader Douglas Julian Sale DSO which was shot down near the small Dutch town of Haaksbergen in Gelderland province near the German border by Oberleutnant August 'Gustel' Geiger of III./NJG1 flying a Bf 110G-4. Julian Sale was blown out of the aircraft when it exploded and he landed in a pine tree. Four of his crew were taken into captivity and the two others were killed but Sale successfully evaded and returned to Graveley where he recommenced operations again until he was shot down on the night of 19/20 February 1944 when four of the missing Halifaxes on Leipzig were on 35 Squadron; one of which exploded over Gohre and another was abandoned near Brandenburg. 'J-Johnny' piloted by Squadron Leader Julian Sale DSO* DFC was hit at 23,000 feet near Beedenbostel in central Germany by a Ju 88 armed with Schräge Musik and flown by Hauptmann Ludwig 'Luk' Meister. Sale was badly injured and he died of his wounds in hospital near Frankfurt on 20 March.

On the night of 23/24 May 1943 the fourth heavy Bomber Command raid of May was on Dortmund. Of 829 aircraft despatched, 38 bombers failed to return. NJG1 was credited with 21 confirmed kills; eighteen of which were achieved over the Netherlands and Dutch coastal waters. Hauptmann August 'Gustel' Geiger claimed Lancaster W4984 SR-J on 460 Squadron RAAF which crashed SSE of Emmen in Holland with the loss of Flight Sergeant Beresford Milton Troy Davis RAAF and five of his crew. Only Flight Sergeant C. Goldthorpe, the Australian flight engineer, survived to be taken prisoner. Oberleutnant Manfred Meurer, Leutnant Heinz Strüning and Hauptmann 'Gerd' Friedrich of I./NJG1 claimed six of the aircraft shot down on the Dortmund raid. Six crews of III./NJG1 destroyed nine bombers. During a patrol in the 'Himmelbett Raum 4C' and being guided by GCI fighter controller Oberleutnant Freudenberg, Hauptmann Wolfgang 'Ameise' ('Ant') Thimmig claimed three aircraft. Wellington X HE290 on 166 Squadron at Kirmington flown by Sergeant Edward Silas Morris came down north-west of Eindhoven. Wellington X HE281 on 426 'Thunderbird' Squadron at Dishforth flown by Sergeant Leslie Gordon Sutherland RCAF crashed southwest of Enschede. There were no survivors on either crew. Halifax II JD122 on 78 Squadron at Linton-on-Ouse crashed at Zuna, west of Almelo between 0108 and 0134 hours. Sergeant Guy Edgar Schubert and his crew were killed. Six crews in IV./NJG1 returned with claims for eight Abschüsse.

On the night of 25/26 May 759 bombers were despatched to bomb Düsseldorf. Twenty-seven bombers (3.6 per cent of the force despatched) were lost, 21 of which were due to night-fighters. The raid was a failure due to the difficulty of marking in bad weather. II./NJG1 crews returned with eight victories, including Major Walter Ehle with claims for four. Oberleutnant Wilhelm Telge and his bordfunker Unteroffizier Walter Telsing of Stab II./NJG1 attacked Halifax II JB837 on 77 Squadron flown by Sergeant Richard Lewis near Jülich at 0140 hours that resulted in a massive explosion, which not only downed the Halifax but also two Stirling IIIs, EF361 on 7 Squadron flown by Flight Lieutenant Joseph Francois Exavier Gilles Berthiaume RCAF (all KIA) and EH887 on 218 Squadron, flown by Sergeant Norman Sidney Collins, who was also killed. Telge claimed a second victim, shooting down Halifax II W7813 piloted by 22-year old Sergeant Lewis William Rees at 0140 hours with the aircraft crashing at Gruitrode, Belgium. There were no survivors.

I./NJG1 at Venlo destroyed ten bombers including Wellington X 'Z-Zebra' on 431 'Iroquois' Squadron RCAF flown by Sergeant Bob Barclay. Sergeant Ken Dix, navigator, had misgivings from the off, as he recalls: 'I was concerned when I saw that our flight path took us one and a half miles north of the German night fighter base at Venlo. I said they could orbit their beacon and pick off bombers behind the main stream but no route change was made. On the runway the port engine would not start and the other bombers went off. As a specially selected crew usually we were the lead-machine. We carried 4,000lbs of incendiaries to drop within less than ten seconds of the flares from the Path Finder Force aircraft going down on the target; usually from as near to 18,500 feet as we could reach with a full bomb load. But it was 22 minutes before we got the port engine going. So it left us well behind the main stream of bombers. The machine did not climb well enough and had not enough speed so we flew to Hornsea on the coast and flew across the North Sea to Ijmuiden. Then we headed between the flak zones of Soesterberg and Hertogenbosch on our way to the Track Indicator Markers laid by the pathfinders. We had just seen it and were on the correct track when Sergeant Harry Sweet in the rear turret shouted, 'FIGHTER!' He immediately fired his four Browning machine guns.'

At the same time as Harry Sweet opened fire, the fighter, a Bf 110 flown by Oberleutnant Manfred Meurer Staffelkapitän, 3./NGJ1, fired his cannons and he hit the Wellington along the starboard beam from the tail as Bob Barclay took evasive action. Ken Dix continues:

'The cannon shells had hit hard. They stopped just by my 'Gee' radar set. The voice intercom failed and then our flashing intercom buttons also went off. Sergeant Jeffries, the WOp/AG, was behind the main spar ready to launch the flare for our picture after the bombing run. He was killed. The aircraft was blazing with the port engine hit and on fire. We were spinning round and down. I managed to get my chest chute into my new harness. I couldn't go back to Sergeant Jeffries because of the fierce flames driving me back. I went to the cockpit. The front hatch was open but Flying Officer Bert Bonner, bomb aimer, and Bob Barclay had bailed out. They could have tried to contact us but the system had been hit. I had flown the aircraft when we were on exercises and I had also been on a pilot's course in Florida before becoming a navigator, so I decided to try and fly the Wellington back to base. I got into the pilot's seat and the Wellington at first answered the controls. I turned to fly northwest back to England then dived to try and put the flames out. It was going well when suddenly the control wires, hit by cannon fire, broke. I had no control so reluctantly I had to bail out. I pulled the ripcord and the turning Wellington just missed me. I saw it hit the ground.'

Wellington X HE990, which crashed at Venray northwest of Venlo, was the first of three Viermots Meurer shot down on 25/26 May. Dix and Barclay were taken prisoner. Meurer went on to claim Lancaster III LM320 on 100 Squadron piloted by Squadron Leader Philip Raymond Turgel DFC at Vlodrop and Lancaster III W5001 on 207 Squadron flown by Wing Commander T. A. B. Parselle at Neerbosch. Turgel and his crew perished. Parselle and one of his crew survived; six others were killed.

When Essen was subjected to a Main Force raid by 518 aircraft on 27/28 May, 23 bombers failed to return. Again, I./NJG1 was successful with seven Abschüsse. III./NJG1 claimed eight victories, which included three Halifaxes and Wellington HE752 on 166 Squadron at Hengelo by Leutnant Hans-Heinz Augenstein. IV./NJG1 claimed four aircraft in quick succession for his first Abschüsse. Born on 11 July 1921, Augenstein first served with 3./NJG1 during mid 1942. He claimed his first victory on the night of 31 July/1 August, a Vickers Wellington downed near Ahlhorn. He joined 7./NJG1 at the end of 1942 with his bordfunker Feldwebel Günther Steins. It was almost six months before Augenstein claimed his first kills on 27/28 May 1943. Unteroffizier Kurt Schmidt joined Augenstein's crew as bordschütze in September 1943 as a precaution when the RAF night intruders began exacting an increasing toll of German night-fighters. Augenstein took command of 7./NJG1 on 31 January 1944 and 12./NJG1 came under his command a month later. Operating as a night fighter ace, he was credited with 46 victories, of which 45 were four-engine bombers. In March 1944 Augenstein was made Staffelkapitän of 12./NJG1 and awarded the Knight's Cross on 9 June.

Minor operations were flown on the night of 28/29 May 1943 with 34 crews, some of them undoubtedly flying their first op sowed mines off the Friesians. The area bombing of the Barman half of the long and narrow town of Wuppertal on 29/30 May involved 719 aircraft and the attack started a large fire area in the narrow streets of the old town centre. Wuppertal had never experienced a major raid before and being a Saturday night, many of the town's fire and air raid precaution officials were absent. About 4,000 houses were burned to the ground and about 3,400 people[103] died as a minor firestorm raged. Thirty-three bombers were lost, 22 of which were shot down by Nachtjäger. I./NJG1 claimed eight aircraft shot down, four of these being credited to Oberleutnant Manfred Meurer Staffelkapitän 3./NJG1: Halifax II HR840 NP-R on 158 Squadron crashed at Swalmen with the loss of Sergeant Charles Kenneth Surgey (a Uruguayan) and crew; Stirling I EF398 AA-A on 75 Squadron at Roermond/Vlodrop, which was lost with Flying Officer Richard Barry Vermazoni RNZAF and crew; Wellington X MS494 on 466 Squadron near Reuver, Limburg with Warrant Officer L. O. Upjohn RAAF and crew being taken prisoner and Lancaster III EE123 KM-K on 44 Squadron at Castenray between 0033 and 0144 hours. All of Flying Officer Peter Grattan Holt RCAF's crew were killed. In May 1943 Meurer claimed thirteen heavies shot down.

Leutnant Wilhelm Beier of 3./NJG1, a successful intruder pilot who had earned the Ritterkreuz in October 1941 with fourteen victories in 3./NJG2, destroyed Halifax HR793 on 35 Squadron at Limbricht. (Beier was awarded the Ritterkreuz. In 1943 he claimed the last of his 38 night victories. At the end of the war he was undergoing night fighter training on the Me 262). Two bombers were credited to Major Walter Ehle and Oberfeldwebel Fritz Schellwat also destroyed two aircraft, including Lancaster DS627 on 115 Squadron near Hechtel, Belgium which was lost with Sergeant Charles Roughead Fleming and crew. Hauptmann Ludwig Meister of I./NJG4 claimed Stirling IV EF349 on 90 Squadron near Cambrai, France. Flying Officer Robert William John Letters and four of his crew were killed. The two others were taken prisoner. Oberleutnant Rudolf Altendorf of the same Gruppe destroyed Halifax II JB805 VR-B on 419 'Moose' Squadron RCAF at Peronnes-les-Binche with the loss of Warrant Officer F. S. Johnson RCAF and crew and Wellington HE212 on 466 Squadron at Vollezele. Pilot Officer Henry Simon Raoul.

Lloyd and crew were all killed. Hauptmann Werner 'Red' Hoffmann, Staffelkapitän 4./NJG5 from Greifswald destroyed a Halifax (possibly W7876 on 35 Squadron) over the Gilbach valley dams. Warrant Officer A. R. Sargent's four crew were taken prisoner; two men were killed. In all 150 individual aircraft were plotted on the Würzburg radars flying through the 'Himmelbett' boxes in eastern Belgium, in which thirteen Bf 110Gs and three Do 217s of II./NJG1 patrolled during the course of the night. For the loss of three aircraft and two aircrew killed, six II/NJG1 crews scored eleven victories.'

Altogether, 167 Nachtjagd victories were recorded in May. These totalled 58 by I./NJG1, 43 by III./NJG1, 24 by II./NJG1 at St. Trond and at least 26 by IV./NJG1. By the early summer of 1943 there was only one effective tactical measure available to Air Marshal Harris and his staff officers to counter the German night fighter defence. This was the saturation of the German GCI system by concentrating the RAF bomber routes through relatively few GCI 'Raume' (boxes) or through 'Gebiete' (zones) in which few or no GCI stations existed. In 1942, when the RAF began attacking targets within a period of thirty minutes the narrow night fighter zone in the west was quickly penetrated and at the same time, only a few fighters came into contact with the bomber stream. Flak, emplaced in single batteries, was unable to cope with the concentrated attacks by the RAF. The carefully practiced system of concentrating several batteries' fire on a single target broke down because so many aircraft appeared over the target at the same time. As a result of all this the night fighter zone in the West had to be rapidly increased in depth and extended to Denmark in the north and to eastern France in the south. Operational control had to be developed whereby two or more night fighters could be brought into action in any one night fighter area at the same time. In addition, bombers over the target had to be attacked by fighters as well as flak, which had to be consolidated into large batteries near the targets and concentrated at the most important targets. Above all, accuracy had to be increased by developing a large number of radar range finders.

In June the Reichsverteidigung 'Himmelbett Nachtjagd' defences claimed a record 223 victories. At least sixty were credited to IV./NJG1, 52 to I./NJG1, 22 to II./NJG1 plus thirteen to ten crews of NJG3, 4 and 5 temporarily attached to the St. Trond Gruppe and twenty to III./NJG1. On 11/12 June when 860 heavies were despatched to bomb Düsseldorf, forty-three aircraft failed to return, 29 of which were shot down by 'Himmelbett'-operating Nachtjäger. Four of the losses can probably be attributed to IV./NJG1 and four Halifaxes and a Lancaster in just thirty minutes to Major Werner Streib, Gruppenkommandeur I./NJG1 who, with Unteroffizier Helmut Fischer as his funker, was flying the first fully operational test sortie in a He 219A-0R2 Uhu (G9+FB). The He 219 might have turned the tide for Nachtjagd had it been introduced in quantity. Fast (670 km/h at 23,000 feet), manoeuvrable and with devastating firepower of four or six forward firing cannon and a twin 30mm Mk.108 'Schräge Musik' installation, the 'Owl', was fitted with SN-2 radar and the world's first operational nose wheel undercarriage and back-to-back 'Katapultsitzen' (ejection seats) for the two crew. I./NJG1 had been equipped with the anti-Mosquito version of the He 219 Uhu, a modified version of the He 219A-2 which was lightened by the reduction in armament from six to four 20mm MG 151/20 cannon and had its performance improved by the installation of a nitrous oxide fuel injection system to its engines. It had FuG 2205-N26 airborne radar system, a service ceiling of 37,000 feet and was one of the few Luftwaffe night fighters fast enough to catch the Mosquito. Streib's victims included Halifax II HR719 NP-M on 158 Squadron near Mook, Limburg at 0155 hours. All seven of Flight Lieutenant Edward Alfred James Laver's crew were killed. Lancaster II DS647 KO-N on 115 Squadron was shot down near Mill at 0216 hours with the loss of Squadron Leader Douglas Park Fox DFC and crew. Halifax II W7932 on 78 Squadron came down at 0222 hours near Sambeek with the loss of Warrant Officer Frank Hemmings' crew. The night's victories took his score to 54. Streib exhausted all his ammunition and approached Venlo with fuel running low and several instruments u/s. On approach his canopy misted over and he was forced to fly on instruments. Streib lowered the electrically-operated flaps to the landing position and then lowered the undercarriage. The flaps did not lock down and they returned to the normal position. The He 219 hit the runway and disintegrated but remarkably, Streib and Fischer escaped almost uninjured.[104]

One of the victories went to Unteroffizier Karl-Georg Pfeiffer of 10./NJG1 who took off for the area 'Hering' at 0115 hours. Earlier that day he had scored his sixth Abschuss when he shot down a B-17 during a daylight sortie. Pfeiffer recalls: 'Oberleutnant Rudolf Sigmund congratulated me on my Abschuss. 'A Boeing is not easy to get,' he said. I appreciated his noble gesture. Once, at 1600 hours on 22 March, I had contact with about sixty Boeings in the vicinity of Terschelling but the defensive fire was too strong and I did not dare to get too close. I fired a couple of bursts at one on the fringe but he did not go down. We always got on well and he was a fine fellow.'

Pfeiffer recalls his night sortie with bordfunker, Unteroffizier Willi Knappe:

'The weather was dreadful with rain, gusting wind and low cloud, all great favourites of pilots. We were sent all over the place by the Jägerleitoffizier without any result as the targets were mostly in cloud, then an order on 270° to the west. Willi, looking into his Lichtenstein, soon said, 'That's an old hand, he's weaving about all the time even though he'll soon be home'. By now we were so far away from area Hering that the voice of the JLO had grown quite faint. There was nothing to be seen. I was in cloud nearly all the time and had to keep my eyes on the artificial horizon. We were just able to make out, 'I cannot guide you any more' then all contact broke off. Willi Knapp was still watching the Lichtenstein and giving me new directions. Then he said, 'He must be somewhere here'. But I could see nothing. As I was worried that I might ram the enemy aircraft in the clouds I went a little lower and searched through the upper part of the windscreen. Willi was no longer able to help me and also stared. Without thinking I happened to take a look directly above me and spotted two tiny flames, the exhaust ports. Two engines? It could only be a Wellington [HE277 on 199 Squadron which was lost with all on the crew of Flight Sergeant Clifford Raymond Andrews RCAF]. This type did not burn easily and was well armoured. However, I had to have a go at it. The red fuel warning lights were already on and blinded me. I had difficulty in matching his weaving about, then, as I had been taught, attacked. A long burst but without effect. A quick breakaway, then the same all over again. This time I fired a little to the left in order to hit an engine. At last there was a small flame, which grew slowly larger. Then it spread to the fuselage and the port wing. I kept my distance as the rear gunner might open fire. A number of crews had been lost this way. At last the burning machine dipped a little, tipped on its nose and went hurtling down into the sea thirty kilometres west of Ijmuiden at 0240. Now quickly homeward, hoping that the fuel would last out. After a while we heard the voice of the Jägerleitoffizier (JLO, or GCI-controller) to whom we reported, 'Sieg Heil' [Bomber destroyed!] We landed happy and proud at Leeuwarden at 0315 hours after exactly two hours flight. Hauptmann Ruppel congratulated us on our seventh Abschuss and he was relieved that the last crew had returned safely. Later I heard him saying to an officer in the operations room: 'The crew Pfeiffer is coming along, they're shooting themselves ahead'. 'But with fortune's powers...' as Schiller says!'

On 12/13 June 24 of the 503 aircraft raiding Bochum were destroyed by the German defences. Nachtjagd was credited with 27 confirmed kills, an unusual over-claiming by three aircraft. Twenty-one Abschüsse went to NJG1. Hauptmann Egmont Prinz zur Lippe Weissenfeld, Kommandeur III./NJG1 destroyed two Halifaxes on 408 and 76 Squadrons. III./NJG1 patrolling the eastern Dutch-German border shot down eight Lancasters and Halifaxes. At 0237 Oberleutnant 'Gustel' Geiger claimed Lancaster III ED584 on 49 Squadron at Luttenberg near Raalte with the loss of Sergeant John Hutchison and his crew. Oberleutnant 'Dieter' Schmidt of NJGl who had claimed his first victory on the night of 24/25 March 1943, a Halifax bomber over Enkhuizen and was promoted to Staffelkapitän 8./NJG1 after his 4th victory in May, recalls that Hauptmann Prinz zur Lippe Weissenfeld was a particularly experienced and successful night fighter: 'The Gruppe received its first distinction with the award of the Ritterkreuz to Lütje and Geiger and the Oak Leaves to Hauptmann zur Lippe, who soon after was posted to NJG6.

Besides Major Prinz zur Lippe, Leutnant Hans-Heinz Augenstein, later successful Staffelkapitän of 12./NJG1 and Oberleutnant Werner Husemann, Kommandeur, 7th Staffel, headed the list. Success for a night fighter did not depend solely on his flying ability. Technical competence and good night vision played a significant part as well and in the summer of 1943 the Gruppe was tested for its ability to see at night.'

IV./NJG1, operating from Leeuwarden and Bergen, claimed three Halifaxes and eight Lancasters destroyed on 12/13 June. These included Halifax DK183 on 427 'Lion' Squadron RCAF by Major Rolf Leuchs of 11./NJG1, who finished the war with ten victories, which crashed near Den Hoorn on Texel Island at 0213 hours. Pilot Officer A. M. Fellner and three of his crew were taken prisoner. The three others were killed. Seven Lancasters were shot down by I./NJG1 during the Oberhausen raid of 14/15 June when the 'Himmelbett' Nachtjagd claimed thirteen Main Force aircraft destroyed. Of 197 Lancasters despatched, seventeen failed to return. Fourteen Lancasters were lost from a force of 212 heavies that raided Cologne on 16/17 June, the number of losses matching exactly the fourteen kills officially credited to Nachtjagd. Three Lancasters - ED840 on 156 Squadron, flown by Squadron Leader John Cameron Mackintosh, who was killed, ED553 on 100 Squadron flown by Sergeant Clifford Boughton (who along with his crew was killed) and ED785 on 49 Squadron piloted by Squadron Leader George Gerard Storey who were also all killed - were shot down by Unteroffizier Rudolf Frank of 2./NJG3 to take his score to twelve kills.

On 21/22 June 705 aircraft - 262 Lancasters, 209 Halifaxes, 117 Stirlings, 105 Wellingtons and twelve Mosquitoes - attacked Krefeld and 44 were lost.[105] I./NJG1 at Venlo in the direct path of the approaching and returning bomber stream, claimed fourteen victories. Hauptmann Hans-Dieter Frank, Staffelkapitän, 2./NJG1 was his unit's top-scoring pilot for the night, returning in his He 219 'Owl' with claims for seven victories: a 100 Squadron Lancaster near Dinter, a 305 Squadron Wellington at Gramersweil, a 158 Squadron Halifax near Kaathoven, a 35 Squadron Halifax at Wamel, an unidentified Halifax near Vechel and two Canadian Halifaxes on 408 'Goose' Squadron near Lopik and Zeist. On 1 July 1943 Frank became Kommandeur I./NJG1

Hauptmann Manfred Meurer of the 3rd Staffel destroyed two bombers on 83 and 77 Squadrons before he was hit by return fire from his second victim and he was forced to bail out wounded. On 27/28 July Ritterkreuzträger Meurer, Staffelkapitän 3./NJG1 claimed his fiftieth victory when he shot down a Mosquito flying a Ju 88R specially prepared for hunting Mosquitoes with much equipment removed to save weight and using GM1 (nitrous oxide, a power boosting device) to increase speed. Meurer was directed to Mosquito IV DZ458 on 139 Squadron flying at 8300 metres in a classic 'Himmelbett' interception. Overtaking the Mosquito from below and behind with a surplus speed of 30-40k/ph, only one of his cannon fired a six-shell burst but his quarry exploded immediately. Flying Officer E. S. A. Sniders and Squadron Leader K. G. Price, who had taken off from Wyton at 2305 hours for a raid on Duisburg, survived to be taken prisoner.

Hauptmann Wilhelm Herget, Kommandeur, I./NJG4 celebrated the Ritterkreuz awarded to him on 20 June having claimed thirty victories by scoring a triple victory: A 619 Squadron Lancaster at Asten, a Wellington on either 166 or 429 'Bison' Squadron RCAF at Neerkant and a 460 Squadron RAAF Lancaster at Leuthlerheide for his 32nd-34th kills. Seven bombers were shot down by IV./NJG1. Feldwebel Rudolf Frank of 2./NJG3 claimed his thirteenth victory, a 305 Squadron Wellington east of Antwerp but he and his crew were forced to bail out due to return fire.

On 22/23 June when 565 bombers raided Mulheim 578 people were killed and 1174 were injured in the twin towns of Mulheim and Oberhausen. Post war the British Bombing Survey Unit estimated that this single raid destroyed 64 per cent of Mulheim.

Thirty-six bombers failed to return, 25 kills being credited to the Nachtjagd. Six of these were claimed destroyed by IV./NJG1 and five by I./NJG1. Two Wellingtons - Wellington X HE326 on 466 Squadron, flown by Pilot Officer Albert Leonard Ford (Ford and two others KIA; one PoW) near Haminkeln at 0133 hours and Wellington X HZ312 on 429 'Bison' Squadron RCAF flown by 22-year old Wing Commander Joseph Logan Savard DFC RCAF (all KIA) near Rees/Niederrhein at 0135 hours - by Oberleutnant August 'Gustel' Geiger. Wellington X HF457 on 429 'Bison' Squadron RCAF skippered by 30-year old Pilot Officer William A. Sneath RCAF was shot down by Oberleutnant Hans Autenrieth of II./NJG1 on detachment to 6./NJG4. Sneath and two of the crew were killed, the Wimpy crashing at 0210 hours at Houthalen in Belgium. Two men were taken prisoner. Stirling III BK656 on 15 Squadron flown by Flying Officer John Vincent Hawkins RNZAF was claimed by Hauptmann Wilhelm Dormann. Stirling I EF399 on 75 Squadron flown by Flight Sergeant Kenneth Alfred Burbidge RNZAF was claimed by Gruppenkommandeur Hauptmann zur Lippe of III./NJG1. There were no survivors on either aircraft. Unteroffizier Karl-Georg Pfeiffer of 12./NJG1 took off from Bergen at 0008 hours and returned at 0152 hours having downed Halifax V DK225 on 427 'Lion' Squadron RCAF flown by Flight Lieutenant Keith Webster at Oost-Mijzen, north-east of Scharmerhorn at 0122 hours. Webster and five crew were killed; one man surviving to be taken prisoner. It was Pfeiffer's eighth victory. He adds:

'During spring-summer of 1943 towards evening, four aircraft were positioned to Bergen am See, which lies further to the west and allowed earlier intercepts. Though mainly responsible for the fighting area Salzhering (over the Zuider Sea) Bergen was the base for the more southerly areas (Zander-Zandvoort). I was one of the pilots who were frequently positioned at Bergen and I always looked forward to it. I was alone for the flight, which took place at low level, in order to avoid detection by the British radar but the best part was flying at about three metres above the dam at the Zuider Sea. Then came the point at Den Helder with the water tower and then into Bergen. A tragic affair took place on one of these positioning flights: the crew of Unteroffizier Ott, flying with the others at about 200 metres, was shot down by two centimetre flak, although information about the flight had previously been given. There was an inquiry but that did not help. A couple of good comrades were dead.

'It was always very cosy at Bergen am See because the senior officers remained in Leeuwarden and four or six crews were able to do their stand-by duty without great military ceremony. We either listened to music on the radio or played cards, chess, 'Skat' and 'Doppelkopf'.[106] Standby duty had another positive side: at this time there were for the first time German airwomen on communications duty, quite a new sight for us. Previously no females had been permitted on the airfield, for security reasons. As long as there were no operations we flirted with the girls and some of us fell in love and even married. Unless there were test flights to be carried out or battle training taking place, crews could nip into town and have an ice cream on the roof terrace of 'Vroom und Dreesmann' or go dancing in the 'Valhalla' and have some fun. But Leeuwarden was a main base of the German defence and when the American bomber attacks on Germany began and the British still came by night this was really the end of our best times, especially for our pilots.'

Wuppertal was the target for 630 aircraft on 24/25 June 1943 when Elberfeld, the other half of the town, unharmed on 29/30 May, was bombed. Thirty-four (or 5.4 per cent) aircraft failed to return. 'Himmelbett' Nachtjagd shot down 28 Main Force aircraft. Twenty-three year old Oberleutnant Gerhard Raht of 4./NJG3 flying a Ju 88C-6 claimed Lancaster III ED595 on 7 Squadron east of Rilland, Zeeland. Wing Commander Robert George Barrell DSO DFC* was killed when his parachute failed to deploy after he bailed out. Hauptmann Werner 'Red' Hoffmann destroyed a Lancaster; probably Lancaster III

GT-R ED858 on 156 Squadron piloted by Pilot Officer Richard Julian Hudson RAAF, which crashed at Erkelenz in the vicinity of Cologne with the loss of all seven crew. Hoffmann also claimed Wellington X HF594 AS-Q on 166 Squadron at Kirmington piloted by Pilot Officer Robert Eldyrn Currie RCAF which crashed at Dessel/Antwerp with the loss of all seven crew. Five Viermots were destroyed by III./NJG1 and one, a 196 Squadron Halifax near Gouda, by Hauptmann Hans-Dieter Frank of I./NJG1. Oberleutnant August 'Gustel' Geiger of III./NJG1 scored a triple victory in 43 minutes. The first of these was Stirling IV EF430 on 218 Squadron at 0126 at Empe which was lost with Squadron Leader D. M. Maw and crew; all of whom were taken prisoner. Halifax II HR731 on 51 Squadron at Snaith was shot down into the Ijsselmeer near Herderwijk at 0200 hours with the loss of Sergeant Anthony Osmond and all his crew. A Lancaster, possibly ED831 on 9 Squadron, which also disappeared into the Ijsselmeer, off Edam, at 0209, was lost with Squadron Leader Alan Murray Hobbs DFC RNZAF and his crew. Sixteen of the bombers lost on the Wuppertal raid were shot down by NJG1, including three Lancasters on 100, 101 and 103 Squadrons which were claimed by Oberfeldwebel Karl-Heinz Scherfling. Born on 6 September 1918 in Gelsenkirchen, he had been posted to III./NJG1 in late 1940 and claimed his first victory on 31 March/1 April 1941; a Vickers Wellington over Groningen. On 9/10 April he recorded his second, a Short Stirling near Lingen. In the spring of 1942 Scherfling transferred to 5./NJG2 and by late 1942 he had a total of six night-Abschüsse.

Unteroffizier Karl-Georg Pfeiffer of 12./NJG1 had mixed fortunes, as he recalls:

'On 25 June we took off alone because according to information from Feldwebel Heinz Huhn at the small operations room a single aircraft was about to pass slowly, apparently damaged, through our area on its way home. I was directed southwards and caught sight of it from quite a distance, crossing my path from left to right. Without waiting for further instructions - I was by now a successful night fighter - I throttled back, put the nose down and placed myself 300-400 metres below the aircraft, a Halifax. There were no signs that we had been spotted. I pulled up to about fifty metres below the long fuselage and was about to pull up in a routine attack from below and behind when Willi suddenly shouted over the intercom:

'Look out; he's coming down on us!'

'I replied quietly: 'If the Tommy is coming down, then we need not go up!'

I throttled back and indeed, the machine went down in front of me. [Halifax JB834 on 102 Squadron crashed in the North Sea at Breez and thirteen kilometres south of Den Helder at 0240 hours but this Abschuss was later credited to Hauptmann Jabs, Staffelkapitän 11./NJG1. It is highly probable that Pfeiffer's claim was subsequently turned down]. But I had pressed the firing button at just the right time and the kite went its full length through my burst. They struck true but a second later a burst rattled through our own machine and I felt a terrible pain in my right thigh close to the hip. I said painfully: 'Willi, I've been hit. Home quickly. Give me a course to Bergen; give me a course for home!' I can still hear him saying continuously '300°' but my brain was unable to do anything with this figure because of the pain. I went into a slow turn to starboard and down. Then suddenly our engine nacelles were lit up from below and I said to Willy, 'Well, at least he's down. What is the course for home?' And he repeated it. I had assumed that the bomber had caught fire below us to light us up from below. I was wrong. Now there was a banging in our machine, the ammunition was exploding because we were on fire ourselves. Willi shouted, I can't stand it any longer, the flames ... we must bail out!'

'Then I heard a bang. He had jettisoned the cabin roof. I got no reply to my calls, 'Willi, Willi'. He had already bailed out and I was alone. I became suddenly aware that we must by now be well out to sea. But just the same, I had no choice but to get out! I opened the roof and it went away with a bang, leaving the side panels flapping. What was it they had said? The pilot had to fly a half roll; push forward and let himself fall out. Easily said.

Stop - first release the straps. So - now the half roll! The flames were getting ever brighter and I could no longer see the horizon. I put the machine on its back, was caught by the slipstream and dragged out - but only half. One of my fur boots was caught between the seat and the starboard panel with the starters and I found myself with my head down half inside and half outside. The machine was hurtling down out of control. For a few seconds I thought, 'So that's what it's like when one dies'. But then the will to live returned.

'Breathing heavily - the slipstream sucked the air from my lungs - I tried to struggle back into my seat, managed it and got hold of the stick. I pulled and it responded. Having levelled out I said to myself quietly: 'Now you must fly the roll of your life, otherwise you will not get out'. I put her slowly on her back, waited until I was certain that I was upside down, then a push forward on the stick and I was flung out like a shot. Now the ripcord handle. Where was it? At last I had it and I pulled it right out until I had it free in my hand. For a few seconds nothing, then a painful jerk and the bright canopy opened up above me. Now all was strangely quiet, while I was swinging to and fro. My wound burned like fire because the parachute straps were tight around it. I felt ill and was sick as I went slowly downward. Thinking that I was still over the sea, I tried to pull the cords on one side to steer closer towards the shore, which I thought to be where the skies were darkest. Then suddenly it collapsed and I dropped like a stone. Startled, I let go and fortunately it opened up again. When I sensed that the ground could not be far away I held my arms in front of my face and there was a heavy bump, which brought a new heavy pain. I lay on the ground, breathing heavily and was unable to move my right leg. It was broken. I must have become unconscious. I awoke some time later and dragged the white silk of the parachute over and laid my head on it. It was freezing cold and my limbs were shaking.

'Suddenly I heard hoof beats and was startled to see cattle charging towards me. I fired some signal lights and the beasts retreated. My watch showed about half past three. In the course of time I fired off all my signal ammunition but no one came to help. At half past six, as the day dawned, a man wearing silk pyjamas came running along. He had been sleeping in a boat, which had been lying at anchor in a Gracht. It was a friendly Dutchman. He tore up his singlet and stuffed it into my wound, which was bleeding strongly. Then he ran off again and brought some farmers who offered me some cigarettes. They had apparently heard me but had not dared to come to help. Shortly after seven a German ambulance, which the man in the pyjamas had called, came and I was carefully laid in it. Now I discovered I was in the vicinity of Leiden. I was taken to the university hospital and operated on straight away. Two days later my radio operator, head and arms bandaged with burns, called. He had no broken bones. He was able to return to Leeuwarden. Some days later Feldwebel Scherfling brought me a new jacket with the epaulettes of a Feldwebel. Major Lent had promoted me. After eleven days Oberleutnant Greiner turned up. He put me with my plastered leg into a car and took me to Bergen. We continued from there in a Fieseler Storch to Leeuwarden where I was taken into the Ziekenhuis in the Troelstrastraat. I had a high temperature but was happy to be 'home'. I was now taken good care of but it was many weeks before I could be discharged. Then I went on home leave. Meanwhile the Gruppe had been transferred from Leeuwarden to Quakenbrück and I was instructed to go there after my leave. After a couple of weeks I was back on operations. During this time I had to be helped into the cockpit and I was only able to walk with the aid of a stick.'

Feldwebel Heinz Huhn who, after his third pilot, Oberleutnant Karl Heinz Vollkopf was killed on 21 June decided, he had had enough and he never flew again. For the remaining years of the war he served as Operations Officer at Bergen/Alkmaar and Sint-Truiden/Sint-Trond airfields.

On 25/26 June 473 bombers attacked Gelsenkirchen. Thirty-one aircraft were lost, including thirteen Lancasters and seven Halifaxes. All told, Bomber command lost 275 bombers shot down in June 1943. Some of the losses were attributed to aircraft missing on 'Gardening' operations whose crews were flying the first operation of their tour as an introduction to combat operations over the Reich. There was no Main Force activity on the night of Sunday 27/Monday 28 June when a Lancaster minelayer was lost from the fifteen Lancasters and fifteen Stirlings that carried out 'Gardening' operations in the Frisians, off La Pallice and in the River Gironde. Flying Officer Frederick Sinclair Buck a Canadian from Toronto, and his crew took Lancaster I ED377 SR-Q, better known as 'Q-Queenie' for their Sunday night 'Gardening' outing to France. A veteran of 186 hours and still flyable after damage in a recent crash landing had been repaired, Buck taxied 'Q-Queenie' out and headed for the 'Gardening' region off La Pallice on the French Atlantic coast. Probably the crew were in a state of high expectancy but this first operation was to be their epitaph. Oberleutnant Erich Gollasch of 11./NJG5 who had four Abschüsse, shot the Lancaster down at 0215 hours at 15,000 feet, 25 kilometres WNW of Angers for his fifth victory. 'Queenie' crashed at Angrie, six kilometres EWE of Cande in the Maine-et-Loire. The six crew who were killed were interred later in the Pont-du-Cens Communal Cemetery in Nantes. Sergeant 'Jimmy' Sparkes, the flight engineer, was the sole survivor. He successfully evaded capture and, with the help of the Marie-Claire escape line, made a 'home run' via Gibraltar. Gollasch was killed on 25/26 September 1943 during aerial combat at Tscherkasy in the Ukraine.

Cologne was subjected to three consecutive heavy raids in late June and early July. On the 28/29 June raid on the city 608 heavies were dispatched. Twenty-five bombers failed to return, all of which were probably destroyed by the 'Himmelbett' Nachtjagd. Eight were claimed destroyed by I./NJG1 and twelve by II./NJG1 over eastern Belgium. Hauptmann Werner 'Red' Hoffmann, Staffelkapitän 4./NJG5 destroyed Stirling BK694 on 15 Squadron flown by Pilot Officer Jack Bradshaw Keen. Only one man on his crew survived to be taken into captivity. Hauptmann Hoffmann became acting Gruppenkommandeur of I./NJG5 in July. On 15 November he was awarded the Deutsches Kreuz in Gold for fifteen victories and by the end of 1943 had a victory total of eighteen.

A follow-up raid on Cologne on 3/4 July 1943 by 653 bombers, cost Harris another thirty aircraft. Twenty-six year old Hauptmann Siegfried Wandam Kommandeur of 1/NJG5, who destroyed a Wellington eight kilometres west of St. Trond followed this by shooting down a Halifax on 35 Squadron flown by Sergeant Donald Milne for his tenth and final Abschuss. Milne's gunners had found their mark however, for Wandam's Bf 110G-4 suffered combat damage and crashed at Hoepertingen on final approach to land at St. Trond on one engine. Wandam and his bordfunker, Feldwebel Alfred Shöpke were killed.

Twelve of the RAF bombers that were lost were claimed shot down over the target by single-engined 'Wilde Sau' ('Wild Boar') fighter pilots of the Nachtjagd Versuchs Kommando (Night Fighting Experimental Command), which were employed for the first time this night. 'Wild Boar' can be attributed to Ritterkreuzträger Oberst Hans-Joachim 'Hajo' Herrmann, a bomber pilot and one of the foremost blind flying experts in the Luftwaffe. Beginning his military career as an infantry officer, he was commissioned in the newly formed Luftwaffe in 1935. From 1936 until 1937, he was a bomber pilot in the Condor Legion. During the Spanish Civil War, Herrmann joined KG4 and wrote several well received tactical reports. When World War II began, he flew Heinkel He 111s in Poland and Norway. By 1940 he was Commander of the 7th Staffel of KG4 and led many attacks on England during the Battle of Britain. In February 1941 his gruppe went to Sicily, where it flew against Malta and Greece.[107] Herrmann had been agitating for a long time, without success, for permission to practice freelance single-engined night-fighting. He had reasoned that the light of the massed searchlights, Path Finder flares and the flames of the burning target below could easily identify enemy bombers over a German city. By putting a mass concentration of mainly single-engined fighters over the target, his pilots could, without need of ground control, but assisted by a running commentary from a lentraler Gefechtsstand (Central Operational Headquarters), visually identify the bombers and shoot them down. A Fuhlungshalter (shadowing) aircraft, usually a Ju 88 or Do 217, would fly in or near a penetrating bomber stream and keep the plotting room at the Zentraler Gefechtsstand informed of course, height and speed of the bombers.

Around May 1943 Hermann had begun trials at Jüterborg in the use of the Bf 109G-6 as a night fighter. On 27 June he transferred his activities to Blind Flying School No 10 at Altenburg, where he gathered together some experienced pilots and began forming a Nachtjagd Versuchs Kommando using a dozen FW 190As fitted with 300 litre (66-gallon) drop tanks. As a result of his suggestion, 'Helle Nachtjagd' was again tried in July and, after, the first trials in Berlin and the Ruhr proved successful. (Twelve Viermots were shot down on 3/4 July over Cologne). 'Helle Nachtjagd' was put into operation over the whole of Germany. This procedure, termed 'Wilde Sau' ('Wild Boar') for short, called for close co-operation by the night fighters and the flak over the target and a dependable control of single-engined night-fighters throughout wide areas. Co-operation was achieved by visual signals and by radio. Flare paths and a system of radio beacons were established. The single engine night fighter was particularly favoured by virtue of its high rate of climb to participate in this primitive form of night fighting the Germans were now forced to adopt. Herrmann's pilots were a motley collection, loosely organized and rather like guerrilla bands in their attitude to authority, composed as they were by volunteers drawn from all sections of the Luftwaffe, including highly qualified ex-bomber pilots and even pilots in disgrace seeking reinstatement. They were equipped with the Focke Wulf 190F-5/U2 and the Bf 109G-6/U4N. Additional FuG 25a and FuG 16zy radio equipment and the FuG 350 'Naxos-Z' radar-receiving set, which could pick up H_2S radar emissions from up to thirty miles away, were installed.

The 'Wild Boar' had to share the victories over Cologne with the local flak defences, who also claimed twelve successes. Twenty-one crews of II./NJG1 at Sint-Truiden/Sint-Trond returned with claims for fourteen 'Himmelbett' Abschüsse. Oberleutnant Heinz-Wolfgang Schnaufer and Leutnant Johannes Hager of Stab II./NJG1 and Oberleutnant Wilhelm Telge, Staffelkapitän, 5./NJG1 each claimed two kills. Schnaufer's claims were for Wellington X HE980 on 196 Squadron at Averbode, seven kilometres (4.3 miles) northwest of Diest at 0048 and Stirling III BF530 on 149 Squadron near Geetbets, nine kilometres (5.6 miles) northwest of Sint-Truiden at 101 hours. Flight Sergeant Paul Gee's and his crew were killed. Pilot Officer George Arthur Cozens DFM and five of his crew died. One evaded and one was taken prisoner.

Flying Officer 'Harry' White and his navigator/radio operator Flying Officer Mike Seamer Allen on 141 Squadron, who had still to claim their first kill, encountered a Bf 110 near Aachen while on patrol in their Beaufighter VIf to the German airfield at Eindhoven. White blasted the night-fighter at 200 yards dead astern in a two second burst. Then he gave the enemy a second burst of cannon and machine-gun fire before diving violently away to port to avoid collision, but the enemy aircraft was not seen again and they could claim only a 'damaged'.

On 8/9 July when Cologne was raided again, 23-year old Eugene Leon Rosner's crew on 106 Squadron at Syerston was on the Battle Order for their 19th operation. On the previous raid on Cologne, on 28/29 June when 608 heavies had been dispatched, Flying Officer Rosner's crew had returned safely from their 18th op. Following interrogation and a bacon and egg breakfast, they all tidied up and headed off on nine day's leave that all the crews were due every six weeks. On returning a week later Rosner told them he would be returning to London to re-muster in the USAAF. He had been pestering the American authorities for weeks to get a transfer to the 8th Air Force. He promised to get the crew some more leave while he was away. Two days later he had returned from London wearing the uniform of a 1st Lieutenant. He had been accepted by the USAAF but he was to complete his tour of operations with the RAF. On 8 July Rosner was told that he would be taking ED720 'R-Robert' and a 'second dickey'. The met forecast was that there would be cumulonimbus clouds up to 20,000 feet over the target.

Twenty-four II./NJG1 crews manned the 'Himmelbett' boxes in eastern Belgium and, despite being hampered by thick layers of cloud, destroyed three Lancasters and claimed seven 'Feindberührungen' ('encounters with the enemy'). Worst hit was 106 Squadron at Syerston, which accounted for three of the losses. Lancaster I R5573 ZB-B piloted by 20-year old Flight Sergeant Kenneth Hector 'Wally' McLean RCAF was shot down NNE of Liège by Oberleutnant Paul Zorner of 3./NJG3 on detachment from 1./NJG1, his ninth victory. There were no survivors. ED360, skippered by Flight Sergeant Arthur George Bristow, crashed northwest of Wisbech killing the pilot and four of his crew.

Warrant Officer Fred Smooker, the 24-year old bomb aimer on ED720, got 'R-Robert's five tons of HE bombs and incendiaries away and the holocaust left behind as they headed south. Rosner turned onto a westerly heading and 'R-Robert' was at 22,000 feet when the starboard outer began heating up. Near Cambrai (Nord) at about 03.30 Oberleutnant Friedrich 'Fritz' Graeff of Stab 1/NJG4 in Bf 110G-4 3C+FB attacked and set the starboard inner on fire but the German pilot failed to pull out in time and he collided with the 'Lanki'. Graef was wounded but managed to bail out. Unteroffizier Heinrich Koehler and Oberfeldwebel Paul Scheuermann died when their aircraft crashed at Wignehies.

On intercom Rosner said: 'Hey you guys, we gotta bail out. Somebody get me my parachute. Bail out, bail out, bail out...' The two screaming port engines suddenly stopped dead and the aircraft went down. Only Fred Smooker got out. Rosner and the five others on his crew, and 21-year old Pilot Officer Geoffrey Disbury flying as the 'second dickie' to gain experience, died in the aircraft. They were laid to rest on 11 July. Smooker was not caught by the Germans until after mid-September and did not arrive in PoW camp until about 15 November. For 56 days he was held in solitary confinement in a Paris prison.

The next Main Force raid was directed to Gelsenkirchen on 9/10 July when seven Halifaxes and five Lancasters went missing from a force of 418 aircraft. Hauptmann August 'Gustel' Geiger of III./NJG1, who was temporarily detached to I./NJG4, destroyed Halifax BB249 on 102 Squadron at Eprave near Dinant, Belgium. Flight Sergeant Albert Thomas Fraser RAAF and three of his crew were killed; three men were taken prisoner.

An area bombing raid on Aachen on Tuesday 13/Wednesday 14 July, which was reported as 'a Terrorangriff of the most severe scale,' officially ended the Battle of the Ruhr. Bombs released by 374 aircraft, mainly Halifaxes, devastated large parts of Aachen, reducing almost 3,000 individual buildings containing almost 17,000 flats/apartments to rubble and killing or injuring over a thousand people. Strong head winds of between 50-90 mph slowed the returning bombers and fifteen Halifaxes, two Lancasters, two Wellingtons and a Stirling were lost. NJG1 and NJG4 were credited with eighteen 'Himmelbett' kills. Both Lancaster losses were from 115 Squadron at East Wretham. Lancaster II DS660 skippered by Flying Officer Rodney Boyd Larson RCAF was claimed by Hauptmann Paul-Hubert Rauh of 3./NJG4 5400 metres over Metz-en-Couture at 0235 hours. The Canadian pilot was the only survivor. Six crew including Sergeant John Albert Thomas Newton, the 19-year old tail-gunner, were killed. Two of the crew bailed out but their bodies were found the following morning. Lancaster II DS690 KO-C flown by 33-year old Squadron Leader The Hon. Robert Alexander Graville Baird was shot down on the homeward leg by Hauptmann August 'Gustel' Geiger of 7./NJG1 and crashed at La Comette in Belgium at 0210. Baird, the 33-year old son of Viscount and Viscountess Stonehaven and five of his crew, including Sergeant Harold Matthews the 19-year old tail-gunner, were killed; the one survivor was taken prisoner. Baird left a widow, Dorviegelda Malvina. This was Gieger's 37th claim, most of which were accompanied by his 22-year old bordshütze, Feldwebel Dieter Koch.

Five bombers - all of them Halifaxes - were destroyed by I./NJG1. Oberleutnant Wilhelm Telge, Staffelkapitän 5./NJG1 and Telsnig his bordfunker shot down two Halifaxes - JD116 on 158 Squadron flown by Squadron Leader Ronald Sidney Williams DFC (Williams and four crew KIA; two PoW) northeast of Gelsenkirchen and an unidentified aircraft that came down at Weissweiler at 0151 hours. Telge was killed on 31 August/1 September 1943 when he rammed a Stirling southwest of Berlin. His bordfunker, Feldwebel Walter Telsing who was with Telge on all his twelve Abschüsse and Signal Officer Oberleutnant Freimann, bailed out and survived after the Bf 110G-4 (G9+AN) sheered a wing. Telsing later took part in eleven victories with Hauptmann Adolf Breves.

In East Anglia meanwhile, a 'Storangriffe' attack by ten Me 410s of V/KG2 operating from bases in Northern France flew in over the east coast and penetrated the defences towards Cambridgeshire to carry out attacks on three airfields. From 2500 metres they dived to 1500 metres and released 31 high-explosive SC50 on Mildenhall, Cambridge and Waterbeach airfields. These raids were no more than nuisance attacks, with little strategic or military value.[108]

On the clear night of 15/16 July, 165 Halifaxes attacked the Peugeot motor factory at Montbéliard suburb of the French town of Sochaux near the Swiss border. The raid killed and injured large numbers of civilian casualties and damage to the plant was minimal. Five Halifaxes were shot down. Feldwebel Helmut Späte of 5./NJG4 was killed in combat with Halifax II JB961 ZA-R on 10 Squadron, which was lost with Flight Sergeant Harry Briggs Mellor and crew at Recey-sur-Ourthe. Unteroffizier Philipps of 6./NJG4 claimed a 'Stirling' at Besancon. Unteroffizier Heinrich Prinz of 5/NJG4 claimed a Halifax at Le Barre, Besancon for his first and only victory before he collided with his victim and was killed.[109] Twenty-nine year old Major Hubert Raüh of 6./NJG4, an Austrian born in Kleinwolkersdorf, claimed a Halifax for his seventh Abschüsse before his Bf 110G-2 was shot down eight miles southeast of Rheims during an 'Intruder' patrol to Juvincourt by Flying Officers 'Harry' White and Mike Allen on 141 Squadron, one of six Beaufighter crews providing Bomber Support for the Main Force. It was their first victory. Raüh bailed out safely but his bordshütze, Obergefreiter Stamm was killed. Raüh was shot down again on 30 December 1943 by a P-47 and again on 21 March 1945 when his aircraft was hit by return fire from a bomber. Raüh was decorated with the Ritterkreuz and he finished the war with 29 Viermot-Abschüsse in 152 combat sorties.[110]

The Battle of the Ruhr was fought over 99 nights and 55 days 5/6 March-23/24 July 1943 and 24,355 heavy bomber sorties were flown. The main Battle of the Ruhr lasted for four months, during which, 43 major raids were carried out. Two thirds of these were against the Ruhr and the rest were to other areas including Stettin on the Baltic, Munich in Bavaria, Pilzen in Czechoslovakia and Turin in Italy. Approximately 57,034 tons of bombs were dropped at a cost of 1038 aircraft (4.3 per cent). Though the flak and searchlight defences around the cities in the Ruhr were by now the most powerful in the Reich, the large majority of these aircraft were destroyed by 'Himmelbett' Nachtjagd.

Endnotes Chapter 9

100   Jordan was awarded an immediate DSO and Paulton and Bigoray received the DFC and DFM respectively. The courage of the crew enabled information to be pieced together on the new radar. As a result, a new, lighter 'Window' was produced.
101   The aircraft is on permanent display at the RAF Museum, Hendon.
102   Since the end of 1942 RAF night-fighters had been able to 'home' onto the radar impulses emitted by the FuG 202/212 Lichtenstein (AI) radars in the 490 Megacycles band by using the 'Serrate' homer, which could only home in on the Lichtenstein AI radar and only if the sets were turned off. 'Serrate' had first been used by 141 Squadron Beaufighter FVIs on 14 June 1943. The first victories to be credited to Mosquitoes fitted with 'Serrate' occurred on the night of 28/29 January 1944 when a Bf 109 and a Bf 110 were shot down. See *Confounding the Reich* by Martin W. Bowman and Tom Cushing Pen & Sword Aviation 2004).
103   Norbert Krüger, *The Bomber Command War Diaries.*
104   On 11 March 1944 Streib was awarded the Swords to his Knights Cross for 66 confirmed victories. On 23 March he was made Inspector of Night Fighters and he would stay in this post as Oberst until the end of the war. Werner Streib was officially credited with shooting down 66 enemy aircraft, with 65 claimed at night.
105   17 Halifaxes, 9 Lancasters, 9 Wellingtons and 9 Stirlings. 38 of these losses were due to Himmelbett night fighters operating mainly over the southern provinces of the Netherlands.
106   'Doppelkopf' ('double-head'), also abbreviated to 'Doko', is a trick-taking card game for four players. 'Skat', which is also played by four players, originally was called 'Schafkopf', a late 18th-century German trick-taking card game most popular in Bavaria, but also played in other parts of Germany.
107   In one such attack, on 6 April 1941 when German forces invaded Greece and Luftwaffe bombers led by Herrmann attacked shipping in Piraeus, the steamship *SS Clan Fraser* was in port still unloading her arms and 200 tons of TNT. At 0315 hours she was hit by a single bomb dropped by Herrmann and destroyed when her TNT exploded. She sank in the harbour, with six killed and nine wounded. Her Master, J. H. Giles, was among the survivors. The shock of the blast was felt fifteen miles away in Athens, where doors were blown in; and in Psihiko, where windows were shattered. White hot debris detonated TNT in other nearby ships, setting them and buildings ashore on fire. The resulting explosion sank eleven ships and made the Greek port unusable for many months. In early 1942 Herrmann was Commander of III./KG30, attacking Arctic convoys from Norway, including the attacks on PQ-17. July 1942 saw him assigned to the general staff in Germany, where he became a close confidant of Hermann Göring. During his career as a bomber pilot, Herrmann flew 320 sorties and sank twelve ships totalling 70,000 tons.
108   *War-Torn Skies of Great Britain: Cambridgeshire* by Julian Evan-Hart (Red Kite 2008).
109   Both he and Major Hubert Raüh claimed a Halifax 500 metres east of Sacquenay at 0130 hours. Halifax II HR752 NP-T on 78 Squadron crashed near Sacquenay. Flight Sergeant Robert Deans and three of his crew were killed. The flight engineer evaded and the other two were taken prisoner.
110   At war's end, he became a British PoW and was released in February 1946. He retired from the Austrian Air Force as an Oberst. He died on 30 August 2005 at Neunkirchen Austria.

Chapter Ten

Gomorrah

In 1943 I was in a children's home run entirely by women, somewhere outside the centre of Hamburg. I don't think the women were in the 'Party' - I think it was just a local authority home. Of course there were pictures of Hitler everywhere and we had to salute the picture and sing Fahne hoch! (Raise the Flag) and Deutschland Uber Alles and we celebrated Hitler's birthday.

Neither my mother nor my grandmother ever visited me in the home before, but a few months after the bombing when my grandmother took me to the station I saw for the first time what had happened to the city, a lot of ruins, a lot of flattened buildings, burned out houses or just rubble. It was sad to see it all gone, but in a way this had all happened as if at another time - I was there but it was as if I wasn't there. It was different being in a 'home', if I'd been at home with my mother and half sisters and brothers I would have felt it all much more directly.

But I do remember one bombing raid in the home. We were woken up at night by one of the 'teachers'; I don't know what time it was, nobody had a watch then. We were just told Schnell, Schnell, out of the beds, everybody down the cellar. Alarm, but quietly, quietly!' Of course, we were all excited, not scared at all, just excited. Everything was dark upstairs, all the lights were off, but there were lights in the cellar. We got used to this, it happened several times, of course, in the home you didn't actually see anything that was going on outside. So, we were taken down to the cellar, settled down there, told to be quiet and of course, you were quiet - there was no answering back in those days - and then you went back up again. In the cellar there were straw sacks, blankets, it was fairly big. There were about thirty kids and the grown-ups.

I don't know how long we were down there. It seemed like a long time. We went back to sleep. I vaguely remember being woken up again, it was still night, it must have been about three in the morning. They told us, when you finish breakfast, get your coats on; you're being taken to another home. I must have heard about this bomb which hadn't exploded from the grown-ups. Of course we were all excited again - this was like a day trip. We didn't have any gear, only one set of clothes and we just put a coat on top and were marched out to the lorries.

I don't actually remember seeing anything outside the building - nor could we see anything out of the lorry. The journey must have been about an hour. I think we were there about three weeks, then went back to the other place - I don't remember seeing anything of the town even then.

Hildegard Teal, nee Burr who was 10 when Hamburg was bombed. As an unwanted child when her mother remarried, she was put in a children's home at the age of two and was moved from one home to another throughout childhood. In the home she was strangely cut off from the bombing. At the start of the Battle of the Ruhr, 'Bomber' Harris had been able to call upon almost 600 heavies for Main Force operations and at the pinnacle of the Battle, near the end of May, more than 800 aircraft took part. Innovations such as Path Finders to find and mark targets with their TIs and wizardry such as 'Oboe', which enabled crews to find them, were instrumental in the mounting levels of death and destruction, but little, it seemed, could be done to assuage the bomber losses, which by the end of the campaign had reached high proportions.

On the very hot, sultry weekend of 24/25 July conditions over Hamburg were clear with only a gentle wind. Feldwebel Hans Meissner a 23-year old Bf 110 pilot in 6./NJG3 patrolled Box 'Kiebitz C' a little to the north of the city and his bordfunker Josef Krinner picked up a bomber on his Li-set. It was P-Peter' the Stirling on 218 'Gold Coast' Squadron flown by the 39-year old CO, Wing Commander Donald Teale Saville DSO DFC, one of 791 bombers dispatched by 'Bomber' Harris in the first of four raids, code-named 'Gomorrah' on Germany's second city. 'Gomorrah' was carefully chosen and had great significance. In biblical times it was one of the two most powerful and wealthy cities in the southern Jordan valley, the other being Sodom. These two cities warred against Abraham and God's chosen people. After the people of Sodom insulted two visiting Angels, God decided to destroy both cities. The Lord rained upon Sodom and Gomorrah brimstone and fire out of heaven and lo the smoke of the country went up as the smoke of a furnace. In his message of good luck to his crews Harris said that 'The Battle of Hamburg cannot be won in a single night. It is estimated that at least 10,000 tons of bombs will have to be dropped to complete the process of elimination. To achieve the maximum effect of air bombardment this city should be subjected to sustained attack. A large number of incendiaries are to be carried in order to saturate the Fire Services.'

Led by H_2S PFF aircraft, 740 bombers rained down 2,284 tons of high explosive and incendiary bombs in two and a half hours upon the suburb of Barmbeck, on both banks of the Alster, on the suburbs of Hoheluft, Eirnsbüttel and Altona and on the inner city. The Rathaus with its copper roof, the Nikolaikirche in Nikolaifleet in the Aldstadt (old town) the Central Police Station, the Long-Distance Telephone Exchange and Carl Hagenbeck's famous Zoo, where 140 animals died, were among the well-known landmarks to be hit. Approximately 1,500 people were killed. Only twelve bombers were shot down[111] (just 1.5% of the force) but bordfunkers had reported several targets at once on their Li sets. Unteroffizier Otto Kutzner of 5./NJG3, piloting a Bf 110G-4 reported that: 'My radar operator suddenly had more targets than could have been possible. I know that I got some directions from him to head on but these were impossible to maintain because we couldn't possibly have overtaken the bombers so fast if they had been real targets. I was picking up targets that didn't exist everywhere. We kept finishing up behind a target but there was never the slipstream of the bomber. In addition to all these troubles, it was my first operational flight. I had no success.'

Another radar operator, Unteroffizier Rolf Angersbach in 3./NJG3 said: 'When we reached our box, we were immediately told by the Jägerleitoffizier (JLO or fighter-control officer) that everything was jammed and that we were simply to fly in the direction of Hamburg. This was unusual; I had never heard this order before. I was surprised. We flew towards Hamburg and soon had many contacts on my radar screen. We thought that we were right in the centre of the bomber-stream. The first impression was that the bombers were heading straight for us. Therefore, we turned, in order to get in behind one of these but, after the turn, they were still coming too fast. I said, 'slow down, slower still, you're too fast'. The pilot said there must be something wrong because he had already let down the flaps and was flying as slowly as possible. We got contact after contact but not one of them was a firm one. We could hear on the radio that the officer on the ground was having trouble too. This went on for a good hour. We saw firing here and there but I couldn't tell whether any aircraft were being shot down. We landed at Stade, instead of our own airfield at Vechta. I seem to remember that we were ordered to land there so that the Gruppe staff could ask us all about the flight. My pilot went into the headquarters and had a conversation with Major Lent, whom he knew very well. He came back and said something like, 'they seem to be all helpless and bewildered'.[112]

In 'Himmelbett' Box 'Tiger' around the Dutch Frisian island of Terschelling Oberleutnant Georg Hermann Greiner of IV./NJG1 at Leeuwarden patrolled well out to sea when a JLO picked up a bomber en route for home. Greiner, born on 2 January 1920 at Heidenheim in the Gunzenhausen region of Mittelfranken, had joined the Luftwaffe on 1 October 1938 as an officer cadet.[113] Greiner was convinced that his victim was a Halifax but it was Lancaster ED878 on 103 Squadron at Elsham Wolds which was being flown by Warrant Officer Felix Francis O'Hanlon whose crew were on their thirteenth operation. Greiner recalled: 'I was controlled from the ground on to this bomber which was crossing 'Tiger' in a north-westerly direction. It was going so slowly that I overshot it on my first run. I soon saw the reason for this was that it had two engines failed, both on one side! It took me - for a combat situation - rather a long time to make up my mind what to do next. I realized that he had probably been damaged over Hamburg and that he had been lucky to get so far towards England. I thought about letting him succeed in this exploit but I had to consider other factors and decided that I had to force a result. I didn't feel too happy about shooting him down though. However, I aimed, as in most other cases, very carefully at the wing tanks to give the crew a chance.'

Unfortunately, despite Greiner's careful aim all seven crew were killed.[114] By the end of September, Greiner would have thirteen victories to his credit. In Box 'Tiger' also Lancaster JA866 piloted by Flight Sergeant Robert Arthur Moore was flying at only 5,000 feet (1600 metres) when it was shot down straight into the sea with one burst of fire by Oberleutnant Ernst-Georg Drünkler of I/NJG5 for his fourth night-Abschuss, which he believed was a Halifax. Drünkler, born on 8 July 1920 at Bernburg, Saale had begun his career with II./ZG2 on the Eastern Front. In November 1942 he had joined I./NJG5. After a spell as an instructor, he became Staffelkapitän of 13./NJG5, which he led until the war ended. As a Hauptmann with forty victories, he was awarded the Knights Cross on 20 March 1945. All seven crew on JA866, who were on their sixth op were killed. A third Lancaster on 103 Squadron which failed to return to Elsham Wolds was ED389 flown by Warrant Officer Gordon Edward Bernard Hardman which was shot down in Box 'Salzhering', probably destroyed by Hauptmann Rudolph Sigmund of IV/NJG1. There were no survivors on the seven man crew, who were on their 17th operation.

In Box 'Kiebitz A' near Scheslwig Leutnant Kurt Böttinger of 6./NJG3 gained his first Abschuss when he shot down a Stirling. Böttinger claimed a second Abschuss, a Halifax at Insel Mano on 24 August, before he was killed in a crash on 26 November at Langendiebach airfield after hitting an obstacle. In Box 'Ameise' ('Ant') north of Sønderborg in Denmark, HR940, a 51 Squadron Halifax flown by 24-year old Sergeant William John Murray who was flying the correct heading but was sixty miles from the bomber-stream, was shot down at 0124 hours by Oberleutnant Günther Köberich of IV/NJG3 flying a Ju 88. Five men were found dead in the wreckage in an orchard on the north bank of the Flensburg Fiord near Sønderborg and the two remaining members of the crew died soon after.[115] Köberich's score had reached fourteen before he was killed on 8 August 1944 at Quakenbrück airfield during a raid by American B-17s. Wellington X HZ314 on 166 Squadron skippered by 21-year old Warrant Officer George Ashplant CGM was claimed shot down by Unteroffizier Walter Rohlfing of 9./NJG3 at 0140 hours at 2500 metres at Buchholz. Ashplant, who had gained his CGM earlier in the year following a mid-air collision with a 166 Squadron Halifax and his crew were killed. This was the second victory for Rohlfing who survived the war with claims for eleven Abschüsse.

'P-Peter' the Stirling on 218 'Gold Coast' Squadron flown by Wing Commander Saville was one of three Stirlings that failed to return. The Australian pilot, born in 1903 at Portland New South Wales and affectionately known as the 'Mad Aussie' had encountered the heavy concentration of flak and searchlights along the banks of the Kiel Canal over which the bomber stream passed. This was a very unpopular area and crews disliked being routed over it. Saville dived and turned to get out of the searchlights but in doing so he left the bomber stream and quickly became vulnerable to the prowling night fighters looking for rich pickings. Feldwebel Hans Meissner set two engines on fire during his initial attack, fifty miles North of Hamburg. Eight kilometres NNW of Neumünster the body of Wing Commander Saville was found at the controls. Six of his crew, most of who were on the 9th operation of their second tour, also died. One man bailed out to be taken prisoner.[116] Meissner could not have known who his victims were but he never set out to kill the crew as he recalls:

'My duty was done when the attacked aircraft went down. The object was not to kill the crew but to destroy engines and tanks. Thus I can say that with the exception of my first kills, when I was rather nervous, large numbers of the bombers' crews always succeeded in descending by parachute. I do not mention this in order to extenuate or glorify. It was a bare fact. Our conversations prior to an action and afterwards were sober, without boasting. All of us, friends and adversaries, had at least one thing in common - death, which might have taken any of us at any time. The Hamburg raid was an horrendous event with vast areas set on fire. No doubt this was a clear signal that as a terror factor we Germans did not have it all our own way in bombing. If we had known the result of our effort I think we would have said that they started it. But we did not know. Our bosses sent us again in the 25th to Essen.'

Reich Minister of Propaganda Dr. Joseph Göbbels wrote in his diary: 'Last night an extraordinarily heavy air raid was made on Hamburg. It had the most devastating consequences both for the civilian population and for armaments production in Hamburg. This raid has finally blown apart the illusions that many people still had about future enemy aerial operations. Unfortunately we shot down remarkably few of the enemy bombers, only twelve in all out of a total of approximately 500; of course this is a woefully inadequate showing. Regrettably, just two days ago, General Weise took the heavy flak guns away from Hamburg to send to Italy. That was the crowning blow.'

On 25/26 July 627 aircraft out of 705 despatched dropped 2,032 tons of bombs upon Essen. The raid caused severe damage to the industrial areas in the eastern parts of the city. Harris was not exaggerating when he said that 'they inflicted as much damage in the Krupps works as in all previous attacks put together'. Fifty-one other industrial buildings were damaged with another 83 heavily damaged. 'The raid' recorded Göbbels in his diary 'caused a complete stoppage of production in the Krupps works. Speer is much concerned and worried'. The areas particularly damaged included, in addition to the Krupps works, Altenessen, Segeroth, Borbeck, Holsterhausen, Rüttenscheid, Frohnhausen, Delbig and Vogelheim. The fire services of the city had to attempt to deal with 270 large and 250 small fires; 340 people lost their lives, 1,128 were wounded and 35,144 rendered homeless: 1,508 houses were destroyed and 1,083 badly damaged. On the morning after the raid, Doktor Gustav Krupp von Bohlen und Halbach came down to his office from the Villa Hügel, where he lived, cast one look upon the blazing remnants of his works and fell down in a fit. This, since he had not recovered from it, saved him in 1947 from being put on trial with other war criminals. Twenty-six bombers or 3.7% of the force failed to return, of which, nineteen were destroyed by night-fighters - fifteen of these to crews of NJG1 and NJG3 manning the 'Himmelbett' boxes in Holland and over the Dutch-German border. 'Wild Boar' single-engined night fighters that engaged the bomber stream over the blazing city of Essen claimed the four remaining aircraft losses. One of these was Lancaster III ED884 on 103 Squadron skippered by 25-year old Flight Lieutenant Harold Frederick Ewer DFC of Westbank, British Columbia, which crashed at Borbeck midway between Oberhausen and Essen with the loss of all seven crew. The aircraft was shot down between 4600 and 7000 metres over Essen at around 0215 hours by either Unteroffizier Wolfgang Knobloch or Feldwebel Horst Heinstein both of 5./JG 300 'Hermann'. It would have been Knobloch's first claim of the war. He was wounded after bailing out of his Bf 109G-6 during air combat with American fighters on 5 August. It would also have been Heinstein's first claim. He was killed on 27/28 August in a crash near Schweinfurt.

Turning his attention to Hamburg once again, Bomber Harris said, 'I feel sure that a further two or three raids on Hamburg, then probably a further six raids on Berlin and the war will finish.'

Bad weather at Hamburg on Monday 26 July prevented a follow-up raid on the German port by the Main Force. Just six Mosquitoes visited Hamburg and three each went to Cologne and Gelsenkirchen. It was enough to permit RAF Headquarters to announce that 'Last night the RAF carried out major raids against Germany. Rapid Mosquito bombers raided Cologne, while Hamburg was bombed for the third time within a 48-hour period.'

On the Tuesday there was something in the air. The early warnings from the 'Freya' radars on the Channel coast indicated a large-scale RAF raid. In the late afternoon of 27 July various flak units, night-fighter gruppes and civilian air raid posts had been given orders to have their full complement at action stations. In all ignorance, the night fighter staffels had taken off against the enemy Viermots whose leaders were reported over Northern Holland. Oberleutnant Wilhelm 'Wim' Johnen, Staffelkapitän 3/NJG1, who was flying his Bf 110 in the direction of Amsterdam, was totally confused. Though the ground stations were giving the night fighters the positions of the bombers Johnen felt that the reports were hasty and nervous. No one knew exactly where the enemy was or what his objective would be. Radio reports contradicted themselves saying that the enemy was over Amsterdam and then suddenly west of Brussels and a moment later they were reported far out to sea. Just like Kuztner and Angersbach two nights before, Johnen was 'helpless and bewildered'. In desperation he flew straight to Amsterdam but he found nothing. It was as if the bad times of the summer of 1942 had returned to haunt him. 'The cities of Münster, Karlsruhe and Essen had suffered grievously' wrote Johnen 'and the whole night defence was crippled by the sheer weight of numbers of RAF Viermots smashing their way through 'like a broad stream driven through a narrow channel. As long as the night-fighter pilot had to rely on a machine being caught in the searchlights and could not find his opponent by his own efforts he was virtually helpless.' But things had then changed dramatically. In December 1942 3/NJG1 had been ordered to Parchim in Mecklenburg which hitherto had been left unscathed by the war. By Christmas I/NJG1 was fully equipped and at full complement. In May 1943 Johnen and his fellow pilots were ordered westwards. Crammed with crates containing wireless sets, washing and toilet utensils a 'Schnapps cupboard' and even a dog, their Messerschmitt 110s looked more like 'furniture vans' than night fighters as they flew off to Holland in search of Gilze Rijin airfield near Breda where Hauptmann Frank, Johnen's Staffelkapitän was an old friend from his Venlo days. Johnen was welcomed by successful pilots like Rolf Bussmann, who would survive the war with a final total of 26 confirmed victories, Oberfeldwebel Paul Gildner and Leutnant Heinz Strüning, or 'Uncle Heini' as he was known because he was older than the rest. Known for his Cologne wit, Strüning told the new arrivals, 'Boys, there are so many Tommies circling the airfield that we could have knocked them out of the skies with our caps.'

But Johnen's and many of his fellow pilots had not always been so cocky and confident. When Risop had been killed and was replaced by Facius, a Viennese bordfunker, Johnen had claimed four Abschüsse over the Netherlands in June but had not added to his score since. But now Johnen's fellow pilots were cocky and confident once more. After the setbacks of summer 1942 salvation had arrived, as Johnen recalled: 'Berlin sent us the first night-fighter machines equipped with their own radar and moreover with an unlimited radius of action. The Lichtenstein apparatus - it was known as 'Li' in night-fighter circles - did not send out death rays; it seized the opponent with invisible arms and drew him towards itself as an octopus catches its prey. The deathblow from the night-fighter's cannon followed.'

In the spring of 1943 the German Kammhuber Line, whose night interception zones stretched from Denmark in the north down to Lake Constance in the south, functioned at its maximum efficiency as it tried to ward off the British bombing offensive against the Ruhr District. In June the German night fighters shot down 235 enemy bombers, which was the greatest success they had ever scored using the 'Himmelbett' system. Bomber Command reported an increasing decline in the morale of its crews.

But now, on the night of 27 July, Nachtjagd was suffering from a reversal of fortunes. Johnen and his crew had begun the night in cheerful mood. Facius had made a final check of his 'Li' set and had reported that he was all set. The ground stations kept calling the night fighters, giving positions of the enemy bombers but Johnen felt that the reports were being given hastily and nervously. It was obvious to him that no one knew exactly where the enemy was or what his objective would be. When Facius reported three or four blips on his Li set Johnen swung the Bf 110 round on to the bearing in the direction of the Ruhr thinking he was bound to approach the stream. Facius continued to read out bearings of 'bombers' but they were travelling at very high speed and Johnen thought that they must be German fighters. Johnen lost his patience but the tense atmosphere was suddenly interrupted by a ground station calling, 'Hamburg, Hamburg. A thousand enemy bombers over Hamburg. Calling all night-fighters, calling all night-fighters. Full speed for Hamburg.' Johnen was speechless with rage. For half an hour he had been chasing an imaginary bomber stream while bombs were falling on Hamburg. By the time he reached the city the dockyards and city districts were blazing like a furnace - 'a horrifying sight'. Incredulously, Johnen turned for home.

Night fighter pilots like 'Wim' Johnen and their bordfunkers were blind but they did not yet know why. On the morning after the first raid shortly after emerging from his party bunker at his headquarters in a beautiful mansion on the Magdalenenstrasse, a fashionable and exclusive street overlooking the gardens on the west bank of the Alster, Gauleiter Karl Otto Kaufmann was handed a 30-centimetre by 1.5-centimetre strip of black paper with aluminium foil stuck to one side by a messenger who had found the item out in the open. Kaufmann was a Rhinelander, a native of Krefeld and he had been in the Nazi Party since 1921. When other strips arrived it was soon realised that they were harmless and children were soon collecting them in bunches and using them as playthings and souvenirs but they had a more sinister intent; perhaps they had something to do with the widespread radar failure that had been reported by General Kammhuber in Berlin who said, '*Die game Abwehr war mit einem Schlag blind*' - 'The whole defence was blinded at one stroke'? The fact was that a simple but brilliant device code-named 'Window' removed the advantages enjoyed by the 'Himmelbett' system, dependent as it was on radar and had wreaked havoc. In 1937, Dr. R. V. Jones, one of the top British radar specialists had been the first to discover the basic principles of radar-jamming using tinfoil strips. After the Ju 88 which had landed at Dyce on 9 May and had given up its secrets the most amazing finding to come out of Dr. Jones' investigation of the German airborne radar system was that the 'Window' tinfoil-strip jamming technique the British had designed to combat Würzburg radar, also neutralized Lichtenstein BC. Although 'Window' had been devised in 1942 its use had been forbidden until now for fear that the Luftwaffe would use it in a new 'Blitz' on Great Britain. Cut to the length equivalent to half the wavelength of the Würzburg ground and Lichtenstein airborne interception, radar, when dropped by aircraft in bundles of a thousand at a time at one-minute intervals 'Window' reflected the radar waves and 'snowed' the tubes with false returns. Walter Knickmeier, the highly skilful JLO in Holland reported: '*Düppel war das Todesurteil fur die gefuhrte Raumnachtjagd*' - 'Window was the death sentence for controlled night fighting in boxes.'[117]

On the night of 27/28 July, 787 aircraft had followed a longer route out to Hamburg and back to include a longer flight over the North Sea with the intention of confusing the

JLOs as to the intended target. This meant that each aircraft had to carry a smaller bomb load than normal and so it was decided to include a higher proportion of incendiaries than usual. A carpet of bombs of unimaginable density caused the almost complete destruction of six districts of the city and of parts of two others. A total of 2,417 tons of bombs was dropped on the districts to the east of the Alster, which included Hammerbrook, Hohenfelde, Borgfelde and others by 739 bombers, and a firestorm was started by the high temperature prevailing (about 30°C at 6 o'clock in the evening). Fires started in the densely built up working class districts of Hammerbrook and those at Hamm and Borgfelde joined together and then became one gigantic area of fire with air being brought into it with the force of a storm. The firestorm raged for about three hours in an area measuring only two miles by one mile, which received between 550-600 bomb loads and only died down when there was nothing left to burn. About 16,000 multi-storeyed apartments were destroyed and 40,000 people died; most of them by carbon monoxide poisoning.

The damage was 'gigantic', reported Generalleutnant Karl Kehrl, the Polizeipräsident (Chief of Police) and Air Protection Leader of the city. 'Before half an hour had passed, the districts upon which the weight of the attack fell; and which formed part of the crowded dock and port area, where narrow streets and courts abounded, were transformed into a lake of fire covering an area of 22 square kilometres. The effect of this was to heat the air to a temperature which at times was estimated to approach 1,000° centigrade. A vast suction was in this way created so that the air stormed through the streets with immense force, bearing upon it sparks, timber and roof beams and thus spreading the fire still further and further till it became a typhoon such as had never before been witnessed and against which all human resistance was powerless. Trees three feet thick were broken off or uprooted, human beings were thrown to the ground or flung alive into the flames by winds which exceeded 150mph. [The trunks of strong trees split and broke, younger trees were bent to the ground like willow rods. Seventy thousand of Hamburg's 100,000 trees were lost to this storm]. The panic-stricken citizens knew not where to turn. Flames drove them from the shelters but high-explosive bombs sent them scurrying back again. Once inside, they were suffocated by carbon-monoxide poisoning and their bodies reduced to ashes as though they had been placed in a crematorium, which was indeed what each shelter proved to be.

'The only people who escaped death were those who had risked flight at the right moment, or who were near enough to the edge of the sea of flame so that there was some possibility of saving them...The overall destruction is so radical that literally nothing is left of many people. The force of the gale tore children out of the hands of their parents and whirled them into the fire. People who thought they had gotten out safely, collapsed in the overwhelming heat and died in seconds. Fleeing people had to work their way over the dead and dying. Seventy per cent of the victims died of suffocation, mostly in poisonous carbon dioxide gas, which turned their corpses' bright blue, orange and green. So many people died of this poisoning that initially it was thought that the RAF had raided us for the first time with poison gas bombs. Fifteen per cent had died more violent deaths. The rest were charred to a cinder and could not be identified.'

Once again 'Window' had rendered the Nachtjagd virtually powerless. Only seventeen bombers were shot down on 27/28 July. The first bomber that was shot down was Lancaster JA709 on 156 Squadron at Warboys piloted by Flying Officer Leonard Robert Crampton. As a 'Blind Marker' it was one of the first to drop a yellow TI as a route marker when the head of the bomber stream crossed the coast at the prominent Sankt Peter Peninsular. Bombers at the front of the stream did not have the full protection of 'Window' and it fell blazing, the remainder of its load of yellow TIs flaring up brilliantly before crashing into the estuary of the River Eider near the small town of Tönning. All seven crew, who were on their 20th operation, were killed.[118]

Oberleutnant 'Dieter' Schmidt, Staffelkapitän, 8./NJG1, comments: 'On the screen of the Lichtenstein radar each such cloud of strips appeared as a target on opposite course and real targets could not be made out at all. Until we received better equipment, the only method we could use was the 'Wilde Sau' ('Wild Boar') tactic.'

'Geschwader Herrmann' (renamed JG300 in August 1943) was equipped with FW 190s and Bf 109s thrown into the fray in 'Wilde Sau' operations on 27/28 July as Oberst 'Hajo' Herrmann recalled.

'Suddenly, while we were still at Bonn, training and expanding, I was called on the phone by Goering. He told me that he wanted us to start operating that night. I said that I couldn't; my unit was not ready. Goering made further calls, telling me that the first Hamburg raid was a catastrophe; he likened it to the earthquake at Lisbon earlier in the century. He asked me to do what I could. So, we flew on the night of the second Hamburg raid even though our training was not complete. It was very dramatic. I told the pilots what Göring had said about Hamburg. I told them that I would fly and they were to follow me. There were about twenty of us from Bonn and others from Rheine and Oldenburg. Many of them failed and had to return to their airfields. You see, it was the first time that these men faced this task and flew in the night without knowing where and when it would be possible to land.

'The clouds of smoke over Hamburg were so dense that it made you shudder. I saw this great column of smoke; I even smelt it. I flew over the target several times and, then, I saw this bomber in the searchlights. He had nearly reached the top of the smoke cloud at the time. I identified the type at the time but I cannot be sure now what it was. I do remember how big it seemed. I think it was a Lancaster. [It was Lancaster JA863 on 101 Squadron at Ludford Magna which was being flown by Flight Sergeant David Picton Phillips Hurst whose crew were on their sixth operation]. The attack was very simple. I went into the searchlights. I was not very experienced; another pilot would have kept in the dark. I was almost level with him, probably just above the turbulence of his propellers. It was like daylight in those searchlights. I could see the rear gunner; he was only looking downwards, probably at the inferno below. There was no movement of his guns. You must remember that, at this time, the British were not generally warned to watch out for us over the target. I had seen other bombers over targets with the gunners looking down. I fired and he burned. He banked to the left and then through 180 degrees to the right. As he fell, he turned and dropped away from the smoke cloud. I followed him a little but, as he got lower and lower, I left him. I watched him burst on the ground. I didn't see anyone bail out but I cannot exclude that. By the light of his explosion, I could see the 'Knicks' - the small walls with bushes built on them against which the cattle found shelter from the sun and wind. That was my homeland - Schleswig-Holstein - as I knew it. Of course, I tried to find some more bombers and I think I shot at some more but there were no more shoot downs.'[119] JA863 crashed into Wellingsbüttel, a northern suburb of Hamburg. All seven crew were killed.[120]

Whilst chasing Halifax DT749 on 408 'Goose' Squadron RCAF, at low level over the North Sea Leutnant Hermann Stock's Ju 88C-6 on IV./NJG3 almost came to grief when the tips of the propellers touched the surface of the sea and as a result they were chopped off. After the crippled Junkers had been safely nursed back to Grove, the Halifax was later shot down by Leutnant Gotthard Sachsenberg of II./NJG3 west of Neumünster. Flight Lieutenant Clifford Campbell Stovel DFC and four of his crew were killed; three were taken prisoner. The crew were on the last of a combined Coastal Command and Bomber Command tour of 42 ops.[121] Stock may also have shot down Lancaster EE169 on 100 Squadron which was on its way home to Grimsby and was piloted by Warrant Officer Roy Gafford. Or it could have been Lancaster ED708 on 106 Squadron piloted by Flight Sergeant John Bennett Charters who was also shot down by a night fighter. In both cases all seven crew were killed. On the other hand, either Lancaster could have been destroyed by Oberfeldwebel

SN-2 equipped Bf 110G-4s of 8./NJG1 or 'Zircus ('Circus') Schmidt' during a daylight training flight over France in the summer of 1944 and taken from the Bf 110 flown by 8th Staffelkapitän Oberleutnant Dietrich Schmidt. (Dr. Schmidt-Barbo via Theo Boiten).

(Right) Hauptmann Georg Hermann Greiner, 47 day and 4 night victories in NJG1 and 2 in 204 sorties.

(Right) Leutnant Norbert Pietrek of 2./NJG4.

(Left) Major Gerhard 'Gerd' Friedrich, 30 night victories in NJG1, 4 and NJG6.

Oberleutnant Heinz-Wolfgang Schnaufer, Staffelkapitän, 12./NJG1 at Leeuwarden points out his 47th Abschuss - he scored his 45th-47th victories on 15/16 February 1944 during a Bomber Command raid on Berlin. (Hans Bredewold via Ab A. Jansen)

(Left) Schnaufer – The 'Night Ghost of St. Trond' - ended the war as the top German night-fighter pilot with 121 Nachtjagd victories (including 114 Viermots) in 164 sorties with NJG1 and 4.

Hauptmann Martin 'Tino' Becker 58 Nachtjagd victories (all Viermots) in 83 sorties with NJG3, 4 and 6.

'Wilde Sau' ('Wild Boar') Messerschmitt Bf 109, a day fighter used for night fighting.

Hauptmann Hans-Heinz 'Honschen' Augenstein, 46 night victories (including 45 Viermots) in NJG1.

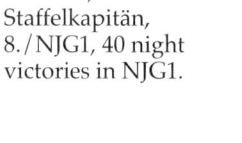

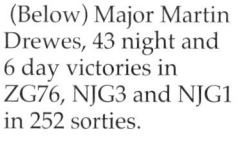

(Above) Oberstleutnant Herbert Lütje, 47 night and 3 day victories in NJG1 and 6.

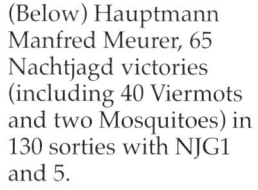

(Above) Oberleutnant Dietrich 'Dieter' Schmidt, Staffelkapitän, 8./NJG1, 40 night victories in NJG1.

(Below) Hauptmann Manfred Meurer, 65 Nachtjagd victories (including 40 Viermots and two Mosquitoes) in 130 sorties with NJG1 and 5.

(Below) Major Martin Drewes, 43 night and 6 day victories in ZG76, NJG3 and NJG1 in 252 sorties.

L-R: Unteroffizier Hans Liebherr (bordfunker); u/k gunner and Major Wilhelm Herget, Kommandeur I./NJG4. 58 Nachtjagd victories in NJG3 and 4, plus 15 day victories in over 700 sorties, sitting in their Bf 110G in 1943.

L-R: Feldwebel Herbert Scholtz, bordfunker; Oberfeldwebel Karl-Heinz Scherfling and Feldwebel Herbert Winkler, bordshütze at General Schmidt's HQ at Jüterborg on 8 April 1944 on the occasion of the award of the Ritterkreuz to Scherfling (33 to 35 night victories in NJG1 and NJG2). (Herbert Scholz via Didier Hindrychx)

Ju 88C-6/R-1 (D5+EV) of IV/NJG3 of NJG3 which was carrying the top secret FuG 202 Lichtenstein BC AI radar set, landed at RAF Dyce in Scotland on Saturday 9 May 1943. The aircraft is now on display at RAF Hendon.

Feldwebel Günther Bahr, 35 night and 2 day victories in SKG210, NJG1, NJG4 and NJG6.

Leutnant Karl-Heinz Völlkopf and Unteroffizier Heinz Huhn of II./NJG2 get into full flying gear prior to taking off on an operational sortie while their Dornier Do 215B-5 is being topped up by one of the ground crew. (Coll. Heinz Huhn via Rob de Visser/Theo Boiten.

Ju 88G-6b with FuG 220 dipoles for SN-2 radar and Schräge Musik installation.

Reichsmarschall Hermann Goering and General Kammhuber inspecting pilots of NJG1 at Leeuwarden airfield on 24 October 1943. Right is Oberleutnant Martin Drewes. (Dr. Schmidt-Barbo via Theo Boiten)

(Below left) Oberleutnant Paul Anton Guido Zorner of 2./NJG3.

(Belowright) Oberleutnant Friedrich Karl 'Felix' or 'Nasen' ('Nose' on account of his aristocratic proboscis) Müller, a pre-war Lufthansa captain and wartime Operations Officer in JG300 destroyed 29 Viermots and a Mosquito in just 52 sorties.

(Above) A mechaniker working on the elevator assembly of Bf 110 D5+GH of 9./NJG3 which has six Abschüsse - victory symbols on the tail. (via Steve Hall)

(Below) Hauptmann Gerhard Raht, 58 Nachtjagd victories (all but one Viermots) in 171 sorties with NJG2 and 3.

(Left) Major Wolfgang Thimmig, 22 night and 1 day victories in NJG1, 2, 3, 4 and NJG101.

(Below) Hauptmann Paul Szameitat, 28 night and 1 day victories in NJG3.

Nachtjäger were unable to prevent RAF area bombing of German cities by night and millions of Germans suffered unimagined catastrophes in Hitler's much-vaunted 'Thousand Year Reich'.

Focke Wulf 190 'Wild Sau' (Wild Boar) crew after returning from a sortie.

(Above) Leutnant Heinz Grimm, 26 night and 1 day victories in NJG1 and NJG2.

Dead Lancaster crew; yet another victim of German night-fighters over the Reich.

Generalmajor Josef 'Beppo' Schmid, commanding I Jagdkorps.

(Above) Oberst Hans-Joachim 'Hajo' Herrmann, a bomber pilot and one of the foremost blind flying experts in the Luftwaffe.

Feldwebel Otto Heinrich Fries and his bordfunker Unteroffizier Fred Staffa of 5./NJG1.

The price of Allied victory was high.

Oberleutnant Rudolf 'Rudi' Schoenert of 4./NJG1 who was credited with 65 Abschüsss, including 35 Soviet aircraft, in 376 combat sorties. He claimed the first aerial victory with upward-firing guns in May 1943.

(Right) Detail from the official handbook showing the installation of a pair of 20 mm cannon in a Messerschmitt 110. 1:MG Ff/M. 2: full ammunition drum. 3: reserve drum. 4: compressed air bottles with pressure reduction unit and cut-off valve. 5: cartridge casing holder. 6: cocking units. 7: weapons mount. 8: weapons bracing truss.

(Below) Bf 110 with crew and Schwarzemänner or 'black men', so-called because of the colour of their tunics. Beneath the cockpit is the 'Englandblitz' diving eagle with its claws on a map of England emblem of the night-fighter arm.

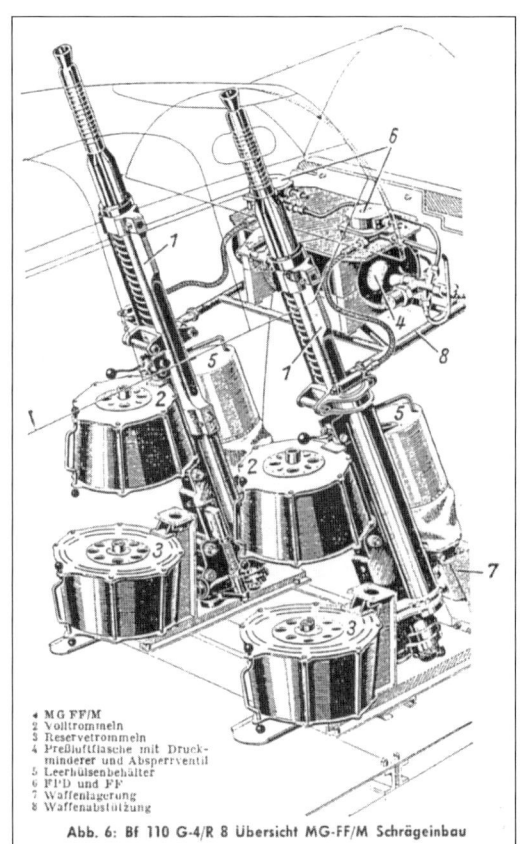

1 MG FF/M
2 Volltrommeln
3 Reservetrommeln
4 Preßluftflasche mit Druck-
   minderer und Absperrventil
5 Leerhülsenbehälter
6 FfD und FF
7 Waffenlagerung
8 Waffenabstützung

Abb. 6: Bf 110 G-4/R 8 Übersicht MG-FF/M Schrägeinbau

Widespread bombing of German cities resulted in large scale death and destruction on both sides.

Air raid search among the rubble after a RAF raid.

(Right) Major Hans-Dieter Frank, 55 Nachtjagd victories in NJG1.

(Left) Oberleutnant Kurt Welter, 56 Nachtjagd victories in JG301, 300, NJG10 and NJG11 (including 33 Mosquitoes), plus 7 day victories in 93 sorties.

German 88mm gun battery and searchlights scanning the night sky during one of the countless raids on Reich towns and cities.

Walter Kubisch, Major Lent's bordschütze in a IV/NJG1 Bf 110 which earned Lent his 64th Abschuss. Lent intercepted his victim when it was on its way back to England at 0237 hours. He manoeuvred into position and opened fire but the bomber did not begin to burn so he broke away and made a second attack, only to experience a complete stoppage of his main armament when he pressed the triggers. He broke off and instructed Kubisch to 'talk' him into position for an attack with the rearward-firing MG 15 machine gun. This Kubisch did, opening fire when the Bf 110 was in position and destroying the Lancaster with his second burst.[122]

Lancaster III EE142 PH-G on 12 Squadron at Wickenby flown by Warrant Officer Wilfred Salthouse whose crew were on their thirteenth operation, was shot down, probably by Oberfeldwebel Wilhelm 'Willi' Schmale of I/NJG3, the aircraft crashing near Vechta. Salthouse and five of his crew were killed; one survived and was taken prisoner. Schmale scored eleven Abschüsse by the war's end. Lancaster I W4962 EM-B on 207 Squadron at Langar flown by Flying Officer Colin Burne was shot down by Major Walter Ehle of II/NJG1, the aircraft crashing at Glinde. Burne and four of the crew, who were on their second operation, were killed; two were taken prisoner.[123] On 467 Squadron RAAF at Bottesford, Lancaster III W5003 PO-H flown by Pilot Officer James Llewellyn Carrington was shot down by fighter attack. Five of the crew, who were on their twelfth operation, were killed; two were taken prisoner. A second Lancaster on the Australian squadron - W4946 flown by Pilot Officer James Thomas Buchanan, was shot down, probably by Hauptmann Hans-Joachim Jabs of IV/NJG1. All seven crew, who were on their first operation, were killed. Wellington X JA114 on 429 'Bison Squadron' RCAF at East Moor flown by Wing Commander James Arthur Piddington DFC was shot down by fighter attack. Three crew were killed; two were taken prisoner. The crew were on the third operation of their second tour. The crew on Lancaster III EE178 GT-R on 156 Squadron at Warboys flown by Flight Sergeant G. W. Wilkins were on their 19th operation and were attacked by a nightfighter. The Lancaster exploded at about 13,500 feet killing six of the crew but Wilkins who was blown out of the aircraft, survived to be taken prisoner.

Stirling III EH893 LS-J on 75 Squadron at Mildenhall which was being flown by Flight Lieutenant John Rowlison Childs whose crew was on their fourteenth operation was damaged by the Hamburg flak and then shot down by Unteroffizier Loeschner of III/NJG3. Seven crew were killed; one was taken prisoner. Two Halifaxes on 102 Squadron at Pocklington were shot down by night fighters. Halifax II JD150 DY-A piloted by Sergeant Gordon Harry Brown was shot down by Feldwebel Hans Meissner of II/NJG3. All seven crew, who were on their third operation, were killed. 'A-Apple' crashed near Rendsburg. The other Halifax, JB864 DY-E flown by Flying Officer George McFerran Clarke, whose crew were on their third operation, was lost with four crew killed and three taken prisoner. Lancaster I ED303 on 106 Squadron at Syerston flown by Sergeant Ellis George McLeod RCAF were probably shot down by fighter attack. All seven crew, who were on their second operation, died.[124]

Peter Spoden, in NJG5, was among the night-fighter pilots who were patrolling in boxes east of Hamburg should part of the Main Force attack Berlin.

'I was in Box 'Reiher' ('Heron') on the Baltic coast east of Lübeck. I was only the new boy in a poor box. I got up to the highest altitude possible - 6000 to 6500 metres - and, from there, I could see these four-engined aircraft. There was a layer of stratus cloud over Hamburg, stretching towards Kiel and I could see these bombers against this layer of cloud. Several times I asked ground control if I could fly to them. 'I can see them. Let me go over there.' But the fighter control officer said that it was not possible. Then, I asked again; I told them to ring up Berlin but I don't think anyone would take the responsibility of leaving Berlin open to a second attack. I even talked to the other pilots in the nearby boxes. They could also see the bombers. We were furious but we couldn't do anything about it. We could see the fire in Hamburg; it was the biggest fire I had ever seen.

'After landing, we went to Hauptmann Schönert in the Gruppe Headquarters. We told him that it was crazy. We had had to watch, helplessly, while they were destroying a German city. We were mad. 'Rudi' Schönert got on the phone to Berlin several times; he even let me and another young fellow who had been flying tell them what was happening. We youngsters were very keen to get our first shoot downs. 'Rudi' Schönert, later Major and highly decorated, was one of the fine officers you can find in every air force. They still thought that there should be a certain kind of chivalry among fighting flyers like in the time of Richthofen 1914-18. So he told us young night fighters when we came into his gruppe: 'Shoot the Viermots between the two engines, there are the fuel tanks, they burn easy and the boys have a chance to parachute!' Schönert had been a sailor on British ships before the war. In the howling storm, when the huge breakers washed the decks and Father Death stood in the bows, was to be found the real League of Nations.

'Maybe my former friends are on board!' he told us.'[125]

One bomber pilot reported after returning to his airfield in England: 'The clouds looked like a blood-soaked cotton swab'. Immediately after the raid about 1,200,000 people fled the city in fear of further raids. In Hamburg, after the raid, Gauleiter Karl Otto Kaufmann declared a 'Situation of Major Catastrophe'. Much later, by order of Doktor Göbbel's Ministry of Propaganda, the word 'catastrophe' was no longer to be used and was to be replaced by 'extreme emergency'.[126]

In London on Wednesday 28 July the Reuters News Agency reported: Here, the present series of air raids on Hamburg is being described as the heaviest ever suffered by any city. Hamburg has been attacked uninterruptedly day and night since Saturday. Well over 5,000 tons of bombs have fallen on Hamburg in these four days. By comparison, the German Luftwaffe dropped a total of 5,800 tons of bombs on Great Britain during the climax of its raids in the months of September, October and November 1940 - that is, approximately the same quantity dropped on Hamburg alone during the past four days.'

On Thursday, 29 July Reich Minister of Propaganda Dr. Joseph Goebbels wrote in his diary: 'Last night the heaviest air raid so far was made on Hamburg. Between 800 and 1,000 British bombers appeared over the city. Our air defence succeeded in shooting down only a few, so we cannot claim that the assailants paid for what they did. Kaufmann is giving me a preliminary report on the effects of the British raid. He speaks of a catastrophe of hitherto inconceivable proportions. We are seeing the destruction of a city of millions of people, an event unparalleled in history. The resultant problems are virtually insuperable.'

The third raid on Hamburg by the Main Force was on the night of Thursday 29/Friday 30 July when the objectives for the 777 aircraft that were detailed were the northern and north-eastern districts, which had so far escaped the bombing. The Main Force was detailed to approach Hamburg from almost due north but the Path Finders arrived two miles too far to the east and marked an area south of the devastated firestorm area. Creepback stretched about four miles along the devastated area and heavy bombing was reported in the residential districts of Wandsbek and Barmbek and parts of the Uhelnhorst and Winterhude. In all, 726 aircraft dropped 2,382 tons on the city and caused a widespread fire area but there was no firestorm. Danish workers arriving at their own frontier from Hamburg's bombed war factories said, according to the Copenhagen correspondent of the Stockholm Aftonbladet that 'Hamburg had ceased to exist as an organised city.'

Twenty-eight bombers were shot down, fourteen of them by searchlight assisted flak. Among the Nachtjäger victors was Unteroffizier Hans Krepp of 1/NJG3 piloting a Bf 110 who probably shot down Halifax II JD309 on 61 Squadron at Snaith captained by 22-year old Flight Sergeant Arthur Fletcher. The attack took place about thirty kilometres west of St. Peter Ording at 0024 hours at a height of 6000 metres. All but one of the crew are commemorated on the Runneymede Memorial. The body of Sergeant Raymond Worrall the 21-year old wireless operator was washed up ashore on 7 August near Katingsiel. This was the first Abschuss for Krepp. He went on to claim one more victory and he survived the war. Unteroffizier Lovenich of II/JG300 piloting a FW 190 claimed a Lancaster, probably JA689 on 460 Squadron RAAF at Binbrook, which was being flown by Flight Sergeant Herbert Leonard Fuhrmann. All seven crew, who were on their eighth operation were killed. Another Lancaster on 460 Squadron, Lancaster ED525 flown by Flying Officer Alan James Johnson, was shot down by Hauptmann Prinz zur Lippe-Weissenfeld of III/NJG1 on detachment with NJG3. Oberleutnant Joachim Wendtland a Jägerleitoffizier (JLO, or GCI-controller) who flew with Weissenfeld as an observer recalled.

'At first we were under the control of Box 2C. The fighter-control officer directed us on to a contact. Then, our radar operator picked up his own contact ahead but we closed on to it very fast and the radar man thought we would ram it. The pilot realized, from the speed of the contact, that it could not be a bomber flying away from us or towards us and must be a little cloud of Window. The pilot held the same course in the hope of following the bundles of Window and finding the bomber dropping them, but the radar operator eventually had to report that he had lost contact. The ground-control officer had kept in touch with his original contact and he directed us again but we had exactly the same experience and remained without a genuine contact.

'We were then ordered to freelance and, while we were doing this, I suddenly saw a large violet-blue exhaust flame shooting over our heads. It was only visible for a split second. Unfortunately, I could only react in astonishment at this sighting by saying, 'There! There!' By the time I had given a more detailed description of what I had seen, it was too late for the pilot to follow it up. Because of this, the pilot insisted most vehemently that, in future, I call out without delay, for example: 'Hard turn starboard!' or 'Reverse course!' He told me he would carry out such an order immediately.

'After a further long zigzag flight, with the ground-control officer giving details of the bomber-stream and being told of bombers here and there, the pilot suddenly spotted a four-engined aircraft against the northerly twilight at a height of 6800 metres and about 150 metres in front and above us to the right. It was a visual sighting with no radar. The eight exhaust flames were, in comparison to the ones I had seen earlier, so small and weak in intensity as to be like 3mm wireless sparks.

'The pilot flew after it straight away, positioned himself about eighty metres underneath, and matched his speed to that of the bomber. The dark shape of the four-engined aircraft was clearly visible against the sky above us. It was a Lancaster.

'The pilot hit its left wing with his first attack and burning pieces of it flew off. The pilot was a little disappointed that the bomber wasn't shot down by this first attack; he had wanted to show me how to hit it between the two engines and finish it off quickly. The Lancaster kept straight and level all the time, without any evasive action.

'On his second attack, Prinz zur Lippe used his special method. He slid under the bomber, pulled up the nose suddenly, fired a burst and dropped away quickly in case the bomber blew up. It didn't, although pieces were still falling off it. We attacked again. The bomber still didn't explode; its pilot was trying to reach some low-lying clouds. I didn't see any return fire but we found four bullet holes in one rudder after we landed. I wasn't used to all these manoeuvres. I wasn't strapped in and I kept being pushed down into the floor and then coming up to hit the cockpit roof.

'We made one more attack and this time his wing started burning after only half a second. We saw the Lancaster go down into a wood near a railway. We started to circle the crash position in the normal manner, so that ground control could fix the position of the success but the radar operator warned the pilot that our petrol was low and we had to leave and land quickly at Stade, actually cutting in front of another fighter that was landing. About fifty metres before we reached the dispersal, the engines cut.'

All seven crew, some of whom were on their second tour, died. It was Prinz zur Lippe-Weissenfeld's forty-third night Abschüsse.

Stirling III BF578 HA-A on 218 Squadron at Downham Market piloted by Sergeant Raymond Stuart Pickard whose crew were on their second operation, was damaged by Hamburg flak and then shot down at Ahrenswohlde by Unteroffizier Walter Rohlfing of III/NJG3. Two crew were killed; five were taken into captivity. Halifax II JB956 KN-O on 77 Squadron at Elvington flown by Flight Sergeant George Henry Sutton was probably shot down by Oberleutnant Gerhardt Raht of II/NJG3 flying a Dornier Do 217. All eight crew who were on their eleventh operation died. Raht is also believed to have shot down Halifax II JD277 NP-G on 158 Squadron at Lissett flown by Flight Sergeant Ninian Robson MacDonald RNZAF and crew who were on their 15th operation. The aircraft crashed between Heids and Tellingstedt. Six of the crew were killed and one was taken prisoner. Halifax II W7883 DY-R on 102 Squadron at Pocklington, flown by Flight Sergeant Thomas Albert Macquarie was probably shot down by Leutnant Gotthard Sachsenberg of II/NJG3 flying a Do 217. All seven crew, who were on their first operation, were killed. Lancaster III ED862 OF-P on 97 Squadron at Bourn was probably shot down by Major Helmut Lent of IV/NJG1, 25 kilometres north of Ameland, for his 65th Abschuss. Pilot Officer Douglas James Marks DFM and his crew, who were on their 30th operation of their tour, were killed. Bf 110G-4 D5+DS flown by Feldwebel Wilhelm Kürreck of 8/NJG3 was shot down by a Mosquito on 605 Squadron flown by Flying Officer Arthur G. Woods as he approached Lüneburg. Kürreck was killed. His radio-operator/gunner Feldwebel Anton Escherle bailed out but became entangled on the tail assembly and may have freed himself but he was too low for his parachute to open and he too was killed.

On Friday 30 July RAF Headquarters announced: 'Last night Hamburg was heavily bombed for the seventh time in six days. Nine thousand tons of bombs have been dropped on Hamburg within the space of 120 hours. Almost 1,000 heavy British bombers took part in the grand assault under the command of Sir Arthur Harris, the Air Chief Marshal of Bomber Command. The bombers approached in five waves and in barely one hour dropped more than 2,000 tons of bombs on the city and its industrial installations. The German Luftwaffe made every conceivable effort to protect Hamburg and deployed more night fighters, flak and searchlights than ever before. As to the consequences of the raid, it is said that it is no longer possible to estimate the number of fires and explosions and the belief is that war production in Hamburg has been eliminated. Airmen report that the city looks as if it had been struck by an earthquake.'

On Sunday 1 August in Stockholm 'Eyewitness reports in the press unanimously indicate that Hamburg has ceased to exist as a city. 'Dante's Inferno is as nothing compared to this hell' stated the captain of a Swedish steamship sunk in the port of Hamburg.'

On 2 August, after a day of heavy thunderstorms, 740 bomber crews were briefed for the fourth raid on Hamburg. They were told that the weather was extremely bad and that cumulonimbus clouds covered the route up to 20,000 feet. Above that height the sky was reported to be clear but the bombing force encountered a large thunderstorm area over Germany and no Path Finder marking was possible. Night fighters and flak shot down thirty aircraft. Hauptmann Jabs, Oberleutnant Georg Hermann Greiner and Oberfeldwebel Karl-Heinz Scherfling, all from IV/NJG1 at Leeuwarden, destroyed six bombers. Jabs was credited with shooting down Stirling EH928 AA-A on 75 Squadron RNZAF at Mepal piloted by Sergeant Cyril Philip Bailie, which crashed twenty-five miles off Terschelling at 0351 hours. All eight crew, who were on their fifteenth operation, were killed. Jabs also probably shot down Lancaster I W4778 KM-T on 44 (Rhodesia) Squadron at Dunholme Lodge, which was being flown by Sergeant Alan Raymond Moffatt on the crew's sixth operation. Six crew died and one was taken prisoner. Jabs shot the aircraft down into the Waddenzee. He is also credited with the probable destruction of Halifax V EB274 NA-H on 428 (Ghost) Squadron RCAF, Middleton St George, which was being flown by Warrant Officer2 Mack Chepil DFM RCAF. All eight crew, who were on their 17th operation, were killed. Oberleutnant Greiner probably shot down Lancaster III ED688 HW-A on 100 Squadron at Grimsby piloted by Warrant Officer Allan Ralph Wilden DFC, which crashed off the Frisian Islands. All seven crew, who were on their 21st operation, were killed. Greiner also shot down Wellington X HE464 AS-W on 166 Squadron at Kirmington piloted by Sergeant Harold Nash, whose crew were on their seventh operation. The aircraft crashed at Ameland. All five crew were killed. Oberfeldwebel Karl-Heinz Scherfling's victim, probably Lancaster III ED493 WS-A on 9 Squadron at Bardney which was being flown by 21-year old Sergeant David Mackenzie of Helmsdale, whose crew were on their seventh operation. There were no survivors, the Lancaster crashing off Bergen-aan-Zee. Sergeant Robert Hugh Jones, flight engineer, and the two gunners, Sergeants Leslie Francis 'Darky' Gilkes, all the way from Siparia, Trinidad, and 27-year old William Miller Welsh, from Tweedmouth are commemorated at Runnymede. Mackenzie, Pilot Officer Thomas McKean McCall, 22, from Muirkirk and Sergeants Robert Reid, 24, from Falkirk and George Arthur Filleul, were laid to rest at Bergen-oop-Zoom War Cemetery.

Lancaster II DS673 KO-V on 115 Squadron at East Wretham flown by Sergeant Robert William Bennett was probably shot down by Oberfeldwebel Heitmann of I/NJG3 flying a Ju 88. All seven crew, who were on their ninth operation were killed. The aircraft crashed off Wilhelmshaven. Halifax HR859 on 51 Squadron at Snaith, flown by Warrant Officer2 Edward Robert Sklarchuk RCAF was probably shot down by a Bf 110 flown by Major Günther Radusch of II/NJG3. All seven crew, who were on their fifth operation, died. Born 11 November 1912, Günther Radusch was the sixth highest-scoring night fighter flying ace in the Luftwaffe. He was also a recipient of the Ritterkreuz des Eisernen Kreuzes mit Eichenlaub. Credited with 65 aerial victories, he claimed one victory during the Spanish Civil War, the remaining 64 victories all being claimed at night in over 140 combat sorties, including the destruction of 57 Viermots. An enthusiastic glider pilot as a student, he had joined the military service of the Heer before transferring to the Luftwaffe. Radusch and nine others, among them Günther Lützow, Wolfgang Falck and Johannes 'Hannes' Trautloft, were recommended for Sonderausbildung (special training) at the Lipetsk fighter-pilot school in Russia.[127]

Lancaster W5000 on 61 Squadron at Syerston, which was being flown by Flying Officer Richard Lyon was probably destroyed in an attack by a Ju 88 piloted by Leutnant Hermann Leube of I/NJG3. All seven crew, who were on their fourth operation, died. Halifax II HR917 LQ-G on 405 'Vancouver' Squadron RCAF at Gransden Lodge, which was being flown by Flight Lieutenant Henry William Julius Dare was probably shot down by a Do 217 flown by Hauptmann Rudolf 'Rudi' Schönert of II/NJG5. All seven crew were killed. Once, Schönert had found true comradeship with 'Britishers, Norwegians, Danes and Germans' on cargo boars before the war. 'We are destroying ourselves' he once said:[128] 'Our fight is not against the powers of nature for the good of humanity but an attempt to destroy life with all the new weapons of science. 'Do not men of our race - perhaps the fair-haired Britishers with whom I sailed in the Bay of Biscay and made friends - sit in their bombers, night after night, turning our cities to ruins? Each does his duty. But don't we thereby aggravate our hatred? At night we see only the enemy bomber and its bright red, white and blue circles. Our cities burn. The bomber must be brought down at all costs and when it crashes we crow. We see only the bomber burning and not the crew. We see only the emblem laid low, not the youngsters hanging on their straps in their death agony. And then perhaps one day you will meet a Tommy who has bailed out. You meet him down below. His eyes have lost the harsh glint of battle. You shake hands and this handshake is the beginning of a comradeship, born of a life and death struggle. Gradually he accepts the cigarette you offer. The barrier that divided us has fallen and two men stand facing each other. Hostility and propaganda have made them enemies but the common danger of battle has made them friends...'[129]

Stirling III BF577 JN-M on 75 Squadron RNZAF piloted by New Zealand Flight Sergeant James Arthur Couper collided with Dornier Do 217N 1419 of II/NJG3 flown by Feldwebel Krauter at Wiemerstedt, ten kilometres north of Heide, killing everyone. Icing (one crew abandoning their Halifax over Sweden) took total losses on the four raids on Hamburg to 79. Three more aircraft crashed on their return.

At Hamburg dawn on 3 August broke upon a city sunk 'in a great silence' after the 'howling and raging of the fire storms' and bathed in the unreal light of rays filtered through a canopy of smoke. Everywhere lay dust, soot and ashes... the streets were covered with hundreds of bodies. 'No worthwhile concentration over the target' had been achieved. (Only scattered bombing took place and 1,426 tons struck the city). But then it was hardly necessary. More than 6,000 acres of Hamburg smouldered in ruins. Over four nights, 3,095 bombers were dispatched, 2,500 attacked and 8,621 tons of bombs were dropped, 4,309 tons of them being incendiary bombs. In these raids, including two minor daylight American attacks, on 25 and 26 July, it was computed by the Police President that 40,385 dwelling-houses and 275,000 flats, representing 61 per cent of the living accommodation of the city, had been destroyed or rendered uninhabitable, 580 industrial and armament establishments were in a similar condition and so were 2,632 shops, 76 public offices, 24 hospitals, 277 schools, 58 churches, 83 banks, twelve bridges and one menagerie, the famous Hagenbeck Zoo, which was wiped out in the first raid. Half the city had been totally devastated. The total population had been reduced by about 30 per cent and the working population by 25 per cent. The number of persons known to have lost their lives was 41,800; the injured, many of whom died, numbered 37,439. To these must be added some thousands more missing.

ACM Sir Arthur Harris said, 'In spite of all that happened at Hamburg, bombing proved a comparatively humane method. For one thing, it saved the flower of the youth of this country and of our allies from being mown down by the military in the field, as it was in Flanders in the war of 1914-1918.'

Gauleiter Karl Otto Kaufmann, in his first report to Doktor Josef Goebbels spoke of a catastrophe, the extent of which simply staggers the imagination. He spoke of about 800,000 homeless people wandering up and down the streets not knowing what to do.' Goebbels wrote 'A city of a million inhabitants has been destroyed in a manner unparalleled in history. We are faced with problems that are almost impossible of solution. Food must be found for this population of a million. Shelter must be secured. The people must be evacuated as far as possible. They must be given clothing.' Generalfeldmarschall Erhard Milch State Secretary of the Reichsluftfahrtministerium (RLM or Reich Air Ministry), went further. 'It's much blacker than [Albert] Speer [the German Armaments Minister] paints it. If we get just five or six more attacks like these on Hamburg, the German people will just lay down their tools, however great their willpower..' (In his speech to a conference of Gauleiters on 6 October, Milch said that in Hamburg particularly the production of variable pitch propellers had suffered very severely because of the loss to these factories of 3,000 skilled workers who are still missing').[130] Up to the time of these attacks, the production of 500-ton U-boats had been between eight and nine a month. After, it fell to between two and three, partly owing to the direct damage inflicted on the yards and workshops and partly because of absenteeism. Speer admitted that 'Hamburg put the fear of God in me - Gauleiter Karl Otto Kaufmann teletyped Hitler repeatedly, begging him to visit the stricken city. When these pleas proved fruitless, he asked Hitler at least to receive a delegation of some of the more heroic rescue crews. But Hitler refused even that.'[131]

During the Battle of Hamburg 24/25 July-3 August, 'Window' prevented about 100-130 potential Bomber Command losses. On 27/28 July, Nachtjäger claimed sixteen bombers shot down, including four by single-engined 'Wild Boars'. During the third raid on Hamburg on 29/30 July the Nachtjagd was credited with 34 kills, equally divided between single-engined 'Wild Boars' and twin-engined crews that were allowed to leave the confines of their 'Himmelbett' boxes for the first time. On 2/3 August, 19 of the 30 bombers that FTR from Hamburg were shot down by the Nachtjagd. Over four nights, 3,000 bombers dropped 10,000 tons of HE and incendiary bombs, to totally devastate half of the city and kill an estimated 42,000 of its inhabitants. After the fourth raid by 740 aircraft on 2/3 August, a million inhabitants fled the city. Thirty bombers were shot down, the bombing force encountered a large thunderstorm area over Germany and the raid was a 'failure'. Albert Speer, Minister of War Production, warned Hitler that Germany would have to surrender after another six of these bombing raids. Paralyzed by 'Window', Nachtjagd and the flakwaffe were unable to offer any significant resistance. On average, British losses during the Hamburg raids were no more than 2.8%, whereas in the previous twelve months, losses had risen from 3.7 to 4.3%. 'Window' neutralized the Würzburg GCI and GL radars and short range AI and completely destroyed the basis of GCI interception. Controlled anti-aircraft fire was almost completely disrupted at night and fixed box barrages only remained possible. The new British tactics also combined the use of PFF, the massed bomber stream and new target finding equipment (H_2S). This combination resulted in total chaos to the German night fighter defence system, which was unable to obtain a true picture of the air situation or control the night fighters in the air.

The report on the raids on Hamburg in July and August 1943 by the Police president of Hamburg on 1 December 1943 painted a grim picture. 'The cause of the enormous extent of the heavy damage and particularly of the high death rate in comparison with former raids is the appearance of firestorms...In Hamburg, the firestorms originated in densely built-up and thickly populated areas, where, therefore, by reason of the type of building and the densely massed houses affected, conditions were favourable for the development of firestorms. In the affected areas in Hamburg there were mostly large blocks of flats in narrow streets with numerous houses behind them, with terraces (inner courtyards), etc. These courtyards became in a very short time, cauldrons of fire which were literally man-traps. The narrow streets became fire-locks through which the tall flames were driven...Only very shortly after the first HE bombs had fallen an enormous number of fires caused by a great concentration of incendiary bombs - mixed with HE bombs - sprang up. People who now attempted to leave their shelters to see what the situation was or to fight the fires were met by a sea of flame. Everything round them was on fire. There was no water and with the huge number and size of the fires all attempts to extinguish them were hopeless from the start... The firestorm raging over many square kilometres had cut off innumerable people without hope of rescue. Only those got away who had risked an early escape or happened to be so near the edge of the sea of fire that it was possible to rescue them. Only where the distance to water or to open spaces of sufficient size was short, was flight now possible, for to cover long distances in the red-hot streets of leaping flames was impossible.

'Many of these refugees even then lost their lives through the heat. They fell, suffocated, burnt, or ran deeper into the fire. Relatives lost one another. One was able to save himself, the others disappeared. Many wrapped themselves in wet blankets or soaked their clothes and thus reached safety. In a short time clothes and blankets became hot and dry. Anyone going any distance through this hell found that his clothes were in flames, or the blanket caught fire and was blown away in the storm.

'Numbers jumped into the canals and waterways and remained swimming or standing up to their necks in water for hours until the heat should die down. Even these suffered burns on their heads. They were obliged to wet their faces constantly or they perished in the heat. The firestorm swept over the water with its heat and its showers of sparks so that even thick wooden posts and bollards burned down to the level of the water. Some of these unfortunate people were drowned. Many jumped out of windows into the water or the street and lost their lives... The scenes of terror which took place in the firestorm area are indescribable. Children were torn away from their parents' hands by the force of the hurricane and whirled into the fire. People who thought they had escaped fell down, overcome by the devouring force of the heat and died in an instant. Refugees had to make their way over the dead and dying. The sick and the infirm had to be left behind by rescuers as they themselves were in danger of burning... Speech is impotent to portray the measure of the horror, which shook the people for ten days and nights and the traces of which were written indelibly on the face of the city and its inhabitants.

'And each of these nights convulsed by flames was followed by a day which displayed the horror in the dim and unreal light of a sky hidden in smoke. Summer heat intensified by the glow of the firestorms to an unbearable degree; dust from the torn earth and the ruins and debris of damaged areas which penetrated everywhere; showers of soot and ashes; more heat and dust; above all a pestilential stench of decaying corpses and smouldering fires weighed continually on the exhausted men.

'And these days were followed by more nights of more horror, yet more smoke and soot, heat and dust and more death and destruction. Men had not time to rest or salvage property according to any plan or to search for their families. The enemy attacked with ceaseless raids until the work of destruction was complete. His hate had its triumph in the firestorms which destroyed mercilessly men and material alike...The streets were covered with hundreds of corpses. Mothers with their children, youths, old men, burnt, charred, untouched and clothed, naked with a waxen pallor like dummies in a shop window, they lay in every posture, quiet and peaceful or cramped, the death-struggle shown in the expression on their faces. The shelters showed the same picture, even more horrible in its effect, as it showed in many cases the final distracted struggle against a merciless fate. Although in some places shelterers sat quietly, peacefully and untouched as if sleeping in their chairs, killed without realization or pain by carbon monoxide poisoning, in other shelters the position of remains of bones and skulls showed how the occupants had fought to escape from their buried prison.

'No flight of imagination will ever succeed in measuring and describing the gruesome scenes of horror in the many buried air raid shelters. Posterity can only bow its head in honour of the fate of these innocents, sacrificed by the murderous lust of a sadistic enemy.'

Endnotes Chapter 10

111 4 Halifaxes, 4 Lancasters, 3 Stirlings and a Wellington, all but one falling to night fighters of NJG3 and IV./NJG1 operating over NW Germany, Schleswig-Holstein and the northern part of the Netherlands.
112 Quoted in *The Battle of Hamburg* by Martin Middlebrook (Penguin 1980).
113 Following four months of basic military training, Fahnenjunker Greiner underwent flying training, initially with the Luftkriegsschule at Berlin-Gatow, qualifying for his pilot's licence on 30 October 1939. He then attended the Flugzeugführerschule C at Alt-Lönnewitz, where he trained to fly multi-engine aircraft types. There followed attendances at the Aufklärungsschule at Grossenhain, Blindflugschule at Neuburg-Donau, Zerstörerschule 2 at Memmingen, Jagdfliegerschule 2 at Schleissheim and Nachtjagdschule at Stuttgart-Echterdingen. In all his flying training had lasted over two years, from March 1939 to September 1941. On 1 October 1941 Leutnant Greiner was posted to II./NJG1 at Stade near Hamburg. He transferred to 4./NJG2 in mid-January 1942. He participated in

Operation 'Donnerkeil', the aerial protection for the *Scharnhorst* and *Gneisenau* and the heavy cruiser *Prinz Eugen* on their Channel dash from France to Germany. On 20 April he was promoted to the rank of Oberleutnant. He achieved his first night victory on the night of 25-26 June when he shot down a Wellington over northwest Holland. On 1 October 4./NJG2 was redesignated 10./NJG1. Greiner recorded his second victory on the night of 6/7 October, by which time he was serving with 11./NJG1. He was transferred to Nachtjagdschule 1 to undertake night fighter pilot instruction on 23 November and on the night of 25/26 February 1943 he claimed a Stirling near Rastatt. On 19 May Greiner returned to combat duty with 10./NJG1.

114   On 4 October 1943 he transferred to I./NJG1 where he assumed command of the Luftbeobachter-Erprobungsstaffel. He returned to 10./NJG1 on 2 December.

115   *The Battle of Hamburg* by Martin Middlebrook (Penguin 1980)/Kracker Archive.

116   According to Martin Middlebrook in *The Battle of Hamburg*, Meissner probably shot down Stirling EE890 on 75 Squadron RNZAF at Mepal flown by Sergeant Henry Nicol. He and three of the crew were killed, 3 PoW. Stirling EE902 on 214 Squadron at Chedburgh flown by Pilot Officer Richard Watt Belshaw DFM was shot down by fighter attack. Belshaw and five killed, 2 PoW. Crew on 16th op. Lancaster W4987 on 460 Squadron RAAF flown by Sergeant Aubrey George Ashley) was shot down by flak at Cuxhaven. 7 killed. Crew on 5th op. Halifax DK187 on 78 Squadron flown by Flying Officer George Such) was shot down by fighter attack and all 7 men perished. The crew were on their 14th op. Halifax JD316 on 102 Squadron flown by Flight Lieutenant Tom Bakewell was shot down by fighter attack. All 8 crew, who were on their 11th op were killed.

117   Quoted in *The Battle of Hamburg* by Martin Middlebrook (Penguin 1980).

118   See *The Battle of Hamburg* by Martin Middlebrook (Penguin 1980).

119   Quoted in *The Battle of Hamburg* by Martin Middlebrook (Penguin 1980).

120   In December 1943 Herrmann was appointed Luftwaffe Inspector of Aerial Defence. By 1944, he was Inspector General of night fighters and received the Knight's Cross with Oak Leaves and Swords. At the end of 1944, he led the 9. Flieger-division (J). At this time he was a leading exponent of the tactical deployment of the so-called Rammjäger Sonderkommando Elbe (ram fighters, task force Elbe), sent into action in April 1945. Pilot volunteers, often aged 18 to 20, were to be trained to be simply competent enough to control specially lightened and unarmoured Bf 109 fighters and charged with downing Allied bombers by deliberately ramming the tail or control surfaces with the propellers of their aircraft and thereafter (hopefully) bailing out. Herrmann's intention was to gather a large number of these fighters for a one-off attack on the USAAF bomber streams, hopefully causing enough losses to curtail the bombing offensive for a few months. Fuel shortages prevented employment of the large numbers necessary, although from one mission of this type of the 138 aircraft thus committed only fifty came back. Herrmann would fly more than fifty night fighter sorties and claim nine RAF bombers destroyed. A new divisional staff, Jagddivision 30, was set up by Oberst Herrmann to control the 'Wild Boars' and operated independently from any other Nachtjagd or flak authorities. Another former bomber pilot, Oberst Viktor von Lossberg, who had flown He 111H bombers in III./KG26 in Norway in 1940 and Ju 88S bombers in II/JG26 before being assigned to the Reich Ministry of Aviation, worked with Generalfeldmarschall Milch as his advisor on night-fighting tactics and advocated strengthening of Herrmann's 'Wilde Sau' units. The force was expanded to three Geschwader with JG300 based around Berlin, JG301 defending the Frankfurt/Main area and JG302 based in the Munich/Vienna area. However, although JG300 and subsequent units raised met with promising initial success, the high wastage of both pilots and aircraft due to high accident rates curtailed extensive use of 'Wilde Sau' beyond the start of 1944. Viktor von Lossberg died on 24 May 1983 at Garmisch-Partenkirchen aged 79.

121   See *Night Airwar* by Theo Boiten.

122   *The Battle of Hamburg* by Martin Middlebrook (Penguin 1980)/*The Lent Papers* by Peter Hichliffe.

123   On 18 November 1943 Walter Ehle's Bf 110 crashed near St. Trond, Belgium. As he was landing his airfield lights were extinguished; his aircraft crashed and he and his crew, Oberfeldwebel Leidenbach, bordfunker and Unteroffizier Derlitzky, bordschütze, perished. Major Ehle was awarded the Knight's Cross on 29 August after 31 victories and at the time of his death he was credited with 39. He shot down a total of 38 enemy aircraft of which 35 were at night.

124   Halifax JD148 on 78 Squadron at Breighton flown by Sergeant Leslie Edward Maidment was shot down by Wilhelmshaven flak. Maidment and one of his crew was killed; one died of wounds and four were taken prisoner. Lancaster R5687 on 50 Squadron, Skellingthorpe flown by Flight

Sergeant Nigel Paul Ivan Castells was shot down by Bremerhaven flak. All seven crew, who were on their second operation, were killed. Stirling BK693 on at 90 Squadron at West Wickham flown by Pilot Officer R. Whitworth suffered flak damage and crash-landed at Stradishall. Halifax DK188 on 76 Squadron at Holme-on-Spalding-Moor piloted by Flight Sergeant W. E. Elder RNZAF crash-landed at Shipdham after fighter combat. One crew member killed in the combat. Stirling EF369 on 7 Squadron at Oakington flown by Pilot Officer G. R. Woodward was written off after crash-landing at Oakington. No casualties.

125   Born 27 July 1911, he had been a sailor who had sailed the seven seas aboard merchant ships before the war. He was the seventh highest scoring night fighter flying ace in the Luftwaffe. He was also a recipient of the Ritterkreuz des Eisernen Kreuzes mit Eichenlaub. At the age of 20 he lived a happy carefree life sailing the seven seas as a ship's boy in the Merchant Navy and learned to appreciate and love other nations. In 1933 Schönert began flight training and went on to fly commercial aircraft for Lufthansa. He was commissioned as a Leutnant in the Luftwaffe's Reserve in 1938 and in June 1941 joined 4./NJG1 at Bergen in northern Holland. He gained his first victories on 9 July 1941 and by 25 July 1942 his total stood at 22 and he was awarded the Knight's Cross. Schönert was the driving force behind the introduction of 'Schräge Musik' upward-firing armament in night fighter aircraft, the first prototype of which he introduced into his own Dornier Do 17 in 1942. Initially, 'Schräge Musik' was rejected by Helmut Lent and Werner Streib. Oberfeldwebel Paul Mahle, an armourer attached to II./NJG5 at Parchim, worked closely with Rudolf Schönert and built his own working prototype of 'Schräge Musik', which was soon fitted to all of the Gruppe's aircraft. Schönert claimed the first aerial victory with upward-firing guns in May 1943. By August he was flying with NJG100 over the Eastern Front, claiming thirty Soviet night raiders by early 1944. Schönert's radio and wireless operator was Oberfeldwebel Johannes Richter.

126   See *The Battle of Hamburg* by Martin Middlebrook (Penguin 1980).

127   Günther Lützow (4 September 1912-24 April 1945) was credited with 110 victories achieved in over 300 combat sorties. During the Spanish Civil War from March to September 1937 Oberleutnant Lützow claimed five victories, including the first ever recorded by the Bf 109. He gained 20 victories over the Western Front, including at least one Viermot and 85 victories over the Eastern Front. Lützow, flying the Me 262 jet fighter for Adolf Galland's JV44, was posted missing on 24 April 1945 while attempting to intercept a USAAF B-26 Marauder raid near Donauwörth. His body was never recovered.

128   *Quoted in Duel Under The Stars* by Wilhelm Johnen.

129   *Quoted in Duel Under The Stars* by Wilhelm Johnen.

130   Milch was born in Wilhelmshaven, the son of Anton Milch, a Jewish pharmacist, on 30 March 1892 in the Kaiserliche Marine, the Imperial German Navy and Clara Milch, née Rosenau. Since his mother was not Jewish, he was not a Jew according to Jewish law. But he was a 'Mischling' ('mixed-race' person) under the Nuremberg Laws introduced by the Nazi regime in 1935. He was one of the few officers in the German high command of Jewish ancestry. In 1933 Milch had taken up a position as State Secretary of the newly formed Reichsluftfahrtministerium answering directly to Hermann Göring. In this capacity, he was instrumental in establishing the Luftwaffe. As such, Milch was in charge of aircraft production. However, the lack of a long-term strategy and a divisive military command structure led to many mistakes in the operational and technical ability of the Luftwaffe in the war and were key to the continued loss of German air superiority as the war progressed. In 1944 Milch sided with Joseph Göbbels, the propaganda minister and Heinrich Himmler, the Reichsführer SS, in attempting to convince Adolf Hitler to remove Göring from command of the Luftwaffe following the failed invasion of the Soviet Union. When Hitler refused, Göring retaliated by forcing Milch out of his position. For the rest of the war, he worked under Albert Speer.

131   *Inside the Third Reich*.

Chapter Eleven

Deadly Nacht Musik

The German Propaganda Ministry would not permit American jazz to be broadcast in Germany. However, the U-boat crews and thousands of young Germans serving in the Wehrmacht in occupied Europe greatly enjoyed it. Many popular German recordings and programmes containing 'American jazz with the German flavour' were broadcast from England over 'Grey' transmitters.

The Black Game **by Ellic Howe (Michael Joseph, 1982)**

During July 1943-early March 1944 'Wild Boar' Geschwader claimed 330 bombers destroyed at night. Such was the immediate success of 'Wilde Sau' that in September they were expanded into three Geschwader named JG300, 301 and 302, under Major Kurt Kettner, Major (later Oberstleutnant) Helmut Weinreich and Major Manfred Mossinger, respectively. JG300, for instance, claimed 173 victories between July 1943-March 1944, including thirteen RAF bombers on 23/24 August, eight on 27/28 August, eleven on 31 August/1 September and sixteen on 5/6 September. Herrmann conducted his operations without the slightest regard for losses. Only when the last of the best pilots had been expended and bad weather set in, late in 1943, it became quite normal for up to 25 'Wilde Sau' aircraft to be lost from sixty engaged. Wastage on this scale continued into the winter of 1943-44. JG301 flew on 21 nights from September 1943, losing 58 pilots killed or severely injured for 87 victories. From November 1943 FW 190s and Bf 109s of JG302 operated on 22 nights, claiming seventy bombers for the loss of 43 pilots. In 1945 General 'Beppo' Schmid estimated 'Wild Boar' losses at 45% between 1 August 1943 and 1 February 1944. Schmid, a Bavarian, born on 24 September 1901, was a close friend of Hermann Göring. Schmid had commanded Abteilung 5, the Luftwaffe's Military Intelligence Branch from 1 January 1938 to 9 November 1942. Adolf Galland later criticized Schmid for doing nothing to upgrade the low quality of the intelligence service. In late 1942 Schmid was put in charge of Division 'General Göring' in Tunisia, known as 'Kampfgruppe Schmid'. On personal orders from Göring, he was flown out of the Tunisian pocket. Promoted to Generalmajor on 1 February 1943 and Generalleutnant on 1 July 1944 he was given command of the I Jagdkorps.

The diminishing 'Wild Boar' results in late 1943 were compensated for by the twin-engined free-lancing 'Tame Boars', which were gradually getting over the shock of 'Window' during the autumn of 1943. On 16 March 1944 Jagddivision 30, the divisional staff, which controlled the three Geschwader was scrapped and shortly afterwards the remnants of Hermann's three Geschwader were subordinated to Jagdkorps 1 and re-trained for day and all-weather fighting.

Of the record 290 Nachtjagd victories achieved in August 1943, only 48 were by the traditional 'Himmelbett' method while the remaining 80% were credited to the 'Wild Boar' units and to twin-engined crews operating in 'Wild Boar' fashion. Nachtjagd lost 61 aircraft in action that same month. Mainly they were flown by green and inexperienced crews. Early 'Wild Boar' successes were undoubtedly achieved by Herrmann's original band of ex-bomber pilots like Oberleutnant Friedrich Karl 'Felix' or 'Nasen' ('Nose' on account of his aristocratic proboscis). Müller, a pre-war Lufthansa captain and now Operations Officer in JG300 destroyed 29 Viermots and a Mosquito in just 52 sorties. Müller received the Ritterkreuz in July 1944 and was the most successful 'Wild Boar' pilot, claiming thirty victories in this fashion. Herrmann claimed nine Viermots shot down in fifty sorties. Another 'Wilde Sau' legend was Oberleutnant Kurt Welter of 5./JG301 who claimed seventeen Viermots in only fifteen sorties between September 1943 and early April 1944. The vast majority of the single-engined night fighter pilots had no such tale of success to tell, but lived on the reputation and glory of the skilful few. Welter, born at Marienbad, Czechoslovakia on 25 February 1916, had joined the Luftwaffe in 1934. He showed a strong natural ability as a pilot and was subsequently selected for flight instructor training and served many years as a flying instructor. In 1943 Welter transferred to an operational night fighter unit flying contemporary piston engine fighter aircraft. On 18 October 1944, after forty combat sorties, Welter was awarded the Ritterkreuz des Eisernen Kreuzes.

Just six victories were credited to night-fighter crews on 9/10 August when 457 aircraft raided Mannheim. Four of these, three Halifaxes and a Lancaster were credited to four crews of the newly formed I./NJG6 at Schleissheim. One of these, Halifax II JD267 on 419 'Moose' Squadron RCAF skippered by 21-year old Flying Officer Michael T. R. Ludlow RCAF was claimed by Oberfeldwebel Richard Launer for his fifth Abschüsse. Ludlow, who was on his 22nd operation, and all six members of his crew, were killed. In fact, Bomber Command lost nine aircraft (six Halifaxes and three Lancasters) or 2% of the force. Two of the missing Lancasters were shot down by Leutnant Norbert Pietrek, a pilot who had become operational in 2./NJG4 in January 1943 flying Bf 110s from Florennes airfield in southern Belgium. He had scored his first 'double' on 16/17 April, his victims being an unidentified Lancaster which flew into a hill surrounding the River Meuse whilst being chased by Pietrek at low level and Stirling BK653 on 214 Squadron, which came down at Bonneuil-les-Eaux in the Oise district at 23.45 (four evaders and three PoWs) after a prolonged battle.

Pietrek recalls the events of 9/10 August:

'We are once again lounging about in our operations hut, wearing our full flying kit. My radio operator Otto had gone down with hepatitis and was in hospital. Unteroffizier Paul Gartig, who at the time had no 'driver', had been assigned to take his place. We had already got to know each other in the course of other operations and I had found him to be a very good radar and radio operator. I called him Paulchen (little Paul), although he was older than me, but he had not taken this badly.

'It is just past midnight. The 'little Kadi' (Hauptmann Wilhelm Herget, Gruppen Kommandeur) had assigned me a few days before to the first wave of his operational area 7B, which had made me feel quite proud (in the first wave, the best and most experienced crews were usually scrambled). In charge of this fighter box's See-burgtisch is Ernschtle, the best JLO (Jager Leit Offizier, or Fighter Controller), which is practically a guarantee for an Abschuss if the Tommies should come. None of us of course want them to come, for we could never shoot down all the bombers but only a small fraction of them, leaving more than enough others to destroy a German city with their bombs.

'Will they be coming tonight and if so, through our sector? The chances are not bad. The Tommies have good weather for taking off and landing, the night is dark with no moon. These are good conditions for us night fighters as well.

'While we are still quietly dozing away we suddenly get the order: 'First wave cockpit readiness!' and we rush out to the bus which brings us to our machines. So they are coming, the Tommies. In no time at all we, Paulchen, Moritz (flight engineer) and I, are on board and are waiting for the order to take off. After only a few minutes it comes.

'The engines fire at once, thanks to the efforts of Moritz, and my ground mechanic Alwin Athen and I take off. I climb, orbiting, with full power, while Paulchen is seeking radio contact with Ernschtle, which isn't easy, for the Tommy's jamming is considerably worse tonight than usual, which almost certainly means that they will be coming through our sector. Then it sounded to me as though the starboard engine wasn't running quite right; in any case its rpm had dropped somewhat and I had to adjust it. I ask Moritz what might be wrong and whether he thought that we should turn back. He asked me for the oil pressure and the oil and cooler temperatures and then thought that we should continue. Without Moritz, I would probably have turned back.

'Now, as I am almost at a height of 6,000 metres, Paulchen got contact with the JLO through the dreadful cacophony of the jammers and he 'serves me up' with a Tommy. He is on a course of around east-south-east and still quite some distance away. I must therefore give chase with full power. We get some minor course corrections and I gradually close with my opponent. He is pretty fast; it must be a new model, perhaps one of the new Lancasters? We should soon find out.

'We have been chasing the Tommy for some minutes and are closing in. He is dead ahead, only 500 metres away and I am straining my eyes to see him. There, or am I mistaken? No, he really is there! The black outline with the four faintly glimming exhausts. I ease a little lower and a little to the right in order to identify him and to get out of the rear gunner's arc of fire with his four machine guns. It is, in fact, a Halifax. Then I slide under the Tommy, adjust to his speed and ease up until I am about twenty metres below him. Now my friend, now you're for it!

'I had decided on his starboard wing as my aiming point, pulled up, rising barely five metres behind the Halifax whilst firing a full burst between the starboard engines where his fuel tanks are and the kite bursts into flames in the starboard wing and plunges burning over his port wing. We follow him down until we see the flash of his crash and report our success to base. After the crash we can hardly believe our eyes: it looks like regular fireworks with variously coloured rockets. We had apparently caught one of the illuminators. He will not be able to set his markers over the city to be attacked. Perhaps we had saved a lot of peoples' lives there. But now back to radio beacon 7B!

'Only now do I realize that my two 2cm cannon had not been fired, only my four machine guns and of these one had failed and cannot be cocked. What's up? Has the armourer, Oberfeldwebel Habermann, made some mistake? Well, I'll give him what for when I get back. Now I'll have to carry on with only three guns!

'Flying westward to the radio beacon we hear from the JLO that he has lost us and cannot find us again because 'the sky is full of Tommies, but none of them are continuing on their way', as good old Ernschtle puts it. He is unable to find me and guide me to another enemy. I make that out through the chatter and noise in my earphones as I notice to our starboard, at about the same height, a small shadow, no larger than a wasp, flit past in the opposite direction at about 500 metres distance. Could that have been a Tommy? Without thinking long about it I swung off to the right and was not a little surprised to find myself exactly fifty metres beneath a Lancaster. Paulchen and Otto behind me were startled by my sudden manoeuvre but

I had had no time to warn them.

'Now I have my second opponent of the night before me. So I am to shoot him down with only three machine guns, but how does one do that? Will I manage it and set him on fire like the Halifax before? Let's try it. Now, as before with the Halifax and at least a hundred times before at practice, I position myself twenty metres beneath him, then I pull up and fire a full burst into the two starboard engines. No success! I must have hit him, but the Lancaster continues steadily on his east-south-east course to bring its bombs to their destination. Now I notice that another gun had failed to fire and that I have only two left. That makes it practically impossible to shoot down a Viermot, but it's worth a try and I want my second victory.

'After my first attack I had placed myself to the right and below, to observe my opponent and consider how I might 'with only two thin squirters' as the Little Kadi expressed it afterwards, sweep him from the sky. To set the engines or tanks on fire is, as the first attack had proved, pointless. That leaves only the fuselage as aiming point and if possible the 4 x 1,000 rounds of ammunition in the rear turret. Normally we don't aim at the fuselage, but only at the tanks and the engines in the wings. The enemy crew should have the chance of escaping with their parachutes. They were only doing their duty, just as we were doing ours and they could not be blamed that 'Bomber Harris' had ordered them to destroy German cities instead of the German industry. But now I have no choice than to try to set fire to the ammunition in the rear turret in order to stop the enemy from reaching his target. That would make it unavoidable that some of the crew would be killed, at least the rear gunner. I feel sorry for him, but how many Germans might be killed by his bombs?

'Now the enemy knows that he is being stalked by a night fighter and he will be very much on the alert. I sneak under him, into the blind spot of his defences, for the second attack. The rear gunner had evidently spotted me, had realized that he no longer had a chance and abandoned his turret to save himself by parachute. But as I am already very close beneath him, which the poor fellow could not have seen, his head hits my port wing, where afterwards we found a scrap of skin with a bunch of red hair. Pity, I would rather have had him land unhurt.

'Now I must try to eliminate the mid-upper gunner; I would have to pursue the Lancaster for some while yet until I should manage, if at all, to set the rear turret ammunition afire and the propeller wash of the four Lancaster engines would fling me several times upwards into the field of fire of the two machine guns of the top turret. I therefore fired, already pulling up, into the area of the mid-upper turret and I must have got him, for he doesn't fire a single shot, although I am thrown about a lot and several times into his field of fire. I am now literally poking around with my two guns at no more than ten metres' range in the bottom right of the rear turret where two of the four ammunition boxes are located and, indeed, after about ten seconds there is a flame. Now the same again in the bottom left with the same result. Then I move off to starboard to observe what happens next.

'At first nothing happens, the Lancaster continues on course to his target. Either those in front have not noticed the fire in the rear turret, or they think that it will burn itself out. I almost thought so myself, for the flame disappeared for a few seconds, only to reappear even larger. It looks as if the Lancaster is alight at the back like a cigar. After five minutes, however, the Lancaster turns back and tries to get away homewards. But after a few minutes the crew must have realized that it was useless, for suddenly the Lancaster dives steeply down and in the bright glare of the crash we see four open parachutes descending. The rest of the crew must have bought it, pity. I have done it, shot down a Viermot 'with only two thin squirters', something not to be emulated easily. But, now that the ammunition for my two guns must be almost exhausted and my fuel too, I report my return and fly home.

'During the chase of the Lancaster we had heard over the radio a succession of fighters leaving Florennes and reporting in 7B, the Little Kadi, my Staffelkapitän 'Rudi' Altendorf, 'Luk' Meister[132] and also Fritz Graff. Would some of those also down one or more Tommies?

'After fifteen minutes I am over the airfield and landing. I taxi over to refuel; I wanted to take off again, should the Tommies return through our area - perhaps I could get a third one! I stop the engines and call for the armourer to give him a ticking off about the cannon which had failed to work. Habermann comes, looks at the guns and then says that both are in order, but that all four machine guns would have to be changed. I then realize that I had not been flying my own 'H', which had all the guns on the trigger of the control column, but 'Rudi' Altendorf's reserve machine 'B' and that one had only the machine guns on the trigger and the cannon separately on a button and I had, as I had been accustomed to do on my 'H', used only the trigger. I feel a fool and apologize to Habermann. So there is no question of another flight. The three of us make our way to the operations room.

'There we get a great welcome and are congratulated on our success. All the others who had taken off for 7B after my first success had now also reported their return. None of them had found an enemy because, as it now became clear, the Tommies had dropped masses of Düppel ('Window') which had so interfered with our radar that neither our ground nor our airborne instruments had been able to make them out and with only the naked eye no enemy aircraft had been spotted. This night, mine had been the only success of the Western defensive chain.'

At 01.00 Leutnant Norbert Pietrek's first victim of the night, Halifax II HR872 LQ-K on 405 Squadron crashed at Awenne, Luxembourg, near the Belgian border. Skippered by Flight Lieutenant Kenneth MacGregor Gray RCAF, it had left Gransden Lodge just over two hours earlier for a raid on Mannheim. All seven crew members, of which six were Canadians, perished and were buried in Florennes. Twenty minutes later Leutnant Pietrek carried out two attacks on Lancaster I W4236 QR-K on 61 Squadron piloted by Sergeant J. C. Whitley. Following the first attack, the bombs were jettisoned but after the second attack Whitley gave the order to bail out before the Lancaster crashed at Marbehan, Luxembourg. Whitley and three others evaded capture. Sergeants John Topham Kendall RCAF, George William Sidney Spriggs and Nevil Temple Holmes were killed. They found their last resting place in Florennes. As Leutnant Pietrek witnessed, the remaining four men in this all-NCO crew bailed out safely, managing to escape capture. Their aircraft was a veteran; it had been on 61 Squadron's strength for almost a year, flying a total of 639 hours 55 minutes. Len Bradfield, bomb aimer on 'J-Johnny' a 49 Squadron Lancaster flown by Johnny Moss reflects:

'When we first began flying ops in March 1943, losses were averaging 5% a night but we believed we were special and would survive. We were sorry other crews didn't make it back but we accepted that this was the way things were. We didn't think it could happen to us. We were an above average crew and expected to go to Path Finders after our tour. On return from leave in August our spirits were high. Casualty figures had got significantly lower. It came as a sharp jolt when the crew we had trained with failed to return from the raid on Mannheim on 9/10 August. Next day, however, was beautiful. The NFT[133] went well. When we saw the fuel and bomb loading we decided it would be a longish operation. After the flying supper we went to briefing. The target was Nürnburg with the MAN diesel factory at Furth being the aiming point. As it was in southern Germany the route was over lightly defended territory as much as possible.

'Climbing to a height of 21,000 feet on track, we crossed the enemy coast at Le Treport and then flew on over France, directly to Nürnburg. 'Window' was dropped at intervals on entering German airspace north of Trier. There was about 8/10ths cloud with tops at 14,000 feet, which meant we would be silhouetted from above by the bright moonlight. We knew we were in trouble and we generally weaved to give a maximum sky search. All of a sudden, at about 0030 hours, near Wolfstein (south of Bad Kreuznach and NNW of Mannheim, where we could see the glow from our bombing the night before), we were attacked by a night fighter. Terry Woods, the mid upper gunner, spotted the incoming attack and shouted,' Bandit 5 o'clock high!'

'I abandoned scrabbling about on the floor dropping 'Window' and stood at my guns (being 6 feet l inch I could work the turret better standing than sitting). Cannon and tracer fire hit our port wing and port outer engine, setting both on fire. Terry returned fire, followed by Ronnie Musson in the rear turret before he was put out of action because of the loss of the port outer, which produced hydraulic power for his turret.

'As our attacker broke away over the nose I got in a burst of thirty rounds from the front guns. Johnny started taking violent evasive action to blow out the fire. Sammy Small, the WOp/AG, was standing in the astrodome coordinating the defences as we had practiced. Almost at once Ron Musson, the rear gunner, called out a second attack. It began at 6 o'clock level, dead aft. All hell was let loose. Shells were exploding 'crunk' 'crunk' 'crunk' against the armoured doors and the 4,000lb cookie in the bomb bay. There was a smell of cordite and fire broke out in the bomb bay and mainplane. I dropped down to the bomb aimer's compartment and could see the fire raging. I told Johnny and he gave the order to jettison. I did. The attack was still in progress. The night-fighter was holding off at 600 yards, blazing away. He didn't close.

'The fire persisted and Johnny gave the order to bail out - 'Abracadabra, Jump, Jump!'

'From beginning to end it had lasted perhaps 1-2 seconds but it seemed like slow motion. The order was acknowledged, except for the rear gunner. I got my parachute on and pulled up, twisted and dropped the front escape hatch in order to bail out. Ernie Roden, flight engineer and David Jones, navigator were coming down the bomb aimer's bay. I dived out and fell clear and delayed opening my chute until I was below the cloud. I could still see red and yellow tracer flying by. It is possible that Ernie and David were hit when they bailed out. As I broke cloud I could see several small fires, which reinforces the idea that 'B-Baker' exploded. On the ground I chucked my lucky woolly golly wog away. It was nothing personal (I had carried him on all my eighteen ops) but I thought it had failed me. He hadn't because later, when I was captured, when I asked about my crew I was told, 'Funf Tot'; (five dead). Johnny Moss was the only other survivor, probably blown clear when the Lancaster exploded. A Luftwaffe NCO told me three four-engined bombers had been brought down in a ten kilometre circle by his unit. At Dulag Luft interrogation centre I thought about the attack and concluded that a professional, a real 'tradesman' had shot us down.'

One of six Lancasters lost 'B-Baker' was shot down by 31-year old Major Heinrich Wohlers, Kommandeur I./NJG6 flying a Bf 110 who claimed a 'Halifax' at Spessbach, northwest of Landstuhl at 0230 and a Stirling at Schaffhausen and a Halifax at Ansbach. Wohlers, a former reconnaissance pilot who had converted to night fighting in 1940, had scored 29 Abschusse by the time he was killed in a flying accident while trying to land in heavy fog on 15 March 1944. Dave Jones died when he landed in a vineyard and was impaled in the throat. Len Bradfield was incarcerated in a PoW camp and in March 1945 he attempted to escape during the forced march through Germany. He hid in a sugar beet field for three nights but both his feet were badly frostbitten and his toes had to be removed later by a Polish surgeon.

On 10/11 August 653 heavies caused widespread destruction in Nürnburg. Seven Halifaxes and three Stirlings also failed to return, making a total of sixteen aircraft lost overall, or 2.4%. Twelve of the losses are attributed to Nachtjagd. Oberleutnant Heinz-Wolfgang Schnaufer, Staffelkapitän II./NJG1 claimed a Lancaster at Hahnlein 25 kilometres (sixteen miles) SSW of Darmstadt. I./NJG6 claimed four victories, Hauptmann Heinrich Wohlers, scoring a triple kill and Oberleutnant Hans Jörg Birkenstock, Staffelkapitän I/NJG6, a Lancaster near Alsenborn. Feldwebel Otto Heinrich Fries and his bordfunker Unteroffizier Fred Staffa of 5./NJG1 shot down Halifax JA716 on 97 Squadron at Hanzinelle, Belgium, southeast of Charleroi for their first kill. Flight Lieutenant W. I. Covington DFC and crew all bailed out safely. On completion of their night fighter training, Otto Fries and Fred Staffa had been posted to II./NJG1 at Sint-Truiden/Sint-Trond in January 1942. Under the prevailing conditions of the 'Himmelbett' GCI system, the green crew had hardly been given a chance to prove their ability in combat, as only the most experienced crews patrolled in the most 'profitable' boxes. Therefore, by August 1943, Fries and Staffa had only had fleeting encounters with a British bomber on two occasions, without being able to score a confirmed kill.

On Sunday 15/Monday 16 August, when 199 Lancasters continued the offensive against Milan (and on the 16/17th when the target for 154 bombers was Turin), there was no Main Force activity over the Reich save for minor operations and minelaying by 63 aircraft on 'Gardening' in the Friesians, off Texel and off all the main Brittany and Biscay ports. Two Wellingtons and Stirling III EE891 on 75 Squadron RNZAF flown by 20-year old Flight Sergeant Neville Bruce Whitta failed to return. There were no survivors on the Stirling. One of the Wellington X's that was lost was HE768 on 300 Polish Squadron flown by Flight Sergeant Maksymilian Rech. He and Flight Sergeant Czeslaw Poddany survived for eight days adrift in a dinghy before being rescued by the Germans. The three other crew members were all killed. Wellington X HF596 on 166 Squadron flown by Flight Sergeant Albert P. Bates who took part in the 'Gardening' operation around the 'Nectarine' region of the Frisian Islands was claimed shot down by Leutnant Heinz Grimm of 12./NJG1 flying Bf 110G-4 G9+CE. 'Bert' Bates, the second eldest of seven children and an accomplished pianist, also excelled at languages and prior to volunteering for the RAF at the start of the war, served in the Grenadier Guards. However, he had a strong desire to become a pilot and his parents had to reimburse the Guards quite a sum of money in order for him to join. His unequal combat with Grimm took place at very low level of eighty metres resulting in the 'Wimpy' crashing into the North Sea eighty kilometres northwest of Vlieland. Bert's death had a devastating impact on his parents and family. They lived in hope that he would return home but his elder brother, Walter, an air gunner on 630 Squadron visited Kirmington, where returning crews confirmed that they had seen the Wellington go down in flames, a fact that he kept to himself rather than cause his parents more pain. Albert would have celebrated his 23rd birthday in November 1943.

Germany's ineffective air defences caused an upheaval in the highest echelons of the German command system. Generalleutnant Josef Schmid, whom it was intended to place in command of the day fighter units of Fliegerkorps XII under Kammhuber, was ordered to report of the state of the fighter defences. Schmid was particularly struck by the eccentric organisation of Command, which seemed to belong to two separate worlds - Luftflotte 3 covering France and Fliegerkorps XII covering Germany and the Low Countries. On 17 August when the USAAF attacked the German aircraft industry for the first time by day, Schmid happened to be at Deelen in Holland, where, owing to the failure of a division in the Luftflotte III area to report the air situation, the target for the RAF heavies that night would not be known until the following day. In Eastern England 596 RAF bomber crews were warned that a special target was to be attacked. Operation 'Hydra' as it was called, was so secret that when the sheet covering the route map was unveiled at each airfield crews were none the wiser as it identified Peenemünde on the Baltic, which meant absolutely nothing to any of them. They had never heard of it!

Endnotes Chapter 11

132   Meister was WIA on 23 March 1944 returning from a sortie in his Bf 110G-4. After shooting down a Lancaster on 514 Squadron near St. Omer Toni Werzinski the bordmeckaniker and bordshütze who had been working on the aircraft throughout the previous night, fell asleep and failed to spot a P-47 flown by Captain Edward H. Spietsma of the 367th Fighter Squadron, 358th Fighter Group who attacked from behind and sent the 110 down. Werzinski was shot in the head but subsequently survived. Meister managed to crash land at Nannine near Namur, but the three crew were injured and trapped in the aircraft. They crashed near a railway line where two German members of the Reichsbahn, working nearby, saw the crash. They arrived at the crash site quickly and ordered the Belgian workforce to remove the crew to safety. The Bf 110 exploded and the crew were put on a train and taken to Namer Lazarett. Meister was hospitalized until August 1944. When he recovered he returned to Florennes to receive the Ritterkreuz for his victories but was still not fit for flying duties, so he organised the evacuation of the airfield in August 1944. At the end of 1944 Meister was promoted to Kommandeur and took command of III./NJG4. He scored his final Abschuss when he shot down a Lancaster on 7 March 1945 near Kassel. Ludwig Meister maintained contact with his two crew members. Werzinski had recovered from the bullet wound to the head and Hannes Forke, whilst on a holiday at Almaar on the coast of the Netherlands in the 1960s, tried to save his daughter and nephew from drowning, but died with them.

133   In ED625 'B-Baker' (the flight commander's aircraft which was fitted with 'Monica' tail warning apparatus.

Chapter Twelve

Hydra

Last night in clear moonlight our bombers undertook a massive raid on Peenemünde approximately sixty miles northwest of Stettin, the largest and most important air research and development institute in Germany. Our aircraft encountered a great many enemy night fighters, several of which we shot down. Mosquito bombers raided targets in Berlin.

RAF Headquarters announcement, 16 August 1943.

The Heeresversuchsanstalt Peenemünde, HVP (Peenemünde Army Research Centre) was founded in 1937 as one of five military proving grounds under the German Army Weapons Office (Heeres Waffenamt). On 2 April 1936 the Reich Air Ministry paid 750,000 Reichsmarks to the town of Wolgast for the whole Northern peninsula of the Baltic island of Usedom. Wernher von Braun was the HVP technical director. The site had been suggested by his mother as 'just the place for you and your friends'. One of his 'friends' - Dr Walter Thiel - the engineer heading the V-2 liquid oxygen propulsion department, was his deputy director. By the middle of 1938, the Army facility had been separated from the Luftwaffe facility and was nearly complete, with personnel moved from Kummersdorf.[134] Several German guided missiles and rockets were developed by the HVP, including the V2 rocket (A4) and the Wasserfall (35 Peenemünde trial firings), Schmetterling, Rheintochter, Taifun and Enzian missiles. The HVP also performed preliminary design work on very-long-range missiles for use against the United States. That project was sometimes called the 'V 3'. The Peenemünde establishment also developed other techniques, such as the first closed-circuit television system in the world, installed at Test Stand VII to track the launching rockets.[135]

In November 1938, Walther von Brauchitsch ordered construction of an A4 Production Plant at Peenemünde and, in January 1939, Walter Dornberger created a subsection of Wa Pruf 11 for planning the Peenemünde Production Plant project, headed by G. Schubert, a senior Army civil servant. By midsummer 1943 the first trial runs of the assembly-line in the Production Works at Werke Süd were made and after the end of July the enormous hangar Fertigungshalle 1 (F-1, Mass Production Plant No. 1) was just about to go into operation. However, in early 1943 two Polish slave janitors at the forced workers camp at Trassenheide more than a mile to the south of Peenemünde had provided maps, sketches and reports to Polish Home Army Intelligence and in June British intelligence had received two such reports which identified the 'rocket assembly hall', 'experimental pit' and 'launching tower'. The Polish janitors were given advance warning of the attack, but the workers could not leave due to SS security and the facility had no air raid shelters for the prisoners.

Bomber crews were told that Peenemünde could alter the whole course of the war and had to be destroyed regardless of losses. Three aiming points, the HVP's 'Sleeping and Living Quarters' (to specifically target scientists), the 'Factory Workshops' and finally the 'Experimental Station' had to be destroyed totally - if not that night, then the next night and the night after if necessary. 'This' recalled Warrant Officer Eddie Wheeler, a WOp/AG on 97 Squadron at Bourn, Cambridgeshire 'did nothing to encourage us especially when we learnt that there would be no cloud and a full moon and the attack would be from as low as 12,000 feet or lower. These conditions would be ideal for the German night fighters so the RAF would adopt 'spoof' tactics by sending a small number of Mosquitoes to Berlin, giving the impression that that was the night's target for the main force. Berlin was high on the RAF priority list and the Germans were very sensitive to attacks on their capital. It was hoped that their fighters would be concentrated nearer to Berlin and that by the time it was established that Peenemünde was to be the main target the first two waves of bombers would have completed their task and been on the way home. The third wave provided by 5 Group could, however, expect to have a hot time.

'We took off at 2108 hours and climbed to 18,000 feet. Our primary target was the scientists' quarters. The whole force would be directed by a Master Bomber, Group Captain John H. Searby on 83 Squadron at Wyton was selected for this task and he was to fly over the target for the whole attack giving a commentary and shifting the attack as was necessary. Forty minutes could elapse from first to last aircraft on target. Some aircraft were fitted with 'Oboe' ground controlled radar, other PFF aircraft with H_2S but the conditions would allow for full visual attacks, providing smoke did not obscure the aiming points. From 08°E we started to throw out 'Window'.

'We began to lose height as we approached Rugen Island and saw many aircraft around us in the almost daylight conditions. Fortunately none were hostile so hopefully the Mosquitoes who had preceded us by one hour had lured the night fighters to the Berlin area. We sighted the target clearly at 11,700 feet. The enemy, in the hope of thwarting the attacking forces, had already started a smoke screen. Light flak started piping up from the target zone as we went in with our green TIs and 7,500lb bomb load. Peter reported direct hits on the living quarters and just then we suffered a direct hit from flak. Johnny shouted that we were going round in circles and could not fly straight and level. If the state of affairs could not be rectified we would have to consider bailing out - a prospect which did not appeal one bit. To jump with the possibility of either landing in the sea or amid a hail of bombs just wasn't on. Bill beckoned me to follow him down the fuselage and with great trepidation I did so, regretting the fact that I was putting distance between me and my parachute. Bill indicated the trimming and aileron cables that had been severed by the impact. He busied himself with lengths of nylon cord and then Johnny said that he had recovered control of the aircraft. By now the target was a sea of flame and high explosions and we were intent on returning from whence we came with all speed.

'The German defences were well alerted by now and fighters would be re-deployed from the Berlin area without delay. We felt sorry for the last wave of bombers entering the scene and who would have to take the full brunt of attacks in ideal night-flying conditions. Several aircraft were seen going down in flames. Seven hours after take-off we had the welcoming sight of Bourn and we hoped that the target had been well and truly plastered and that it would not be necessary to return again the next night, when the Luftwaffe would be ready and waiting to wreak their revenge.'

Pilot Officer John A. Martin DFC navigator on Pilot Officer 'Mac' McDonald's Stirling crew on 218 Squadron at Chedburgh recalled:

'During the attack we had a master bomber directing the dropping of the bombs. His call sign to us was 'Raven' and as soon as we were getting ready to do our run in to drop the bombs, he would call, 'Raven aircraft, Raven aircraft, don't drop the bombs, the TIs (target indicators) are falling into the sea.' Because of this we had to go around and start our bomb run again. The next number of crews had had the TI problem rectified, by the time it came our turn the target indicators were again falling into the sea so we had to abort our bomb run and again go around to start our bomb run again. On our next approach I was in the astrodome looking out, when suddenly this fighter came up dead astern. I shouted 'Rear gunner, fighter, dead astern.' The rear gunner fired at the fighter and shot it down. I was still in the astrodome and saw the glow of engines coming towards us and shouted, 'Rear gunner there is another one coming in.' The rear gunner started shooting. We then heard, on the radio, 'Saint, saint'. It was a Halifax that we were shooting at. We dived and got away from it. We dropped our bombs on target and returned back to base. We had a second pilot with us that night, Bunse was his name. I was sitting in the mess the next morning when Bunse came over to me and said: 'Would you read that there, Paddy.' The report was of a Halifax crew, being attacked from below and the flight engineer lost his foot in the incident. It seemed like the incident we had been involved in. That was an awful night, the night of that Peenemünde raid. Can you visualise 700 aircraft going round and round, aircraft here and aircraft there, TI going off in the middle of it. During the bomb runs there was radio silence, apart from the Master Bomber. The Master Bomber shouted over the radio, 'Raven aircraft, Raven aircraft: don't bomb now the TIs are falling into the sea.' A wee voice from somewhere came up on the radio, 'Raven, Raven, we're Raven mad, would you drop those TIs.' Target indicators were big flares which were dropped on the target and provided an easier located target, for the other aircraft on the raid, on which to aim their bombs. I can still see that fighter as if it was only yesterday, coming up and showing his belly to us, and air gunner McIlroy pumped his rounds into it and down he went. I can still see that fighter over Bremen with the bullets coming out of his main plane and I can still see Gamble throwing out the propaganda leaflets. He was quite a character.'

After dropping his bombs Sergeant John Anthony Logan 'Jack' Currie, the 21-year old pilot of Lancaster 'George 2' on 12 Squadron at Wickenby climbed away smoothly and headed to the west. 'We had no way of knowing that the Nachtjagd controllers, aware now that the Berlin raid was no more than a feint, had redirected all their available Messerschmitts and Junkers to our homeward route.

'The Lancaster's electronics included a receiver that picked up transmissions from the Lichtenstein radar sets in the German fighters. The radar device was code-named Boozer, perhaps because the red lamp it lighted on the panel was reminiscent of a heavy drinker's nose. At 18,000 feet over Stralsund, thirty miles west of Peenemünde, the roving eye picked the glow up straight away.

'Rear gunner from pilot, I have a Boozer warning.'

'Rear gunner watching out astern.'

'Boozer also read transmissions from the ground-based Würzburg radars, which could be quite a nuisance when you were flying in the stream; at all times, however, you had to heed the signal. It was as well we did: seconds later, Lanham spoke again. 'Fighter at seven o'clock low. Stand by to corkscrew.'

'Standing by.'

'Mid-upper from rear gunner. There could be a pair. I'll take care of this one, you watch out.'

'I didn't like the sound of that remark. I would be difficult enough to evade one fighter in the moonlight, let alone two. I sat up straight and gently shook the wheel. Don't get excited, George 2, but you might be doing some aerobatics any minute now.

'Prepare to corkscrew port, Jack... corkscrew port... go!'

'Going port.'

'I used heavy left aileron and rudder, elevators down, held the diving turn through fifteen degrees, I pulled out sharply and turned hard to starboard halfway through climb. George 2 responded like a PT-17 - a PT-17 weighing twenty-five tons.'

'Foxed him, Jack. He's holding off, level on the starboard quarter.'

'Protheroe then came through. 'Another bandit, skipper, four o'clock high, six hundred yards. It's an Me 210...'

'Lanham broke in. 'Watch him, George here comes number one again. Corkscrew starboard ... go!'

'According to the navigator's log, the combat continued for another eight minutes: to me it seemed longer. After each frustrated pass, the attacker held off, content to occupy the attention of one gunner, while his partner came on in. I longed to have the heat turned down - the sweat was running down my face - but I dared not interrupt the gunners' running commentary. The sound of heavy breathing was sufficiently distracting and I knew that it was mine.

'My wrists and forearms were reasonably strong, but I was no Charles Atlas and 'George 2' wasn't feeling like a Stearman anymore. It occurred to me that these two fighter pilots were just playing games with us, biding their time until I was exhausted. Then they would rip the Lancaster to shreds. The sheet of armour plate behind me seemed pitifully small and there was a lot of me it failed to shield. If only our Brownings had a greater range; if only I could find a layer of cloud to hide in; if only the moonlight wasn't quite so bright...

'Corkscrew port... go!'

'Throwing George 2 into another diving turn, I looked back through the window. There was the Messerschmitt again, turning steeply with me as the pilot tried to bring his guns to bear. I could see his helmet and his goggles, looking straight at me. Staring back at him I felt a sudden surge of anger and a change of mood. You're not good enough, Jerry, I thought, to win this little fight. You're a bloody awful pilot and a damn poor shot. 'Well, for Christ's sake, George,' I squawked into the microphone, 'shoot that bastard down.'

'Instantly the Lancaster vibrated. At first the flashed dazzled me, but when Protheroe fired a second burst I saw the streams of tracer make a sun-bright parabola between George 2 and the fighter's nose. The Messerschmitt rolled over and went down. The last I saw of that bloody awful pilot was a long trail of smoke, ending in the stratus far below.

'I think you got him,' I said. 'Where's the other one?'

'Falling back astern,' said Lanham.

'He's clearing off. Probably out of ammo or fuel.'

'Good shooting, George. What kept you?'

'Sorry, skipper. I had my sights on him all the time. I guess I just forgot to pull the trigger.'

'Pilot from nav; let me know when you're back on course.'

'Roger.'

'Bomb-aimer, skip. I was ready for the buggers, but they never came in bloody range of the front bloody guns ...'

Although the ground controllers were fooled into thinking the bombers were headed for Stettin and a further 'spoof by eight Mosquitoes on 139 Squadron led by Group Captain 'Slosher' Slee aiming for Berlin drew more fighters away from the Peenemünde force, forty Lancasters, Halifaxes and Stirlings (6.7% of the force) were shot down. In the wild mêlée over the target, Nachtjagd actually claimed 33 aircraft, total claims from the Peenemünde force amounting to 38 victories.

One of the victors was Hauptmann Peter Spoden of 5./NJG5 whose first victory between Hanshagen and Greifswald was Lancaster III JA897 on 44 Squadron at Dunholm Lodge piloted by Flight Sergeant Johnnie Drew (KIA). Spoden would become one of Germany's leading 'Tame Boar' pilots.

'I was still in high-school in early 1940 when a few RAF aircraft bombed the surroundings of my home-town Essen in the industrial Ruhr-district. My parents, sisters and relatives were living in Essen and as a young man of 18 years I had to become a soldier anyhow. My father, a former soldier and wounded in 1914-1918, was against the National Socialist party and any militarism and told me: 'Don't go to the infantry, you have no chance.' So I decided to volunteer for the Luftwaffe, to become a Night fighter hoping to protect my hometown. Like many young men I was impressed by the strong army and the Luftwaffe. In October 1940 my application for the Luftwaffe was accepted, also because I was a glider pilot in the time before the war. The training for a night fighter pilot lasted 27 months including blind-flying and radar exercises on many aircraft like the FW 158, Ju 52, He 111, Bf 109 and mostly Bf 110. The training was excellent and helped me very much after the war when becoming an airline pilot. Early in summer 1943 (21 years old) after having finished the night fighter training I joined II/NJG5 in Parchim, Mecklenburg for protection of Berlin. Hauptmann Rudolf Schönert was my Gruppenkommandeur. Essen was already heavily bombed by the RAF, our house damaged, my mother, two little sisters and grandma evacuated to South Germany.'[136]

In his first attack on the night of the Hamburg raid, 27/28 July, 22-two-year-old Leutnant Peter Spoden of 5./NJG5 at Parchim airfield could not find anyone in his Bf 110 because of 'Window'. Now, at Peenemünde it seemed that he might be frustrated again by the enemy's clever 'Spoofing' tactics, as he recalls.

'The British tricked us. There were 200 fighters over Berlin being held by six Mosquitoes. I was there. Then we saw that it was on fire in the north but it wasn't Berlin. They had ordered us to stay in Berlin and it had started to burn in Peenemünde. We flew there very fast. I shot one down. At that particular moment you do not think about the other crew. You have to shoot between the two engines and we had been trained to do that. It was said, 'Shoot between the two engines, it will go on fire and they will have a chance to bail out.' So I shot between the two engines to give them a chance to bail out. When I shot somebody down I was so excited. I landed and went to the crash site and spoke to the only survivor [Sergeant William Sparks, bomb aimer]. I felt free, as if I had achieved what I had been trained to do. How can I explain how I felt? Like an avenger for Essen.'

Two crews flying Bf 110s fitted with 'Schräge Musik' found the bomber stream and destroyed six bombers. Unteroffizier Holker of 5./NJG5 shot down two Viermots and Leutnant Peter Erhardt destroyed four within half an hour. Towards midnight, thirteen II./NJG1 crews left Sint-Truiden/Sint-Trond for the Gruppe's first 'Wild Boar' operation of the war. They returned with claims for thirteen victories, mainly over Peenemünde, nine of which were consequently confirmed by the Reichsluftfahrtministerium (RLM or Reich Air Ministry). These included five 'Schräge Musik' kills by 20-year old Leutnant Dieter Musset and his bordfunker Obergefreiter Helmut Hafner of the 5th Staffel, which were their first (and last) victories of the war. Whilst attacking their sixth bomber of the night Musset's cannon jammed and their Bf 110G-4 G9+JN, was subjected to ferocious return fire. Wounded, Musset and his bordfunker bailed out to the north of Gustrow. Musset's ankles had been broken. When he had recovered from his injuries he joined Stab II./NJG1. He was severely injured in a crash in bad weather on 7 February 1945, crashing at Harderode. Oberfeldwebel Otto Moll, bordfunker and Feldwebel Willi Heizmann, bordshütze were killed. Musset died of his injuries two days later. Leutnant Helmut Perle of Stab NJG2 in a Bf 110G-4 claimed a fighter ten kilometres north of Peenemünde. He was killed on the night of 30/31 August after scoring a double victory southwest of Mönchengladbach.

Nachtjagd also successfully employed 'Zahme Sau' ('Tame Boar') free-lance or Pursuit Night Fighting tactics for the first time since switching its twin-engined night-fighting crews from the fixed 'Himmelbett' system. 'Zahme Sau' had been developed by Oberst Victor von Lossberg of the Luftwaffe's Staff College in Berlin and was a method used whereby the ('Himmelbett') ground network, by giving a running commentary, directed its night fighters to where the 'Window' concentration was at its most dense. The tactics of 'Zahme Sau' took full advantage of the new RAF methods. Night fighters directed by ground control and the 'Y' navigational control system[137] were fed into the bomber stream (which was identified by tracking H_2S transmissions) as early as possible, preferably on a reciprocal course. The slipstream of the bombers provided a useful indication that they were there. Night fighters operated for the most part individually but a few enterprising commanders led their Gruppen personally in close formation into the bomber stream, with telling effect (Geschlosser Gruppeneinsatz)-Night-fighter crews hunted on their own using 'SN-2' AI radar[138] 'Naxos Z' (FuG 350)[139] and Flensburg (FuG 227/1).[140]

'SN-2' recalls Oberleutnant 'Dieter' Schmidt, Staffelkapitän, 8./NJG1 'was a great improvement on Lichtenstein, which worked on a wavelength of 53 centimetres, had a search angle of 24° and a maximum range of 4000 metres. SN-2 worked on a wavelength of 330 centimetres had a search angle of 120° and a maximum range of 6500 metres! With this equipment, wide-ranging night fighting, independent of the target being attacked and dependent solely on general reports of the situation and one's own navigation, again became possible. For the individual crews, 'Zahme Sau' frequently involved more than one sortie per night. Almost invariably landings were away from base; such as take-off at Laon, an approach via Osnabrück to Frankfurt and landing at Mainz-Finthen, or take-off at Laon, attack over Berlin, Abschuss of a departing bomber after three hours flight and landing after three and a half hours at Erfurt. (The usual airborne time was only three hours). The early finding and infiltrating of the bomber stream, whose progress was soon marked by Abschüsse of other crews but occasionally also by turning-point markers or the dropping of incendiaries was decisive. Now, during all major attacks, all available night fighters were whenever possible assembled over radio or light beacons to be directed early on into the bomber stream. Although there was no traffic control at these assemblies - an unthinkable procedure in peacetime - resulting losses were rare.'

Out of the total of 606 aircraft assigned, twenty-three Lancasters, fifteen Halifaxes, two Stirlings and one of the Mosquitoes were lost (6.7%); 32 suffered damage. In England initial reports on the morning of the 18th indicated that the raid had been a complete success achieved through the element of surprise, the decoy raid on Berlin and the sheer audacity of operating under a full moon and clear skies. In the daylight reconnaissance twelve hours after the attack, photographs revealed 27 buildings in the northern manufacturing area destroyed and forty huts in the living and sleeping quarters completely flattened. The foreign labour camp to the south suffered worst of all. The whole target area was covered in craters. The initial marking over the residential area went awry and the TIs fell around the forced workers camp at Trassenheide where 500-600 foreign workers, mostly Polish, were trapped inside the wooden barracks. Once rectified Operation 'Hydra' went more or less according to plan and a number of important members of the technical team were killed. They included Dr. Walther Thiel. 1 Group's attack on the assembly buildings was hampered by a strong cross wind but substantial damage was inflicted and this left only 5 and 6 Groups to complete the operation by bombing the experimental site.

'It was inconceivable that the site could ever operate again' recalled Eddie Wheeler 'and at least we had gained valuable time against V1 and V2 attacks on London and our impending second front assault forces. This raid probably gave us our most satisfaction against all other targets attacked.'

On 26 August Albert Speer called a meeting with Hans Kammler, Dornberger, Gerhard Degenkolb and Karl Otto Saur to negotiate the move of A4 main production to an underground factory in the Harz mountains.[141] Another reaction to the aerial bombing was the creation of a back-up research test range near Blizna, in southeastern Poland. Carefully camouflaged, this secret facility was built by 2,000 prisoners from the Pustkow concentration camp, who were killed after the completion of the project. 'Armia Krajowa' the Polish resistance movement, succeeded in capturing an intact V2 rocket there in 1943. It had been launched for a test flight, failed but did not explode and was retrieved intact from the River Bug and transferred secretly to London.[142]

In what was to be his first and last Geschlossener Gruppeneinsatz using the Y-Verfahren (Y-Control) system, on 17/18 August Oberleutnant Heinz-Wolfgang Schnaufer and three other Bf 110s of the unit took off from Leeuwarden airfield. Soon after take-off Schnaufer and Oberfeldwebel Karl-Heinz Scherfling had to break off the operation, as they suffered engine failures. Schnaufer made an emergency landing at Wittmundhafen in northwest Germany and the flak defences shot at him. It was a bad omen for what was to come for the crews of IV./NJG1. Two other Bf 110s flown by Feldwebel Heinz Vinke and 22-year old Unteroffizier George 'Schorsch' Kraft pressed on to intercept what they thought were RAF heavies. They arrived north of Schiermonnikoog around 2300 hours. Ten of 141 Squadron's Beaufighter VIfs patrolled German night fighter bases in Germany and Holland this night. One of them was flown by the CO, Wing Commander J. R. D. 'Bob' Braham DSO DFC** and his radar operator, Flight Lieutenant 'Jacko' Jacobs DFC[143] whose Beaufighter VIf was fitted with the 'Serrate' homer. Braham bounced Kraft's Bf 110 (G9+E7) and shot it down in flames. Unteroffizier Rudolf 'Rudi' Dunger, radar operator, bailed out into the sea and was rescued two hours later by a German flak trawler but Kraft's body was washed ashore four weeks later on the Danish coast near Heidesande (Esbjerg), where he was interred. Kraft had shot down fifteen Allied bombers in a period of only seven months.

Immediately after shooting down Kraft's Bf 110 Braham got onto the tail of the second Bf 110G-4 of IV./NJG1 flown by Feldwebel Heinz Vinke, a night fighter 'Experte' with over twenty victories. Unteroffizier Johann Gaa, the gunner, spotted the attacker and Vinke immediately turned away sharply. The German crew had already assumed that they had shaken off the Beaufighter, yet only moments later Braham's attack from below and behind caught the German crew completely by surprise. Vinke's control column was shot out of his hands and the burning aircraft plunged down out of control with a severely injured gunner. Vinke and Feldwebel Karl Schodl, his radar and radio operator, who was injured, bailed out. Landing in the North Sea Vinke inflated his one-man dinghy. While he floated under the star-lit expanse of the night sky he was appalled to hear the desperate calls for help from his friend Schodl. This continued for quite some time but Vinke was unable to do anything to rescue his friend, who drowned. Next day, a ship sailed past quite close to Vinke's dinghy but the crew did not notice him. Only eighteen hours after he was shot down by Braham and Gregory he was picked up by a Dornier Do 18 floatplane of the German ASR service. The bodies of both Gaa and Schodl were never recovered. Unteroffizier 'Rudi' Dunger crewed up with Feldwebel Vinke and with their gunner, Unteroffizier Rudolf Walter they became a most successful team. After scoring 27 Night Abschüsse, Vinke was awarded the Ritterkreuz on 19 September 1943 and the Oak Leaves followed in April 1944. The Eichenlaub were awarded posthumously because on 26 February 1944 two Typhoons on 198 Squadron (Flight Lieutenant R. A. Cheval L'Allemand and Flying Officer George E. A. Hardy) shot down Vinke while flying Bf 110G-4 during an ASR operation fifteen kilometres northwest of Dunkirk. Vinke, Dunger and Walter had scored 54 victories in about 150 sorties. Dunger and Unteroffizier Walter were also killed.

The third Bf 110 lost to a Beaufighter crew on 141 Squadron on 17/18 August was a Bf 110 of 9./NJG1 flown by Hauptmann Wilhelm Dormann, who had by now fourteen victories. The victory was later credited to Flying Officers 'Harry' White and Mike Seamer Allen, their second of the war. Dormann's radar operator, Oberfeldwebel Friedrich Schmalscheidt was killed when his parachute did not fully open. Despite his wounds Dormann also bailed out, near Klein-Dohren and he suffered severe head injuries and burns. He never flew operationally again. Shortly after midnight White and Allen intercepted a Bf 110 of 12./NJG1 flown by Leutnant Gerhard Dittmann, a 20-year-old pilot and his bordfunker, Unteroffizier Theophil Bundschuh, also twenty years of age. After raking the 110 with gunfire it plunged down steeply. Dittmann may have tried to crash-land Bf 110 G9+FZ on the Friesian coast but the Bf 110 exploded near Marrum at 0015 hours. Both crew were killed. Dittmann had claimed no night kills during his short time with 12./1 NJG1 but he had claimed two B-17s on 25 and 26 July 1943. For once the tables had been turned. It had been a very black night for the night fighters from Leeuwarden.[144]

Flying back to the General Staff HQ in East Prussia on 20 August Generalleutnant Josef 'Beppo' Schmid learned that the Chief of Staff, Generaloberst Hans Jeschonnek had died overnight (he had committed suicide by shooting himself because Hitler and Göring held him responsible for the deterioration of the Luftwaffe). Schmid therefore approached Göring directly with his proposals that the conduct of the entire defence of the Reich both by day and night should be placed in one pair of hands and that France, the territory of Luftflotte 3, should be incorporated into the defence of the Reich. He seems also to have convinced Göring that he was the man for the task. In any event Kammhuber was in disfavour because his night fighting system showed few signs of success. Göring gave Schmid command of Fliegerkorps XII on 15 September. Kammhuber remained General der Nachtjagd for two months longer but fell into disfavour when he continued to press for a new dedicated night-fighter design, eventually selecting the Heinkel He 219 'Uhu' after seeing it demonstrated in 1942. During the first ten days of operations in June 1943 with I./NJG1 which operated from Venlo and Münster, the 'Owl' proved the only Luftwaffe piston-engined night-fighter capable of taking on the Mosquito on equal terms, the unit claiming six Mosquitoes destroyed (plus claims for 25 Viermots). But, like the Me 262 jet fighter in the day-fighter arm, was never available in sufficient numbers to have a significant effect on the course of the air war. In late May 1944 the 'Uhu' was abandoned in favour of the Ju 88G series, an aircraft that had sufficient performance to take on Viermots but was incapable of combating the 'Wooden Wonder'. By the time the first He 219A-6 Mosquito hunters (with all engine and ammunition tank armour and oblique armament removed) was delivered, use of the 'Uhu' against the Wooden Wonder had officially been banned. Only 268 'Uhu's were built, 195 of which were delivered to operational units. The majority went to I./NJG1 and to NJGr10, a specialist anti-Moskito Gruppe at Werneuchen near Berlin. He 219 production ceased in favour of the Ju 88G (Gustav) series by January 1945.

When Generalfeldmarschall Erhard Milch the Air Inspector General, had decided to cancel the 'Uhu' there was disagreement. Milch, had overseen the development of the Luftwaffe as part of the re-armament of Germany following World War I and served as founding Director of Deutsche Luft Hansa. At the outbreak of World War II Milch commanded Luftflotte 5 during the Norwegian campaign. In November 1943 he had Kammhuber transferred to Luftflotte 5 in Norway, which now was equipped with a handful of outdated aircraft. After the reorganization of the Luftwaffe in Scandinavia and the dissolution of Luftflotte 5, Kammhuber became commanding general of the Luftwaffe in Norway (September-October 1944). In 1945 he was re-appointed to command of the night fighters, at this point a largely ceremonial position considering the state of the Third Reich at that time.[145]

With Kammhuber's departure, the title of General der Nachtjagd was dropped, the relevant functions being taken over by a newly instituted Inspekteur der Nachtjagd, subordinated to the General der Jagdflieger. This was a great blow to the prestige of night fighting and resulted, according to General 'Beppo' Schmid, in considerable neglect of night fighting interests. The change in the night fighter command had immediate repercussions. Schmid described the Divisional Operations Rooms, as they were when he took over command as 'Richard Wagner theatres.' They were, he said: 'Oversized, overstaffed, over-equipped and utilizing every device of electrical engineering, optics and cartography for the sole purpose of fixing the position of the enemy and one friendly night fighter on large scale maps, they were built almost as an end to themselves. They ceased completely to function when the British tactics of flying in a narrow stream deprived the 'Himmelbett' system of its effectiveness.'

Schmid reduced the personnel of each Division by 75 officers, fourteen officials, 3,290 NCOs and men and 2,630 female employees. On 1 October, in an extensive re-organisation, Fliegerkorps XII was split into three separate commands: Jagdkorps I, II and 7. This signalled the end of unified night fighter control and the adverse effect on night fighter efficiency was so great that Schmid, in command of Jagdkorps I, had no difficulty in obtaining the re-subordination of 7 Jagddivision on 1 February 1944.

Since the introduction of 'Window', few of the traditional 'Himmelbett' GCI patrols were flown. The twin-engined German night-fighters thus released from GCI activity were employed at first on Objektnachtjagd (target interception). The Jagd-division carried out control, all the aircraft of a Geschwader operating as a unit, with no limitation of the area of activity. High power light beacons and radio beacons were set up and used as assembly and waiting points. At the same time single engined night-fighters were also employed in fairly small numbers on Objektnachtjagd.

The simultaneous operation of several bomber streams, the jamming of the Lichtenstein AI and the Mosquito screening of the bomber formations resulted in the splitting up of German night fighter forces and reduced (it) to a minimum the chances of success of individual 'Zahme Sau' tactics. Indeed, owing to the inability to overcome RAF jamming, the 'Zahme Sau' technique never reached its full development but it was used to great effect during the Battle of Berlin and remained the main night attack tactic until the end of the war. General Schmid thought that had the Jagdschloss 'Panorama' ground radar set been perfected early enough, events might have taken a different course. Schmid concluded that in view of the high standard of RAF Bomber Command tactics, the Germans acted correctly in not depending on one method of night fighting alone but in employing the different methods singly and in combination in accordance with the situation. i.e. 'Zahme Sau' against the massed bomber stream, 'Himmelbett' against loose formations or single aircraft, Objektnachtjagd in the case of surprise attacks and against Mosquito formations.

Endnotes Chapter 12

134   There were nine major departments. Technical Design Office (Walter J. H. 'Papa' Riedel); Aeroballistics and Mathematics Laboratory (Dr Hermann Steuding); Wind Tunnel (Dr Rudolph Hermann); Materials Laboratory (Dr Mäder); Flight, Guidance and Telemetering Devices (German: BSM) (Dr. Ernst Steinhoff); Development and Fabrication Laboratory (Arthur Rudolph); Test Laboratory (Klaus Riedel); Future Projects Office (Ludwig Roth); Purchasing Office (Mr. Genthe). The Measurements Group (Gerhard Reisig) was part of the BSM and additional departments included the Production Planning Directorate (Detmar Stahlknecht), the Personnel Office (Richard Sundermeyer) and the Drawings Change Service.

135   The supersonic wind tunnel at Peenemünde's 'Aerodynamic Institute' eventually had nozzles for speeds up to the record speed of Mach 4.4 (in 1942 or 1943), as well as an innovative desiccant system to reduce the condensation clouding caused by the use of liquid oxygen, in 1940. Led by Rudolph Hermann who arrived in April 1937 from the University of Aachen, the number of technical staff members reached two hundred in 1943 and it also included Hermann Kurzweg of the (University of Leipzig) and Walter Haeussermann. Initially set up under the HVP as a rocket training battery (Number 444), Heimat-Artillerie-Park 11 Karlshagen/Pomerania (HAP 11) also contained the A-A Research Command North for the testing of anti-aircraft rockets. The chemist Magnus von Braun, the youngest brother of Wernher von Braun, was employed in the attempted development at Peenemünde of anti-aircraft rockets but their development as practical weapons took another decade of development in the United States and in the USSR.

136   *Enemy in the Dark; The story of Luftwaffe Night Fighter Pilot* by Peter Spoden (Cerberus Publishing Ltd).

137   Which escaped jamming throughout the war but owing to its limited number of channels was restricted to use by individual reconnaissance aircraft and formation leaders.

138   whose longer wavelength, unlike early Lichtenstein AI, could not be jammed by 'Window'.
139   A device which homed onto the H_2S navigation radar.
140   Which homed onto the 'Monica' tail warning device widely used of Bomber Command heavies.
141   Kammler suggested moving the A4 Development Works to a proposed underground site in Austria. After a site survey in September by Papa Riedel and Schubert, Kammler chose the code name 'Zement' (cement) for it in December and work to blast an underground cavern into a cliff at Lake Traunsee near Gmunden commenced in January 1944. In early 1944 construction work started for the test stands and launching pads in the Austrian Alps (code name Salamander), with target areas planned for the Tatra Mountains, the Arlberg range and the area of the Ortler mountain. In early September Peenemünde machinery and personnel for production (including Alban Sawatzki, Arthur Rudolph and about ten engineers) were moved to the Mittelwerk, which also received machinery and personnel from the two other planned A4 assembly sites. On 13 October the Peenemünde prisoners from the small F-1 concentration camp boarded rail cars bound for Mt. Kohnstein. As with the move of the V2 Production Works to the Mittelwerk, the complete withdrawal of the development of guided missiles was approved by the Army and SS that same month. Other evacuation locations included: Hans Lindenmayr's valve laboratory near Friedland moved to a castle near the village of Leutenberg, 10 km (6 miles) south of Saalfeld near the Bavarian border. the materials testing laboratory moved to an air base at Anklam; the wind tunnels moved to Kochel (and then after the war, to White Oak, Maryland); Engine testing and calibration to Lehesten.
142   A year later on 18 July, 4 August and 25 August, the US 8th Air Force carried out three additional Peenemünde raids to counter suspected hydrogen peroxide production. The last V2 launch at Peenemünde happened in February 1945 and on 5 May 1945 the soldiers of the Soviet 2nd Belorussian Front under General Konstantin Rokossovsky captured the seaport of Swinemünde and all of Usedom Island. Soviet infantrymen under the command of Major Anatole Vavilov stormed the installations at Peenemünde and found '75 percent wreckage'. All of the research buildings and rocket test stands had been demolished.
143   The son of a World War I RFC pilot, Braham shot down his first aircraft during the Battle of Britain and at 23 had become the youngest wing commander in the RAF. An outspoken individualist, unsurpassed in his sheer aggressive fighting spirit and relentless determination, Braham was already a living legend when he assumed command of the Squadron in December 1942, having shot down 12 e/a, 11 of them at night. 'The Night Destroyer', as he was dubbed in the press, had an overdeveloped sense of modesty and could see no reason for the press having an interest in him. On 9/10 August 1943 Braham notched his 4th victory since joining 141 Squadron and his 16th overall, when he destroyed a Bf 110 on a patrol to the German fighter a/f at St Trond in Belgium. Flying Officer William J. 'Sticks' Gregory DFC DFM who as usual flew as his navigator and operated the radar, was then rested and replaced by Flight Lieutenant H. 'Jacko' Jacobs DFC who had been instructing at 51 OTU Cranfield. Gregory earned his nickname as a result of having been a drummer in Debroy Somer's band.
144   Flight Lieutenant Harry White DFC** and Flight Lieutenant Mike Allen DFC** finished the war with 13 victories and 3 damaged.
145   Following Hitler's suicide, Milch attempted to flee Germany, but was captured by Allied forces on the Baltic coast on 4 May 1945. On surrendering, he presented his baton to the Commando Brigadier Derek Mills-Roberts, who was so disgusted by what he had seen when liberating the Bergen-Belsen concentration camp that he broke the baton over Milch's head. In 1947 Milch was tried as a war criminal by a US Military Tribunal in Nuremberg. He was convicted and sentenced to life imprisonment at Landsberg prison. His sentence was commuted to 15 years imprisonment in 1951, but he was released in June 1954. He lived out the remainder of his life in Düsseldorf, where he died in 1972.

After the fall of the Reich in May 1945 Kammhuber was held by the United States, but he was released in April 1948 without charges being brought against him. He wrote a series of monographs for the US Department of Defense on the conduct of the German defences against the RAF and USAAF. These were later collected into book form. In 1953 he published a definitive work on what he learned during the war as *Problems in the Conduct of a Day and Night Defensive Air War*. He later spent time in Argentina, helping to train the air force under Juan Perón. Josef Kammhuber returned to Germany and joined the German Air Force while it was being formed. He was promoted to Inspekteur der Bundesluftwaffe (West German Air Force), serving in that role between 1956 and 1962. Kammhuber died in Munich in January 1986 aged 89 in Munich and is buried there.

Chapter Thirteen

The 'Zahme Sau'

After the air raids on Hamburg, authoritative sources believe that other similar operations will be carried out, probably against Berlin. It has been noted that extensive preparations are already underway at a number of new airfields that are used exclusively by heavy four-engined RAF bombers. The predicted raids on Berlin will be mainly RAF night operations. The date of the raids will depend on the length of the nights, which now is increasing by half an hour per week. This means that each week the heavy bombers can penetrate fifty miles deeper into Germany. In two or three weeks the RAF will be able to reach Berlin just as easily as it can reach Hamburg because Berlin is only 130 miles farther away. In several weeks' time the Americans may also begin daylight raids on Berlin. The 8th Air Force has already made daylight flights into Germany as far as Warnemünde, which is the same as the distance to Berlin.

The Reuters News Agency 4 August 1943, London

At Parchim airfield on the night of 23/24 August Wilhelm Johnen, his bordfunker Facius and bordmechaniker Paul Mahle and their fellow crews on 1/NJG1 rushed to their Bf 110s at 2306 hours, took off and headed towards Berlin. The 'Big City' as the RAF called the Reich capital, was the target for 710 Lancasters, Halifaxes and Stirlings and seventeen Mosquitoes. Mahle had every right to be worried; his wife lived in Berlin. The night was bright and, at 18,000 feet over Hannover, he could see for 350 miles the Hamburg flak in action and bombs dropping on Berlin, fires in Leipzig and incendiaries falling on Cologne. Shortly before the raid the Jagddivision ordered its night-fighters to pursue the enemy to the capital and to ignore their own flak, which had permission to fire as high as 24,000 feet. Johnen loaded his guns and just as he was about to go into the attack, Facius reported that his SN-2 was out of action. The only solution was to fly with the bomber stream over the city and try to spot the 'furniture vans' with their naked eyes. No one lacked a target. Red, yellow and green tracers tore through the air past Johnen's cockpit. Shortly after 0100 hours a Halifax crossed Johnen's path. He attacked immediately with no fear for the defence and fired at the Viermot's petrol tanks in the wings. The bomber exploded and fell to earth in a host of burning fragments. It was 01.03. Five minutes later he saw a Stirling. The huge Viermot grew larger in his sights and he sprayed the rear gunner with his guns and silenced them just as he opened fire. The rest was merely a matter of seconds. At 01.08 the Stirling fell like a stone out of the sky and exploded on the ground.

'The nightmare ended. The Britishers were on the way home. I circled over the burning city waiting for stragglers. The flak guns fell silent. Huge fires lit up the night. The crew was silent. We could not get it into our heads that our capital - Berlin - was doomed.'[146]

Bomber Command suffered its greatest loss of aircraft in one night in the war so far. The flak and night fighter defences were extremely fierce and 63 aircraft were lost or written off. Among them was Lancaster ED328 SR-S on 101 Squadron at Ludford Magna. Twenty-three year old Flight Sergeant Robert Clarence Naffin RAAF and his crew were killed. Sergeant John Henry Phillips, the nineteen-year old mid-upper gunner, had walked twenty miles from Crewe to Stoke with his friends to sign up when he was told his apprenticeship would exclude him from being called up. He had trained as a pilot in Winnipeg, Canada but lost his wings after a brawl and ended up as an air gunner. He had flown over twenty ops. It appears that they were attacked by two or three night-fighters and ED328 exploded in mid-air scattering them and the Lancaster over a one kilometre area. The Abschuss was claimed by 23-year old Oberleutnant Werner Husemann of Stab NJG1 at 0050 hours over Biesenthal with the aircraft coming down at Lanke for his ninth victory. Naffin and crew were buried with full military honours in the local cemetery in Beisenthal and were re-interred at the Berlin 1939-1945 War Cemetery. Stirling III BF564 on 75 Squadron RNZAF captained by 20-year old Pilot Officer Alan J. L. Sedunary DFC is thought to have been shot down by Oberleutnant Heinz Ferger of 3./NJG3 at 0051 hours southwest of Berlin at 3000 metres. All eight crew were killed. Ferger had 23 confirmed Abschüsse and three probables by the time he was killed on 13/14 April 1945 when he was shot down by a Mosquito on finals to Lübeck airfield.

For some, the night was not yet over. Near Shouldham on the return over Norfolk 'Q-Queenie', flown by Sergeant Cliff Chatten, was attacked by Oberleutnant Wilhelm Schmitter, Staffelkapitän of 15./KG2 flying a Me 410A-1 Intruder. Unnoticed by the crew of the Lancaster, Schmitter, an experienced bomber pilot and a holder of the Ritterkreuz, closed in on his target and his bordfunker opened fire with the twin 13mm remotely controlled MG 131 guns fitted in the fuselage barbettes and controlled from the cockpit. Shells exploded in the Lancaster's fuselage and starboard wing. Flight Sergeant John Robert Kraemer RAAF the mid-upper gunner was killed and Chatten was wounded in his legs and chest. He ordered the rest of the crew to bail out and left it late to get out. As he came down in his parachute he was injured when the Lancaster exploded below him. After this experience three of the crew refused to fly again but Chatten, a confirmed teetotaller, recovered to fly a full tour of operations. Just four minutes after his attack on Chatten's Lancaster, Schmitter dropped eight bombs on an airfield west of Cambridge and head for base at Soesterberg in Holland. Eight kilometres off Zeebrugge, Belgium Schmitter's Me 410 became the target for an RAF night fighter and was so damaged in its fuselage and one of the engines that he and his bordfunker, Oberfeldwebel Heinz Gräber were forced to bail out into the sea. Gräber was unlucky and hit the 410's tail as he jumped clear, breaking both his legs. Exhausted and unable to climb into their dinghies, the two men fired flares into the sky and they were fortunate that a flak post at Zeebrugge spotted them. Schmitter and Gräber were picked up by a rescue boat from the Marine Untergruppe Zeebrugge one and a half hours later. On 8 November 1943 Schmitter and his bordfunker Unteroffizier Felix Hainzinger were killed when their Me 410 was shot down near Eastbourne by Squadron Leader William Hudson Maguire and Flying Officer W. D. Jones on 85 Squadron flying a Mosquito XII. It was Maguire's fifth victory. Before the war he had worked in the millinery business. He and Jones were both awarded the DFC at the end of the year and in November they destroyed a He 111. Bill Maguire crashed and was killed on 17 February 1945 when he was performing aerobatics to test a new altitude indicator. Schmitter was posthumously promoted to Major and awarded the Oak leaves to his Ritterkreuz.[147]

Five missing Halifaxes were on 158 Squadron at Lissett. Pilot Officer H. B. Frisby RAAF the pilot of 'C for Charlie' bailed out safely and he and five other members of his crew who also survived, were taken prisoner. (Later, in Stalag Luft III at Sagan, Frisby earned a reputation as a very skilful forger and map maker and his efforts were rewarded when, in March 1944, his fake identity cards and maps were used by the escapers after the Great Escape). Following the loss of 'K-King' Flying Officer F. A. Unwin and five of his crew survived and they were captured. 'A-Apple' flown by Sergeant Tom Edwards crashed near Döberitz where the pilot's body and two of his crew were recovered from the wreckage. Four other men who had bailed out were rounded up and taken into captivity. A fourth

Halifax was lost when 'E-Easy' piloted by Flight Sergeant William Arnold 'Bill' Burgum RAAF was attacked just north of Berlin by Oberleutnant Rudolf 'Rudi' Altendorf of 2./NJG4. Burgum, whose crew had flown their first sortie on the Peenemünde raid, turned and flew south to what looked like an open field but it was a swamp and the Halifax crashed into it after part of the wing broke off on the approach. All seven crew were killed in the crash.

Five Luftwaffe fighters were lost to return fire and to flak. A sixth force-landed at Hannover after a combat with a bomber on the inward flight and a seventh, a 'Naxos'-equipped Bf 109 of II./JG300, crashed in Sweden. Another six Bf 110s of NJGs 1, 2 and 3 carried out emergency landings at Berlin-Werneuchen airfield with flak damage.

Leutnant Peter Spoden experienced his first 'Wild Boar' sortie Berlin. 'I was ordered to take off on a mission over Berlin in Bf 110 CA+KP. After being in the air for around one hour I saw a Viermot with two tail fins which was illuminated by searchlights. I fired several bursts from a distance of 200 metres and as a result the aircraft plunged down in flames. I next engaged an enemy aircraft over the city at a height of 4000 metres [13,000 feet]. The results of my bursts of fire however could not be observed. The last enemy aircraft I could determine was a Short Stirling, which turned into me and so I was forced to attack it from head-on. My bursts of fire were aimed so well that the aircraft dived down steeply and approached the ground fast. In the meantime, the enemy rear gunner fired at my own aircraft and inflicted a number of clearly audible hits in the fuselage, so that it started to burn.'

Spoden was hit in the upper left leg and he immediately checked if his crew were all right, but received no reply. When the heat from underneath him became unbearable, he loudly and clearly ordered them to bail out four or five times. After some more time had expired, he jettisoned the cockpit canopy and got out. He hit the tailplane and whilst exerting all his strength, being hampered by his injured upper thigh and the speed of the aircraft pinning him for some time, he eventually broke free and pulled the ripcord at a height of 1000 metres [3,250 feet]. Spoden lost consciousness and came to in an air-raid shelter at Grunewalddamm 69 where German civilians thinking that he was an RAF airman, attacked him. But when he spoke to them in German they stopped. His bordfunker Unteroffizier Rüdke survived but Unteroffizier Franz Ballweg, his bordmechaniker, was killed. The bullet which had hit Spoden in the left leg shattered his femur and he underwent surgery in hospital. Following a long period of convalescence and despite the surgeons' opinion that he would never walk again, Spoden only returned to action again in early November 1943. (Ballweg was replaced by Feldwebel Schmiedler).

Peter Spoden described the mental and physical burdens experienced by RAF aircrew on a long range flight of eight hours or more as 'unimaginable'.

'The British crewmen often saw comrades flying nearby go down in flames. The fighters were faster and more manoeuvrable. The German two-centimetre cannon shells were more lethal than the machine-gun bullets of the RAF. On rare occasions when our cannon jammed a single two-centimetre shell in a fuel tank was enough to shoot the bomber down. The British navigators, flight engineers and air gunners had to move around in very restricted space in their heavy flying suits, in aircraft without pressurised cabins and without heating. Unlike our practice, their parachute was not worn all the time but had to be clipped on when an emergency occurred. Just like us, they also had their idealism and love for their country. They had volunteered for the RAF out of the spirit of adventure and they enjoyed flying. Only comparatively few RAF aircrew reached their statutory thirty operations. Bomber losses often amounted to five percent per operation, which statistic implies that to survive more than twenty sorties was a matter of chance. For us German aircrew there was no limit set to the number of night-time operations. A hundred or two hundred operations against the enemy, repeated wounds, four or more descents by parachute, were not a rarity in the German night-fighter force. The crew and our comrades in the Squadron in England or in the Staffel in Germany were like a secret society and we stuck together through thick and thin. Flying for hours through the darkness, the ever-present fear of sudden attacks out of the blackness of the night, the searchlights groping for us fliers like the fingers of a corpse, the turbulence, the weather with its icing and its thunderstorms, injured or wounded comrades in the aircraft - all this welded us together. And then, suddenly, they were no longer there, they would never return. Missing, nowhere to be found, mutilated, burnt to death. What monsters we human beings are! On many occasions the RAF crews impressed us night fighters very much. On the night of 23 August 1943 there was a terrible turmoil over Berlin where the Bomber Command lost 62 four engine aircraft. It was one of these nights you never forget your whole life. On the ground in the 'Great City' fierce fires were blazing: first of all the high-explosive bombs and then the phosphorous incendiary dropped into the shattered ruins of the buildings. It was an inferno without equal. Hundreds of searchlights rose up towards us, sweeping the heavens like the fingers or corpses and the hands of ghosts, dazzling friend and foe alike. The anti-aircraft guns fired a furious barrage up to ten thousand feet and above that were the 'Wild Boars' (single engine aircraft) and the 'Tame Boars' (twins). At times I could see between thirty and forty aircraft at once milling around. Tracer cannon and bullets, cascades of flares of every colour, night fighters' recognition signals when the flak had fired in one of them. Huge clouds of smoke, garishly illuminated, rising into the sky. White condensation trails everywhere and down below fearful explosions. A Lancaster attempting to escape from a cone of searchlights did a full loop. I got the impression that everyone was firing at everyone else. And I was in the very middle of it all. It was hell - Dante's Inferno!

'At the end of the war the RAF crews received a lot of respect by us when they were flying the 'corkscrew', a kind of aerobatics. As a night fighter you had to get away immediately otherwise you were crashing with that big plane. My good friend 'Gerd' Friedrich, just married a few days earlier, collided with a Lancaster on the night of 16 March 1945 near Stuttgart....friend and enemy united in death. Not a single case.'[148]

On the night of 27/28 August 1943 when 674 heavy bombers attacked Nürnburg, the marking of this raid was based mainly on H2S. 47 of the Pathfinders H$_2$S aircraft were ordered to check their equipment by dropping a 1,000lb bomb on Heilbronn while flying to Nuremburg. Twenty-eight Pathfinder aircraft were able to carry out this order. Heilbronn reports that several bombs did drop in the north of the town soon after midnight. The local officials assumed that the bombs were aimed at the industrial zone; several bombs did fall around the factory area and other bombs fell further away. No industrial buildings were hit, one house was destroyed but there were no casualties. Nuremburg was found to be free from cloud but it was very dark. The initial Pathfinder markers were accurate but a creep-back quickly developed which could not be stopped because so many Pathfinder aircraft had difficulties with their H$_2$S sets. The Master Bomber could do little to persuade the Main Force to move their bombing forward, only a quarter of the crews could hear his broadcasts. Bomber Command estimated that most of the bombing fell in open country SSW of the city but the local reports say that bombs were scattered across the southeast and eastern suburbs. The only location mentioned by name is the Zoo, which was hit by several bombs. Ten German night fighters were claimed shot down during a fierce battle over the bombing area which lasted over thirty minutes.

Leutnant Norbert Pietrek of 2./NJG4 piloting Bf 110F-4 3C+BK was ordered to take off for a 'Zahme Sau' pursuit sortie. Free-lancing single-engined 'Wild Boars' often obtained successes in good visibility, which favoured searchlight operations. Sometimes, when twin-engined night-fighters were illuminated by searchlights in the hectic and whirling chaos over the German cities under attack, a twin-ruddered Bf 110 was mistaken for a Halifax or Lancaster and paid the price, as Pietrek recalls:

'The Tommies were attacking Nürnburg. Unteroffizier Paul 'Paulchen' ['Little Paul'] Gartig was still flying with me [Otto Bauchens, his original radio operator having been hospitalised with hepatitis] together with my rear gunner Moritz. We were off at full throttle in the direction of Nürnburg and after about an hour we were in the vicinity of the city. The weather had created excellent defensive conditions, a so-called 'shroud'. This was a thin, high-level cloud layer on which, when illuminated by searchlights and fires from below, one could see the attacking Tommies crawling like bugs across a bed sheet. As we arrived we could see that the attack had already begun. A horrid-beautiful and colourful spectacle was presented to us. Seeking searchlights, exploding shells of the heavy flak, multi-coloured tracer of the medium flak, the brilliant white, red, yellow and green 'Christmas trees' of the attacking Tommies, the explosions of the bombs below, the expanding rings around an exploding heavy mine, the bright white lanes of igniting incendiaries and the terrible multi-coloured fires raging in the city. And added to all this, Tommies, who had been shot down by night fighters, going down in flames and the fires as they crashed. All very fascinating but bitter for those in this hell below. A spectacle which no painting could ever portray.

'The searchlights had caught a Tommy and they waited for a night fighter to shoot him down. The flak was only permitted to fire to 4000 metres. We arrived and I made for the Tommy twisting about in the searchlight cone. Range 800 metres, 600 metres, 400 metres. But one went much closer in order to conserve ammunition and be more certain of a hit and that was a range of less than fifty metres! Then I was suddenly fired at from behind. A burst hit my starboard engine and I had to feather it. What rotten luck. Damn it! I had my fifth night Abschuss certain in my sights and then this had to happen! Moritz said it was a Wilde Sau! The 'Wild Boar' was the single-engined night fighter unit of Major Herrmann, stationed at Bonn-Hangelar. The pilots were from bomber and reconnaissance units, which had been disbanded and converted to Bf 109 and FW 190 fighters. Whether this fellow had, after firing at me, realized that it was not a four-engined Tommy but a twin-engined night fighter he had attacked, or whether he had fired at a range of 600-800 metres at the Tommy in the searchlights before me, remained a mystery. I think it had been the latter. No more hunting now and off I went to find a place for a single-engined landing.

'Now the weather conditions were not favourable for me, for the 'shroud' hid my view of the ground. On feathering the engine I turned off to the west, for the port engine proved too powerful until I trimmed the kite and now I did not know my position. I asked Paulchen for a QDM to Stuttgart. The machine maintained height well on one engine and the new trimmers on the rudders made it easy to maintain course. I could therefore look forward to a single-engined landing with confidence. After all, it would be my fourth (the third by night) and it would not be the last by a long chalk. Then suddenly I saw an airfield through a gap in the cloud almost directly below me, so power off and down. From only 2500 metres I could clearly see flying activity only there was no sight of a Morse identification beacon. Had that become unserviceable? Paulchen was continuously firing the colours of the night plus a red, indicating an aircraft in emergency, until the trigger of his signal pistol failed and I circled, losing height.

'The landing as such presented no problem for me. The only snag was that the starboard engine operating the hydraulic system had failed and with it the extension and retraction of undercarriage and flaps. I could extend both pneumatically but then no longer retract. At a strange airfield by night, one is not familiar with local conditions and one could make considerable errors in one's judgement. Get too high or too low, with unpredictable consequences for survival. As I was responsible not only for my own life but also for that of my crew I decided on a belly landing, which would cause no problems but I did not want to interfere with the flying activities, especially landings, so I aimed fifty metres to the right and had Moritz continuously firing reds. We were still thirty metres high and 500 metres from the threshold when the runway controller fired two reds at us, meaning that we should go round again. But that was quite impossible on one engine. We were just past the threshold. I eased my straps a little and about to switch off the ignition of the port engine when there was a terrible crash and my head struck against the reflector sight, which broke off. I jettisoned the cabin roof at once and I found myself up to my belly in gravel and the tail unit of my machine hurtling forward above my head. The port engine and wing were torn off at the first impact. At the second the starboard wing with the stationary engine folded vertically upwards, then the third impact followed and then there was silence. Only the cockpit was left and that lay on the tip of a heap of gravel. I released my straps, jumped down the heap of gravel and drew my signal pistol, which was always loaded with a red, when I saw Moritz standing beside the pilot's seat shouting, 'The boy has gone!'

'No, here I am,' I replied and fired off my signal pistol. Then we got Paulchen out of the cockpit. He had struck his head against the radio equipment and had received a gaping wound like a parting. An ammunition drum from the rearward facing machine gun had been torn free and had also struck his right upper arm and fractured it. Moritz had only sprained the little finger of his left hand. My collision with the reflector sight had punctured my right eyelid and if I pulled it down a little, I could see through it. It could have been much, much worse. Everyone who looked at the wreckage later could hardly believe that the three of us were alive. It had been particularly fortunate that the still hot port engine, together with the wing and the fuel tanks, had broken away at the first impact; otherwise the kite could have caught fire and then what would have happened to us? I preferred not to think about it.

'Having got Paulchen out of the machine we plodded towards the sick quarters. Reaching the first building, I went down to the air raid shelter in order to report to the operations room. Women and children - dependants of the station personnel - sat in the cellar and cried out in alarm as I entered. At first I did not understand why. Then I looked down at myself and realized that my face and overalls were covered in blood from my injured eyebrow. We went to the sick quarters where we got first aid for our injuries. There we discovered that we were in Kitzingen, an airfield which was closed for night landings because of repair work on the runway. We knew that, for it was mentioned at each briefing but how was I to recognize it from above with no Morse recognition beacon operating? Then we boarded the ambulance which would take us to hospital in Würzburg but before we left I had us driven to the operations room in order to phone my unit in Florennes and inform them what had happened. The commander of the night fighter school at Kitzingen must have heard and he raged at me.

'What do you mean by landing here when you know that it is closed for night landings!'

'I replied, 'Because some idiot had turned on the airfield lighting and switched off the recognition beacon.'

'That idiot was me!'

'You said it!' I replied. 'How could I, in my situation, urgently needing an emergency landing ground and happening to see one, know that it is Kitzingen when the beacon is not operating? It could be any open field whose beacon had gone unserviceable for some unknown reason.'

'The Major remained unconvinced and I left the fellow standing there. We went to the ambulance which got us to Würzburg towards five o'clock in the morning. I insisted on Paulchen being treated first. His head was terribly swollen and the doctor pressed hard a couple of times against the sides of the gaping wound, causing almost a litre of blood to spurt out. The swelling was gone and the wound sown up. His upper arm was also seen to, the bone being drilled in several places and then bandaged.

'Then it was my turn and my right eyebrow was stitched up. On my way to my sick room I passed a clock. It was 7.45. After the strain of the past weeks, during which we had to fly almost daily with up to five sorties by day or by night with hardly any sleep, I was so exhausted that I slept for ten days. Apart from my eye injury I had also suffered severe concussion.'

Barely recovered from his wounds, Leutnant Norbert Pietrek suffered further head injuries when Bf 110G-4 3C+DJ crashed at Bieul near Dinant, Belgium on 1 October 1943 and he never flew again.

Twin-engined Nachtjagd crews operating in 'Tame Boar' fashion claimed twelve of the 33 bombers shot down on 27/28 August 1943. Total Nachtjagd claims were 28 kills this night. One of the missing aircraft was Stirling III EE942 QS-R on 620 Squadron piloted by Flight Sergeant John Francis Nichols, which was shot down at Halbersdorf, west of Mains by Leutnant Werner Baake for his twelfth Abschuss. There were no survivors. Baake, born on 1 November 1918 at Nordhausen, Harz, was another rising star in the Nachtjagd. Halifax II JD406 on 78 Squadron skippered by 27-year old Flying Officer Richard Herbert Orr RCAF was shot down at 0142 hours by Oberfeldwebel Reinhard Kollack of 8./NJG4 for his 29th Abschüsse. Sergeant W. A. Dunleavy RCAF the mid-upper gunner was the only survivor. Halifax II JD368 on 10 Squadron captained by Sergeant G. Baker was returning from Nürnburg when attacked and shot down at a height of 3800 metres over Estinnes, North Saarlouis in Belgium at about 0336 hours by Hauptmann Fritz Söthe of 3./NJG4. It is almost certain that Sergeant George Warren RCAF the 19-year old rear gunner was killed in the initial attack from the rear. The other seven crew parachuted to safety and six of them evaded capture. Two young boys sleeping in a haystack in a field had a narrow escape when they heard the bomber approaching at low level and saw it crash in front of them. Söthe had a total of 18 Abschüsse by the time he was shot down and killed by a Mosquito at Lambrecht-Neustad on 28/29 September 1944. Stirling III EH985 on 15 Squadron captained by Flying Officer Lionel J. Jefferies RAAF was probably shot down by Oberleutnant Manfred Tischtau of Stab (staff flight) 1./NJG5 at 0208 hours. Flying Officer O. E. A. Nestor the navigator stated:

'I was sitting alongside the captain who gave the order 'prepare to abandon aircraft'. I unplugged my intercom and went back to the navigation table to get Jeffries parachute from the stowage. I gave it to him and then collected my own. Sergeant Taggart, the air bomber who was in the front part of the fuselage, had opened the escape hatch and was awaiting the order to abandon. Sergeant 'Bill' Bailey the wireless operator passed me and went to this escape hatch. Just after this the fuselage was filled with flames and I jumped down to the hatch and found it had closed. I opened it and threw myself out. I don't know what went on in the rear part of the fuselage. While at Dulag Luft however, I was told by the German authorities that Sergeant Donald Malley, the rear gunner, Sergeant William Duncason, the mid-upper gunner and Sergeant Gunn, the 19-year old flight engineer, were dead.' The pilot suffered a broken leg during the landing, also suffering burns to his hands and face and on landing shouted his surrender to the local inhabitants. Some offered assistance to the injured pilot - these were threatened with jail for their efforts. This was the first Abschuss for Oberleutnant Manfred Tischtau and he had six victories by the time he was shot down and killed on 20/21 April 1944 at Altenkirchen probably by a Mosquito on 169 Squadron flown by Flight Lieutenant Gordon D. Cremer and Flying Officer R. W. 'Dick' O'Farrell.

Stirling III EE913 on 199 Squadron at Lakenheath, skippered by 19-year old Pilot Officer Thomas Rex Odgers RAAF, was shot down by Oberleutnant Albert Walter of 1./NJG6 piloting a Bf 110, this being his first confirmed kill of the war. Combat took place over Geiselwind, 25 kilometres northeast of Kitzingen at 0215 hours. EE913 EX-F crashed at Futtersee, thirteen kilometres NNE of Scheinfeld and about forty kilometres northwest of Nuremburg, killing all seven crew. It was reported by the Burgomeister of Fuettersee that the aircraft was seen approaching from the east on fire at 0300 hours and that the Stirling crashed just outside the village and burnt for seven hours. The Luftwaffe from Illesheim transported the wreckage away. Odgers left a widow, Marjorie Joyce Odgers of Castlemaine, Victoria. Flight Sergeant Roland Ernest James Rees the 35-year old navigator also left a widow, Ivy Muriel Rees of West Bromwich, Staffordshire.

On 30/31 August 660 heavies targeted the cities of Mönchengladbach and Rheyd. Approximately half of the built-up area in each town was destroyed for the loss of 25 aircraft, 22 of which were shot down by the 'Tame Boars'. II./NJG1 claimed five victories whereas I./NJG1 destroyed eight bombers, including a triple victory by Gruppenkommandeur Hauptmann Hans-Dieter Frank: a Stirling over Monchengladbach, a Wellington (JA118 on 432 'Leaside' Squadron RCAF, which crashed at Siggerath near Mönchengladbach with the loss of Flight Sergeant James Edward Pendleton and crew) and a Lancaster that came down at Brüggen, west of Mönchengladbach. Halifax V LK629 on 427 'Lion' Squadron RCAF, skippered by 21-year old Flight Sergeant Bernard Buxton was possibly shot down by Leutnant Walter Schön of Stab 1./NJG1 who engaged the bomber at a height of 4200 metres and the aircraft crashed at 0350 hours ten kilometres southwest of Antwerp. None of the crew survived. Oberstleutnant Schön was killed on 20/21 October 1943 at Gross-Ballersetd near Stendal airfield after air combat. It was claimed that the bombers shot down eight night fighters during the raid and that they were attacked a further 33 times after the raid had been completed and on their return leg.

The very next night, 622 bombers assembled in a giant stream and headed for the 'Big City' once more. Three heavy bombing raids in ten days by RAF Bomber Command on Berlin resulted in the loss of 137 aircraft and great loss of life to Berliners in the Siemensstadt and Mariendorf districts and also to Lichterfelde. It was but a prelude to the Battle of Berlin, which would open with all ferocity in November. On the 3/4 September raid, twenty out of 316 Lancasters were lost, twelve (possibly even fifteen) of which were destroyed by Nachtjäger. On 5/6 September a force of 605 aircraft was despatched to bomb Mannheim and Ludwigshafen. The raid was successful but thirteen Halifaxes, thirteen Lancasters and eight Stirlings, or 5.6% of the force were lost. III./NJG1 claimed four of these aircraft over Germany, including a Lancaster (W4370 on 12 Squadron) by Hauptmann August 'Gustel' Geiger, which crashed at 0024 hours near Oppau/Stutenheim. Five men bailed out safely but Flying Officer Derek George Leader-Williams and Sergeant John Harding his rear gunner were killed. Geiger went on to claim a Halifax at 0045 hours at Rheinhausen. Leutnant Hans-Heinz Augenstein also scored a double victory shooting down Stirling IV EH878 on 623 Squadron at 0045 hours at Rodem/Schonborn and a Lancaster 22 minutes later at Boechingen near Landau. The Stirling crashed at Schonberg with the loss of the skipper Flying Officer Noel Robert Shakespeare Humphreys MiD RNZAF, and five crew. One man survived to be taken prisoner. II./NJG1 operating from St. Trond claimed a Stirling and a Lancaster destroyed and Hauptmann Hans-Dieter Frank, Kommandeur of I./NJG1 shot down an unidentified Lancaster northeast of Pirmasens. I./NJG6 at Mainz-Finthen was credited with seven Stirlings and Halifaxes. German losses amounted to four single-engined 'Wild Boars' and three twin-engined aircraft; three crew were killed. One of these was Oberfeldwebel Willi Bleier, Oberleutnant Heinz Strüning's (Staffelkapitän 3./NJG1) bordfunker. Their He 219A-0 (G9+FB) was damaged by return fire during a sortie in the Ludwigshafen-Mannheim area and a bullet severed the control cable from the fuel tank selector lever and during the flight back to Venlo, Strüning was unable to switch to Tank One. Operation of the fuel system required tanks 2 (centre) and 3 (rear) to be used initially until half-empty (i.e. about 1000 litres remaining), thereafter switching to the forward or No 1 tank until its contents were exhausted. The He 219's engines quit one after the other and Strüning and Bleier decided to abandon the aircraft. However, the 'Katapultsitzen' (ejection seats) refused to fire and so both men climbed out. Strüning hit the antenna mast and tail surfaces of his Uhu and suffered bruised ribs and contusions. Willi Bleier probably also hit the machine and he was found dead the next day with an unopened parachute. At the time of his death Bleier had participated in the destruction of forty RAF bombers.

Hannover was the target for 711 bombers on 22/23 September. At least twenty bombers were shot down over the target by single-engined and twin-engined night fighters that engaged the bomber stream en masse and in 'Wild Boar' fashion over the burning city under attack. Lancaster I W4948 on 57 Squadron, which was one of 21 aircraft that had taken off from East Kirkby and was returning from Hannover, was attacked by Major Wolf Dietrich Meister of 14./KG2 at 0043 hours over Driby in Lincolnshire. Pilot Officer Gordon Alexander Duff RAAF's aircraft was set on fire whilst in the circuit. Only two men managed to bail out before the Lancaster, crashed on the outskirts of Spilsby. Among the claimants over the Reich this night were 25-year old Feldwebel Anton Benning of 8./JG300 who destroyed two Lancasters, one twenty kilometres southeast of Bremen, the other northeast of Verden for his first two Abschüsse. He would finish the war with 28 victories. Feldwebel Kurt Emler of 7./JG300 claimed a Lancaster southeast of Bremen and 25-year old Feldwebel Heinz Gossow of the same unit claimed two Lancasters south of the city. Emler was killed on 3 January 1944 during aerial combat near Mattershausen, ten kilometres west of Jüterbog. He had twelve Abschüsse. Gossow, who ended the war flying the Me 262 on JG7 finished with a total of twelve Abschüsse. Oberfeldwebel Ernst Fleishmann of 7./JG300 claimed a Mosquito at Oldenburg and 23-year old Leutnant Klaus Bretschneider of 5./JG300 a Lancaster for his fourth victory. Fleishmann was killed in his Bf 110E-3 on 5 January 1943. Bretschneider was killed on 24 December 1944 in combat with a Mustang of the 357th Fighter Group. He had 31 Abschüsse.

Leutnant Hermann Stumpe and 26-year old Feldwebel Hermann Wischnewski - both of 3./JG300 - each claimed a Viermot at Hanover. Stumpe was killed in October 1943 after he crashed at Werl, near Hamm, following an engine fire. He had three victories. It is thought that Wischnewski shot down Lancaster I R5700 on 9 Squadron skippered by 21-year old Pilot Officer Edward Jeptha Crabtree RAAF at a height of 2500 metres at 2237 hours over the target area. Crabtree, who was from Surrey Hills in Victoria and his six crew were killed. Wischnewski was wounded on 29 July 1944 when his Bf 109G-6 'Red Two' was shot down by a P-51. He bailed out safely at Gelbstadt/Apolda. Feldwebel Gerhard Pietsch of II./JG302 claimed two Halifaxes at Hanover for his first victories. Pietsch was killed on 24 December 1943 at Jüterbog-Waldlager airfield. Feldwebel Erich Teubner of 8./JG301 claimed a Lancaster forty kilometres west of the city and another northwest of Hanover. Leutnant Heinz Grimm of 12./NJG1 claimed a Lancaster at Braunstedt for his 25th Abschüss. Halifax V LK909 on 434 'Bluenose' Squadron RCAF skippered by 23-year old Pilot Officer Herbert Green was shot down by Leutnant Heinz Bock of 8./NJG1 at a height of 4500 metres at 2240 hours over Ströhen, South Barenburg for his third Abschüss. All eight crew were killed. Boch was killed shortly afterwards in a crash landing at Bad Aibling airfield after being hit by flak.

On the night of 23/24 September 627 bombers attacked Mannheim when 42 bombers were lost, 21 of them to twin-engined night fighters and thirteen to 'Wilde Sau' single-engined fighters of all three 'Wild Boar' Geschwader that operated in force over Mannheim. Seven bombers were shot down before they reached the target zone and another twenty were shot down over the target area. During the many engagements, seven German fighters were claimed destroyed. Twenty-nine year old Hauptmann Ewald Janssen of JG300 claimed a Viermot for his second victory. He ended the war with three Abschüsse and died in Brazil in 1985. Feldwebel Ullrich Veh of 3./JG300 claimed a Viermot (Lancaster III JA708 on 97 Squadron) south of the city for his fourth victory. Flight Lieutenant Robert A. Fletcher and three crew were taken into captivity. Veh was killed in a crash on 8 March 1944. Unteroffizier Anton 'Toni' Gaissmayer of 6./JG300 claimed a Lancaster fifteen kilometres northwest of Mannheim for the second of his eventual nine Abschüsse. Oberfeldwebel Günther Migge and Feldwebel Willi Rüllkotter of 2./JG300 claimed Viermots at Mannheim. Rüllkotter was killed in action on 2 October 1943. Oberleutnant Robert Plewa of 9./JG300, Oberleutnant Rudi Hoffmann of II./JG300 and Oberfeldwebel Walter Mackens of 1./JG300 each claimed a Viermot near Mannheim. Plewa was killed in a crash on 29/30 September. Mackens was killed in combat on 5 January 1944. He had eight Abschüsse. Oberfeldwebel Artur Gross of 2./JG302 shot down a Lancaster at Mannheim for the first of his ten Abschüsse. Oberleutnant Gerhard 'Gerd' Stamp, Staffelkapitän, 3/JG300 destroyed a 'Lanki' ten kilometres west of Mannheim. He was injured when he overturned on landing at Biblis airfield. A year later he was shot down with wounds in his Bf 109G-6/U2 on 29 June 1944 at Lodersleben. He finished the war with four victories. Oberfeldwebels Kurt Greineisen and Norbert Graziadei both of 5./JG300 each claimed a Lancaster. Graziadei, who ended the war with ten victories, died in 1999. Feldwebel Theo Hans Kugler claimed a Lancaster five kilometres southeast of Mannheim for the fourth of his five victories. He was killed on 20 June 1944 near Potsdam.

Leutnant Friedrich Hans Kröner of 10/NJG1, flying a Bf 110, was killed while attempting to land at Mainz-Finthen by a Mosquito on 605 Squadron flown by Flight Lieutenant C. E. Knowles. Unteroffizier Josef Brunner and his radar operator Siegfried Beugel of 2./NJG1 claimed two 'Lanki's' for his second and third victories. His first Abschuss, at Bad Dürkheim at 2250, was Lancaster JB152 on 103 Squadron flown by Flying Officer D. W. Finlay DFC whose crew was nearing the end of its tour of duty, having been together since April and having completed 23 attacks on the Ruhr, Dortmund, Hanover and Turin among other targets. The raid of 23 September 1943 was the crew's first to Berlin. They were scheduled to be in the front of the first wave of the stream of bombers. This was as they wanted it for they firmly believed this was the safest position for a bomber to be in, getting away from the target before the night-fighters could gather. Unfortunately engine trouble delayed them and they arrived some ten minutes behind schedule. Sergeant J. H. McFarlane, the navigator, was completing his final calculations to take the Lancaster over the aiming point, when Brunner dived on the bomber, spraying cannon shells into the port wing. The fuel tank immediately caught fire, illuminating the black crosses on the fighter as it swept past. The bomber was clearly doomed, so Finlay ordered the crew to bail out. Two men died, but the other five landed safely. Being so deep inside Germany they had no hope of escape and were duly taken prisoner. Brunner's second victim eight kilometres south of Edenkoben near Koblenz at 2256 was Lancaster JA708 on 97 Squadron piloted by Flight Lieutenant R. A. Fletcher DFM, who with three of his crew were taken into captivity. Two crew were killed.

A few nights later, on 27/28 September, Hannover was the target for 678 aircraft although of these only 612 dropped their bombs, but scattering them in open country. RAF crews were not yet expert with the new H_2S navigational radar, which showed up an expanse of water very well but the Steinhuder See, a large lake, which was used as a way point, had been almost completely covered with boards and nets. Millions of strips of 'Window' were dropped but 38 heavies were lost; 33 of these for five aircraft missing were claimed by 207 twin-engined 'Tame Boars'. Wing Commander Bertie Rex 'Sammy' Hoare on 605 Squadron claimed a 'Dornier Do 217 during aerial combat one kilometre west of Abbensen for his fourth victory. His victim was actually Bf 110G-4 G9+EN flown by Hauptmann Hans Werner Rupprecht of 5/NJG1, who was killed. Seven victories were credited to III./NJG1. Hauptmann August 'Gustel' Geiger scored a triple victory destroying a Lancaster at 2210 over the Ijsselmeer, Halifax LWE230 on 78 Squadron at 2330 at Hattendorf, Germany and at 0001 a Halifax (possibly HR907 on 35 Squadron) went down at Wippingen. 22-year old Hauptmann Heinz Martin 'Hannibal' Hadeball of 3./NJG6 claimed Halifax HX159 on 10 Squadron thirteen kilometres northeast of Minden at 2335 hours. Hadeball became an 'Experte' with 33 night kills with NJG1, 4, 6 and 10 and he was awarded the Ritterkreuz in July 1944.

Oberleutnant Heinz Knigge of 2./NJG6 claimed a Stirling twenty kilometres northeast of Hanover at 2308 for his first Abschuss. After an uneventful trip to the target, Stirling III EF118 on 199 Squadron, skippered by 21-year old Pilot Officer Maurice A. Hodson, was just starting its bombing run when it was coned by searchlights. Hodson tried to lose the searchlights by putting the aircraft into a series of violent corkscrew turns but it was to no avail. The gunners reported two night fighters closing in and at 5000 metres there was a large explosion causing the aircraft to go out of control. The Stirling crashed at a farm near the village of Ramlingen about ten miles northeast of Hanover. Robert Taylor the air bomber managed to escape from the front hatch before the aircraft crashed. He was the only survivor on the eight man crew which included a second pilot on his 'second dickie' trip. Knigge claimed Halifax at Hohensülzen on 18 November for his second victory. He was killed on 18/19 March 1944 during aerial combat near Kellmüz/Memmingham.

Eighteen Halifaxes were lost and ten Stirlings, a Wellington on 432 'Leaside' Squadron RCAF and ten Lancasters were also missing. Wellington X HE817 skippered by 20-year old Pilot Officer Stanley Atkinson RCAF, a veteran of 25 sorties, was brought down by a combination of flak and fighter action, the kill being claimed by Oberfähnrich Siegfried König of 9./NJG3 for his second 'Anerkennung' but this is disputed by the rear gunner, Master Sergeant Shelton C. Bybee USAAF, one of two survivors who were thrown clear. In a letter to the family of the pilot he stated: 'We reached the target in good condition, a little ahead of time. We were the only plane over the target at the time. The Jerries picked us up in the searchlights. A fighter came up from the front and underneath, hitting my turret. I was wounded at the time but did not know it. My communication was cut from the rest of the plane; therefore I did not know what happened in the front... who was wounded. Another fighter came in on me from the tail. I shot him and he ran into us, hitting us in the mid-section. It turned the plane upside down, threw the turret with me inside away from the plane that was about 18,000 feet. I bailed out about 2,000 feet. The two planes were stuck together and came down in flames. Bill Grant, who was the bombardier, was thrown clear of the plane, came down unconscious, landing on a building, fell off and broke his leg. Bill and I landed about two blocks apart. There were six of us on the plane. To the best of my knowledge, we two are the only ones that survived...'

The German fighter pilot shot down by Shelton Bybee was Feldwebel Heinz Radloff of 1./JG301. He crashed with his Bf 109G in the List district of Hannover, approximately two kilometres from the crash site of HE817. Little is known about Radloff. He scored one previous victory on the night of 30/31 July 1943 when he shot down a Viermot at Remscheid. HE817 was his second victim on this, his final combat sortie.

Stirling III EF515 on 76 Squadron captained by Flight Sergeant R. E. Martin RNZAF was intercepted and shot down by Unteroffizier Emil Heintelmann of 8./NJG1 at 2330 hours 5500 metres over Haverbeck, five kilometres northwest of Hamelin. Sergeant Archie Bangs the 18-year old mid-upper gunner, who it is believed lied about his age when he volunteered for the RAFVR, was the only casualty. Although Sergeant Charles A. Smith, the 36-year old flight engineer, survived the crash and was taken prisoner, he died in captivity on 8 April 1944. EF515 was the fifth and final Abschuss for Heintelmann. He was killed on 13/14 October 1944 after a failed belly landing during a practice flight after an engine fire. Stirling EF495 QJ-R on 149 Squadron at Lakenheath, piloted by Flight Sergeant George Stuart Hotchkis RAAF which ditched in the North Sea, was probably the victim of an intruder flown by Oberleutnant Rudolf Abrahamczik of 14./KG2 who claimed a Viermot off Cromer. Hotchkis and three of the crew were killed; three survived to be taken prisoner.

In a separate intruder action, Abrahamczik shot down the Lancaster flown by Pilot Officer Desmond Wallace Skipper on 101 Squadron in flames near Wickenby after he had been refused permission to land back at Ludford Magna and was told to head for Lindholme. There were no survivors. Seven other aircraft crashed or crash-landed at bases on their return claiming the lives of sixteen crew and injuring five. 101 Squadron was the only one of its kind to combine 'Airborne Cigar' (ABC) electronic countermeasure duties[149] with regular bombing operations, which meant that the squadron flew on almost every major bombing raid until the end of the war. Consequently, 101 Squadron lost 113 Lancasters on 308 raids, plus another 33 destroyed in crashes on the British mainland. It was a particularly bad night for 428 Squadron at Middleton St. George which lost five aircraft this night. Halifax II JB968 skippered by 24-year old Flight Lieutenant Ronald H. Sherback was hit by flak and finished off by Leutnant Josef Kraft of Stab II./NJG5, a 21-year old Viennese pilot ten kilometres southwest of Hannover at 2326 hours. All seven crew died.

Major Hans-Dieter Frank, Kommandeur, I./NJG1 with 55 night victories was killed at Heese, approximately 25 kilometres north-west of Celle when his He 219A-03 (G9+CB) collided with Bf 110G-4 G9+DA flown by Hauptmann Günther Friedrich of the Geschwaderstab/NJG1. As they went down, the two aircraft separated and crashed five kilometres south of Bergen near Meisendorf. Friedrich and his funker, Oberleutnant Werner Gerber and Obergefreiter Weisske, bordshütze, were killed. They had shared in four victories. Frank, who three months earlier had received the Ritterkreuz while Staffelkapitän of 2./NJG1 was most likely being pursued by John Randall Daniel 'Bob' Braham DSO DFC** CO of 141 Squadron before the collision. He ejected from the Uhu and landed safely but he was choked to death by the cable of his radio helmet, which he had omitted to disconnect and which compressed and crushed his larynx. His bordfunker, Oberfeldwebel Erich Gotter was either thrown from the aircraft or he bailed out without the aid of his 'Katapultsitzen', which was found in the wreckage with the seat harness undone. Frank, who had 55 victories, was posthumously awarded the Eichenlaub.

On 29/30 September, 352 aircraft raided Bochum. Leutnant Nikolas Volkmar of IV/NJG3 at Grove in Denmark was injured when his Ju 88C-6 (D5+FE) was shot down while attacking Lancaster 'P' on 207 Squadron flown by the CO, Squadron Leader David M. Balme. The return fire from the Lancaster, possibly by Les Mitchell, the rear gunner who was on his first tour with David Balme and who would fly with him on a second tour on 227 Squadron, set the Ju 88's starboard engine on fire and Volkmar, his bordfunker, Unteroffizier Heinz Bankowski and bordmechinker, Unteroffizier Helmut Grubendorf and Unteroffizier Willi Hanrat bailed out safely. Volkmar, Bankowski and Grubendorf were killed in aerial combat on 24 February 1944 when their Ju 88R-2 (D5+FE) crashed at Ettischleben east of Arnstadt/Thüringen. David Balme completed a tour on 207 Squadron and was promoted Wing Commander, taking command of 227 Squadron in March 1945. After the war he resumed his academic career at Cambridge, founding the University College of The Gold Coast, being awarded the CMG and, in 1964, he was appointed as Professor of Classics at Queen Mary College, London University. Wing Commander Balme DSO DFC CMG died on 2 February 1989, aged 76.

Hauptmann August 'Gustel' Geiger, Staffelkapitän, 7./NJG1 and Feldwebel Dieter Koch, his bordfunker, were attacked by Wing Commander 'Bob' Braham in a Beaufighter VIf over the Zuider Zee. It took Braham ten minutes of fierce manoeuvring before he could finally out-turn the Bf 110 and, five miles west of Elburg, the 'Night Destroyer' gave Bf 110G-4 G9+ER a three-second-burst from astern. Geiger and Koch parachuted into the Zuider Zee and were drowned. Hauptmann Geiger had become Nachtjagd's highest-scoring 'Experte' March-September 1943 with 41 'Himmelbett' victories, which took his final total to 54 Abschüsse. It was Braham's twentieth victory and the eighth while on the squadron.[150] The Bochum raid cost the RAF nine bombers, seven of which were claimed destroyed by the Nachtjagd.

Feldwebel Karl-Georg Pfeiffer of 12./NJG1 was airborne once again this night after having bailed out and broken his leg in June:

'It was a lovely moonlight night with nothing much going on. We had just passed over the two lakes to the east of Leeuwarden. Suddenly the pointer of the boost gauge of the port engine began going to and fro, although the engine continued to run normally.

Carefully I throttled back, waited, then pushed the lever forward again, when suddenly the cowlings flew off and flames came from the rear, close to the wing. I tried to extinguish the fire and shut the engine down but all to no avail. The fire got stronger. I said to my crew (apart from Willi, Gefreiter Bauernfeind, a gunner, was with us because of the presence of many long range night fighters) 'We must bail out!' They had seen for themselves why. Based on our own experience, we had explained to the gunner the important points. I heard them jettisoning the roof and then felt a strong impact on the machine, as if someone had kicked the port rudder pedal. Unfortunately Gefreiter Bauernfeind had opened his parachute too soon and his head had struck the rudder. But we only discovered this afterwards after Willi and I had landed safely and the third man had been found dead. I had again done a half roll, like the first time, and had almost been trapped by my fur boot. But this time I had not been wounded and had managed the roll so that I was flung out. I opened my parachute and landed at 2200 hours precisely in a meadow beside a road. I took my parachute under my arm and started walking, meeting two Dutchmen, one with a bicycle, who accompanied me to the nearest village. I waited there with a Dutch family until I was picked up from Leeuwarden. There, in the operations room, I met Willi again and we heard the sad story that our companion had not reached the ground alive. As far as I know he came from Berchtesgaden and I later sent a letter of condolence to his mother but what use were words. Her boy had been killed. The following day Oberleutnant Greiner took me back to Leeuwarden but Willi had had enough and, although his wife visited, he preferred to go by train and did not arrive until two days later. I took his wife to the cinema in the evening to keep her company.'

A total of 178 victories were credited to Nachtjagd in the Reichsverteidigung for September. The arm was now in a downwards spiral that was not halted until the end of the year when the 'Tame Boar' force had been fully built up and trained to counter the strategic night bombing offensive effectively.

When a bombing force of 294 Lancasters set out for Munich on the night of 2/3 October (8 Lancasters were shot down by night fighters) Warrant Officer Eddie Wheeler DFC WOp/AG, 97 Squadron had no prior knowledge that this would be his crew's final operation together:

'Perhaps it was just as well as we might have been even more nervous in our anxiety to survive. As it was, the trip was largely uneventful except that we coaxed Hitch, our navigator to leave his seat and take up position in the astrodome to see what was going on over the target area. His remarks over the intercom brought smiles to our faces when he said, 'Christ! Does this sort of thing go on every night?' Seeing the mass of fires in the target area he considered it was 'sheer bloody murder.' Ginger too was on this raid and he was to be involved in five further operations against Berlin. Our crew was stood down for a few days after this until Johnny called us together and said, 'Well lads, do we want to go on, or for some of us at least, shall we call it a day?' For Johnny, Hitch, Jackie Blair and myself we had done our quota and would ask to be relieved of further operational duty. Bill (flight engineer), Peter (air bomber) and Geoff (rear gunner) had no option but to continue. Peter anxiously cleaned his pipe, Bill kept shuffling his feet and Geoff nervously fingered his lanyard whilst the rest of us tried to reach a decision. If we old-stagers decided to finish, then Bill, Peter and Geoff would be assigned to a new crew to finish their first tour. Whilst they were hopeful that the crew would not split up, they recognized that we had done our fair share of ops over a long period and in similar circumstances they would say, 'enough is enough.' Johnny posed the question to us again and there seemed a reluctance to reply. Finally, I said that the last half dozen trips had been a nightmare for me and I had been getting progressively more nervous, so I was going to call it a day. Hitch said he agreed with me and so it was decided to tell the CO, Wing Commander Alabaster, we had made up our minds. Naturally, the other three lads were disappointed but they thanked us for the happy times we had enjoyed at Bourn and we wished them all the luck that was going.'

On the Kassel raid of 3/4 October seventeen heavies were claimed shot down from a force of 547 aircraft and for nine 'Tame Boar' losses. At Haste three kilometres north of Osnabrück, 32-two year old Oberleutnant Fritz Lau of 9./NJG1 destroyed Stirling III BF470 on 15 Squadron at Mildenhall flown by Flight Sergeant A. V. Wood, who survived, and he and three of his crew were taken into captivity. The three other crewmembers were killed. Lau, who was born at Stettin on 23 September 1911, was a former Lufthansa pilot and after flying Ju 52 transports in the Poland campaign, he was an instructor at Instrument Flying School. He was wounded shooting down the Stirling and safely bailed out at Bohmte near Wittlage. It was not the first time he had been wounded in action. On 10 March his Bf 110G-4 (5339) had been damaged in combat and his bordschütze, Obergefreiter Erwin Weber had been killed. Leutnant Hans-Heinz Augenstein shot down Stirling EF158 on 623 Squadron at Downham Market to crash at Windhausen, Germany. The skipper, Pilot Officer Keith Fred Shaw RNZAF and his crew including two fellow New Zealanders and his Canadian flight engineer were killed. The Stirling crashed east of Kassel. Hauptmann Walter Milius of 1./NJG3 was wounded in action after he was rammed by a RAF night-fighter and bailed out safely at Schwaneburger Moor. Milius had scored three victories in one day, 17 December 1942 and three more in June-July 1943, to add to two Abschüsse in 1941. He would finish the war with eight victories.

Halifax V EB213 on 428 'Ghost' Squadron RCAF skippered by 21-year old Pilot Officer Francis Bernard Edwards was possibly shot down by 30-year old Hauptmann Ernst Zechlin of 4./NJG5 at 2239 hours for his first Abschuss of the war. The Halifax crashed at Hofgeismer. The navigator, Sergeant F. Gration RCAF was the only survivor on the eight man crew. Zechlin, who was wounded during a low level attack on Langensaltza, Germany, survived the war with a total of eight Abschüsse. Oberfeldwebel Wilhelm Engel of 3./NJG6 destroyed Halifax V LK925 on 431 'Iroquois' Squadron RCAF at Tholthorpe, the aircraft crashing near St. Vith in Belgium at 2315 hours. Pilot Officer J. Reynoldson RCAF and three of his crew survived and were taken into captivity. The three other crewmembers were killed. Sergeant Ray A. C. De Pape RCAF who was flying as the 'second dickie' on his first trip recalled: 'About ten minutes off target on the way home we were warned of an approaching fighter. We took evasive action. After four successive blasts of flak the plane dived, covered in smoke. The intercom was broken and the captain tapped me on the shoulder and indicated the escape hatch. I was unable to locate the district where I fell. It was probably somewhere in between Prüm and Schleiden because the first town I reached after walking for four days [in a westerly direction, deeper into Germany] was La Roche-en-Ardenne, Belgium.' De Pape was moved along the Comète escape line with other evaders and in November crossed the Pyrenees into Spain. He was escorted across the border into Gibraltar on 14 December and flown back to England with two fellow evaders. During his absence, the crew he left behind in England teamed up with Flight Sergeant Freddie F. E. Rein RCAF and were lost on their first operation, on 20/21 January 1944 when their Halifax was hit in the fuel tanks by flak twenty minutes short of Berlin, the target. Another burst caused more leakage as they were heading for home. With only ten minutes or so of fuel remaining, Rein gave the order to bail out. Six of the crew, including Rein, evaded capture, with the seventh being taken prisoner.[151]

Hauptmann Rudolf Sigmund, who had 27 Abschüsse in 150 sorties; 26 victories at night - was also on the hunt for Viermots attacking Kassel. Sigmund, who had been given command of III./NJG3 on 15 August, was born on 5 March 1915 at Hardheim in Nordbaden. He joined NJG1 in spring 1941 and gained his first victory on the night of 24/25 August, when he shot down a Whitley near Wavre. The following spring Oberleutnant Sigmund was appointed Adjutant of II./NJG2. By the end of the year he had increased his victory total to seven. On 1 October Sigmund was appointed Staffelkapitän 10./NJG1. On

26 February 1943 he shot down a USAAF B-24 Liberator by day to record his tenth victory. He recorded another day victory on 17 April when he shot down a B-17 for his thirteenth Abschuss. Sigmund then claimed four Viermots on each of the nights of 21/22 June (18-21) and 25/26 June (22-25) and he was awarded the Ritterkreuz on 2 August for 26 victories. On the night of 25/26 July Sigmund and his bordfunker were wounded in aerial combat with RAF aircraft. Sigmund, Feldwebel Hugo-Albert Bauer his funker and Unteroffizier Johannes-Max Dittrich the bordschütze did not return from the sortie on the night of the Kassel raid. They were killed when their Bf 110 (G4+U7) was hit either by flak or by return fire southwest of Gottingen.

On 4/5 October, when 406 aircraft attacked Frankfurt, 'Tame' and 'Wild Boars' claimed twelve victories. On the other hand, the raid by 343 Lancasters against Stuttgart on 7/8 October resulted in claims by Nachtjagd for only two kills but on the Bremen and Hannover raids of 8/9 October, Nachtjagd claimed 37 of the 623 bombers that were lost. Lancaster III JB181 on 7 Squadron was the first to be shot down on the outbound route to Hannover and was claimed by Oberfeldwebel Heinz Vinke of 11./NJG1 over Norg at 0027 hours while at 5000 metres. There were no survivors on the seven man crew skippered by 21-year old Flying Officer Bruce E. C. Macpherson. Leutnant Erwin Ernst of 6./NJG1 and Leutnant Hans-Heinz Augenstein and Unteroffizier Heinz Amsberg both of 9./NJG1 were among the successful 'Tame Boar' crews. Ernst destroyed Halifax II LW236 on 78 Squadron, captained by Sergeant William Henry Scott. All the crew were killed. Augenstein shot down a Stirling south-southwest of Hannover at 0142 and Amsberg claimed a 'Lancaster' at Schwarmstedt. Amsberg shot down Lancaster A4-K LL693 over Stuttgart on the night of 15/16 March 1944, just after it had dropped its bomb load. It crashed at Gallenhof in the north east Stuttgart area. Pilot Officer James Menzies Rodger and crew were all killed.

Flying instructors of II./NJG101 operating from Deelen in Holland scored three 'Wild Boar' victories. Two German aircraft were lost and Leutnant Heinz Grimm of Stab IV./NJG1, who had 27 victories, was mistakenly shot down by German flak over Bremen. He escaped by parachute, but died on 13 October from severe burns, aged 23 and is buried in Bergen op Zoom War cemetery. He gained a total of 25 night kills and a further single daylight claim. Three more large-scale 'Tame Boar' operations were mounted by First Jagdkorps during October. On the 18/19th, when Bomber Command attacked Hannover with 360 Lancasters, 190 twin-engined aircraft claimed fourteen victories for two own losses, JG300 and JG301 claiming seven Viermot kills.

On the 20/21st I Jagddivision scrambled 220 aircraft, which claimed eleven Lancasters destroyed from 358 sent to raid Leipzig for nine own losses. Three victories went to III./NJG1. Lancaster II DS686 OW-D on 426 'Thunderbird' Squadron RCAF, skippered by 27-year old Flying Officer Frederick J. Stuart CGM, was one of fourteen aircraft loaded with one 4,000lb bomb and 3,120lbs of incendiaries. Stuart was born and raised in Newcastle upon Tyne. He worked as a solicitor's clerk and met and married Constance Howey, another solicitor's secretary. DS686 was halfway to Hanover from Bremen when they were repeatedly attacked by a Bf 109. The enemy aircraft attacked four times hitting the tail plane and fuselage, disabling the mid-upper turret and wounding its gunner, Sergeant McGovern. Stuart flew corkscrews and diving turns while the gunners returned fire, in particular Flight Sergeant George Andrew, the twenty-year-old old rear gunner, who warned his pilot of each attack. Several minutes later, a Junkers 88 appeared on the starboard quarter below and began its attempt to bring down the bomber. This time the enemy managed three attacks before Stuart lost them in the clouds. The Lancaster was badly damaged. Only the pilot's skilful flying and the rear gunner's marksmanship and lightning reactions saved it from certain destruction. Not only was the mid-upper turret disabled, but two of the rear turret guns were also inoperable, one with a link stoppage and the other with a round jammed in the serve mechanism. Despite these problems, Andrew had fired 2200 rounds during the seven attacks. Other damage included a smashed pilot's windscreen, a hydraulic-system failure, many bullet holes in the top of the starboard side of the fuselage and wing, shot-up navigation and wireless equipment, the trailing aerial shot away, a failure in the boost gauge of the starboard outer engine and bullet holes in the starboard inner fuel tank. Despite all the damage, Stuart chose to press on and bomb the target, which was still 140 miles away.

With most of his instruments destroyed, Flying Officer Roderick James Dunphy, the twenty-year-old navigator, directed the aircraft to the target and home again. For his part, he received the DFC. McGovern suffered wounds in the arms, legs and chest and was temporarily blinded in one eye, but after four months rejoined the Thunderbirds and later received a commission and the award of a DFC. Flying Officer Freddy Stuart and crew were shot down and killed on 20/21 December when their Lancaster II (LL630 OW-D) was the second of two Abschüsse claimed by Leutnant Ludwig Würtz of I.NJG.7 at Frankfurt which he shot down at 5400 metres above Güls near Koblenz at 2030 hours. Stuart was a veteran of 23 operations, Andrew 22 operations and Dunphy 21 operations. Conny, who had given up her job to be near her husband while he was stationed at Linton, was lodging near York. After his death, she moved in with her parents in Newbrough and gave birth to a daughter a month later. Würtz was killed on the 8 January 1944 when the controls of his FW 190 became blocked shortly after take-off from Venlo airfield. He had two night kills to his credit and a further daytime kill.

On 22/23 October, a clear, moonless night, but with ominous black clouds to the west marking the approach of a cold front, 36 heavies set out to bomb Frankfurt as a diversion for 569 Lancasters and Halifaxes heading for Kassel. They subjected Kassel to an exceptionally accurate and concentrated raid, which created a firestorm destroying 63% of all living accommodation. I Jagddivision action was hampered by strong 'Window' jamming of the Fighter R/T Frequency and the diversionary raid on Frankfurt but the 194 'Tame Boars' dispatched made forty kills, mainly in 'Wild Boar' fashion in the target area and to the north of the target, for the loss of only six fighters. Altogether, the RAF lost 43 aircraft. Hauptmann Manfred Meurer of Stab I./NJG1 claimed one victory, Lancaster W4357 on 61 Squadron flown by Pilot Officer R. D. Truscott that crashed at Buhne-Haarbrück, north of Kassel at 2120 hours. All seven crew survived and were taken into captivity.

Northwest of Mindenat at 2130 hours, 23-year old Oberleutnant Werner Husemann of 7./NJG1 claimed Lancaster DS778 on 408 Squadron. Flight Lieutenant Arthur James Whiston RCAF and his crew were killed. Husemann was born on 10 November 1919 in Schötmar/Lippe. From 1941 until late 1942 he had served with a weather reconnaissance squadron before transferring to the Stab of NJG1. He claimed his first aerial victory on the night 17/18 August 1942. His number of victories had increased to seventeen by the end of 1943; among them three Lancasters shot down on the night of 25/26 June. He was appointed Staffelkapitän of 7./NJG1 on 1 October and was awarded the German Cross in Gold on 24 October and the Ehrenpokal der Luftwaffe on 1 November. He became commander of I./NJG3 in January 1944. Husemann was awarded the Knight's Cross on 30 September after he was credited with thirty aerial victories. In total he claimed 34 Night-Abschüsse in over 250 combat sorties. The last thirteen victories were claimed with Oberfeldwebel Hans-Georg Schierholz as his bordfunker.

Leutnant Otto Fries of 5./NJG1 and his Funker, Alfred Staffa, had taken off in the early evening in their Bf 110G-4 from Sint-Truiden/Sint-Trond flying 'Tame Boar' under 'Ypsilon'[152] control in search of their second Abschüsse. They had been vectored first north, then south-east and then south, but had had no contact with the enemy. In the short breaks between jamming, Fries picked up a few sentences of the broadcast and managed to make out an instruction to turn on to a north-westerly heading, but could not hear the estimated height of the approaching bombers. He climbed to 6000 metres (20,000 feet), getting nearer and nearer to the bank of clouds to the west. On the aerials Fries and Staffa saw the flickering lights of St. Elmo's fire. The airscrews, too, showed circles of flame and the Bf 110 lurched and swayed in the turbulence of the cold front they were flying into. Fries turned on to a reciprocal heading and began to lose height. Then he heard a message from the ground, another breakthrough in the jamming:

'Adler 98 from Eisvogel, head 300°. Bombers approaching. Height 4 to 4500 metres.'

Fries turned and Staffa peered at his Lichtenstein screen. At first he saw nothing, not even 'Window' returns, but very soon there was a response. 'I've got a blip! Coming in very fast. Probably Düppel. Climb a bit higher just in case!'

At that very moment a dark shadow flashed past on a reciprocal heading and Fries flung his Messerschmitt around in a steep turn. Once on a south-easterly course he opened the throttles. His air speed indicator showed 430 kph. At first Staffa could see nothing on his radar and then he yelled: 'The bloody fool! It's a classic example! He's got the idea there's a night-fighter hanging around and he's trying to camouflage himself. He's chucking Düppel out every few seconds and he's leaving us a splendid trail we just can't miss! We'll catch him! He's only two kilometres in front!'

Fries closed in on their prey. It was a Lancaster III - EE175 EM-R on 207 Squadron at Spilsby flown by Canadian Squadron Leader Alexander Lyons McDowell. Soon Fries could see a shadow which quickly consolidated into the shape of a '4-mot'. Fries continues: 'The shadow grew bigger and bigger, until at last we could make out quite clearly the glowing exhausts of the four motors. We were scarcely a hundred metres away. 'Open fire, before he sees us! Take it easy - just a bit closer.' Then suddenly there were flashes from the rear of the bomber and like a concentrated beam of light the bullets from the four-gun turret swept around the machine. There was a loud banging noise and I felt a piercing pain in my left calf. I reacted instinctively, pushing the control column to the right and kicking hard right on the rudder bar. Then I pulled back gently on the control column so that the bomber's turret moved slowly across my sight. A short burst put the rear guns out of action. It was the first and only time that I fired directly at the fuselage of a bomber.'

Peeling off to port, Fries fired a second burst into the port wing root of his target. Despite the dazzling effect of his own tracer he could clearly see his cannon shells hitting home. The wing of the 'Lanki' broke off and the fuselage spiralled down to crash in a great explosion. Fries saw the severed, burning port wing fluttering down until, almost a minute later, it too hit the ground. The main part of the Lancaster, with its bomb-load still on board, came down near Nettersheim in the Eifel region at 2030 hours, carving out a crater 25 feet deep and 75 feet in diameter. Squadron Leader McDowell and his crew are buried at Rheinberg War Cemetery. Fries was uninjured. A bullet from the bomber's rear turret had penetrated a joint between two armoured plates and struck a signal cartridge in a belt attached to his left flying boot. Fortunately for Fries and Staffa the cartridge had not exploded.[153]

During October 1943, 149 RAF bombers were destroyed by Nachtjagd but despite its best efforts there seemed no way that the German pilots could halt the tide and the RAF bomber onslaught on German cities was inexorable. On Saturday 23 October RAF Headquarters announced: 'Last night a large number of RAF wings attacked the Henschel locomotive-engine plant (the largest of its kind in Europe) and the Fieseler plant (the manufacturers of Focke-Wulf fighter planes) in Kassel, while other formations bombed the city's rail installations. The Luftwaffe made every effort to prevent the raid but was unable to keep the bomber wings away from the city. Visibility over Kassel was extremely clear and the bombers had an accurate view of their targets. One of the Mosquito pilots reported: 'Kassel was a single sheet of flame from which violent explosions were continuously erupting. You could see the smoke up to an altitude of 16,000 feet. We approached the city repeatedly from different directions, but after the raid we found no opportunity to take aerial photographs due to the dense clouds of smoke. The rising wind caused the sea of flame to spread more and more. Now the extent of the destruction in Kassel must virtually match that in Hamburg.'

Aircraft of I Jagddivision flew 728 sorties during November 1943 but scored only 22 victories for 24 fighters lost. Total Reichsverteidigung Nachtjagd claims for November amounted to 128. Night-fighters destroyed all of the eighteen heavies that failed to return from Düsseldorf on the night of 3/4 November when the city was raided by 577 bombers and twelve Mosquitoes after a lapse of almost five months. Against all odds Acting Flight Lieutenant William 'Bill' Reid RAFVR and his crew of Lancaster III LM360 'O-Oboe' on 61 Squadron returned after being shot up by a twin-engined night fighter which killed his navigator. Despite being badly wounded and with a damaged aircraft, Reid carried on to Düsseldorf where eighty fighters were reported over the city, as many as 55 of these being twin-engined and bombed the target before making for home. Fourteen returning bombers were damaged by the fighters while three enemy fighters were claimed destroyed, two Ju 88s to Halifaxes of 4 Group over Düsseldorf and a Me 210 to a 5 Group Lancaster near Gilze-Rijen. Bill Reid was given a blood transfusion and spent four days at the Norfolk and Norwich Hospital before being transferred to a military hospital. It was while convalescing that he was told he had been awarded the Victoria Cross.

Altogether, eighteen bombers or 3.1 per cent of the attacking force were lost on the night of 3/4 November while 37 were damaged. Three German fighters were claimed destroyed. I./NJG6 and II./NJG101 were credited with a victory apiece. Leutnant Otto Fries of 5./NJG1 at Sint-Truiden/Sint-Trond shot down Halifax LK932 MP-X on 76 Squadron near the Dutch village of Opgrimby near the border with Belgium for his third Abschüsse. The skipper, Flight Lieutenant Dennis G. Hornsey evaded but Sergeant R. W. Glover was caught on the French-Swiss border on 23 December. The rest of the crew were taken prisoner. At Lanaken (Limburg), 22 kilometres south-east of Genk, Belgium, Fries' Gruppe were credited with five Lancasters and Halifaxes in all. Halifax LW298 on 158 Squadron, which crashed thirteen kilometres north-east of Tongeren, Belgium was piloted by Sergeant V. E. Horn and was one of twenty crews on 158 Squadron at Lissett bound for Düsseldorf. Sergeant Robert Coats Graham perished and was later buried in Heverlee War Cemetery. Two of the crew, including the skipper, evaded; four others were taken prisoner. The Gruppe's four other victories were awarded to Leutnant Wilhelm 'Willy' Henseler of 4./NJG1 (Halifax LK948 on 76 Squadron piloted by Flight Lieutenant Donald Elliott Hicks RCAF southeast of Rheydt with the loss of the skipper and four crew); Hauptmann Manfred Meurer of I./NJG1 (Halifax JD321 on 77 Squadron which crashed at Helvoort with the loss of Pilot Officer Robert John Jones and crew) and Oberfeldwebel Becker and Feldwebel Günther Bahr of I./NJG6 claimed a Lancaster at Düsseldorf and a Halifax 25 kilometres south of Düsseldorf respectively. Lancaster I W4822 on 57 Squadron, skippered by 25-year old 1st Lieutenant Donald R. West USAAF of Fresno, California was intercepted and shot down at 1936 hours by Oberleutnant Werner Baake of 3./NJG1 for his twentieth Abschüsse of the war, the aircraft crashing at Hechtel, Belgium. West had joined the RCAF on 27 August 1941 and later transferred to the USAAF who allowed the experienced Lancaster pilot to remain with his parent squadron. He and four of his crew were killed. In a letter to Floyd and Maybelle West, the pilot's parents, after returning to England, Jim Elliott the 22-year old air bomber, who evaded, said:

'Even on that terrible night, when we were under the maximum of strain with both gunners dead and Don at the controls of a burning plane, there was no panic because the skipper was calm. In his quiet tone he told two of the crew to go back with extinguishers and try to control the fire. Without hesitation or question they did so and worked heroically amid the smoke and exploding ammunition, but all in vain, using all of the extinguishers without controlling it. Then came the order from Don to abandon the aircraft. As bombardier and nearest the bomb hatch, I went first, so from then on my information ceased... Don had his parachute on, but knowing him as I did, I'm certain he would wait until everyone had left before moving. It grieves me to say it, but I'm afraid Don made the supreme sacrifice for our united cause that night. In a vain attempt to save the remainder of the crew (one other member was left) he hadn't left himself enough time to get out before the crash came.'

The navigator, Pilot Officer Norman Buggey, who had safely parachuted from the Lancaster but had been captured by the Germans, wrote after the war: 'The complete calm and self possession of Don West and his refusal to leave the controls while there was still remote possibility of saving some of the crew was superb. I am afraid his action cost him his life.' For his actions, Donald West was posthumously awarded the British Distinguished Flying Cross and the California Air Medal.

One of the Halifaxes that was lost on Düsseldorf was credited to Oberleutnant Dietrich Schmidt, Staffelkapitän, 8./NJG1, who was flying his seventieth operational sortie, for his seventh confirmed victory. Schmidt's graphic account reveals the chaotic conditions in which the Nachtjagd crews had to hunt for Bomber Command at this time:

'We took off from St. Trond for a 'Wild Boar' sortie. Utter confusion reigned. We had only just arrived and had to collect our flight documentation first. Willi Schlosser, bordschütze, accompanied me for the first time. We flew towards radio beacon 'Kurfurst'. Nothing was going on. On a silly hunch I flew to the south again. There was a bright moon in the southwest and a thin cloud layer at 5000 metres. Suddenly I saw four exhaust flames below to port. Then they were gone again. Then two of them drew away up ahead. We were right in the bomber stream! Then I saw a third - four-engined, twin fins - a Halifax - ahead and a little above. At the same time Schlosser saw one over to port. I closed in, fired into the fuselage and starboard wing, saw the shells hit and broke off! He burned very bright and white in the starboard wing. He returned fire and I heard a distinct 'click'. We'd caught one too! Schlosser was struck on the cheek but did not bleed. I fired at him again, scoring hits. Burning bits flew off and he entered the clouds to port. I fired again. More hits. No return fire. A brief bright glow and then we were in the clouds.

'I pulled up straight away. There was nothing to see above but below us there was a bright fire-glow. I went through the clouds again. There was one down below. Impact at 1936 hours. We must have been in the area Mönchengladbach-Aachen-Maastricht. It was 060° to the target (Düsseldorf). One hit in our machine went through a piece of equipment on the starboard wall. Willi Schlosser got a splinter in the earpiece of his helmet. A second hit in the tail unit, the skin near the landing light was damaged by wreckage. Confirmation of my eighth Abschuss was finally given by the Reichsluftfahrtministerium (RLM or Reich Air Ministry) in February 1945.'

On the night of 4/5 November the RAF carried out mining of the western Baltic, with a Mosquito 'spoof' towards the Ruhr. At 1819 hours German radar picked up fifty to sixty RAF aircraft between Cap Griz Nez and the Westerschelde River at 23,000 to 30,000 feet. Their further course was southeast into the southern Ruhr area. As their speed at first was only about 250mph they were taken to be '4-mots' but later, taking headwinds into consideration, the defences identified them as Mosquitoes. Several aircraft of 1 Jagddivision for 'Himmelbett' night fighting in the area of the western Ruhr were ordered to take off but the operation was abandoned after the approaching aircraft were identified as Mosquitoes. Meanwhile, at 1802-1840 hours, thirty to fifty aircraft at heights between 3,300 feet and 5,000 feet flying at 200 mph were picked up by German radar approaching the northern part of west Jutland. They were a force of 36 minelayers carrying out 'Gardening' operations at various places from Lorient to the Kattegat. 2 Jagddivision occupying two night fighter boxes in Jutland scrambled 10, 11 and 12./NJG3 to take on the heavies. They engaged sixteen bombers and shot down four Stirlings without loss. Oberleutnant Hans-Hermann

Müller of 11./NJG3 claimed Stirling III EE897 on 75 Squadron RNZAF at 1500 metres in the 'Silverstone' area at 2002 hours for his tenth confirmed claim.[154] Flying Officer Norman Wilson the 23-year old pilot and his seven crew were lost without trace and are commemorated on the Runnymede Memorial.

Leutnant Karl Rechberger of 12./NJG3 claimed his fifth Abschüsse, shooting down Stirling III BF461 on 75 Squadron RNZAF whose rear gunner, Sergeant Reggie Ingrey hit the attacking pilot in the thigh. The skipper, Pilot Officer G. K. Williams RNZAF and five of his crew bailed out before the Stirling crashed at Kallerup southwest of Thisted and were taken into captivity. Sergeant William James Champion was the only casualty. There was a degree of over claiming on the part of the Nachtjäger. Twenty-two year old Oberleutnant Hans-Hermann Müller of 10./NJG3 claimed two Stirlings (ending the war with total claims for eighteen Abschüsse), as did Oberleutnant Johannes 'Hans' Hiendmayr of 11./NJG3 who had scored three victories during September-October. (Hiendmayr was killed on 4/5 December when his Ju 88C-6 crashed northeast of Veddel near Hamburg after engine failure following combat with a Lancaster). Twenty-two year old Oberleutnant Werner Speidel also claimed a Stirling and a Wellington. He was killed on 31 January 1944, crashing at Epe near Hesepe. (His total score was ten Abschüsse). Oberleutnant Günther Rogge of 12./NJG3 flying a Bf 110 claimed a Halifax for the second of his eventual four Abschüsse.

On 8 November 100 Group (Special Duties, later Bomber Support) was created to consolidate the various squadrons and units using the secret ELINT and RCM in the war against the German night fighter air and defence system. In tandem with this electronic wizardry, 100 Group also accepted 'spoofing' as a large part of its offensive armoury and it also controlled squadrons of Mosquitoes engaged purely on 'Intruder' operations over Germany. It would need to hone and refine all of these techniques if it were to be of any value against the German night fighter defences. Early in November about fifty German night fighters were equipped with the improved SN-2 radar, which was relatively immune to 'Window' but only twelve night fighters and crews were operational, mainly because of the delay in training suitable operators to use the complicated and sensitive radar equipment.

Endnotes Chapter 13

146 *Duel Under The Stars* by Wilhelm Johnen.
147 *Intruders over Britain: The Luftwaffe Night Fighter Offensive 1940 to 1945* by Simon W. Parry (ARP 2003).
148 *'Enemy in the Dark, The story of Luftwaffe Night Fighter Pilot'* by Peter Spoden (Cerberus Publishing Limited).
149 Airborne Cigar (ABC) was a device consisting of six scanning re¬ceivers and three transmitters designed to cover the VHF band of the standard German R/T sets and to jam 30-33 MHz (Ottokar) and later 38-42 MHz (Benito. R/T and Beam).
150 On 25 June 1944 Braham and his navigator Flight Lieutenant D. C. Walsh DFC RAAF flew a 'Day Ranger' to Denmark and Braham scored his 29th and final victory. Braham had just completed an attack of a German Staff car on a road on Fyn Island when 2 FW 190s, one flown by Leutnant Robert Spreckels, attacked and set the Mosquito's port wing and engine on fire. Braham tried to crash-land on the shore of a fiord when he was attacked again but he managed to set it down and fortunately the aircraft did not explode. Walsh and Braham made a run for it and got behind sand dunes. Troops from a nearby radar station advanced towards them and opened fire with automatic weapons. Unhurt, Braham and Walsh were marched away into captivity.
151 *RAF Evaders* by Oliver Clutton-Brock (Grub St 2009).
152 Ypsilon, Y-Verfahren, Ypsilonverfahren: Luftwaffe ground-controlled navigation by means of VHF.
153 See *The Other Battle* by Peter Hinchliffe.
154 He survived the war with a total of 11 night-Abschüsse and a further five during day operations. It is understood that as at January 2014 he was still living in Germany. See Aircrew Remembered, Kracker Archive.

Chapter Fourteen

Once The Most Beautiful City In The World

In January 1944 the Battle of Berlin reached its peak. On 27 January the Met reported a cloud ceiling of 150 feet with solid cloud up to 13,000. From 3,000 feet there was danger of icing. 'You're not thinking of taking off in this are you sir? Even the Chief's left his bicycle at home and has come on foot.' We had to laugh as we climbed into the cockpit. I switched on all my instruments and gave them a thorough check-up. Facius fiddled with his apparatus and tuned in to the notorious Calais station. The sugary-sweet music was suddenly interrupted by the well known 'V for Victory and we heard the announcer say; 'Berlin, you were once the most beautiful city in the world. Berlin, look out for eleven o'clock tonight!' We were dumbfounded.

Duel Under The Stars **by Wilhelm Johnen**

From 18/19 November 1943 to 24/25 March 1944, Berlin was subjected to sixteen major raids, which have gone into history as the Battle of Berlin. During the 18/19 November raid, only nine out of 440 Lancaster were lost. An effective 'Tame Boar' operation was mounted against a second force of 395 aircraft simultaneously raiding Ludwigshafen-on-Rhine, a handful of crew shooting down the majority of the 23 aircraft that failed to return from this raid. Six crews of I./NJG6 destroyed eight Viermots, Hauptmann Franz Evers of the Gruppenstab claiming one Viermot (Lancaster DS784 on 115 Squadron) shot down at 2210 hours at Assesse. On Friday 19 November, RAF Headquarters reported: last night Bomber Command sent to Germany the largest contingent of heavy bombers ever deployed in a single night. It divided up into two formations which operated independently. One formation attacked Ludwigshafen, the other Berlin, which lay under a pall of cloud so that the damage could not be accurately observed. A stream of several hundred four-engined bombers reached the German capital along the Havel river (in eastern Germany) and then split into groups that bombed Siemensstadt, Neukolln, Mariendorf, Steglitz, Marienfelde and other districts of Berlin. Tens of thousands of incendiaries and 2- and 4-ton high-explosive bombs, dropped on Berlin within a period of barely thirty minutes. The reflection of huge fires lit up the clouds, revealing that severe damage must have occurred in the industrial districts.'

The Air Ministry added: 'More than 2,500 tons of bombs were dropped in the raids on Berlin and Ludwigshafen. Two important targets were raided simultaneously; simultaneous raiding is a new tactic of Bomber Command. Recently the German Luftwaffe has concentrated extremely strong formations of night fighters around probable target zones. Aerial reconnaissance informs Bomber Command of the positions of the German night fighters and Bomber Command then tries to strike at places where there is inadequate fighter protection. For example, last night the RAF deployed its formations simultaneously over two cities approximately 300 miles apart, so that the German night fighter defences found it impossible to adequately protect both targets. Naturally these new tactics require the deployment of formations that are as large as possible, because, despite everything, the German Luftwaffe remains a formidable enemy that is quite capable of warding off twin attacks of limited force.'

On the 19th, of 266 aircraft which were despatched to Leverkusen, just four Halifaxes and a Stirling were lost, as very few Nachtjagd fighters were operating, probably because of bad weather at their airfields. At Sint-Truiden/Sint-Trond Leutnant Otto Fries and Unteroffizier Alfred Staffa were one of the NJG5 crews that did get airborne. Fries had scored his first three victories during the chaotic months following the Hamburg disaster and had recently been appointed Technical Officer of II./NJG1.

'At briefing, the type of tactic to be used had been left open; should there be an attack, the fighter division wanted to leave the decision whether to use 'Himmelbett' or 'Zahme Sau' ('Tame Boar') to the last moment - the development of the weather conditions would also partly influence this decision. At briefing, the weather conditions did not look particularly good: heavy haze, complete darkness, the cloud ceiling was at 200 metres, the tops of cloud unknown. The weather wizard assumed, however, that the clouds would extend up to at least 4000 metres, probably with zones of icing. But during the night, a considerable improvement in the weather could be expected, at the Channel coast the cloud was already broken with the ceiling at about 1,000 metres.

'The approach of the bomber stream was reported shortly after briefing, but in the north, far outside of their operational sector, probably through that of the fourth Gruppe of our Geschwader which was stationed at Leeuwarden.

'Towards 1800 we went to cockpit readiness. At first we thought it was for the approach of another bomber stream, but then we were told by fighter division that it was for the return of the bombers which had flown in, in the north. We were always amazed that the British did not return the way we had come. The night fighter units who had borne the brunt of the approach were generally unable to combat the returning bombers in full strength. Some of the machines dropped out during the first attack and the returning aircraft had to be refuelled and possibly rearmed before we could be used again.

'We had taken off at 1816 in G9+EM, a machine borrowed from the 4th Staffel, with orders for a 'Himmelbett' hunt in area 6C. Meanwhile the weather had improved, the cloud ceiling was a little over 500 metres and their altimeter showed 1000 metres as we emerged from the murk. We had noticed no icing. Above a starry sky, completely free of cloud or haze.

'Ten minutes after take-off the radio operator had established contact with the operations room of 6A. We had been ordered to a height of 7000 metres and we had been wandering around on varying headings, guided by Würzburg Riese blue. I was on a course of 090 when the controller came on the air:

'Adler 98 from Feuerwerk ['Firework'] - Adler 98 from Feuerwerk - Kurier approaching - continue 80 - go to Kirchturm [Church Tower'] 50 - question Viktor.'

'Viktor-Viktor.' I pulled the throttles right back, turned propeller pitch to automatic and pushed the stick forward. The rate of descent indicator went to the bottom stop. I looked at the clock - it was 19.41. I raised my seat until my eyes and the reflector sight were on one level, switched on the sight's light and adjusted its intensity. Then I turned over the gun switch; I was always surprised at the noise the repeating mechanisms of the guns made. The red indicators glowed: all guns cocked!

'Adler 98 from Feuerwerk - make Salto Lisa to 270 - go Express to Kirchturm 40 - question Viktor.'

'Viktor-Viktor - 270 and 40.'

'The altimeter showed 5500 metres and as I turned off the autopilot, all I had to do was to slide my left hand down the control column. I flung the machine in a steep turn to port until the compass approached a course of 270. As I levelled out, the altimeter showed the required height - the machine had slid down over its left wing. I was very fast and could feel the vibration of the wings, so I opened the throttles only very slowly. I switched the autopilot back on, for now it was important to follow the instructions of the controller very precisely until either my radio operator had the enemy aircraft on his radar or I could see it myself.

'Adler 98 from Feuerwerk - make twice Rolf.'

'Viktor - twice Rolf.'

'I applied aileron and turned the course indicator on the stick until the pointer on the compass indicated 290. 'What does your magic lamp say, Fred, no blips yet?'

'None.'

'Adler 98 from Feuerwerk - make three times Lisa.'

'Viktor - three times Lisa? I turned 30 degrees to port.

'I have a blip on the screen; distance 2000 metres, slightly left, higher.' 'Feuerwerk from Adler 98 - contact with Emil-Emil!'

'Viktor - contact - good hunting - out.'

'I eased the aircraft up and turned off the autopilot. I did not require it any more for now my bordfunker would guide me with the Lichtenstein radar set - it was really amazing that it was not getting any interference. A little higher, distance 1,200, closing fast.' I took off a little power. 'Higher, port a little, distance 500 - you are much too fast!' I pulled the throttles back to idling. I searched the horizon. 'Where is he exactly - what distance?'

'Slightly left, slightly higher - 300 metres.'

'There he is! A Short Stirling - on the port bow and just above the horizon!' I saw the tall rudder, the squat fuselage; the wings narrow like the back of a knife and on each side two engines with faintly glowing exhausts. I was much too fast for a sensible attempt. Although I had spontaneously attacked when much too fast the last time - and it had worked. But one could not be so lucky every time! And especially with the Short Stirling I had to be particularly careful. I remembered only too well my first meeting with this type of bomber. I had, without matching his speed, spontaneously attacked when much too fast - and it had all gone wrong! On no account should it be so tonight! I slunk off to the right and kicked alternately the rudder pedals without using aileron. Although it was unpleasant being pushed sideward right and left, it was an old proven method to 'tail away' speed.

'There, suddenly, the bomber dived away to starboard! He must have realized that a night fighter was clinging to his tail. There had been rumours that the British bombers had an acoustic warning device installed which sounded an alarm on being approached from the rear but there was no real knowledge about it. As the Stirling dived away it went right through his sights. I could not resist and spontaneously pressed the trigger - it was like some reflex action. Only a short burst though. I had a feeling of having hit the bomber, but it showed no effect.

'Fred, note the time! It's 1953.'

'I dived in order to keep the bomber above me, so I could keep the Stirling in sight against the lighter sky. 'Feuerwerk from Adler 98 - have made Pauke-Pauke - Kurier shows no effect - keeping contact.'

'Viktor-Viktor - Weidmannsheil!'

'The Stirling twisted like mad, down and up, did what they called a 'corkscrew'. I followed the corkscrew, but less violently. 'He'll soon have a bellyful of his twisting and turning! What do you think; will the pilot now hear from his crew - especially from the rear gunner!' We called that man in the rear turret with his quadruple machine guns 'sniper' or 'tail-end Charlie' and we treated him with respect.

'Some minutes had passed since the first attack; the Stirling gradually ceased its twisting about and resumed its steady flight. We surely thought to have shaken him off. I was under the bomber to starboard, about 200 metres below and slightly behind. Slowly I rose, very slowly. When I was to starboard of the bomber, at almost the same height and about seventy metres behind, I kicked into the rudder and slunk to port. I gave a burst of fire as the starboard wing passed through my sights and then a second into the port one. Then I peeled off to port to get out of the rear gunner's arc of fire. The tracers flashed past my stern like maddened glow worms - like a fiery fan!

'I saw a faint glow in the Stirling's port wing, which suddenly spread like an explosion and then encompassed the fuselage. Single parts detached themselves and flew off - were they crew members who had jumped? I could not be sure. Within seconds the whole bomber was aflame - it reared up, fell over on its port wing and then plunged down like a stone streaming flames like the tail of a comet. The flames disappeared in the clouds, which moments later were lit by a red flash, to be followed by a steady red glow. The clock showed 19.59. 'Feuerwerk from Adler 98 - report Sieg-Heil - note position - over!'

'Adler 98 from Feuerwerk - Viktor-Viktor - position noted - congratulations!'
'Thank you!'[155]

A teleprinter message received by II./NJGl at Sint-Truiden/Sint-Trond the following day revealed that Leutnant Fries' fourth Abschuss had crashed near Horrues, 35 kilometres south-west of Brussels. The markings on the fuselage were still clear, reading JN-F and it was identified as Stirling III LJ442 JN-F on 75 Squadron RNZAF which Flight Sergeant N. N. Parker RAAF had taken off from Mepal, north of Cambridge at 1701. Four crew members were found dead at the crash site: Sergeant Michael Irvine Ryder Day, rear gunner, whose name was found on an envelope, Sergeant Stanley 'Tuffy' Watkins, flight engineer, who was identified by his clothing card and two others (later identified as Pilot Officer William Robert 'Bill' Kell RNZAF, WOp and Sergeant William 'Jack' Gilfillan, mid-upper gunner. The crew's bomb-aimer, Sergeant Jack Hyde RNZAF - an Australian by birth - had bailed out only moments before the aircraft exploded in mid-air. He landed heavily, fracturing his pelvis and spitting out two teeth and losing one of his eyelids. He was taken to the Luftwaffe hospital in Brussels-Sint Gilles. Flight Sergeant Parker the experienced Australian captain and his navigator, Sergeant Robert E. Griffith evaded capture after bailing out of their crashing aircraft and reached England early the following year. Four crew were killed and one was taken prisoner. Parker received a commission, subsequently volunteered for the Pathfinder Force and survived another fifty operations, acting on some as Master Bomber.[156]

On the night of Monday 22nd/Tuesday 23rd November when 764 bombers raided Berlin, Nachtjagd largely remained grounded due to adverse weather conditions. Only an estimated four out of the twenty-six bombers that failed to return were claimed by night-fighters. The first Path Finders arrived over the 'Big City' just before 2000 to find the city covered by ten-tenths cloud. The forecast had been for clear conditions over the home airfields, broken to medium-level cloud over Berlin and low cloud or fog over much of the rest of Germany. Three of the five Lancasters equipped with the new 3cm H_2S Mk.III sets had to turn back after their equipment failed but the two blind markers accurately dropped four red TIs at the AP, slightly to the east of the centre of the capital. Fifteen year old Gerda Kernchen who lived with her parents in a cottage in the Kleingarten (small garden) area called Wittenau on the northwest edge of the capital recalled, 'When the final alarm sounded, you could already see 'the Christmas trees,' the coloured flares being dropped by the Pathfinders to mark the target for the bombers. You could see the searchlights streaming up from the ground, searching for the aircraft.

The city was surrounded by a ring of white light.'

More than 2,000 tons of blast bombs and approximately 150,000 incendiaries were dropped on Berlin in barely 35 minutes. Air crews reported large fires spreading through the city and that they lit the sky a fiery red. Approximately twenty minutes after the first bomb was released, there was a gigantic explosion whose effects were clearly visible from an altitude of over 21,000 feet. Hundreds of air crews confirmed that they had never seen such a severe explosion or felt such a shock wave, on any previous operation. The explosion was the huge Neuköln gasworks blowing up. A vast area of destruction stretched across the capital caused mainly by firestorms as a result of the dry weather conditions. At least 3,000 houses and 23 industrial premises were completely destroyed with thousands of other buildings damaged. It was estimated that 175,000 people were bombed out. An estimated 2,000 people were killed.[157]

Gerda Kernchen remembered the raid so well because it was the first time she saw a dead body. 'We were in our cellar and we heard a tremendous crash and the whole house shook. The biggest bomb, called an air mine, or blockbuster, had landed in our neighbourhood. The earth was soft peat, so most of the houses just moved on their foundations, but the houses closer to the blast were destroyed. When we left our cellar, we went to see where the bomb had landed. Then we saw one of the neighbours. He was dead. It was a really frightening sight, because the percussion had mutilated him and his eyes were hanging out of his head. It was one of those images I will never forget. Everyone was so shocked and horrified by the first big raid, because we had been assured that Berlin was safe. My mother said: 'We must keep our faith in Herr Hitler. He will protect us!' My father, who was a first war veteran and had refused to join the Nazi Party, never said a word. I suspect that he knew that things were not going well. From then on, everyone was too frightened to stay at home and we headed to the neighbourhood bunker when the alarm sounded. The bunker had been built earlier in 1943 and it was just two blocks away. Our bunker could accommodate two hundred people. It contained a honeycomb of small rooms, each with a pair of bunk beds and two benches for sitting. There were also full kitchens and bathrooms. As the raids continued, some people lived there full-time because they had no homes. The maximum length of a raid was two hours. After it was over, people would go back to sleep. In the morning, I would go off to work although I never knew whether my factory where I sewed uniforms for the Luftwaffe would still be standing.'[158]

On the night of the 23rd/24th 383 bombers again made the long haul to the 'Big City'. A handful of experienced Nachtjäger braved the elements, twelve 'Tame Boar' crews shooting down thirteen of the twenty bombers that were lost. One of these was Lancaster III JA865 on 166 Squadron captained by Warrant Officer E. F. Grove which had taken off from Kirmington at 1702 hours. It is thought probable that this Lancaster was shot down forty kilometres west of Berlin at 6000 metres by Leutnant Peter Spoden who had recently joined 5./NJG5 after a long period of convalescence despite the surgeons' opinion that he would never walk again. He was still very angry at being shot down and wounded over Berlin on 23 August and was ashamed to say that he aimed not for the normal point of the wings, but into the fuselage. Spoden fired a long burst with his forward firing weapons, the salvo resulting in an explosion sending countless chunks of burning debris and wreckage down to earth.[159]

Sergeant Alan C. Smith the navigator recalled: As we were approaching Berlin the plane was hit by two bursts of flak; the first of which came between my legs which were apart due to the fact that I had my parachute on the floor between my feet because the wireless operator [Sergeant S. G. Patterson] had put his rations bag in my parachute stowage container. As I bent down to look under the navigation table, the second burst of flak came and the blast caught me in the eyes, face, under the chin and on the back of the left hand, resulting in superfluous cordite burns and cuts. The intercom and hydraulic systems were rendered u/s so therefore the bomb doors could not be opened or the bombs released. The two port engines were on fire and the Incendiary bombs were ignited. I was ordered to bail out three times by the flight engineer on the instructions of the pilot, but I had seen that the wireless operator was in a state of shock and as he wasn't wearing his parachute harness I stayed behind to fit it on him which was a bit of a struggle as his legs were rigid and I had to force them apart to get the harness straps to the front. Meanwhile the plane had lost height from 21,500 feet to 13,000 feet and kept veering and tipping over to port trying to go into a spin. By this time the W/Op had come round so I gave him his parachute to put on and I went to the pilot who had now put the plane on automatic pilot. I wanted to open the bomb doors manually and for him to put the plane in a dive to try and extinguish the flames, but he said there wasn't time and told me bail out and stop arguing otherwise we would all get killed. I then said I would go down the aircraft and see if the mid-upper gunner [Sergeant John Davies] and rear gunner [Sergeant James Iverson] were out and I would then bail out of the rear exit, but he ordered me to get out the front exit and said that he was going out the rear exit and he would see if they had gone on his way down. (Later when I saw him in Berlin he told me he couldn't get down the aircraft because of the flames, so he had helped the W/Op to clip his chute on and they bailed out of the front exit. The two gunners were never seen again).

During this period my parachute which had caught some of the flak and flames from the incendiary bombs was smouldering a little, so that when I jumped, quite a bit of the chute was burnt and torn, so I dropped faster than normal and made a very heavy landing, which resulted in a severe pain from the right ankle, along the leg to the small of my back. Next day when I had been captured, a German officer asked me if I was wounded as he could see I was having trouble walking. Thinking I would be sent to hospital and have to face the wrath of the civilians of which we had previously been warned about in England, I told him that I had just bruised my leg.'[160]

Next day RAF Headquarters announced: 'Last night Berlin was again the target of a grand assault by the RAF. This time the attack concentrated mainly on the western part of the capital with its three large rail installations: Westend, Bahnhof Zoo and Bahnhof Charlottenburg. The night was clear and there were only a few clouds to hinder visibility, so that operational conditions were far more favourable to the German air defence than on the previous night. From a distance of thirty miles the British air crews could see the fires that have continued to smoulder since Monday. Finally in the fire-glow over Berlin they were able to observe many details of the destroyed city districts. The whole complex around the Wilhelmstrasse, the Brandenburg Gate area and the Tauentzienstrasse, Potsdam Square, the Anhalter Strasse and many other building-lined streets have been completely destroyed. On Tuesday night leading into Wednesday, the western part of Berlin suffered more than in all the previous raids. On Wednesday afternoon, Mosquitoes flew over the capital and reported having observed well over 200 giant conflagrations.'

Reich Minister of Propaganda Doktor Joseph Goebbels noted in his diary on Wednesday 24th November: 'Early in the morning I am already at work. Straightaway Schaub gives me a report on the situation in Berlin, which is very sad. It is inexplicable how the British were able to destroy so much of the capital in one air raid. The Wilhelmsplatz is truly the picture of desolation. It is still blazing from end to end. The Propaganda Ministry has mainly been spared... Now and then I am able to snatch half an hour's sleep; but then I am called back to work. Large formations of British aircraft are again set on an obstinate course for Berlin... The raid begins shortly after the alarm siren. This time there are more blast bombs than incendiaries. Once again it is a first-class grand assault... Mines and explosive bombs hail down incessantly on the government district. One after another the most important buildings start to burn. After the raid when I take a look at the Wilhelmsplatz, I find that the ghastly impression of the previous evening has grown even worse. I pass on into the Propaganda Ministry. The offices are burning in two places on the side of the Wilhelmsplatz.' At noon, a spokesman for the German Armed Forces High Command (the Wehrmacht) stated to representatives of the foreign press concerning the raid on Berlin: 'These terrorist raids on German cities have expanded to such an extent that regrettably we are forced to deploy our retaliatory weapon.' However, when questioned by journalists, the spokesman expressed no details about the method or date of German retaliatory measures.

Privately, Goebbels for one knew that the writing was on the wall. On Thursday 25th November he wrote in his diary: 'Now we are gradually learning again to get used to a primitive pattern of life. Mornings in the Göringstrasse there is no heat, no light, no water. One can neither shave nor wash. One has to leave the bunker with a burning candle. At the crack of dawn I get up with the worst headache of my life. I am plagued with headaches non-stop. But what does that matter; it's time to get to work. I drive straight to the office where I can shave and wash... Most of the Kaiserdamm is still burning; but the fire department hopes to get the fires under control in the course of the night. Isolated clumps of people flit over the streets making a genuinely ghostly impression. Your heart is wrenched when you drive through areas like this. How beautiful Berlin was once and how wretched and dilapidated it looks now.'

RAF Headquarters was more clinical. It announced: 'Although Berlin has already been bombed more heavily than Hamburg, the damage is comparatively less because the built-up area of Berlin is substantially larger. It would take approximately 50,000 to 60,000 tons of bombs to destroy the German capital to the same extent as Hamburg.'

On the night of Thursday 25th/Friday 26th November, 262 Halifaxes and Lancasters attacked Frankfurt, for the loss of twelve of their number. At least six Halifaxes were destroyed by as many crews of NJG3, NJG4, NJG5 and NJG6. Hauptmann Leopold 'Poldi' Fellerer of 5./NJG5 claimed two Lancasters to take his score to sixteen. Leutnant Heinz Rolland of 12./NJG1 claimed a 'Lanki' and a Stirling minelayer to take his score to seven Abschüsse. Stirling III EF202 on 149 Squadron was shot down at Ste-Etienne-de-Montluc. Sergeant K. C. Richardson and four of his crew evaded capture. Two others were taken prisoner. Major Wilhelm Herget Staffelkapitän NJG4 shot down the Halifax on 35 Squadron captained by Pilot Officer Desmond Lander four kilometres east of St. Vith for his 33rd Abschüsse. Lander and five of his crew survived and were taken prisoner. Hauptmann Eckart-Wilhelm 'Hugo' von Bonin, Gruppenkommandeur 6./NJG1 claimed three Viermots to take his score to 26. One of these was Halifax V LK946 on 76 Squadron at Holme-on-Spalding Moor in the direction of Stuttgart, which crashed at 1930 hours in Malborn. Eighteen-year-old Canadian Evan James Berndt, one of the youngest Canadian airmen who fell in 1943 is buried at the Cologne Southern Cemetery. The others on Flying Officer N. W. Mann's crew were taken prisoner. One of the other of von Bonin's victims that night was the Lancaster on 97 Squadron skippered by Flight Lieutenant Carlos Brown CdG RCAF, an American; all of whom were killed.

Oberleutnant Hans-Heinz Augenstein of 9./NJG1 claimed his sixteenth victory, shooting down Halifax V LK995 on 429 'Bison' Squadron RCAF, piloted by Warrant Officer2 David Smith DFM at Frankfurt-am-Eder. Smith was to recall: 'After setting course, I checked D/R compass with Pip and found a difference of several degrees from the navigator's figures and we had some difficulty in getting it settled. On crossing the French coast we were port of track and the navigator suggested greater alteration to starboard. When I saw other aircraft crossing in front I resumed course. In fifteen minutes we were port of track again when we were attacked. I had every confidence in Flying Officer Thurmeier as a navigator and believe that the P.4 compass was unserviceable. We were attacked with only a pip or so from 'Monica' just before being hit. The rear gunner saw and I believe fired in exchange to two bursts from the fighter which severed all controls and set incendiaries afire in centre and port bays. I gave the order to prepare to abandon, when attempts to jettison failed (circuit cut) and then almost immediately I ordered to abandon the aircraft, to which only the navigator was heard to acknowledge as intercom faded out. I had made an attempt to hold the aircraft straight and level while the others got out but the controls were dead and useless. There seemed to be some delay as others were waiting to leave. Since I had on a seat type chute, I stood up in the seat and had the fantastic idea of sliding down the fuselage. Of course I was gone immediately I felt the slipstream. There was only one crew member that I could see and about to leave the aircraft (Warrant Officer2 Douglas Nelson, the air bomber who was last to leave the aircraft) when I had left. There was no word from the rear gunner and call light received no reply. I found my chute split in several places and almost severed when I attempted to stop turning. I landed safely but sprained my ankle and wrenched my back.'

Smith and Sergeant J. A. Renton RAFVR, the flight engineer, were captured and sent to PoW camps. Flight Sergeant Robert Davis, the 21-year old Canadian rear gunner, was the only fatality. Flying Officer Jacob John Thurmeier, the 27-year old navigator, successfully evaded. Flight Sergeant Randolph 'Randy' Thadius Abbott, the 26-year old West Indian wireless operator, and Flying Officer Manuel Rabinovitch, the mid-upper gunner, went on the run. Abbott was hidden in a cellar in Brussels by the Resistance but was captured and taken to the notorious St. Gilles prison and he and Manuel Rabinovitch, who was arrested in Brussels on 10 February 1944, were later transported to PoW camps in the Reich. Doug Nelson had been held by the ankle when the trap door in the aircraft fell down and he hung underneath the bomber until it disintegrated and let him fall. Because of this delay in getting out he landed in France, where, helped by the French Resistance and dressed as a civilian he reached Paris. It was all to no avail however. He and his rescuers were betrayed and picked up by the SS and Nelson was treated as a spy. After a period of incarceration and torture, Nelson was finally released into the hands of the Luftwaffe and taken into captivity for the remainder of the war.

Other Nachtjagd claimants included 21-year old Leutnant Guido Krupinski of 11./NJG1 who claimed a Halifax for his first victory. Krupinski was killed in a crash in his Bf 110 on 25/26 February 1944 at Maldeghem after running out of fuel. Oberleutnant Gustav Tham of 11./NJG5 claimed a Viermot at Frankfurt-am-Main for his sixth victory. Feldwebel Johann 'Hans' Kissel of 7./NJG5 claimed a '4-mot' west of the city for his first and only Abschuss. Kissel was killed when his Bf 110F-4 (4686) was shot down by return fire from the doomed Halifax. Oberleutnant (later Hauptmann) Fritz Brinkman of Stab I/NJG3 and Unteroffizier Robert Krohn of 5./NJG6 claimed their first Abschüsse. Krohn was killed in action on 29 January 1944 during combat with US fighters near Cochem. Leutnant Wilhelm Henseler claimed his fourth Abschüsse when he shot down a Halifax northeast of St. Vith.

By now Doktor Goebbels in Berlin was inconsolable. 'Your heart is wrenched when you see all that has fallen victim to the air raids… At last I have got the Führer to allow us two types of air raid siren, at least for Berlin: that is one genuine alarm siren to signal that bomber formations are approaching the city and a mere warning siren to warn of isolated offensive aircraft. This is essential because I cannot throw a city of four and a half million people into a violent turmoil every evening for the sake of two Mosquitoes. So far the Führer has given permission for these two distinct types of air siren only in

Berlin; but I hope that they can soon be transferred to other districts as well. Also, in future the radio transmitters will no longer be turned off when individual offensive aircraft fly in.'

A raid by 450 bombers on Berlin and 178 on Stuttgart on the night of Friday 26th/Saturday 27th November was met by a combined operation of target area and 'Himmelbett' night-fighting under difficult weather conditions, which resulted in only the best German crews being ordered to take off. Even so, 84 fighters engaged the RAF formations. 1 Jagddivision shot down most of the 28 Main Force bombers that failed to return while from the smaller force six aircraft were lost. Major Wilhelm Herget claimed three Viermots to take his score to 36 Abschüsse. Just two German night fighter aircraft were lost. Oberleutnant Eckart-Wilhelm 'Hugo' von Bonin claimed a Lancaster and a Halifax to take his score to 29. Oberleutnant Albert Walter of I./NJG6 claimed a Halifax one kilometre north of Winkel to take his score to four victories. Walter went on to claim a total of ten night-Abschüsse before he was killed on the 24/25 February 1944 near Egenhausen/Calw, almost certainly by return fire from Halifax LW427 on 420 'Snowy Owl' Squadron, which was also his last kill.

Leutnant Wilhelm Engel of 1./NJG6 claimed a Halifax at Burg Grafenrode to take his score to eight victories. Leutnant Josef Kraft of 6./NJG5 destroyed a 'Lanki' at Berlin for his sixth victory. Oberleutnant Dieter Schmidt claimed a Lancaster at Emlichheim for his eighth Abschüsse. Oberleutnant Hans-Joachim Witzleb of III./NJG1 claimed a Lancaster for his second victory. Unteroffizier Heinz Amsberg of 9./NJG1 claimed a Lancaster for his third victory. (He and his bordfunker were killed in action on the night of 7/8 February 1945, when their Bf 110G-4 was shot down by a Mosquito).

That Saturday the German News Bureau reported: 'Yesterday evening the British made another terrorist raid on the German capital. Partly for reasons of weather, partly to mislead the German air defence, they chose to make a detour across south-western Germany. German night fighter aircraft fought the enemy along his lengthy run-in route and involved him in heavy aerial combats especially in the Berlin area, with support from German flak guns. Reports received so far indicate that 15 bombers were observed to go down before this new raid began. We are still receiving reports of further shoot-downs.'

Reich Minister of Propaganda Dr. Joseph Goebbel's only concerns were the destruction in Berlin: 'I travelled through the damaged areas with Naumann and Schaub. We also stopped at several ration distribution stations... The misery one sees is indescribable. It breaks one's heart to see it; but all the same we must clench our teeth [and bear it]. Sometimes one has the impression that the mood of people in Berlin is almost religious. Women walk over to me and make signs of blessing and pray God to keep me safe. All this is very moving... The food [being distributed to the people] is praised everywhere as excellent... You can wrap these people around your little finger with small tokens of kindness. I can hardly believe that this city led a revolt in 1918. Under my leadership that would never have happened... Another grand assault comes due on the city. This time it is not the turn of the city centre so much as of the Wedding and Reinickendorf districts; the main target in Reinickendorf is the big industrial munitions plant... Back to the bunker in the Wilhelmsplatz. The situation has taken a more threatening turn as one industrial plant after another has gone up in flames. The sky arches over Berlin with a blood-red eerie beauty. I can no longer stand to look at it.'

He wrote in his diary on Monday 29 November: 'I went to Reinickendorf and especially to Wedding [in Berlin]. I took part in a public meal at the Gartenplatz. Male and female workers here received me with an enthusiasm that was as incredible as it was indescribable. Once that was the Reddest [most Communist] part of Wedding, around the Ackerstrasse. I would never have believed it possible for such a change in attitude to take place.

'The people made me eat with them. I was lifted onto a box to speak to them. I gave a very passionate and unrestrained talk that spoke to the hearts of the workers. Everyone addressed me in the familiar and called me by my first name. The people wanted to carry me across the square and I managed only with difficulty to prevent them. Women embraced me. I was forced to give out autographs. Cigarettes were handed out; we smoked one together. In short, everything was as jolly as an amusement park.

'Naturally the destruction is enormous. But as far as the public themselves are concerned, they are taking it in good humour... In an extended discussion with Dr. Ley [Robert Ley, head of the German Labour Front and one of Hitler's inner-circle] I considered how we can get the workers to go back to the factories; because for the most part they have not returned there... Tobacco is now the most approved luxury; a Berliner will stand on his head for a cigarette.'

Predominantly crack night fighter crews again were sent to intercept the bombers on 16/17 December when RAF Bomber Command made yet another night attack on Berlin. They were met with a combination of 'Zahme Sau', 'Objektnachtjagd' (Target Area night fighting) and (in the Schleswig-Holstein and Jutland areas) 'Himmelbett' night fighting tactics. German radar began picking up J beams from 1800 hours and the assembly of the RAF formations, their leaving England and approach, were all plotted correctly by H_2S bearings. Mosquito 'spoof' attacks on Kassel and Hannover were clearly recognized as such. Large scale jamming of German radio and radar was carried out.

First Jagdkorps VHF was jammed by bell sounds, HF was jammed by quotations from Hitler's speeches and R/T traffic was rendered almost impossible. First Jagdkorps alternate frequency and Division frequencies also were strongly jammed and there was a very sudden jamming of the Soldatenrundfunksender (Forces Broadcasting Station) 'Anne Marie' by continuous sound from a strong British jamming station. Widespread mist and fog at 150-300 feet in the North German plains reduced the overall effectiveness of the fighter defence and 23 aircraft, mostly Bf 110s, had to abandon their sorties prematurely. The thirty night fighters engaged in Target Area Night Fighting, 28 for 'Zahme Sau' and 34 for 'Himmelbett' (over Jutland) shot down twenty bombers. 'Wilde Sau' night fighters and flak brought down another five. Heinz-Wolfgang Schnaufer, Staffelkapitän, 12./NJG1 shot down four Lancasters during a classic 'Himmelbett' sortie over Friesland Province to take his total to forty victories. Only three German aircraft were lost.

After a certain initial success 'Objektnachtjagd' proved to have weaknesses easily exploitable by Bomber Command. It was not until the twin engined night-fighters were used for route interception that the Luftwaffe could begin to inflict heavy losses again. This technique was subsequently improved to such an extent that deep raids into Germany could only be carried out at a heavy price in bombers. However, Bomber Command's new tactics of multiple raids and shallow raids on invasion targets in France combined to offset the development of route interception.

Despite atrocious winter weather Nachtjagd claimed 169 victories during the final month of 1943 against 28 lost, 23 of which were written off I Jagdkorps' strength. I./NJG1 claimed four aircraft destroyed, including a Mosquito by Hauptmann Manfred Meurer flying a He 219A-0 Uhu ('Owl') on the 12/13th. DZ354/D on 105 Squadron crewed by Flying Officer Benjamin Frank Reynolds and Flying Officer John Douglas Phillips crashed near Herwijnen in Holland on the North bank of the Waal River. Both were later buried in the Herwijnen General Cemetery.

During the 20/21 December raid on Frankfurt by 650 aircraft Hauptmann Major Wilhelm Herget, Gruppenkommandeur of I./NJG4 at Florennes claimed no less than eight Viermots. The little Kadi's first was a Halifax at Münstermaifeld at 1927 hours. Five minutes later he claimed another Halifax at Wiesenheim. A third Halifax followed at Florsheim just two minutes later. Then at 1943 hours he claimed a Viermot twelve kilometres west-southwest of Frankfurt. Four minutes later he claimed a Lancaster northeast of Hanau. At 1957 he claimed a Halifax at Hanau. Then at 2000 hours he shot down a second Lancaster at Rossdorf. Finally, a third Lancaster followed fifteen minutes later west of Schwalbach. Fifty-eight of the 73 victories Herget gained were at night with his bordfunker, Hans Liebherr, who was awarded the Knight's Cross.

I./NJG6 destroyed ten Lancasters and Halifaxes. They included triple victories by Feldwebel Günther Bahr (three Halifaxes between 1924 and 2000 hours, two of which were possibly Halifaxes on 10 Squadron) and Oberleutnant Martin 'Tino' Becker. Becker was born on 12 April 1916 at Wiesbaden in Hesse. His service with the Luftwaffe began in 1940, flying with an unknown reconnaissance unit. He flew 27 reconnaissance sorties. In early 1943 Becker transferred to the Nachtjagd, to 11./NJG4 (which on 1 August became 2./NJG6). At Bodenrode/Bad Nauheim, Becker shot down Lancaster III DV234 VN-M on 50 Squadron piloted by Wing Commander Edward Pullen, who was killed along with three of his crew; Halifax V LK644 on 427 'Lion' Squadron RCAF, flown by Flying Officer John Melrose Grieve RCAF, which was lost with all the crew at Weilmünster/Hessen and a unidentified Halifax at Ellar/ Hintermeilingen. Becker destroyed them all in just six minutes between 1950 and 1955 hours.

II./NJG1 was credited with three Halifax kills. Two of these, LK928 on 428 'Ghost' Squadron RCAF whose skipper, Flight Sergeant J. L. Keighan RCAF was the only survivor and LK732 on 76 Squadron piloted by 22-year old Flight Sergeant William Douglas Vernon Cable who, with two others, were killed; three surviving to be taken prisoner, were shot down by Gruppenkommandeur Oberleutnant Eckart-Wilhelm 'Hugo' von Bonin. By the end of 1943 von Bonin's victories had increased to 31 Abschüsse. He is credited with shooting down 37 enemy aircraft claimed during 150 combat sorties. Almost all of these victories he achieved with his bordshütze Feldwebel Johrden. His father, Luftwaffe Oberst Bogislaw von Bonin, was taken prisoner of war in March 1945 and declared missing. His brother, Jürgen-Oskar von Bonin was killed in action as an observer in Jagdgeschwader 52 in Russia. Another brother, Oberstleutnant Hubertus von Bonin (Knight's Cross recipient) was killed in action on 15 December 1943.

In December II./NJG1 was credited with four victories. III./NJG11 claimed four victories on the night of 16/17 December and a Lancaster over Frankfurt by Oberleutnant Hans-Heinz Augenstein on the 23/24th. Feldwebel Karl-Georg Pfeiffer of 12./NJG1 who, flying from Bergen on 4 December 1943 shot down Stirling III LK387 on 623 Squadron into the Waddensea at 0303 hours for his ninth confirmed victory. Pilot Officer Neville John Veech RAAF and his crew were killed. On 16 December Pfeiffer had to make a belly landing at Bergen with engine trouble:

'One shook wildly and would take more petrol. I therefore did not dare to risk landing on my wheels and put the machine down on its belly beside the runway. They were not very happy about this at Leeuwarden and hinted that this had not been necessary, although there was a regulation about a situation such as this. I was annoyed about this but my life was more valuable to me.

'Our next sortie, on Christmas Eve, was criminal. We had hoped that the British would leave us alone. The worst of it was that on this night [23/24 December] only the northwest corner of Holland remained free of fog. All the airfields, even those in the Reich were already closed at mid-day. Against our wishes, the British had sent out several hundred bombers. They flew far to the south along the French west coast to bomb targets in southern Germany (Munich, as it transpired later) (sic). From Bergen or Leeuwarden the fuel was just sufficient to fly there and back, without time to fight over the target. We had just reached the area around Stuttgart, when we heard that Munich had already been hit (sic).[161] There was no point in trying to get the returning aircraft because we were in cloud at whatever height we flew. We headed for the radio beacon Rhein-Main and from there to Bonn-Hangelar. That was as far as the fuel would last. I had already shut down one engine to save fuel. The cloud base was reported to be 120 metres but it was not enough because of the Siebengebirge where many crews had struck the ground in bad weather and exploded. I said so to Willi and had him enquire what the visibility was at St. Trond. 'Cloud base 80 metres and very hazy!' In spite of this I decided on St. Trond because it is flat and I knew the field very well. I flew on using the minimum of fuel and could see the place from afar. All the field's searchlights had been set vertically, brightly illuminating the cloud tops above. At least we knew where the field was but going down into this bright murk I could hardly make out my wing tips. But all went well. Bathed in sweat and with our last drops of fuel we touched down heavily on the runway after a confused blind-landing procedure and were safe. When the dawn broke the fog had become thicker and they would not let us go. But Willi wanted to get engaged to his girl friend and he kept urging me so hard until midday that I decided on a blind take-off on my own responsibility. All went well and as we got closer to Bergen the clouds broke up and we landed in bright sunshine. The following party with the happy couple was one of the highlights of our flying life.'

On 23/24 December Flying Officer Howard Charles Kelsey and Sergeant E. M. Smith on 141 Squadron in Beaufighter VIF V8744 1943 scored the first kill in 100 Group when they claimed a Ju 88 near Düren. Their victim was actually Bf 110G-4 740139 of 4/NJG1[162] piloted by Oberleutnant Lenz Finster, who had ten victories. He was killed, his funker was wounded and his bordshütze bailed out safely. It was Kelsey and Smith's fourth victory on Beaufighters. They had destroyed a Bf 110 at Rijssen on 22/23 June and on the 25/26th they shot down Bf 110G-4 5319 of 12/NJG2 at Hardenburgh. Leutnant Robert Denzel was killed and his bordfunker was wounded when they crashed northeast of Vollenhove. Kelsey and Smith destroyed a Ju 88 at Étampes on 16/17 August when they were also awarded a Bf 110 'probable' and a Ju 88 'damaged'. Flying Mosquito NF.IIs the two men destroyed a further four enemy aircraft in the air and four on the ground, including the final victory in 100 Group, on 24/25 April 1945.

Leutnant Otto Fries, Unteroffizier Fred Staffa and their gunner Unteroffizier Konrad Deubzer were again on readiness at St. Trond on 29/30 December when Bomber Command attacked Berlin with 709 heavies and three Mosquitoes:

'During briefing for the mission, the codeword 'Temporary Crow' was given. This meant that due to adverse weather conditions we should not expect an order to take off for the time being. In case of an expected improvement of the weather at a later stage the codeword 'Pheasant' might be given to order us to take off on the mission. On the other hand, in the case of lasting bad weather over the 'drome or even further deteriorating weather conditions, the codeword 'Definitive Crow' might be issued to announce the end of our state of immediate readiness.

'By 1700 hours the first enemy aircraft were reported flying in. This was far off to the north in the operational area of the Fourth Gruppe, but these comrades were not able to take off either due to the bad weather. Thus, the whole Geschwader had to sit and wait at their bases for the bombers coming back in some three or four hours, silently hoping that by that time the weather conditions would have improved so much that they would be able to start.

'The Operations Room regularly announced the position of the front of the bomber stream - they assumed that Berlin must be the target for the night. The weather intelligence people affirmed that the weather was gradually improving from north-west to south-east. Nevertheless, this didn't show at the 'drome yet. From the Jagddivision HQ they learnt that the units in northern Holland would be able to take off and land shortly.

'Shortly after 2000 hours the crews who were on the battle order to patrol in both the northern night fighting boxes were taken by surprise by the order for cockpit readiness, even though the codeword 'Temporary Crow' was not yet cancelled. On this night, [Fries and] his crew were allocated to the wave to patrol in box "Gemse' ('Chamois')'.

'The crew bus drove six of them over to the dispersal area, where they immediately boarded their aircraft. All the checks before take-off, already carried out hundreds of times before, were performed with the confidence of a sleepwalker. Having completed the check list and having been strapped in, they sat and waited in their machines. The NCO Schwarzemänner sat and waited with them on the edge of the narrow cockpit rim. In the end, he got a sore behind and he slid down onto the wing.

'Cockpit readiness is a nerve-wracking business. The more unfavourable the weather conditions on take-off and landing are, the stronger is the tension and the greater the pressure on the nerves. Still, once the machine is in the air and the props are turning quietly and smoothly, the pressure is gone and left behind on the ground. The fascination of night flying is always a new and wonderful experience!

'Then, all of a sudden, the green lamp on the front edge of the hangar is blinking: the order to take off!

'The NCO Schwarzemänner jumps up and shuts the cockpit roof; he [Fries] locks it from the inside. On the seat of his pants, the 'black man' slides down from the wing and runs towards the battery trolley, which he plugs in. One after the other, the engines burst snorting into life. Cable removed - battery trolley rolled aside - chocks away - aircraft free! He [Fries] cautiously taxies out of the camouflaged hangar and turns off towards the taxi track whilst applying a bit of extra power.

'Eagle 98 taxies to starting point - switch on flare path!'

'Roger-Roger - you may proceed!'

The moment he arrived at the take off point he turned sharply to the left and paused for a few seconds to check the time of take-off on the clock in the instrument panel. It indicated 2042 hours.

'Eagle 98 taking off - will go on small lantern right away!'

'Roger-Roger - Horrido and good hunting!'

'Horrido - thanks!'

'Taking off was done in the same way as on that afternoon when they had tested the aircraft, with the difference that now complete darkness prevailed. This meant that after lifting off, he had to change over to flying on instruments immediately and complete the take off procedure quickly, in order to have his eyes and brains free for blind flying.

'Changing over from flying on sight to flying on instruments is always a battle between feeling and reason. The feeling points out that the aircraft is listing to the left, so push the stick to the right to restore level flight again! The reason responds: no way, the instruments indicate that the machine is flying in a completely normal fashion! Many a young and less experienced pilot has met his fate as a result of this internal conflict, by reacting instinctively and causing the aircraft to slip down over one wing and smash to pieces on the ground.

Even before the lamps of the second artificial horizon (which were positioned five kilometres [three miles] beyond the end of the runway to ease the switching over from visual flight to instrument flying) had disappeared below his wings, he went into a flat curve and set course for the radio beacon in box 'Gemse'. When he had reached a height of 80 metres [260 feet] the machine was swallowed up by the clouds. The Funker pulled in the transmitter and aligned the bearing loop aerial diagonally - this was the simplest method finding the shortest route to the waiting position in the box.

The needle of the altimeter had almost reached the 2000 metres [6,500 feet] mark when they surfaced from the clouds and had a brilliantly clear starry sky over them. They concluded that the upper limit of the cloud layer had sunk considerably since that afternoon, a clear sign of the forecast improvement in the weather. Only the lower limit of the clouds had not lifted yet. He had not noticed any icing up.

'Eagle 98 to Barrabas - we're approaching, please come in!'

In answer he heard only a mutilated rasping.

'Eagle 98 to Barrabas - I cannot understand you - please come in - please come in!'

There was a murmuring and hissing in their headphones and then, still a bit faint, box 'Gemse' responded: 'Barrabas to Eagle 98 - please come in!'

'Eagle 98 is approaching.'

'Roger - ask heading - ask altitude.'

'Head eight-five - height three-two.'

'After a short break, 'Gemse' came in again:

'Turn ten degrees starboard, ten degrees port!'

'Roger.' He alternately banked to the left and right several times.

'Barrabas to Eagle 98 - I have established contact - head nine-zero and climb to height four-five.'

'Roger-Roger!' He turned onto a course of ninety degrees. When the needle on the altimeter indicated 4000 metres [13,000 feet], he clipped on his oxygen mask and ordered both his crew members to do the same. A few minutes later, he had reached the demanded height. He stopped climbing, changed over to level flight and throttled back to economic cruising speed. He then trimmed the aircraft and synchronized the engines.

He was well aware of the fact that they had only been scrambled as a precautionary measure and that the British aircraft coming back took a much more northerly route. Still, possibly one bomber or another might stray towards his area, as perhaps its compass had been damaged by shrapnel - this did happen once in a while.

They received instructions to orbit the beacon and change course every eight to ten minutes by 90 degrees. He didn't feel very well physically. For lunch he had enjoyed a nourishing pea soup with bacon; and for supper a farmer's meal, richly laced with onions, had been dished up. Now the peas battled with the onions for the available space in his intestines, but he was firmly strapped into his confined cockpit and was suffering. It felt as if it would tear him apart. He tried everything to distract himself from the pain, but just didn't succeed: the piercing pain in his bowels became more unbearable every minute. When he indicated to his crew that he might have to break off the mission and also told them why, he received some sniggering remarks. He had no choice but to suffer in silence.

In the course of the next half-hour, he talked with the ground station several times on the whereabouts of the Kuriers. And always, he got the same stock answer: 'Please wait - Kuriers are still on their way'. Thus, he felt ever more and more that no enemy aircraft would stray into their hunting grounds this time - by now, they had been airborne for more than an hour. He took the decision to break off the mission, since the revolt in his bowels had become unbearable.

Just when he intended to press the microphone to announce his decision and ask for a course home, the excited voice of the fighter control officer came in: 'Barrabas to Eagle 98 - I have a Kurier for you - steer eight-zero - target at height six-three - increase speed - increase speed.'

He glanced at his clock: it was exactly 2200 hours.

The pain had instantly disappeared - at last, he could get into action again; what a stroke of luck! He pushed the throttle forward and adjusted the propellers to fine pitch. He steered onto the indicated course in a steep curve. From the variometer he read off a climbing speed of between seven and nine metres per second. When he had reached the operational height, he throttled back a little.

'Barrabas to Eagle 98 - turn 360 degrees port at two-eight-zero - increase speed - increase speed!'

He went to a reciprocal course in a steep left-hand turn. During the turn he switched on his weapons systems. As soon as the machine was heading on the new course, he raised his seat and switched on the lighting in the reflector sight.

'Target height six-three - ten degrees starboard - target range three-five-zero - increase speed - increase speed!'

'What does your SN-2 indicate? Don't you have an echo yet?' he asked his Funker.

'One moment, there's a lot of jamming, the tubes are flickering considerably!'

'Barrabas to Eagle 98, twenty degrees port -target height six-three unaltered - target range three-zero-zero.'

'Yes, I have him in my set - the large echo there, must be it, range three Ka-Em.'

'Eagle 98 to Barrabas - I have contact on Emil-Emil - over and out!'

'Roger-Roger - good hunting!'

The bomber was flying three kilometres [1.9 miles] in front of him. It was amazing that it was flying at such great height, normally they cruised at between 4000 and 5000 metres [13,000 and 16,200 feet] high, at times even at 5500 metres [18,000 feet], but over 6000 metres [19,500 feet], he had never experienced this before.

'A bit to the right - a little higher - distance nineteen hundred.'

He steered ten degrees to the right and pulled the machine up a bit.

'Target dead ahead - almost same height - distance twelve hundred.'

They approached rapidly, so he throttled the engines back a little.

'Left a bit - little higher - distance seven hundred.'

The expanse of the star-spangled sky hung brilliantly clear over them, only the horizon was a bit indefinite through a thin bank of haze, which defined the clear sky from the darker depth.

'Slightly left - a bit higher - distance four hundred - we're approaching rather fast!'

He throttled back even a bit more.

'Tell me his exact position!'

'He is now immediately ahead - just a little over us - drifting a bit to the left - distance three hundred.'

He screwed up his eyes and peered intensely forward. He scanned the horizon from right to left. There he is! Just a shadow, thin like the back of a knife, just above the layer of mist which outlines the horizon. He distinguished the four engines, the relatively slender fuselage and the double tail unit - Lancaster or Halifax? Probably Lancaster - the Halifax was more cumbersome. He came in a bit closer and clearly saw the engines protruding from the front of the wings and their weakly glowing exhausts. It definitely was a Lancaster! [It was Lancaster II DS834 KO-F on 115 Squadron, which had left Witchford at 1728 hours. Flight Sergeant J. Y. Lee and his crew were on their way back from Berlin.]

'I can see it - you can switch off your set! A Lancaster - make a note of the time, it's 2205 hours.'

'Eagle 98 to Barrabas - I engage!'

'Roger-Roger - Horrido!'

The 'Lanki' flew 150 metres in front of him and slightly to the left. He removed the safety lid from the control column and moved in a bit closer. Just when he wanted to launch his attack, the Lancaster turned sharply to the right and flew exactly through his sights - its crew must have spotted him. Almost automatically his right forefinger bent and all the machine guns and cannons blazed away. He didn't register any hits - it had all gone much too quickly. 'Write down the time! It's 2207 hours.'

'Eagle 98 to Barrabas; have made Pauke-Pauke - will keep in visual contact!'

'Roger-Roger!'

The tail gunner had simultaneously opened fire, he saw the muzzle fire flashing up in the turret and how the lines of tracer of the four machine guns fanned out against the night sky through the wild manoeuvres of the bomber. The tail gunner hardly had a chance to score any hits on his machine during such extreme manoeuvres.

He swiftly pulled the throttle back and plunged down to the right and after the bomber, always endeavouring to stay below the aircraft so as to be able to keep an eye on it against the clearer sky.

All of a sudden, the Lancaster pulled up to the right and just as unexpectedly slid down again to the left, followed by sharply pulling up to the left and plunging down to the right again. Both the bomber and fighter aircraft rapidly lost height and accelerated very fast.

'Keep your eyes on the needle of the speedometer Fred and tell me when it approaches the red mark! I have to keep my eyes glued to this lad up front, otherwise he's gone!'

The Lancaster danced the corkscrew and he danced with it - it was a foolish game, which not only took a lot of nerves but also sheer strength. He felt sweat pouring from his temples and he started to steam all over his body. Behind him, the two men were roaring, but he could not understand them as they both shouted at the same time. The gunner's makeshift light folding chair had collapsed. Depending on the manoeuvres of the machine, he was glued to the cockpit roof or the next moment he was pressed to the floor through the centrifugal forces. Fred's bordfunker case had unlocked and its contents were flying through the cabin. The ammunition belts of Konrad's twin-machine guns had crept out of their boxes and hissed through the cabin like crazy snakes. The chaos was complete!

'Let him go and take the next one - you're not going to get this one, the way he's turning - everything is in a mess here with us in the back!'

'Not now!' he muttered.

All of a sudden the Lancaster slid down over its left wing - this had nothing to do with a corkscrew! He dived down after it, they raced down steeply. He had almost lost the bomber in the darkness.

'Are you crazy? We almost have 700 on the clock!' his Bunker yelled! He glanced at the speedometer and indeed, they travelled far beyond the 600 mark! Almost as suddenly as the bomber had plunged down, it pulled up again, it zoomed up all but vertically. Taken by surprise by this manoeuvre, he pulled the stick against his breast and stalled his machine so badly that it sheered off to the side. The Lancaster had already disappeared from his view, when he saw it sliding past, only a few metres over his machine. The bomber pilot had stalled his machine as well. He immediately went after it and wondered how one could cut such capers in a heavy kite like the Lancaster.

'What bloody game are you playing!' the Bunker exclaimed, 'cut this damned dog fighting now, you can't win!

He was right; it was an idiotic game, in which the bomber undoubtedly held the best cards. Its pilot laid down the rules of play; he knew what he intended to do the next second, which flying manoeuvres he wanted to perform. The chasing hunter always hobbled split seconds, if not whole seconds, after it, as the pilot had to adapt to the next manoeuvre of the bomber and react accordingly. Whilst he was twisting and turning, he pondered on how to get into a firing position. He only saw one possibility: when the bomber had reached the highest point in the corkscrew and prepared to roll to the other side, it hung still in the air for one short instant - he had to seize this opportunity. It would undoubtedly be hard and the chance to hit the bomber squarely at this moment surely was not big, but he had to try! The game could not go on for much longer as they steadily lost height and if the Lancaster succeeded in reaching the safety of the clouds, it would escape for certain!

He concentrated fully on the movements of the bomber and at the next moment when it hung as if suspended, he fired a burst into its left wing. He believed he saw a hit, but no fire erupted. The tail gunner replied with a volley but the tracer flew past their machine. Aiming accurately was hardly possible for the British gunner in the wild manoeuvring of the bomber.

'2212 hours - height 4,200', reported the funker.

The corkscrewing of the Lancaster became even more feverish. It also lost height rapidly and he had the impression that it wanted to reach the layer of clouds at all cost - he would have done the same in their position.

With his third burst of fire, he got it in its right wing - the right inner engine was on fire, it trailed a banner of smoke like a ribbon.

'2214 hours - height three-three - you had better watch your speed!'

The bomber's corkscrew flattened out; it was quite clear that the 'comrades from the other side' desperately wanted to reach the safety of the cloud layer. They were certainly travelling much faster than was permitted in the type's manuals. Now that the Lancaster was hardly curving any more, he could quietly aim. Very slowly he approached the aircraft - the bomber's pilot must have pushed the throttles through the gate, he noticed the vibration of his wings - and he let the crossing lines of the reflector sight wander between the engines in the right wing. A short burst set the wing on fire - it was like an explosion, he must have hit the fuel tanks squarely.

He rolled away to the right and then went over into a sharp left hand turn. He saw how the Lancaster plunged down over its right wing. The fire reflected in the clouds and disappeared.

Moments later the layer of clouds lit up as if illuminated by a flashlight. All that remained was the typical dull red burning spot.

'Height 2,800 - time 2216 hours - I have made full notes for the combat report. Congratulations! That really was a tough cookie!'

'Ugh! Indeed it was!'

'Eagle 98 to Barrabas - have Sieg-Heil! - do you have position?'

'Barrabas to Eagle 98 - congratulations -Roger-Roger - position is noted.'

Fred got a little overconfident: 'Eagle 98 to Barrabas - next one please!'

'Roger-Roger - we do our best - proceed to height five-five - head nine-zero.'

He increased the manifold pressure, steered a course of 90 degrees and with eight metres per second he started climbing. He was exhausted! His arms and legs trembled from the strains of the combat. Never would he have suspected that a bomber could twist and turn like that - perhaps its pilot had been the aerobatics champion of England! He was bathing in his own sweat really; he had had enough for one day! Yet, perhaps another one would stray into their box, who knows?

When they had reached a height of 5000 metres [16,200 feet] he attained level flight again and throttled back to economic cruising speed. They had used up a lot of fuel in the combat, but there was still enough left for another one and a half hours. They flew squares again over box 'Gemse'.

'Barrabas to Eagle 98 - Kuriers have gone to bed - return to base - head two-five-zero - good night - over and out.'

'Roger-Roger - good night - over and out.'

He steered the indicated course, throttled back a bit and trimmed the elevator so that they headed for base whilst descending some three to five metres per second. The Funker picked up the radio beacon of the home base in the bearing receiver. After having been on their way for some ten minutes, the Funker called the Operations Room of their Gruppe.

'Eagle 98 to 'Tango' - come in please - come in please!'

'Tango to Eagle 98 - Roger-Roger - come in!'

'Eagle 98 returning to base - switch on flarepath in ten minutes.'

'Tango to Eagle 98 - you cannot come to garden fence - head for Home 46 - garden fence has thick soup!'

'Oh damn it! That's what we need! Where is Home 46 - surely somewhere in Holland?'

'One moment - Konrad, hold the lamp please!'

The Funker thumbed through his documents. With his finger, he ran through a table.

'It's Leeuwarden!'

'On no, that's the other end of the world! Well, let's see.' He checked the remaining fuel.

'We won't make it; in the combat we've used rather too much juice. As a last resort I would perhaps risk it, but what the heck, the weather can't be that bad! If it's the same as on take-off, we'll make it! So, let's go home!' He pressed the microphone on his stick: 'Eagle 98 - are very thirsty - cannot go to Home four-six - must come to garden fence - switch on flarepath in five minutes!'

'Roger-Roger - curtain at zero-seven - nothing else changed!'

'Well, the lower limit of the clouds at seventy metres [230 feet], weather otherwise unaltered, hardly a problem!' He had always found that landing in bad weather at night was less complicated than at daytime, as the lamps were more visible - and after all, flying on instruments was their nightly bread!

On approach to the base radio beacon, their machine dived into clouds at 1000 metres [3,200 feet]. He concentrated completely on his instruments. With the aid of the radio altimeter he felt his way toward the ground using the Roland system. The needle of his altimeter was between the seventy and eighty mark when he finally saw the flickering of the lamp on top of the radio beacon. Whilst holding his altitude, he carefully curved until he was on course of 270 degrees, then he levelled the machine and throttled back a little. When the first lamp of the flare path turned up, he pulled back the throttle and lowered the undercarriage and the flaps. With a speed of 300kph [186mph] he headed towards the 'drome along the path of lights whilst taking great care to hold his altitude. The first and outer artificial horizon turned up - another five kilometres, then the arrow to indicate the right direction came into view. When the inner artificial horizon disappeared beneath his wings, he fully throttled back and lowered full flaps. Just like in training, he put down the machine on the concrete runway with a three-point landing. The clock indicated 2255 hours.

'Tango from Eagle 98 - Luzie-Anton completed!'

'Roger-Roger' - congratulations!' 'Thanks!'

'My congratulations too!' said the Funker. 'This time on a perfect landing!'

'Thank you too - practice makes perfect!'

'He rolled his aircraft on to the end of the runway and then turned off to the right onto the taxi tracks leading to the dispersal area of his Staffel. In front of his hangar he switched off the engines.

'The Schwarzemänner of the Staffel who were on night duty came walking towards them and climbed onto the wings. With a hearty 'Hallo' they congratulated the crew on their victory. He was barely able to get out of his machine; his knees were very shaky from the strain of the mission and from the nervous tension of the landing.

'They just set off to walk over to the operations room of the Staffel to report their return and give a first account of their mission, when they heard the noise of engines over the 'drome, which seemed to come from the direction of the approach route. There, from the haze a Me 110 turned up with its landing light blazing and navigation lights switched on. It glided in much too high and touched down far too late, almost in the middle of the runway, its speed much too high. 'This is definitely going wrong!' The wheels only just touched the concrete and the machine bounced high into the air again. Brakes were squeaking, the aircraft raced towards the fence. They instinctively ducked - presently there would be an excruciating cracking and tearing! Still, only a muffled sound was heard, a grinding and rasping - then it became deathly quiet. Seconds later, one heard a canopy roof slammed open. Loud and clear, it resounded in the quiet: 'Shit, damn it!'

'His friend Willi had also landed!'

The wreck of the Lancaster was found near the Dutch village of Tungelroy eighteen kilometres (eleven miles) west of Roermond. The HQ at Venlo airfield laconically reported on the fate of the bomber crew: four men dead, one man prisoner; rest probably on the run. Flight Sergeant J. Y. Lee and Sergeant H. L. Pike, navigator were taken prisoner whilst Sergeant A. F. Gunnell the flight engineer evaded capture. The four other members of the crew who had put up such a brave fight were less fortunate. Flight Sergeant Keith Selwyn Bell RAAF, the 23-year old bomb aimer, and Sergeants Laurens H. Jones, wireless operator and Arthur M. Wilkinson RCAF, mid-upper gunner and Sergeant Graham Johnson, the 19-year old rear gunner, were killed and are buried in Weert Roman Catholic Churchyard. Otto Fries and Fred Staffa would add another thirteen victories to their tally before the end of the war.

The adverse weather had prevented more night-fighters from taking off and intercepting the Berlin force. Nachtjagd lost three aircraft shot down or crashed in bad weather. Among the forty-three Bomber Support sorties despatched there were no losses. Bomber Command lost twenty-one Lancasters and Halifaxes on the raid, of which at least six were destroyed by night fighters. One of these was Lancaster III ED713 *Nulli Secondus* (Latin for 'Second to None') on 576 Squadron captained by Pilot Officer Richard Lloyd Hughes which was shot down by Oberleutnant Paul Zorner of 8./NJG3 who claimed three 'Lankis', one east of Geissen, another south of Diepholz and one at Cloppenburg to take his score to twenty Abschüsse. Hughes and three crew, including Sergeant Frank Rivett the 19-year old mid-upper gunner were killed. ED713 crashed into deep snow in a thickly wooded area near Hannover. Sergeant Frank Lanxon the rear gunner, who with two others managed to bail out of the stricken Lancaster, landed close by and despite losing blood from his wounds, carried out a search of the wreckage in the hope of finding survivors. Exhausted and without his flying boots, which had been ripped off as soon as his parachute opened, he had to give himself up to local villagers.

In London, a city ravaged by German bombing in the early years of the war, Lord Sherwood, undersecretary of state in the Air Ministry stated, concerning the air war against Germany: 'In the past Berlin expressly ordered Warsaw, Rotterdam and Belgrade to be levelled. In their enthusiasm the Germans even made documentary films of these great deeds of the German Luftwaffe so that they could be suitably admired. Now they are being paid out in the same coin. The crocodile tears in the eyes of so many Germans can awaken no pity. The blows now being dealt to Germany are merely punishment for the crimes that the Third Reich has committed against small nations, their unprotected cities and minority groups in many states. We can make Germany only one promise: our blows will increase in power until the military capacity of the Nazi Reich has been broken.'

Endnotes Chapter 14

155   *Night Airwar* by Theo Boiten (The Crowood Press 1999).

156   Three crews of NJG1 and NJG5 were credited with three Halifax kills. *Night Airwar* by Theo Boiten (The Crowood Press 1999).

157   *The Bomber Command War Diaries: An Operational reference book 1939-1945* by Martin Middlebrook and Chris Everitt (Midland 1985).

158   From a story on the web site of Elinor Florence.

159   By the end of 1943 Spoden had raised his victory total to four. In January 1944 Spoden claimed five victories, including two in a night on 14/15 January and 27/28 January, to raise his victory total to nine. During early 1944 he also participated in daylight sorties intercepting USAAF bomber raids. On 6 March, the first American daylight raid on Berlin, he engaged the formation north of Rostock and claimed a B-17 - probably unconfirmed - but his Bf 110 was hit in the port wing and engine. Spoden nursed his damaged aircraft back to Parchim and was forced to carry out a belly landing because his undercarriage had also been damaged in the incident. Oberfeldwebel Walter Kammerer and his bordfunker of 16/NJG5 flying a Bf 110G were killed by P-51 Mustangs near Berlin. On the night of 26/27 March Spoden was shot up again by an unknown assailant in the Stettin area. He force-landed his damaged Bf 110 out of fuel at Kornwestheim near Stuttgart. Spoden and his crewmen all received injuries in the incident resulting in several weeks in hospital. Shortly after returning to combat duty in late March 1944, Spoden was assigned to the Stabs Staffel of III./NJG6 and relocated to Steinamanger in Hungary. The transfer also resulted in a change of equipment with the Gruppe re-equipping with the Ju 88 night-fighter. Spoden recorded one victory with the unit when he shot down a Wellington bomber near Neunkirchen that was targeting the oilfields at Pardubice for his tenth victory. In August 1944 Spoden was transferred to the Stabs Staffel of II./NJG6 at Swäbisch Hall. On 5 October, he was awarded the Ehrenpokal

160   Sergeant Alan Smith, Warrant Officer Grove, Sergeant A. Rossi the flight engineer, Sergeant Patterson and Flight Sergeant E. W. D. B. Hunt RNZAF the air bomber were held in captivity until the end of the war.

161   379 bombers including 364 Lancasters were headed for Berlin but Pfeiffer might have received confused signals from the German controller who was temporarily deceived by a diversion by seven Mosquitoes at Leipzig and possibly by other Mosquitoes heading for Aachen and Duisburg.

162   Research by Theo Boiten.

Appendix One

German Ranks and Their Equivalents

German Ranks	US equivalent	RAF equivalent
Reichsmarschall	no equivalent	no equivalent
Generalfeldmarschall	General (5-Star)	
Generaloberst	General (4-Star)	
General der Flieger	Lieutenant General	
Generalleutnant	Major General	
Generalmajor	Brigadier General	
Oberst	Colonel	Group Captain
Oberstleutnant	Lieutenant Colonel	Wing Commander
Major	Major	Squadron Leader
Hauptmann	Captain	Flight Lieutenant
Oberleutnant	1st Lieutenant	Flying Officer
Leutnant	2nd Lieutenant	Pilot Officer
Stabsfeldwebel	Flight Officer	Warrant Officer
Oberfahnrich	no equivalent	no equivalent
Oberfeldwebel	Master Sergeant	Flight Sergeant
Fahnrich	Officer candidate	no equivalent
Feldwebel	Sergeant	Sergeant
Unteroffizier	Staff Sergeant	Corporal
Obergefreiter	Corporal	Leading Aircraftsman
Gefreiter	Private First Class	Aircraftsman 1
Flieger	Private Second Class	Aircraftsman 2

Appendix Two

The 100 Highest Scoring Nachtjagd Pilots

1. Major Heinz-Wolfgang Schnaufer, 121 Nachtjagd victories (including 114 Viermots) in 164 sorties with NJG1 and 4. Ritterkreuz with Eichenlaub, Schwerter and Brillanten. Died in car accident 13 July 1950.
2. Oberst Helmut Lent, 102 Nachtjagd victories (including 61 Viermots and 1 Mosquito) in 396 sorties with NJG1, 2 and 3, plus 8 as Zerstörer in 3./ZG76. Ritterkreuz with Eichenlaub, Schwerter and Brillanten. Died after landing accident at Paderborn 7 October 1944.
3. Major Heinrich Prinz zu Sayn-Wittgenstein, 83 Nachtjagd victories (including 23 on the Eastern Front) in 170 sorties with NJG2, 3 and 5. Ritterkreuz with Eichenlaub and Schwerter. KIA 21/22 January 1944 by Lancaster return fire or by Mosquito E of Magdeburg.
4. Oberst Werner Streib, 67 Nachtjagd victories (including 30 Viermots) in 150 sorties with NJG1, plus 1 as Zerstörer in I./ZG1. Ritterkreuz with Eichenlaub and Schwerter. After the war he worked in the grocery business before joining the Bundeswehr on 16 March 1956. For three years he commanded the pilot school A in Landsberg am Lech, equipped with the T-6 Texan was responsible for training the beginner pilots in the Luftwaffe. Streib's military career ended with his retirement on 31 March 1966. His last position was Inspizient Fliegende Verbände (Inspector of Flying Forces). He died on 15 June 1986 and is buried in Munich.
5. Hauptmann Manfred Meurer, 65 Nachtjagd victories (including 40 Viermots and two Mosquitoes) in 130 sorties with NJG1 and 5. Ritterkreuz with Eichenlaub. KIA 21/22 January 1944 by debris from his final Lancaster victim 20 km E of Magdeburg.
6. Oberst Günther Radusch, 64 Nachtjagd victories (including 57 Viermots) in over 140 sorties with NJG1, 2, 3 and 5, plus one victory in Spain with 2./Jgr.88. Another 14 of his Nachtjagd victories were allotted to other pilots. Ritterkreuz with Eichenlaub. Survived war, died 29 July 1988.
7. Major Rudolf Schönert, 64 Nachtjagd victories (including 36 on the Eastern Front) in 376 sorties with NJG1, 2, 5 and 100. Ritterkreuz with Eichenlaub. Survived war, died 30 November 1985 in Canada.
8. Hauptmann Heinz Rökker, 63 Nachtjagd victories (including 55 Viermots and one Mosquito), plus one in daylight in 161 sorties with NJG2. Ritterkreuz with Eichenlaub. Survived war.
9. Oberstleutnant Walter Borchers, 43 night and 16 day victories in NJG1, 3 and 5 and ZG76, KIA 5/6 March 1945, shot down by 239 Squadron Mosquito North of Altenburg.

10 Major Paul Zorner, 59 Nachtjagd victories claimed in 272 sorties, including 110 at night with NJG2, 3, 5 and 100. Decorated with the Ritterkreuz mit Eichenlaub. He claimed his 59th and last victory on 5/6 March 1945, a B-24 near Graz. Zorner surrendered his Gruppe to US troops near Karlsbad on 10 May 1945. He was then handed over to Soviet Forces on 17 May. He returned to Germany after years of incarceration in December 1949. Zorner studied mechanical engineering in Stuttgart and entered the field of refrigeration engineering before he rejoined the Bundesluftwaffe in 1956. He was not passed fit to fly jet fighters and returned to civilian life in May 1957. He was employed within the chemical industry. He retired in 1981 as a chief engineer with Hoechst near Frankfurt. He died on 27 January 2014.

11 Hauptmann Martin Becker, 58 Nachtjagd victories (all Viermots) in 83 sorties with NJG3, 4 and 6. Ritterkreuz mit Eichenlaub. Survived war.

12 Hauptmann Gerhard Raht, 58 Nachtjagd victories (all but one Viermots) in 171 sorties with NJG2 and 3. Ritterkreuz mit Eichenlaub. Survived war, died 11 January 1977 in Rheinfeld/Holstein.

13 Major Wilhelm Herget, 58 Nachtjagd victories in NJG3 and 4, plus 15 day victories in over 700 sorties. Ritterkreuz mit Eichenlaub. Survived war, Died 27 March 1974 in Munich.

14 Oberleutnant Kurt Welter, 56 Nachtjagd victories in JG301, 300, NJG10 and NJG11 (including 33 Mosquitoes), plus 7 day victories in 93 sorties. Ritterkreuz mit Eichenlaub. Survived war, died in car crash at a railway crossing on 7 March 1949 at Leck/Schleswig-Holstein.

15 Hauptmann Heinz Strüning, 56 Nachtjagd victories in NJG1 and 2 in 250 sorties, shot down by Mosquito on 157 Squadron and killed hitting tail unit of his Bf 110G-4 on bailing out on 24/25 December 1944 near Bergisch-Gladbach. Ritterkreuz mit Eichenlaub.

16 Oberleutnant Gustav Eduard Francsi, 56 Nachtjagd victories in NJG100 (including 49 on Eastern Front) in 150 sorties. Ritterkreuz. Survived war, drowned in Spain, 6 October 1961.

17 Major Hans-Dieter Frank, 55 Nachtjagd victories in NJG1. Ritterkreuz mit Eichenlaub. KIA after colliding with other night fighter of Stab I NJG1 on landing NW of Celle 27/28 September 1943.

18 Oberfeldwebel Heinz Vinke, 54 victories in NJG1, Ritterkreuz mit Eichenlaub, KIA 26 February 1944, shot down by 198 Squadron Typhoons.

19 Hauptmann August 'Gustel' Geiger, 53 victories in NJG1, Ritterkreuz mit Eichenlaub, KIA 29 September 1943, shot down by Beaufighter of 141 Squadron in Ijsselmeer NW of Harderwijk.

20 Major Werner 'Red' Hoffmann, 51 victories in NJG3 and 5, plus 1 Zerstörer victories in ZG2, Ritterkreuz, survived war. After the war he studied pharmacy and opened a dispensary in Goslar. In 1957 Hoffmann was engaged by Hoechst AG in Bremen in an advisory role. Hoffmann was credited with 51 aerial victories, 50 of them at night in 192 sorties. He recorded one victory by day and four were recorded over the Eastern front. He died on 8 July 2011.

21 Major Egmont Prinz zur Lippe-Weissenfeld, 51 victories in NJG1 and 5, Ritterkreuz mit Eichenlaub, KIA 12 March 1944 in flying accident near St. Hubert, Ardennes.

22 Oberstleutnant Herbert Lütje, 47 night and 3 day victories in NJG1 and 6, Ritterkreuz mit Eichenlaub, survived war.

23 Hauptmann Josef Kraft, 56 victories in NJG1, 4, 5 and 6, Ritterkreuz mit Eichenlaub, survived war. Died 16 October 1994.

24 Hauptmann Georg Hermann Greiner, 47 day and 4 night victories in NJG1 and 2 in 204 sorties. Ritterkreuz mit Eichenlaub, survived war. He went on to study law and

returned to service in the West German Luftwaffe in 1957, retiring with the rank of Oberstleutnant in 1972.

25 Major Martin Drewes, 43 night and 6 day victories in ZG76, NJG3 and NJG1 in 252 sorties, Ritterkreuz with Eichenlaub. He was captured by British forces at the end of the war. In 1949 Drewes emigrated to Brazil, where he built a career as an entrepreneur and married a Brazilian woman. The long marriage ended only in 2010 by the death of his wife. He returned at least once each year on visits to Germany. He died on 13 October 2013 in Blumenau, southern Brazil, of natural causes.

26 Oberstleutnant Hans-Joachim Jabs, 28 night and 22 day victories in ZG76, NJG3 and NJG1, Ritterkreuz with Eichenlaub. He became a businessman in Westphalia after the war. Jabs died on 26 October 2003.

27 Stabsfeldwebel Reinhard Kollak, 49 night victories in NJG1 and NJG4, Ritterkreuz. After the war he found it difficult to adjust to civilian life before he rejoined the newly founded Bundeswehr in 1956. He retired in 1967 as a Hauptfeldwebel. On 6 February 1980 he died at the age of 65.

28 Hauptmann Ernst-Georg Drünkler, 45 night and 2 day victories in NJG5, NJG1 and NJG3, Ritterkreuz, survived war. Died 1970.

29 Hauptmann Hans-Heinz Augenstein, 46 night victories (including 45 Viermots) in NJG1, Ritterkreuz, KIA 6/7 December 1944, shot down by 85 Squadron Mosquito near Münster-Handorf.

30 Hauptmann Alois Lechner, 45 or 46 night victories in NJG2, NJG5 and NJG100, MIA 23 February 1944, shot down by Russian ack-ack, force-landed Brigade Leonow airfield.

31 Major Paul Semrau, 46 night victories in NJG2 and NJG6, Ritterkreuz with Eichenlab, KIA 7/8 February 1945, when shot down by a Spitfire flown by Flight Lieutenant K. S. Sleep on 402 'Winnepeg Bear' Squadron RCAF on landing at Twente airfield.

32 Leutnant Rudolf Frank, 45 night victories in NJG3, Ritterkreuz with Eichenlaub, KIA 26/27 April 1944, crashed after being hit by debris from a 12 Squadron Lancaster.

33 Oberleutnant Paul Gildner, 43 night and 2 day victories in ZG1, NJG1 and NJG2, Ritterkreuz with Eichenlaub, KIA 24/25 February 1943 in failed forced landing near Gilze-Rijen airfield after engine failure.

34 Hauptmann Reinhold Knacke, 44 night victories in NJG1, Ritterkreuz with Eichenlaub, KIA 3/4 February 1943 by return fire from 75 Squadron Stirling.

35 Hauptmann Ludwig Becker, 44 night victories in NJG1 and NJG2, Ritterkreuz with Eichenlaub, MIA 26 February 1943 N of Schiermonnikoog during daylight sortie.

36 Hauptmann Johannes Hager, 42 night victories in NJG1, Ritterkreuz, survived war. Died, 2 September 1993.

37 Hauptmann Werner Baake, 41 night victories from 195 sorties in NJG1. All his victories were recorded at night and include 37 Viermots and one Mosquito. At least nine victories were achieved when he flew He 219A. Ritterkreuz, survived war. He died piloting Lufthansa B-720-030 D-ABOP when it crashed at Heilsbronn on 15 July 1964.

38 Hauptmann Leopold 'Poldi' Fellerer, 39 night and 2 day victories in NJG2, 1, 5 and NJG6. 32 were Viermots. Awarded the Ritterkreuz. Survived war. During the 1950s, he served with the Austrian Air Force, becoming Commander of the Langenlebarn Airbase in Tulln on the River Donau, retiring as an Oberstleutnant. Leopold Fellerer died on 15 July 1968 in an air crash, his Cessna L-19 coming down near Krems.

39 Oberleutnant Wilhelm Beier, 37 to 40 night victories in NJG2 and NJG1, Ritterkreuz, survived war. He died in July 1977.

40 Hauptmann Dietrich 'Dieter' Schmidt, 40 night victories in NJG1, Ritterkreuz. Died 6 March 2002.

41 Major Walter Ehle, 35 night and 4 day victories in ZG1 and NJG1, Ritterkreuz. On

17/18 November 1943 30-year old Ehle and his crew were on finals to St. Trond when the flarepath was suddenly extin¬guished and Bf 110G-4 G9+AC crashed near Horpmoel killing all on board.

42 Hauptmann Ludwig 'Luc' Meister, 38 night and 1 day victories in NJG1 and NJG4, Ritterkreuz, survived war. He died on 26 November 2011, 18 days before his 92nd birthday.
43 Hauptmann Helmut Bergmann, 36 night victories in NJG4, Ritterkreuz, KIA 6/7 August 1944 in area Avranches-Mortain, shot down by 604 Squadron Mosquito.
44 Oberfeldwebel Günther Bahr, 35 night and 2 day victories in SKG210, NJG1, NJG4 and NJG6, Ritterkreuz, survived war. Died 29 April 2009.
45 Oberfeldwebel Karl-Heinz Scherfling, 33 to 35 night victories in NJG1 and NJG2, Ritterkreuz, KIA 20/21 July 1944 near Mol, shot down by 169 Squadron Mosquito.
46 Oberleutnant Günther Bertram, 35 night victories in Nachtjagd Schwarm Luftflotte 6 and NJG100, Deutsches Kreuz, survived war.
47 Major Werner Husemann, 34 night victories in NJG1 and NJG3, Ritterkreuz, survived war. He died on February 2014.
48 Hauptmann Wilhelm Johnen, 34 night victories in NJG1, 5 and 6, Ritterkreuz. Postwar, Johnen attended university and gained an Engineering degree. In 1952 he worked with Professor Willy Messerschmitt before taking up construction engineering, successfully running his own business. He also wrote his biography, Duel under the Stars, one of the first English language books about the Luftwaffe. He died aged 80 on 7 February 2002 at Überlingen.
49 Hauptmann Ernst-Wilhelm Modrow, 34 night victories in NJG1, Ritterkreuz, survived war. In the 1950s he joined Bundeswehr and retired 1964 as an Oberstleutnant. He died on 16 September 1990.
50 Hauptmann Heinz-Horst Hissbach, 29 night and 5 day victories in KG40 and NJG2, Ritterkreuz, KIA 14/15 April 1945 near Gelnhausen, shot down by American ack-ack.
51 Oberleutnant Klaus Bretschneider, 14 night and twenty day victories in JG300, Ritterkreuz, KIA 24 December 1944 near Oberaula, Kassel area, in air combat with P-51 Mustangs.
52 Hauptmann Heinz-Martin Hadeball, 33 night victories in NJG1, 4, 6 and NJG10, Ritterkreuz, survived war.
53 Major Eckart-Wilhelm von Bonin, 32 night victories in NJG1, Ritterkreuz, survived war. He died on 11 January 1992 in Luhmühlen in Lower Saxony.
54 Major Hubert Rauh, 31 night victories in NJG1 and NJG4, Ritterkreuz, survived war.
55 Hauptmann Hans Schmidt, 16 night and 15 day victories in ZG, NJG3 and NJG100, survived war.
56 Leutnant Josef Kociok, estimated to have scored 21 to 24 night victories and nine to twelve night victories in SKG210, ZG1 and NJG200, Ritterkreuz, KIA 26/27 September 1943 in collision with Russian DB-3.
57 Hauptmann Heinz Ferger, estimated to have scored 30 night victories in NJG3 and NJG2, KIA 13/14 or 14/15 April 1945, shot down near Lübeck airfield by Mosquito.
58 Major Friedrich-Karl Müller, 30 night victories in JG300, NJGr 10 and NJG11, Ritterkreuz, survived war. He died on 2 November 1987.
59 Major Gerhard 'Gerd' Friedrich, 30 night victories in NJG1, 4 and NJG6, Ritterkreuz, KIA 16/17 March 1945 near Bonlanen (near Stuttgart) in collision with a 576 Squadron Lancaster.
60 Major Hans-Karl Kamp, estimated to have scored 28 night and 2 day victories in ZG76, NJG1, 4 and JG300, KIA 31 December 1944 north of Hamburg.
61 Hauptmann Otto-Karl Klemenz, estimated to have scored 29 night victories in NJG1 and NJG5, survived war.

62 Major Heinrich Wohlers, 29 night victories in NJG2, 1, 4 and NJG6, Ritterkreuz, KIA 15 March 1944 in crash near Echterdingen airfield.
63 Hauptmann Eduard Schröder, 24 night and 5 day victories in NJG3, survived war.
64 Oberleutnant Erich Jung, 28 night victories in NJG2, survived war.
65 Hauptmann Hans Krause, 28 night victories in NJG3, NJG101, Ritterkreuz, survived war.
66 Oberfeldwebel Karl Maisch, estimated to have scored 28 night victories in NJG5 and NJG100, survived war.
67 Hauptmann Paul Szameitat, 28 night and 1 day victories in NJG3. Ritterkreuz, Ritterkreuz. Killed 1/2 January 1944 while trying to make an emergency landing in a plantation of firs near Bückeburg in the Weser Mountains after an air combat at Obernkirchen.
68 Hauptmann Fritz Lau, 28 night victories in NJG1, Ritterkreuz, survived war. Died 1 January 2003 aged 91.
69 Hauptmann Rudolf Altendorf, 24 night and 4 day victories in NJG3, 4 and 5, Deutsches Kreuz, survived war.
70 Leutnant Heinz Grimm, 26 night and 1 day victories in NJG1 and NJG2, Ritterkreuz, died 13 October 1943 after being shot down by flak over Bremen four nights previously.
71 Oberleutnant Lothar Linke, 24 night and 3 day victories in ZG76, NJG1 and NJG2, Ritterkreuz, KIA 13/14 May 1943 near Lemmer due to engine failure.
72 Hauptmann Rudolf Sigmund, 25 night and 2 day victories in NJG1, NJG2 and NJG3, Ritterkreuz, KIA 3/4 October 1943 at Fassberg southwest of Gottingen, probably shot down by flak.
73 Oberleutnant Hans Gref, 24 or 25 night and 2 day victories in NJG3, 5, 100 and NJG1, Deutsches Kreuz, KIA January 1944, or 26 March 1944.
74 Oberleutnant Josef Putzkuhl, 26 night victories in NJG5 and NJG100, survived war.
75 Hauptmann Alfons Koster, 25 night and 1 day victories in NJG2, NJG1 and NJG3, Ritterkreuz, KIA 6/7 January 1945 near Varel in landing accident.
76 Oberleutnant Walter Briegleb, 25 night victories in NJG3 and NJG2, Deutsches Kreuz, survived war.
77 Hauptmann Helmuth Schulte, 25 night victories in 180+ combat sorties with NJG5 and NJG6, being awarded the Ritterkreuz on 17 April 1945. Died 9 July 1982.
78 Leutnant Herbert Altner, 24 night and 1 day victories in NJG3, NJG5 and NJG11, Deutsches Kreuz, survived war.
79 Hauptmann Rolf Bussmann, 24 night and 1 day victories in NJG2, 3, 1 and NJG5, Deutsches Kreuz, survived war.
80 Oberleutnant Peter Erhardt, 24 night and 1 day victories in NJG1, NJG5 and NJG11, survived war.
81 Hauptmann Fritz Söthe, 24 night and 1 day victories in NJG4, KIA 28/29 September at Lambrecht-Neustadt, shot down by Mosquito.
82 Hauptmann Peter Spoden, 24 night and 1 day victories in NJG5 and NJG6, Deutsches Kreuz. He finished the war as Gruppenkommandeur of I./NJG6. He entered university where he studied mechanical engineering and was later employed as a technical advisor with the Bundesbahn in Essen. In 1951 he resumed glider flying although it was prohibited to fly motor-powered aircraft. By travelling to Holland, Belgium and England, Spoden was able to fly powered aircraft. In 1954 he was accepted for a Lufthansa training programme to become an airline pilot. He completed the course on 20 July 1955. On his retirement in 1981 Spoden had flown 22,147 hours. When he applied for his war pension he discovered he had been promoted to the rank of Hauptmann on 20 April 1945!

83 Oberleutnant Reinhold Eckardt, 22 night and 3 day victories in ZG76, NJG1 and NJG3, Ritterkreuz, KIA 29/30 July 1942 after combat with a 102 Squadron Halifax at Kampenhout, 9 km N of Melsbroek, near Brussels after his third Viermot victory of the night. He had to bail out and became entangled in the tailplane. His bordfunker, Feldwebel Frank, bailed out safely. Three Day victories as a destroyer pilot plus 17 aircraft destroyed on the ground.
84 Oberfeldwebel Helmut Dahms, 24 night victories in NJG100, survived war.
85 Oberleutnant Klaus Scheer, 24 night victories in NJG100, survived war.
86 Oberfeldwebel Karl Strohecker, 24 night victories in NJG5 and NJG100, survived war.
87 Oberfeldwebel Hermann Wischnewski, 16 or 17 night victories and 8 day victories in JG300, Ritterkreuz, WIA 29 July 1944 in air combat at Gelbstadt.
88 Hauptmann Erhard Peters, 22 night & 2 day victories in NJG3, KIA 19/20 February 1944 at Brandenburg-Briest, shot down by Wild Boar night fighter.
89 Oberfeldwebel Wilhelm Glitz, estimated to have scored 23 night victories in NJG2, Deutsches Kreuz, survived war.
90 Hauptmann Dr. Horst Patuschka, 23 night victories in NJG2, Ritterkreuz, KIA 6/7 March 1943 near Bizerta/Tunisia in flying accident.
91 Oberfeldwebel Ernst Reitmeyer, 23 night victories in NJG5. Died on 6 November 1998 in St. Leonard, Austria.
92 Oberfeldwebel Hans Schadowski, 23 night victories in NJG3, survived war.
93 Oberfeldwebel Rudolf Mangelsdorf, 19 night and 4 day victories in NJG3 and NJG2, survived war.
94 Oberleutnant Helmut Woltersdorf, 15 night and 8 day victories in ZG76 and NJG1, KIA 1/2 June 1942 in crash at Twente airfield, shot down by 3 Squadron Hurricane.
95 Major Wolfgang Thimmig, 22 night and 1 day victories in NJG1, 2, 3, 4 and NJG101, survived war. Died 6 November 1976 in Stockholm, Sweden.
96 Oberleutnant Jakob Schaus, 21 night and 2 day victories in NJG4, KIA 2/3 February 1945 at KIA 2 Rockenhausen/Pfalz, near Bad Kreuznach; shot down by a Mosquito intruder on 239 Squadron.
97 Hauptmann Herman Leube, 22 night victories in NJG3, KIA 27/28 or 28/29 December in crash-landing at Reeuwijk near Gouda.
98 Hauptmann Franz Brinkhaus, 21 night victories in NJG1 and NJG2, survived war.
99 Hauptmann Werner Hopf, 21 night victories in NJG1 and NJG5, survived war. Died in Heidelberg in 1970
100 Hauptmann Hans Autenrieth, 22 night victories in NJG1 and NJG4. Was shot down and taken prisoner on 6 August 1944 northeast of Rennes. He remained in captivity in the US until March 1946. Upon release Autenriech joined the Bundersluftwaffe and he ended his career as an Oberleutnant. He died on 8 June 1996.

Appendix Three

Glossary

*: (Medal) and Bar (second award of the medal specified) A/c: abbreviation for aircraft
AA: Anti-Aircraft
AAA: Anti-Aircraft Artillery
Abschuss: Claim for a victory in air combat
Abschüsse: Claims for air combat victories
Abschussbeteiligung: Contribution to a claim for a victory in air-combat
AFC: Air Force Cross
AI: Airborne Interception (radar)
Alarmstart: 'Scramble'
Anerkannter Abschuss: Officially confirmed air-combat victory claim
AOC: Air Officer Commanding
ASH: AI Mk.XV narrow-beam radar used for low-level operations
ASR: Air-Sea Rescue
ATS: Air Training Squadron
BBC: British Broadcasting Corporation
BEM: British Empire Medal
Blip: Radar echo or response
bordmechaniker: flight engineer (German)
Bogey: Unidentified aircraft
bordfunker or **Funker**: German radar/radio operator
bordshütze: air gunner
BSDU: Bomber Support Development Unit (RAF)
CCU: Combat Crew Unit
CoG: Centre of Gravity
CRT: Cathode Ray Tube
C-scope: CRT showing frontal elevation of target
Day Ranger: Operation to engage air and ground targets within a wide but specified area, by day
DCM: Distinguished Conduct Medal
Deutsches Kreuz: German Cross
Deutsches Kreuz im Gold; German Cross in Gold
'Dicke Autos': 'Fat Cars' (Four engined heavy bombers)
DFC: Distinguished Flying Cross
DFM: Distinguished Flying Medal
Diver: V-1 flying bomb operation
Drem lighting: System of outer markers and runway approach lights
DSC: Distinguished Service Cross
DSO: Distinguished Service Order
Düppel: German codename for Window after a town near the Danish border where RAF metal foil strips were first found.
Eichenlaub: (Knight's Cross with) Oak Leaves
Einsatz: Operational flight
Eisernes Kreuz I, II (EK I, EKII): Iron Cross (1st and 2nd Class)
Emil Emil: German codename for AI
Ergdnzungsgruppe: Replacement or complement wing
ETA: Estimated Time of Arrival
Experte(n): Expert. An ace/aces (five or more confirmed victories)
Express-Express: German R/T code for 'hurry up'
FF: Flugzeugführer (pilot)
Feindberuhrung: Contact with an enemy aircraft
FIDO: Fog Investigation and Dispersal Operation
Firebash: 100 Group Mosquito sorties using incendiaries/napalm against German airfields
Flak (Flieger Abwehr Kanone(n): Anti-Aircraft Artillery

Flensburg: German device to enable their night fighters to home on to Monica
FNSF: Fast Night Striking Force
Freelance: Patrol with the object of picking up a chance contact or visual of the enemy
Frontflugspange für Kampfflieger im Gold: Front Flying Clasp of the Luftwaffe for Bomber crews in Gold
FTR: abbreviation for failed to return
Führer: Leader
Gardening: Mine laying
GCI: Ground Control Interception (radar)
Gee: British medium-range navigational aid using ground transmitters and an airborne receiver
Geschwader: Roughly equivalent to three RAF wings. Comprises three or four Gruppen containing three or four Staffeln, eg: IV./NJG1 (the fourth Gruppe in Nachtjagd Geschwader 1), 12./NJG1 (the 12th Staffel (in the fourth Gruppe) of Nachtjagd Geschwader 1)
GP: General Purpose bomb
Gruppenkommandeur: Commander or Captain, a Gruppe command position rather than a rank
H$_2$S: British 10-cm experimental airborne radar navigational and target location aid
HE: High Explosive (bomb)
HEI: High Explosive Incendiary
'Heavies': RAF/USAAF four-engined bombers
Helle Nachtjagd: illuminated night fighting
Herausschuss: Claim for a bomber shot out of formation
HMS: His Majesty's Ship
Horrido!: The victory cry of the Luftwaffe fighter pilots. Also a greeting and parting word among friends and comrades of the Luftwaffe
IAS: Indicated Air Speed
IFF: Identification Friend or Foe
Intruder: Offensive night operation to fixed point or specified target
IO: Intelligence Officer
Jagdbomber (Jabo): Fighter-bomber
Jagdgeschwader: Fighter wing, includes three or four Gruppen
Jagdwaffe: Fighter Arm or Fighter Force
Jager: Fighter
Jagerleitoffizier: JLO, or GCI-controller

Kampfgeschwader (KG): Bomber Group
Kommandeur: Commanding officer of a Gruppe
Kommodore: Commodore or Captain, a Geschwader command position rather than a rank
KUFlGr: Kilstenfliegergruppe: Coastal Flying Wing (German)
Kurier: German R/T code for 'Allied heavy bomber'
Lichtenstein: Early form of German AI radar
LMF: Lack of Moral Fibre
LNSF: Light Night Striking Force
LORAN: Long-Range Navigation
Luftflotte: Air Fleet
Luftwaffe: Air Force
M/T: Motor Transport
Mahmoud: British High-level bomber support sortie
Mandrel: American airborne radar jamming device
Maschinen Gewehr (MG): Machine gun
Maschinen Kanone (MK): Machine cannon
MC: Medium Capacity bomb
MCU: Mosquito Conversion Unit
Met.: Meteorological
MiD: Mention In Dispatches
Monica: British active tail warning radar device
MTU: Mosquito Training Unit
Nachtjagdgeschwader: (NJG) Night fighter Group
Nachtjäger: Nightfighter
NCO: Non-Commissioned Officer
NFS: Night Fighter Squadron
Night Ranger: Operation to engage air and ground targets within a wide but specified area, by night

Noball: Flying bomb (V-l) or rocket (V-2) site

OBE: Order of the British Empire
Objektnachtjagd: Target Area Night Fighting
Oberkommando der Wehrmacht: High Command of the Armed Forces
Oboe: Ground-controlled radar system of blind bombing in which one station indicated track to be followed and another the bomb release point

Op: Operation (mission)
OSS: Office of Strategic Services. The US intelligence service activated during the Second World War and disbanded on 1 October 1945
OTU: Operational Training Unit
Pauke! Pauke!: 'Kettledrum! Kettledrum!' (R/T code for 'Going into attack!')
PFF: Path Finder Force
PoW: Prisoner of War
PRU: Photographic Reconnaissance Unit
R/T: Radio Telephony
RAAF: Royal Australian Air Force
RAE: Royal Aircraft Establishment
RAFVR: Royal Air Force Volunteer Reserve
RCAF: Royal Canadian Air Force
RCM: Radio Counter Measures
Reflex Visier (Revi): Gunsight
Reichsluftfahrtministerium (RLM): German Air Ministry
Reichs(luft)verteidigung: Air Defence of Germany
Ritterkreuz (träger) (RK/RKT): Knight's Cross (holder)
RN: Royal Navy
RNorAF: Royal Norwegian Air Force
RNVR: Royal Naval Volunteer Reserve
Rotte: Tactical element of two aircraft
Rottenflieger: Wingman, the second man in the Rotte
RP: Rocket Projectile
SAAF: South African Air Force
SAS: Special Air Service
SASO: Senior Air Staff Officer
Schlachtgeschwader: Ground attack Group
Schräge Musik: 'Slanting Music'; night fighters' guns firing upwards
Schwarm: Flight of four aircraft
Schwarmführer: Flight leader
Schwarzemänner: ground crew or 'black men', so-called because of the colour of their tunics
Schwerten: (Knight's Cross with Oak Leaves and) Swords
SD: Special Duties
Serrate: British equipment designed to home in on Lichtenstein AI radar.
SKG: Schnelles Kampfgeschwader: Fast Bomber Group
SOE: Special Operations Executive
Stab: Staff flight

Staffel: Roughly equivalent to a squadron, designated sequentially within the Geschwader by Arabic figures, e.g.: 4./NJG1
Staffelkapitän: Captain, a Staffel command position rather than a rank
TIs: Target Indicators
TNT: TriNitroToluene
Transportgeschwader: Transport Group
UEA: Unidentified Enemy Aircraft
U/S: Unserviceable
UHF: Ultra-High Frequency
Uhu: 'Owl' Heinkel He 219 night fighter aircraft
USAAF: United Sates Army Air Force
VC: Victoria Cross
VHF: Very High Frequency
Viermot (4-mot): Four-engined bomber abbreviation of viermotorig.
Viktor: R/T code for 'have received and understood message'
WAAF: Women's Auxiliary Air Force
Wilde Sau: 'Wild Boar': Free-lance night fighting, originally by single-engined aircraft, mainly over the RAF's target, relying on freelance interceptions from a running commentary aided by the lights from fires and from searchlights
Window: Metal foil strips dropped by bombers to confuse German radar
Y-Service: Ypsilon, Y-Verfahren, Ypsilonverfahren: Luftwaffe ground-controlled navigation by means of VHF
Zahme Sau: 'Tame Boar': Tactic of feeding German twin-engined fighters into the bomber stream as soon as its track was properly established on the way to or from the target and by means of broadcast running commentary on situation in the air
Zerstörer: 'Destroyer', heavy twin-engined fighter-bomber aircraft (Bf 110/210/410)
Zerstörergeschwader (ZG): Bf 110 unit roughly equivalent to four RAF squadrons (Geschwader consisted of 100-120 a/c; each Geschwader had a Geschwader Stab and three or four Gruppen, with 25 to 35 a/c each; each Gruppe had three Staffeln of ten a/c each).
Zweimot: Twin-engined aircraft

Bibliography

Gebhard Aders, *Geschichte der deutschen Nachtjagd 1917-1945* (Stuttgart 1978)
Anonymous, *Extract from I. Jagdkorps War Diary, 15.9.43 to 20.5.44* (ADIK Report No. 416/1945, at National Archives, Washington DC, USA)
Michael Balss, *Deutsche Nachtjagd. Personalverluste in Ausbildung und Einsatz -fliegendes Personal* (Eich 1997)
Jack Bennett, *Jack's Wartime RAF. Exploits* (privately published Biggleswade 1997)
Herbert Bethke & Friedhelm Henning, *Jagdgeschwader 300. The Wild Huntsman* (Volume 1, 2000)
Theo Boiten, *Nachtjagd. The night fighter versus bomber war over the Third Reich 1939-1945* (Crowood Press Ramsbury, Marlborough 1997)
Theo Boiten, *Bristol Blenheim* (Crowood Press Ramsbury, Marlborough 1998)
Theo Boiten, *Night Airwar. Personal recollections of the conflict over Europe, 1939-1945* (Crowood Press Ramsbury, Marlborough 1999)
Martin W. Bowman & Theo Boiten, *Raiders of the Reich; Air Battle Western Europe: 1942-1945* (Shrewsbury 1996)
Martin W. Bowman, *The Men Who Flew The Mosquito* (Pen & Sword 2003)
Martin W. Bowman, *Moskitopanik!* (Pen & Sword 2004)
Martin W. Bowman *Wellington The Geodetic Giant.* (Airlife 1998)
Martin W. Bowman, *Confounding the Reich* (Pen & Sword 2004)
Martin W. Bowman, *Mosquito Fighter/Fighter-Bomber Units of WW2.* (Osprey 1998)
Martin W. Bowman, *Mosquito Bomber/Fighter-Bomber Units of WW2.* (Osprey 1998)
Martin W. Bowman, *RAF Bomber Stories.* (PSL 1998)
Chaz Bowyer, *The Wellington Bomber* (London 1986)
Chaz Bowyer, *For Valour. The Air VCs* (London 1992)
W. R. Chorley, *To see the dawn breaking. 76 Squadron operations* (Ottery St. Mary 1981)
W. R. Chorley, *In Brave Company. 158 Squadron operations* (Salisbury 1990)
W. R. Chorley, *Royal Air Force Bomber Command Losses of the Second World War* (six volumes. Midland Counties, Leicester 1992-1998)
Coen Cornelissen, *Van Grasmat tot Fliegerhorst* (Oldenzaal 1998)
Alan W. Cooper, *Bombers over Berlin. The RAF offensive, November 1943-March 1944* (PSL Wellingborough 1989)
Wolfgang Dierich, *Die Verbdnde der Luftwaffe 1935-1945* (Stuttgart 1976)
Julian Evan-Hart, *War-Torn Skies of Great Britain: Cambridgeshire* (Red Kite 2008).
Jonathan Falconer, *Stirling at War* (London 1991)
John Foreman, Johannes Matthews, Simon Parry, *Luftwaffe Night-Fighter Combat Claims 1939-45* (Red Kite. 2004)
Norman L. R. Franks, *Forever Strong. The Story of 75 Squadron RNZAF 1916-1990* (Auckland 1991)
Norman L. R. Franks, *Claims To Fame: The Lancaster.* (Arms And Armour. London, 1994)
Norman L. R. Franks, *RAF Fighter Command Losses of the Second World War. Vol.3. 1944-45.* (Midland Publishing 2000)
Roger A. Freeman, *Raiding the Reich. The Allied Strategic Bombing Offensive in Europe* (London 1997)
Mike Garbett and Brian Goulding, *The Lancaster at War* (Ian Allan London 1971)

Bryce B. Gomersall, *The Stirling File* (Tonbridge 1987)
Alex H. Gould DFC, *Tales from the Sagan Woods* (Bundanoon 1994)
J. J. Halley, *The Lancaster File* (Tonbridge 1985)
Werner Held and Holger Nauroth, *Die deutsche Nachtjagd.Bildchonik der deutschen Nachtjdger bis 1945* (Stuttgart 1982)
Georg Hentschel, *Die geheimen Konferenzen des General-Luftzeugmeisters* (Koblenz 1989)
Peter Hinchliffe, *The Other Battle. Luftwaffe night aces versus Bomber Command.* (Airlife Shrewsbury 1996)
Harry Holmes, *Avro Lancaster, The Definitive Record.* (Airlife Shrewsbury 2001)
Ab A. Jansen, *Wespennest Leeuwarden* (3 Vols) (Baarn 1976-1978)
Werner Kock, *Das Kriegstagebuch des Nachtjagdgeschwaders 6* (Wittmund 1996)
Michel Marszalek, *L'Odyssee du Halifax DT 775. Anoux - 11/04/43* (private publication, Woippy 1995)
Merrick, K. A., *The Handley Page Halifax* (Aston 1990)
Martin Middlebrook, *The Nuremberg Raid* (London 1973)
Martin Middlebrook & Chris Everitt, *The Bomber Command War Diaries. An operational reference book, 1939-1945* (Harmondsworth 1985)
Martin Middlebrook, *The Berlin Raids* (London 1988)
Harry Moyle, *The Hampden File* (Tonbridge 1989)
Holger Nauroth & Werner Held, *Messerschmitt Bf 110 Zerstörer an alien Fronten 1939-1945* (Stuttgart 1978)
Heinz J. Nowarra, *'Uhu' He 219, best night fighter of World War II* (West Chester 1989)
Simon W. Parry, *Intruders over Britain. The Luftwaffe Night Fighter Offensive 1940-45* (Surbiton 1987)
Richard Pape, *Boldness Be My Friend.* (Elek 1953)
Brian Philpott, *RAF Bomber Units 1939-1945* (2 Vols) (London 1977-1978)
Mark Postlethwaite *Lancaster Squadrons In Focus.* (Red Kite 2002)
Ron Pütz, *Duel in de Wolken. De luchtoorlog in de gevarendriehoek Roermond-Luik-Aken* (Amsterdam 1994)
Rapier, Brian J., *Halifax At War* (Ian Allan Ltd, 1987)
John D. Rawlings, Fighter Squadrons of the RAF and their aircraft (Macdonald & Janes London 1978)
Robert S. Raymond, *A Yank in Bomber Command.* (Pacifica Press 1998)
Ron Read DFC, *'If You can't take a joke' An every night story of bomber folk.'* (Snell Print 1995)
Roland Remp, *Heinkel He 219: An Illustrated History of Germany's Premier Nightfighter.* (Schiffer 2000)
Hans Ring & Werner Girbig, *Jagdgeschwader 27. Die Dokumentation Über den Einsatz an alien Fronten 1939-1945* (Stuttgart 1994)
Anthony Robinson, *Night Fighter. A concise history of nightfighting since 1914* (London 1988)
Heinz Rökker, *Chronik I. Gruppe Nachtjagdgeschwader 2* (Zweibrücken 1997)
Major Heinz-Wolfgang Schnaufer, *Nachtjagd Leistungsbuch* (book of night-fighting achievements, unpublished)
Jerry Scutts, *Luftwaffe Night Fighter Units 1939-1945* (London 1978)
C. Martin Sharp & Michael J. F. Bowyer, *Mosquito* (London 1971)
J. R. Smith & Antony L. Kay, *German aircraft of the Second World War* (London 1972)
Martin Streetly, *Confound and Destroy.* (Macdonald and Jane's, London, 1978)
Colonel Raymond F. Toliver and Trevor J. Constable, *Horrido!* (Bantam 1968).
Christiaan Vanhee and Peter Celis, *Vinnige Valken, Vlammende Bliksems. De Vliegbasis van Sint-Truiden 1941-1945* (Luxembourg 2000)
Edwin Wheeler DFC, *Just to Get a Bed* (privately published 1990)
Dennis A. Wiltshire, *Per Ardua Ad Infinitum* (unpublished autobiography, Filton 1999)